Baumgarten's Aesthetics

Global Aesthetic Research

Series Editor: Joseph J. Tanke, Professor,
Department of Philosophy, University of Hawaii

The Global Aesthetic Research series publishes cutting-edge research in the field of aesthetics. It contains books that explore the principles at work in our encounters with art and nature, that interrogate the foundations of artistic, literary and cultural criticism, and that articulate the theory of the discipline's central concepts.

Titles in the Series

Early Modern Aesthetics, J. Colin McQuillan
Foucault on the Arts and Letters: Perspectives for the 21st Century,
    Catherine M. Soussloff
Architectural and Urban Reflections after Deleuze and Guattari, Edited by
    Constantin V. Boundas and Vana Tentokali
Living Off Landscape: or the Unthought-of in Reason, Francois Jullien, Translated by
    Pedro Rodriguez
Between Nature and Culture: The Aesthetics of Modified Environments, Emily Brady,
    Isis Brook and Jonathan Prior
Reviewing the Past: The Presence of Ruins, Zoltán Somhegyi
François Jullien's Unexceptional Thought: A Critical Introduction, Arne De Boever
Figural Space: Semiotics and the Aesthetic Imaginary, William D. Melaney
Eroticizing Aesthetics: In the Real with Bataille and Lacan, Tim Themi
Baumgarten's Aesthetics: Historical and Philosophical Perspectives, Edited by
    J. Colin McQuillan

Baumgarten's Aesthetics

Historical and Philosophical Perspectives

Edited by
J. Colin McQuillan

ROWMAN & LITTLEFIELD
Lanham • Boulder • New York • London

Published by Rowman & Littlefield
An imprint of The Rowman & Littlefield Publishing Group, Inc.
4501 Forbes Boulevard, Suite 200, Lanham, Maryland 20706
www.rowman.com

6 Tinworth Street, London SE11 5AL, United Kingdom

British Library Cataloguing in Publication Information Available

Library of Congress Cataloging-in-Publication Data

Names: McQuillan, J. Colin, editor.
Title: Baumgarten's aesthetics : historical and philosophical perspectives / edited by
     J. Colin McQuillan.
Description: Lanham : Rowman & Littlefield, [2021] | Series: Global aesthetic research |
     Includes bibliographical references and index.
Identifiers: LCCN 2021015931 (print) | LCCN 2021015932 (ebook) |
     ISBN 9781538146255 (cloth) | ISBN 9781538146262 (epub)
Subjects: LCSH: Baumgarten, Alexander Gottlieb, 1714-1762—Aesthetics. | Aesthetics.
Classification: LCC B2637.Z7 B385 2021 (print) | LCC B2637.Z7 (ebook) |
     DDC 111/.85092—dc23
LC record available at https://lccn.loc.gov/2021015931
LC ebook record available at https://lccn.loc.gov/2021015932

Contents

Acknowledgments   vii

Introduction   1
J. Colin McQuillan

1 Baumgarten's Invention of Aesthetics   27
   Ursula Franke

2 Baumgarten's *Aesthetics:* Topics and the Modern
   Ars inveniendi   71
   Stefanie Buchenau

3 Beauty and Appearance in Baumgarten's Metaphysics
   and Aesthetics   85
   Matthew McAndrew

4 Baumgarten's Conception of Aesthetic Truth in the *Aesthetics*   105
   Angelica Nuzzo

5 Pietist *Aisthēsis* and Moral Education in the Works of
   Alexander Gottlieb Baumgarten   125
   Simon Grote

6 Wolffian Rationalism and Baumgarten's Aesthetics   149
   J. Colin McQuillan

7 The Cofounding of Aesthetics: Baumgarten and Meier   171
   Alessandro Nannini

8 An Exercise in Humanity: Baumgarten and Mendelssohn on
       the Importance of Aesthetic Training   193
       Anne Pollok

9 Herder's Engagement with Baumgarten   213
       Hans Adler

10 The Majesty of Cognition: The Sublime in Baumgarten,
       Mendelssohn, and Kant   241
       Robert R. Clewis

11 The Discipline of Aesthetics Is the Aesthetics of Discipline:
       Baumgarten from Foucault's Perspective   273
       Christoph Menke

12 The Happy Aesthetician and the Feminist Killjoy:
       Baumgarten and Ahmed   283
       Amelia Hruby

Permissions   303

Bibliography   305

Index   339

About the Contributors   363

Acknowledgments

Contracts for this book were signed in February 2020. The chapters were written and translated during the COVID-19 pandemic that followed. The pandemic lasted into the first months of 2021, when I submitted the manuscript to the publisher. It is my hope that, by the time this volume appears in print, vaccines will have been distributed to the public and the pandemic will have begun to recede.

I am thankful for the hard work and dedication of all the contributors, each of whom showed great dedication to this project during a very difficult time. Every single one of the authors and translators who agreed to contribute to this volume was able to finish their work, despite lockdowns and quarantines that restricted travel; limited access to offices, libraries, and other research materials; and filled our lives with stress, anxiety, and loss. I would especially like to thank Alessandro Nannini for reading a draft of the introduction; Matthew McAndrew and Robert Clewis for comments on a draft of my chapter; and Mauricio González for his help with the notes and bibliography.

I am also grateful for the support of my friend, Joseph Tanke, editor of the Global Aesthetic Research series in which this volume appears. It was Joseph who first suggested that I take on this project and encouraged me to submit a proposal to the publisher. Frankie Mace and Scarlet Furness, the editors at Rowman & Littlefield, have been extremely helpful throughout the entire publication process. I appreciate their kindness, patience, and professionalism.

Several of the chapters included in this volume have been previously published elsewhere. A German version of Hans Adler's chapter is included in his book *Die Prägnanz des Dunklen. Gnoseologie – Ästhetik – Geschichtsphilosophie* (Hamburg: Felix Meiner Verlag, 1990, 63–87). Stefanie Buchenau's chapter was originally part of her book *The Founding of Aesthetics in the German Enlightenment: The Art of Invention and the Invention of Art* (Cambridge University Press, 2013, 137–151). Ursula Franke's chapter was first published in German in *Baumgartens Erfindung der Ästhetik* (Münster: Mentis Verlag, 2018, 9–52). Simon Grote's chapter appeared in German in *Alexander Gottlieb Baumgarten: Sinnliche Erkenntnis in der Philosophie des Rationalismus*, edited by Alexander Aichele and Dagmar Mirbach (Hamburg: Felix Meiner Verlag, 2008, 175–198). Christoph Menke's Chapter was published in German in *Baumgarten-Studien*, edited by Rüdiger Campe, Anselm Haverkamp, and Christoph Menke (August Verlag, 2014, 233–247). I would like to thank the authors, translators, and publishers for permission to reprint and translate this material.

Finally, I would like to thank the Office of Sponsored Projects, Academic Research, and Compliance at St. Mary's University for awarding me a faculty research grant that paid for the translations.

Introduction

J. Colin McQuillan

This volume is the first collection of essays devoted to Alexander Gottlieb Baumgarten's aesthetics to be published in English. Although it is well known that Baumgarten introduced aesthetics as a new part of philosophy in Germany in the eighteenth century, and some scholars are aware that he provided a unique account of its subject matter, his aesthetics has generally been neglected by anglophone philosophers.

First and foremost, Baumgarten's aesthetics has been neglected because there is as yet no complete English translation of Baumgarten's *Aesthetics* (*Aesthetica*)—an incomplete work that was published in Latin in two volumes in 1750 and 1758. An English translation of Baumgarten's *Reflections on Poetry* (*Meditationes philosophicae de nonnullis ad poema pertinentibus*, 1735) was published in 1954 by Karl Aschenbrenner and William B. Holther. Courtney Fugate and John Hymers have also recently published translations of Baumgarten's *Metaphysics* (*Metaphysica*, 1739, trans. 2013) and *Elements of First Practical Philosophy* (*Initia Philosophiae Practicae*, 1760, trans. 2020), along with the notes that Kant wrote in his copies of these texts and used in his lectures. Translations of Baumgarten's *Aesthetics* have appeared in French, German, and Italian, but so far only short translations of the opening sections of the *Aesthetics* have appeared in English.[1] This leaves most of

---

[1] A partial French translation, *Esthétique*, was published by Jean-Yves Pranchère in 1988 by L'Herne. A complete Italian translation by Francesco Caparrotta, Anna Li Vigni, and Salvatore Tedesco appeared as *L'Estetica* in 2000, published by Aesthetica Edizioni. A new edition by Alessandro Nannini and Salvatore Tedesco has just appeared with Mimesis in 2020. Selections of the *Aesthetics* were translated into German by Hans Rudolf Schweizer and published as *Texte zur Grundlegung der Ästhetik* (1983) and *Theoretische Ästhetik* (1988) by Felix Meiner Verlag. A complete German translation by Dagmar Mirbach was published by the same press in 2007. A second Latin-German edition, translated by Constanze Peres, is scheduled to be published by Wilhelm Fink Verlag at the end of 2023. English translations of the beginning of the *Aesthetics* have also been

the work inaccessible to anglophone readers and those for whom English has become an academic lingua franca.

Earlier generations of anglophone scholars would have had greater facility with Baumgarten's Latin than contemporary readers, but they were less receptive to his aesthetics for other reasons. Many believed that Baumgarten's contributions to aesthetics were, in the words of Katharine Everett Gilbert and Helmut Kuhn's *A History of Esthetics* (1939), "nominal rather than substantial."[2] This claim has its origins among German historians of philosophy in the nineteenth century. Recent scholarship has exposed the biases many of these historians shared, including the sexist, racist, national-ist, and religious prejudices that influenced their conception of philosophy and their accounts of its origin and past.[3] Although he was white, German, and Protestant, these historians dismissed Baumgarten and disparaged his aesthetics because they were associated with the Leibnizian-Wolffian ratio-nalism that Kant and Hegel were supposed to have overcome. Baumgarten's aesthetics did not fit neatly into the Hegelian and Neo-Kantian frameworks that nineteenth-century German historians of philosophy presupposed, so they were not taken seriously. Contemporary historians of philosophy have begun to recognize the limitations of these frameworks, as well as the ben-efits of exploring different philosophical traditions, including the Leibnizian-Wolffian school. So, instead of being condemned as a dogmatic rationalist who "moves with glacial celerity" and "ruthlessly bores," Wolff is now seen by many historians of philosophy as a dynamic, modern thinker whose works ranged from metaphysics and empirical natural science to epistemology and psychology, as well as law, politics, and theology.[4] That aesthetics would emerge within a philosophical tradition as sophisticated and expansive as the Leibnizian-Wolffian school should not be surprising.

The ahistorical character of Anglo-American philosophy in second half of the twentieth century also contributed to the neglect of Baumgarten's aesthetics. During the postwar period, it was not uncommon for analytic philosophers to draw sharp disciplinary distinctions between history and philosophy. Some even suggested that historical accuracy could and, indeed, should be subordinated to "the articulation of philosophical ideas" in histories of philosophy.[5] But new research on the history of early modern

---

published in two anthologies. See Harrison, Wood, and Gaiger, *Art in Theory, 1648–1815* (2000); and Tanke and McQuillan, *The Bloomsbury Anthology of Aesthetics* (2012).

[2] Gilbert and Kuhn, *A History of Esthetics*, 289.

[3] See Park, *Africa, Asia, and the History of Philosophy* (2013).

[4] White Beck, *Early German Philosophy*, 258. For a more contemporary perspective on German philosophy prior to Kant, see Dyck, *Early Modern German Philosophy*, 1–11. See also the updated entry on Wolff in the *Stanford Encyclopedia of Philosophy*. Hettche and Dyck, "Christian Wolff," (2019).

[5] Williams, *Descartes*, 9.

philosophy and science has led to a greater appreciation of otherwise obscure figures and works that played important roles in the development of modern physics, biology, and psychology. Much of this scholarship depends on a greater sensitivity to the historical contexts in which philosophers and scientists thought and wrote. So, instead of rejecting historical accuracy as an impediment to the articulation of philosophical ideas, historians and philosophers of science have come to understand that historical accuracy is actually an important condition of the articulation of philosophical ideas, which are confused and misunderstood when they are reconstructed in supposedly rational but anachronistic ways.[6] Aesthetics is rarely thought to be as important as the history and philosophy of science, or as central to philosophy as a discipline, so there has been less incentive to conduct historical research on neglected figures and works in the history of aesthetics. Yet there is still a great deal of contextualist scholarship being published on early modern aesthetics, including Baumgarten's aesthetics.[7]

Another reason Baumgarten's aesthetics was often neglected has to do with the status of aesthetics within Anglo-American philosophy. During the twentieth century, analytic philosophy came to dominate academic philosophy in the English-speaking world. New aesthetic theories were developed by analytic philosophers during this time; yet they remained marginal with respect to philosophy as a discipline, never attaining the prestige of analytic metaphysics, epistemology, philosophy of language, or philosophy of science—the core of the discipline, according to many analytic philosophers.[8] Aesthetics occupied a more central place in continental European philosophy, but the canons of continental philosophy were drawn from nineteenth-century French and German traditions—traditions that were founded by the same Hegelian and Neo-Kantian historians of philosophy that dismissed Baumgarten as a dogmatic rationalist metaphysician.[9] Baumgarten's aesthetics was, as a result, rarely mentioned by continental philosophers and never received the kind of interpretive commentaries that were devoted to Kant or Hegel. The opposition between analytic and continental philosophy has, thankfully, declined somewhat in recent years, which seems to have facilitated a greater interest in otherwise marginal parts of philosophy as well as greater recognition for noncanonical figures and works. It should come as no surprise, then, that we find renewed interest in Baumgarten's aesthetics among philosophers trained in both schools. One of the goals of

[6] See Mercer, "The Contextualist Revolution in Early Modern Philosophy," 529–548.
[7] See, for example, Beiser, *Diotima's Children* (2009); Buchenau, *The Founding of Aeshetics in the German Enlightenment* (2013); Guyer, *A History of Modern Aesthetics* (2014); McQuillan, *Early Modern Aesthetics* (2015); and Grote, *The Emergence of Modern Aesthetic Theory* (2017).
[8] See Lamarque, "Analytic Aesthetics," 770–794.
[9] See Wicks, "Nineteenth- and Twentieth-Century Continental Aesthetics," 51–61.

this volume is to encourage that interest by making recent scholarship on Baumgarten's aesthetics accessible to anglophone readers.

Ultimately, I believe the interest scholars have shown in new editions and translations of Baumgarten's works, their rejection of traditional narratives about the history of modern European philosophy, the development of contextualist approaches to the history of philosophy, and their appreciation for the place of aesthetics within philosophy all mean that the time when anglophone readers were unaware of Baumgarten's aesthetics is ending. We may not yet have a complete translation of his *Aesthetics*, but I hope this book, the chapters it contains, and the ongoing research of the contributors, as well as others, will continue to make Baumgarten's aesthetics more accessible to anglophone readers.

ALEXANDER GOTTLIEB BAUMGARTEN, 1714–1762

Alexander Gottlieb Baumgarten was born in Berlin in 1714, the fifth of seven sons in a devout Lutheran family. His mother died when he was only three years old. His father began educating Baumgarten according to the precepts of Locke's *Some Thoughts on Education* (1693) but died when Baumgarten was eight.[10] After his father's death, the young Baumgarten was placed in the care of his grandmother and educated by Martin Christgau, who taught him classical languages, including Hebrew, and helped to cultivate his interest in Latin poetry.[11] In 1727, when he was thirteen, Baumgarten fulfilled one of his father's last wishes by following his older brothers to Halle and enrolling in August Hermann Francke's *Pädagogium*.[12]

Francke had been a friend of the Baumgarten family, but he was also the leader of the Pietists in Halle. Pietism is perhaps best understood as a protest against orthodox Lutheranism and the institutionalized Lutheran Church, inspired by works like Philipp Jacob Spener's *Pious Longing* (*Pia Desideria*, 1675). Spener was careful to affirm the theological correctness of the doctrines contained in the *Lutheran Confessions* (*Konkordienbuch*,

---

[10] Fugate and Hymers joke that it is not known whether, in keeping with Locke's educational theories, "the young Alexander was denied fruit, made to sleep on a hard bed, and forced to wear wet shoes," but they also suggest that Baumgarten's Lockean education indicates "that he was raised not only in a pious, but also in an 'enlightened' household, one in which reason was highly prized in religious and secular matters alike." I am not sure I agree with this assessment, but see Baumgarten, *Metaphysics*, 5. For more on Locke's theory of education, see Ezell, "John Locke's Images of Childhood," 139–155.

[11] Baumgarten pays homage to Christgau in the preface to the *Reflections on Poetry*. See Baumgarten, *Reflections*, 35.

[12] Baumgarten's father indicated, in his will, that his sons should study with Francke in Halle. See Meier, *Baumgartens Leben*, 358. See also Baumgarten, *Metaphysics*, 5.

1580), but he also warned that the practices of the Lutheran Church were beginning to resemble those of the Roman Church that Luther had so vehemently opposed.[13] Spener called for a renewal of Christian practice within the Lutheran Church, promoting the study of the Bible, the priesthood of the laity, moral conduct, and the reform of schools and universities. He insisted that schools and universities should become "workshops of the Holy spirit," advancing the faithful practice of Christianity as well as theological knowledge.[14] Francke was an early follower of Spener and eagerly took up his cause. In the 1690s, Francke founded an orphanage and charity school, known as the *Waisenhaus*, that included the *Pädagogium* where Baumgarten and his brothers were educated. Francke also joined forces with the jurist and philosopher Christian Thomasius to found the University of Halle (1694), known at the time as the *Fridericiana*, after Friedrich III, Elector of Brandenburg, who later became Friedrich I, King in Prussia.[15] By the time Baumgarten enrolled in the university in 1730, it had become one of the most modern and dynamic academic institutions in Germany.

Baumgarten and his brothers arrived in Halle and studied at the university at a time when Francke's followers were engaged in a vigorous campaign against the philosopher Christian Wolff. Wolff had been appointed *Professor Ordinarius* of mathematics at the university in 1706, but soon began lecturing on other subjects in the philosophy faculty.[16] He also began publishing a series of popular textbooks, first in German and only later in Latin, on subjects ranging from mathematics to logic, metaphysics, ethics, political philosophy, and natural science.[17] Wolff became convinced that philosophy would benefit from the application of the mathematical methods he employed in his textbooks, because he thought "the rules of philosophical method are the same as the rules of mathematical method."[18] In practice, this meant that philosophers should only use terms that have been accurately defined, carefully distinguish the subjects and predicates of their judgments, affirm as true only what has been demonstrated to be true, and organize everything so that premises precede the conclusions that are derived from them.[19] This might not

---

[13] On the context of Spener's Pietism, see the helpful introduction to the English translation of the *Pia Desideria* by Theodore G. Tappert in Spener, *Pia Desideria*, 1–28.

[14] Spener, *Pia Desideria*, 103.

[15] Friedrich I's title was "King in Prussia" (*König in Preußen*) and not "King of Prussia" (*König von Preußen*) because of the peculiar political status of his territories. Friedrich could only be King "in" Prussia because Prussia was not a part of the Holy Roman Empire. Another part of Friedrich's territory, the Electorate of Brandenburg, was a part of the Empire, which prevented him from claiming the title of "King" within Imperial lands. Friedrich I's grandson, Friedrich II, was the first to claim the title of "King of Prussia" in 1772, after the First Partition of Poland.

[16] See Gottsched, *Life of Baron Wolfius*, viii and Kertscher, *Er brachte Licht*, 104.

[17] Kertscher, *Er brachte Licht*, 101–103.

[18] Wolff, *Preliminary Discourse*, §139.

[19] Wolff, *Preliminary Discourse*, §139.

seem like a terribly novel method, much less a controversial one, but Wolff still managed to make enemies of both Pietist theologians and Thomasian philosophers in the university. The Pietist theologians saw Wolff's rationalism as a threat to divine revelation, the authority of scripture, and religious faith, while the Thomasian philosophers tended to be more eclectic, more empiricist, and less invested in modern philosophy and science than their rigorous, methodical, modernist colleague. Wolff gave the theologians even more reason to oppose him when, at the end of his term as pro-rector of the university in 1721, he delivered his lecture *On the Practical Philosophy of the Chinese* (1723), in which he used the teachings of Confucius as an example of moral and political philosophy that is grounded in reason, rather than revelation, scripture, or theological doctrine.[20] By suggesting that ethics and politics could leave religion behind, Wolff had crossed a line—it also did not help that he insulted Joachim Lange, the Pietist theologian who was to be Wolff's successor as pro-rector, during his introductory remarks.[21]

Francke, Lange, and other Pietist theologians had Wolff expelled from the university, the city of Halle, and the kingdom of Prussia in 1723. They accused him of atheism and fatalism, even warning King Frederick Wilhelm I that Wolff's philosophy could be used to justify desertion from the army, because it (allegedly) denied free will and moral responsibility.[22] Baumgarten and his brothers were personally supported by Francke, who had taken them into his home and fed them at his table.[23] Their academic careers were also promoted by Lange, who continued to engage in public polemics against Wolff throughout the 1720s and 1730s. Yet it was not long after he arrived in Halle that Baumgarten began to show an interest in Wolffian philosophy. Wolff's works were still banned by the university at the time, but Baumgarten was encouraged to study them by his oldest brother, Siegmund Jakob, who had taught Latin in Francke's *Pädagogium* before becoming *Privatdozent* in the theology faculty of the university in 1732 and then being appointed *Professor Ordinarius* of theology in 1734. The young Alexander even traveled to Jena to attend lectures by professors like Jakob Carpov, Heinrich Köhler, Georg Erhard Hamberger, and Johann Peter Reusch. Reusch had been Wolff's student before Wolff was expelled from Halle. Carpov had sided with Wolff against Lange and the Pietists in the controversies that followed his expulsion.[24] The Wolffians in Jena also seem to have shown a

---

[20] See Wolff, "Discourse on the Practical Philosophy of the Chinese," 145–186.

[21] See Holloran, *Professors of Enlightenment*, 297.

[22] Holloran, *Professors of Enlightenment*, 365.

[23] Meier, *Baumgartens Leben*, 355.

[24] Carpov's commentary on Wolff's *German Ethics*, published in 1735, is meant to defend Wolff's ethics from Lange's claim that Wolff's philosophy is mechanistic, fatalistic, and Spinozistic. See Carpov, *Ausführliche Erläuterung*, 5, 9–17.

special interest in humanistic subjects like grammar and rhetoric, producing works like Reusch's *Dissertation on the Beauty of Speech* (*Dissertatio de eo, quod pulchrum est in eloquentia eiusque potissimum rationibus*, 1724) and Carpov's *Critical-Philosophical Meditation on the Perfection of Language* (*Meditatio critico-philosophica de perfectione linguae, methodo scientifica proposita*, 1735). The degree to which these works influenced Baumgarten's aesthetics remains unclear; yet the time he spent studying Wolff in Halle and Jena seems to have been an incredibly formative one.[25]

His former student and friend, Georg Friedrich Meier, paints a compelling portrait of this time in his biography of Baumgarten (*Baumgartens Leben*, 1763). Meier casts Baumgarten as an earnest young philosopher, a lover of truth who heard others criticize Wolff, but withheld judgment until he had carefully examined Wolff's philosophy for himself.[26] When he had finished his rigorous study of Wolff's philosophy, Meier tells us that Baumgarten did not find anything about Wolff's mathematical method to be particularly dangerous.[27] Yet the "Preface" to the third (1750) edition of Baumgarten's *Metaphysics* (*Metaphysica*, 1739) tells a slightly different story. There Baumgarten says he is thankful "for having grown up surrounded by others hostile to this way of philosophizing" and that he "first imbibed almost exclusively whatever could be objected to it, rather than its own doctrines."[28] Baumgarten then confirms that he "made some—no, on the contrary, many—of these same teachings my own, but only after an intense and careful investigation of the truth," indicating that he studied Wolff's philosophy and carefully examined the objections raised by his opponents before embracing many aspects of Wolff's philosophy himself.[29] His upbringing among Wolff's Pietist critics and his sympathy for some of their objections to Wolff also helps to explain why Baumgarten says, in his *Philosophical Letters from Aletheophilus* (*Philosophische Brieffe von Aletheophilus*, 1741), that he laughed when he found his *Reflections on Poetry* listed "in a catalog of Wolffian texts"—Carl Günther Ludovici's *Newest Curiosities of the Leibnizian-Wolffian Philosophy* (*Neueste Merckwürdigkeiten aus der Leibnitz-Wolffischen Weltweisheit*, 1738).[30] Baumgarten suggests that Ludovici included his *Reflections on Poetry* in his catalog simply because "I had divided my text into §s and referred in each [section] to the previous one."[31] Far from being proof of Baumgarten's

---

[25] Baumgarten cites Carpov's work on the perfection of language in the *Reflections on Poetry*. See Baumgarten, *Reflections*, §10.

[26] Meier, *Baumgartens Leben*, 356.

[27] Meier, *Baumgartens Leben*, 356.

[28] Baumgarten, *Metaphysics*, 77.

[29] Baumgarten, *Metaphysics*, §77.

[30] Ludovici, *Neueste Merkwürdigkeiten*, §232.

[31] Baumgarten, *Philosophische Brieffe*, 3. See also Grote, *The Emergence of Modern Aesthetic Theory*, 71.

Wolffianism, the form of Baumgarten's works—their division into §s—simply reflects their academic context. Wolff's works and those of his Pietist critics, even the ones who most vehemently rejected the mathematical method that structured Wolff's textbooks, appear to be very similar, because they were all products of the same academic culture and institutions.

Despite his interest in poetry and the theological controversies that raged in Halle, Baumgarten remained an academic philosopher. His *Reflections on Poetry*, the work in which he first introduces aesthetics, was submitted to the faculty of philosophy in Halle as a dissertation for the *venia legendi*, or license to teach, in 1735.[32] It was on the strength of this dissertation that Baumgarten was appointed *Privatdozent* in philosophy at Halle in 1737. There he taught a wide variety of different subjects—history of philosophy, logic, metaphysics, natural law, and natural theology, but also Latin poetry, Hebrew grammar, and the Book of Isaiah.[33] Two years later, in 1739, Baumgarten published the first edition of his *Metaphysics*, which would go through four different editions (1739, 1743, 1750, 1757) during his lifetime, along with a German translation by Meier that appeared in 1766.[34] In 1740, Baumgarten published another textbook, *Philosophical Ethics* (*Ethica Philosophica*), which explains "the science of human obligations" through a distinction between religious duties, duties to oneself, and duties to others.[35] That same year, Baumgarten was appointed Professor of Philosophy at the University of Frankfurt an der Oder—a small city in Brandenburg about 50 miles East of Berlin. His inaugural lecture was a guide to academic acclaim (*Einige Gedancken vom vernünfftigen Beyfall auf Academien*, 1740). According to Baumgarten, academic acclaim is rational when students appreciate the benefits of a professor's lectures.[36] The best lectures are, Baumgarten argues, a combination of intellect, sensibility, and utility—they should be thorough, beautiful, and practical.[37] Shortly after he received his appointment, in 1741, Baumgarten also undertook his only nonacademic, German-language publishing venture, the *Philosophical Letters from Aletheophilus*. The *Philosophical Letters* consists of thirty-four letters, published in twenty-six issues of a journal modeled on the "moral weeklies" of Gottsched and his followers, which were themselves modeled on English publications like *The Tatler* (1709–1711)

---

[32] Baumgarten, *Aesthetica/Ästhetik*, xvii.

[33] Baumgarten, *Metaphysics*, 7.

[34] Baumgarten, *Metaphysics*, 53–60. A fifth (1763), sixth (1768), and seventh (1779) edition of the *Metaphysics* were published after Baumgarten's death, though these are essentially reprints of the fourth edition. See Baumgarten, *Metaphysics*, 54–55.

[35] Baumgarten, *Ethica Philosophica*, §1. See also Schwaiger, *Baumgarten*, 128–143 and Osawa, *Perfection and Morality*, 74–210.

[36] Baumgarten, *Gedancken vom vernünfftigen Beyfall auf Academien*, §5.

[37] Baumgarten, *Gedancken vom vernünfftigen Beyfall auf Academien*, §6–§9. See also Grote, *The Emergence of Modern Aesthetic Theory*, 117–118.

and *The Spectator* (1711–1712).[38] These writings differ from Baumgarten's academic writings in certain ways, though they are perhaps not as different as they might seem. While they are intended for a popular audience, and do not proceed as systematically as his textbooks, they show the same concern for scientific rigor, vivid expression, and practicality that Baumgarten promoted in his inaugural lecture. His desire to combine these qualities, and to instruct the public as well as his students, suggest that Baumgarten was a proponent of the German Enlightenment, despite his Pietism, and the modern assumption that reason and religion are somehow incompatible.

It was also during his first years in Frankfurt, in 1742–1743, that Baumgarten began lecturing on aesthetics. He apparently shared the text of these lectures with Meier, who used them as the basis for his own *Foundations of All Beautiful Sciences* (*Anfangsgründe aller schönen Wissenschaften*), which appeared in three volumes between 1748 and 1750.[39] Baumgarten published the first volume of his *Aesthetics* shortly thereafter, finally giving a systematic presentation of the new science he had announced in his *Reflections on Poetry* fifteen years earlier. The second volume of the *Aesthetics* appeared in 1758, though, as we will see in the next section, it did not even come close to completing the plan Baumgarten laid out in the synopsis that he included in the first volume. The incompleteness of Baumgarten's aesthetics is no doubt a consequence of the scope of Baumgarten's ambitions, and the extent of his plans, but perhaps some blame can also be placed on his divided attention. Before his death in 1762, Baumgarten published another textbook on ethics, the *Elements of First Practical Philosophy* (*Initia Philosophiae Practicae*, 1760), lectures on Christian Wolff's logic (*Acroasis Logica*, 1761), and a text on natural law (*Ius Naturale*, 1763) that was published posthumously. After his death, a number of Baumgarten's philosophical and theological texts were also edited for publication by others, including his *Outline of Philosophical Encyclopedia* (*Sciagraphia encyclopaedia philosophicae*, 1769), *General Philosophy* (*Philosophia generalis*, 1770), *Lectures on Dogmatic Theology* (*Praelectiones theologiae dogmaticae*, 1773), and *Thoughts on the Speeches of Jesus* (*Gedanken bei den Reden Jesu*, 1796–1797). These works do not contribute directly to the exposition of Baumgarten's aesthetics, but they do help us to understand where his new science fits into philosophy as a system and how it relates to the other parts of philosophy. The *Lectures on Logic* contains a few remarks about the relation between logic and aesthetics that Baumgarten does not address in his other writings.[40] Both the *Outline* and *General Philosophy* help us appreciate Baumgarten's understanding of

---

[38] See Mirbach and Allerkamp, "Ale.Theophilus Baumgarten," 317–340.
[39] Meier, *Anfangsgründe*, Vol. 1, §6.
[40] Baumgarten, *Acroasis Logica*, §7.

philosophy as a science and academic discipline, while also explaining how aesthetics fits into philosophy as a system.[41] Finally, Baumgarten's *Thoughts* contains a number of important remarks on hermeneutics, which was closely associated with aesthetics for both Baumgarten and Meier.[42]

Baumgarten died in Frankfurt in 1762, when he was only forty-eight years old. He had been sick for most the 1750s, probably suffering from tuberculosis. His illness prevented him from reading, writing, and teaching for extended periods, though he did publish a number of works during this time and even managed to record a series of meditations on the Gospels in anticipation of his death.[43] Baumgarten's condition worsened in the spring of 1762 and he was forced to give up his academic activities. During the same period, Meier tells us that Baumgarten committed himself to dying in a way that would be exemplary for "a Christian philosopher" (*ein christlicher Weltweiser*).[44] According to Meier, Baumgarten spoke often about the joy of death, even declaring "*Serenitas animi est demonstratio demonstrationum.* Christ alone has this, reason knows nothing of it."[45] Meier also says that, shortly before his death, Baumgarten "banished all learnedness from his bed" and declared that "whoever says anything about it to me, he will have my hatred."[46] In the end, he concluded that "neither philosophy, nor theology, but faith alone" could bring him peace.[47] These remarks were praised by a number of his followers, including Meier, who describes Baumgarten as a "Christian Socrates" in *Baumgarten's Life* (1763).[48] In *The Characters of Three Famous Philosophers of Modern Times* (*Charactere dreyer berühmter Weltweisen der neuern Zeiten*, 1765), Johann Christian Förster also declares that "the death of a righteous man is a crown on his life" and then argues that the peace and happiness with which Baumgarten faced death proves that he was a greater philosopher than either Leibniz or Wolff.[49] However, this view of Baumgarten's death was not universally shared. His colleague Thomas Abbt notes in *Baumgarten's Life and Character* (1765) that while some, like Meier, may have regarded Baumgarten's death as "the triumph of the Christian religion," others took it as evidence of "feeble-mindedness and

---

[41] Baumgarten, *Sciagraphia*, §25; Baumgarten, *Philosophia generalis*, §147.

[42] See, for example, Baumgarten, *Gedanken*, Vol. 1, 24–26. On the relation between aesthetics and hermeneutics, see Makkreel, "The Confluence of Aesthetics and Hermeneutics in Baumgarten, Meier, and Kant," 65–75 and Nannini, "From the Density of Sense to the Density of the Sensible," 163–186.

[43] Meier, *Baumgartens Leben*, 361. See also Baumgarten, *Gedanken*, Vol. 1, Vorrede, 2–4.

[44] Meier, *Baumgartens Leben*, 361.

[45] Meier, *Baumgartens Leben*, 361.

[46] Meier, *Baumgartens Leben*, 362.

[47] Meier, *Baumgartens Leben*, 363.

[48] Meier, *Baumgartens Leben*, 366.

[49] Foerster, *Charactere*, 3.

hypocrisy" for a philosopher to renounce reason for the sake of his faith—especially because Baumgarten's *Lectures on Dogmatic Theology* promoted the harmony of faith and reason.[50] Moses Mendelssohn takes Abbt's suggestion a step further, denouncing Baumgarten's misological death and wondering why Baumgarten had ever bothered with philosophy at all if he believed his soul could only find peace in faith.[51] Modern readers may be inclined to side with Abbt and Mendelssohn, but we should not overlook the tension between philosophy and religion, reason and faith, that the different judgments of Baumgarten's death represent.[52] This tension was a persistent feature of the German Enlightenment, from the conflict between Wolff and the Pietists in the first half of the eighteenth century to the Pantheism controversy near the end of the century.

BAUMGARTEN'S AESTHETICS, 1735–1758

As we can see from his biography, Baumgarten first introduced aesthetics in his dissertation, *Reflections on Poetry*, at the very beginning of his academic career. He began lecturing on aesthetics a few years later, when he was appointed to his position in Frankfurt an der Oder. And he published the first two volumes of a systematic treatise on the subject, the *Aesthetics*, during the 1750s, shortly before his death. Even if this seems relatively straightforward, it is important to understand the nature of the new science Baumgarten proposed, the different contexts in which he discussed aesthetics before the publication of his treatise, and the incompleteness of the account Baumgarten managed to present in the two volumes of the *Aesthetics* that he published.

To begin, I think it is important to recognize that Baumgarten's *Reflections on Poetry* is not actually about aesthetics. In the 'Preface,' Baumgarten explains that his goal is to show that "many consequences can be derived from a single concept of a poem which has long ago been impressed on the mind, and long since declared hundreds of times to be acceptable, but not once proved," in order to show that "philosophy and the knowledge of how to construct a poem, which are often held to be entirely antithetical, are linked together in the most amiable union."[53] These remarks indicate that Baumgarten's dissertation is intended as a contribution to poetics. This is confirmed by the first paragraphs of the *Reflections on Poetry*, where Baumgarten

[50] Abbt, *Vermischte Werke und Briefe*, Vol. 4, 236. This remark is not included in the original, 1765 edition of Abbt's text. See Abbt, *Baumgartens Leben und Charakter*, 25–26.
[51] Mendelssohn, *Gesammelte Schriften*, Vol. 12.1, 32.
[52] Nannini, "How a Philosopher Dies," 51. For a contemporary philosopher who sides with Abbt and Mendelssohn, see Look, "Baumgarten's Rationalism," 12.
[53] Baumgarten, *Reflections on Poetry*, 36.

presents definitions of a poem ("a perfect sensible discourse"), poetry ("the state of composing a poem"), the poet ("the man who enjoys that state") as well as poetics ("the body of rules to which a poem conforms") and philosophical poetics ("the science of poetics").[54] It is not until the very end of the *Reflections on Poetry*, after extensive discussions of other topics in poetics, that Baumgarten introduces aesthetics and explains its relation to the subject matter of his dissertation. According to Baumgarten, philosophical poetics presupposes that the poet possesses "a lower cognitive faculty," since poetic representations are "sensible" and "sensibility" is the lower cognitive faculty.[55] Baumgarten rejects the idea that logic could guide sensible, poetic discourse to perfection, so he proposes aesthetics as a new science, grounded in psychological principles, that might "improve the lower faculties of knowing and sharpen them, and apply them more happily for the benefit of the whole world."[56] The manner in which Baumgarten distinguishes logic and aesthetics depends on a distinction between "things known" and "things perceived," in which logic remains the science of "things known . . . by the superior faculty," the intellect, and aesthetics becomes "the science of perception," or things "known by the inferior faculty," sensibility.[57] Poetics and rhetoric are subordinated to aesthetics, in the sense that they are specific parts of aesthetics, dealing with different ways of presenting sensible representations. Poetics deals with the perfected presentation of sensible representations, because poetry is metered, while rhetoric deals with the unperfected presentation of sensible representations, because it is unmetered. The way that Baumgarten distinguishes poetics and aesthetics in the *Reflections on Poetry* is technical, but it is important to recognize the systematic relationship between them in order to understand the nature of the Baumgarten's aesthetics.

Several of the works that Baumgarten published in the years following the publication of his dissertation elaborate on the remarks at the end of the *Reflections on Poetry*, though they do not yet constitute a formal presentation of Baumgarten's new science. In the *Metaphysics*, for example, Baumgarten defines aesthetics as "the science of knowing and presenting with regard to the senses."[58] He adds, parenthetically, that aesthetics is "the logic of the inferior cognitive faculty, the philosophy of graces and muses,

[54] Baumgarten, *Reflections on Poetry*, §9.
[55] Baumgarten, *Reflections on Poetry*, §115.
[56] Baumgarten, *Reflections on Poetry*, §115.
[57] In Wolff's *German Metaphysics* (*Rational Thoughts on God, the World and the Soul of Man, and on All Things in General; Vernünftige Gedanken von Gott, der Welt und der Seele des Menschen, auch allen Dingen überhaupt*, 1720), the inferior and superior cognitive faculties are identified as *Sinn* and *Verstand*, which is typically rendered as "sensibility" and "understanding" in English translations of Kant. However, these terms are translated into Latin, in Wolff's and Baumgarten's works, as *sensus* and *intellectus*, which are more literally translated as "sense" and "intellect."
[58] Baumgarten, *Metaphysics*, §533.

inferior gnoseology, the art of thinking beautifully, the art of the analogue of reason."[59] These definitions confirm that aesthetics is a science, that it is concerned with sensibility, the inferior cognitive faculty, which is distinct from, but analogous to, reason, the superior cognitive faculty, and its science, logic. The context in which Baumgarten situates these definitions is also significant. The location of his definitions makes aesthetics a part of metaphysics and, more specifically, psychology (Part III), which is, according to Baumgarten, "the science of the general predicates of the soul."[60] Aesthetics is a part of empirical psychology (Part III, Chapter 1), which is the division of psychology that "deduces its assertions based upon experience that is nearest to hand."[61] Within empirical psychology, aesthetics concerns the inferior cognitive faculty (Part III, Chapter 1, Section II), which Baumgarten defines as "the faculty of knowing something obscurely and confusedly, or indistinctly."[62] This might seem like a strange definition of sensibility to modern readers, but it would have been perfectly comprehensible to Baumgarten's contemporaries. Indeed, it had become conventional for philosophers associated with the Leibnizian-Wolffian school to distinguish the inferior and superior cognitive faculties, sensibility and the intellect, by the clarity and distinctness of their cognition.[63] Clear and distinct cognition was, for these philosophers, intellectual, while indistinct cognition was sensible, whether it was obscure or confused. Baumgarten distinguishes himself from other members of the Leibnizian-Wolffian school by insisting that distinctness was not the only perfection cognition could possess. In the *Reflections on Poetry*, he argues that "extensively clear" representations were more poetic than obscure representations or clear and distinct representations, because they represent more than obscure representations, but do so in a way that is less dry and more lively than the clear and distinct representations found in logical demonstrations.[64] By combining a number of clear representations, poetry can achieve the same degree of clarity as logical demonstrations, even if all of the sensible representations they contain are indistinct. In the *Metaphysics*, Baumgarten extends his account of extensive clarity from poetic representation to sensible cognition, arguing that extensively clear cognition derives its clarity from "the multitude of notes" it contains, as opposed to the "the clarity of the notes" themselves, the latter being associated with the intensive clarity of logic and the intellectual cognition of the superior cognitive faculty. Even though Baumgarten does not appeal to the concept of extensive clarity in his

---

[59] Baumgarten, *Metaphysics*, §533.
[60] Baumgarten, *Metaphysics*, §501.
[61] Baumgarten, *Metaphysics*, §503.
[62] Baumgarten, *Metaphysics*, §520.
[63] See McQuillan, "Clarity and Distinctness in Eighteenth Century Germany," 149–159.
[64] Baumgarten, *Reflections on Poetry*, §13–§17.

later works, and it is not mentioned in his *Aesthetics*, the account he presents in the *Metaphysics* is, nevertheless, an important step in the development of his new science, because it helps to define the difference between sensible and intellectual cognition, as well as the perfection of sensible cognition.

Baumgarten's *Philosophical Letters* contains several passages that are similarly helpful for understanding his aesthetics. For instance, in the second letter, Baumgarten addresses the relationship between philosophy, logic, and aesthetics. He begins with a distinction between organic philosophy and logic, which acknowledges that "organic" philosophy can be identified with logic "in a broader sense," but also suggests that they should be distinguished, since the name "logic" as well as "the habits of most logicians" confirm the objection that they are primarily concerned with distinct cognition and the superior cognitive faculties.[65] Objecting to the narrowness of this conception of logic, as he had in the *Reflections on Poetry*, Baumgarten notes that human beings possess "many more faculties in our souls that serve for cognition than just the understanding or reason."[66] For this reason, he continues, "logic seems to promise more than it can deliver, if it wants to improve cognition in general, but only concerns itself with distinct insight and its proper demonstration."[67] For philosophy to be truly organic, or systematic, logic would have to be supplemented by a special science that would articulate "the laws of sensible and lively cognition."[68] Identifying aesthetics as this special science, Baumgarten divides it into two parts.[69] The first (theoretical) has to do with "cognition itself," while the second (practical) part concerns "lively presentation in general."[70] Baumgarten briefly discusses theoretical aesthetics, which includes the art of attention, memory, abstraction, as well as the "aesthetic empiric" or "art of improving one's experience."[71] He distinguishes the latter from the "logical empiric," which is solely concerned with drawing general conclusions from distinct concepts, judgments, and explanations. Baumgarten spends some time enumerating the benefits of these arts, but says at the end of the letter that he does not have time to discuss the second, practical part of aesthetics. Another one of the *Philosophical Letters* extends this discussion, though, again, Baumgarten does not have much to

---

[65] Baumgarten, *Texte zur Grundlegung der Ästhetik*, 69. Baumgarten's reference to "organic" philosophy in this passage suggests that he is referring to his own *Outline of Philosophical Encyclopedia*, whose first chapter is devoted to "organic" philosophy. See Baumgarten, *Texte zur Grundlegung der Ästhetik*, 98, n. 218 and Baumgarten, *Sciagraphia*, §7.

[66] Baumgarten, *Texte zur Grundlegung der Ästhetik*, 69.

[67] Baumgarten, *Texte zur Grundlegung der Ästhetik*, 69.

[68] Baumgarten, *Texte zur Grundlegung der Ästhetik*, 69. Kant also refers to the critique of pure reason as a "special science." See Kant, *Critique of Pure Reason*, A11/B24.

[69] Baumgarten, *Texte zur Grundlegung der Ästhetik*, 69.

[70] Baumgarten, *Texte zur Grundlegung der Ästhetik*, 69.

[71] Baumgarten, *Texte zur Grundlegung der Ästhetik*, 70.

say about practical aesthetics.[72] Instead, he discusses some of the antecedents of aesthetics, including works by Aristotle and Cicero, Bouhours and
Crousaz, Bodmer and Breitinger, and especially Bilfinger, whose elucidations of Wolff's metaphysics (*Dilucidationes philosophicae de Deo, anima
humana, mundo et generalibus rerum affectionibus*, 1725) had sought to do
for "the faculties of sensation, imagination, attention, abstraction, and memory" what Aristotle's logic had done for the understanding.[73] Baumgarten
treats his aesthetics as an extension of Bilfinger's project, though he also
plans to include "a treatise on the improvement and use of the faculties of
invention, wit, astuteness, taste or the sensible power of judgment, foresight,
anticipation, and faculty of designating one's thoughts," as well as an account
of "the method of beautiful, lively, sharp thinking" and "the conventional
signs for beautifully represented things."[74] Baumgarten indicates that all of
this material would belong to the first, theoretical part of aesthetics, which
could be presented in a short volume on the "wealth, nobility and greatness,
probability, liveliness, persuasiveness, movingness and stirringness" (*dem
Reichtum, dem edlen und großen, dem wahrscheinlichen, dem lebhaften,
dem überredenden, dem bewegenden und rürenden*) of "beautiful thoughts"
(*schöner Gedancken*). The second, practical part of aesthetics would have to
"interpret the general theory of beautiful cognition in an accurate way" and
then distinguish several other, more specific parts of aesthetics, insofar as
they are "expressed either in bound or unbound discourse, so that the former
would be thoroughly examined by poetics and the latter by rhetoric."[75] This
distinction corresponds to the divisions Baumgarten proposed in the last section of his *Reflections on Poetry* and could even be taken to imply that the
Reflections on Poetry was already a contribution to practical aesthetics, since
poetics is the part of practical aesthetics that concerns "bound" or "perfect"
discourse.[76]

The publication of the *Aesthetics* was also preceded by a series of lectures
that Baumgarten delivered in Frankfurt an der Oder starting in 1742–1743.
While the contents and organization of these lectures remain uncertain, we
know that Baumgarten shared the text of his lectures with Meier, perhaps
as early as 1745.[77] Meier used this text as the basis for his own lectures on
aesthetics in Halle in 1745–1746, as well as his *Foundations of All Beautiful
Sciences*, which appeared in three volumes in 1748–1750—even before

---

[72] This letter was only recently discovered and published. See Kliche, "Über einen Fund," 54–65. See
also Nannini, "Baumgarten and the Lost Letters of Aletheophilus," 23–43.

[73] Kliche, "Über einen Fund," 58. See also Bilfinger, *Dilucidationes philosophicae*, §268.

[74] Kliche, "Über einen Fund," 59.

[75] Kliche, "Über einen Fund," 59.

[76] Baumgarten, *Reflections on Poetry*, §117.

[77] Bergmann, *Die Begründung*, 23.

Baumgarten's *Aesthetics* was published. There are important differences
between Meier's *Foundations* and Baumgarten's *Aesthetics*, particularly
regarding their structure. However, if Baumgarten's *Lectures on Aesthetics*
(*Kollegium über die Ästhetik*) is any indication of the contents of his lectures,
we can probably attribute these differences to Meier's reorganization of the
material with which Baumgarten provided him. The text of these *Lectures*
was published by Bernard Poppe at the beginning of the twentieth century,
based on student transcripts from around 1750.[78] Like the *Reflections on
Poetry* and *Metaphysics*, Baumgarten's *Lectures* identifies aesthetics as a
science of the indistinct, sensible cognition of the inferior cognitive faculty
(sensibility) and distinguish it from logic as the science of the distinct cognition of the superior cognitive faculty (intellect). Like the *Philosophical
Letters*, they also discuss a number of antecedents for the science of aesthetics, tracing its emergence from the ancient Egyptian, Chaldean, and Celtic
sources, through classical Greek and Roman thought, as well as modern philosophers like Descartes, Leibniz, Wolff, Bilfinger, Bouhours, and Crousaz.
However, there are also a number of important differences between the
Lectures and Baumgarten's earlier works. Unlike the *Reflections on Poetry*
and *Metaphysics*, the *Lectures* does not appeal to the concept of extensive
clarity. Instead, it identifies the perfection of sensible cognition with "beauty"
and its imperfection with "ugliness."[79] According to the *Lectures*, there are
three aspects of the beauty of cognition: the beauty of thoughts, their order,
and their expression or designation.[80] The first, the beauty of thoughts, has
to do with the beauty of the cognition itself, rather than any object it might
represent, since beautiful things can be cognized in ugly ways and ugly things
can be thought in ways that are beautiful. The second, the beauty of order,
concerns the agreement of thoughts with one another and with their objects.[81]
The third, the beauty of expression or designation, uses signs to represent the
beauty and order of thoughts. These signs may be linguistic, as in a poem, or
visual symbols used by painters, but they must be beautiful, and beautifully
disposed, in order to represent beautiful things and thoughts in a beautiful
way.[82] In a subsequent passage, Baumgarten also notes that there are six
"characteristics" (*Kennzeichen*) of beautiful cognition, which include richness, nobility, truth, light, thoroughness, and life (*Reichtum, Adel, Wahrheit,
Licht, Gründlichkeit, und Leben*), although he alternates between "certainty"
(*Gewissheit*) and "thoroughness" (*Gründlichkeit*) at different points in the

[78] See Poppe, *Baumgarten*, 61–258. The beginning of the *Lectures* has also been republished in
Baumgarten, *Texte zur Grundlegung der Ästhetik*, 79–83.
[79] Poppe, *Baumgarten*, 80 (§16).
[80] Poppe, *Baumgarten*, 81 (§17).
[81] Poppe, *Baumgarten*, 82 (§19).
[82] Poppe, *Baumgarten*, 82–83 (§20).

same passage.[83] This list is similar to, but not the same as, the list of qualities that Baumgarten includes in his discussion of theoretical aesthetics in the *Philosophical Letters* as well as his enumeration of the perfections that constitute beautiful cognition in the *Aesthetics*. Yet their differences suggest that Baumgarten was still working through some aspects of his new science.

The first two volumes of Baumgarten's *Aesthetics* adhere closely to the plan laid out in his *Lectures on Aesthetics*.[84] Like the *Lectures on Aesthetics*, the *Aesthetics* defines Baumgarten's new science as "the science of sensible cognition," where "sensible cognition" is understood as "the entirety of all representations which remain below the level of distinctness."[85] This is a consistent feature of Baumgarten's aesthetics from the *Reflections on Poetry*, *Metaphysics*, and *Philosophical Letters*, as well as the *Lectures on Aesthetics*. However, the *Aesthetics* is similar to the *Lectures on Aesthetics*, and different from Baumgarten's earlier works, because it identifies the perfection of indistinct, sensible cognition as "beauty" without referring to extensive clarity.[86] Baumgarten also retains the distinction between theoretical and practical aesthetics that he had proposed in his *Philosophical Letters*. He continues to employ the three-part division of theoretical aesthetics that he had proposed in his *Philosophical Letters* and *Lectures*, though he gives them different names. Baumgarten now calls the first part of theoretical aesthetics "Heuristic" and charges it with prescribing rules for "things and thinking of things."[87] The second part, "Methodology," sets the rules for "clear order."[88] The third part, "Semiotic," addresses "the signs of beautiful cognition and order."[89] This structure corresponds to the distinction between the beauty of thoughts, the beauty of order, and the beauty of expression that Baumgarten had drawn in his *Lectures*. Baumgarten includes a similar distinction in the first chapter of the *Aesthetics*, though they are now identified as three parts of the "universal beauty of sensible cognition."[90] A few paragraphs later, however, Baumgarten says, "the richness, greatness, truth, clarity, certainty, and life of cognition comprise the perfection of every cognition, insofar as they are in agreement with each other in a representation" and, as such,

---

[83] Poppe, *Baumgarten*, 83 (§22).
[84] This should not be surprising, since the text of the *Lectures* published by Poppe likely dates from the same year that the first volume of the *Aesthetics* was published. See Poppe, *Baumgarten*, 61–64.
[85] Baumgarten, *Aesthetica/Ästhetik*, §1, §17.
[86] It is sometimes argued that richness (*ubertas*) is a substitute for extensive clarity, since it also pertains to the "copiousness" and "abundance" of the notes contained in sensible cognition. See Gregor, "Baumgarten's Aesthetics," 381, n. 33 and Guyer, *A History of Modern Aesthetics*, Vol. 1, 332.
[87] Baumgarten, *Aesthetica/Ästhetik*, §13.
[88] Baumgarten, *Aesthetica/Ästhetik*, §13.
[89] Baumgarten, *Aesthetica/Ästhetik*, §13.
[90] Baumgarten, *Aesthetica/Ästhetik*, §18–§20.

constitute the "universal" beauty of sensible cognition.[91] It seems reasonable to treat richness, greatness, truth, clarity, certainty, and life as characteristics of the first part of the "universal beauty of sensible cognition," namely, "the beauty of things and thoughts."[92] Yet it should also be noted that the list of characteristics is somewhat different from the list Baumgarten includes in his *Lectures*. There, he had mentioned richness, nobility, truth, light, thoroughness, and life, but, in the *Aesthetics*, he replaces nobility (*Adel*) with greatness (*magnitudo/Größe*), light (*Licht*) with clarity (*claritas/Klarheit*), and settles on certainty (*certitudo/Gewissheit*) rather than thoroughness (*Gründlichkeit*). This framework seems to hold until the second volume, where Baumgarten adds a discussion of aesthetic light (*lux aesthetica/ästhetisches Licht*) and aesthetic persuasion (*persuasio aesthetica/ästhetische Überredung*), instead of proceeding to the sections on clarity, certainty, and life that one would expect.[93] Baumgarten was unable to complete these sections before his death and did not come close to finishing the chapters on methodology and semiotics. Consequently, the *Aesthetics* remains incomplete as a formal presentation of the first, theoretical part of Baumgarten's new science. Nor does it have anything to say about the second, practical part of aesthetics that he envisioned.

Despite its incompleteness, Baumgarten's *Aesthetics* remains an important text. Within the context of the German philosophy in the eighteenth century, Baumgarten's *Aesthetics* represents an intriguing synthesis of Pietism and Wolffianism, religion and philosophy, sensibility and reason. It is also an important source for the history of aesthetics, which would remain incomplete without a careful examination of Baumgarten's *Aesthetics*. Meier's *Foundations* may have been the first systematic treatise on aesthetics to be published; yet the *Aesthetics* is still the first attempt at a formal presentation of Baumgarten's new science of aesthetics by the philosopher who coined the term and introduced aesthetics as a new part of philosophy. The distinction between theoretical and practical aesthetics that Baumgarten uses to structure his treatise was a familiar way of distinguishing the parts of logic in eighteenth-century Germany, though Baumgarten uses this distinction to a very different end, limiting the scope of logic and carving out a space for

---

[91] Baumgarten, *Aesthetica/Ästhetik*, §22.
[92] Baumgarten, *Aesthetica/Ästhetik*, §18–§20.
[93] For the original play of the *Aesthetica*, see the synopsis in Baumgarten, *Aesthetica/Ästhetik*, 4–11. On the rushed publication of the second volume of the *Aesthetics*, see Baumgarten, *Aesthetica/Ästhetik*, 597–599. It is particularly unfortunate that Baumgarten never completed the sections on the "life" of aesthetic cognition, since he calls life the "foremost" (*primariam*) and "loveliest" (*venustae*) beauty of cognition. See Baumgarten, *Aesthetica/Ästhetik*, §36, Vol. 2, 597–598. See McQuillan, "The Aesthetic Perfection of Life in Baumgarten, Meier, and Kant," (Forthcoming).

a new kind of cognitive perfection.[94] Instead of treating the clear and distinct cognition of the superior cognitive faculty as the standard of perfection for all cognition, the theoretical part of the *Aesthetics* presents an alternative account of the perfection of sensible cognition. The aesthetic perfection of sensible cognition is analogous to the logical perfection of intellectual cognition, but it is carefully distinguished from logic and the distinct, intellectual cognition with which it is concerned. It is also noteworthy that Baumgarten identifies the perfection of indistinct, sensible cognition with beauty. Indeed, this constitutes a genuinely new conception of beauty, which cannot be reduced to proportion, harmony, symmetry, or any of the other conceptions of beauty, such as unity in variety, with which philosophers are familiar. The *Aesthetics* defends an epistemic conception of beauty, which primarily refers to the perfection of a particular kind of cognition—indistinct sensible cognition. Baumgarten's claim that the perfection of sensible cognition consists in, or is characterized by, some combination of richness, nobility, greatness, truth, light, clarity, thoroughness, persuasion, certainty, and life is innovative, even though his treatment of these characteristics is incomplete. The fact that he planned to follow his treatment of these characteristics with chapters on methodology and semiotics, as well as a separate section on practical aesthetics, also suggests that Baumgarten's *Aesthetics* was not merely a theoretical exercise. Baumgarten thought his insights had practical applications, which could be used to improve poetry and rhetoric, the other arts, and, indeed, all sensible cognition. For these reasons, and many others, Baumgarten's *Aesthetics* should be carefully studied.

OUTLINE AND OVERVIEW

The chapters included in this volume are meant to serve three purposes. First, they are meant to introduce readers to Baumgarten's aesthetics and highlight some of its most distinctive features. Second, they are intended to situate Baumgarten's aesthetics within its historical and philosophical context, emphasizing important precedents for Baumgarten's aesthetics as well as its reception among other eighteenth-century German philosophers. Third, and finally, they establish connections between Baumgarten's aesthetics and contemporary philosophy, proving that interest in this subject is not merely antiquarian.

---

[94] Thomasius's *Introduction to the Doctrine of Reason* (*Einleitung zur Vernunftlehre*, 1691) and *Practice of the Doctrine of Reason* (*Ausübung der Vernunftlehre*, 1691) are helpful examples of the distinction between theoretical and practical logic in early modern Germany. Wolff also appeals to this distinction in a discussion of his *German Logic*. See Wolff, *Ausführliche Nachricht*, §55.

The first two chapters of the volume provide a general overview of Baumgarten's new science from different but complementary perspectives. Chapter 1, "Baumgarten's Invention of Aesthetics," is a translation by Mauricio González of an essay by one of the most renowned Baumgarten scholars of the twentieth century, Ursula Franke. Franke's earlier book, *Art as Cognition: The Role of Sensibility in the Aesthetics of Alexander Gottlieb Baumgarten* (*Kunst als Erkenntniß: Die Rolle der Sinnlichkeit in der Ästhetik des Alexander Gottlieb Baumgarten*, 1972), is a standard reference for Baumgarten scholars around the world. Franke updates the argument of *Art as Cognition* in "Baumgarten's Invention of Aesthetics," contending that "in Baumgarten's *Aesthetics*, there emerges for the first time an understanding of art as the presentation or representation of the absolute, which would then, with its own claim to truth, come expressly into play in the philosophies of art in German idealism and have a lasting influence on modern philosophy of art to this day."[95] In addition to surveying the recent scholarly literature on Baumgarten's aesthetics, and situating it in relation to Leibniz, Wolff, and the rationalist, academic philosophy of the German Enlightenment in the eighteenth century, Franke looks forward to the philosophy art that would rise to prominence with the German idealists in the nineteenth century. Stefanie Buchenau's chapter, "Baumgarten's *Aesthetics*: Topics and the Modern *Ars Inveniendi*," takes a different approach, relating Baumgarten's aesthetics to the search for a new "art of invention" (*ars inveniendi*) among early modern European philosophers. In the classical Aristotelian tradition, *inventio* refers to "the finding of topics to be treated or arguments to be used."[96] Early modern European philosophers from Francis Bacon to Christian Wolff sought to systematize this process and generate a reliable method of invention, which would aid in the discovery of new truths and the generation of new knowledge. Baumgarten took up this project, Buchenau argues, by looking back to Cicero's rhetoric and using it as a model for his aesthetics.

Chapters 3 and 4 deal with central issues in Baumgarten's aesthetics—beauty and truth. In the third chapter, Matthew McAndrew attempts to solve the "riddle" of Baumgarten's aesthetics—the apparently different, and possibly conflicting, definitions of beauty that Baumgarten presents in the *Metaphysics* and *Aesthetics*. Baumgarten defines beauty as "the perfection of an appearance" (*perfectio phaenomenon*) in §662 of the *Metaphysics*, but he says beauty is "the perfection of sensible cognition" (*perfectio cognitionis sensitivae*) in §14 of the *Aesthetics*. Scholars have debated whether the definition in the *Metaphysics* refers to the objective perfection of a beautiful object, whether the definition in the *Aesthetics* refers to a subjective perfection of

---

[95] Franke, "Baumgarten's Invention of Aesthetics," 29.
[96] Buchenau, *The Founding of Aesthetics in the German Enlightenment*, 18.

cognition, and whether these definitions are contradictory or compatible.[97] McAndrew maintains that Baumgarten is describing the perfection of sensible cognition as beautiful, rather than defining beauty, in §14 of the *Aesthetics*, so that the definition of beauty in §662 of the *Metaphysics* remains the only definition of beauty in Baumgarten's works. McAndrew elucidates this definition and highlights Baumgarten's conception of "appearance" (*phaenomenon*), which he takes to refer to the object of sensible cognition, that is cognized confusedly and indistinctly, in keeping with the Wolffian definition of sensibility. Angelica Nuzzo focuses on the "truth" of this confused, indistinct, sensible cognition in chapter 4. Against those who would subordinate "aesthetic truth" (*veritas aesthetica*) to logical truth or truth in general, Nuzzo argues that Baumgarten's "pluralization" of truth is, in fact, one of his most important contributions to philosophy. By pluralism, Nuzzo means that that there is no single, unqualified truth, but different, specifically determined, and irreducible kinds of truth. Baumgarten's conception of aesthetic truth checks the privilege that Wolff and other early modern rationalists had afforded the higher cognitive faculties—the understanding and reason—in the cognition of truth. But it also binds together a theory of cognition and a theory of the liberal arts, so that the beauty of sensible cognition is embodied in beautiful works of art that possess their own, aesthetic truth. Baumgarten typically draws his examples of this kind of truth from poetry and rhetoric, but Nuzzo shows that aesthetic truth is an expression of the reality of human cognitive experience, in all its specificity and concreteness, so it is certainly not limited to these particular arts.

Chapters 5, 6, and 7 help to situate Baumgarten's aesthetics in its historical context by looking at some of the sources from which it was drawn and the ways in which it was first articulated and defended. In chapter 5, "Pietist *Aisthēsis* and Moral Education in the Works of Alexander Gottlieb Baumgarten," Simon Grote explores the theological sources of Baumgarten's aesthetics— a context that is often neglected by historians of philosophy, though it is especially important for understanding Baumgarten. Grote shows that, while Baumgarten is often credited with coining the term "aesthetics," the word had already been used by Lutheran and Pietist theologians, including August Hermann Francke, decades before Baumgarten published his *Reflections on Poetry*. These theologians used the term in order to explain "the means by which God communicates with human beings" and "the involvement of human affects in that process of communication."[98] They maintained that the interpretation of scripture is not a purely intellectual exercise, but depends on *aisthēsis* as a kind of "spiritual sensation" that allows the "sanctified souls"

---

[97] See McAndrew's survey of the scholarly literature in McAndrew, "Beauty and Appearance," 85–86.
[98] See Grote, "Pietist *Aisthēsis* and Moral Education," 130.

of those who have been "reborn" to grasp both the literal and the spiritual meaning of the Bible. Grote argues that there is both biographical and textual evidence that Baumgarten was familiar with this conception of *aisthēsis* and that it is closely related to the new science that he proposed in his *Reflections on Poetry*. This might be surprising to those who regard Baumgarten as a Wolffian and a rationalist, but J. Colin McQuillan suggests, in chapter 6, that Baumgarten may not have been the Wolffian rationalist that he is often supposed to be. There can be little doubt that Baumgarten's study of Wolff during his time in Halle and Jena was intellectually transformative for him. And he clearly embraces some of the most important doctrines of Leibnizian-Wolffian rationalism, including the theory of monads and the universality of the principle of sufficient reason. McQuillan points out, however, that Baumgarten seems to limit the application of Wolff's mathematical method to the "presentation" of philosophical doctrines. He also restricts the scope of logic in a way that undermines the "marriage of reason and experience" (*connubium rationis et experientiae*) that Wolff sought to promote by introducing a qualitative difference between sensible and intellectual cognition—a difference that cannot be resolved through analysis. This difference is essential to Baumgarten's aesthetics, because it defines the object of aesthetics—sensible cognition—and distinguishes its perfection—beauty—from the perfection of clear and distinct, intellectual cognition, with which logic is concerned. In chapter 7, Alessandro Nannini reconstructs the two paths through which Baumgarten's aesthetics was initially articulated and defended.[99] Baumgarten himself blazed one of these trails in his lectures in Frankfurt an der Oder and his published writings; yet we should not forget the contributions of Georg Friedrich Meier, who Nannini calls the "co-founder" of aesthetics. Unlike Baumgarten's *Aesthetics*, Meier's *Foundations of All Beautiful Sciences*, is complete—though there is some debate about how faithfully it represents Baumgarten's plan and which aspects of the *Foundations* are original to Meier. Nannini also emphasizes Meier's polemical contributions to aesthetics, especially his defense of Baumgarten's definition of poetry and his criticism of Gottsched's poetics, which helped to establish the place of aesthetics within philosophy and the legitimacy of philosophical inquiry into the liberal arts and fine arts.

Chapters 8–10 address the early reception of Baumgarten's aesthetics. In chapter 8, "An Exercise in Humanity: Baumgarten and Mendelssohn on the Importance of Aesthetic Training," Anne Pollok focuses on Moses Mendelssohn's appropriation of Baumgarten's conception of "aesthetic training" (*exercitatio aesthetica*). Pollok argues that Baumgarten's conception of

---

[99] Nannini, "The Co-Founding of Aesthetics," 179.

aesthetic training was important for Mendelssohn because it takes up one of the central concerns of German philosophers in the eighteenth century—the perfection of the whole human being.[100] This concern led philosophers like Mendelssohn to see Baumgarten's aesthetics as a contribution to psychology and a guide to the improvement of all of humanity's mental faculties—the lower cognitive faculty of sensibility as much as the higher cognitive faculties of understanding and reason. For Mendelssohn, humanity can only make progress toward perfection, and achieve its vocation, if it cultivates all of these faculties. Johann Gottfried Herder takes a different approach, which is described in chapter 9, "Herder's Engagement with Baumgarten," by Hans Adler. Unlike Mendelssohn, who stresses the complementarity of the higher and lower faculties, and the necessity of cultivating all the powers of the human mind, Herder treats sensibility as the source of the obscure cognition that constitutes the "ground" or "foundation" of the human soul (*fundus animae*)—all other cognition, no matter how clear, distinct, abstract, and intellectual it might be, ultimately derives from this "dark region" of the soul. Baumgarten's aesthetics is important for Herder precisely because it values sensible cognition and makes it the object of an authentically human philosophy, grounded in psychology and anthropology. Yet he still sees Baumgarten as a "second rate" philosopher, who remained too closely bound to tradition, particularly in his academic Latin and in the Wolffian form he imposed on his works. More pressing is Herder's complaint that Baumgarten "built his aesthetics back to front by taking the foundational concepts as given without testing their reality," that is, their foundation in sensibility.[101] Herder's teacher, Immanuel Kant, presents a related critique of Baumgarten's aesthetics in a footnote to the 'Transcendental Aesthetic' of the *Critique of Pure Reason*. Although he calls Baumgarten an "excellent analyst," Kant also thought Baumgarten's Wolffian rationalism had led his aesthetics astray, because he did not realize that judgments of taste are grounded in merely empirical principles.[102] And while Kant often reiterated this judgment, and presented a profoundly different account of the relationship between sensibility and beauty in his *Critique of the Power of Judgment*, Robert R. Clewis calls our attention to a point of agreement among Baumgarten, Mendelssohn, and Kant in chapter 10, "The Majesty of Cognition: The Sublime in Baumgarten, Mendelssohn, and Kant." Clewis points out that Kant was not the first philosopher to connect sublimity and morality in his aesthetics. Although it has received little

---

[100] Pollok, "An Exercise in Humanity," 194.

[101] Adler, "Herder's Engagement with Baumgarten," 226.

[102] Kant, *Critique of Pure Reason*, A21/B35. Kant later rejected the view that the principles of aesthetic judgment are "merely empirical," but still denied the possibility of a science of aesthetics. See McQuillan, "Kant's Critique of Baumgarten's Aesthetics," 69–80 and McQuillan, "Kant on the Science of Aesthetics and the Critique of Taste," 113–132.

attention until now, Baumgarten's *Aesthetics* contains an extensive discussion of the sublime, which is closely related to the practical aims of his new science, the cultivation of moral virtue, and the constitution of the "happy aesthetician" *(felix aestheticus)*. Clewis notes that Baumgarten conceives of sublimity as a perfection of sensible cognition, while Mendelssohn regards it as the perfection of certain kinds of objects, which reveals the goodness and perfection of the world. Kant rejects the perfectionism of Baumgarten's and Mendelssohn's accounts of the sublime, but he seems to agree that virtue is sublime, and arouses moral feeling, even if he does not specifically distinguish the moral sublime from the mathematical and dynamical sublime in the *Critique of the Power of Judgment.*[103]

Chapters 11 and 12 are a departure from the previous chapters, because they extend beyond the eighteenth century and place Baumgarten's aesthetics in dialogue with contemporary philosophers. In chapter 11, "The Discipline of Aesthetics Is the Aesthetics of Discipline: Baumgarten from Foucault's Perspective," Christoph Menke contends that aesthetics is "the model after which Foucault thinks disciplinary power in *Discipline and Punish.*"[104] Foucault's *Discipline and Punish* (*Surveiller et punir*, 1975) is usually regarded as a study of the transformation of punishment in Europe and North America during the seventeenth, eighteenth, and nineteenth centuries—a time when elaborate public executions, meant to display the might and majesty of the sovereign, were replaced by more humane punishments behind the walls of the prison. In fact, Foucault argues, the disciplinary practices that were employed in prisons during this time were also used in the military, in hospitals, in factories, and in schools. Together, these institutions constituted a disciplinary regime that sought to create a new kind of subject—one that would be capable of governing itself, while remaining sufficiently docile and appropriately productive. This might seem far removed from aesthetics, but Menke reminds us that "aesthetic discipline" (*disciplina aesthetica*, translated into German by Mirbach as *ästhetische Lehre*) is an important part of Baumgarten's new science.[105] Baumgarten's discussion of aesthetic discipline follows his treatment of "aesthetic exercise" (*exercitatio aesthetica*) near the beginning of the *Aesthetics*, leading into his account of the "happy aesthetician" (*felix aestheticus*). While Mendelssohn saw this part of the *Aesthetics* as a valuable contribution to the enlightenment project of perfecting the whole

---

[103] Clewis points out that Kant distinguishes between the mathematical, dynamical, and moral (*edel*, "noble") sublime in an earlier work, his *Observations on the Feeling of the Beautiful and Sublime* (1764). Clewis thinks there is good evidence from Kant's examples that he still regarded morality as a special kind of sublimity in the third *Critique*, even if he does not explicitly identify it as such. See Clewis, "The Majesty of Cognition," 263–264.

[104] Menke, "The Discipline of Aesthetics is the Aesthetics of Discipline," 275.

[105] See Baumgarten, *Aesthetica/Ästhetik*, §62–§77.

human being, Menke highlights the ways in which it constitutes a particular kind of modern subjectivity, which cannot be separated from power and ideology. Amelia Hruby also focuses on Baumgarten's conception of the *felix aestheticus* in chapter 12, "The Happy Aesthetician and the Feminist Killjoy: Baumgarten and Ahmed." Hruby uses the work of feminist philosopher Sara Ahmed to ask what kind of "happiness" (*felicitas*) Baumgarten attributes to his "happy" aesthetician. After surveying Baumgarten's sketchy accounts of happiness in works preceding the *Aesthetics*, Hruby focuses on the definition of happy aesthetician as "the one who thinks beautifully" in *Aesthetics* §27. To think beautifully is to perfect one's sensible cognition by bringing different perfections that constitute beauty into a harmonious relationship. Hruby also points out that there is a moral dimension to this conception of happiness, emphasizing the goodness and desirability of beautiful thinking. Against this tendency in Baumgarten's thought, Hruby emphasizes the ways in which his aesthetics can perform a function similar to Ahmed's "feminist killjoy." While the feminist killjoy exposes a "fantasy" of happiness that uses "the language of civility and love" to obscure "violence and power," Baumgarten's aesthetics challenges the privilege that logic, truth, the understanding, and reason have been granted in other philosophical systems, while dignifying faculties, cognitions, and representations that have been considered "lower" or "inferior," and creating a space for difference within philosophy.[106]

---

[106] Hruby, "The Happy Aesthetician and the Feminist Killjoy," 299–302.

Chapter 1

Baumgarten's Invention of Aesthetics

Ursula Franke

In the past decades, Baumgarten research has experienced an extraordinary flourishing. For a long time, the epoch between Wolff and Kant was terra incognita. Since the philosophical revolution that began with Kant, the philosophy of the German Enlightenment and especially its rationalist academic philosophy has more or less fallen into oblivion. If one asks for reasons for the increasing interest in Baumgarten's aesthetics since the 1970s and 1980s, one can cite the crisis of aesthetics at the end of last century as what made it seem necessary to turn back to its historical presuppositions.[1] But above all, the critical confrontation with the hermeneutic situation of that significantly rationalist philosophy stimulated, so to say, the interest in an alternative aesthetic thinking which, not without reason, demanded an updated and ongoing engagement with the founder of philosophical aesthetics, most especially today. For example, the multifaceted contributions to an anthology published in 2016 entitled *Schönes Denken* show the wide range of the concept of sensible cognition that characterizes Baumgarten's invention of aesthetics: "Baumgarten's *ars pulchre cogitandi* captures the border-crossing, interdisciplinary dynamics of the reciprocal relationships between aesthetics, metaphysics, ethics, logic, poetics, rhetoric and law, and thus contains a great potential of scientific references and connections."[2]

It was precisely with this intention that Baumgarten raised an "objection against a unilateral, rationalistic concept of cognition." He was concerned with demonstrating the independence of sensible cognition and complementing the rationalist concept of cognition with the concept of "cognition guided

---

[1] Cf. Caygill, "Erfindung und Neuerfindung der Ästhetik," 233–241. See also Scheer, "Baumgartens Ästhetik und die Krise der von ihm begründeten Disziplin," 108–119.
[2] Allerkamp and Mirbach, *Schönes Denken*, 9.

27

by sensibility."[3] Martin Seel, who follows the trace of philosophical aesthetics in the interconnections between sensibility and the construction of sense, emphasizes: "The career of aesthetics since Baumgarten stems not least from the need to gain freedom of movement in the face of Enlightenment's rationalism, which had become narrow or was perceived as such."[4]

Characterized by the conception of an eclectic nexus between the Leibniz-Wolffian school philosophy and the rhetorical-poetological tradition, Baumgarten's aesthetics exceeds the theoretical framework of poetry, as it is still binding, for instance, in Johann Christoph Gottsched's determination of "poetic words," "poetic writing," and so on.[5] Baumgarten refers to Georg Bernhard Bilfinger, whose *Dilucidationes philosophicae*—a popular textbook of Wolffian philosophy published in Tübingen in 1725—had announced the desideratum of a logic of imagination and had further thought of a philosophical poetics in the track of the Swiss theorists of poetics Bodmer and Breitinger.[6] According to Herder's characterization of the starting point of Baumgarten's "way of thinking," nothing was believed to be more contrary to one another than philosophical reflection and the questions of art and taste.[7] Baumgarten's philosophical program consists in bringing them together and relating them to one another. Baumgarten must have been at least interested in this connection as he was educated in the pietistic orphanage in Halle, which was known for combining philosophical studies with belletrist study of the *schönen Wissenschaften*,[8] that is, rhetoric and poetics. This unusual connection also distinguished Baumgarten's own academic teaching, which he first practiced in Halle in 1737, and then at Viadrina in Frankfurt an der Oder from 1740 onward, where he lived and worked until his death in 1762.[9]

---

[3] On the "critical potential" of philosophical aesthetics and its denunciation of the "absolutization" of the "traditional logocentric concepts of rationality," see Scheer, *Einführung in die philosophische Ästhetik*, specially 1–5 (here 1).

[4] Seel, *Die Kunst der Entzweiung*, 28 and 172; see also Raulet, *"Logica inventionis und episteme esthetike."*

[5] Gottsched, *Versuch einer Critischen Dichtkunst*, I.VII–XII. See also Reiss, "Die Einbürgerung der Ästhetik," 110–138.

[6] Cf. Piselli, "Einige philologische und theoretische Überlegungen zu A.G. Baumgartens *Aesthetica*," 67–70. On the problematic concerning the object of aesthetics, see Franke, *Kunst als Erkenntnis*, 3–14.

[7] Cf. Herder, "Begründung einer Ästhetik," 65–192. The rapport between philosophy and art continues to occupy philosophy; cf. Neumaier, *Grenzgänge zwischen Wissenschaft und Kunst* (2015).

[8] Cf. Strube, "Die Geschichte des Begriffs Schöne Wissenschaften," 136–216.

[9] Cf. Franke, "Baumgarten, Alexander Gottlieb," 367–371—An incomparable portrait of Baumgarten, the "Viadrina's philosophical star," as a teacher was proposed by Louis de Beausobre, who studied law at the Viadrina between 1749 and 1752, and who obviously took part in Baumgarten's lectures. Beausobre is credited with the first French use of the word "esthétique," dating from 1753, according to the *Littré* (https://www.littre.org/definition/esthétique). Cf. Fontius, "Baumgarten und die Literaturbriefe," 571f. and 559 n. 18. On the Viadrina, see also Blänker, "Die Viadrina und Alexander Gottlieb Baumgarten," 299–316.

As to how Baumgarten managed to invent aesthetics in this way, this was for a long time only comprehensible for specialists familiar with the Latin text of Baumgarten's *Aesthetics*, which in spite of its unfinished form, however fragmented, remained voluminous. This has changed fundamentally since 2007, as Dagmar Mirbach published a bilingual [Latin-German] edition, offering for the first time a complete German translation of the *Aesthetics*. Mirbach's edition also contains a detailed introduction that provides comprehensive biographical information about Baumgarten, the history of publication of the *Aesthetics* in the eighteenth century and of its previous editions in the twentieth century, as well as the current state of research, particularly in Italy and Germany.[10] The critical apparatus of their edition should be highlighted; for in addition to the paragraphs of the *Metaphysics* and *Ethics* to which Baumgarten refers in his *Aesthetics*, and a substantial index of research literature and a register of subjects and names, it also contains a very complete glossary of terms and phrases used in the *Aesthetics*.[11] Moreover, further impulses for Baumgarten research should follow from the critical Latin-German edition of the *Aesthetics* that Constanze Peres has been preparing for some time; this ought to contain also a complete translation and additional texts, in part newly translated, that the research has been using for the interpretation of the *Aesthetics* for decades.[12]

In a trivial sense, the fact that Alexander Gottlieb Baumgarten invented aesthetics is a commonplace in the history of philosophy: not only as the title of his work, the *Aesthetics*, but also as designation of a subdiscipline of philosophy, the term "aesthetics" emerges for the first time in Baumgarten. However, this study seeks at the same time to understand and ground the thesis of Baumgarten's invention of aesthetics in a more demanding sense: according to my reading, in Baumgarten's *Aesthetics* there emerges for the first time an understanding of art as the presentation or representation of the absolute, which would then, with its own claim to truth, come expressly into

---

[10] Especially instructive are Mirbach's analyses of the relationship between Baumgarten's *Aesthetics* and his *Ethica*, which has remained until now quite disattended, and on which she deepened in a study devoted to it (Mirbach, "Ingenium venustum und magnitudo pectoris").

[11] For the Mirbach edition (= Baumgarten, *Aesthetica/Ästhetik*, 2007) cf. moreover, the very informative review by Armin Emmel ("Alexander Gottlieb Baumgarten, *Ästhetik*")—Already after the First World War, the *Kantgesellschaft* planned a German translation of the *Aesthetics*, which was not carried out; see the notes in *Kant-Studien* 20 (1915), 137 and 22 (1918), 201.

[12] The edition prepared by Constanze Peres with the collaboration of Peter Witzmann is intended to provide a comprehensive text commentary and, in addition to the *Aesthetics* (bilingual edition and in a new translation), also parts of Baumgarten's *Metaphysica* (after its seventh edition from 1779), *Acroasis logica* (1761), *Ethica* (after its third edition of 1763), *Philosophia generalis* (1770), *Sciagraphia encyclopaediae philosophicae* (1769), as well as excerpts of the *Philosophische Briefe von Aletheophilus* (1741); it intends to include also a complete version of the *Kollegnachschrift* of Baumgarten's lectures on aesthetic edited by Bernhard Poppe and excerpts from Georg Friedrich Meier's *Anfangsgründen aller schönen Wissenschaften* (after its second edition from 1754).

play in the philosophies of art in German idealism and have a lasting influence on modern philosophy of art to this day.[13]

This reading, which I already defended in my dissertation entitled *Kunst
als Erkenntnis* in 1972, diverges from the interpretation of Baumgarten's
aesthetic theory in the context of an understanding of aesthetics as *aisthesis*.
My reading is understood against the background of the philosophical
interest of cognition in the unity of reason, which had been sharpened by
Kant's critical philosophy, as well as modern European philosophy of art
and art theory, which developed from the Renaissance to the early nineteenth
century, bringing about a change in the concept of art—one whose emergence
exposes the central problem of modern aesthetics and its historiography.[14]

In order to justify this reading, the following section deals with sensible
cognition and its function in the overall context of aesthetics as well as the
peculiar form of sensible representation that is the source of artistic cognition
and its expression in the arts.

In this study I assert that sensibility is the source of artistic cognition and
its expression in the arts, which is due to my understanding of Baumgarten's
aesthetic theory as the philosophical foundation of art as cognition. In
the overall context of the *Aesthetics*—this is my thesis—Baumgarten's
conception of sensibility and sensible cognition only attains its full brisance
when due attention is paid to the noteworthy rank of poetry, music, and the
visual arts [*bildende Kunst*] as the prominent objects of sensible cognition as
artistic cognition. It will have to be asked whether, in the end, the intention
of the founding father of aesthetics—as Baumgarten could in fact be called in
the sense described above—is in this way fully acknowledged.

In what follows, I begin by considering sensible cognition as the theory
of sensible perception, recalling Baumgarten's own explanation of the word
"aesthetics"; then I consider his understanding of aesthetics as an "art of the
analogue of reason" [*Kunst des Vernunftähnlichen*] (*ars analogi rationis*) and
move on to the peculiar form of perception proper of sensible cognition as a
cognitio clara et confusa. Then, I put together those bricks that form the basis
for my interpretation of the epistemological function of sensibility in the overall
context of the *Aesthetics*: the role of art and the arts, which is to be seen in light
of the unity of reason, while removed from the cognitive interest of the sciences

---

[13] As for the "aesthetics of truth," which, "prepared by Baumgarten's teaching of the 'veritas aesthetica,' is first developed by Schelling and Hegel," see Schmücker, *Was ist Kunst?* 23–49, here 28.
Modern aesthetics of truth understands truth "neither as an *adequatio rerum et intellectus* nor as a
judgment's agreement with an objective state of affairs [*Sachverhalt*]. Nor does it use the concept
of truth in the sense of formal logic or of consensus theory. In the eyes of the aesthetics of truth,
this concept rather characterizes a metaphysical idea, whose outstanding or even unique form-of-
presence [*Präsenzform*] are works of art" (Schmücker, *Was ist Kunst?* 29).

[14] See Franke, "Zeichenkonzeptionen in der Kunstphilosophie und Ästhetik . . ." esp. 1232 f. et
passim.

of art [*Kunstwissenschaften*], both of rhetoric and poetics. As a next step, I discuss the significance of beauty, in view of Baumgarten's reception of Leibniz's determination of the soul as a force or power [*Kraft*] to represent the universe (*vis repraesentativa universi*). After that, the metaphysical reconstitution of aesthetic theory in Baumgarten can be asserted; and further, in connection with the interpretation of the *Aesthetics*, the transformation of rhetoric in particular is to be elaborated. Furthermore, I assert the cultural-theoretical implications that result from the interweaving of philosophical aesthetics and cultural sciences [*Kulturwissenschaften*]. Finally, I take issue with the function of Baumgarten's aesthetic theory (which has so far been neglected) as a second instrumental philosophy alongside logic, as well as its relationship to the *Aesthetics*, and problematize their connections and differences. In order to stimulate further research, I propose some concluding considerations with questions regarding the applicability of Baumgarten's aesthetics with regard to current discourses. In this context, I deal not only with efforts of actualization in the recent Baumgarten research, which I believe require a critical comment. Instead, I am particularly interested in the possible relevance of Baumgarten's aesthetics for philosophy of culture, for art studies, and not least for contemporary literary history and its potential for stimulating and orientating art today.

On the one hand, the course of my considerations takes as its point of departure the determinations of aesthetics, which its inventor explained by way of synonyms in the "Preliminary Remarks" (*Prolegomena*) to his *Aesthetics*: "Aesthetics (theory of the liberal arts [*freien Künste*], lower doctrine of cognition, art of beautiful thinking [*schönen Denkens*], art of the analogues of reason) is the science of sensible cognition."[15] On the other hand, a guideline for my interpretation is the aim stipulated for the "science of sensible cognition," which Baumgarten also formulates in the "Prolegomena," in reference to his *Metaphysica*: "The purpose of aesthetics is the perfection of sensible cognition as such. This, however, is beauty. And what ought to be avoided is its imperfection as such. This, however, is ugliness."[16]

AISTHESIS, THE ORIGIN OF "AESTHETICS" AND AESTHETIC THINKING

The first translation of parts of the *Aesthetics* into German, carried out by Hans Rudolf Schweizer, was published in 1973. Schweizer's attempt to make

---

[15] See Baumgarten, *Aesthetica/Ästhetik*, §1: "AESTHETICA (theoria liberalium artium, gnoseologia inferior, ars pulchre cogitandi, ars analogi rationis) est scientia cognitionis sensitivae."
[16] See Baumgarten, *Aesthetica/Ästhetik*, §14: "Aesthetices finis est perfectio cognitionis sensitivae, qua talis, §1. Haec autem est pulcritudo, *Metaphysic.* §521, §662, et cavenda eiusdem, qua talis, imperfectio, §1. Haec autem est deformitas, *Metaphysic.* §521, §662."

the *Aesthetics* more accessible to today's German readers, of which René Wellek said that Baumgarten moves within a "well-defined theoretical framework, but awkwardly, as if in heavy armour,"[17] came at a time—stimulated, among other things, by Joachim Ritter's article in 1971[18]—when the possibility and meaning of philosophical aesthetics were regaining increasing attention. However, Schweizer leaves in the shadows what made Baumgarten's invention of aesthetics programmatically fruitful for contemporary aesthetic and philosophical discourse. He sees his task as an interpreter primarily in elaborating on Baumgarten's conception of sensibility and sensible cognition, detaching it as much as possible from its rhetorical-poetic context. Schweizer therefore expressly opposes the "limitation" of philosophical aesthetics to the "phenomenon of art" as well as the "identification of the aesthetic with the artistic sensibility [*künstlerischen Empfinden*] and creativity."[19] In doing so, he moves Baumgarten's thought close to Heinrich Barth's *Philosophy of Appearance* (*Philosophie der Erscheinung*, 1947/1959), which in his view "[seems to] build the most honest basis for an aesthetics that takes aesthetic experience seriously, not primarily in the encounter with the work of art, but already in the ordinary situation."[20]

The explicitly textual-immanent considerations of Schweizer, which gradually follow the unfolding of thoughts, concentrate on the difficult determination of an aestheticological truth, in which Baumgarten combines the logical and aesthetic possibilities of cognition. Schweizer emphasizes the need to complement intellectual cognition and stresses the self-reliance and autonomous lawfulness of aesthetic cognition. He sees Baumgarten's decisive conceptual approach in an antagonism of logical and aesthetic truth, which is based on the relation, both of logical (formal) cognition and of aesthetic (abstract-individual) cognition, to metaphysical (material or concrete-individual) truth, in contrast to which both of them are fundamentally imperfect.[21]

As a consequence of his inquisitive interest, Schweizer stands by his thesis of an antagonism between logical and aesthetic truth that is to be settled. Hence, he loses sight of Baumgarten's own achievement, which derives

---

[17] Wellek, *A History of Modern Criticism, 1750–1950*, 154.

[18] See Ritter, "Ästhetik, ästhetisch," 555–580. See also his *Vorlesungen zur Philosophischen Ästhetik* (2010).

[19] Schweizer, *Ästhetik als Philosophie der sinnlichen Erkenntnis*, 73f. See also the review by Wolfhart Henckmann ("Neue Ausgaben von Baumgartens Ästhetischen Schriften," 422f.) and my own review (Franke, "Ist Baumgartens Ästhetik aktualisierbar?" 272–278 et passim).

[20] Schweizer, *Ästhetik als Philosophie der sinnlichen Erkenntnis*, 98f.—Schweizer took up this approach again in his book *Vom ursprünglichen Sinn der Ästhetik* (1976) and expanded it through rather popular scientific considerations.

[21] See the schematic presentation by Adler, "Was ist ästhetische Wahrheit?" 49–66 and also Emmel, "Logische, ästhetische und metaphysische Wahrheit bei Alexander Gottlieb Baumgarten," 209–242.

from the complementarity of logical and aesthetic cognition, a foundational function of sensible cognition for the arts. What logical truth means for the constitution of the sciences is analogously achieved by aesthetic truth in regard to the foundation of the arts. The fact that Schweizer abstains from reconstructing the history of the problem, in whose context Baumgarten's *Aesthetics* belongs, thus affects the approach and results of his interpretation, including his translation of central terms of the *Aesthetics*.[22]

Although Karlheinz Barck and Dieter Kliche also put Baumgarten's *Aesthetics* in an aesthetic context—equally inspiring and idiosyncratic— they mainly understand it as theory of sensible perception.[23] Yet, in current German-language aesthetics, an effort to enlist Baumgarten as forefather of a general doctrine of perception not specifically focused on the arts—along the lines of Schweizer's arguments—has been pursued above all by Wolfgang Welsch, since his habilitation *Aisthesis: Foundations and Perspectives on the Aristotelian Doctrine of the Senses* (*Aisthesis. Grundzüge und Perspektiven der Aristotelischen Sinneslehre*, 1987). For Welsch, aesthetics was "initially— since 1750—the title of a philosophical discipline that sought knowledge of the sensible [*Wissen vom Sinnhaften*] and was, therefore, designated by its founding father, Baumgarten, as *episteme aisthetike*, in short, aesthetics." By contrast, "only afterwards it narrowed mainly to art or even to beauty." This ought to be "reversed today" in view of a determination of aesthetics as "aesthetic," that is, "as thematization of all kinds of perceptions, sensible as well as intellectual, ordinary as well as sublime, mundane as well as artistic."[24]

At first glance, Baumgarten's explanation of the word "aesthetics" seems indeed to suggest such a "*de*differentiation of *aisthesis* and aesthetics."[25] As it has been handed down in transcripts, probably dating from 1750, Baumgarten explains the "origin" of the word "aesthetics" to his audience in this way:

> It ["aesthetics"] actually comes from *aisthanomai*; this word describes what *sentio* means in Latin, namely all clear sensations. Since the sensations are divided into external and internal ones, into those that act consciously in my body and relate to all the senses, and those that only act in my soul, this word designating the clear sensations in general concerns both. Furthermore, since the

[22] More extensively on this issue, Franke, "Ist Baumgartens Ästhetik aktualisierbar?" 272–278.
[23] Cf. Barck/Kliche, "Ästhetik/ästhetisch," 308–400, esp. 327. As I have shown elsewhere in detail, this interpretation remains too narrow, see Franke, "Baumgarten, Alexander Gottlieb," esp. 77–80 and 94–98.
[24] See Welsch, *Ästhetisches Denken*, 9–40, here 9f., as well as the review of Liebsch, "Ästhetische Grundbegriffe," esp. 140f. See also Welsch, *Blickwechsel*, and along this same line, the similar position of Gernot Böhme, *Ästhetik*.
[25] See Ehrenspeck, "Aisthesis und Ästhetik," 208.

word *sentio* designates the sensible perception of something, to which the Greek wholly accords, so it will designate also sensible representations.[26]

Baumgarten uses, therefore, the expression *sentire* (to sense) in order to designate the inner and outer sensations of the soul as well as sensible perception based on our five senses,[27] a difference between inner and outer perception that was for him overtly important. If this difference is often ignored or even leveled,[28] it should also be noted that perception and sensation are not clearly distinguishable from the perspective of their conceptual history.[29] For instance, in 1764 Thomas Reid attempted to approach the complex character of perception, by distinguishing *perception* [*Wahrnehmung*] and sensation [*Empfindung*] from one another.

In fact, "the equivocations arising in the aesthetic field under the motto aesthetics evoke associations, rhizomatic" in the sense of Wittgenstein's "family resemblance, interconnected to one other."[30] The ambiguity of sensible and aesthetic perception or sensation that informs the Greek words *aisthanomai* and *aisthesis* (perceiving and perception)—according to Wolfhart Henckmann's fitting diagnosis—hinders "to this day any agreement concerning the object and task of aesthetics, especially if aesthetics is defined as a science of sensible perception, due to a reductive reception of Baumgarten's aesthetics."[31] Thus, Christoph Menke has rightly underlined the "dual character of aesthetics as a philosophical discipline" since its "systematization by Baumgarten": "Since the middle of the 18th century, philosophical aesthetics has always been a theory of beauty in art and nature, but at the same time it has always formulated a more general far-reaching theory of human performances and practices—first in concepts of sensibility, then in those of the intellect, presentation or language."[32]

---

[26] Baumgarten, "*Kollegium über die Ästhetik*," 65 (§1); on the epistemo-psychological and epistemo-theoretical aspects of difference between the "sensual" and "sensible," see Franke, *Kunst als Erkenntnis*, 39–42.

[27] An aesthetic project related to sensible perception, which he then did not pursue, is described in his *Philosophical Letters of Aletheophilus* (*Philosophische Brieffe von Aletheophilus*). There, Baumgarten speaks of an aesthetic *art* of experience [*ästhetischen Erfahrungskunst*]. With this, he refers to the five senses, that is, to visual, auditive, olfactory, gustatory, and tactile perception. The aesthetic art of perception should deal with the means by which the senses could be expanded, by the use of weapons of the senses, glasses, binoculars, but also barometers, thermometers, and so on.

[28] See, for example, Kliche, "'Ich glaube selbst Engel können nicht ohne Sinnlichkeit sein,'" 485–505.

[29] See Fontius, "Wahrnehmung," 420–421.

[30] According to Kliche, "Sinnliche Erkenntnis," 53. See also Kliche, "Ästhetik und Aisthesis," 492–494.

[31] Henckmann, "Wahrnehmung, ästhetische," 386.

[32] Menke, "Wahrnehmung, Tätigkeit, Selbstreflexion," 39.

In view of the dual character of the new philosophical discipline sketched
out in the horizon of logic,[33] which is not least based on its eclectic approach,
and of the equivocations under the heading of aesthetics, the question
emerges concerning Baumgarten's understanding of sensible cognition, as
acutely as the question of what should be understood under sensible cognition in the overall context of the *Aesthetics*. For the time being, this much
can be stated: that in the *Aesthetics* Baumgarten sees the expression of artistic cognition as a result of a methodical process which he calls a "beautiful
thinking" [*Schöndenken*], a *pulchre cogitare*, a thinking that would be as
such supplied by the human sensible capacities as a gnoseologically determined *cognitio clara et confusa*. Baumgarten determines the ensemble of the
sensible capacities of the human being as *analogon rationis*—a concept that
he takes up from the realm of animal psychology.[34] In the ensemble of these
capacities, the poetic faculty [*Dichtungskraft*] (*facultas fingendi*) and the
power of judgment [*Urteilskraft*] (*judicium sensitivum*) are guidelines for
artistic cognition.

a) If the discourse of understanding denotes the rational capacity for
abstraction and for discursive thinking, then *analogon rationis* means those
capacities which are constitutive for the concretizing, complex thinking.
According to Georg Friedrich Meier, this "epitome [*Inbegriff*] of all the sensible powers of the soul"[35] is, for Baumgarten, *per definitionem* an analogue
of reasotxn. "That which resembles reason," as he translates it,[36] is formed
from the following capacities: wit (*ingenium*), acuteness (*acumen*), memory
(*memoria*), poetic faculty (*facultas fingendi*), power of judgment (*facultas
diiudicandi*), the capacity to expect similar cases (*expectatio casuum similium*) and the faculty of characterization (*facultas characteristica*).

If the discursive, clear, and distinctly cognizing understanding penetrates
the nexus of the things in the concept (*perspicere*), so is this nexus in the
medium of the "epitome of the sensible powers of the soul," in an intuitively differentiated but conceptually undiscerned fullness, "muddled [*kon-
fus*]" (*confuse*) brought to presence [*vergegenwärtigt*] (*repraesentare*).[37]

---

[33] See Adler and Wolff, *Aisthesis und Noesis* (2013).
[34] See Franke, "Analogon rationis," esp. 229 f. See also Buchenau, "Sinnlichkeit als Erkenntnisvermögen," 191–206.
[35] Meier, *Anfangsgründe aller schönen Wissenschaften*, Vol. 3, §541.
[36] See Baumgarten, *Metaphysica* (4th Ed.), §640.
[37] Cf. Baumgarten, *Metaphysica* (4th Ed.), §640: "Nexum quorundam confuse, quorundam distincte
percipio. Ergo habeo intellectum nexum rerum perspicientem i.e. RATIONEM, et facultates nexus
confusius cognoscentes, quales inferior facultas identitates rerum cognoscendi, quo ingenium
sensitivum; inferior facultas diversitates rerum cognoscendi, quo acumen sensitivum pertinet;
memoria sensitiva, facultas fingendi, facultas diiudicandi, quo iudicium sensitivum, et sensuum;
expectatio casuum similium. Hae omnes, quatenus in repraesentando rerum nexu rationi similes
sunt, constituunt ANALOGON RATIONIS (*das der Vernunft aehnliche*), complexum facultatum
animae nexum confuse repraesentantium."

Therefore, the unfolding of the laws of sensation pertains to the doctrine of sensibility (*gnoseologia inferior*) along with the gnoseological determination of sensible representation.

In the vocabulary of animal psychology, from which the expression *analogon rationis* derives, this is used to denote an instinctive behavior proper to the situation, which is chiefly understood as characteristic of animal mode of behavior. It consists in an empirical inferential capacity based on sensible memory. Leibniz says of this inferential capacity that it bears "some resemblance to reason" (*quelque ressemblance avec la Raison*),[38] and Christian Wolff calls it an "*analogon rationis.*"[39] In contrast, Baumgarten gives the concept a seemingly epistemological meaning, as he uses it to determine an organon of sensible representation nourished by inner perception (*sensus internus*).[40] This organon of reason-like cognition essentially differs from the understanding as an organon of rational cognition, with respect to two capacities: on the one hand, through the poetic faculty based on the faculty of imagination (*imaginatio, phantasia*); on the other, through the capacity for aesthetic judgments (*iudicium sensitivum*) about the beautiful and the ugly. In Baumgarten, these determinations are important for aesthetic theory, which he consequently specifies in the *Aesthetics* (§1) through the synonym of an "*ars analogi rationis.*"

If one considers the constituents of the analogue of reason in the light of Christian Wolff's empirical psychology, it is striking that wit (*ingenium*) and acuteness (*acumen*), in the meaning of capacities to uncover similarities or distinctions among things,[41] are addressed by Wolff as intellectual

---

[38] Leibniz, *Philosophical Essays,* 208–209, 216–217.

[39] Wolff, *Psychologia Rationalis,* §765.

[40] The indication found in Riemann (Riemann, *Die Ästhetik A.G. Baumgartens,* 41) according to which the "doctrine of *analogon rationis*" is to be found already in Leibniz, who touches upon it "albeit too fleetingly," ignores the fact that Leibniz does not relate the "similar to reason" to cognition, as Baumgarten does, but refers it to action, as a synonym for the "*expectatio casuum similium.*" If reason then infers from rational causes [*aus Gründen*], so its analogue draws consequences based on experience: animals (*bêtes*) as well as humans, insofar as they purely empirically proceed (*agir*), have an inferential capacity [*Schlussfolgerungsvermögen*] that imitates reason (cf. Leibniz, *Theodicy,* §65). Leibniz attributes this inferential capacity to memory. He illustrates this "*imiter la raison*" on the basis of once felt sensations (*sentiments*), using the example of dogs that were shown the stick; they remember the pain inflicted on them and they shout, even flee—Arguing in terms similar to Leibniz, Christian Wolff (Wolff, *Psychologia Rationalis,* §765) ascribes to animals an inferential capacity similar to reason: "*Bruta habent analogum rationis*"; it is formed by power of imagination (*imaginatio*) and memory (*memoria*). Wolff puts forth also the example of the dog, while declaring that the same can be shown *per* analogy of other animals too.

[41] See Baumgarten, *Metaphysica* (4th Ed.), §572: "Habitus identitates rerum observandi est ingenium strictius dictum." And §573: "Habitus diversitates rerum observandi acumen est. Acutum ingenium est perspicacia." That is, in Baumgarten's own German translation, "a refined or subtle insight" (*eine artige oder feine Einsicht*).

attitudes (*habitus*),[42] whereas Baumgarten ascribes them not only to intellectual cognition but also to sensible cognition: "I perceive agreements
[*Übereinstimmungen*] and differences among things either distinctly or
sensibly. Consequently, the capacities to perceive agreements and differences, and further to perceive wit, acuteness, and perspicaciousness [*Witz,
Scharfsinnigkeit und Feinsinnigkeit*] are either sensible or intellectual. The
AESTHETICS OF PERSPICACIOUSNESS is the part of aesthetics that
deals with ingeniously witty and acute thinking and performing."[43] The same
applies to memory, to the powers of judgment and to the denotative faculty,
as well as to the capacity for expecting the future, even to presage [*vorherzu-
empfinden*] it (*praesagitio*).[44]

These capacities are, therefore, no less indispensable for reason-like
cognition (as *cognoscere per analogon rationis*)[45] as they are for rational cognition,[46] because cognition in general consists of finding nexuses
and the previously mentioned capacities have the function of unlocking
certain temporal and factual connections. *Memoria* helps to recognize
(*recognoscere*) as such previously held ideas (*repraesentationes*).[47] Its
law consists in bringing a series of successive representations into connection, in order to let their partial commonality emerge—their partial
being-contained in one another.[48] The faculty of expectation is directed
toward the future and represents representational contents, insofar as
they are present, agree with previous ones, not only as contained in the
preceding representation but also in the subsequent one.[49] In turn, the
faculty of characterization makes it possible "to represent the sign in
unity with the signified" (*signa cum signatis una percipere*); it concerns
the nexus between signs and designated things (*nexus significativus*).[50]
Finally, the capacity to judge is defined in such a way that judgment
means, for Baumgarten, the fact that I represent things according to their
perfection and imperfection (*perfectionem imperfectionemque rerum*

---

[42] Wolff, *Psychologia empirica*, §332 and §476 deal with it within the section "De facultatis cognoscendi parte superiori" as well as in the chapters "De tribus intellectus operationibus in specie" and
"De dispositionibus naturalibus et habitus intellectus."

[43] Baumgarten, *Metaphysica* (4th Ed.), §575: "Identitates diversitatesque rerum vel distincte percipio,
vel sensitive. Hinc facultates identitates, diversitatesque percipiendi, adeoque ingenium, acumen et
perspicacia vel sensitiva sunt vel intellectualia. AESTHETICA PERSPICACIA est aesthetices pars
de ingeniose et acute cogitando et proponendo."

[44] Cf. Baumgarten, *Metaphysica* (4th Ed.), §579 (*memoria*), §607 (*facultas diiudicandi*), §610 (*praesagitio*), §619 (*facultas characteristica*).

[45] Cf. Baumgarten, *Metaphysica* (4th Ed.), §640.

[46] Cf. Baumgarten, *Metaphysica* (4th Ed.), §641.

[47] Cf. Baumgarten, *Metaphysica* (4th Ed.), §579.

[48] Cf. Baumgarten, *Metaphysica* (4th Ed.), §580.

[49] Cf. Baumgarten, *Metaphysica* (4th Ed.), §611.

[50] Cf. Baumgarten, *Metaphysica* (4th Ed.), §619.

percipio),[51] that is, that I cognize the manifold, the fullness of a thing, as harmonious or disharmonious.[52]

Seen in this way, "wit," "acuteness," "memory," as well as the "faculty of denotation [*Vermögen der Zeichen-Kunde*]," the "faculty of expecting something," and the faculty to "judge"[53] are constitutive for cognition as such. It is first the poetic faculty that distinguishes sensible from intellectual cognition; it manifests itself in the free assembling and mutual detachment of the imagination: "By joining and SEPARATING images, i.e., by attending only to one part of a representation, I POETIZE [*DICHTE ICH*]."[54] On the one hand, as a capacity for combining, for representing unity in the multiplicity, it is akin to wit [*Witz*].[55] On the other, insofar as it is imaginations (*phantasmata*) that mutually join one another, this capacity is essentially based on the power of imagination [*Einbildungskraft*] (*facultas imaginandi, seu phantasia*): "Hence I have the faculty of poetry, POETIC FACULTY."[56] Baumgarten comprehends imagination in an Aristotelian way as representations of absent things that were formerly present to the senses. If it could be said of the imaginative capacity that shrinks into the power of poetry [*Dichtungskraft*] that "there is nothing in the imagination that was not previously in the senses" (*nihil est in phantasia, quod non ante fuerit in sensu*),[57] this is because Baumgarten understands the exclusively sensibly determined[58] phantasy [*Phantasie*] as reproductive.[59] In contrast, he describes the power of poetry as a productive faculty. For him, the power of poetry is creative [*schöpferisch*], not in the sense that it could generate a growth into new elements, but rather insofar as it can, out of already given singular representations, and with the help of wit, come up with or invent [*ausdenken, erfinden*] a new whole that was not there before. Its rule of action states: "Parts of imaginations are perceived as

---

[51] Cf. Baumgarten, *Metaphysica* (4th Ed.), §606.

[52] Cf. Baumgarten, *Metaphysica* (4th Ed.), §607.

[53] According to the German translations Baumgarten proposes in his *Metaphysics*, cf. Baumgarten, *Metaphysica* (4th Ed.), §572, §573, §579, §606, §610, §619.

[54] Baumgarten, *Metaphysica* (4th Ed.), §589: "Combinando phantasmata et PRAESCINDENDO i. e. attendendo ad partem alicuius perceptionis tantum, FINGO."

[55] Cf. Baumgarten, *Metaphysica* (4th Ed.), §589.

[56] Baumgarten, *Metaphysica* (4th Ed.), §589: "Ergo habeo facultatem fingendi, POETICAM."

[57] Cf. Baumgarten, *Metaphysica* (4th Ed.), §559.

[58] Cf. Baumgarten, *Metaphysica* (4th Ed.), §570: "omnis imaginatio est sensitiva, formanda per facultatem cognoscitivam inferiorem."

[59] Cf. Baumgarten, *Metaphysica* (4th Ed.), §559. Baumgarten determines a *phantasma*, an imagination [*eine Einbildung*], as "reproduction of sensory perceptions [*Sinnewahrnehmungen*]," as a reproduction of that "which we have imaginatively [*bildhaft*] represented ourselves"; see Baumgarten, *Reflections on Poetry*, §28.

a whole."[60] The creative moment of sensible cognition gains special significance for aesthetic truth.[61]

b) As similar to reason, sensible cognition is gnoseologically determined by its fullness of marks: aesthetic thinking is identified as *cognitio
clara et confusa*. As far as the cognition of the understanding is concerned,
Baumgarten deals with gnoseology essentially in the scholastic way,[62] while
his determinations of indistinct cognition, although they remain within the
conceptual framework of tradition, show certain terminological shifts that
allow the modification of the gnoseology through detailed reflection to be
summoned by the perceptual form of sensible cognition. In this modification,
the gnoseology of scholastic philosophy narrows in the *Aesthetics* into the
determination of the complexity of the sensible as a clear representation, in
which the marks remain interconnected (*cognitio clara et confusa*).

Baumgarten thus determines the sensible representation marked as indistinct (*repraesentatio non distincta*) by the gnoseological criterion of the interconnectedness of marks [*Merkmale, notas*]. But to think something in such a
way that its marks are not differentiated means to think it "con-fused"[63]—or
positively formulated: to represent it in the fullness of its marks. With this
determination, Baumgarten takes up the logical criterion that would attain
great importance for his aesthetics, with the help of Leibniz's critical differentiation of the Cartesian axiom of *clare et distincte cognoscere*.[64] We have
to start from this differentiation in order to uncover the modification that
Baumgarten introduced into gnoseology concerning the mediating function
of sensibility.

Descartes held the truth of clear and distinct representations to be evident;
he affirmed their provenance from a perfect God, who could not deceive
because of his supposed perfection, and explained the confusion and obscurity
of a representation from their participation in nothingness.[65] Thus, Descartes
argues metaphysically and even theologically. Leibniz, on the other hand,
develops a logical criterion as a mark of conceptual clarity: the analyzability

---

[60] Baumgarten, *Metaphysica* (4th Ed.), §590: "*Phantasmatum partes percipiuntur ut unum totum*"—
See the rich material on the capacity constituted by the *analogon rationis* in Baeumler, *Das Irrationalitätsproblem*, esp. 141–166 on power of imagination, wit, and poetic power.

[61] On the truth of art, see Franke, *Kunst als Erkenntnis*, 88–116, esp. 104–116.

[62] Cf. Baumgarten, *Metaphysica* (4th Ed.), Ch. XII.

[63] Cf. Baumgarten, *Metaphysica* (4th Ed.), §510: "Some things I think clearly, some others con-fused.
Whoever thinks something con-fused does not distinguish its marks but represents it or perceives it.
[*Quaedam distincte, quaedam confuse cogito. Confuse aliquid cogitans eius notas non distinguit,
repraesentat tarnen, seu percipit*]."

[64] Cf. Descartes, *Philosophical Writings*, Vol. 1, 207–208.

[65] Cf. Descartes, *Philosophical Writings*, Vol. 1, 116–122.

of a representation.[66] With this criterion as his starting point, indistinct representation is for Leibniz determined by the fact that it eludes analysis, that is, that it cannot be sufficiently dissected into its conceptual components and, therefore, remains conceptually indistinct.[67] For Leibniz, however, this cognition is also clear. For our question, the decisive characteristic of the gnoseological aspect of the sensible making-present of the world is this: although it is confusing for the understanding, it is still clear to the senses.[68]

For Leibniz, therefore, the following applies: a concept that remains indistinct for the understanding, due to its being incapable of analysis because of the indissolubility of its marks [*Merkmale*], nevertheless is clear to the senses, regardless of the confusion of the marks contained in it, insofar as it suffices for distinguishing something [*ein Etwas*] from another and thus, also, for recognizing it.

Thus, the mixture of marks [*Vermengung der Merkmale*] characteristic of Leibniz's determination of indistinct cognition (*cognitio clara et confusa*) is, for Baumgarten, determined by the logical criterion of simultaneity between conceptual indistinctness and sufficient sensible clarity for the recognition of an object. Hence, Baumgarten can characterize the sensible making-present of the world [*empfindende Weltvergegenwärtigung*] as a kind of thinking, for which this simultaneity is constitutive. However, Baumgarten grasps such sensible making-present of the world as a complex cognition that drops out of logic and is, therefore, considered a *gnoseologia inferior*.

c) In view of founding a gnoseology of sensibility, Baumgarten expands in two directions Leibniz's criterion of non-analysability, which epitomizes the fullness of a sensible representation. On the one hand, he advances positive determinations for obscure representation (*cognitio obscura*); on the other, for sensible clarity, which Leibniz and Wolff connected to the problem concerning the mark of recognizability (which they posed otherwise), without distinguishing it any further.

In the first place, Baumgarten speaks with Wolff of the "realm of darkness," and like Wolff he contrasts it with the "realm of light."[69] However, he

---

[66] Cf. Leibniz, *Philosophical Essays*, 26: "Saepe enim clara et distincta videntur hominibus temere judicantibus, quae obscura et confusa sunt. Inutile ergo axioma est, nisi clari et distincti CRITERIA adhibeantur, quae tradidimus."

[67] Cf. Leibniz, *Philosophical Essays*, 24: "Confusa, cum scilicet non possum notas ad rem ab aliis discernendam sufficientes separatim enumerare, licet res illa tales notas atque requisita revera habeat, in quae notio ejus resolvi possit."

[68] Heimsoeth, *Die Methode der Erkenntnis bei Descartes und Leibniz*, 256.

[69] Cf. Baumgarten, *Metaphysica* (4th Ed.), §518: "The state of the soul in which the ruling perceptions are obscure is the KINGDOM OF DARKNESS, whereas the state of the soul in which the ruling perceptions are clear is the KINGDOM OF LIGHT. [Status animae, in quo perceptiones dominantes obscurae sunt, est REGNUM TENEBRARUM, in quo clarae regnant, REGNUM LUCIS est]." As Wolff emphasizes (*Philosophia rationalis*, §34–§36), the metaphorics of light and darkness is not to be understood here in the sense of its theological use, but in *sensus philosophicus*:

takes his distance from Wolff in a decisive way, not in the determination of their relation to one another,[70] but in the evaluation of these fields of representation. While Wolff sees obscurity only in its "defectus perceptionum,"[71] in Baumgarten those marks that remain obscure, as components of sensible representation,[72] gain the positive meaning of a "*fundus animae*," as he himself translates, a "ground of the soul."[73]

With this determination, which is reprised in the *Aesthetics*, obscure representations attain the function of an association principle: they are frequently attached to the clear ones, so that "things are evoked" which one had "forgotten," and this way the "realm of clarity" and the "field of obscure representation gathered together" give as a result "a wider field" for nonconceptual thinking.[74] Before the "enhancement of psychology,"[75] the ground of the soul had been disregarded as such by many philosophers.[76] They might not have noticed, Baumgarten says, alluding to Leibniz's doctrine of those "sensations (*perceptions*) which one is not aware of,"[77] that our soul is constantly filled with an "astonishing multitude" of obscure representations.[78]

By reassessing these obscure representations, Baumgarten certainly does not intend to plead for obscurity or even for linguistic *ambiguitas*, for a sense-obscuring polysemy [*sinnverdunkelnde Mehrdeutigkeit*] that was once praised by Leibniz as "a superlative clarity, so to speak."[79] In the context of his question about the significance of sensible representations

---

"The clarity of a representation can be called the light of the soul [Claritas perceptionum est id, quod *Lumen animae* appellare solemus]" (§35); "In contrast to it, the obscurity of a representation is that which reaches into the soul under the name of darkness [Ex adverso obscuritas perceptionum est id, quod *Tenebrarum* nomine in anima venit]" (§36).

[70] Cf. The schema in Menzel, *Der anthropologische Charakter des Schönen bei Baumgarten*, 30.

[71] Cf. Wolff, *Philosophia rationalis*, §36. See also Wolff, *Ausführliche Nachricht von seinen eigenen Schriften*, Ch. 7, §91: "The obscure representations don't confer any cognition, and therefore we don't deal very much with them."

[72] Cf. Baumgarten, *Metaphysica* (4th Ed.), §522: "Perception of this sort is distinct with regard to the clear marks {*Merkmale*, notas}, and it is sensitive perception with regard to the obscure marks [Eiusmodi perceptio, qua notas claras, distincta est, qua obscuras, sensitiva]."

[73] Cf. Baumgarten, *Metaphysica* (4th Ed.), §511: "There are obscure perceptions [perceptiones obscurae] in the soul (§510). The collection of these perceptions is called the GROUND OF THE SOUL [FUNDUS ANIMAE]."

[74] Baumgarten, "*Kollegium über die Ästhetik*," 116 (§80).

[75] Baumgarten, "*Kollegium über die Ästhetik*," 116 (§80).

[76] Cf. Baumgarten, *Aesthetica/Ästhetik*, §80.

[77] Leibniz, *Philosophical Essays*, 214–215. Leibniz reproaches the Cartesians that they consider those petites perceptions, which we are not aware of, "to be nothing." In contrast, he is gladly willing to distinguish between perception and "apperception or consciousness."

[78] Cf. Baumgarten, "*Kollegium über die Ästhetik*," 116 (§80).

[79] Cf. Leibniz "Preface to an Edition of Nizolius," 121. See also Leibniz, *Die philosophischen Schriften*, Vol. IV, 139: "Claritati, sive notitiae significationis, duo vitia opposita sunt, *obscuritas*, et ut sie dicam nimia claritas seu *ambiguitas*, illic nulla significatio nota est, hic plures simul apparent, sed quae sit vera incertum est."

(*repraesentationes sensitivae*) for poetry, he rejects the opinion of those who believe that the more obscurely and intricately (*quo obscurius et intricatius*) they speak, the better the poem.[80] The plenitude of a poetic cognition demands rather a well-balanced relation of clarity and obscurity—an indispensable condition of its communicability, which is indeed hindered, or even made impossible, by the prevalence of obscure moments in a representation.[81]

The following applies, then: "Through the multitude of marks, clarity increases."[82] Departing from this point, a distinction is to be made: "Greater CLARITY due to the clarity of the marks can be called INTENSIVELY [greater], due to the multitude of marks EXTENSIVE GREATER."[83] He distinguishes the intensive clarity of the marks due to conceptual analysis in what is "sufficiently cognized" (*satis cognitum*) from an extensive clarity due to the multitude of marks,[84] Baumgarten distinguishes between a conceptual thinking that abstracts from the complexity of the object and a full making-present [*vollen Vergegenwärtigung*] of something in sensible cognition. Non-distinction means for him positive plenitude of cognition, logically determined by the negative criterion of the complexity of the marks.[85]

Sensible representing has its plenitude to thank [*verdankt*] for a remarkable pregnancy. In contrast to the univocity of abstract representation, it displays itself as "perceptio praegnans,"[86] as "evocative representation [*vielsagende Vorstellung*]."[87] According to Georg Friedrich Meier, in this evocative trait lies "the inner kernel of our thoughts,"[88] a sensible pregnancy that constitutes

[80] Cf. Baumgarten, *Reflections on Poetry*, §13. Here it must be asserted, against Kuno Fischer, that Baumgarten breaks with Leibniz by also demanding clarity from poetic representation. See Fischer, *Leibniz*, 491f.
[81] This issue plays a decisive role in connection with aesthetic truth. See Franke, *Kunst als Erkenntnis*, 88–116 (The Truth of Art).
[82] Baumgarten, *Metaphysica* (4th Ed.), §531: "[. . .] multitudine notarum augetur claritas."
[83] Baumgarten, *Metaphysica* (4th Ed.), §531: "Claritas claritate notarum maior intensive, multitudine notarum extensive maior dici potest." Cf. Baumgarten, *Acroasis Logica*, §51.
[84] Cf. Baumgarten, *Reflections on Poetry*, §16.
[85] Instead of the misleading translation of "confuse" as "verworren," the editors of the English edition of the *Reflections on Poetry* have proposed a more fitting translation as "fused to one another" ["miteinander verbunden"], in contrast to "sharply separated from one another" (distinct). The difference can be quite perspicuously expressed: "The Reader must be careful to keep fusion foremost here and not confusion in the derogatory sense" (see Baumgarten, *Reflections on Poetry*, 21). In order to express the characteristic confusion of many marks as their being-fused-to-one-another [*Miteinanderverbundensein vieler Merkmale*], already Karl Heinrich von Stein (Stein, *Die Entstehung der neuern Aesthetik*, 338) translated "confuse" as "bunt."
[86] Cf. Baumgarten, *Metaphysica* (4th Ed.), §517: "representations, which contain within them multiple (marks) are called VIELSAGENDE VORSTELLUNGEN. [*PERCEPTIONES plures (notas) in se continentes PRAEGNANTES vocantur.*]"
[87] Baumgarten, *Metaphysica* (4th Ed.), §517:
[88] Meier, *Anfangsgründe*, Vol. 1, §126.

both the liveliness (*vividitas*) of nonconceptual thinking[89] as well as its force[90] that puts the mind [*Gemüt*] in motion.[91] With this significance, sensible representation, terminologically seized as "aesthetic wealth" (*ubertas aesthetica*), becomes the foundation of an aesthetic theory of art as it unfolds in Baumgarten's *Aesthetics*.

If this thinking, which penetrates into things and fathoms them through analysis, dissecting each concrete figure that has coalesced from many into one, is in this way counterposed by Baumgarten to the form of intuition of its plenitude (*cogitio clara et confusa*), then the consequence that follows from here is this: not that this thinking is inferior to conceptual cognition (*cognitio clara et distincta*), but that it is a different kind of cognition, which is independent in its own field, namely, that of the liberal arts [*freie Künste*]. Thus, Baumgarten acknowledges that a mode of representation, which, due to its complexity, is rejected by a conception of cognition restricted to the understanding, may well have its place in "learned cognition," that is, in philosophy (as one of his students already emphasized in a little-noticed treatise).[92]

---

[89] Cf. Baumgarten, *Metaphysica* (4th Ed.), §517: "Extensive clarior perceptio est vivida."

[90] Cf. Baumgarten, *Metaphysica* (4th Ed.), §517: "The more marks a perception embraces, the stronger it is. Hence, an obscure perception comprehending more marks than a clear one is stronger than the latter, and a con-fused perception comprehending more marks than a distinct one is stronger than the latter. Perceptions containing several ones in themselves are called PREGNANT PERCEPTIONS {VIELSAGENDE VORSTELLUNGEN = EVOCATIVE REPRESENTATIONS}. Therefore, pregnant perceptions are stronger. [Quo plures notas perceptio complectitur, hoc est fortior. Hinc obscura perceptio plures notas comprehendens, quam clara, est eadem fortior, confusa plures notas comprehendens, quam distincta, est eadem fortior. Perceptiones plures in se continentes praegnantes vocantur. Ergo PERCEPTIONES PRAEGNANTES fortiores sunt.]"

[91] If one brings, as it has repeatedly happened (cf. e.g., Bergmann, *Die Begründung der deutschen Ästhetik*, 163–165), Baumgarten's concept of a *perceptio praegnans* in connection with Kant's concept of the aesthetic idea, "a representation that gives lots to think of," which contains a huge "multiplicity of partial ideas" and, thus, "much unnamable" [*viel Unnennbares*], and for which no concept can be fit [*angemessen*] (cf. Kant, *Critique of the Power of Judgment*, 194/ AA 5: 316, §49), it should be noted that Kant provides a transcendental grounding of the aesthetic idea; it cannot become cognition because "it is related to an intuition according to a merely subjective principle of the agreement of the cognitive faculties (of imagination and understanding)" (Kant, *Critique of the Power of Judgment*, 217–219/AA V: 341–344, §57, *Anmerkung* I). By contrast, Baumgarten's concept of the sensible representation as a nondistinct and, therefore, evocative representation (*vielsagenden Vorstellung* = *perceptio praegnans*) is ontologically grounded. In reference to the different problems here related, see Vogt, *Die ästhetische Idee bei Kant*, esp. 51–56. See also Franke, *Kunst als Erkenntnis*, 44–46.

[92] See Winkelmann, "Von der ohnlängst erfundene Ästhetik," 149 and 152: "[through] the science that is called aesthetics, and which should contain in itself the principles the liberal arts [*freyn Künste*], the limits of learned cognition are expanded. Yes, their grounds [*Gründe*] have been fixed in such a way that one can now safely build upon them further." Bergmann (*Die Begründung der deutschen Ästhetik*, 176) saw in this treatise by the rector of the school of Sorau, Georg Conrad Winkelmann, "the only successful (contemporary) attempt to penetrate into Baumgarten's aesthetics."

d) The peculiarity of sensible cognition as not dry but vivid cognition full of splendor and without the thorns of abstraction that hurt the concrete—thus comparable to the *bon sens vif et brillant* cited by Bouhours[93]—reflects itself philosophically in the gnoseological mark of complexity. However, the question remains open concerning a principle that lends order and shape to this plenitude [*Fülle*], if it should not remain chaotic. This principle could not come into view when considering the gnoseological component of sensible cognition; it only arises from the metaphysical component of sensible cognition. It is first from the metaphysical relevance that Baumgarten ascribes to sensibility that its mediating function can ultimately be inferred, and along with it the cognitive relevance of the arts, which are grounded in it.

The doctrine of sensibility, therefore, not only defines the gnoseological component of the sensible but also ascribes to it; moreover, in the determination of *vis repraesentativa universi*, a metaphysical-cognitive component that will be later discussed. The latter implies a principle that is suitable to arrange in a fundamental way the gnoseologically characterized plenitude of a sensible representation. But this very representation, as it was explained above, derives from the *analogon rationis* that particular source of sensible cognition which differs from the understanding.

As an artistic cognition, sensible cognition is an effect of beautiful thinking [*Schönendenken*], an *effectus pulchre cogitantis*, as it attains acute expression in poetry, painting, sculpture, or music. Hence, it is important to take a closer look at the role of art and the arts in this regard.

THE ROLE OF ART AND THE ARTS
AND THE UNITY OF REASON

For a long time, research has openly assumed, more or less explicitly, that the part of philosophical aesthetics that allows for testing upon examples does not have much to offer. For instance, in his edition of Hegel's *Aesthetics*, Rüdiger Bubner only included from its material parts the section on poetry. Moreover, Bubner also leaves Hegel's discussion of the symbolic art form aside, on the basis that Hegel regards it only as mere 'pre-art' [*Vorkunst*].[94] A simple

---

[93] See Bouhours, *La manière de bien penser, Avertissement*, 341–402.

[94] According to Bubner, Hegel would have "made use of contemporary sources of information and the available literature on the science of arts [. . .], in order to give the audience [of his lessons] or his readers the greatest possible clarity." However, given the expansion of art history and archaeological knowledge, the "material parts [. . .] do not maintain their old function unchanged today" (Bubner's "Einführung" in Hegel, *Vorlesungen über die Ästhetik*, 32). For criticism of this claim, see Kwon, *Hegels Bestimmung der Kunst*, 13 n. 7 et passim.

look at the bibliography added by Wolfhart Henckmann to his edition of the introduction to Hegel's *Aesthetics* shows how rare, in spite of the prosperous reception of Hegel in the twentieth century, are the works dedicated not just to Hegel's aesthetic theory, but also to the arts within this theory.[95]

However, the arts and their works play no secondary roles in philosophical aesthetics. Not only Hegel and Schelling, who expressly refer to their aesthetics as philosophies of art, but also Baumgarten and Kant incorporate into the systematic philosophical reflection on art the empirical knowledge of their time about the arts, which is transmitted by rhetoric and/or the sciences of art.

The interweaving of the ideal point of view—to speak with Hegel—with the empirical one emerges as a transformation of rhetoric, art theory, art history, or artistic doctrine into differently structured and accentuated aesthetics [*Ästhetiken*], as a result of which the arts and their works are regarded, on the basis of their beauty, as media of transcendence. The category of beauty comes here to play a key role—especially in view of the transformation of rhetoric and the art sciences, a transformation that inevitably follows from the metaphysical framing of rhetoric in Baumgarten's *Aesthetics*.[96]

This horizon of the problem, to which the philosophies of art from Kant to Schelling and Hegel are indebted, is already fundamentally anticipated in Baumgarten's aesthetics. Like Baumgarten before them, Kant, Schelling, and Hegel translate into aesthetics the inquiry of what their object (art and the arts) in the medium of their works contribute to the cognition of the idea or the absolute, the end and unity of thinking. This cognitive interest determines both the philosophical perspectives in which not only art but also the arts and their works are viewed and methodologically reflected, as well as the way in which cognition in the realm of the sciences of art is incorporated and processed, and in particular the transformation of poetics and rhetoric.[97]

What did Baumgarten's *Aesthetics* and philosophical aesthetics from Kant to Hegel contribute to the exploration of art, the arts, and their works? What should they contribute to it, according to the self-conception of these authors? Anyone looking for an answer must see the development of the philosophical concept of art in Baumgarten, Kant, Schelling, and Hegel in connection with the problem to which it is committed both methodologically and in terms of content. Therefore, it is important to see the theory and the understanding of art in philosophical aesthetics at that time in the context of the problem of the

---

[95] Hegel, *Einleitung in die Ästhetik*, 152 f.
[96] See Piselli, "Ästhetik und Metaphysik bei Alexander Gottlieb Baumgarten," 101–116, esp. 103 f., and 107–111.
[97] See Niehues-Pröbsting, "Rhetorische und idealistische Kategorien der Ästhetik," 94–110. He deals with the consequences of such interweaving, while also including Nietzsche and Adorno.

unity of reason and reason's need (according to Hegel's diagnosis) to restore unity to shattered experience.

In his treatise on *The Difference between Fichte's and Schelling's Systems of Philosophy* (1801), his first publication at the age of thirty, Hegel asserted the problem of the unity of reason as an inevitable necessity of reason and, therefore, as the end of all philosophizing of his time. Reason, which has to do only with itself in philosophy, divides itself from itself in the course of the history of philosophy. The grounding figure of the divide, understood as the antithesis between the finite and the infinite—that is how Hegel describes the development of philosophy until the turn of the eighteenth to the nineteenth century—has stiffened into various forms of opposition:

> Antitheses such as spirit and matter, soul and body, faith and intellect, freedom and necessity, etc. used to be important; and in more limited spheres they appeared in a variety of other guises. The whole weight of human interests hung upon them. With the progress of culture of human interests hung upon them. With the progress of culture they have passed over into such forms as the antithesis of reason and sensibility, intelligence and nature and, with respect to the universal concept, of absolute subjectivity and absolute objectivity. . . . The sole interest of reason is to suspend such rigid antitheses.[98]

In this respect, the cognitive interest of philosophical aesthetics is fundamentally different from the questions posed by the disciplines of the sciences of art and must be distinguished from them.

Just like the beginnings of art history, those of *art theory* articulated within the horizon of western intellectual history lead back to antiquity and the Middle Ages. However, it was not until the eighteenth century that it gained clear contours as the discipline charged with analyzing the specificity and limits of individual arts as well as their modes of configuration, and as the discipline that seeks to establish the laws in their development. With this, in turn, art theory is intertwined with both art history and aesthetics.

Only in the second half of the nineteenth century was *art history* first established in German universities as an independent discipline that goes back to antiquity.[99] Already in the early modern period, the artist's biographies, the so-called *Lives* of Giorgio Vasari (1550, 1568) and art historiography as well,

[98] Hegel, *The Difference between Fichte's and Schelling's System of Philosophy*, 90. Cf. Zimmerli, *Die Frage nach der Philosophie*, esp. 7–11 et passim.

[99] Cf. Dilly, *Kunstgeschichte als Institution* (1979). See also Jahn and Haubenreisser, "Kunstgeschichte."

offered rich materials for art history.[100] As is well known, only since Johann Joachim Winckelmann's *History of Ancient Art* (1764), whose observations of the historical development of art also take into account the political and general cultural conditions of a people, is there art history in the proper modern sense of the word. Since then, the view of art's cultural and intellectual history is not least influenced by Hegel.[101]

Compared to the empirical view of the arts (for instance, that of their historical development) in the context of art history, and in contrast to the subject-specific and in particular the form-analytical research in art theory, the interest of philosophical aesthetics is oriented toward a concept of art that is coined by the philosophical efforts to solve the problem of the unity of reason, which was brought sharply into focus by Kant's critique of reason. The interest in regaining the unity of reason determines the construction of theory in philosophical aesthetics, insofar as art as well as the arts and their works (on the basis of the beauty that manifests within them) are believed to be responsible and expected to overcome the division between reason and sensibility as well as between intelligence and nature—whether that happens through the beauty of the artwork, through art as *representation of the whole, of the world's perfection and completeness* (Baumgarten), or as *cipher of the supersensible* (Kant), or as a *counterimage of the absolute* (Schelling) or as *sensible appearance of the idea* (Hegel), and that, in this way, the significance of art and the arts for human life can be estimated as well.[102]

THE FUNCTION OF THE *VIS REPRAESENTATIVA* AND THE IMPORTANCE OF BEAUTY

Behind Baumgarten's bonding of art (and thus of artistic cognition) to beauty, one finds Leibniz's metaphysics of the best possible world.[103] This is shown by the fact that the determination of the soul as a "power to represent the universe" (*vis repraesentativa universi*) is the starting point for

---

[100] Cf. Waetzoldt, *Deutsche Kunsthistoriker* (1986).

[101] Cf. Gombrich, "Hegel und die Kunstgeschichte," 202–219. See also Siebert, "Jacob Burckhardts Konzeption einer historisch fundierten Kunstgeschichtsschreibung," 107–119.

[102] Cf. Paetzold, *Ästhetik des deutschen Idealismus* (1983). See also Gethmann-Siefert, *Einführung in die Ästhetik*, esp. 27–31 and 136–148.

[103] See chapter 2 ("From Metaphysics to Aesthetics") in Franke, *Baumgartens Erfindung der Ästhetik*, 53–64. As a consequence of the dependence of artistic cognition on metaphysics lies a verdict of the absurd, which Baumgarten formulated with Horace as follows: "that painters and poets have whatever they can and whatever is in their power to be dared, if only they did not force the incompatible together, that one did not mix snakes with the birds, lamb and tiger" (cf. Horace *The Art of Poetry*, v. 8–12; cf. Franke, *Kunst als Erkenntnis*, 78–85). Already the verdict of the absurd, which results from the metaphysical presuppositions of the *Aesthetics*, forbids any unrestricted actualization of Baumgarten's aesthetics (cf. Franke, "Ist Baumgartens Ästhetik aktualisierbar?" 272–278).

Baumgarten's considerations.[104] On the basis of this determination, which Baumgarten establishes through repeated references to his *Metaphysics*,[105] artistic cognition is able to express the perfection of the world (not least in its Christian understanding) in the beauty of artworks, their *pulchritudo* in the sense of an appearing, eye-catching perfection (*perfectio phaenomenon*), and is able to make it intuitable and sensible to experience. Hence, artworks mirror the order of our world; and what philosophers think of the world also applies to the order of the art-world.[106] Like intellectual cognition, the artistic as sensible cognition also achieves a presentation [*Vergegenwärtigung*] of the universe. Insofar as its perfection, which (viewed as a whole) is still out of the question for Baumgarten, attains intuition in the beauty of the artworks, the perfection of the world is not only thought but also aesthetically present. In this way, the intersection between the ideal point of view of art's metaphysical grounding and the empirical point of view becomes apparent as Baumgarten sets the criterion of artistic beauty in the agreement (*consensus*) of signs (*signa*), their nexus and their expression (*elocutio*), and thus resorts to ancient rhetoric, by transforming its categories in the problem horizon of the *Aesthetics* and reformulating them philosophically[107]—a transformation that presupposes an understanding of the *Aesthetics* as a philosophy of art.

The great tradition of philosophical aesthetics that followed Baumgarten, from Kant to Hegel, holds fast to the bonding of art to the beautiful as well as to its metaphysical determination, which ultimately leads back to Plato. Thus, in precisely this respect, the different philosophical aesthetics offer a philosophical grounding for the specifically modern conception of the autonomy of

---

[104] Cf. Baumgarten, *Metaphysica* (4th Ed.), §507: "My soul, at the very least, thinks about some parts of this universe (§354). Therefore, my soul is a power for representing this universe, at least partially (§155). [*Cogitat anima mea saltim quasdam partes huius universi. Ergo anima mea est vis repraesentativa huius universi.*]" See Leibniz, *Philosophical Essays*, 223–224. On this context, see also Franke, *Kunst als Erkenntnis*, 67–72.

[105] Cf. Baumgarten, *Aesthetica*, §28–39; see also Franke, "Baumgarten, Alexander Gottlieb," esp. 80–84—The artistic cognition that is nourished by the sensible abilities [*sinnlichen Fähigkeiten*] Baumgarten understands as the analogue of reason is, in this determination, a complement of the cognition of understanding [*Verstandeserkenntnis*] (see Franke, "Ein Komplement der Vernunft," 131–148).

[106] Cf. Baumgarten, *Reflections on Poetry*, §68 as well as the review of this selection by Henckmann, "Neue Ausgaben von Baumgartens Ästhetischen Schriften," 420–423. See also Franke, *Kunst als Erkenntnis*, 76–85.

[107] Cf. Baumgarten, *Aesthetica*, §18–§21—On the topical transformation, see the chapter "From metaphysics to aesthetics. The step from Leibniz to Baumgarten," in Franke, *Baumgartens Erfindung der Ästhetik*, 53 ff. On the transformation of ulterior rhetorical categories in the context of Baumgarten's *Aesthetics*, let me remit to the studies of Pietro Pimpinella ("Truth and Persuasion," 21–49), Hans Carl Finsen ("Evidenz und Wirkung im ästhetischen Werk Baumgartens," 198–212), Salvatore Tedesco (*L'estetica di Baumgarten*, 2000), Rüdiger Campe ("Bella Evidentia," 243–256), Eberhard Ortland ("Ästhetik als Wissenschaft der sinnlichen Erkenntnis," 1–18), and Eberhard Ostermann (*Die Authentizität des Ästhetischen*, 2002).

art, which, from the point of view of the aesthetics of artworks, is essentially based on the bonding of the arts and their works to the beautiful.[108] Thus, since ancient times, the metaphysically and theologically accentuated meaning of "beauty" and "beautiful" in opposition to the ugly comes into play whenever philosophers talk about art.[109]

Since early modern times, more precisely since the early Italian Renaissance, when the Platonic-Christian theory of beauty was bound to the theory of art, art has become the place of beauty par excellence. It is first the modern bonding of art to the beautiful that leads to a distinction between the visual arts [*bildende Kunst*] (architecture, sculpture, painting), poetry and music from the sciences and the arts of handicraft.[110] As is well known, in antiquity and in the Middle Ages, the visual arts, just like music and poetry, were assigned to the various sciences as well as handcrafts and other human activities. Art was understood as a canon of rules that should guide some kind of production. In this sense, the shoemaker's handcraft, the art of cooking and the art of juggling, grammar and arithmetic were no less arts (and in no other sense) than painting or sculpture, poetry and music.

But the representation of art, which (with the accentuation of the beautiful) puts at the center of attention its aesthetic value and thus displaces the historically earlier religious function of art, in other words, the rise of autonomous aesthetic art, has also detached the work of art from its social context, the life-nexus of human beings in which they originated and which coined them.[111] Also Christian art is now more or less subordinated to its aesthetic reception and interpretation in terms of its aesthetic value.[112] But this is associated with a loss of its original function. Recall Hegel's famous dictum: the most excellently portrayal of God the Father does not move us to bend our knees in front of Him.[113]

---

[108] Cf. Haller, "Das 'Zeichen' und die 'Zeichenlehre' in der Philosophie der Neuzeit," esp. 123–131. See also Meier-Oeser, *Die Spur des Zeichens* (1997). On the sign-theoretical realization [*zeichentheoretischen Realisierung*] of the criterion of beauty, see Franke, "Zeichenkonzeptionen in der Kunstphilosophie und Ästhetik," 1232–1262.

[109] Cf. Franke, "Jenseits von schön und häßlich," esp. 290–294. Reviewed in Blaschke, "Leuchttürme und Irrlichter des Hässlichen" (2006). See also Rosenkranz, *Ästhetik des Hässlichen*, esp. 5–56 and 458–485.

[110] Cf. Jäger, *Die Theorie des Schönen in der italienischen Renaissance*, 38–81 and Eco, *On Beauty* (2004).

[111] Although in a critical intent, this has been recently stressed above all by Wolterstorff, *Art Rethought* (2015).

[112] Cf. For a renewed discussion, see Strube, "Ästhetische Wertäußerungen," 240–257.

[113] Cf. Hegel, *Aesthetics*, Vol. 1, 103. On this, see also Franke, "Nach Hegel," esp. 306, and Belting 1993.

CONSEQUENCES FOR THE INTERPRETATION
OF THE *AESTHETICS*

With the interpretation of sensibility as the source of artistic cognition and
its expression, Baumgarten's *Aesthetics* comprises the determination of
aesthetics as *scientia cognitionis sensitivae*; thereby, the *pulchre cogitare*, a
beautiful thinking [*Schöndenken*] or poetic thinking is conceived as a process
of artistic cognition.[114] Accordingly, in the overall context of the *Aesthetics*,
the understanding, as well as the function of sensibility and of sensible cognition, gains their proper brisance if the outstanding rank of art and the arts as
privileged objects of sensible cognition is adequately considered as the basis
of artistic cognition and its expression. For the artistic as sensible cognition,
epistemologically determined as *cognitio clara et confusa*, proves itself—as
it was already revealed—in the epistemological problem horizon of the philosophical question of the unity of reason as a first and essential step toward the
concept of art as the representation of the absolute. Here, a guiding thread is
the—metaphysically grounded—connotation of art and beauty as well as the
semiotic aspect [*zeichentheoretische Aspekt*] of the modern concept of art, to
which I will return later.

This interpretation gives an account of the overall context of the *Aesthetics*,
especially since it is only from this perspective that it becomes clear that and
how key terms of rhetoric and poetics are philosophically reformulated or
transformed by Baumgarten.[115] In this way, the topic is expanded to become
an instrument for the invention of aesthetic arguments[116] and the philosophical

---

[114] In this regard, Eberhard Ortland ("Ästhetik als Wissenschaft der sinnlichen Erkenntnis,"), in an
important confrontation with the positions of Hans Rudolf Schweizer (*Ästhetik als Philosophie der
sinnlichen Erkenntnis,* 1–18) and Wolfgang Welsch (*Grenzgänge der Ästhetik,* 1996 and "Erweiterungen der Ästhetik," 39–67), both of whom elaborate on a sublation of the boundary between
art and life, attempts a symbol-theoretical reformulation of Baumgarten determination of sensible
cognition. Ortland connects the mark of a complex of representation that remains below the clarity [*Deutlichleit*] with which Baumgarten characterizes the *cognitio sensitiva* with the properties
of density, plenitude or repleteness, exemplification, which Nelson Goodman (*Languages of Art,*
252ff.) identifies as "symptoms of the aesthetic" and so describes it as the aesthetic difference of
a world-production through art. On this subject, see also Gabriel, "Nelson Goodman, Weisen der
Welterzeugung," 48–55; Gabriel, *Logik und Rhetorik der Erkenntnis,* 356–401. See also Peres,
"Komplexität und Mangel ästhetischer Zeichen," 215–236.

[115] On this point, see Ostermann, *Die Authentizität des Ästhetischen,* 71–88. Although he does not
account for the transformation of rhetoric, Horst-Michael Schmidt located Baumgarten's aesthetics in the "philosophical and poetological context of the German Enlightenment" and examined
especially the rhetorical-poetic conception of aesthetics (Ch. IV), while characterizing Baumgarten's aesthetics from a "philosophical-literary" perspective as a "concluding systematic summary"
of the poetics of the German enlightenment (Schmidt, *Sinnlichkeit und Verstand,* 236).

[116] Salvatore Tedesco (*L'estetica di Baumgarten,* 108–111) described in detail the transformation of
the topic, having in view the function of the aesthetic arguments that account for the perfection of
sensible cognition. On this transformation of the topic, see Franke, *Baumgartens Erfindung der
Ästhetik,* 67 ff.

formulation of the *signficatio aesthetica* is reshaped into a semiotics in the determination of an aesthetic propaedeutic;[117] such a transformation has also been elaborated upon in regard to the rhetorical concepts of *evidentia* and *persuasio*.[118]

In view of these findings, even if it does not take Baumgarten to be "too modern," not detached from the tradition of rhetoric and his still "pre-modern" concept of art is not whisked away [*eskamotiert*]," it appears somewhat surprising to assume that his "modern approach" shows itself to be more fruitful. This view is just as unconvincing as the underlying view that Baumgarten goes beyond the framework of rhetoric and poetics, insofar as he considers "sensible modes of apperception as an essential presupposition for a balanced [. . .] image of humanity."[119] If the double character of Baumgarten's aesthetic theory is not adequately taken into account, as is here proposed, then the aesthetic transformation of rhetoric in particular remains underemphasized, even disregarded, so that the overall context of aesthetics is whisked away. The anthropological interpretation and the understanding of sensibility, in connection with the vision of a new image of humanity according to the building block borrowed from empirical psychology, owe their place to the double character of Baumgarten's aesthetic theory. In Baumgarten's dry conceptual determinations of sensible capacities, as he treats them in his textbook on metaphysics, following Christian Wolff's empirical psychology, the ideal of the formation [*Bildung*] of the integral human being can be discerned. Thus, Baumgarten more or less expressly anticipates the idea of an aesthetic education [*ästhetischen Erziehung*], which is meant as a cultivating of our sensibility rather than as its disciplining. This thought can only be rightly dignified, if one keeps in mind that not only a logical but also a moral prejudice lays beneath sensibility. Some "catonic moral teachers [*catonische Sittenlehrer*]," according to Baumgarten's pupil and friend Georg Friedrich Meier, could only think of the word sensibility "as original sin and what the Scripture calls flesh."[120]

---

[117] See Franke, *Baumgartens Erfindung der Ästhetik*, 81 ff.

[118] Rüdiger Campe ("Bella Evidentia," 243–256) elaborates on the philosophical reshaping of *evidentia*. The rhetorical category that is meant as convincing speech is reshaped in the *Aesthetics* into a category that verbally encompasses the aesthetic appearance: "One is confronted with an aesthetic rhetoric or an aesthetics that is to be rhetorically produced, with the interpretative transfer of rhetoric into aesthetics: under the guiding perspective of 'sensible cognition' and at once with the rhetorical staging of aesthetics and its guiding category 'sensible cognition' itself" (Campe, "Bella Evidentia," 254). The reshaping takes place in the way of a connection with what Baumgarten calls the *lux aesthetica*, a constellation whose conceptual history Campe traces back to the connection between *lumière* and *evidence* in D'Alembert's *Discours preliminaire* (1751)—See also Pimpinella, "Truth and Persuasion," 21–49; Finsen, "Evidenz und Wirkung im ästhetischen Werk Baumgartens," 198–212, as well as the schemata in Adler, "Was ist ästhetische Wahrheit?" 49–66.

[119] See Barck and Kliche, "Ästhetik/ästhetisch," 327.

[120] Meier, *Anfangsgründe*, Vol. 1, 35. See also Franke, "Bildung/Erziehung, ästhetische," esp. 703–707 and the review by Liebsch, "Karlheinz Barck u.a. (Hrsg.), Ästhetische Grundbegriffe," 141 f.

In the *Aesthetics*, this foundation has the function of describing the natural disposition of a *felix aestheticus* or *esprit createur*, as Baumgarten also says, which however does not mean for Baumgarten, as Dieter Kliche assumes in his plea for aesthetics,[121] that by this one should understand every human being. As far as I am concerned, the attribution of a *felix aestheticus* to all of us[122] is simply not tenable, since this attribution flattens out the difference that Baumgarten expressly asserts in the scientific language of his time as he distinguishes between *dispositio* and *habitus*. Nature must be trained, so that it does not "consume" us. However, the question remains as to what object sensibility can use to measure its own powers. The answer reads: the nonmechanical arts.

It is an issue on its own to comprehend the steps in the formation of natural dispositions "for the gradual acquisition of every capacity for beautiful thinking" ("ut habitus pulc[h]re cogitandi sensim acquiratur"),[123] as well as to integrate these building blocks picked up from the rhetoric into the overall structure of the *Aesthetics*, with whose help Baumgarten grasps the practice of aesthetics more expressly than had hitherto been done. It is first in the performance of beautiful thinking [*Schönendenken*], *pulchre cogitare*, that the creative capacities—imagination and the poetic faculty, wit, acuteness, the power of judgment, as well as the faculty of characterization—become habitual, namely, through exercise (*exercitatio*), correction (*correctio*), enthusiasm (*impetus aesthetica*), and by taking orientation from beautiful learnedness (*pulchra eruditio*).[124]

After the first complete German translation is available of the (difficult to follow) Latin text of the *Aesthetics*, hopefully these sections as well as the second part (which has so far hardly been recognized) will come into the focus of research, so that the function of sensibility as a source of artistic cognition can be further elucidated in the overall context of the *Aesthetics*.

CULTURAL-THEORETICAL IMPLICATIONS

Furthermore, the cultural-theoretical implications of the connection between philosophical aesthetics and the science of art have to be considered, on

---

[121] See Kliche, "Ästhetik und Aisthesis," 308–400.

[122] See also Gross, *Felix Aestheticus*, 163–174, as well as the critical review by Stöckmann, "Steffen W. Groß, Felix aestheticus," 294–298.

[123] Baumgarten, *Aesthetica/Ästhetik*, §47. See also Frey, "Zur ästhetischen Übung," 171–181.

[124] Cf. Baumgarten, *Aesthetica*, §62–§103—The difference between the disposition and the habituation of creative abilities based on sensibility is left out of the picture, when Arbogast Schmitt suggests that Baumgarten expects "not little" from the "power of sensible cognition." See Schmitt, "Die Entgrenzung der Künste durch ihre Ästhetisierung bei Baumgarten," 56.

the one hand, the relevance for popular education, which is attributed to art by Baumgarten and Kant as well as by Schelling and Hegel, and, on the other hand, the conception of the autonomy of art, which is solidified in the formation of theories of philosophical aesthetics, although it is controversial today,[125] as it has shaped the modern concept of art in connection with the connection of art to the beautiful.[126]

For Schelling and Hegel, as for Baumgarten and Kant, the idea and the hope that the reception of art promotes the education of humanity as human beings [*die Bildung des Menschen zum Menschen*], humanity is in the foreground; they are based on the idea of the perfection of human beings and humanity, not least due to Rousseau,[127] an idea which for them is beyond doubt—however deceptively this hope may be assessed today.

In connection with the reevaluation of sensibility, Baumgarten takes up the idea of human education and perfection, which, since Schiller and Humboldt, constitutes an essential aspect of the concepts of aesthetic education and training that are still relevant today.[128] Because and insofar as the sensible abilities of the human beings complement their intellectual powers, reception of the arts and their works significantly contributes to human sensibility.

Philosophical reflection on the art-world aimed at the education of humanity presupposes the thought of a controversial autonomy of art, which is founded and reflected in what bounds the arts and their works to the beautiful, in connection with the philosophical discourse about art that is shaped by metaphysics. This aspect distinguishes both Schelling's and Hegel's self-conception, according to their two aesthetics, from "theories of fine arts and sciences, the principles of which were the psychological principles of the English and French." According to Schelling, the latter sought "to explain the beautiful in empirical psychology."[129] Philosophical aesthetics therefore also distinguishes itself from the psychological method of German popular aesthetics, as represented, for example, by Moses Mendelssohn. According to Hegel, this approach only examines the "*sensation* of the beautiful."[130]

---

[125] See, for example, Schmücker, "Funktionen der Kunst," 13–33.

[126] Still relevant Perpeet, *Das Kunstschöne* (1987) and Perpeet, *Vom Schönen und von der Kunst* (1997). See also Garin, *Die Theorie des Schönen im Humanismus und in der Renaissance* (1969); Assunto, *Die Theorie des Schönen im Mittelalter* (1963); Grassi, *Die Theorie des Schönen in der Antike* (1980); Oelmüller, Dölle-Oelmüller, and Rath, *Diskurs: Kunst und Schönes* (1982)— Winfried Menninghaus examines the connection between evolution theory and philosophical aesthetics; see Menninghaus, *Das Versprechen der Schönheit*, esp. 216–233 (on sexual 'choice' and philosophical aesthetics).

[127] See Hornig, "Perfektibilität II," 241–244. For Rousseau's influence on Kant, cf. Recki, *Ästhetik der Sitten*, 26–32.

[128] See Franke, "Bildung/Erziehung, ästhetische," esp. 703–707.

[129] Schelling, *Philosophie der Kunst*, 362.

[130] Hegel, *Aesthetics*, Vol. 1, 32–33, here 33 (translation modified/emphasis added). See also Parret, "De Baumgarten à Kant: sur la beauté," 87 and 317–343.

This difference is also leveled when Christoph Menke[131] "extracts," as if from a quarry, the determination of force from texts by popular philosophers, but also from Baumgarten and Kant, so that "the aesthetics of force is a science of the nature of human beings—of their aesthetic nature as distinct from the culture, acquired by practice, of their practices." In his book, which is as provocative as it is stimulating, Menke "hardly pays attention to the classic discussion of aesthetic theories in which the content of works of art and their social relevance is negotiated."[132]

Although the criteria of the beautiful and the autonomy of art, which are at the center of modern theories of art and philosophical aesthetics, may seem subordinate or subordinate to the description and evaluation of works of art from an art-historical perspective,[133] the contribution that philosophy makes to the education and self-understanding of humanity should not be overestimated—a contribution that Hegel summed up in the first third of the nineteenth century when he interpreted works of art like philosophical texts that deal with and speak of the absolute. Although discursive, intellectual thinking cannot grasp the fullness of aesthetics, philosophy, through its own thinking and discourse about art, is able to discover a work of art in an excellent way and make it speak because, according to Hegel, "its standing is of such a kind that, though sensuous, it is essential at the same time for *spirit* [*für den Geist*]; *spirit* [*Geist*] is meant to be affected by it and to find some satisfaction in it."[134]

Wherever the view of the arts and their works as media of transcendence arises in philosophical aesthetics that seek to take account of the works of the arts, the view that art transcends limited reality is still alive, even though it no longer appears as a demand for the aesthetic realization of the metaphysically conceived original perfection of the world. However, this thought still reverberates as it did in the twentieth century when Ernst Bloch discovered the appearance of a better world in old works of art and thus asserted the utopian

---

[131] Cf. Menke, *Kraft*, 9 and Menke, *Kraft der Kunst*, xi.

[132] As Werner Köhne aptly indicates about Menke's book *Kraft*. See Köhne, "Das letzte Wort der Ästhetik ist die menschliche Freiheit" (2009). The problem here in question is the separation of philosophical aesthetics from metaphysics. Already in 1967, Gerd Wolandt ("Zur Aktualität der Hegelschen Ästhetik," esp. 229f. and 233f.) underlined how questionable it is the attempt to detach aesthetics from metaphysics; see also Kulenkampff, "Metaphysik und Ästhetik: Kant zum Beispiel," 49 and 80. In his clever *artnet*-review from January 22, 2009 ("Dry swimming against the stream"), Michael Mayer sees in turn a deficiency in the book, in the fact that "Menke's concept—to speak with Kant—is simply in lack of the intuition, which means that there is no confrontation with that specific kind of sensibility that we call art." According to Mayer, Menke should have "put to test his thesis on selected examples of contemporary art [. . .] productions." I'm not quite sure whether Menke's study from 2013, *Die Kraft der Kunst*, compensates for this deficiency.

[133] See Franke, "Nach Hegel," esp. 82–85.

[134] Hegel, *Aesthetics*, Vol. 1, 35 (translation modified).

character of art, true to the motto of the Russian writer Nikolai Gawrilowitsch Tschernyshevskij: "Beauty is life as it should be in all its reality."[135]

The philosophically-based and art-theoretically formulated idea of the work of art as a perfectly shaped, harmoniously beautiful object is also suggested to today's viewer by the great works of the old masters as well as the classic moderns that can be seen in museums. However, we also come across works of art in museums today that are no longer considered beautiful by art history and which were so named after the Second World War and increasingly brought into focus.[136]

Change testifies to the need of humanity to become aware of the world so that it recognizes itself in it: humanity "doubles" itself by looking at its spiritual world in a work of art. It therefore sounds very modern when Hegel says that every work of art is "a dialogue with everyone confronts it."[137]

Last but not least, Hegel's historical-philosophical interpretation of the history of the arts and their works also opens up a perspective on the cultural-theoretical potential of his aesthetics.[138] The potential of Baumgarten's philosophy should be opened in relation to the determination of his aesthetics as "instrumental philosophy," which has so far been neglected, and in view of which the basic features of the *Aesthetics* are outlined and problematized.

AESTHETIC THEORY AS INSTRUMENTAL PHILOSOPHY

If the *Reflections on Poetry* is satisfied with calling for a scientific investigation of our ability to cognize something sensibly (*scientia sensitive quid cognoscendi*) for the foundation of poetics, and if this early writing already has something more in view,[139] it is then the second letter of the *Philosophical Letters from Aletheophilus*, a really "interesting document from the history of the emergence of aesthetics,"[140] that fulfills this promise. It not only leads to a more detailed definition of the new science but also

---

[135] Bloch, *Das Prinzip Hoffnung*, 959. See Gawrilowitsch, *Die ästhetischen Beziehungen der Kunst zur Wirklichkeit* (1954).

[136] See Eco, *On Ugliness* (2007); see also Stemmrich, *Das Charakteristische in der Malerei* (1994).

[137] Hegel, *Aesthetics*, Vol. 1, 263–264: The work of art "exists not for *itself* but for *us*" and we should be at home in it. "The actors, for example, in the performance of a drama do not speak merely to one another, but to us," and all works of art do that.

[138] See Franke and Gethmann-Siefert, *Kulturpolitik und Kunstgeschichte* (2004), especially the introduction by the editors and the contributions by Jeong-Im Kwon, Elisabeth Weisser-Lohmann, Annemarie Gethmann-Siefer, and Bernadette Collenberg-Plotnikov. See also Schnädelbach, "Geist als Kultur?" 187–207.

[139] Cf. Baumgarten, *Reflections on Poetry*, 5.

[140] See Bergmann, *Die Begründung der deutschen Ästhetik*, 15. For what follows, see Baumgarten, *Philosophische Brieffe*, 5–8.

explains the place it should occupy within the system of scholastic sciences. This is done in an *Outline of Philosophical Encyclopedia* that Baumgarten wrote for the use in his lectures[141] and about which he allows the anonymous author of the *Philosophical Letters* to report.

Aletheophilus describes the philosophical encyclopedia designed in the *Outline* in contrast to the famous *Encyclopaedia* by Johann Heinrich Alsted[142] and mentions that "Baron von Leibnitz" would have "approved of a work of this kind, revised and expanded to include new contributions, being supplied to the learned world."[143] A "work of this kind," a systematic compendium of the entirety of all sciences,[144] which, according to Baumgarten, "can hardly be given birth by a single head," is not what the *Outline* intends to offer. He merely introduces "the whole of sciences belonging to philosophy in their connection."

The main thought concerns the abandonment of the common synonymy of organic philosophy and logic, in favor of an expansion of the concept of organic philosophy in view of a new science. This science, which should serve to "improve sensible cognition" and which Baumgarten expressly calls "aesthetics" in this context,[145] is reserved for "the laws of sensible and vivid cognition." In this function, aesthetics acts as a further instrumental philosophy alongside logic, which serves to improve the cognition of the understanding [*Verstandeserkenntnis*].

If, according to Baumgarten's thesis, we cognize not only through the understanding but also through sensibility, then the thing itself, namely, the

---

[141] Baumgarten, *Sciagraphia* (1769). On the place of the *Sciagraphia* in the "system" of Baumgarten, cf. Peres, "Die Doppelfunktion der Ästhetik im philosophischen System A. G. Baumgartens," 89–116. The question remains open, whether the encyclopedic arrangement can be in fact "systematically understood," as Peres suggests.

[142] Alsted, *Encyclopaedia*. Alsted († 1638) was a philosophy professor and later theology professor in Herborn, where he was the teacher of the great pedagogue Jan Amos Komenský (Comenius).

[143] Baumgarten, *Philosophischer Brieffe*, 6. Evidently, Baumgarten has here in mind Leibniz's methodological considerations, *De Ratione perficiendi et emendandi Encyclopaediam Alstedii*, which were edited in 1718 and 1738. Cf. Franke, *Kunst als Erkenntnis*, 23.

[144] Cf. Walch, *Philosophisches Lexicon*, Sp. 737: "Ἐγκυκλοπαίδεια, from ἐγκύκλος, circularis, is indeed a compendium [*Zusammen-Begriff*] or a body [*Cörper*] of all sciences, which the antique brought together in unity due to the kinship they had among them, in order to represent their arrangement as how they follow one another."

[145] See Baumgarten *Philosophische Brieffe*, 7. Baumgarten allows here his pseudonym to hint at his *Reflections on Poetry* (§116): as Aletheophilus explains, the name "aesthetics" seems to him to be all the more appropriate for the new science, since he has already found him in "academic writings." One may assume that thereby Baumgarten's own determination of aesthetics is meant, since we find indeed an academic writing before us in the *Reflections* with which he disputed *pro loco*. The allusion could also go to a member of Plato's academy. Kristeller ("The Modern System of the Arts II," 17–46) refers the assignment of intellectual representations, on the one hand, and sensible representations, on the other, each to a special science, to a distinction made by Speusippus and reported by Sextus Empiricus (*Adversus Mathematicos* VII, 145)—See also Baumgarten, *Aesthetica/Ästhetik*, §631ff., and Allerkamp and Mirbach, *Schönes Denken* (2016).

task of organic philosophy to guide knowledge, demands such an extension. Later on, in his lectures on aesthetics, Baumgarten turned against the equation of organic philosophy or instrumental philosophy and logic, which he wanted to invalidate by establishing aesthetics. Since the "sciences of cognition [. . .] should be counted as *philosophia instrumentali* or *organica*," aesthetics as a science mediated by sensible cognition also belongs to instrumental philosophy, so that both terms are "no longer to be regarded as synonyms."[146] Aesthetics is assigned its own object and has the improvement of sensible cognition as its task.

With the help of the *Outline*,[147] the position of aesthetics as an instrumental philosophy within the academic sciences can now be determined. As it should first be noted, since the beginning of his teaching career, Baumgarten's interest followed the trend of the time by making the encyclopedic accomplishment of knowledge prevail. Already in his inaugural lecture *Thoughts on Rational Acclaim from Academies* (*Gedancken vom vernünfftigen Beyfall auf Academien*, 1740/1741)[148] he had emphasized the organic character of his aesthetics.[149] In the *Outline* he then elaborates on the distinction between a general encyclopedia as a collection of disciplines that encompasses everything that can be known by human beings, an encyclopedia at the basis of all branches of learning, and a special philosophical encyclopedia.[150] The latter is characterized by the fact that its disciplines have a scientific character in the sense that they try to conceive the quality of things "sine fide," that is, without resorting to religion, especially Christian beliefs.[151] In doing so, he adopts the for him "usual"[152] Aristotelian division according to which instrumental

---

[146] See Baumgarten, *"Kollegium über die Ästhetik,"* 71 (§1). On the scholastic understanding of instrumental philosophy, see, for example, Heineccius, *Elementa philosophiae*. According to Heineccius, Baumgarten lectured in Halle before using Wolff's *German Logic* as a basis for his lectures.

[147] Ernst Bergmann (*Die Begründung der deutschen Ästhetik*, 17–20) apparently has no qualms about going into more detail about the *Sciagraphia*, in contrast to Paul Menzer ("Zur Entstehung von A. G. Baumgartens Ästhetik," 294), for whom it can "hardly be used as a source" because the editor Johann Christian Foerster has compiled it "out of different notebooks from different times" (Baumgarten, *Sciagraphia*, 1769). However, Menzer notes that aesthetics appears in the *Sciagraphia* as "comprehensive science," as we are particularly interested in here.

[148] See the edition of the *Gedancken* by Alexander Aichele, in Aichele and Mirbach, *A. G. Baumgarten: Sinnliche Erkenntnis in der Philosophie des Rationalismus*, 271–304.

[149] This, according to Dagmar Mirbach in the introduction to her translation of *Aesthetics*; see Baumgarten, *Aesthetica/Ästhetik*, B. 1, xxix–xxxii. Thomas Abbt also gives testimony: "For the sake of our times, it is still worth mentioning that, in 1737, he already gave the current fashion lectures, namely encyclopedic, about everything that is not related to the three higher faculties. (the natural theology, jurisprudence, medicine)" (Abbt, *Vermischte Werke*, Vol. 4, 225).

[150] See Baumarten, *Sciagraphia*, §1.

[151] See Baumarten, *Sciagraphia*, §2. In addition, see Aichele, "Wahrheit — Gewißheit — Wirklichkeit," 15–18.

[152] See Baumgarten, *Sciagraphia*, §6.

philosophy together with theoretical and practical philosophy make up the field of philosophical science in general.[153]

Baumgarten thus assigns "the place of aesthetics in the philosophy of the time,"[154] by inserting into the collection of philosophical disciplines a science that trains the faculty of sensibility, in the sense of an instrument of sensible cognition. From the perspective of the theory of science, organic philosophy thus receives the meaning of a common heading for logic and aesthetics, and a new organon of sensibility appears alongside the classic organon of the understanding.

According to an indication incidentally given in the context of the *Outline*, this organon serves a "philosophical theory of the beautiful sciences."[155] "So called for a long time," they can finally become sciences, since "from them certain general grounds should be proven to be justified."[156] This does not only apply to poetics and rhetoric, but moreover Baumgarten, "when giving lectures on his doctrine, constantly looked at the connection between the beautiful sciences and fine arts."[157]

For Baumgarten, however, the liberal arts [*freie Künste*] expressly include not only rhetoric and poetics, already mentioned in *Reflections on Poetry* as beneficiaries of aesthetics, but also philology, hermeneutics, music, and so on,[158] that is, all those arts whose common mark, according to Karl Friedrich Flögel, an epigone of Baumgarten, is communication through sensibly articulated signs, or which serve to interpret such communications.[159]

---

[153] Baumgarten, *Sciagraphia*, §5: "Sciagraphia encyclopaediae philosophicae si sequatur ordmem, quo a pluribus tractandae sunt principales philosophiae partes, aget 1) de logica, 2) de metaphysica, 3) de philosophia practica, 4) de physica, et propius cum qualibet connexis." On this division, see also Franke, *Kunst als Erkenntnis*, 25.

[154] See Nivelle, *Kunst- und Dichtungstheorien zwischen Aufklärung und Klassik*, 10.

[155] See Baumgarten Baumgarten, *Sciagraphia*, §25, §109.

[156] See Meier, "Baumgartens Leben," 357.

[157] See Abbt, *Vermischte Werke*, Vol. 4, 229ff.—Even Meier ("Baumgartens Leben," 357) underlines and defends this aim of his teacher: "And if philosophical heads who understand the music, painting art, and all other fine arts apart from speech and poetry, apply the aesthetic principles to the same: so the only objection that has been made against the aesthetic with flattery and lots of appearance will be completely eliminated"; it is, namely, the objection that "Baumgarten's aesthetics only contains the first principles of speech and poetry" because: "anyone who sees this aesthetic properly is convinced tby the contrary."

[158] Baumgarten, *Aesthetica/Ästhetik*, §4: "Hinc usus speciales, 1) philologicus, 2) hermeuticus, 3) exegeticus, 4) rhetoricus, 5) homileticus, 6) poeticus, 7) musicus e.c."

[159] See Flögel, *Einleitung in die Erfindungskunst*, §118: "The signs by which we express our interiority must also be felt with the senses; for a sign is something sensible, whereby the thought is excited by a thing. Hence, the signs through which we let others know our thoughts fall either in the feeling or in the face or in your ears," while one cannot "make his thoughts cognizable through smell or taste," we may add, just as little as we can understand the thoughts of others—I draw Flögel's art of invention [*Erfindungskunst*], from which Baeumler (*Das Irrationalitätsproblem*, 177 n. 4) rightly says that it contains "nothing but classifications in the manner of Baumgarten," precisely because of its epigonal character, as attested by Baumgarten's biographers. Also for Thomas Abbt (*Briefe die neueste Literatur betreffend*, 194; letter from May 7, 1761), Flögel's

As an instrumental philosophy, aesthetics is therefore dependent on training and perfecting the "art of signs" [*Zeichenkunde*], which Baumgarten also calls a *facultas signatrix*. Baumgarten is thinking here of a theory of signs (*scientia signorum*) in the sense of a canon of rules, a guideline that he introduces as "semiotics" and also as "philosophical semiology"—a determination that Baumgarten obviously gained in parallel to logic;[160] for he distinguishes between a logical and an aesthetic characteristic. Both are intended to serve the invention as well as the interpretation of signs. The logical doctrine of the sign is, on the one hand, concerned—as a heuristic characteristic—with primitive signs and has to do with derived signs as a combinatorial [*Kombinatorik*] in Leibniz' sense; on the other hand, it is concerned—as a hermeneutic characteristic—with recognizing what is designated by signs (*de cognoscendis signorum signatis*).[161] Accordingly, aesthetic semiotics is understood as an instrument for the invention and interpretation of signs insofar as they are an expression of sensible cognition.[162]

In the sense of his determination of aesthetics as an instrumental philosophy, Baumgarten primarily conceives aesthetic sign theory as a characteristic of discourse and understands it as philology. Since it specifies rules that apply to many languages, it can also be called a grammar in a broader sense. Orthography, etymology, syntax, prosody as well as the lexicographical meaning of word-signs [*Wortzeichen*] or the art of fine writing (*Philologia graphice*) are assigned to the aesthetic characteristic. However, aesthetic characteristic as a canon of eloquence (*eloquentia*) particularly concerns prosaic and metered poetic speech. Also assigned to aesthetics is the theory of signs that Baumgarten submits to an encyclopedic division into disciplines that, in addition to grammar, rhetoric, and poetics, also includes emblematics [*die Emblematik*] with its particular subdivisions.[163] Baumgarten subordinates

---

book is only "a Germanized Baumgartian Collegium," which "would have never been developed without Baumgarten's lectures." And Johann Christian Foerster asserts that "one can get an idea" of Baumgarten's philosophical encyclopedia "through by Mr. Flögel's art of invention" (Foerster, *Charaktere dreier berühmter Weltweisen der neueren Zeit*, 39).

[160] See Baumgarten, *Metaphysics*, §349. This meaning has not yet been recorded in Walch, *Philosophisches Lexicon*, col. 2369 ("Semeiotic"). The latter only knows semiotics in the old meaning of a "science [. . .] of the characteristics [*Kennzeichen*]" from which the doctors reveal a person's state of health, as well as in the sense of a symptomatic of the "moral state of souls."

[161] See Baumgarten, *Metaphysica* (4th Ed.), §349.

[162] Baumgarten's determination came along, evidently, in connection with the elaboration of his aesthetic theory. It can only be found in Baumgarten's *Metaphysica* (2nd Ed.), as a supplement to §622.

[163] Baumgarten, *Metaphysica* (4th Ed.), §622. See Baumgarten, *Philosophia generalis*, §147: "[. . .] ars signandi et ex signis cognoscendi, CHARACTERISTICA (Semiotica, Semiologia, Symbolica) [. . .] tractat [. . .] orationem, PHILOLOGIA universalis [. . .]."

rhetoric as well as poetics to eloquence [*Beredsamkeit*], which he conceives as the doctrine of discourse.[164]

Baumgarten himself did not discuss the aesthetic characteristics in its hermeneutic determination, but it was Georg Friedrich Meier who carried this out, in connection to Baumgarten, in his *Attempt at a General Art of Interpretation* (1757). Meier subordinates hermeneutics to characteristics, namely, the "science of rules, through the observation of which meaning is cognized from signs."[165] Since it is concerned with signs, it presents a "part of characteristic."[166] As Meier points out, interpretation means nothing other than "to see clearly the connection of the marked thing with its signs." A distinction is made between a "learned," "rational" philosophical interpretation, which uses the means of logic and finds its application in conceptual-scientific discourse, and an aesthetic interpretation (*interpretatio aesthetica*) as appropriate for "meaningful" or "sensibly rich" [*sinnreichen*] writings.[167]

Following Baumgarten, Meier grounds aesthetic interpretation in cognitive-psychological as well as cognitive-metaphysical terms, on the basis of the power of representation through the sensible cognitive abilities.[168] Their resemblance to reason [*Vernunftähnlichkeit*] guarantees the interpretation of the meaning [*Sinns*] of an aesthetic speech (*sensus orationis sensitivae*),[169] which presents a "series of words," "which signify representations that are connected with each other,"[170] and whose meaning [*Sinn*] must be discerned from "signs," whose expression (*terminus*) "usually consists in a human voice," for which it is called "word" [*"Wort"*] (*vocabulum*).[171]

Since no one is able to understand and interpret signs, who has not mastered the art of characterization, interpretation—a kind of hermeneutic circle—presupposes the "theory of the characteristic art of invention." A theory is needed for both inventing and interpreting signs, from which the principles of the "beauty of signs" can be derived.[172]

Such a theory was first developed in a philosophical framework in Baumgarten's *Aesthetics* and then also in Meier's *Foundations of All*

---

[164] In the eighteenth century, these disciplines were seen in different functions and relationships to one another; see. Ueding, *Einführung in die Rhetorik*, esp. 100–102. See also Ch. 4 of Franke, *Baumgartens Erfindung der Ästhetik* ("Der Abschluss der Ästhetik"), 81–98 esp. 87 (Figure 3).

[165] Meier, *Versuch einer allgemeinen Auslegungskunst*, 3, §1.

[166] Meier, *Versuch einer allgemeinen Auslegungskunst*, §3.

[167] Meier, *Versuch einer allgemeinen Auslegungskunst*, §9.

[168] Lutz Geldsetzer rightly sees this as a peculiarity of Meier's theory of interpretation. See the reprint (ed. 1965) supervised by Geldsetter: Meier, *Versuch einer allgemeinen Auslegungskunst*, XXIII. See also Scholz, "Die Allgemeine Hermeneutik bei Georg Friedrich Meier," esp. 175–181.

[169] Meier, *Versuch einer allgemeinen Auslegungskunst*, §29.

[170] Meier, *Versuch einer allgemeinen Auslegungskunst*, §105.

[171] Meier, *Versuch einer allgemeinen Auslegungskunst*, §103.

[172] Meier, *Anfangsgründe*, Vol. 2, §516.

Beautiful Sciences.[173] Still in 1742, Johann Martin Chladenius, in his *Introduction to the Correct Interpretation of Rational Writings* (an important document for the history of hermeneutics), overlooks an explanation of "meaningful" thoughts and writings, above all those coming from the power of imagination. The "new Philosophy" would have "provided a ground" for such an explanation.[174]

Therefore, it is first of all clear that the determination of aesthetics as instrumental philosophy exhaustively takes into account the intention of the founding father of aesthetics. And how does the determination of aesthetics as an instrumental philosophy relate to the *Aesthetics*?

If one makes it clear that Baumgarten does not intend to sharpen sensibility for its logical use, that he did not intend aesthetics to serve this function, but rather to promote its possible autonomy [*Eigenständigkeit*], then the juncture shows itself here: the systematic connection between aesthetics as the science of sensible cognition, on the one hand, and as a theory of the liberal arts, on the other. Aesthetics applies the laws and the peculiar form of sensible representation to the nonmechanical, free arts, of which it considers itself their theory—from this scientific-theoretical point of view, Baumgarten can speak of a "marriage" (*connubium*) of science and art.[175]

BAUMGARTEN AND HIS INVENTION TODAY

While the growing interest in Baumgarten initially focused primarily on the founding father of aesthetics, in the past two decades research has increasingly turned its attention to the function of sensible cognition and its connection with ethics,[176] natural law,[177] and natural theology, to which Baumgarten—following the tendency of his time—dedicated textbooks of his own, on which he based his lectures as an academic teacher at the *Fridericiana* University in Halle and at the *Viadrina* University in Frankfurt an der Oder.[178] Contemporary Baumgarten research especially seeks to

---

[173] Meier's *Anfangsgründe* refers back to Baumgarten's notebook, which Meier followed as he lectured on aesthetics in Halle as early as 1745/1746. In his preface, he calls Baumgarten the "main founder" of aesthetics; see Meier, *Anfangsgründe*, Vol. 1, 1. See also Bergmann, *Die Begründung der deutschen Ästhetik*, 141–143.

[174] See Chladenius, *Einleitung zur richtigen Auslegung vernünftiger Schriften*, §63–§65; see also Pimpinella, "Hermeneutik und Ästhetik bei A. G. Baumgarten," 265–283.

[175] See Franke, *Kunst als Erkenntnis*, 85–87.

[176] In addition, see Schwaiger, "Ein 'missing link' auf dem Weg der Ethik von Wolff zu Kant," esp. 252 ff. and 256–259.

[177] See Aichele, "Sive vox naturae sive vox rationis sive vox Dei?" 115–135. See also Aichele, "Die Ungewißheit des Gewissens," 3–30.

[178] "The large number of subjects about which Baumgarten lectured at the time makes it clear what would still be included under the concept of Philosophical Faculty by the middle of that century.

interpret Baumgarten's approach to sensibility by locating it in the constellation of the philosophy of art, epistemology, and anthropology.

Notably, Italian research, in whose context the first complete modern translations of *Aesthetics*, associated with the names of Francesco Piselli and Salvatore Tedesco, emerged,[179] displays an extraordinary and multifaceted number of philological and philosophical-historical studies, which permit a more precise understanding of the concept of sensible cognition as well as the place of Baumgarten's aesthetic theory and its problem history within European intellectual history.[180]

In the German-speaking context, the history of aesthetic problems is approached from the perspective of the present, which involve Baumgarten's aesthetic theory in the contemporary horizon of philosophical questions. From this perspective, it is less concerned with an exegesis of Baumgarten as with consequences of a structural kind: "They consist in a different understanding of the constitution of sensible cognition and presentation, which Baumgarten no longer thinks of as representation, but begins to understand as activity."[181] Baumgarten's conception of sensibility and sensible cognition are not least thematized with regard to poetics and rhetoric, in relation to which Baumgarten unfolded his aesthetics. This way, the structure-forming and shaping power of rhetoric[182] in the *Aesthetics* is integrated into the determinations of sensible cognition and beautiful thinking [*schönen Denkens*]. Such a thinking, a *pulchre cogitare*, joins aesthetics to both rhetoric and poetics.[183]

Already Alfred Baeumler called attention to the problem of the relation of Baumgarten's aesthetics to rhetoric and poetics, and also to the question of their transformation, which he emphasized with regard to the function of sensible cognition: the question of rhetoric, namely, of "how a thought that

---

At the same time, it is easy to see how the Prussian prescriptions for lecturing about certain textbooks in connection to the necessary oral corrections could be a school for independent thinking." See Fontius, "Baumgarten und die Literaturbriefe," 573—On the old Viadrina, see Heinrich, "Frankfurt an der Oder. Universität," 335–342.

[179] See Baumgarten, *L'estetica di Alexander Gottlieb Baumgarten* (ed. Tedesco, 2000) and Baumgarten, *Estetica* (ed. Piselli, 1992). [See also *Alexander Gottlieb Baumgarten, Estetica*, ed. Salvatore Tedesco and Alessandro Nannini, 2020—ed.]

[180] See Mirbach, "Neue Beiträge der italienischen Forschung zu Alexander Gottlieb Baumgartens Ästhetik," 606–621.

[181] Menke, "Schwerpunkt: Zur Aktualität der Ästhetik von Alexander G. Baumgarten," 230. Unlike Menke, I believe that, although Baumgarten begins to understand the constitution of sensible cognition and presentation as an activity, he still thinks of it *also* as representation, as it was previously.

[182] On this see Bender, "Rhetorische Tradition und Ästhetik im 18. Jahrhundert: Baumgarten, Meier, Breitinger," esp. 481–494; see also Bezzola, *Rhetorik bei Kant, Fichte und Hegel* (1993).

[183] See Allerkamp and Mirbach, *Schönes Denken*, passim.

can be expressed, which surpasses the scope of the concept, is answered by Baumgarten's aesthetics."[184]

It seems then consistent that rhetoric stands at the core of the *Baumgarten-Studien* on the "genealogy of aesthetics," which was published in 2014 on the occasion of Baumgarten's 300th birthday by Rüdiger Campe, Anselm Haverkamp, and Christoph Menke. The contributions of the editors themselves are as worthy of discussion as they are debatable. They postulate the shaping power of rhetoric as if it were absolute, so that the question of a transformation of the rhetorical categories to which Baumgarten expressly refers does not come to the fore. In this way, what I believe to be the crucial point of the *Aesthetics*—probably not inadvertently—is left out of the picture and becomes a blind spot. As stated at the beginning of the volume, the authors are engaged in a renewal of interest in Baumgarten's aesthetics.[185] This new interest responds to "another history of literary studies and philosophy," whose "interplay" in Baumgarten's aesthetics ought to be developed by the *Studien*. The "legend of the invention [. . .] of the aesthetics" that is "attached" to Baumgarten is expressly rejected—a position already suggested by the subtitle of the volume, *Genealogy of Aesthetics*. For, since Foucault, we have reckoned the concept of genealogy as the name of a specific form and a specific program of (social) criticism.[186]

The arc of genealogical tension drawn by the *Baumgarten-Studien* collected in the volume ranges from Erasmus's *On the Abundance of Words and Ideas* (*De copia rerum et verborum*, 1512) to Kant and finally Michel Foucault's *The Order of Things* (*Les mots et Les choses*, 1967). In this genealogy focused on rhetoric, which results in the rejection of the alleged "legend of the invention of aesthetics" by Baumgarten, nevertheless, Baumgarten is assigned the key function for a new reading of history of philosophy and literary history. To what extent the interplay between literary history and philosophy has been brought to a "new stage" in Baumgarten's aesthetics—this is what the articles want to present with "justificatory examples," for example, in view of Gottsched or Vico, that would have opened up a "constellation of increasing interest in Baumgarten," namely, in close relation to rhetoric. The crucial question for the authors is the "survival of rhetoric," which in Germany would have been completely precluded by Kant, while rhetoric remained "more relevant" in the English and French traditions.[187]

---

[184] Baeumler, *Das Irrationalitätsproblem*, 210. See also Niehues-Pröbsting, "Rhetorische und idealistische Kategorien der Ästhetik," 94–110.

[185] See Campe, Haverkamp, and Menke, *Baumgarten-Studien*, 9f.

[186] See Foucault, "Nietzsche, Genealogy, History," 369–392.

[187] Campe, Haverkamp, and Menke, *Baumgarten-Studien*, 9–12.

In one of his contributions to this volume, entitled "The Discipline of Aesthetics is the Aesthetics of Discipline," Christoph Menke reads "Baumgarten from Foucault's Perspective." Menke rightly attaches great importance to Baumgarten's considerations regarding the training of creative capacities that are naturally given to us. In this regard, Baumgarten speaks of exercise (*exercitatio*). Menke, however, regards *exercitatio* from the perspective of Foucault's *Discipline and Punish* as disciplining and subjection, while he claims that "aesthetics is the thinking of disciplines, of disciplinary power." This interpretation culminates in the thesis: "the model after which Foucault thinks in *Discipline and Punish* disciplinary power is aesthetics." However, as Menke notes, Foucault refers nowhere explicitly to aesthetics as "the new way of thinking of the arts," nor does he have to, "for aesthetics models Foucault's analysis of the disciplines."[188]

For Menke, Foucault's analysis of "disciplinary power" and "thinking of aesthetics" operates on the "same conceptual foundation"—whatever that may mean. If, as Menke points out, "force and capacity, of dynamics and development" are the central concepts through which Foucault determines disciplinary power,[189] Baumgarten's determination of force is allegedly put on the level of the same conceptual foundation. However, Baumgarten understands force, with Leibniz, as the determination of the soul to represent the universe, as it is said in the *Metaphysics*,[190] to which Baumgarten expressly refers in the *Aesthetics*. But this determination is hardly likely to accord with the concept of force in *Discipline and Punish*. In any case, only in this determination (that of representing the universe) is force (*vis*) a concept of Baumgarten's aesthetics.

Menke dedicates another contribution in the *Baumgarten-Studien* to the determination of force, where he interprets force [*Kraft*] from the perspective of Herder's debate with Baumgarten. There Baumgarten's insight comes to the fore, according to which there are "dark representations" in the soul, which he calls *fundus animae*.[191] Menke does not "explicitly" follow Baumgarten's considerations here, "but rather the step Herder takes in his

---

[188] See, in this volume, Menke, "The Discipline of Aesthetics is the Aesthetics of Discipline," 275.
[189] Menke, "The Discipline of Aesthetics is the Aesthetics of Discipline," 275.
[190] See Baumgarten, *Metaphysica* (1st Ed.), §527 ("anima mea est vis repraesentativa universi"). See also Mirbach, "Die Rezeption von Leibniz' Monadenlehre bei Baumgarten," esp. 376–379—Whereas Haverkamp and Menke leave metaphysics more or less explicitly aside, and then, to a large extent, ignore as impertinent a central aspect of the *Aesthetics* to which the "Prolegomena" are dedicated, Rüdiger Campe explicitly engages with Baumgarten's metaphysics. Of his three contributions to the volume, let me highlight here Campe's study "Effekt der Form," 117–144, which particularly raises clarity upon the connection of agency or effect [*Wirkung oder Effekt*] and form.
[191] See Baumgarten, *Metaphysica* (1st Ed.), §510–§514.

criticism of Baumgarten." From this perspective, according to Menke, aesthetics ought to be unfolded anew as anthropology.[192]

Baumgarten and his invention today—this means, last but not least, to pose anew the question concerning the grounds and the conditions for the emergence of aesthetics as a new philosophical discipline. The Baumgarten research of the late twentieth and early twenty-first centuries looks for an answer, on the one hand, in the perspective of a possible connection between aesthetics and anthropology; on the other hand, in view of Baumgarten's character, shaped through his youth and the education he received at the orphanage from August Hermann Francke, that is, at the center of eighteenth-century Pietism.[193] With this, Baumgarten's determination of aesthetics as a science of sensible cognition, which has its own aesthetic truth, stands at the center of attention.[194]

a) The birth of aesthetics is discussed in connection with the emergence of anthropology as a new philosophical discipline in the eighteenth century, for instance, from the perspective of a "generation of the whole human being." This way, in reference to its central determination of sensible cognition, Baumgarten's aesthetics is associated with the modern life sciences, especially to medicine and biology. However, this perspective seems to be fruitful at best in terms of a reflection upon the development of biology (and medicine) as a science, whereas the connection to Baumgarten's aesthetics remains less plausible.[195]

b) There is the attempt to account for Baumgarten's pietist character, in view of his "education and training by pietist theologians in Halle," which "provided him with many of the pieces" that shape his aesthetic theory.[196] However, this reading neglects the difference between Baumgarten's aesthetic theory and his theologically accentuated works and considerations and, therefore, mostly relies on arguments from his older brother, the theologian Siegmund Jacob Baumgarten, than on documented views of the inventor of aesthetics.[197]

---

[192] See Menke, "Das Wirken dunkler Kraft," 104. See also Menke, *Kraft*, 99 n. 97, as well as the extended study by Zelle, "Sinnlichkeit und Therapie," 5–24.

[193] See, in this volume, Grote, "Piestist *Aisthesis* and Moral Education," 125 ff.

[194] See Fritz, *Vom Erhabenen*, 248–283 and 284–355.

[195] See already Adler, "Aisthesis, steinernes Herz und geschmeidige Sinne," 96–111 and above all Borchers, *Die Erzeugung des ,ganzen Menschen'*, esp. 136–155 (The Birth of Aesthetics—Convenentalist-theological anthropology in Baumgarten's aesthetics).

[196] See Schwaiger, *Alexander Gottlieb Baumgarten*, esp. §5 (Baumgarten as "Pietist enlightener"), as well as 116f. and 140f. Grote indicates relations, but also differences between the so-called spiritual and good taste; see Grote, "Vom geistlichen zum guten Geschmack?" 365.

[197] See, for example, Bahr, *Darstellung des Undarstellbaren*, esp. 11–45.

In contrast, one ought to emphasize Baumgarten's defense against a sensibility like the one bound to pietist devotion. Baumgarten had explicitly rejected this connection in the prolegomena to his *Aesthetics*, on the basis of "the aesthetic program for the training of sensible cognition" that he had already developed in the *Reflections on Poetry* and later in the *Aesthetics*.[198]

If, as evidence of its pietist foundations, recourse is taken to concepts such as *vita, aedificatio*, or *fundus animae*,[199] these determinations can certainly be found in the lexicon of German Pietism;[200] however, between the pietist use of these words, on the one hand, and the use of words in Baumgarten's aesthetic theory, on the other, conceptual shifts can be clearly read, which distinguish them from their pietist meaning: *Fundus animae*, for example, in the pietist theology is thoroughly determined as the ground of the soul, in the sense of a foundation for the "elevation of the soul" toward God; in Baumgarten, on the other hand, *fundus animae* is—as already stated—the place for those obscure ideas to which sensible cognition owes its conciseness.[201]

c) The cultural-philosophical potential of Baumgarten's aesthetic theory,[202] which Ernst Cassirer has already highlighted,[203] is emphasized by questions such as those concerning the relationship between aesthetics and literary history[204] or aesthetics and visual art[205] or the never-ending questions about the experience, meaning, and justification of beauty.[206]

---

[198] "Concomitantly thought in Baumgarten's aesthetic critique of knowledge is thus, at once, an aesthetic criticism of the Pietist theory of experience"; Baumgarten introduces "the unprocessed field of sensibility as one indispensable for rationality and its equivalent to a human cognitive force in the field," and asserts "against the pietistic repression of evil sensibility" a "rightful use of this divine talent of men." See Federlin, *Kirchliche Volksbildung und Bürgerliche Gesellschaft*, 85.

[199] See Schwaiger, *Alexander Gottlieb Baumgarten*, 29.

[200] See the entries on these keywords in Langen, *Der Wortschatz des Deutschen Pietismus* (1968).

[201] Well elaborated are these and other meaning shifts in Martens (*Literatur und Frömmigkeit*, esp. 76–81); see also Adler, "Fundus Animae—Der Grund der Seele," 197–220 and Bahr, *Darstellung des Undarstellbaren*, 78–85.

[202] See Gross, *Felix Aestheticus: Die Ästhetik als Lehre vom Menschen*, Th. 3; Gross, "*Felix Aestheticus und animal symbolicum*," 275–298. See also Haverkamp, "Wie die Morgenröte zwischen Nacht und Tag," 3–26 and Stöckmann, "Steffen W. Groß, *Felix aesthicus*," 294–298. See also Spree, "Cassirers Baumgarten," 410–420.

[203] See Cassirer, *Freiheit und Form*, esp. 79–86; Cassirer, *Die Philosophie der Aufklärung*, 288–375, esp. 353–372—See also Orth, "Ernst Cassirer als Kulturwissenschaftler," 269–291.

[204] Berndt, *Poema/Gedicht*, esp. 12–126. See also Berndt, "Die Kunst der Analogie," 183–199; Gaede, *Poetik und Logik*, esp. 106–114; Buchenau, "Die Einbindung von Poetik und Ästhetik," 81–84; Neumann, *Präsenz und Evidenz fremder Dinge im Europa des 18. Jahrhunderts* (2015); Trop, *Poetry as a Way of Life* (2015); Haverkamp, "Alexander Gottlieb Baumgarten als Provokation der Literaturgeschichte," 35–48.

[205] See Berndt, "Ex marmore," 73–96. See also Haverkamp, "Metaphora Dis/continua: Figure in De/construction," 29–45.

[206] See Schmitt, "Schönheit: Gegenstand der Sinne oder des Denkens?" 49–70.

If these questions already show a continuing or renewed interest in research on Baumgarten's aesthetic theory for its cultural-scientific and cultural-philosophical applicability[207] from Cassirer's perspective, they must be linked then to aesthetics as an instrumental philosophy, which Baumgarten, as already explained, assigns to all those disciplines that make use of sensibly rich signs [*sinnreicher Zeichen*].[208] Today, this includes cultural studies as well as the humanities and social sciences, which, depending on how "cultural studies" is understood, are considered as separate disciplines or as part of the science of culture.[209] Sensibly rich signs are nonpropositional signs;[210] they structure texts in the fields of cultural science, the humanities and social sciences, for they play a role in the understanding, interpretation, and performance of texts.[211]

If, on the basis of its hermeneutical aspect,[212] Baumgarten's aesthetic theory can be seen to provide a tool or an instrument for today's debates in the sciences of arts and culture, from a methodological perspective the question arises, concerning the points of contact between his aesthetic theory and the language-analytical aesthetics, specifically with regard to his understanding of aesthetics as *ars pulchre cogitandi*, that is to say, in the sense of a "technique of beautiful thinking."[213] Even though the answer should/must be left to further research, it ought to be emphasized that the question concerning such points of contact is thoroughly discussed in aesthetic discourse in relation to aesthetic judgment in Kant.[214]

d) Finally, Baumgarten's aesthetics undoubtedly offers an orientation with regard to the currently much-discussed topic of art as research. There, it is discussed whether and in what respect we can speak of art as research at all, as well as under which conditions in the humanities and cultural sciences, and

---

[207] See Sonderegger, "Die Kunst als Sphäre der Kultur," 50–65.

[208] See Baumgarten, *Philosophia generalis*, §147. Among those disciplines of a *Philosophia Organica*, Baumgarten counts not only philology, grammar, and emblematics, but also the mantic or divination with a number of subordinates. The particular disciplines of the *Philosophia Organica* are assigned to the various capacities that constitute the *analogon rationis*; Philology, grammatic, and emblematics become the "ars signandi et ex signis cognoscendi," for which they count among the characteristics or the semiotics (respectively, semiology)—On mantic, see Allerkamp, "*Onirocritica und mundus fabulous*," 201–221.

[209] See Nünning, *Grundbegriffe der Kulturtheorie und Kulturwissenschaften*, 125–130. See also Rüsen, "Sinnverlust und Transzendenz," 533–544.

[210] Mersch, "Nicht-Propositionalität und ästhetisches Denken," 28–55. See also Assmann, *Einführung in die Kulturwissenschaft*, 31–51.

[211] See Meier, *Versuch einer allgemeinenAuslegungskunst* (ed. 1965).

[212] See Schurz, "Erklären und Verstehen," 156–175. See also Aichele, "Die Grundlegung einer Hermeneutik des Kunstwerks," 82–90.

[213] See Bühler, "Ein Plädoyer für den hermeneutischen Intentionalismus," 178–198 See also Reicher, *Fiktion, Wahrheit, Wirklichkeit*, esp. 16–18 and Franke, *Kunst als Erkenntnis*, 81–85.

[214] See Zimmermann, *Sprachanalytische Ästhetik*, esp. 179 and 195; see also the review by Werner Strube, "Jörg Zimmermann, Sprachanalytische Ästhetik," 157–160.

in what sense, this topic should be problematized.[215] Here, orientation may be gained from Theodor W. Adorno's aesthetic theory and, moreover, from Baumgarten's invention of aesthetics, because in Baumgarten the central determination of sensible cognition (*cognitio sensitiva*) is directed toward the cognition of the individual, to which he ascribes an independent, specifically aesthetic truth.[216]

"Intuitive cognition" comes into focus as a crucial aspect of Baumgarten's view of sensible cognition. Baumgarten's notion is pointedly opposed to the "classical concept," which "has been problematic since the Enlightenment," because "in this version, cognition is bound to rational-conceptual argumentation, subject to the rules of logic and, in this way, what counts as cognition is restricted at once to what can be grasped in the medium of such proof." So that "what has been called intuitive cognition" only applies "as preliminary stage of an actual cognition." Against this background, the "concept of cognition as it was conceived in aesthetics" is of considerable "significance" for the question of an artistic researcher.[217]

e) If further questions concerning the empirical aesthetics of Baumgarten's aesthetic thinking come into focus,[218] then perhaps the decisive question of its applicability, as I see it, relies in a possible orientation that Baumgarten's aesthetics may offer for the valuation and criticism of art today. Can Baumgarten's aesthetic theory provide guidance in this regard or not?[219]

From my point of view, it all depends on what it means or should be meant by "orientation." If one takes the rules or criteria of "beautiful thinking," that is, wealth (*ubertas*), magnitude (*magnitudo*), truth (*veritas*), clarity (*claritas*), certainty (*certitudo*), and life (*vita*), as they are treated in the *Aesthetics* in view of the perfection of sensible cognition (*scientia cognitionis sensitivae*) and its expression in the (beautiful) work of art,[220] as a means through which to appreciate and reflect upon art and artistic ends and objectives today, against this background, then the emancipation of today's art from tradition becomes clearly evident. The emancipation of sculpture, painting, and architecture from traditional bounds can be described as an example of a point of

---

[215] See the critical considerations of Daniel Hornuff, "Kann Kunst forschen?" 225–233.

[216] See Schmücker, "Künstlerisch forschen," 131–136.

[217] See Badura, "Erkenntnis (sinnliche)," 43–48. See also Lange and Neumeyer, *Kunst und Wissenschaft um 1800*, passim.

[218] See Kater, "Brückenschläge," 171–176. See also Kleinschmidt, "Die Vermessung des Sinnlichen," 37–39.

[219] Groundbreaking for the question of the possible actualization of Baumgarten's aesthetics is Spree, "Die Aktualität der Ästhetik Baumgartens," 155–165.

[220] See Franke, *Kunst als Erkenntnis*, 81–83.

departure for a progressive break with tradition. The departure goes hand in hand not only with an expanding of boundaries of art, not just with a cross-over between the arts and the media, but also between art and life, public and private.[221] But this is a new topic—and an extensive field that is at best only partially suggested by this indication.

Translated by Mauricio González

---

[221] See Franke, "Was sie verbindet und was sie trennt" (2014).

Chapter 2

Baumgarten's *Aesthetics*

Topics and the Modern Ars inveniendi

Stefanie Buchenau

Undoubtedly, one major difficulty that Baumgarten met in his efforts toward a reform of logic was linguistic. Confronted with the philosophical terminology of his time, Baumgarten was, in a sense, speechless. He lacked the words to allow him to articulate his own critical viewpoint, because these words did not exist; they needed to be created. Baumgarten's addition of "extensive clarity" in his *Reflections on Poetry* was a major verbal invention, indicating a fundamental redistribution of functions: as Baumgarten was the first to point out, philosophical thought and discourse aim merely at logical transparency; they can remain intuitively poor, symbolic, and indifferent, and thus represent a deficient form of logic. Poetry, in contrast, aims at conveying a maximum number of characteristics and represents a different, auxiliary, or complementary kind of logic. This, in a nutshell, is the argument: innovative in Baumgarten's rationalist age and echoing the ancient, larger view on reason. In his 1750/1758 *Aesthetics*, Baumgarten rendered his account of "extensive clarity" more generally comprehensible by adding a couple of new attributes and categories borrowed from the rhetorical tradition. More directly than in the *Reflections on Poetry*, he returned to Cicero, whose viewpoint in various respects resembles his own.

CICERO AND BAUMGARTEN: ELECTIVE AFFINITIES

Although separated from the German philosopher by more than 1,700 years, and arguing from radically different philosophical and political premises, Cicero expresses a "holistic" view of philosophy and rhetoric and a criticism of the philosophy of his contemporaries similar to Baumgarten's. In fact, Cicero, provoked by Socrates' categorization of philosophy as an art of

71

thought, and rhetoric as an art of discourse, denounces the impoverishment of philosophy:

> Whereas the persons [the pre-Socratic philosophers] engaged in handling and pursuing and teaching the subjects that we are now investigating were designated by a single title, the whole study and practice of the liberal arts being entitled philosophy, Socrates robbed them of this general designation, and in his discussions separated the science of wise thinking from that of elegant speaking, though in reality they are closely linked together.[1]

In his *De oratore*, Cicero works to overcome this ill-advised Socratic division and proclaims a return to the original, pre-Socratic view of wisdom as constituting a "method of attaining and of expressing thought and a faculty of speaking" (*cogitandi pronuntiandique rationem vimque dicendi*).[2] More than merely knowledge of the object, such wisdom also demands "the art of speaking fluently about it."[3] What Cicero calls wisdom, or true oratory, strives for "a style that is dignified and graceful and in conformity with the general modes of thought and judgment,"[4] and encompasses philosophy and, more particularly, all the practical disciplines of philosophy, such as morals, politics, law, and an art of style. True oratory constitutes

> so potent a force that it embraces the origin and operation and development of all things, all the virtues and duties, all the natural principles governing the morals and minds and life of mankind, and also determines their customs and laws and rights, controls the government of the state, and expresses everything that concerns whatever topic in a graceful and flowing style.[5]

Such oratory pursues both a theoretical and a practical aim. It employs thought and speech as cognitive and "pragmatic" instruments. The orator cannot achieve his effect unless he "has gained profound insight into the characters of men, and the whole range of human nature, and those motives whereby our souls are spurred on or turned back."[6] Ultimately, nevertheless, the orator's philosophical knowledge serves a practical aim. It enables him to employ his thoughts and words as efficient weapons of action, deploying the

---

[1] Cicero, *On the Orator (De oratore)*, Bk. III, 60.
[2] Cicero, *On the Orator*, Bk. III, 56 (translation modified).
[3] Cicero, *On the Orator*, Bk. I, 63.
[4] Cicero, *On the Orator*, Bk. I, 54.
[5] Cicero, *On the Orator*, Bk. III, 76.
[6] Cicero, *On the Orator*, Bk. I, 53–54.

full power of oratory to "calm or kindle the feelings of the audience,"[7] and influence their biases and inclinations.

There is no doubt that Baumgarten finds in Cicero a soul mate and a model; in fact he reproduces Cicero's rhetorical turn in the philosophy of his age. He emphasizes the practical and political urges of his age, sketches a "rhetorical" ideal of philosophy, highlights the "rhetorical" and practical shortcomings of his predecessors' philosophy—and the necessity to complement philosophy with rhetoric and poetry. In the terminology of the *Aesthetics*, philosophy falls short insofar as it does not by itself respond to the perfection of all cognition: "Abundance, magnitude, truth, clarity, certainty and life, insofar as they are in accordance with each other in one perception, constitute the perfection of all cognition."[8] In consequence, poetry and art are better than philosophy: they represent an alternative and in some respects superior mode of thought and speech.

ATTRIBUTES OF PARTICULAR
BEAUTY IN THE *AESTHETICS*

As mentioned earlier, the chapter divisions in the *Reflections on Poetry* already reflect Baumgarten's formal debt to Cicero. The *Aesthetics* essentially takes over the same outline. As commentators as various as Marie Luise Linn,[9] Heinz Paetzold,[10] and Salvatore Tedesco[11] have recognized, Baumgarten's "theoretical" aesthetics (*aesthetica docens*) is in three parts: one concerning invention or "heuristics" (*heuristica*); a second concerning arrangement or "method" (*methodologia*); and a third concerning expression or "semiotics" (*semiotica*). The unfinished *Aesthetics*, offering long developments on inventio, simply does not get as far as to give an account of the second and third parts on *elocutio* and *semiotica*. Moreover, Baumgarten reintroduces the same Ciceronian tripartite arrangement in his very first chapter by distinguishing between the beauty of things and thought (*cogitationum*), the beauty of order and disposition, and the beauty of expression. Finally, Baumgarten obviously decides to employ Cicero's terminology better to explain the new, modern, and broad definition of poetry that in the *Reflections on Poetry* he calls "extensively clear" speech and at the beginning of the *Aesthetics* he

---

[7] Cicero, *On the Orator*, Bk. I, 17 (translation modified).
[8] Baumgarten, *Aesthetica/Ästhetik,* §22.
[9] Linn, "A.G. Baumgartens Aesthetica und die antike Rhetorik," 108.
[10] Paetzold, "Rhetorik-Kritik und Theorie der Künste in der philosophischen Ästhetik," 14.
[11] Tedesco, *L'Estetica di Baumgarten*, 81.

calls beauty: "The end of aesthetics is the sensible perfection of a cognition in itself . . . which is beauty" (*pulchritudo* or, less frequently, *venustas*).[12]

The particular components that compose general beauty—namely "abundance, magnitude, truth, clarity, certainty and life, insofar as they are in accordance with each other in one perception"—echo Cicero, who employs these attributes to characterize the virtues of a good argument. A statement in Book III of *De oratore*, for instance, contains an almost complete enumeration of the above attributes: "Who is thought to be so to say a god among men? It is those whose speeches are clear [*distincte*], explicit [*explicate*] and full [*abundanter*], perspicuous (*inluminate*) in matter and language, and who in the actual delivery achieve a sort of rhythm and cadence—that is, those whose style is what I call artistic (*ornate*)."[13] Baumgarten simply confers a more technical meaning on these attributes and updates the Ciceronian argument by relating it to the perspectives and the terminology of his time.

CHARACTER AESTHETICI

Chapter (a) of the *Aesthetics* presents a preliminary discussion of the poet's natural requisites: Baumgarten employs a Ciceronian terminology and takes up central elements from Cicero's description of the orator's natural *ingenium*. This description is completed in later sections by a discussion of further requisites cited by Cicero: ardor, exercise, imitation, discipline, impetus, and correction. The chapter on *ingenium* is followed by a series of chapters on abundance, magnitude, truth, light, certainty, and life. In the revised 1758 synopsis, the last two chapters are replaced by a chapter on persuasion.

Ubertas and *Brevitas*

The subject matter of Chapter (b) dealing with *ubertas* seems to concern mainly the first part of Ciceronian invention, namely, the finding of evidence. *Ubertas*, as opposed to *brevitas*—discussed in two separate sections of Chapter (b)—qualifies the abundance, amplification, and variety of the orator's argument: according to Cicero, quoted by Baumgarten,[14] the "complete and finished orator is he who on any matter whatever can speak with

---

[12] Baumgarten, *Aesthetica/Ästhetik*, §14.
[13] Cicero, *On the Orator*, Bk. III, 53.
[14] Baumgarten, *Aesthetica/Ästhetik*, §125 and, on *brevitas*, Baumgarten, *Aesthetica/Ästhetik*, §161; Baumgarten, *Kollegium über die Ästhetik*, §161. Baumgarten's reference to Cicero's *On Invention* (*De inventione*) I.28 is erroneous.

fullness and variety"[15] while respecting the principle of brevity, that is, the order and unity of his argument and the sobriety and parsimony of means. Like the remaining categories, *ubertas* refers to both content[16] and form: the orator must have at his disposal ample knowledge of every discipline in order to speak with great variety on different subjects. In contrast to Cicero, however, Baumgarten associates *ubertas* (and *brevitas*) not with an amount of knowledge but with extensive clarity of cognition, as he defines it in the *Reflections on Poetry*. The aesthetic type of abundance relates to the kind of cognition through which one can conceive of more things beautifully.[17] In other words, while both philosopher and poet can speak about a subject with some variety, each will opt for a different form of amplification or elaboration.

Magnitudo (*Dignitas* and *Magnamitas*)

Cicero appears to rank dignity highest in the hierarchy of qualities.[18] Most often, he notes, the object with the greatest dignity or practical relevance is also the most beautiful.[19] Dignity obviously relates more to the second part of Ciceronian invention, to the raising of sympathy. A poet cannot be convincing unless he wins the heart of the audience through his moral attitude or ethos, his dignity. "Feelings are won over by a man's merit, achievements or reputable life."[20] This perspective on invention, generally absent from the earlier logical tradition, reemerges in Baumgarten, who views magnitude as qualifying an argument that provides weighty or practically relevant reasons,[21] and calls "dignity" the "moral," as opposed to the "natural," type of "magnitude." Devoting some 250 paragraphs to the question, Baumgarten also adopts a Ciceronian[22] view when associating magnitude and magnanimity (the personal magnitude qualifying the speaker) with the orator's moral attitude or ethos,[23] and, more particularly, with his practical

[15] Cicero, *On the Orator*, Bk. I, 59.
[16] Cicero, *On the Orator*, Bk. III, 76 and, in particular, 120.
[17] Baumgarten, *Aesthetica/Ästhetik*, §116.
[18] Cicero, *On the Orator*, Bk. II, 334.
[19] Cicero, *On the Orator*, Bk. III, 178.
[20] Cicero, *On the Orator*, Bk. II, 182.
[21] For a definition of "magnitude," see Baumgarten, *Metaphysics*, §151; and *Aesthetica/Ästhetik*, §177. Baumgarten proposes a series of synonymous or at least related terms for *magnitude*, namely, *foecunditas*, productivity; *dignitas*, dignity; *gravitas*, gravity; *pondus*, weight; *nobilitas*, nobility. See Baumgarten, *Metaphysics*, §166. For a more detailed analysis of *magnitude*, see Mirbach, "Ingenium venustum und magnitude pectoris," 199–218.
[22] Cicero. *On Ends (De finibus)*, Bk. V, 57.
[23] See Baumgarten, *Aesthetica/Ästhetik*, §191–§201. Baumgarten also quotes Quintilian, *The Orator's Education (Institutio oratoria)*, Bk. VI, 3. For a short discussion, see Tedesco, *L'Estetica di Baumgarten*, 194.

and political engagement: "Hence the abler and more accomplished a man is, the less he would care to be alive at all if barred from taking part in affairs, although allowed to batten on the most exquisite pleasures." Baumgarten finally takes up Cicero's division of "relative magnitude," that is, his division of styles into "high," "medium," and "low." His discussion of Longinus and the sublime comes in here, and bears marks of the ancient tradition.[24]

Veritas/Falsitas/Verisimilitudo

The chapter on truth has been widely discussed in secondary literature and has given rise to a series of misunderstandings. Almost every commentator reduces Baumgarten's concept of truth to its strictly cognitive components.[25] In fact Baumgarten seems rather be referring to a Ciceronian perspective on truth[26] and to a set of Ciceronian categories such as *sinceritas, aptum, congruentia* that are far wider than cognitive categories[27] and pertain to all three parts of Ciceronian invention: *instruere, conciliare,* and *movere,* as well as to content and form. The gist of Baumgarten's argument on truth is that domains in which philosophical distinctness is unavailable— the practical and political sphere—require a different form of reflection than does philosophy[28] on truth and on possibilities. First of all, a poem cannot be called true unless it presents its author as a sincere and dignified man. Truth in the wider sense of the term rests upon both the plausibility of the argument and the "accordance between the signs and our mind,"[29] or on the poet's sincerity, as opposed to his loquacity.[30] In addition, the truth of the poem must appeal to the reader's imagination and desires. Like his predecessors in the Wolffian School, Baumgarten points out that the poet describes particular objects and characters rather than general notions by inserting the former into a wider order of elements. The order (or the *inseparabilitas determinationum in cogitandis*) constitutes the unity and harmony of the poem, comprising both the unity of action and the unity of place and time. In Baumgarten's view, the destiny of the courageous

---

[24] See Tedesco, *L'Estetica di Baumgarten,* 111.

[25] For example, Baeumler, *Das Irrationalitätsproblem,* 225.

[26] Baumgarten, *Aesthetica/Ästhetik,* §426; see also Cicero, *On Duties (De Officiis),* II.18. It is true that Baumgarten, in conformity with his wider modern perspective described earlier, departs from Cicero insofar as he assigns these virtues to one *truth* faculty in the human soul. In other words, Baumgarten refuses Cicero's skepticism and probabilism (Baumgarten, *Aesthetica/Ästhetik,* §479).

[27] Cicero, *On the Orator,* Bk. III, 53.

[28] Baumgarten, *Aesthetica/Ästhetik,* §431f.

[29] "Convenientiam signorum cum mente nostra." For a wide definition of *congruentia,* see Baumgarten, *Philosophica generalis,* §147.

[30] Baumgarten, *Aesthetica/Ästhetik,* §435f.

but tough and haughty Coriolan, who did not abandon his fight against the Romans although his mother implored him to do so, illustrates the harmony of the poem. The poet also reveals the gap between wishful thinking and reality: he shows us better worlds, presenting not just any kind of imagination but an imagination that affects us because it contains premonitions or divinations.

The truth of poetry thus rests on the "propriety" of the argument (according to the principle of contradiction), its consequences (according to what Baumgarten introduces as the principle of consequence),[31] and its causes (according to the principle of sufficient reason). After providing the general definition of aesthetic truth, Baumgarten uses the remaining chapter to explain its particular aspects, beginning with the poet's conformity to the principle of contradiction. Baumgarten's use of this principle depends upon an untraditional division of truth into metaphysical, objective, and subjective kinds of truth, introduced at the very beginning of the chapter: he explains that "one could call the metaphysical truth the objective truth, and the representation of the objective truth in a given soul the subjective truth."[32] Aware that he is advancing an original distinction, Baumgarten adds a more detailed explanation: the metaphysical or objective truth either reveals itself to the intellect in the strict sense of the term—when it is in an object that is perceived intellectually, through distinct perception—in which case it is called logical truth; or it is the object of the "lower" cognitive faculties, when it is called "aesthetic truth."[33] Both together make up the "aestheticological" truth.[34] For Baumgarten, who in part follows Gottsched's line of argument, "aesthetic truth is essentially verisimilitude."[35] The poet respects the principle of contradiction when he avoids plain contradictions and impossibilities,[36] and when he considers what is naturally and morally possible. In particular, good poetry takes a hero's or protagonist's moral possibilities into account, that is, the plausibility of his or her actions.[37]

---

[31] Baumgarten adds the "principle of consequence" to the Leibnizian principles of contradiction and sufficient reason in Baumgarten, *Metaphysics*, §23; he appears to deduce the principle of consequence from the principle of sufficient reason, arguing that any possible thing must be a sufficient reason for something else and that nothing can be completely sterile or without consequences.

[32] Baumgarten, *Aesthetica/Ästhetik*, §424.

[33] Baumgarten, *Aesthetica/Ästhetik*, §424.

[34] Baumgarten, *Aesthetica/Ästhetik*, §427.

[35] Baumgarten, *Aesthetica/Ästhetik*, §483.

[36] Baumgarten, *Aesthetica/Ästhetik*, §483.

[37] The wider perspective on truth and verisimilitude allows us to understand what Baumgarten means in the following section, on *falsitas*. Baumgarten here also relies on Cicero. He quotes Antonius, one of Cicero's spokesmen in the *De oratore*, to argue that, under certain circumstances, the orator has the right to lie (Baumgarten, *Aesthetica/Ästhetik*, §445).

Lux

In the section on light Baumgarten elaborates on the analogy between poetry and painting that was already part of the earlier debate on rhetoric.

While Cicero employs expressions such as *lux*, "light"; *plane*;[38] *illuminate* [*dicere*];[39] and *aperte dicere*[40] as more or less synonyms, Baumgarten associates "light" with clarity and perspicuity,[41] that is, some sort of "splendor" in respect of both content and form.[42] Light, whose opposites are obscurity, fog, and shadow,[43] comprises colors or shades.[44] Baumgarten calls the deficient kind of "color," "make-up," or "dressing-up," *fucus*. *Fucus* is obviously closely related to what Baumgarten's predecessors in the Wolffian School called baroque *Schwulst*. According to the argument already sketched in the *Reflections on Poetry*, the poet's use of induction and of particular examples contributes to the "light" that reigns in poetry. Light also appears to be closely linked to the issue of "enlightenment" discussed earlier.

Persuasio

In *Persuasio* can be found the most comprehensive description of beauty; here Baumgarten finally discusses the life, *vita*, or practical value of poetry. In his account of "persuasion," Baumgarten includes even more references to Cicero than in the preceding sections. The orator should not only instruct but move, exert an emotional effect on the audience, so as to give a practical impulse to action.[45] Since even poetry communicates and "demonstrates" some kind of truth, Baumgarten draws only a relative distinction between persuasion in poetry and persuasion in philosophy. "The distinct kind of consciousness of truth is conviction, the indistinct and sensible kind is persuasion."[46] Baumgarten emphasizes that persuasion is a condition for the "life" or practical efficacy of the discourse.[47] In a section entitled *evidentia*, Baumgarten finally introduces the fundamental distinction, already mentioned above, between two kinds of "evidence": the more formal and symbolic type,

---

[38] Cicero, *On the Orator*, Bk. III, 50.

[39] Cicero, *On the Orator*, Bk. III, 53.

[40] Cicero, *On the Orator*, Bk. II, 329.

[41] Baumgarten, *Aesthetica/Ästhetik*, §614.

[42] See Baumgarten, *Metaphsyics*, §518. Light is closely linked to what Baumgarten calls "brightness," that is, *nitor*, and *splendor* (See §515 of the 1743 and subsequent editions of his *Metaphysics*; and Baumgarten, *Aesthetica/Ästhetik*, §618–§622, and, in particular §619), but it is not to be conflated with *vita* (Baumgarten, *Aesthetica/Ästhetik*, §620).

[43] Baumgarten, *Aesthetica/Ästhetik*, §631–§634.

[44] Baumgarten, *Aesthetica/Ästhetik*, §688.

[45] Cicero, *On the Orator*, Bk. I, 202.

[46] Baumgarten, *Aesthetica/Ästhetik*, §832.

[47] Baumgarten, *Aesthetica/Ästhetik*, §829.

which prevails in philosophy, and the more intuitive and practical type, or "clarity" and "beauty," which prevails in poetry and the semantic arts.[48] As I have already indicated, Baumgarten's distinction between these two types of persuasion and evidence is notably crucial, for it allows him to include poetry within the sphere of logical invention, and to distinguish between two spheres of invention and argument, and two standards of perfection of speech.

THE CONSTRUCTION OF A SECOND
METHOD OF INVENTION

In Baumgarten's view, his distinction between two forms of invention—namely, poetry and philosophy—justifies (1) the implementation of two sets of cognitive faculties—the faculty of poetry, or sensibility, and the faculty of philosophy (analysis), or reason; and (2) the construction of two methods of invention: aesthetics and logic. Both are arts grounded in a natural creative faculty of the human mind, and possess natural and artificial forms.

First, Baumgarten's distinction between two standards of perfection, pertaining respectively to poetry and to philosophy, allows him to propose a new circumscription and separation of two sets of rational faculties, namely, the faculty of poetry and the faculty of philosophy in the narrow sense. In conformity with the Wolffian line of argument, Baumgarten appears to contend that, as empirically observed, the difference in effect justifies an adjustment of the doctrine of faculties; and the distinction, within the unique force of the soul, between two types of discursive and rational faculties.

Baumgarten's move may be characterized as "genetic," "gnoseological," or "critical," according to whether one prefers Baumgarten's terminology in the *Aesthetics* or his more Kantian terminology in the *Acroasis Logica*. As Franke has pointed out, the term "gnoseology," which occurs in Baumgarten's definition of aesthetics as a *gnoseologia inferior*, refers to a method that allows one to determine the *scibile quatenus scibile*. Baumgarten appears to have borrowed the term from such older authors as Valentin Fromme and Abraham Calov. More directly, however, Baumgarten is clearly making reference to Wolffian logic (and also to Tschirnhaus's "genetic" method of invention).[49] Wolff's logic includes separate chapters on "the art of examining whether or not one's cognitive faculties are sufficient to analyze a truth"[50]—an art that Baumgarten in his own Logic calls "dynamics."[51]

---

[48] Baumgarten, *Aesthetica/Ästhetik*, §847.
[49] See Buchenau, *The Founding of Aesthetics in the German Enlightenment*, 28–30.
[50] Wolff, *German Logic*, Ch. 8; see in particular §1.
[51] Baumgarten, *Acroasis Logica*, Ch. 8; see Baumgarten, *Kollegium über die Ästhetik*, §60.

Second, our preceding analysis has shown that Baumgarten's gnoseological and dynamic move affects both philosophy/logic and poetry/aesthetics, insofar as it implies a radical redistribution of their respective functions. Baumgarten reduces the scope of philosophical and logical cognition in order to carve out a space for poetry and sensibility. While the faculty of philosophical cognition shrinks to a faculty of symbolic, abstract, and indifferent cognition—a truth faculty in the poorest sense of the term—the faculty of poetic cognition expands to become a faculty of intuitive and pleasurable cognition, a faculty of truth and beauty. Reference to a faculty of beauty allows Baumgarten to transpose the modern methodological paradigm from invention in mathematical philosophy to poetry, and to replace the former Aristotelian and Ciceronian *ars inveniendi* or *topica* with more productive methods. As a matter of fact, Baumgarten expresses a criticism of the old *topica* similar to the one advanced by the early moderns. The crucial difference, though, is that Baumgarten applies his criticism to the rhetorical form of the art of invention. In the chapter on *ubertas*, Baumgarten expounds his criticism of the ancient Aristotelian and Ciceronian *ars inveniendi* or *topica* in greater detail. The topics served Cicero and Aristotle as an art of invention or of finding arguments. Baumgarten cites the second section of Cicero's *Topica*, where the heuristic function of the topics is outlined. In this passage Cicero explains:

> It is easy to find things that are hidden if the hiding place is pointed out and marked; similarly, if we wish to track down some argument, we ought to know the places or topics: for that is the name given by Aristotle to the "regions," as it were, from which arguments are drawn. Accordingly, we may define a topic as the region of an argument, and an argument as a course of reasoning which firmly establishes a matter about which there is some doubt.[52]

Baumgarten overtly rejects the Aristotelian and Ciceronian interpretation of the art of invention. He argues that the art considered there is not a true *ars inveniendi* but an *ars revocandi*, an "art of recalling predicates of a certain subject according to a certain order of associated notions."[53] His criticism reveals his modern stance on the question, positioning himself on the side of the Baconians and the post-Baconians. He takes over the Baconian argument outlined earlier. The Aristotelian *topica* cannot fulfill the function of a true art of invention because no rules are offered there for original inventions. The topics concern only the reception of what is already known. Nevertheless,

---

[52] Cicero, *Topics (Topica)*, Bk. II, 7 in Cicero, *On Invention*, 387. See also Buchenau, *The Founding of Aesthetics in the German Enlightenment*, 18.

[53] Baumgarten, *Aesthetica/Ästhetik*, §130.

considered in detail, Baumgarten does not altogether reject the use of topics
and, in particular, Aristotelian topics. In fact he ascribes greater value to the
Aristotelian tradition than to its succession from the hands of Raymond Lull
and Peter Ramus. Whereas Baumgarten views the Lullian art as an "artifice
that a sensible person will soon put away," he grants that the Aristotelian categories—*subiectum, quantitas, qualitas, relatio, actio, passio, ubi, quando,
habitus*—may serve as a heuristic tool for the beginner.[54] The student can
also turn to the traditional verse *Quis?, quibus auxiliis?, quid?, quomodo?,
cur?, ubi?, quando?* to reproduce particular qualities of what he is concerned
with. In principle, however, the art of invention cannot be based on the traditional catalog; it must be founded on the gnoseological method. Invention
in aesthetics requires one to reflect on and measure one's natural faculty of
poetry. Constant reflection on one's powers allows one to invent by an *actus
iudicii* (act of judging), not an *actus compilationis* (act of compiling).[55] In
other words, it is necessary to replace the traditional topics with more modern
versions, and to respect "particular topics" for invention in aesthetics.[56] The
particular topics comprise the six components of aesthetic cognition named
above: *ubertas, magnitudo*, and the rest. Nevertheless, topics even in their
more sophisticated, modernized form afford only a formal technique, constitute merely a part or the term of the art of invention. The methodical cultivation of the *felix aestheticus* comprises various further aspects.

Baumgarten subscribes essentially to Cicero's articulation of art and
nature, their order or priority, and the individual stages of the learning process: exercise, imitation, discipline, divine breath (*impetus*), and correction.[57]
Poets first created great works of art and later extracted rules from them.
Creative expression comes first, rules come second. Homer and Pindar thus
represent archetypes and models, rather than ectypes, for the *eruditio*.[58]
More than Cicero, Baumgarten offers a detailed enumeration of the required
faculties, and he employs Wolffian psychological categories to describe
them. He spells out the required natural and innate faculties in the section
on natural aesthetics and the *felix aestheticus* in his *Aesthetics*.[59] He again
adopts a twofold perspective, both theoretical and practical, by distinguishing between the faculties of cognition that comprise the *ingenium*, or genius,
and the faculties of desire that make up the "temperament." He affirms that
each set of faculties requires the harmonious interaction of a range of more
particular faculties. *Ingenium*, to begin with, comprises acuity, imagination,

---

[54] Baumgarten, *Aesthetica/Ästhetik,* §130–§133.
[55] Baumgarten, *Aesthetica/Ästhetik*, §144.
[56] Baumgarten, *Aesthetica/Ästhetik*, §135f.
[57] See Cicero, *On the Orator*, Bk. I, 148f.
[58] Baumgarten, *Aesthetica/Ästhetik*, §53.
[59] Baumgarten, *Aesthetica/Ästhetik*, §28–§37.

perspicuity, the faculty of recognition, memory and the *facultas fingendi* (the ability to combine and separate figments), taste or a lower form of judgment, a faculty of foreseeing and foretelling things, and finally a lower form of *facultas characteristica*. Furthermore, *ingenium* involves to a certain extent the higher faculties of cognition, reason, and understanding. In addition, the acquisition of an aesthetic habit requires a certain innate temperament, depending in turn upon the harmonious interplay of the faculties of desire. Such a temperament depends on a natural magnanimity. Natural faculties, namely, genius and temperament, condition the acquisition of the aesthetic habit. The acquisition of such a habit can be either purely empirical and imitative, or rational. Empirical exercises—improvisations and imitations— come first in the pedagogical *curriculum*. The student begins his training with a number of exercises. Through the repetition of improvisations, which teach the student to focus on one theme, the student progressively trains his faculties and develops a harmonious interplay between them. Baumgarten insists that such improvisations already contribute to the cultivation of the aesthetic mind. They in fact first create the necessary disposition,[60] or habit,[61] of beautiful thinking. Within the modern perspective on originality defended by his Wolffian contemporaries, Baumgarten ascribes great significance to the spontaneity and creativity of exercise. Exercises must leave space for creative, playful expression of the natural faculties, giving rise to one's first reflections on the scope of these natural faculties, or, as Baumgarten terms it, one's "aesthetic horizon."[62] The student must discard not only the subject matters that fall outside the general horizon of beauty but also those that fall outside his or her individual horizon. The state of his or her faculty must determine his choice of subject matter. At the same time, he or she must be aware that this faculty is open to development, parallel to the expansion of his or her horizon. After having improvised exercises, the student will turn to the imitation of models. It is notable that Baumgarten lays particular emphasis on the creative aspect immanent to imitation. Like the architect described by Wolff in his *Psychologia empirica*, the student of aesthetics studies models in order to extract rules of invention from them. Baumgarten insists that the student should not only express a judgment of taste and affirm that the model is pleasant and beautiful, but also reconstruct the process of invention manifest in the model and *reinvent* the work. By doing so, he will simultaneously train his faculties of judgment and invention, that is, cultivate his own creativity, so that in the third and highest type of exercise the student may depart from the model and attempt to produce original exercises, *autoskediamata heuristica*,

---

[60] Baumgarten, *Metaphysics*, §577.
[61] Baumgarten, *Metaphysics*, §650.
[62] Baumgarten, *Aesthetica/Ästhetik*, §119.

spontaneously, by the force of his own mind (*"proprio marte fundit animus automatos"*). Having appropriated the existing inventions and creative habits for him- or herself, he or she will be able to develop them further, surpassing the ancient models and creating original and novel works of art.[63] The practice of imitation allows the poet to acquire an empirical and "confused" knowledge (*eruditio*) of the rules of poetry. While such practical knowledge cannot be qualified as "blind," insofar as it allows the student to recognize and apply rules of invention, it nonetheless remains "one-eyed," to borrow Baumgarten's terminology from the preface of the *Reflections on Poetry*, for as long as the student remains unable to articulate the rules. The discipline or method represents "a more perfect theory of the more direct influences on the material and form of beautiful cognition."[64] While the particular model represents the rules in an indistinct form, the discipline represents them in a distinct form: it includes articulated rules, and shows how they are related to and grounded in higher philosophical principles. Since the rules need to be deduced from a higher principle, they constitute not only a (polyhistorical) discipline, as in Cicero, but also a *scientia*, a *mathesis aesthetica*.

In conformity with the modern pre-Kantian stance on creativity, Baumgarten believes in the compatibility of the idea of exercise and method with genius, or, as he names it, "impetus," "enthusiasm," or "divine breath."[65] Methodical exercise is first of all what *awakens* the poet's divine spirit. Baumgarten again formulates the idea in the terminology of Wolffian metaphysics. Poetry, as an active faculty (*potentia activa*), is grounded in what he calls a natural receptivity (*possibilitas patiendi*), which requires some sort of external solicitation to manifest itself, that is, to change from the state of a "dead" force to that of a "vivid" force. The poet possesses either a natural or a divine gift, depending on whether the external solicitation is natural or supernatural. Moreover, method helps not only to awaken but also to correct the poet's genius. The direct function of artificial aesthetics is correction and emendation insofar as it helps to correct and straighten the natural expressions of the *ingenium*; to reduce confusion and uncertainty; and to attain greater completeness, exactitude, and certainty. Its direct function is therefore "critical" and negative, but more indirectly it possesses a positive heuristic function. The artificial art of aesthetics contributes to the awakening and cultivation of the poet's genius, to a bringing of the rules to greater perfection, to sharpening the poet's judgment and consolidating his habits.

---

[63] Baumgarten, *Aesthetica/Ästhetik*, §56f.
[64] Baumgarten, *Aesthetica/Ästhetik*, §62.
[65] Baumgarten, *Aesthetica/Ästhetik*, §78.

Chapter 3

Beauty and Appearance in Baumgarten's Metaphysics and Aesthetics

Matthew McAndrew

Baumgarten appears to have two competing definitions of beauty. In §662 of the *Metaphysics*, he defines beauty as the "perfection of an appearance" [*perfectio phaenomenon*].[1] However, in §14 of the *Aesthetics*, Baumgarten states that beauty is the "perfection of sensible cognition" [*perfectio cognitionis sensitivae*].[2] There is an important difference between these two statements. An appearance or phenomenon is an object of sensible cognition. In the *Metaphysics*, Baumgarten ascribes beauty to an *object* of cognition. Conversely, in the *Aesthetics*, he attributes it to cognition itself.

Eleven years elapsed between the publication of the *Metaphysics* (1739) and the first volume of the *Aesthetics* (1750). Albert Riemann has argued that during this period Baumgarten's thinking about aesthetics underwent a crucial "turn" [*Wendung*] and shifted from a "rational-objective" definition of beauty to a "rational-subjective" one.[3] However, there is a problem with this thesis. When Baumgarten supposedly redefines beauty as the "perfection of sensible cognition" in the *Aesthetics*, he cites §662 of the *Metaphysics*. This section contains the definition of beauty from that earlier work. The citation suggests that Baumgarten did not actually reject the *Metaphysics*' definition of beauty and that he regarded it as compatible with his position in the *Aesthetics*.

A number of scholars have tried to explain the relationship between Baumgarten's two definitions of beauty and how they might be compatible with each other. This question is often described in the scholarly literature

---

[1] Baumgarten, *Metaphysics,* §662.
[2] Baumgarten, *Aesthetica/Ästhetik*, §14.
[3] Riemann, *Die Ästhetik A.G. Baumgartens,* 37.

as the "riddle" [*Rätsel*] of Baumgarten's aesthetics.[4] Beginning with Alfred
Baeumler, a number of scholars have rejected the premise that Baumgarten's
definition of beauty can be characterized as either objective or subjective.[5]
For example, Ursula Franke claims that Baumgarten's aesthetics is grounded
on a metaphysical concept of perfection. Beauty is the appearance of this
perfection and, as such, it is mediated by the subject's sensible cognition.
Consequently, Baumgarten's definition of beauty is neither strictly objective
nor strictly subjective.[6] Dagmar Mirbach makes a similar argument in the
introduction to her translation of the *Aesthetics*.[7] Hans Rudolf Schweizer and
Friedhelm Solms both argue for the compatibility of Baumgarten's two definitions by equating the terms "appearance" and "sensible cognition."[8] Mary
Gregor also regards the definitions as compatible. She argues that the difference between them can be explained by the different aims of the *Metaphysics*
and the *Aesthetics*.[9] Frederick Beiser has expressed a similar view.[10]

In this chapter, I am going to attempt to solve the riddle of Baumgarten's
aesthetics by challenging a basic assumption made by all of these scholars;
namely, that he defines beauty as the "perfection of sensible cognition." In the
Aesthetics, Baumgarten writes, "The purpose of aesthetics is the perfection of
sensible cognition as such. However, this is beauty."[11] This passage has been
interpreted as a definition of beauty. However, I am skeptical that this was
actually Baumgarten's intention. Instead of offering a definition, he is claiming that the perfection of sensible cognition *is beautiful*. Baumgarten has just
a single definition of beauty and it is found in §662 of the *Metaphysics*. He
did not consider the perfection of sensible cognition to be the definition of
beauty, but rather an example of it. It is something that is beautiful, not the
essence of beauty.[12]

This interpretation is plausible for several reasons. First, Baumgarten
describes perfect sensible cognition as "beautiful cognition." If he defined
beauty as the "perfection of sensible cognition," as is generally assumed,

---

[4] See, for example, Peters, *Studien über die Ästhetik des Alexander Gottlieb Baumgarten*, 13;
Franke, *Kunst als Erkenntnis,* 88; Solms, *Disciplina aesthetica*, 51; Mirbach, "Einführung" in
Aesthetica/Ästhetik, LIII.

[5] Baeumler, *Das Irrationalitätsproblem,* 231.

[6] Franke, *Kunst als Erkenntnis*, 88–90.

[7] Mirbach, "Einführung," LIV–LV.

[8] Schweizer, *Ästhetik als Philosophie der sinnlichen Erkenntnis*, 82–83; Solms, *Disciplina aesthetica*, 51–57.

[9] Gregor, "Baumgarten's Aesthetica," 376–377.

[10] Beiser, *Diotima's Children*, 146.

[11] Baumgarten, *Aesthetica/Ästhetik*, §14.

[12] I want to acknowledge from the outset what I believe is the strongest objection to the interpretation
that I will be advancing; namely, that it is not supported by the grammar of the passage in question. Baumgarten writes, "Haec autem est pulcritudo" (ibid., §14). If he wanted to assert that the
perfection of sensible cognition is beautiful, which is my contention, then presumably he would
have used the adjective *pulcra*, rather than the noun *pulcritudo*.

then this expression would be redundant. There would be no beauty other than that of cognition. However, this cannot be Baumgarten's view because he refers explicitly to the beauty of objects.[13] Second, this interpretation solves the puzzle of Baumgarten's reference to the definition of beauty in the *Metaphysics*. He cites this definition to justify his claim that the perfection of sensible cognition is beautiful. The perfection of this cognition fits the definition of beauty that he cites. Third, Baumgarten's student and protégé, George Friedrich Meier, makes this same argument about the beauty of perfect sensible cognition in his own work on aesthetics. Meier starts with a definition of beauty that is very similar to Baumgarten's definition in the *Metaphysics*. He then argues that this definition applies to the perfection of sensible cognition and that this perfection is therefore beautiful.

Meier's aesthetics consists of three volumes and is entitled *Foundations of All Beautiful Sciences* (*Anfangsgründe aller schönen Wissenschaften*, 1748–1750). It is based on Baumgarten's teachings. In the preface, Meier explains that Baumgarten gave him access to his lecture notes. He writes,

> When the professor [Baumgarten] was called to Frankfurt, he had the opportunity to further realize his plan for an aesthetics, which he had already conceived here in Halle. He worked out in short Latin paragraphs the first principles of beautiful thinking in a lecture notebook about aesthetics. I asked for these notes and read them several times, until I now, with the professor's permission, have delivered to the press the first part in the present form.[14]

It would be a mistake to conclude that Meier's *Foundations* is entirely derivative. He writes in the preface, "I can still boldly say that I have done more than a mere translator and paraphrast. I have still never succumbed to the temptation to do nothing further than translate another man's writing."[15] Nonetheless, Meier possessed extensive, firsthand knowledge of Baumgarten's views.[16] My assumption in this chapter is that, unless there is evidence indicating otherwise, Baumgarten and Meier are likely in agreement.

This chapter consists of four parts. In part one, I clarify some of Baumgarten's terminology, including his definitions of "appearance" and "perfection." In part two, I discuss his definition of beauty in the *Metaphysics*: the perfection of an appearance. Next, I pivot to Meier's *Foundations*. Part

---

[13] Baumgarten, *Aesthetica/Ästhetik*, §18.

[14] Meier, *Anfangsgründe*, Vol. 1, a3.

[15] Meier, *Anfangsgründe*, Vol. 1, a4.

[16] During the eighteenth century, the *Foundations* achieved a wider readership than the *Aesthetics*. Its first volume was published two years before the first volume of the *Aesthetics*. Meier also had the advantage of writing in German, whereas Baumgarten wrote in Latin (Mirbach, "Einführung," xx–xxii).

three sets forth his argument, in §27–§28, that the perfection of sensible cognition is beautiful. This argument relies on a premise that Meier fails to adequately explain. He asserts that the perfection of sensible cognition is itself something that is cognized without distinctness. My view is that Meier is referring to inner sense. Finally, in part four, I turn to Baumgarten's *Aesthetics*. I defend my thesis about the meaning of §14 and argue that Baumgarten does not offer a new definition of beauty in this section. Instead, he claims that the perfection of sensible cognition is beautiful. Baumgarten's argument for this conclusion is located in §18–§20. I reject the thesis that Baumgarten uses the term "appearance" as a synonym for sensible cognition and argue that it consistently refers, in both the *Metaphysics* and the *Aesthetics*, to objects of sensible cognition. I show that Baumgarten's argument for the beauty of sensible cognition is very similar to Meier's argument in the *Foundations*. He also repeatedly draws on his definition of beauty in the *Metaphysics* to justify his claims.

SENSIBLE COGNITION, APPEARANCES, AND PERFECTION

Baumgarten accepts the standard Leibnizian definitions of conceptual clarity and distinctness. Representations can be classified as either clear or obscure. Things that are represented obscurely blend together because one cannot distinguish them from each other. A representation is clear if one can recognize its object and distinguish it from other things. Clear representations can be further classified as either confused or distinct. A representation is confused if one can recognize its object without being able to articulate the marks that distinguish it. The term "mark" [*nota, Merkmal*] denotes a characteristic or predicate. A representation is distinct if one can identify the marks that distinguish its object from other things.[17]

Baumgarten uses the term "sensible" [*sensitiva*] to describe representations that lack conceptual distinctness, that is, that are obscure or confused. It applies to all representations that are conceived through the soul's lower faculty of cognition. Baumgarten writes, "A representation that is not distinct is called a SENSIBLE REPRESENTATION. Therefore, the power of my soul represents sensible perceptions through the inferior faculty."[18]

---

[17] Leibniz, "Meditations on Knowledge, Truth, and Ideas," 23–24. See also Christian Wolff, *German Logic*, Ch. 1, §9, §13.

[18] Baumgarten, *Metaphysics*, §521. I have modified Fugate and Hymers's translation. They translate *sensitiva* as "sensitive" rather than "sensible."

The Latin term *phaenomenon* is often translated as appearance. Baumgarten's employs it to refer to an object of sensible cognition. In the *Metaphysics*, he writes, "We call OBSERVABLE (appearance) that which we are able to know (confusedly) through the senses."[19] In this passage, Baumgarten claims that an appearance is an object of the senses. He also reminds the reader that sensations are confused representations; they are an example of sensible cognition. This passage is consistent with Wolff's definition of the term *phaenomenon* in his *Latin Logic*: "that which we observe to be, but of which we nevertheless have a confused concept."[20]

Baumgarten defines perfection in terms of agreement or harmony. He writes, "If several things taken together constitute the sufficient ground of a single thing, they AGREE. The agreement itself is PERFECTION, and the one thing in which there is agreement is the DETERMINING GROUND OF PERFECTION (the focus of the perfection)."[21] According to Baumgarten's definition, something is perfect if its parts are in agreement with each other. Moreover, the parts are in agreement with each other when they all collectively serve as the sufficient reason for a single thing. Baumgarten thinks that things are primarily related in terms of grounds and consequences.[22] If all of something's parts constitute the sufficient reason for the same thing, then they are all related to that thing. This shared relationship unites them and brings them into agreement with each other. Baumgarten calls the thing that unites them in this way the "determining ground" of the perfection.

Baumgarten's definition of perfection in the *Metaphysics* is consistent with Wolff's definition of this concept.[23] Wolff writes, "The harmony

---

[19] Baumgarten, *Metaphysics*, §425. For the sake of consistency, I have slightly modified Fugate and Hymers's translation. They translate the term *phaenomenon* as "phenomena" rather than "appearance."

[20] Wolff, *Philosophia rationalis sive logica*, §610.

[21] Baumgarten, *Metaphysics*, §94.

[22] Baumgarten, *Metaphysics*, §14.

[23] Clemens Schwaiger argues that there is a difference between Baumgarten's concept of perfection and that of Wolff. Wolff's conception of perfection is implicitly teleological, but this vanishes from Baumgarten's account (Schwaiger, *Alexander Gottlieb Baumgarten—Ein intellectuelles Porträt*, 158–163). Wolff's examples of perfection in the so-called *German Metaphysics* have the teleological character that Schwaiger notes. Wolff claims that the perfection of a clock is assessed in terms of how clearly and accurately it displays the time. Ideally, all of its parts should serve this end and none of them should hinder its achievement. When this occurs, the parts are in harmony with each other and the clock as a whole is perfect. Wolff also explains that the way of life [*Wandel*] of a multitude of people consists in their many actions. If all of their actions pursue a single intention or purpose [*Absicht*], then their actions are in harmony and their way of life is perfect (Wolff, *German Metaphysics*, §152). Schwaiger is correct that Baumgarten does not identify the determining ground of a thing's perfection with its purpose. However, if Baumgarten eliminates the teleological aspect of Wolff's account of perfection, his student Meier reintroduces some of it. In the *Foundations*, Meier claims that, in aesthetics, the determining ground of something's perfection is its purpose. He writes, "There must be something that one calls one thing [*Eins*], the focal point, or the determining ground of the beauty. In aesthetics, one can maintain without error that

[*Zusammenstimmung*] of the manifold constitutes the perfection of the thing."[24]
In the preface to the second edition of the *Metaphysics* (1743), Baumgarten
acknowledges that he shares Wolff's definition of perfection and defends it
against an objection, namely, that some things, which appear to be imperfect,
nonetheless consist of harmonious parts. He writes, "I should explain here why
I have not changed the definition of *the illustrious Wolff*."[25] Leibniz also shares
this understanding of perfection. In 1714, Wolff wrote to Leibniz and asked
him to explain his definition of perfection.[26] Leibniz responded, "*Perfection*
is the harmony of things, or the state where everything is worthy of being
observed, that is, the state of agreement or identity in variety."[27] As we have
seen, Wolff and Baumgarten accept this definition of perfection.

BAUMGARTEN'S DEFINITION OF
BEAUTY IN THE *METAPHYSICS*

In the *Metaphysics*, Baumgarten defines beauty as follows: "The perfection
of an appearance, or the perfection observable by taste in the broader sense,
is BEAUTY."[28] Baumgarten uses the term "appearance" to refer to objects of
sensible cognition. Beauty is the perfection of such an object. It is perfection
that is represented without distinctness, via a sensible cognition. As I noted
earlier, Hans Rudolf Schweizer and Friedhelm Solms argue that Baumgarten
equates the term "appearance" with sensible cognition. I consider and reject
this thesis in part four. However, in the meantime, we can be certain about the
meaning of Baumgarten's definition of beauty because he also claims that it
is "perfection observable by taste in the broader sense."

The expression "taste in the broader sense" refers to the lower or sensible
faculty of judgment. Baumgarten defines the faculty of judgment in general
as one's capacity to represent "the perfection and imperfection of things."[29]

---

this focal point is a purpose" (Meier, *Anfangsgründe*, Vol. 1, §24). The caveat "in aesthetics" is
significant because in his metaphysics, Meier acknowledges that not everything has a purpose and,
consequently, perfection is not always grounded in a purpose. He writes, "Not every perfection
consists in the agreement of the manifold with the purpose because not everything has a purpose"
(Meier, *Metaphysik*, Vol. 1, §94). Meier's position seems to be that anything beautiful must have
a purpose and that this purpose is the determining ground of its perfection. However, this is not
necessarily the case for the things that are incapable of beauty or ugliness and that fall outside
scope of aesthetics.

[24] Wolff, *German Metaphysics*, §152. See also Wolff, *Philosophia prima sive ontologia*, §503.
[25] Baumgarten, *Metaphysics*, 87. Baumgarten responds to the objection by clarifying that the determining ground of something's perfection must be real and that the agreement that it grounds is
necessarily an agreement among real things (ibid., 88).
[26] Leibniz, "From Letters to Wolff," 230.
[27] Leibniz, "From Letters to Wolff," 233–234.
[28] Baumgarten, *Metaphysics*, §662.
[29] Baumgarten, *Metaphysics*, §606.

He divides this faculty into two parts based on the confusion or distinctness of one's representations. The intellectual faculty of judgment is the capacity to represent perfection and imperfection with distinct concepts. It belongs to the higher faculty of cognition. The sensible faculty of judgment is the capacity to represent perfection and imperfection without distinctness, and belongs to the lower faculty of cognition. Baumgarten identifies the sensible faculty of judgment with "taste in the broader sense." He writes, "Since this occurs either distinctly or indistinctly, the faculty of judging and hence judgment, is either sensible or intellectual. Sensible judgment is TASTE IN THE BROADER SENSE (flavor, palate, smell)."[30] Baumgarten claims that beauty is perfection that can be perceived through the sensible faculty of judgment. This is equivalent to saying that beauty is a sensible cognition of perfection or that it is perfection that is cognized without distinctness. If the "perfection of an appearance" is "observable by taste in the broader sense," then the term "appearance" refers to an object of sensible cognition.

Baumgarten's definition of beauty in the *Metaphysics* is fully consistent with Wolff's account of this concept in his empirical psychology.[31] According to Wolff, beauty is perfection that is represented without distinctness. I will refer to this as the "Wolffian theory of beauty." This theory was shared by Gottsched, Meier, and Mendelssohn, among others.[32] For example, Gottsched writes, "If such a perfection comes under the senses and is perceived clearly but without distinctness, then it is called beauty."[33] Likewise, Meier writes in the *Foundations*, "That beauty in general is perfection, insofar as it is cognized indistinctly or sensibly, is nowadays such a sure thing among all experts about beauty that it seems unnecessary to offer an extensive proof of it."[34] Mendelssohn writes, "Beauty rests, in the opinion of every philosopher, on the indistinct representation of a perfection."[35] It is only later that Kant will reject the Wolffian theory of beauty in §15 of the *Critique of the Power Judgment*. He writes that perfection "has therefore been held to be identical with beauty even by philosophers of repute, though with the proviso if it is

---

[30] Baumgarten, *Metaphysics*, §607.

[31] Wolff, *Psychologia empirica*, §544. For a discussion of Wolff's account of beauty, see Beiser, *Diotima's Children*, 60–64.

[32] Baeumler points out that Baumgarten's definition of beauty in the *Metaphysics* was not original and that it was shared by Wolff and others: "One usually regards Baumgarten as the originator of the definition: beauty is the sensible appearance of perfection. This is a mistake. This definition is not only to be found in Wolff, but also in Gottsched" (Baeumler, *Das Irrationalitätsproblem*, 113). See also Beiser, *Diotima's Children*, 144–145.

[33] Gottsched, *Erste Gründe der gesamten Weltweisheit*, §249. It is worth noting that the first edition of Gottsched's *Erste Gründe* was published in 1733. This was six years prior to the first edition of Baumgarten's *Metaphysics* (1739).

[34] Meier, *Anfangsgründe*, 38, §23. See also Meier, *Metaphysik*, Vol. 3, §659.

[35] See *On Sentiments* in Mendelssohn, *Philosophical Writings*, 12. See also "On the Main Principles of the Fine Arts and Sciences" in Mendelssohn, *Philosophical Writings*, 172.

thought confusedly."[36] Baumgarten's definition of beauty in the *Metaphysics*, the "perfection of an appearance," can be regarded as an example of the Wolffian theory of beauty that Kant rejects.

MEIER'S ACCOUNT OF BEAUTIFUL COGNITION IN THE *FOUNDATIONS*

Before I turn to Baumgarten's *Aesthetics*, I want to address Meier's argument for the beauty of perfect sensible cognition in the *Foundations*. As we will see in part IV, Baumgarten makes a very similar argument in the *Aesthetics*. Meier's text provides some valuable clues that will subsequently help us to understand Baumgarten's position in the *Aesthetics*.

Meier defines beauty as perfection that is represented without distinctness through sensible cognition.[37] This is typical of the Wolffian theory of beauty and it is consistent with Baumgarten's definition in the *Metaphysics*. In §27–§28 of the *Foundations*, Meier applies this definition to the perfection of sensible cognition. He writes, "We now want to apply these universal concepts to cognition."[38] The "universal concepts" to which he refers are the concepts of beauty and ugliness. Meier proceeds to argue that the perfections of a sensible cognition fit his definition of beauty and that they are therefore beautiful. He writes, "All sensible cognition is cognized by us indistinctly. Consequently, all perfections of this cognition, insofar as it is a sensible cognition, are perfections that are cognized indistinctly. However, one calls these perfections beauties."[39] Meier's argument in this passage can be summarized as follows:

P1. All sensible cognition lacks distinctness.
P2. The perfections of a sensible cognition are themselves cognized without distinctness.
P3. Beauty is perfection that is cognized without distinctness.
∴.   The perfections of a sensible cognition are beautiful.

The first premise follows from Wolff's and Baumgarten's psychology, in which the absence of conceptual distinctness is the defining characteristic of sensible cognition.[40]

---

[36] Kant, *Critique of the Power of Judgment*, 111 (AA 5: 277, §15).
[37] Meier, *Anfangsgründe*, Vol. 1, §23. See also Meier, *Metaphysik*, Vol. 3, §659.
[38] Meier, *Anfangsgründe*, Vol. 1, §27.
[39] Meier, *Anfangsgründe*, Vol. 1, §28.
[40] Meier, *Anfangsgründe*, Vol. 1, §27.

However, premise two is more difficult to understand. Meier writes that the perfections of a sensible cognition are "perfections that are cognized indistinctly." The implication is that cognitive perfection is itself an object of cognition. Moreover, if the perfection belongs to a sensible cognition, then it too will be cognized without distinctness. How does Meier arrive at this premise?

To answer this question, we should start with Meier's definition of cognition [*Erkenntniß*]. He claims that this term has a twofold meaning. It refers to both the *act of representing* something and the *representation* itself. For example, he writes in the *Foundations*, "One may now say that we cognize something if we make a representation of it actual in us or that the cognition consists in a totality [*Inbegriffe*] of representations and concepts."[41] He repeats this definition in his *Doctrine of Reason* (*Vernunftlehre*, 1752), "We understand cognition to be either a complete totality [*Inbegrif*] of many representations or the action through which a representation of a thing [*Sache*] is affected."[42]

Like Baumgarten, Meier defines perfection as the harmony of something's parts.[43] A cognition, understood in the sense of a representation, consists of a manifold of simpler representations. In both of the passages that I quoted above, Meier claims that a cognition is the "totality" [*Inbegriff*] of multiple representations. These representations can be regarded as the cognition's parts. The perfection of a cognition consists in the agreement of the manifold of representations that compose it.

Meier indicates that the agreement of the manifold in a perfect cognition is itself something that is cognized. He writes, "Consequently, the beauty of cognition consists in that agreement of the manifold in this cognition, *which can be cognized sensibly*."[44] How does the agreement of the manifold become an object of cognition? Unfortunately, Meier does not answer this question. Since he does not explain his reasoning, I am going to reconstruct what I think his answer would be.

Like Kant, Baumgarten draws a distinction between inner sense and outer sense. Outer sense represents the body and by extension the external objects that interact with it. Inner sense represents the soul. Baumgarten writes, "I have a faculty of sensing, i.e. SENSE. SENSE either represents the state of my soul, which is then INTERNAL SENSE, or the state of my body, which is then EXTERNAL SENSE."[45] Meier also distinguishes between inner sense and outer sense. He writes, "Consequently, we have two kinds of sensations

---

[41] Meier, *Anfangsgründe*, Vol. 1, §27.
[42] Meier, *Vernunftlehre,* §25.
[43] Meier, *Anfangsgründe*, Vol. 1, §24. See also Meier, *Metaphysik*, Vol. 1, §94.
[44] Meier, *Anfangsgründe*, Vol. 1, §28 (emphasis added).
[45] Baumgarten, *Metaphysics*, §535.

[*Empfindungen*]. The first represents the current state of our soul and these
are inner sensations. The other, however, represents the current state of our
body and they are called outer sensations."[46]

Inner sensation can be described as a kind of cognition. Indeed, this
description is consistent with Meier's terminology. He writes, "If I represent
to myself what I am now thinking or that I am sad, joyful, etc., then this is an
inner sensation."[47] Here Meier characterizes an inner sensation as a *representation* of what one is currently thinking or feeling.[48] Moreover, a representation is one of the two senses of the term "cognition." In the *Foundations* he
writes, "We can, without fear of a noticeable error, use the words 'representation,' 'concept,' and 'cognition' without distinction."[49] In other words, he
claims that these terms can be used interchangeably. Thus, it would not be
incorrect to describe inner sensations as "cognitions."

Meier claims that the perfections of a sensible cognition are cognized without distinctness. He writes, "All perfections of this cognition, insofar as it is
a sensible cognition, are perfections that are cognized indistinctly."[50] I would
like to propose that Meier is referring to the inner sensation of the cognition's
perfections. The perfection of a cognition consists in the harmony of the
manifold of representations that are its parts. The harmony of this manifold
is perceptible to inner sense. Moreover, the lack of distinctness with which it
is cognized is consistent with Meier's account of inner sense. All sensations,
including those of inner sense, lack distinctness and are sensible cognitions.
Meier writes, "All our sensations are either entirely sensible representations,
in which there is not any distinctness or, if certain sensations should also be
distinct, plenty of obscurity and confusion will be found in them."[51] Thus, the
inner sensation of a cognition's perfection could be accurately described as
a sensible cognition.

Meier defines beauty as the sensible cognition of perfection. He concludes on the basis of this definition that the perfections of a sensible cognition are beautiful, because these cognitive perfections are themselves things
that are represented without distinctness. I have argued that this occurs

---

[46] Meier, *Metaphysik*, Vol. 3, §529 "Inner sense" [*innerlicher Sinn*] is a faculty of the soul. "Inner
sensations" [*innerliche Empfindungen*] are the representations that are conceived through this faculty. Baumgarten and Meier use both of these expressions.

[47] Meier, *Metaphysik*, Vol. 3, §529.

[48] Tetens considers the question of whether inner sensations are representations in the typical sense
at some length and ultimately concludes that they are. He writes, "Thus, we have representations
of sensations [*Empfindungsvorstellungen*] of the individual acts of thinking in precisely the sense
in which we have them of the corporal objects that act on our external sense organs [*Sinnglieder*]"
(Tetens, *Philosophische Versuche*, Vol. 1, 50.

[49] Meier, *Anfangsgründe*, Vol. 1, §27.

[50] Meier, *Anfangsgründe*, Vol. 1, §28.

[51] Meier, *Metaphysik*, Vol. 3, §542.

by means of inner sense. Since the perfections of a sensible cognition are perfections that are represented without distinctness, via sensible cognition, they fit Meier's definition of beauty. Meier concludes that these perfections are beautiful, and he describes perfect sensible cognition as "beautiful cognition." As we will see, Baumgarten makes a similar argument in the *Aesthetics*.

BAUMGARTEN'S ACCOUNT OF BEAUTIFUL COGNITION IN THE *AESTHETICS*

Baumgarten begins the first chapter of the *Aesthetics* with the following statement: "The purpose aesthetics is the perfection of sensible cognition as such. This however is beauty."[52] If Baumgarten is offering a definition of beauty in this passage, as is often thought, then it differs from the Wolffian definition that he endorses in the *Metaphysics*. However, this is a misreading of the passage. Baumgarten is not offering a definition; he is claiming that the perfection of sensible cognition is beautiful. It is beautiful because it fits the definition of beauty that he set down in the *Metaphysics*: the perfection of an appearance. That is why he follows this claim with a citation that refers to §662 of the *Metaphysics*, which contains his definition of beauty.

Baumgarten does not initially explain why his definition of beauty in the *Metaphysics* applies to the perfection of sensible cognition. He merely asserts that it is beautiful and cites the relevant section of that work. Baumgarten later explains his reasoning in §18–§20. Here he discusses the "universal beauty of sensible cognition" [*pulcritudo cognitionis sensitivae erit universalis*]. This expression refers to the beauty exhibited by perfect sensible cognition.

Baumgarten divides the beauty of sensible cognition into three components: (1) the "beauty of things and thoughts" [*pulcritudo rerum et cogitationum*], (2) the "beauty of order" [*pulcritudo ordinis*], and (3) the "beauty of signification" [*pulcritudo significationis*]. Each of these beauties corresponds to a perfection that is related to sensible cognition. The "beauty of things and thoughts" is based on the perfection of a single cognition. The "beauty of order" concerns how multiple cognitions are combined. It is the perfection of their sequence or order. The "beauty of signification" is based on the linguistic signs through which a sequence of cognitions are expressed. In each case, Baumgarten claims that the perfection is beautiful. It is a perfect appearance and hence fits his definition of beauty in the *Metaphysics*.

---

[52] Baumgarten, *Aesthetica/Ästhetik*, §14.

The Beauty of Thoughts and Things

The expression "thoughts and things" refers to two aspects of a single representation or cognition. "Thought" refers to the representation itself, and "thing" refers to what is represented. Baumgarten's choice of the term "thing" [res] is significant. In the *Aesthetics*, Baumgarten draws a distinction between the terms *res* and *obiectum*.[53] He claims that these terms are often conflated.[54] They denote a weaker and a stronger sense of objectivity. *Res* is the weaker sense. It refers to what we might now call an "intentional object," or an object of thought. *Obiectum* is ontologically stronger. It refers to a mind-independent object.[55] The "things" in the "beauty of thoughts and things" are what is represented by the thoughts. They are not *obiecta*, at least in the sense that Baumgarten uses this term.[56]

Baumgarten writes, "The BEAUTY OF THOUGHTS AND THINGS must be distinguished from the beauty of cognition, whose first and primary part it is, and from the beauty of objects and materials, with which they are often, but wrongly, confused, due to the assumed meaning of 'thing.'"[57] In this passage, Baumgarten distinguishes the "beauty of thoughts and things" from the beauty of cognition in general. It is different than the beauty of cognition because it is one component, and not the entirety, of beautiful cognition. Baumgarten also distinguishes the "beauty of thoughts and things" from the "beauty of objects and materials." An object, understood in the strong sense that Baumgarten reserves for the term *obiectum*, can have features that are beautiful or ugly. It also can be represented in a manner that is beautiful or ugly. The thing [res] that one thinks or cognizes can be beautiful even if the underlying object [obiectum] is not. Baumgarten writes, "What is ugly as such can be thought beautifully, and what is more beautiful can be thought

---

[53] Baumgarten, *Aesthetica/Ästhetik*, §18. In her German translation of the *Aesthetics*, Mirbach translates *res* as *Sache* and *obiectum* as *Gegenstand* (see Baumgarten, *Aesthetica/Ästhetik*, 1163, 1173). Baumgarten does not draw this terminological distinction in the *Metaphysics*. Moreover, in the 1773 edition of the *Acroasis logica*, edited by Töllner, the term *obiectum* is used to refer to an object of cognition (Baumgarten, *Acroasis logica* (1773), §6). This is not consistent with the distinction that Baumgarten draws in the *Aesthetics*. An object of cognition should be a *res*, not an *obiectum*.

[54] Baumgarten, *Ästhetik*, §18.

[55] Baumgarten's distinction between *res* and *obiectum* is comparable to the distinction that Henry Allison draws between the terms *Objekt* and *Gegenstand* in the first edition of *Kant's Transcendental Idealism* (Allison, *Kant's Transcendental Idealism*, 135). Allison does not draw this distinction in the second edition (idem, *Kant's Transcendental Idealism (Revised & Enlarged Edition)*, 476n).

[56] Thus far, I have employed the term "object" rather loosely and not in the specialized sense that Baumgarten denotes with the term *obiectum*. For example, I define the term "appearance" [phaenomenon] as an object of sensible cognition. However, an appearance is not a mind-independent object, or what Baumgarten would call an *obiectum*. Going forward, I will specify when I am using the term "object" in this precise sense. Otherwise, the reader can assume that I am still employing it as before.

[57] Baumgarten, *Aesthetica/Ästhetik*, §18.

as ugly."[58] An object that is ugly can be represented as something beautiful, and vice versa.[59]

The "beauty of thoughts and things" consists in the agreement, or harmony, of the manifold of representations that compose a single cognition. Baumgarten explains that it is "the agreement [*consensus*] of the thoughts, insofar as we disregard their order and signs, among themselves towards one thing, which is an appearance."[60] Here he employs the same conception of perfection that he defines in the *Metaphysics*: the agreement or harmony of something's parts.[61] The "thoughts" that he refers to are the manifold of representations that compose a cognition. They are the cognition's parts. Since these parts are in agreement with each other, the cognition as a whole is perfect.

Baumgarten writes that the thoughts agree "among themselves towards one thing [*ad unum*]." This "one thing" is the determining ground of the cognition's perfection. This interpretation is consistent with Baumgarten's definition of perfection in the *Metaphysics*, which includes the following: "The one thing [*unum*] in which there is agreement is the DETERMINING GROUND OF PERFECTION" (Emphasis in the original).[62] According to Baumgarten, something's parts agree with each other because they all serve as the sufficient reason for the same thing. He calls this grounded thing the "determining ground of the perfection."

What is the "one thing" that serves as the determining ground of a cognition's perfection? Baumgarten writes nothing further about it. However, I want to propose that it is the thing that is represented by the cognition. The manifold of representations that compose the cognition are collectively the sufficient reason for the representation of this "one thing." This interpretation is supported by Meier. In the *Vernunftlehre*, he writes, "Thus, the perfection of cognition is when that which can be differentiated from each other in a cognition, agrees [*zusammenstimt*] with the intention [*Absicht*], or when the

[58] Baumgarten, *Aesthetica/Ästhetik*, §18.
[59] Gerard David's *The Flaying of Sisamnes* vividly illustrates this principle. The painting depicts the torture and execution of Sisamnes, a corrupt judge. Its subject matter is objectively ugly, even revolting, and yet the artist paints the scene with great skill.
[60] Baumgarten, *Aesthetica/Ästhetik*, §18.
[61] J. Colin McQuillan draws a distinction between two conceptions of aesthetic perfection. The first is metaphysical and is the perfection of a beautiful object. The second is epistemic and is the perfection of sensible cognition (McQuillan, "Baumgarten, Meier, and Kant on Aesthetic Perfection," 15–17). I am skeptical that, at least in regard to Baumgarten's philosophy, this distinction can be drawn as cleanly as McQuillan thinks. The epistemological perfection that Baumgarten pursues in his aesthetics is based on a metaphysical conception of perfection: the agreement or harmony of something's parts. This will become clear through my analysis of §§18–20 of the *Aesthetics*. Ursula Franke also claims that Baumgarten's aesthetics is grounded on a metaphysical concept of perfection (Franke, *Kunst als Erkenntnis*, 78–82).
[62] Baumgarten, *Metaphysics*, §94.

cognition, through the manifold that it contains in itself, is skillfully made to achieve its intention."[63] In this passage, Meier explains that the perfection of a cognition consists in the agreement of the manifold of representations that it contains. Moreover, these representations are in agreement when they all contribute to the achievement of the cognition's intention. This intention is the determining ground of the cognition's perfection, as the representations are collectively the sufficient reason for its achievement. Meier defines the term "intention" [*Absicht*] as the representation of a purpose [*Zweck*].[64] What is the intention of a cognition? I take it to be the representation of the cognition's object.

Baumgarten claims that the "agreement of the thoughts" [*consensus cogitationum*] is an appearance [*phaenomenon*]. The pronoun *qui* in the phrase *qui phaenomenon sit* is masculine and, as such, it has only one possible referent: the word *consensus* or "agreement."[65] Schweizer and Solms both conclude from this that Baumgarten equates sensible cognition with appearances. For example, Solms writes, "The sensible cognition is itself the 'phaenomenon'"[66] The "agreement of the thoughts" is the harmonious manifold of representations that constitutes a perfect cognition. Since Baumgarten identifies this manifold with an appearance, the term "appearance" must refer to a kind of cognition. Schweizer and Solms, quite reasonably, assume that it is a synonym for sensible cognition.

However, there is a problem with this interpretation. The aim of Baumgarten's arguments in §18–§20 is to demonstrate that the perfection of sensible cognition is beautiful. In §18, he explains that "the beauty of thoughts and things" consists in the agreement of the manifold of representations that compose a cognition, insofar as this harmonious manifold is an appearance. This is immediately followed by another citation directing the reader to §662 of the *Metaphysics*. Baumgarten's intention is that the reader will recall his definition of beauty and recognize that it applies to the harmonious manifold that he has just described. The harmonious manifold is a perfect cognition. If the perfect cognition is also an appearance, then, by definition, it is beautiful. However, if Schweizer and Solms are correct, and Baumgarten is employing the term "appearance" as a synonym for sensible cognition, then the argument is fallacious. In the *Metaphysics*, Baumgarten uses this term to denote

---

[63] Meier, *Vernunftlehre*, §36.

[64] Meier, *Metaphysik*, Vol. 1, §267. See also Baumgarten, *Metaphysics*, §341.

[65] This important grammatical point is not captured by Mirbach's translation of the *Aesthetics*. The neutral pronoun *das* refers to *Einem*, rather than to *Übereinstimmung*. In other words, it refers to the "one thing" instead of the "agreement of the thoughts" (Baumgarten, *Aesthetica/Ästhetik*, §18). Cf. Schweizer, *Ästhetik als Philosophie der sinnlichen Erkenntnis*, 117.

[66] Solms, *Disciplina aesthetica*, 57. See also Schweizer, *Ästhetik als Philosophie der sinnlichen Erkenntnis*, 39.

an object of sensible cognition. This includes his definition of beauty in §662. If Baumgarten employs the term "appearance" ambiguously, if it refers to things in the *Metaphysics* and cognition in the *Aesthetics*, then his argument for the beauty of perfect sensible cognition will be invalid.

It is quite possible that Baumgarten actually makes this error. However, it also possible to interpret him in a way that avoids this equivocation. The reading that I am about to propose assumes that he uses the term "appearance" consistently and that, in both the *Metaphysics* and *Aesthetics*, it refers to an object of sensible cognition.

As we learned in part three, Meier's definition of beauty is quite similar to Baumgarten's definition in the *Metaphysics*. They are both consistent with the Wolffian theory of beauty. Moreover, Meier argues on the basis of this definition that the perfections of a sensible cognition are beautiful. He argues that these cognitive perfections fit his definition of beauty. Baumgarten makes the same argument in the *Aesthetics*. Furthermore, Meier's argument for the beauty of perfect sensible cognition relies on a curious premise. He claims that the perfections of a sensible cognition are themselves objects of cognition and that they are represented without distinctness. For example, Meier writes, "all perfections of this cognition, insofar as it is a sensible cognition, are perfections that are cognized indistinctly."[67] Finally, if the term "appearance" denotes an object of sensible cognition, then claiming that something is cognized without distinctness is equivalent to describing it as an appearance.

If Meier and Baumgarten make the same argument for the beauty of perfect sensible cognition, then we should expect Baumgarten to assert that the perfection of a sensible cognition is itself something that is cognized without distinctness. Baumgarten actually does this when he claims that the "agreement of the thoughts" is an appearance. In the *Foundations*, Meier writes, "Consequently, the beauty of cognition consists in that agreement of the manifold in this cognition, which can be cognized sensibly."[68] In the *Aesthetics*, Baumgarten writes that the "beauty of thoughts and things" consists in "the agreement of the thoughts [. . .] among themselves towards one thing, which is an appearance."[69] These two passages are roughly equivalent. Interpreting them in the way I have proposed has the advantage of attributing a consistent meaning to the term "appearance." It allows Baumgarten to use his definition of beauty from the *Metaphysics* to justify his claim in the *Aesthetics* about the "beauty of thoughts and things" without equivocation.

One important question remains: how does a harmonious manifold of representations, that is, the "agreement of the thoughts," become an object of

---

[67] Meier, *Anfangsgründe*, §28.
[68] Meier, *Anfangsgründe*, §28.
[69] Baumgarten, *Aesthetica/Ästhetik*, 22, §18.

sensible cognition, or appearance? Meier does not explain the reasoning that justifies this premise in the *Foundations* and, unfortunately, Baumgarten is also silent about this question. In part three, I argued that Meier is referring to inner sense. The perfection of a cognition is perceived through inner sense and the inner sensation of this perfection can be accurately described as a sensible cognition. This thesis is fully consistent with Baumgarten's account of the senses in the *Metaphysics*. He claims that inner sense is "consciousness, more strictly considered" [*conscientia sensu strictiori*].[70] He also claims that all sensations are sensible cognitions. Baumgarten writes, "Every sensation is a sensible perception that must be formed through the inferior cognitive faculty."[71] One's consciousness of a cognition can extend to the manifold of representations that it contains. Since inner sense is "consciousness, more strictly considered" and one can be conscious of the "agreement of thoughts" in a cognition, it follows that this "agreement" can be perceived through inner sense. It is also consistent with Baumgarten's terminology to describe the inner sensation of the "agreement" as a sensible cognition. Therefore, the "agreement of the thoughts" can be an object of sensible cognition, or an appearance.

There is a potential objection to the interpretation that I have just proposed. Baumgarten is supposed to be arguing that the perfection of *sensible* cognition is beautiful. However, the argument that I have attributed to him never specifies that it applies only to sensible cognitions. The agreement of any manifold of representations could be beautiful, provided that their harmony is represented without distinctness through inner sense. My response to this objection is that the "beauty of thoughts and things" is one component of the "universal beauty of sensible cognition." It is likely that Baumgarten simply took it for granted that the thoughts, whose agreement constitutes the "beauty of thoughts and things," are part of a sensible cognition. They are confused or sensible representations. If Baumgarten made this assumption, then his argument in §18 of the *Aesthetics* would be consistent with Meier's argument for the beauty of perfect sensible cognition in the *Foundations*.

The Beauty of Order

There are two further components of beautiful cognition: the "beauty of order" and the "the beauty of signification." The "beauty of order" is based on the order or sequence in which a series of sensible cognitions are

---

[70] Baumgarten, *Metaphysics*, §535.

[71] Baumgarten, *Metaphysics*, §544. In the *Acroasis logic*, Baumgarten equates the term "cognition" [*cognitio*] with "perception" [*perceptio*] (Baumgarten, *Acroasis logica* (1773), §4).

considered. Baumgarten argues, on the basis of his definition of beauty from the *Metaphysics*, that the perfection of this order is beautiful.

The "beauty of order" consists in "the agreement of the order, in which we think about the beautifully thought things, both in itself and with the things, insofar as it is an appearance."[72] In this passage, Baumgarten makes two claims about the "beauty of order." First, the cognitions are ordered in such a way that they agree both with each other and with the things that they represent. This is equivalent to asserting that the order of the cognitions must be perfect. Second, the order of the cognitions is an appearance. It is not difficult to grasp why Baumgarten would make this claim. If the order of a series of cognition is both perfect and an appearance, then it will be a perfect appearance, which would fit his definition of beauty in the *Metaphysics*.

According to Schweizer, the fact that Baumgarten applies the term "appearance" to the order of multiple cognitions confirms that he equates it with sensible cognition.[73] On this reading, Baumgarten is asserting that the "beauty of order" consists in the perfect ordering of a series of sensible cognitions. The problem with this interpretation is that it commits Baumgarten to an obvious fallacy. He would not choose to describe sensible cognitions as "appearances" unless he wanted to draw on his definition of beauty in the *Metaphysics*. However, he would then be equivocating between two different senses of this term. There is an alternative to this unsympathetic reading: we can attribute a consistent meaning to the term "appearance." In the *Metaphysics*, it does not refer to sensible cognition, but rather to things that are cognized without distinctness. If Baumgarten continues to employ the term in this sense in the *Aesthetics*, then the "beauty of order" consists in the perfect ordering of a series of cognitions, insofar as their order is itself cognized without distinctness. The order of the cognitions can be cognized in this way through inner sense.

It might be objected that this interpretation fails to specify that the perfectly ordered cognitions, which constitute the "beauty of order," are *sensible* cognitions. However, Baumgarten claims that the "beauty of order" is "the order in which we think about the beautifully thought things."[74] The beautiful thoughts that he refers to here are perfect sensible cognitions. Consequently, it is not necessary to interpret the term "appearance" in the manner of Schweizer and Solms in order to specify that the "beauty of order" is based on sensible cognitions. Baumgarten makes this clear when he claims that it is the order of a series of beautiful thoughts. Moreover, the interpretation that

---

[72] Baumgarten, *Aesthetica/Ästhetik*, §19.
[73] Schweizer, *Ästhetik als Philosophie der sinnlichen Erkenntnis*, 39.
[74] Baumgarten, *Aesthetica/Ästhetik*, §19.

I am advancing has the advantage of not attributing a fallacious argument to Baumgarten.

The Beauty of Signification

The "beauty of signification" is the third and final component of beautiful cognition. In the *Metaphysics*, Baumgarten defines "signification" [*significatus*] as the connection between a sign and what it signifies. He writes, "The nexus between the sign and the signified is the nexus of SIGNIFICATION, which is called MEANING (power, potency) when attributed to the sign."[75] According to Baumgarten, words [*termini*] are signs that denote mental representations. They are combined to create speech [*oratio*], which he defines as "a series of words signifying connected representations."[76]

The "beauty of signification" is based on agreement or harmony between words and the representations that they signify. Ideally, these signs should agree with both the order of the representations and the things that are represented. Baumgarten writes that the "beauty of signification" is "the inner agreement of the signs both with the order and with the things, insofar as it is an appearance."[77] As I explained earlier, signification is the relationship between a sign and its referent. If words agree with both the order and the content of the representations that they signify, then this relationship is completely harmonious. Baumgarten defines perfection in terms of harmony. Hence, in the passage above, he is describing the perfection of signification. It is the agreement between signs and their referents.

Baumgarten claims that the "beauty of signification" consists in this perfection, "insofar as it is an appearance." He is again drawing on his definition of beauty from the *Metaphysics*. If the perfection of signification is also an appearance, then this definition entails that it is beautiful. Although Baumgarten's reasoning is straightforward, it raises an obvious question: how can signification, that is, the connection between a sign and what it signifies, be an appearance?

Fortunately, Baumgarten's psychology provides a clear answer to this question. He claims that the soul has a capacity to represent the connection between signs and their referents. He calls it the faculty of characterization [*facultas characteristica*]. Baumgarten writes, "I perceive signs together with the signified, and therefore I have a faculty of joining signs together

---

[75] Baumgarten, *Metaphysics*, §347.

[76] Baumgarten, *Metaphysics*, §350. In his dissertation, *Meditationes philosophicae de nonnullis ad poema pertinentibus*, Baumgarten defines poetry as "perfect sensible speech" [*oratio sensitive perfecta*] (Baumgarten, *Reflections on Poetry*, §9). Sensible speech consists of words that designate sensible representations (Baumgarten, *Reflections on Poetry,* §4).

[77] Baumgarten, *Aesthetica/Ästhetik*, §20.

in a representation with the signified, which can be the FACULTY OF CHARACTERIZATION."[78] Baumgarten divides the faculty of characterization into a higher and a lower faculty. The higher or intellectual faculty of characterization is the capacity to distinctly represent the connection between a sign and its referent. The lower or sensible faculty of characterization is the capacity to do so without distinctness. Thus, Baumgarten's psychology allows for the representation of what he calls "signification," that is, the connection between a sign and its referent. Insofar as it is represented without distinctness, through the sensible faculty of characterization, it can be accurately described as an "appearance." Signification is a legitimate object of sensible cognition.

CONCLUSIONS

In §18–§20 of the *Aesthetics*, Baumgarten discusses three perfections that are related to sensible cognition: the perfection of a single cognition, the perfection of the order in which multiple cognitions are thought or conceived, and the perfection of the linguistic signs through which these cognitions are expressed. In each case, he makes a similar argument. He argues that the perfection in question is beautiful insofar as it is an appearance. We can draw several conclusions from this line of reasoning.

First, Baumgarten remains committed to his definition of beauty in the *Metaphysics*: the perfection of an appearance. This definition justifies his claims that the cognitive perfections that he discusses are beautiful. Indeed, in §18, which is about the "beauty of thoughts and things," Baumgarten explicitly cites §662 of the *Metaphysics*.

Second, if this argument is to be valid, then Baumgarten must employ the term "appearance" consistently. When Baumgarten defines beauty as the "perfection of an appearance" in the *Metaphysics*, he uses this term to denote an object of sensible cognition. We can be certain of this because he also claims that beauty is "perfection observable by taste in the broader sense." According to Schweizer and Solms, Baumgarten treats the term "appearance" as a synonym for sensible cognition. However, this would entail that Baumgarten's arguments in §18–§20 are invalid, as he would be equivocating between two different senses of this term.

Third, if the term "appearance" is interpreted in the consistent manner that I have advocated, then Baumgarten's arguments in §18–§20 share an important premise with Meier's argument for the beauty of perfect sensible cognition in

---

[78] Baumgarten, *Metaphysics*, §619.

§27–§28 of the *Foundations*. They both claim that the perfections of sensible cognition are themselves objects of cognition that are represented without distinctness. As Meier puts it, "All perfections of this cognition, insofar as it is a sensible cognition, are perfections *that are cognized indistinctly.*"[79] When Baumgarten applies the term "appearance" to perfections of sensible cognition, he is claiming that these perfections are cognized without distinctness.

The riddle of Baumgarten's aesthetics concerns the relationship between his two definitions of beauty. In this chapter, I have challenged a central assumption made by this debate, namely, that Baumgarten redefines beauty in the *Aesthetics*. It is my view that he does not offer a new definition of beauty in this work. Instead, he asserts that the perfection of sensible cognition is beautiful. He justifies this claim by citing his definition of beauty in the *Metaphysics*.

My analysis of §18–§20 supports this thesis. In these sections, Baumgarten explains why the perfection of sensible cognition fits his definition of beauty. It is noteworthy that he does not cite his supposed definition in §14 and instead repeatedly appeals to his "old" definition from the *Metaphysics*. It is also noteworthy that his protégé, Meier, makes more or less the same argument in the *Foundations*. Meier starts with a definition of beauty that is very similar to Baumgarten's definition in the *Metaphysics*. They are both variations on the standard Wolffian theory of beauty. He then applies this definition to the perfections of sensible cognitions and concludes that they are beautiful. It is likely that Meier, who was well acquainted with Baumgarten's views and had access to his notes, learned this argument from him.

---

[79] Meier, *Anfangsgründe*, Vol. 1, §28 (emphasis added).

Chapter 4

Baumgarten's Conception of Aesthetic Truth in the *Aesthetics*

Angelica Nuzzo

The idea of "aesthetic truth"—or *veritas aesthetica*—fits squarely within Baumgarten's much-praised chief contribution to the incipient history of the discipline of aesthetics. As the art of "knowing" aesthetically and "thinking beautifully" (*ars pulcre cogitandi*) is famously introduced by Baumgarten as the sister discipline to logic—logic being now regarded as the "older sister" to aesthetics[1]—it is only fair that "truth" should find its place not only in logic but in aesthetics as well. And yet, that at stake in the new discipline should be "truth" specifically qualified as "*aesthetic* truth" is neither as evident nor as simple a matter as it may at first sight appear. In fact, quite generally, on the scholastic rationalist paradigm that constitutes the backdrop of Baumgarten's reflection, sensible representations and perceptions may be seen as instrumental to the attainment of the clear and distinct knowledge of (unqualified) truth but not necessarily as endowed with truth themselves. Further assumptions that significantly determine the nature of the new discipline as well as the conception of truth itself must be put in place in order to justify Baumgarten's notion of *veritas aesthetica* or, differently put, in order to get from that general rationalist paradigm accounting for the nature of perception and sensible cognition to Baumgarten's own position.

To be sure, the qualification of truth as "aesthetic truth" next to "logical truth" is only one of the many qualifications that articulate Baumgarten's rich concept of truth. Indeed, Baumgarten offers not only a multiplication of truths differently specified but also a wide array of degrees and levels in which each truth is differently exhibited.[2] These qualifications go from the commonly

---

[1] Baumgarten, *Aesthetica/Ästhetik*, §13.
[2] See Baumgarten, *Aesthetica/Ästhetik*, §441 in which Baumgarten speaks of representation "*veri*, [. . .] *veriori*, [. . .] *verissimi*." Hans Adler speaks of a "Kaskade von Wahrheitsgraden, -dimensionen und -stufen" in Adler "Was ist ästhetische Wahrheit," 56.

scholastic (*veritas metaphysica, subjectiva, objectiva*), to the novel yet more or less unsurprising to our modern ear (*veritas aesthetica, aestheticologica*), to the intriguingly far-fetched to that same modern sensibility (*veritas heterocosmica*). But it is the very act of qualifying truth in multiple ways or, more accurately, the very act of pluralizing truth in many irreducible truths and degrees of truth that is relevant and worth a closer inspection. Thus, what I want to call the "pluralism" of truth characterizing Baumgarten's position is one of the central issues that I set out to explore in this chapter. On what ground is truth not one but many for Baumgarten—not (only) one absolute, unqualified truth but (also) many specifically determined and irreducible kinds of truths? And what are, in the particular case of *veritas aesthetica*, the consequences that arise from this pluralistic position both with regard to the nature of truth and with regard to aesthetics as an approach to truth in cognition as well as in art?

Historically, Baumgarten's introduction of *veritas aesthetica* next to *veritas logica* brings to the fore his stance toward Leibniz's own recognition of a specific cognitive value proper to the senses as well as the innovation over Christian Wolff's rationalism whereby the new discipline of aesthetics uniquely displaces the privilege Wolff uncompromisingly grants to the "higher" cognitive faculty with regard to truth.[3] As science of the perceptions of the "lower" cognitive faculty or science of what he now calls "sensible cognition," Baumgarten's aesthetics upholds the worthiness of such lower faculty while still maintaining the ranking of mental powers proper of scholastic psychology. Thereby, however, he importantly begins the process of destabilization to which such a ranking is increasingly subjected from now on. Because of the mono-dimensionality of truth they uphold, neither Leibniz nor Wolff nor the entire rationalist tradition could make systematic room for a conception of truth alternative to and independent of logical truth, itself topic of an alternative and complementary science to logic—its younger "sister," as it were. On the other hand, the dominance of the mathematical ideal of cognition inherited from Descartes and generally pervading the rationalist tradition, explains why, within this tradition, art and its productions are not recognized as having either cognitive value or a systematic philosophical significance of their own. Art's function is accordingly confined to being a pedagogical tool subservient to furthering moral precepts and aims. Art is, at the most, a tool of morality not the site or the carrier of a truth of its own, deserving independent treatment in a science in its own right.[4]

---

[3] See Franke "Von der Metaphysik zur Aesthetik," 272–278 and Casula, "A. G. Baumgarten entre G. W. Leibniz et Ch. Wolff," 547–574.
[4] See Gregor, "Baumgarten's Aesthetica," 363.

Baumgarten's innovation with regard to all these points generally characterizing the rationalist tradition is encapsulated in the much-commented definition that opens the *Aesthetics* (1750). It is a famous definition: "Aesthetics
(the theory of liberal arts, inferior gnoseology, the art of thinking beautifully,
the art of the analogue of reason) is the science of sensible cognition."[5]
To be sure, we are presented herein with two definitions joined together
in an identity relation. The first is the direct definition, which concerns the
new science that is now named, for the first time, "*aesthetica*" as "*scientia
cognitionis sensitivae.*" The second is the parenthetical definition, which is
instead the one that points to all the disciplinary branches and the more or
less common denominations that Baumgarten gathers together, again for the
first time, under the name and the task of that new science. Accordingly,
the new discipline called aesthetics is a theory of cognition and a theory of
the liberal arts in one; it is *scientia* and *ars* in one. It is *gnoseologia*, albeit
inferior; it addresses reason, albeit as an *analogon*; and it is a philosophical
theorization of the liberal arts and the *ars* of thinking beautifully. While the
first, explicit definition is seemingly straightforward in its conciseness—aesthetics is the "science of sensible cognition"—none of those parenthetical
characterizations, let alone their connection, is self-evident. Baumgarten is
well aware that along with their unification under the new title of aesthetics,
they certainly require further elaboration and justification. My point in this
regard is limited to drawing attention to the relation that Baumgarten establishes from the outset between the two definitions. I shall argue in this chapter
that this starting point is relevant to his peculiar conception and presentation
of the notion of aesthetic truth. Since aesthetics is a theory of cognition *and*
a theory of the liberal arts *in one*, the innovation that the notion of aesthetic
truth carries vis-à-vis the tradition is twofold as it extends *both* to the theory
of cognition *and* to the theory of the arts.

In what follows, I begin with a discussion of Baumgarten's presentation
of aesthetic truth in section XXVII of the *Aesthetics*.[6] In this connection, I
also briefly outline some of the implications of this notion with regard to
the idea of truth in general. In the second part of the chapter, I concentrate
on what strikes me as a peculiarity of Baumgarten's presentation. This
is an aspect of Baumgarten's work that hinges, in part, on the nature and
historical time of his treatise, but more importantly, is directly connected
to the complex view of the new science of aesthetics presented above: the
theory of sensible cognition is, at the same time, a theory of cognition and a
theory of art, *scientia* and *ars*. Aesthetics is a theory of the peculiar cognition
(or truth) conveyed by sense perception and, in particular, is a theory of the

---

[5] Baumgarten, *Aesthetica/Ästhetik,* §1.
[6] Baumgarten, *Aesthetica/Ästhetik,* §423–§444.

cognition (or truth) conveyed, sensibly and "beautifully," by the arts. In this second part of the chapter, then, I will examine some of the examples with which Baumgarten illustrates specific aspects of his notion of aesthetic truth. Significantly, almost all Baumgarten's examples are taken from poetry, not directly from sense perception as such as is instead the case for most of the other rationalists for whom the "aesthetic" or rather "sensible" realm never includes the arts.[7] What is relevant, even surprising, in Baumgarten's examples is how little self-evident they are; how difficult it is to find in them the purported illustration of the theory of aesthetic truth (at least, again, this is the predicament of the contemporary reader). My claim herein is that the way in which poetry embodies and uses aesthetic truth is crucial to the understanding of how this notion or *tertia cura* of aesthetics works in the activity of "beautifully thinking." In other words, the idea of aesthetic truth cannot be fully understood when "aesthetic" is limited to the sensible or perceptual in cognition since such truth is embodied, specifically and necessarily, in the arts and their productions.[8] At issue, then, is the peculiar way in which poetry uses the sensible element in order to produce cognition. This connection is addressed by Baumgarten both in examples in which the artistic effect of poetry is brought to light and in examples in which instead the contrast between abstract intellectual ideas and their aesthetic expression is used to elucidate the validity (and the limits) of aesthetic truth.

BAUMGARTEN'S *VERITAS AESTHETICA* AND ITS SYSTEMATIC PLACE IN THE ORDER OF TRUTH

The systematic place that "aesthetic truth" occupies in the universe of Baumgarten's pluralistic conception of truth is crucial to the understanding of its specificity and irreducibility but also to the appreciation of its interconnectedness with the other forms of truth—first and foremost, with metaphysical truth and logical truth, and with the novel notion of "aestheticological truth (*veritas aestheticologica*)."[9] The very fact that truth is plural characterizes, for Baumgarten, the human standpoint. Baumgarten's peculiar attention to this fact, then, is a consequence of the anthropological turn

---

[7] Other examples are taken from Cicero, Livy, and the Latin classics—their tone is, rather, philosophical.

[8] Baumgarten's aesthetics is usually examined either with regard to his novel perspective on the lower cognitive powers or with regard to the theory of the arts: see Adler, "Was ist ästhetische Wahrheit," 51; Gregor, "Baumgarten's Aesthetica," 357–385; Franke, *Kunst als Erkenntnis* (1972); McQuillan, "Baumgarten, Meier, and Kant on Aesthetic Perfection," 13–27 (these latter for the cognitive perspective). My suggestion is that in order to understand the notion of aesthetic truth the two perspectives must be connected together.

[9] Baumgarten, *Aesthetica/Ästhetik*, §427.

initiated by and nested within his new science. As one of the *transcendentalia* or universal predicates of being (*unum, verum, bonum*), metaphysical truth is one and indicates "the unity of many in one." "Transcendental truth" is the order of the manifold determinations and attributes of a being.[10] The unity of metaphysical truth is thought, traditionally, according to the "catholic" principles of noncontradiction and sufficient reason.[11] "*Veritas metaphysica*" is truth qualified as "*realis, obiectiva, materialis.*"[12] Metaphysical truth is one and applies both to individual beings or things in their individuality and to the cosmic order as a whole. Cosmologically, the truth of the individual is and reflects the order of the universe. Cognitively, according to the scholastic definition of truth as *adaequatio rei et intellectu*, in the case of metaphysical truth the relation between the order of being and that of thinking is a relation of immediate identity and congruity. The intellectual grasp of the thing and the thing's being are one and the same. Precisely for this reason, however, metaphysical truth is constitutively inaccessible to the human mind.[13] Metaphysical truth in its uniqueness and objectivity, in the perfect identity of representation and being, is only in God. In the human case, by contrast, truth denotes, in general, how aptly and felicitously a representation (intellectual or sensory and perceptual) renders the material or real being of things.[14] It is a designation of both the degree and the type of adequacy that connects the mental representation to the thing's reality. Accordingly, truth is necessarily plural as plural are the degrees and the modes in which a presentation can aptly capture the thing's being (and different aspects of such a being). Offering a variation on a successful Leibnizian imagery (i.e., the image of the theater or the city and the different perspectives they afford)[15] Baumgarten maintains that, metaphysically, truth expresses the way in which the one cosmos is reflected in manifold possible ways in the *fundus animae*.[16] Anthropologically, such a reflection implies a necessary pluralization—the pluralization already entailed in that Leibnizian imagery.

While metaphysical truth is "objective," its human approximation is "subjective"—it is the truth of the subjective representation of things; it is the truth of the possibly plural reflection of objective truth in the *fundus animae* (i.e., in the collection of the soul's obscure perceptions). "The representation of

---

[10] Baumgarten, *Metaphysics,* §89.

[11] Baumgarten, *Metaphysics,* §92.

[12] Baumgarten, *Metaphysics,* §89.

[13] See the discussion below and Baumgarten, *Aesthetica/Ästhetik,* §557.

[14] See Baumgarten, *Aesthetica/Ästhetik,* §423.

[15] See, for example, *Monadologia,* §57. Baumgarten takes up Leibniz's theater image in the *Vorlesungsnachschrift* to Baumgarten, *Aesthetica/Ästhetik,* §427. According to this image, truth (i.e., metaphysical truth) is one, pluralized in the manifold different standpoints or representations.

[16] Baumgarten, *Aesthetica/Ästhetik,* §80; Baumgarten, *Metaphysics,* §511: *fundus animae* is the "collection" of all the "obscure perceptions in the soul."

the objective truth in a given soul can be called the subjective truth," explains Baumgarten.[17] In its subjectivity and in contrast with God's unique objective truth, human truth is plural in the sense of being pluralized in different kinds, degrees, and perspectives. Such pluralization is due, first, to truth's connection to different mental faculties (first and foremost, higher and lower faculties); and it is due, second, to the manifold psychological and anthropological relations that the workings of these faculties have with the body and its states.

Subjective truth is, to begin with, either "aesthetic" or "logical" truth. In this bifurcation lies Baumgarten's innovation in relation to the tradition, an innovation that he proposes by distinguishing a "logical truth in the broader sense" from a "logical truth in the narrower sense," and introducing the notion of "aesthetic truth" to complement the latter.[18] The insertion of the new notion of aesthetic truth *within* the order of logical truth (namely, as part of logical truth in the broad sense) produces the additional new concept of "aestheticological truth."[19] Subjective truth, Baumgarten argues, is what we can call, "with the majority," "logical truth"—but logical, he underscores, "in the broader sense (*latius*)."[20] This logical truth broadly construed renders the way in which the metaphysical, objective truth is represented, subjectively, in a given soul so as to produce "within it" "the subjective truth belonging to that soul."[21] Thus, logical truth *latius dicta* is the way in which the soul makes metaphysical truth subjectively its own in and through a given representation. Now, on Baumgarten's view, this process connecting the objective metaphysical truth to the subjective truth in a (human) soul can take place in two different ways according to the mental powers respectively involved in the representation (hence according to the type of representation produced). When the metaphysical truth is rendered subjectively "mainly through the intellect" and is contained "in that which is known distinctly by the intellect," then the subjective truth is "logical truth in the narrower sense (*veritas logica strictius dicta*)."[22] When, by contrast, the metaphysical truth is rendered subjectively "mainly or exclusively through the analogue of reason and the lower cognitive faculties," then the subjective truth is "aesthetic truth."[23] Herein, Baumgarten's division of what is generally called logical truth—and is now, more precisely, logical truth *latius dicta*—in logical truth in the stricter sense and aesthetic truth is brought back to the fact that the higher and the lower cognitive powers are endowed with a distinctive way of

---

[17] Baumgarten, *Aesthetica/Ästhetik*, §424.
[18] Baumgarten, *Aesthetica/Ästhetik*, §424.
[19] Baumgarten, *Aesthetica/Ästhetik*, §424.
[20] Baumgarten, *Aesthetica/Ästhetik*, §424.
[21] Baumgarten, *Aesthetica/Ästhetik*, §424.
[22] Baumgarten, *Aesthetica/Ästhetik*, §424.
[23] Baumgarten, *Aesthetica/Ästhetik*, §424.

subjectively re-producing in the soul (and for the soul) the one metaphysical truth. In particular, the introduction of the notion of *veritas aesthetica* reveals the fact that the confused and obscure representations of the analogue of reason (or the lower cognitive faculties) have a unique and indeed irreducible way of bringing the metaphysical truth subjectively to light. This is precisely what the arts (and poetry in particular) accomplish. Moreover, Baumgarten underlines the fact that the distinction between logical truth (*strictius dicta*) and aesthetic truth is not a nonnegotiable dichotomy (resembling, e.g., Kant's separation of the sensible and the intellectual sources or "branches" of human knowledge),[24] and that while each truth may be completed and sufficient in its own right it may also complement (and be complemented by) the other. Accordingly, the lower cognitive powers may work together with the intellect or may be "exclusively" in charge of the new truthful aesthetic representation.[25] Importantly, there is nothing in the way Baumgarten introduces the notion of aesthetic truth in relation to logical truth to suggest that the truth achieved by the *analogon rationis* is "inferior" or lower than the one achieved by reason or the intellect itself—nothing except his following the terminology of traditional scholastic psychology in designating the mental powers that produce such truth. Indeed, while the mental faculties seem to obey the traditional ranking (higher and lower), their respective truths are viewed as largely equipollent.

"Common (*communis*)" to the aesthetic and the logical "consideration (*meditatio*)" of things is, quite generally, the attempt at grasping what is "truthful and not falsified" in the object according to the principles of noncontradiction and sufficient reason.[26] The way such *"meditationes"* accomplish this, however, is different and is ultimately guided by different concerns even when they apparently thematize the same object.[27] Significantly, the difference is not simply a varying degree of clarity and distinctness in the representation of objects. For, the diverging modality of representation (i.e., aesthetic and logical) produces the specific "horizon" proper, specifically, to aesthetic truth and logical truth.[28] Such horizon demarcates the respective spheres of competence and legitimacy in which different truths affirm their validity—each horizon, in turn, being oriented according to a higher and a lower edge. In other words, while the traditional hierarchy between clear and distinct and obscure and confused representations (and the higher and lower cognitive powers presiding over them) covers the spectrum of a progression

---

[24] As claimed, famously, in Kant, *Critique of Pure Reason,* A15/B29, for example.
[25] See the *"vel unice, vel potissimum"* in Baumgarten, *Aesthetica/Ästhetik,* §427.
[26] Baumgarten, *Aesthetica/Ästhetik,* §426.
[27] Baumgarten, *Aesthetica/Ästhetik,* §428.
[28] Baumgarten, *Aesthetica/Ästhetik,* §429; §119.

that is, by and large, linear and one-dimensional in its orientation to the one metaphysical truth, Baumgarten complicates the picture by proposing a pluralistic universe of truths coordinated rather than subordinated, each with its own sphere of competence, but also with possibly intersecting horizons. While the logical consideration works to produce a "distinct and intellectual" grasp of things, the aesthetic *meditation*, remaining within its own "horizon," is concerned with the intuitive grasp of those same things through the senses and the analogue of reason.[29] Importantly, Baumgarten's point is that in order to produce aesthetic truth, the aesthetic consideration only needs to dwell within its own "horizon." It does not need to be lifted higher to logical perspicuity in order to achieve truth. On the other hand, aesthetic thinking should also *not* aim at a realm that "transcends" its sphere of competence. It should, instead, dwell precisely within the realm populated by those things that (for an average "aesthetic spirit") cannot be "deduced" from the distinct and adequate cognition of the higher sciences but are instead illuminated by that "beautiful light" that pleases "the eye of the analogue of reason." Indeed, "*Carmina vel caelo possint deducere lunam*," offers Baumgarten, quoting Virgil.[30]

The concept of "horizon" aptly renders Baumgarten's view of the human cognitive endeavor, hence of human subjective truth. In the *Aesthetics*, this concept is discussed in connection with the "richness" of material proper of the aesthetic consideration ("*ubertas aesthetica*"). Generally, the "horizon" is the "territory and sphere" of "human cognition," which is constitutively finite with regard to the matter it encompasses. The horizon implies the sensible and material limitation of the overall universe to which human cognition is confined in its capacity to apprehend things in a clear representation. Cognitively, aesthetics and logic operate within distinct horizons. The "logical horizon" concerns the activity of reason and the intellect, and covers that which an "average philosophical spirit" can grasp. The "aesthetic horizon" is instead the "territory and sphere" of the "beautiful analogue of reason." This is the sphere that occupies the average "aesthetic spirit."[31] On Baumgarten's view, truth, in its plural constitution, is rooted in and justified by a plurality of "horizons."

Now, the respective horizons of logical and aesthetic truth may be diverging, in which case the two truths instantiate the bifurcation within subjective truth (truth in the soul or the mind); or they may be converging and

---

[29] Baumgarten, *Aesthetica/Ästhetik*, §426.

[30] Baumgarten, *Aesthetica/Ästhetik*, §121. See also Virgil, *Eclogues*, 60.

[31] Baumgarten, *Aesthetica/Ästhetik*, §119; §121. Much is usually—and rightly—done of the "geography" of the human mind that Kant sketches out in the Introduction to the *Critique of Judgment*. Baumgarten's similar language and intentions in the *Aesthetica* should be considered an important precedent.

overlapping.[32] For this latter case, Baumgarten introduces the novel notion of *veritas aestheticologica*. Thereby he achieves an important expansion of the notion of *logical* truth itself, an expansion that should be appreciated in addition to the more often underlined operation that recognizes an independent cognitive value to sensible perception as such. "Aestheticological truth," Baumgarten suggests, "has been *heretofore* characterized *only* as logical."[33] Now, by reclaiming an independent truth for the aesthetic realm, Baumgarten further grants it a place *within the province of the logical itself* (not just next to it). The example provided by Baumgarten is a verse by Lucretius in which the poet presents the *truthful* "fiction" that lends to Nature the divine voice explaining the necessity of death to a human being who is instead set to reject it. Herein, argues Baumgarten, the poetic fiction converges with the (logical) truth. In this example, everything that is aesthetically true is also logically true.[34] Joining forces in the aestheticological truth, the aesthetic and the logical provide the human equivalent—or the "*analogon*," as it were—of God's metaphysical truth. While this latter is inaccessible to the human mind due to the unavoidable "defect" of human truth (a defect rooted in the *malum metaphysicum*),[35] aestheticological truth is the highest mark to which our human "aesthetic striving"[36] should be positively and successfully directed. Indeed, metaphysically, the beauty captured by the highest degree of aesthetic truth is the human analogon of the perfect unity and totality of the cosmos. In this connection, Baumgarten cites a Platonist-sounding Shaftesbury: "all beauty consists in truth," and "even in poetry, where everything is fable, truth dominates and constitutes the perfection of the whole."[37]

There is a difference, however, in whether subjectively the truth captured in the representation of things concerns the individual or the universal order of things as a whole (or even something in-between). In this regard, aesthetic and logical representations (and truths) diverge. In general, and due to the different aptitudes proper to the respective mental powers, aesthetic thinking and cognizing concern the individual while logical thinking and cognizing concern the universal. From the standpoint of the aestheticological truth (in which aesthetic and logical truth are coordinated) Baumgarten expresses this predicament in the following disjunction, whereby the bifurcation between aesthetic and logical truth is now established *within* the new notion of aestheticological truth, which is accordingly twofold: "The aestheticological truth

---

[32] Baumgarten, *Aesthetica/Ästhetik*, §427; §123.

[33] Baumgarten, *Aesthetica/Ästhetik*, §427 (emphasis added).

[34] Baumgarten, *Aesthetica/Ästhetik*, §427, citing Lucretius, *On the Nature of Things* (*De rerum natura*), Book III, v. 950f.

[35] Baumgarten, *Aesthetica/Ästhetik*, §557.

[36] Baumgarten, *Aesthetica/Ästhetik*, §555.

[37] Baumgarten, *Aesthetica/Ästhetik*, §556.

is either that of the universal, the concepts, and the universal judgments; or that of the individual and of the ideas. The former is the *universal*, the latter the *individual* aestheticological truth."[38] Baumgarten claims that often the aesthetic truth renders the logical truth of the whole as it is captured in individual parts that are beautifully represented. Given the fact that the whole itself can be grasped only once all its individual parts are known, and given that the complete enumeration of the parts constitutes a task humanly impossible to fulfill, then it becomes clear that on this point aesthetic truth is the only access the human mind has to the whole. Aesthetically, the whole is captured, albeit imperfectly and indeed indirectly, as reflected or embodied in the beauty of its parts.[39] Furthermore, additionally underscoring the ways in which aesthetic truth may exceed logical truth, Baumgarten maintains that "in an object of universal truth is never encompassed as much metaphysical truth—at least sensibly—as in an object of individual truth."[40] Aesthetic truth renders the truth of the individual (in its "complete determination," as it were),[41] which is, instead, as such logically inaccessible to the human mind. This is, Baumgarten maintains, the sensible "representation of the widest metaphysical truth."[42] Indeed, he underscores that the more universal the aestheticological truth is, the less metaphysical truth it contains and makes present to the mind.[43] Hence, conversely, because of its sensible concreteness, in this regard the aesthetic truth (or individual aestheticological truth) is closer to metaphysical truth than the logical. Indeed, if the aim of the "*aestheticus*"—that is, the one who thinks aesthetically and beautifully—is "the highest truth," then, as suggested above,[44] he should dwell within the aesthetic horizon and privilege "the more determinate, less universal, less abstract truths over the more universal, highly abstract, and universal truths."[45] This confirms, yet again, that far from being itself "inferior" or "lower" than logical truth, aesthetic truth is endowed with a sphere (or a horizon) of validity of its own which, in determinate cases, may in fact surpass the amount of metaphysical truth that the logical consideration can intellectually grasp.

I want to make a final point regarding the truth of the individual or "*veritas singularis*" and its aesthetic or sensible significance beyond the mind's intellectual grasp. "The truth of the individual," explains Baumgarten, "is either the truth of the internal determinations of the best and highest being

---

[38] Baumgarten, *Aesthetica/Ästhetik,* §440.
[39] Baumgarten, *Aesthetica/Ästhetik,* §428.
[40] Baumgarten, *Aesthetica/Ästhetik,* §440.
[41] See Baumgarten, *Metaphysics,* §148–§149.
[42] Baumgarten, *Aesthetica/Ästhetik,* §441.
[43] Baumgarten, *Aesthetica/Ästhetik,* §440.
[44] Baumgarten, *Aesthetica/Ästhetik,* §426.
[45] Baumgarten, *Aesthetica/Ästhetik,* §440.

(*entis optimi maximi*) or the truth of absolutely contingent things (*absolute contingentium*)."[46] Metaphysically, the truth of the individual spans the onto-logical extremes represented by the highest necessary being (on the highest end) and utterly contingent things (on the lowest end). Theology and aesthet-ics address these ontologically opposite dimensions respectively.[47] Broaching a crucial metaphysical constellation made prominent by Leibniz, Baumgarten claims that the representation of contingent things takes place as they are framed as possible parts within a determinate universe or world. In this regard, two possibilities stand open. On the one hand, things may be repre-sented "as possible and as parts of this world." But contingent things may be also considered and represented "as possible and as parts of another world."[48] The former is "truth in the strictest sense" (*veritas strictissime dicta*); the lat-ter is "*veritas heterocosmica*" and concerns the "human middle knowledge" (*cognitio media*).[49] Baumgarten refers at this juncture to *Metaphysics* §876, which explains God's "middle knowledge," that is, his knowledge of things and connections of things in other possible worlds than the actual (or his pre-volitional and counterfactual knowledge of things independently of the act of creation). In this passage of the *Aesthetics*, however, Baumgarten deals with the *aesthetic* representation—and the aesthetic truth—of contingent things as possible parts of other worlds—a representation and truth that is now the object of "*human* middle knowledge."[50] Thereby *aesthetic* "human middle knowledge" appears as a sort of an *analogon* of divine middle knowledge.

There is indeed a sense, we can suggest departing, perhaps, from Baumgarten's metaphysical speculation but invited to it by the connections he establishes, in which art imagines an alternative universe, and imagines it as endowed of a truth of its own instantiated, concretely, in individual things, events, and deeds interconnected in the unity of a world. At stake herein are a truth—indeed an "aesthetic truth" but also an "heterocosmical truth"—and a universe that are, in fact, connected to the actual world in the same way in which alternative possible worlds are, metaphysically (and in God's mind), counterfactual variations of the actual one. In this respect as well, then, the artist's (or the *aestheticus'*) knowledge can be said to operate analogously to God's middle knowledge.[51] In fact, this is a thought that is not straying that far from the systematic development of the *Aesthetics*. Already

---

[46] Baumgarten, *Aesthetica/Ästhetik*, §441.

[47] Significantly, next to aesthetics is history in its attention to individuality. Herein the Leibnizian tra-dition diverges from Aristotle's famous and influential judgment in the *Poetics* (1451b). Aristotle views poetry as more "philosophical" than history because more universal.

[48] Notice Baumgarten's variation on Leibniz's terminology: the modality—actual vs. possible world—is replaced by the distinction between "this" and "another" world.

[49] Baumgarten, *Aesthetica/Ästhetik*, §441.

[50] Baumgarten, *Aesthetica/Ästhetik*, §441 (emphasis added).

[51] The additional notion of aesthetic "creation" can be further brought to bear on this analogy.

in *Aesthetics* §444, in bringing aesthetic and heterocosmical truth together to the extent that at stake are "true things" represented in sense perception, through the imagination, and generally through the *analogon rationis*, Baumgarten references Leibniz as a precedent but immediately overrides him by quoting instead Tibullus's poetry. In the two verses from the *Elegies*, truth of fact (in the actual world) is set next to the truth of fiction (*fabula*) or the heterocosmical truth of the poetic universe. These are Tibullus's two verses rendering Odysseus travels: "*Atque haec seu nostras intersunt cognita terra*" (whether all this happened in the lands known to us) to which Baumgarten adds, "*strictissime vera*" (i.e., true in this actual world); "*Fabula sive novum dedit his erroribus orbem*" (or whether the fiction created for his [Odysseus'] travels a new world), to which he adds: "*heterocosmice vera.*" Poetic fiction is able to create "a new world" thereby achieving its own "truth." Indeed, Baumgarten's treatment of aesthetic truth in the section examined above[52] is followed not only by the treatment of "*falsitas aesthetica*" but also, among the main headings, of "*fictiones*" (and, specifically, *fictiones poeticae*) and "*fabulae.*"[53]

AESTHETIC TRUTH, POETRY, POETIC EXPERIENCE—BAUMGARTEN'S EXAMPLES

On Baumgarten's view, "truth" is the "third concern" or "*tertia cura*" in thinking of matters of taste and beauty and the arts. Accordingly, this is a concern that does not regard things as such but the act of thinking beautifully about them, their sensible cognition, as it were. But it is also a crucial concern in evaluating and appreciating beautiful things or the productions of art, and specifically, given the examples provided by Baumgarten, the works of poetry. This third concern is "*veritas*" specifically characterized as "*aesthetica*," that is, as we have amply discussed above, "truth insofar as it is to be sensibly cognized."[54] *Veritas aesthetica* is preceded by the first "concern" in thinking of matters of taste, which is the "*ubertas aesthetica*," that is, the richness in notes characterizing the sensible presentation of beautiful things;[55] and by the second "concern," which is the "*magnitudo aesthetica*," that is, the "dignity" and "gravity" and "meaningfulness" proper both to the objects and to the thinking of the objects in the sensible aesthetic realm.[56] These

---

[52] Baumgarten, *Aesthetica/Ästhetik*, §§423–444.
[53] Respectively, Baumgarten, *Aesthetica/Ästhetik*, Sections XXVIII, XXX–XXXI, XXXII.
[54] Baumgarten, *Aesthetica/Ästhetik*, §423.
[55] Baumgarten, *Aesthetica/Ästhetik*, §115.
[56] Baumgarten, *Aesthetica/Ästhetik*, §177.

three features or requirements of aesthetic thinking and knowing should be seen as working together. Indeed, the richness, magnitude, and dignity of the aesthetic representation all contribute to the idea of aesthetic truth, that is, ultimately, to the way the aesthetic consideration achieves sensible cognition—in particular the sensible cognition of individual concrete things. Considering now the examples that Baumgarten uses in order to illustrate the theoretical points defining the notion of aesthetic truth, it is relevant that the majority of them are taken from classical Latin poetry. Philosophical and rhetorical writings of the same tradition, on the other hand, are often used as counterparts to poetry in order to bring to light, alternatively, the convergence or divergence between logical and aesthetic truth as well as the value of aestheticological truth. While aesthetic truth is defined, apparently quite simply, as truth "sensibly cognized," that is, as truth apprehended through the medium of sense perception, Baumgarten's examples make clear that at stake is something more complex than, generally and generically, the capacity of sense perception as such to yield "sensible cognition" and a type of truth of its own. At stake is the type of sensible cognition specifically at work in the determinate ways in which poetry embodies (and triggers) the activity of "thinking beautifully," or, alternatively, the type of sensible cognition in the beautiful works of poetry. Recall, at this point, the definition of the new science of "aesthetics" that Baumgarten presents at the outset of his work.[57] *Aesthetics* is a theory of cognition and a theory of the liberal arts—*scientia* and *ars*—in one so that both aspects must converge in the idea of aesthetic truth.

In order to highlight my point, let me begin with an example that does not invoke poetry as an art directly but refers, rather, to something like poetic thinking or a poetic attitude or disposition of the subject (and not to simple or pure sense perception and its peculiar cognitive validity). To be sure, Horace's poetry is in the background here as an inspiration (to the contemporary reader), although none of his verses is explicitly quoted. We have seen in the previous discussion that Baumgarten underlines the independence of logical truth and aesthetic truth from each other, at the same time insisting that the two considerations (or *meditationes*) may indeed refer to different aspects of the same thing or connection of things, and accordingly, subjectively capture different aspects of the objective truth proper to the reality at hand. In the case of certain objects, argues Baumgarten, there may very well be one truth (logical truth in the strict sense) accessible only through the intellect as the power that yields intellectual cognition. And yet, under certain circumstances, the mental disposition of the subject may go in a very different

---

[57] Baumgarten, *Aesthetica/Ästhetik*, §1.

direction than intellectual cognition, that is, the subject may be inclined to think aesthetically or poetically. In this case, logical truth yields to aesthetic truth—the latter being, under the given circumstances, the only truth capable of rendering the present state of affairs and the nature of the object at hand. In this case, explains Baumgarten, the logical truth "lies above the aesthetic horizon and is rightfully left aside, at least in the present moment."[58] The notion of "horizon" is appealed to herein in order to circumscribe a specific human *experience*, namely, the *poetic experience*. While logical truth is constitutively unable to render such experience as it lies "above" the horizon in which the subject's experience takes place, aesthetic truth captures its full validity. This shows that, in its plural specifications, for Baumgarten truth is a contextual concept that in its subjective validity (as aesthetic and/or logical truth) describes a certain type of experience of the human subject and her mental states. The horizon that demarcates truth's sphere of validity is the horizon of an experience—it is, anthropologically, an experiential horizon (it is not, directly, the object's metaphysical truth). This, then, is the example or rather the thought-experiment with which Baumgarten makes his point: "Think"—he invites the reader—"of the sun's circular eclipse of the last year as you are in the company of physical and mathematical astronomers; and then, think of it imagining that you are a shepherd, either directing your thoughts to your companions or to your Neaira. Oh! How much truth have you thought before that now must be completely left aside!"[59] The starting point is a "truth of fact," namely, the sun eclipse of July 25, 1748, observable in certain parts of Germany. At stake, however, in the concept of truth are two different subjective experiences of the same fact—experiences that cannot coexist (or, rather, cannot be simultaneous). This is what Baumgarten summons us to distinguish. On the one hand, there is the scientific, astronomical, and mathematical account and experience of that fact, while on the other hand, there is the poetic account and experience of that same fact. The point is that in order to access the latter, the reader—or, rather, the contemporary audience familiar both with that eclipse and with Horace's verses—must forget or "leave aside" all the mathematical and scientific truths she may have apprehended and rather follow her poetic thinking or be inspired by poetry in order to do justice to the "truth" of the present experience which is an *aesthetic experience*.

It is clear from this example that at stake in aesthetic truth is not simply the cognitive value of sense perception as such but rather, in a more complex way, the irreducible truth of a specific human experience that is expressed by poetic thinking, that is, that is expressed either directly by determinate poetic

[58] Baumgarten, *Aesthetica/Ästhetik*, §429.
[59] Baumgarten, *Aesthetica/Ästhetik*, §429.

verses or by the poetic inspiration to which the subject "decides" to heed.[60] It is also important that such an experience is construed as contextual: the reader is invited to imagine herself in different companies, surrounded by different familiar objects, addressing different interlocutors, and the like. It is the changing context that lends to the same "fact" a different experiential validity, hence, ultimately, a different truth.

The peculiarity of Baumgarten's position in this regard can be appreciated when compared with the example that Descartes uses in *Meditatio III* to illustrate the different "ideas" of the sun produced, respectively, by the senses and by the intellect. In dwelling on the different description of the two ideas (the sensory one, which presents the sun as quite small; the intellectual one, which presents it as "several times larger than the earth"),[61] Descartes's point is to show that only one of those ideas is true, namely, the one produced by the mathematical and astronomical science. The one derived by the senses, by contrast, is proven false upon further examination. In Baumgarten's example, instead, at stake is not the contrast between the mathematical-astronomical concept of the sun's eclipse and the representation produced by sense perception. Indeed, the sense perception of the eclipse is not even brought up in §429. It is not the sensory perception of the object *per se* but its poetic representation and meaning within the horizon of the subject's experience that interests Baumgarten when discussing the relation between logical and aesthetic truth. And in this regard the poetic meaning is channeled not so much by the senses *simpliciter* but by the imagination and by the imaginative transfiguration of the context in which the subject's mind operates. Baumgarten's example is meant to underline the way in which different truths—namely, logical in the strict sense and aesthetic truth—pertain to different "horizons" of experience; and is meant to make the further point that in order for aesthetic truth to be appreciated, the logical or intellectual concept that lies "above" the aesthetic horizon *must* be utterly ignored.

In another example, taken from Vergil's epic poem, Baumgarten makes a connected point, this time, however, showing the need for the aesthetic consideration to ignore certain logical truths, in this case, some necessary law that regulate the way things happen in reality since these truths "lie under the aesthetic horizon."[62] For, despite being truths, they do not contribute to the

---

[60] Baumgarten, *Aesthetica/Ästhetik,* §429.

[61] Descartes, *Philosophical Writings,* Vol. 2, 24ff. Joachim Ritter refers to the passage in *Meditationes III* in order to underline how Descartes is already "distinguishing" the two concepts (the small sun and the big sun) the same way that Baumgarten distinguishes the two truths regarding the sun's eclipse. My point, by contrast, is that Baumgarten's example illustrates a position that is very different from Descartes's. See Ritter, *Subjektivität,* 156, quoted in Mirbach's introduction to Baumgarten, *Aesthetica/Ästhetik,* xlix, n. 63.

[62] Baumgarten, *Aesthetica/Ästhetik,* §430.

"*aesthetic* truth" of the situation poetically represented. At stake herein are some "small truths" (*veritates parvae*) that even the "historian," Baumgarten suggests, is allowed to ignore.[63] At the beginning of Book VI of the *Aeneid*, Vergil describes Aeneas's very first act of setting foot in Italy: "The pious Aeneas ascends the sacred hill where the high Apollo dominates, and the cave that the terrifying Sybil makes her abode."[64] Baumgarten's claim is that these verses *completely* render the "truth" of the moment (Aeneas's first touching Italy's shore). And since this is an *aesthetic* truth, the poet "neither cares about nor thinks of (*nec curat, nec cogitat*) with which foot Aeneas first touched the Italian shore."[65] The poet is entirely justified in his not bringing up the "small truth" (indeed, a strictly logical truth) contained in the necessary fact that Aeneas must have treaded the shore either with the left or with the right foot first (or, Baumgarten suggests, maybe even with both feet, although this may have been of "*minus decorus*"). Although, with Cicero, Baumgarten agrees that "nothing true should go unmentioned," i.e., that all truth must be reported, he claims that these "infinitely small truths" which lie "below" the aesthetic horizon far from contributing to or enhancing the aesthetic truth of the situation described, take away from its "aesthetic magnitude."[66] In this example as well, the point is not the way sense perception as such constitutes aesthetic truth. At stake is instead the much more complex way in which the truth of the imagined narrative situation is rendered poetically in verse; at stake is the truth of the imagined object and the poetic experience—neither historical nor factual truth as such but the poetic rendering of Aeneas arriving in Italy. Baumgarten's example implies that Aeneas's aiming toward Apollo's rock and the Sybil's cave is somehow essential to the aesthetic effect, hence constitutive of the aesthetic truth and poetic magnitude of the reality under consideration; whereas the mention of the hero's touching the shore either with the left or the right foot is not (although it is true that he must have touched it either with the left or right foot). It is not immediately clear, though, that "sensible cognition" stands here in contrast to intellectual cognition—or, rather, that this opposition does anything to the explanation of Baumgarten's specific poetic example. It is rather the appeal to the ways (or the *ars*) of "*pulcre cogitandi*" as embodied in the medium of poetry that is more helpful.

Finally, I want to bring one last example to discussion. This is an example in which Cicero's *Tusculan Disputations* are commented on in order to illustrate the relation between universal and individual truth as it is differently instantiated logically and aesthetically in the balance of aestheticological

---

[63] Baumgarten, *Aesthetica/Ästhetik*, §430.
[64] Baumgarten, *Aesthetica/Ästhetik*, §430.
[65] Baumgarten, *Aesthetica/Ästhetik*, §430.
[66] Baumgarten, *Aesthetica/Ästhetik*, §430.

truth.[67] This time, however, it seems that at stake is the way in which the aesthetic perspective distracts from a clear insight into what is a fundamentally intellectual—and, in fact, a properly moral—point. At issue in Baumgarten's discussion is *veritas strictissime dicta*, namely, what he has just explained is the truth of the individual (which, he has claimed, regards either the *ens necessarium* or utterly contingent things).[68] In the case of the aesthetic truth, the individual is represented as possible either in this actual world (as its part or as part of its connections) or in another possible world (*veritas heterocosmica*). The latter, I suggested above, can be considered the world imagined by the poetic work. But the aesthetic presentation may also concern the abstract and the universal and, in this case, the question is whether and in what sense the sensible aesthetic expression can be considered the best form to convey truth. Cicero's example is herein relevant because with it Baumgarten can be seen addressing an entire philosophical tradition that uses "aesthetic" fictions and imagination in order to render some point of moral theory "sensible."

Referring to Cicero's text, Baumgarten now identifies "truth in the strictest sense" as the "truth by which that which is or was or will be is represented unchanged (*immutata*)."[69] While in this definition something like a "truth of fact" seems to be addressed, the example that follows concerns an apparently abstract point of moral philosophy. It is only at the end of Baumgarten's discussion that it may become clear how the two standpoints are in fact connected. This definition, explains Baumgarten, can be illustrated by the following passage by Cicero: "When that chorus of virtues (consistency, dignity, courage, wisdom, and the usual virtues) is committed to the rack" (either on the basis of a universal or a particular truth, Baumgarten adds), "it presents such dignified images to view that happiness seems to hasten toward them"—or so it seems, at least, to "middle knowledge," interjects Baumgarten—"and not to suffer them [i.e., the virtues] to be deserted by her [i.e., happiness]."[70] At stake in this passage is the way in which the aesthetic presentation is brought to bear, this time, on a philosophical and intellectual issue—or, perhaps, on a moral experience (as a "fact" that ought to be presented "unchanged"). Or, to put this point differently, this is an example in which the aesthetic presentation (the dignified image of the virtues that constitute a chorus; the expedient whereby they are committed to torture, etc.) creates a universe of meaning that is alternative to the actual one (hence offers a heterocosmical truth). It creates, essentially, a "fiction." Now the beauty and dignity of the (aesthetic) portrait of the chorus of virtues leads one to assume

---

[67] Baumgarten, *Aesthetica/Ästhetik,* §430. See also Cicero, *Tusculan Disputations,* V, 13f.
[68] See our discussion above and *Baumgarten, Aesthetica/Ästhetik,* §441.
[69] Baumgarten, *Aesthetica/Ästhetik,* §442.
[70] Baumgarten, *Aesthetica/Ästhetik,* §430.

that happiness cannot possibly desert them (and should indeed be and remain necessarily bound with them, no matter what). Hence it suggests the (factually false) idea that the virtuous man is and must be happy. So here comes the important remark: "But when you take your mind (*animum*) off *this picture and these images* of the virtues (*picture imaginibusque virtutum*) and direct it instead to *the truth and reality* (*ad rem veritatemque*), what remains without disguise (*nudum*) is the question whether anyone can be happy in torment."[71] The contrast set up by Baumgarten in his use of Cicero's passage concerns the "pictures and images" on the one hand, and the "truth and reality" on the other—the "images" may be general and abstract, they are, however, still sensible images embedded in a sensible, that is, aesthetic narrative. While the imaginative presentation of the virtues allegedly expresses a truth somehow sensibly covered up (*non nudam*, as it were) and aesthetically fictionalized, the point is that precisely this aesthetic presentation seems to turn the mind away from the "truth and reality" of the matter at hand (namely, the relation between the virtues and happiness). In other words, what is problematic (or, perhaps, simply "heterocosmical") in the aesthetic presentation is not the content (which is indeed abstract, i.e., philosophical, and may well be "true") but the kind of thoughts and inferences it elicits. For, following the "beauty" of the presentation, the reader seems to be taken away from the true and real question, namely, how can one be happy in torment (which is precisely what awaits the virtues on the rack)? Or, how can it be that the virtuous person is, in fact, very often deserted by happiness? At stake herein is both a philosophical idea (abstract and universal) and a moral experience—an experience that may be indeed rendered concretely and individually as well. The connection between virtue and happiness can be addressed as an *experience*, hence as a truth of fact pertaining to this actual world. The issue, then, is the different way this "fact" is, respectively, rendered aesthetically and intellectually. In this case, the aesthetic representation is considered such as taking the mind away from the truth and reality of our human experience in this world in the suggestion that the virtues, on the ground of their dignified image, cannot possibly be deserted by happiness. In its "naked" exposition, by contrast, the merely intellectual-logical presentation goes, directly, to the "truth and reality" of the moral question.

So here, by way of conclusion, are some final reflections on Baumgarten's idea of "aesthetic truth." It is by now a largely acknowledged and often remarked contribution of Baumgarten's philosophy that with the introduction of the new science of aesthetics he has promoted the realm of the "sensible" to a cognitive and psychological validity of its own. Thereby, he has indeed

---

[71] Baumgarten, *Aesthetica/Ästhetik*, §442 (emphasis added).

filled a gap in the German rationalist speculation and paved the way to Kant's unique transcendental theory of the human mental powers. On the other hand, however, the theory of aesthetics is for him a theory of the liberal arts. And herein lies Baumgarten's further contribution to a discipline that is found here at its very inception. It is less clear, in the discussion taking place in the secondary literature, how the two characterizations of the new discipline are connected. There is, however, no doubt that Baumgarten considered them to go seamlessly hand in hand. In the course of this chapter, I suggested that this is reflected in the examples he generally uses to illustrate the theoretical points made in the *Aesthetics*—in particular with regard to the central notion of "aesthetic truth." I have examined three of these examples. In them, I argued, the way in which aesthetic truth is embodied, respectively, in the poetic mental attitude of the subject, directly in the works of poetry itself, and in the contrast between poetic or aesthetic presentation and intellectual presentation is more difficult to grasp than one may prima facie assume in a cursory reading of Baumgarten's text. And yet, these examples make clear that the "sensible" cognition brought forth by aesthetic truth is not simply and directly the cognition channeled by the senses and by perception. It is, instead, the complex cognition produced by the way in which perception, along with the imagination and feeling, is employed and shaped and triggered by the artistic work of the poet. Aesthetic truth is, accordingly, poetic truth. It is the truth of the poetic "fiction" through which reality is subjectively—and indeed, sensibly, individually, and concretely—apprehended. Ultimately, aesthetic truth conveys the reality of a human cognitive experience—experience being a way of our being part of the actual world even though this experience may be channeled by the picture of another world. I have also suggested that Baumgarten's idea of aesthetic truth is inscribed in the "pluralism" of truth—and truths—that pervades his philosophy and is paradigmatically expressed in the relationship between logical, aesthetic, and aestheticological truth. The important upshot of this pluralism is in the way truth is characterized as circumscribing a "horizon" of experience. Ultimately, the pluralism of truth is the pluralism of human experiences.

Chapter 5

Pietist *Aisthēsis* and Moral Education in the Works of Alexander Gottlieb Baumgarten

Simon Grote

It is hardly a secret that Alexander Gottlieb Baumgarten (1714–1762) spent eight formative years as a student among Pietist theologians in Halle (Saale) before issuing his influential call for an "aesthetic" philosophy in 1735. His biographers attest that he attended one of August Hermann Francke's (1663–1727) orphanage schools (the Latin School) from 1727 to 1730, and that he studied theology and philosophy at the University of Halle from 1730 to 1735, hearing lectures by several of Halle Pietism's greatest luminaries. It is moreover attested that his theological and philosophical education was guided by his older brother, Siegmund Jacob Baumgarten (1706–1757). Siegmund Jacob had himself attended Francke's schools and studied theology under Pietist professors at the University of Halle. He had been close to the older and younger Franckes since his arrival in Halle in 1722, served as inspector of the Latin School during Alexander's time there as a student, became adjunct on the Halle theology faculty in 1732 and then Professor *ordinarius* in 1734. It was he who encouraged Alexander to teach in the orphanage schools while studying at the university.[1] These biographical facts make it seem obvious that Alexander Baumgarten's philosophical projects, above all his reasons for calling for and developing an aesthetic philosophy, had roots in Halle Pietism. And yet while Baumgarten's debts to another Halle luminary, Christian Wolff (1679–1754), have been and continue to be investigated with great diligence, our understanding of what Baumgarten

---

[1] Abbt, "Leben und Charakter Alexander Gottlieb Baumgartens," 218–223; Meier, *Baumgartens Leben,* 5–19; Zedler, *Grosses vollständiges Universal-Lexicon*, s.v. "Baumgarten, Siegmund Jacob."

learned from his theological studies and of the influence of his Pietist teachers remains deficient.[2]

One of the most recent gestures toward increasing that understanding underscores the paucity of basic research. In an article of 2002, Steffen Gross asserts that Baumgarten's aesthetic theory represents his response to the two very different but equally "one-sided" theories of knowledge that he encountered in Halle. "On the one hand," Gross writes, "the rationalist stream in the Enlightenment," represented above all by Christian Wolff,

> established a clear hierarchy among human faculties and capacities, privileging one-sidedly logical thinking and seeing human emotionality primarily as a darkening threat to clear thinking. On the other hand, Pietism concentrated on inner feelings, placed them at the top of the hierarchy, and showed hostility towards logical thinking and abstractions in general.[3]

"No doubt Baumgarten," Gross continues, "was in search of a third position beyond the traditional division and vertical hierarchization of human faculties, namely the division of man, as such, into a rational or intellectual and a sensual side."[4] Gross's schematic characterization of the influence of Pietism on Baumgarten is by no means implausible, but nor is it fully persuasive. Baumgarten may very well have adopted an interest in "inner feelings" from Halle Pietists, but Gross subjects no Pietist texts to examination, and his assertion that "Pietism . . . showed hostility towards logical thinking and abstractions in general" is scarcely defensible. Among the many facts that contradict it is the presence of mathematics and logic in the curriculum of Francke's orphanage schools, taught with reference to textbooks by Christian Wolff (extracts from *Anfangs-Gründe aller Mathematischen Wissenschaften*) and Johann Gottlieb Heineccius (*Elementa philosophiae rationalis*).[5]

A fuller discussion of the connection between Baumgarten and his Pietist teachers is to be found in Wilhelm Ludwig Federlin's *Popular Religious Education and Civil Society* (*Kirchliche Volksbildung und Bürgerliche Gesellschaft*, 1993). In an attempt to correct an "ignorance of Baumgarten . . . in the area of theology," Federlin draws attention to the theological aspects and implications of Baumgarten's aesthetic philosophy, asserting that Baumgarten's reaction to his Pietist teachers was partly receptive and partly critical. On the one hand, Baumgarten's Pietist upbringing "undoubtedly left

---

[2] The clearest recent example of an otherwise useful analysis of Baumgarten's *Reflections on Poetry* that describes Baumgarten's debts to Wolff but makes no significant mention of Baumgarten's theological studies in Halle is Strube, "Alexander Gottlieb Baumgartens Theorie des Gedichts," 1–25.
[3] Gross, "Neglected Programme," 407.
[4] Gross, "Neglected Programme," 408.
[5] Freylinghausen and Francke, *Ausführlicher Bericht*, 99.

a lasting mark.["][6] Federlin notices this mark in Baumgarten's description of aesthetics as "the science of improving sensible cognition" (*Wissenschaft der Verbesserung sinnlicher Erkenntnis*), to which the "art of awareness" (*Kunst der Aufmerksamkeit*) is indispensable. Baumgarten himself notes the commands by which his Pietist teachers attempted to encourage children to cultivate an awareness of their own inner psychological state: "Concern yourself only with this! Consider why you are here! Watch out! Pay attention!" (*beschäftige dich nur hiermit! bedenke, warum du hier bist! gib acht! merk auf!*).[7] On the other hand, Federlin asserts that Baumgarten did not devise his aesthetic theory as simply an elaborate philosophical exposition of a Pietist regimen for training the sensible cognitive faculties of the soul. Rather, Baumgarten's aesthetic theory represents a theological critique of the Pietist "doctrine of experience" (*Erfahrungslehre*) and "suppression of evil sensuality" (*Unterdrückung der bösen Sinnlichkeit*). Whereas Francke and other Pietists typically invoked darkness as a metaphor for the soul's defectiveness before conversion, according to Federlin, Baumgarten saw the soul's sensible cognition of "dark" ideas as potentially constructive and warned against underestimating its value.[8]

Federlin's observations draw attention to aspects of Baumgarten's writings that have otherwise gone more or less unnoticed, but they are not the last word on the subject. Shedding light on Alexander Baumgarten's call for an aesthetic philosophy by understanding his connection with Pietists in Halle is a time-consuming and unfinished project. It requires a reconstruction of Baumgarten's intellectual and personal relationships with individual teachers and colleagues in Francke's orphanage schools and with professors at the University of Halle, many of whose biographies, let alone their intellectual projects, remain largely or wholly unknown. This reconstruction is made especially difficult by a relative dearth of detailed research into the history of theological and philosophical discussion in Halle among August Hermann Francke and his colleagues (including Alexander's father, Jacob Baumgarten) before Francke's death in 1727, and, still more importantly, in the 1730s, when Alexander Baumgarten began to publish his first aesthetic writings. In the absence of an adequately detailed account of the contemporary intellectual background, Federlin's analysis must be treated with caution. Moreover, one of the texts to which Federlin devotes considerable attention has still more to reveal about the connection between the Pietist background

---

[6] Federlin, *Kirchliche Volksbildung*, 61, 67: "Zweifellos hatten die pietistische Erziehung mit Liebe und Rute, aber auch ein ausgeprägter lebenskluger und dialektischer Selbsterhaltungstrieb ihre bleibende Spuren hinterlassen."

[7] Baumgarten, *Philosophische Brieffe*, quoted in Federlin, *Kirchliche Volksbildung*, 75.

[8] Federlin, *Kirchliche Volksbildung*, 84–85.

and Baumgarten's call for an aesthetic philosophy, and much of what it reveals cannot be construed as critical of Pietist theology in the way Federlin suggests.

The text is Baumgarten's well-known *Reflections on Poetry* (*Meditationes philosophicae de nonnullis ad poema pertinentibus*, "Philosophical considerations of some things pertaining to poetry"). Baumgarten wrote it in 1735 as a *Habilitationsschrift*, allegedly stimulated by his work as a teacher of poetry and logic to students in the most advanced Latin class of Francke's orphanage schools.[9] Baumgarten claims to have seen it as the duty of a philosopher not simply to repeat the rules of writing poetry, appealing to the authority of others in order to justify what he himself had learned by practice and imitation, but rather to prove those rules himself:

> What was more reasonable in this situation than to put into practice the principles of philosophizing, since the first opportunity was presenting itself? Indeed, what can I say is less worthy or more difficult for a philosopher than to pledge allegiance to the words of others and to recite the words of one's teachers with a stentorian voice? I needed to be ready to reconsider those things that I had learned, as was the custom, in the historical way: through practice, imitation (if not blind, then one-eyed), and the expectation of similar cases.[10]

Baumgarten therefore set out

> to demonstrate that many things which have been said a hundred times but scarcely ever proven can be proven from the single concept of a poem that has been firmly in my mind for a long time.[11]

The fulfillment of this intention constitutes most of the rest of the *Reflections on Poetry*. Baumgarten begins his proof with a definition of a poem as "perfect sensible discourse" (*oratio sensitiva perfecta*).[12] From this

[9] Baumgarten, *Meditationes philosophicae*, 3–4; Meier, *Baumgartens Leben*, 13–14. In translating Baumgarten's Latin, I have consulted the (sometimes unreliable) English translation by Aschenbrenner and Holther (Baumgarten, *Reflections on Poetry*, 1954), as well as German translations by Albert Reimann (Reimann, *Die Ästhetik Alexander Gottlieb Baumgartens*, 1928/1973) and Heinz Paetzold (Baumgarten, *Philosophische Betrachtungen über einige Bedingungen des Gedichtes*, 1983).

[10] Baumgarten, *Reflections on Poetry*, 36: "*Quid hic erat aequius, quam praecepta philosophandi transferre in usum, qua se prima nobis offerebat occasio? Quid vero indicius dicam, an difficilius philosopho, quam iurare in verba aliorum, & scripta magistrorum stentorea voce recitare? Accingendus eram ad meditationem eorum, quae de more cognoveram historice, per usum, imitationem, nisi c[a]ecam, luscam tamen, & exspectationem casuum similium.*"

[11] Baumgarten, *Reflections on Poetry*, 36: "*ut enim ex una, quae dudum mente haeserat, poematis notione probari plurima dicta iam centies, vix semel probata posse demonstrarem.*"

[12] Baumgarten, *Reflections on Poetry*, §9.

definition, Baumgarten deduces the general characteristics of a perfect poem. The principal characteristic of such a poem, according to Baumgarten, is its tendency to produce, to the greatest extent possible, "sensible ideas" (*representationes sensitivae*) in the mind of its reader.[13] Applying terms influentially described by Gottfried Wilhelm Leibniz in 1684 and in common use by the 1730s, Baumgarten calls those ideas "clear" (*clarae*) and "confused" (*confusae*).[14] An idea is clear in so far as it allows one to recognize what thing is being represented, because it contains representations of the characteristics of the thing that distinguish it from other things.[15] An idea is confused, as opposed to *distinct*, in so far as those distinguishing characteristics are not made explicit, so that the thing represented cannot immediately be classified according to a definition.[16] Unlike a logical proof, in other words, a poem does not contain words and phrases that denote general concepts and correspond obviously to definitions; rather, it contains words and phrases that represent particular objects of the senses.[17] But Baumgarten adds that these words should not simply convey "dead mental images" (*phantasmata mortua*).[18] From the principle that the perfect poem produces as many sensible ideas in the mind of its reader as possible, Baumgarten concludes that the most perfect poems produce imagined not only sense impressions of particular objects but also another kind of sensible idea, namely, ideas of "momentary changes" (*mutationes praesentes*) in the human mind.[19] Baumgarten's term is "sensual ideas" (*repraesentationes sensuales*), and he includes among them ideas of "affects" (*affectus*), which he calls "noticeable degrees of pain and pleasure" (*notabiliores taedii et voluptatis gradus*) in a person confusedly representing something to themselves as bad or good.[20] The most perfect poems, therefore, arouse in their readers as many and as strong affects as possible.

After explaining the various rules for choosing and arranging the contents of a poem so as to produce as many sensible ideas as possible, Baumgarten calls for the philosophical treatment of a new type of knowledge, which is to say, he calls for the creation of a new "science" or branch of philosophy, one that teaches the perception of truth not through the "higher" cognitive faculties of the soul, such reason, whose improvement has traditionally been considered the ambit of logic, but through the "lower" faculties, such as the

[13] Baumgarten, *Reflections on Poetry*, §8.
[14] Baumgarten, *Reflections on Poetry*, §12–§15.
[15] Baumgarten, *Reflections on Poetry*, §13. C.f. Leibniz, "Meditations on Knowledge, Truth, and Ideas," 24.
[16] Baumgarten, *Reflections on Poetry*, §14; Leibniz, "Meditations on Knowledge, Truth, and Ideas," 24.
[17] Baumgarten, *Reflections on Poetry*, §25.
[18] Baumgarten, *Reflections on Poetry*, §29.
[19] Baumgarten, *Reflections on Poetry*, §24.
[20] Baumgarten, *Reflections on Poetry*, §25–§27.

imagination and memory, which play a more direct role in the generation of sensible ideas and therefore a more direct role in the creation of and response to poetry as Baumgarten defines it. As a name for this new branch of philosophy, Baumgarten suggests "aesthetics" (*aesthetica*).[21] In Baumgarten's choice of this word, the connection between his call for a new, "aesthetic" philosophy and the Pietist background can be seen particularly clearly. The connection moreover reveals precisely what has tended to be overlooked and what even Federlin does not emphasize, namely, the ethical dimension of Baumgarten's early aesthetic project. Like many Halle Pietists, Baumgarten was advancing a conception of moral education as requiring the improvement of the human affects through the correct exercise of the sensible faculties of the soul.

Baumgarten has occasionally been honored as the coiner of the term *aesthetics*,[22] but Baumgarten himself declines this honor, referring explicitly to the ancient use of the Greek word *aisthētikē* (printed by Baumgarten's publisher in Greek as αἰσθητική) among "the Greek philosophers and the Church Fathers," for whom its cognate *aisthēta* referred to sensible things perceived by means other than reason.[23] Baumgarten does not mention, but must have been aware of, the currency of another Greek cognate among his contemporaries: *aisthēsis*. Already for several decades, Halle theologians had been deploying this word in connection with a debate over the means by which God communicates with human beings, and over the involvement of human affects in that process of communication. One of these theologians was August Hermann Francke himself, who had given *aisthēsis* (consistently printed in Greek as αἴσθησις) a significant place in his hermeneutic theory, above all in his *Outline of Doctrine Concerning Affects* (*Delineatio doctrinae de affectibus*), an addendum to his *Guide to Reading Holy Scripture* (*Manuductio ad lectionum scripturae sacrae*), first published in 1693.[24]

Francke mentions *aisthēsis* in connection with what he calls "expository" (*exegetica*) reading of the Bible, one of the seven types of biblical reading that altogether constitute a "complete study of divinity" (*solidum Theologiae studium*) and one of four types that aim at understanding the "core" (*nucleus*) of the text, as opposed to the "shell" (*cortex*).[25] According to Francke, an expository reading of a biblical text expounds "the literal sense as intended by the Holy Spirit" (*sensum literalem, ab ipso S[ancto] intentum*). The meaning at which it aims is simple (*simplex*) and is communicated without need of

---

[21] Baumgarten, *Reflections on Poetry*, §115–§116.
[22] Aschenbrenner and Holther, *Reflections on Poetry*, v.
[23] Baumgarten, *Reflections on Poetry*, §116.
[24] See Erhard Peschke's introduction to Francke, *Manuductio ad lectionem scripturae sacrae*, 28–30. Francke himself appears to have given lectures on the *Manuductio* in Halle from 1698 through 1702. Later editions appeared in 1700 (Halle), 1706 (London), and 1709 (Halle).
[25] Francke, *Manuductio*, 36–37, 61.

"labored interpretations" (*sine operoso interpretationis molimine*). The general hermeneutical techniques by which one arrives at this meaning are many. They include the purpose (*scopus*) of the passage in question; the context; parallelisms, that is, the use of similar expressions elsewhere; the so-called analogy of faith (*analogia fidei*); the order in which the biblical authors typically expound their subjects; the circumstances to which the passage refers; and the affects or emotional state of the author.[26] In the course of explaining this last consideration, Francke directs his readers to the much more extensive discussion of it in his *Delineatio*, where he invokes *aisthēsis* by name.

In applying the term, Francke no doubt had in mind Paul, whose Letter to the Philippians he more or less quotes. Paul prays "that your love may overflow more and more with knowledge and full insight [εὐ ἐπιγνώσει πάσῃ αἰσθήσει] to help you determine what is best."[27] On Francke's account, *aisthēsis* is what allows a reader of the Bible to perceive the affects of a sanctified soul, and therefore the affects of the sanctified people whose words the Bible records. It is not available to everyone. The only people who seriously strive to attain *aisthēsis* and are capable of it, according to Francke, are those people who have themselves been "reborn" (*rennatus*), and who have therefore personally experienced the "*habitus* of a soul that has been sanctified and endowed with divine wisdom" (*illum animae sanctificatae & sapientia divina donatae habitum*).[28] This *habitus* is the essential distinguishing mark of rebirth. It is the predominance of "spiritual" (*spiritualis*) over "natural" (*naturalis*) affects. Humility, serenity, love of God, and a desire to seek God's glory and the edification of mankind, for example, outweigh the perversely self-interested, turbulent desire for one's own private pleasure.[29] This experience of moral reform among the reborn is the precondition of *aisthēsis*.

According to Francke, insight into the affects of a sanctified soul is important because it allows a reader of the Bible to understand two elements of a passage's "core": the literal meaning and the spiritual truths to which the passage refers.[30] That the literal meaning cannot be understood reliably without *aisthēsis* follows largely from two premises. The first premise derives from the nature of verbal discourse: affects are what cause people to make statements, and they are therefore inseparable from language and its meaning.[31] "Everyday experience in familiar discourse," Francke writes, "attests . . . how

---

[26] Francke, *Manuductio*, 61–71.
[27] Paul, *Letter to the Philippians*, 1: 9–10: ". . . ἵνα ἡ ἀγάπη ὑμῶν ἔτι μᾶλλον καὶ πάσῃ αἰσθήσει, εἰς τὸ δοκιμάζειν ὑμᾶς τὰ διαφέροντα. . . ." Francke reproduces Paul's pairing as "*solida* . . . ἐπιγνώσει, & αἰσθήσει" in his *Manuductio,* 92.
[28] Francke, *Manuductio*, 91–92.
[29] Francke, *Manuductio*, 93–94.
[30] Francke, *Manuductio*, 88.
[31] Francke, *Manuductio*, 88.

the same words, uttered differently on account of a different affect, differ in meaning." One must therefore perceive the affects of an author in order to ascribe the correct meaning to the author's utterance.[32] The second premise is of course that the authors of the words recorded in the Bible indeed had affects like those of the reborn, such that the reborn can apply an understanding of those authors' affects, derived from their own experience, to the interpretation of biblical passages.

That a biblical passage's spiritual meaning, too, cannot reliably be grasped without *aisthēsis*, follows not only from these two premises but also from Francke's concept of a text's spiritual meaning. In the important case of interpreting the divine commandments, grasping the spiritual meaning comprises not only identifying a precept issued by God and being able to apply it to oneself but also understanding and striving to attain the spiritual *habitus* to which the precept ultimately refers. Francke's final exhortation in the *Delineatio* summarizes this idea as it applies to biblical interpretation in general:

> Rule XI: *And so, in examining affects, we profit most of all by an imitation and pious emulation of those affections that we have perceived in the holy authors.*
>
> For the more we adopt the same affect, the more skillfully and deeply we will be able to seek it, assess it, and show it in the holy texts. And so whenever an affect of the holy authors presents itself to us, let us diligently try under the same circumstances to obtain the same affect in ourselves, and indeed the same degree of the affect, if possible; and let us try, with the help of God's grace, to correct every faulty [affect] we have discovered. The meaning of scripture, grasped in this way by the heart rather than the head, will penetrate to the very marrow of our bones, and will transform our souls "from glory to glory" [ἀπὸ δόξης εἰς δόξαν],[33] and we will experience truly that the word of God is effective, and sharper than any two-edged sword, piercing all the way to the division of mind and spirit, of joints and marrow, and that it discerns the thoughts and intentions of the heart.[34]

---

[32] Francke, *Manuductio*, 66: "*Testis etiam est quotidiana in famiari sermone experientia, quantum pondus addat, ad recte comprehendum sensum dicentis, affectus, & quam varium eadem verba, diversimode ob diversum affectum pronunciata, sortiantur sensum.*" C.f. Francke, *Einleitung zur Lesung Heiliger Schrift*, 141.

[33] Paul, *II Corinthians*, 3:18.

[34] Francke, *Manuductio*, 98: *Reg. XI. Tandem in scrutinio affectuum potissimum proficimus imitatione, piaque aemulatione eorum, quos in Scriptoribus S. semel perspexerimus affectuum. Quo enim magis eundem induerimus affectuum, eo solertius, ac profundius eum in Textibus sacris rimari, perpendere, ac demonstrare poterimus. Quoties itaque affectus se nobis sistet Scriptorum S. toties posito vel ficto eodem casu, eundem in nobis ipsis affectum, imo eundem affectus gradum, quoad ejus fieri potest studiose quaeramus, deprehensumque defectum per gratiam Dei auxiliatricem corrigere studeamus. Sic Scripturae sensus, corde potius quam cerebro comprehensus, ad medullas usque ossium penetrabit, nostramque animam transformabit ἀπὸ δόξης εἰς δόξαν,*

On Francke's account, grasping the spiritual truth of a biblical text means engendering a personal, moral transformation, not only on the level of behavior but also on the deeper level of one's own affects. To be sure, experience of spiritual affects on the part of the reader is a precondition of understanding the spiritual meaning of the text, but it is also the result. Recognizing the spiritual affects of the holy authors is the indispensable means of further strengthening those affects in oneself by a process of "imitation and holy emulation" at the expense of the "faulty" natural affects that they outweigh. This is the theory of moral education implicit in Francke's hermeneutic discussion of *aisthēsis*.

Francke was neither the originator nor the only representative of the view that understanding the affects of biblical authors is essential to understanding the literal and spiritual meanings of their words. As authorities for his view, he cites Martin Luther, Wolfgang Franzius, and Philip Jakob Spener, among others.[35] Nor did Francke stand alone among his contemporaries in this regard. A view very similar to his, also with explicit reference to *aisthēsis*, can be found in two hermeneutical texts by Johann Jacob Rambach (1693–1735): Rambach's 1723 *Institutes of sacred hermeneutics* (*Institutiones sacrae hermeneuticae*) and, more elaborately, Rambach's German commentary on his own *Institutes*, published posthumously in 1738 under the title *Elucidation of his own institutes of sacred hermeneutics* (*Erläuterung über seine eigene Institutiones hermeneuticae sacrae*).[36] Rambach was Francke's student, colleague, and successor in the Halle Theology Faculty, and he expounded basic principles essentially in agreement with Francke's. The differences are minor. Rambach adduces more and different authorities, including Francke himself and Longinus.[37] He also explains the principles somewhat more elaborately

---

& revera experiemur, sermonem DEi esse efficacem, & penetrantiorem quovis gladio, utrinque incidente, ac pertingente usque ad divisionem animae simul ac Spiritus; compagumque ac medullarum, & discretorem cogitationum & intentionum cordis.

[35] Francke, *Manuductio*, 88–89.

[36] The relationship between Francke and Rambach was relatively close. Born in Halle in 1693, Rambach attended Francke's orphanage schools from 1708 to 1712 and then studied theology until 1715 at the University of Halle, where he is attested to have studied hermeneutics with Francke. After several years working on a new edition of the Hebrew Bible with Francke's colleague Johann Heinrich Michaelis and then studying in Jena, Rambach returned to Halle in 1723 to take up an adjunct position in the Halle theology faculty and an inspectorship at Francke's schools. Upon Francke's death in 1727, Rambach became ordinarius professor of theology. He left Halle again in 1731 to take up a professorship in Giessen. Zedler, *Universal-Lexicon*, s.v. "Rambach, (Joh. Jac.)"; Strieder, *Grundlage zu einer hessischen Gelehrten-und-Schriftsteller-Geschichte*, s.v. "Rambach, Johann Jacob."

[37] Rambach, *Institutiones hermeneuticae sacrae*, 123, 128; Rambach, *Erläuterung über seine eigene Institutiones hermeneuticae sacred*, 381. To the best of my knowledge, Rambach's reference to Longinus has not been noticed until now. His connections to Immanuel Jacob Pyra (1715–44), who studied in Halle and translated Longinus, deserve investigation.

and occasionally with a slightly different emphasis. More explicitly than Francke, for example, Rambach asserts not simply that utterances cannot be understood without an understanding of their author's affects, but that the utterances are a means of communicating those affects. "Our thoughts," Rambach writes, "are almost always bound up with particular private affects, ... so that by means of words we are causing others to understand not only our thoughts, but also the affects of ours that are bound up with them."[38] Rambach calls affects "the soul of discourse" (*anima sermonis*), the transmission of which gives the utterances of biblical authors their morally edifying power: "We must attempt to profit from not only the words but also the affects of the holy men, and must therefore read the Bible to this end, so that our hearts are filled with good and holy affects."[39] Like Francke, Rambach calls the capacity to perceive these affects *aisthēsis*, which he translates as "spiritual sensation" (*geistliche Empfindung*) and ascribes to the reborn alone.[40]

Francke and Rambach's conception of divine communication and moral education through the arousal of human affects, with its stress on the indispensability of *aisthēsis*, was clearly controversial. Two objections to Francke and Rambach's position, dealt with explicitly and at some length both by Francke in 1693 and by Rambach decades later, reveal one of the points at issue: the nature of divine inspiration or *theopneustia*, and more specifically, whether God's direct communication with human beings through inspiration by the Holy Spirit involves a dampening of the prophets' human affects. The first objection, as Francke puts it, is that "one who attributed affects to the theopneustic or divinely inspired authors would be doing an injustice to the Holy Spirit, since the holy scripture must be credited not to the holy authors, but to the Holy Spirit, speaking through their mouth[s]."[41] The alleged danger is that attributing human affects to the authors of scripture excludes the possibility that those authors were divinely inspired, because inspiration necessarily involves the suppression of human affects by the Holy Spirit. To this objection, Francke and Rambach give similar answers: the inspired authors clearly did not write the biblical texts "like blocks, without sense or *aisthēsis*" (*ut truncos, & sine sensu, ac*

---

[38] Rambach, *Erläuterung*, 374: "*Unsere Gedancken . . . sind fast allezeit mit gewissen geheimen Affecten verknüpft . . . daher geben wir durch die Rede nicht nur unsere Gedancken, sondern auch unsere damit verknüpften Affecten andern zu verstehen.*"

[39] Rambach, *Erläuterung*, 377–378: "*[W]ir müssen nicht nur von den Worten, sondern auch von den Affecten der heiligen Männer zu profitiren suchen, und müssen daher die Schrift auch um deswillen lesen, damit . . . unser Hertz mit guten und heiligen Affecten erfüllet werde.*"

[40] Rambach, *Erläuterung*, 388–389.

[41] Francke, *Manuductio*, 90: "*Existimare aliquis posset, illum fore in ipsum Spiritum S. injurium, qui Scriptoribus θεοπνεύστοις sive ex afflatu divino scribentibus affectus tribuerit; neque enim Scripturam S. esse Scriptoribus S. sed Spiritui S. per ipsorum os loquenti acceptam ferendam.*"

αἰσθήσει).[42] (Rambach writes, "completely without sensation" (*ohne alle Empfindung*).[43]) To the contrary, the authors' wills were stirred up (*concitata*) "with pious, holy, and ardent emotions" (*piis, sanctis, ardentibusque motibus*).[44]

A second objection, according to Francke and Rambach, is that considering the affects of scriptural authors renders their utterances ambiguous, such that a reader can derive from them whatever meaning he likes.[45] The alleged danger again appears to be that assuming the utterances of biblical authors to be laden with affects excludes the possibility that they were divinely inspired, since divinely inspired utterances must by their nature be unambiguous and affect-laden utterances are not. To this objection, Francke and Rambach offer a simple rebuttal: experience with everyday language confirms that the meaning of an utterance depends on the affects of the utterer. Paying attention to those affects is therefore the only way to eliminate ambiguity.[46]

Francke and Rambach's controversial insistence on the importance of perceiving and imitating the affects of divinely inspired biblical authors as a means of moral improvement appears to have implied a similarly controversial defense of poetry as a verbal means of communicating divine truths and improving the affects of a reader or listener. Hints of the character of this defense can be found in a slim booklet of poems and poetic fragments by Martin Luther, published in 1729 in Magdeburg by Johann Justus von Einem (1685–1762), who had studied biblical hermeneutics and rhetoric with Francke in Halle between 1706 and 1708.[47] In defense of reading and writing poetry as activities worthy of a holy person, Einem asserts that Luther himself took delight in reading ancient poets, whose style he compared to that of the moving poetic passages in scripture. In withdrawing to the monastery in Erfurt, Einem claims, Luther left behind all his books except the poetry of Vergil, whose "affect was not engendered by nature or by the common virtue of the Muses, or by their ordinary inspiration, but rather indeed is an extraordinary gift of the spirit and is loftier, inspired by heaven."[48]

Einem's characterization of Luther as an admirable poet and lover of poetry implies that poetry should not be condemned as a gift merely of the Muses, but rather ought to be admired as—at least in some cases—a gift of the Holy

---

[42] Francke, *Manuductio*, 90.
[43] Rambach, *Erläuterung*, 378.
[44] Francke, *Manuductio*, 90; cf. Rambach, *Erläuterung*, 377, 389, 411.
[45] Francke, *Manuductio*, 90; Rambach, *Erläuterung*, 378.
[46] Francke, *Manuductio*, 90; Rambach, *Erläuterung*, 374–379.
[47] Trinius, *Beytrag*, Vol. 1, s.v. "Einem, Johann Justus von"; Einem, *Martini Lutheri poemata, Vorrede*; Meier, *Baumgartens Leben*, 10.
[48] Einem, *Martini Lutheri poemata*, 8: "*affectus non a natura, nec ex vulgari Musarum virtute venit, aut earum adflatu solito concipitur, sed revera donum novum est spiritus, & altior a coelo adflatus.*"

Spirit, capable of moving human beings in a salutary way. This view finds much more elaborate and explicit articulation in Johann Jacob Rambach's preface to the 1727 collection of his own poems, *Poetic Thoughts in Celebration of God's Supreme Benefactions* (*Poetische Fest-Gedancken von den höchsten Wohlthaten Gottes*). In discussing the "abuse and correct use of poetry," Rambach condemns in no uncertain terms all poetry that is used "as an instrument of the three most prominent sinful predilections: carnal desire, love of honor, and love of money [*Wohllust, Ehrgeiz und Geldgeiz*]."[49] He condemns the poems of Anacreon, Ovid, Catullus, Tibullus, and Propertius for undermining their readers' "chastity, self-control, decency, and fear of God" (*Keuschheit, Zucht, Ehrbarkeit und Gottesfurcht*).[50] The danger of such poems arises, according to Rambach, on account of their words' capacity to affect the character of their readers; they awaken feelings by causing the reader to imagine the things to which the words refer. The more frequently one imagines things that arouse a particular desire, the deeper such desire impresses itself into the reader's heart.[51] Dangerous poems describe "things that violate the purity of one's character" (*Sachen, die die Keuschheit des Gemüths verletzen*), in so far as those things arouse a "carnal desire for pleasure" (*fleischliche Wohllust*).[52] Poetry itself, however, Rambach calls an "honorable gift of God" (*eine edle Gabe des Höchsten*), capable also of being used as an instrument for moral edification. Poems must be written

> to honor God, to sing of his boundless perfections, his most lovable qualities, his venerable majesty, which the prophets describe in a style so sublime that the reader cannot but be overcome by holy trembling.[53]

The effect of poems that fulfill Rambach's conditions is that readers'

> hearts can be awakened to reverence for God, to love of Jesus Christ, to praise of the creator, to recognition of their own insignificance, to longing for his holy community, and to holy conduct and godly life.[54]

---

49 Rambach, *Poetische Fest-Gedancken*, Vorrede, §2.
50 Rambach, *Poetische Fest-Gedancken*, Vorrede, §1–§3.
51 Rambach, *Poetische Fest-Gedancken*, Vorrede, §6.
52 Rambach, *Poetische Fest-Gedancken*, Vorrede, §6.
53 Rambach, *Poetische Fest-Gedancken*, Vorrede, §11: "*zur Ehre GOttes, zur Besingung seiner unendlichen Vollkommenheiten, seiner liebenswürdigsten Eigenschaften, seiner unanzubetenden Majestät (deren Beschreibung die Propheten mit einer so erhabenen Schreibart verrichten, daß dem Leser dabey ein heiliger Schauer überfallen muß).*"
54 Rambach, *Poetische Fest-Gedancken*, Vorrede, §11: "*daß ihre Herzen dadurch zur Ehrfurcht vor GOtt, zur Liebe JEsu Christi, zum Lobe des Schöpfers, zur Erkäntniß ihrer Nichtigkeit, zum Verlangen nach seiner seligen Gemeinschaft, zum heiligen Wandel und gottseligen Leben erwecket werden können.*"

This attitude toward poetry as an instrument of moral edification whose effectiveness derives from its power to awaken spiritual affects in its readers by means of a sublime style, like the power of the affect-laden words uttered by biblical authors, must have been familiar to Alexander Baumgarten.

Baumgarten's acquaintance with the debate over poetry's usefulness as an instrument of divine communication and edification is strongly suggested by a reference in his *Reflections on Poetry* to a 1710 dissertation written under the supervision of the Helmstedt theologian (and one-time teacher of Johann Justus von Einem) Johann Andreas Schmidt (1652–1726), entitled *On the Method of Propagating Religion by Means of Poems* (*De modo propagandi religionem per carmina*).[55] Baumgarten invokes the dissertation as an authority for his claim that virtue and religion have long been promoted by means of poems (*carmina*). The dissertation itself describes "poetic theology" as having flourished in various ancient communities, and it describes poems as having been the standard vehicle of transmitting divine law and true religion before Moses.[56]

Baumgarten must also have known that Francke and Rambach had invoked *aisthēsis* in their account of divine inspiration as elevating rather than suppressing the human affects of biblical authors. Although Francke's *Manuductio* does not seem to have been assigned to students in his orphanage schools during Baumgarten's time there, all students in the Latin School—attended by Baumgarten from 1727 to 1730—were required to read Francke's *Introduction to the Reading of Holy Scripture* (*Einleitung zur Lesung Heiliger Schrift*), in which the *Manuductio* is explicitly mentioned.[57] Nor would the Latin of Francke's *Manuductio* have been a barrier to the young Baumgarten; upon enrollment in the Latin School at age thirteen, he was placed in the second-most-advanced Latin class, showing a linguistic ability very rare among classmates his age.[58] His knowledge of Rambach's *Institutes* could have come from several sources. One likely source is Christian Benedict Michaelis (1680–1764), Professor *ordinarius* of theology and philosophy at the University of Halle, a friend of August Hermann Francke's and a respected philologian who taught biblical languages and biblical interpretation to two generations of theology students at Halle. Baumgarten is attested to have attended his lectures as a student of theology between 1730

[55] Schmidt, praes., *Dissertatio historico-theologica de modo propagandi religionem per carmina*, def. Ludovicus Guntherus Gelhud. A second edition of the dissertation appeared in 1728. Einem is attested to have studied under Schmidt in 1705. See Trinius, *Beytrag*, s.v. "Einem, Johann Justus von."

[56] Baumgarten, *Reflections on Poetry*, §58; Schmidt, *Dissertatio*, for example, §3, §5, §6, §9.

[57] *Album scholae latinae* (1712–1729), AFSt/S L2, fols. 331–332; Freylinghausen and Francke, *Ausführlicher Bericht*, 97–99; Francke, *Einleitung*, 133.

[58] *Album scholae latinae*, fols. 331–332.

and 1735.[59] Between 1731 and 1732, Michaelis taught biblical hermeneutics from Rambach's *Institutes*.[60] Baumgarten is also likely to have learned about Francke's and Rambach's hermeneutics from his brother, Siegmund Jacob, who is alleged to have guided Alexander's education.[61] Having attended Francke's orphanage schools and studied theology in Halle with Rambach and Michaelis, among others, Siegmund Jacob was appointed Professor *ordinarius* of Theology in 1734 and gave lectures on Rambach's *Institutiones* in 1735.[62] In his 1745 *Instruction in the Exegesis of Holy Scripture* (*Unterricht von Auslegung der heiligen Schrift*), he recommends, among other books on hermeneutics, Francke's *Manuductio* and parts of Rambach's *Institutes*.[63]

Baumgarten's acquaintance with Francke's and Rambach's engagement in the controversy over *aisthēsis* and the role of the human affects in the conveyance of divine truths, as well as the related controversy over the suitability of poetry as a means of divine communication and of moral edification, can also be inferred from Baumgarten's own involvement in another, larger polemical effort, well under way in Halle in the 1730s, to which Francke's and Rambach's controversial positions contributed. This larger polemical effort aimed at proving that the authors of biblical texts were divinely inspired at all. Its connection with the controversy over affect-laden divine communication finds a particularly vivid illustration in hermeneutical writings by Siegmund Jacob Baumgarten. According to Baumgarten, many passages in the Bible appear to make no sense to any reader who does not keep in mind that divine inspiration put the human authors of those passages in a state of "strong, sensible emotion" (*starke sinnliche Gemüthsbewegung*). This included passages where

> general truths are uttered in a very concrete way; . . . fully equivalent or at least very similar and interchangeable expressions are repeated; . . . absent people and even unthinking and lifeless objects are spoken to; . . . short, broken-off sentences and comments appear; . . . dedicatory words appear, which the context and the integrity of the meaning didn't call for; . . . the discussion is interrupted by ideas that do not add to the comprehensibility of the things being discussed . . .

and so on.[64] For Baumgarten, it seems, the danger was that the divine inspiration of biblical authors could be called into question if apparently senseless or

---

[59] Meier, *Baumgartens Leben*, 10.
[60] [Anonymous,] *Catalogus lectionum aestivalium* (Halle, April 1732).
[61] Meier, *Baumgartens Leben*, 11.
[62] [Anonymous,] *Index acroasium ex omni scientiarum et disciplinarum bonarum genere* (Halle, September 1735).
[63] Baumgarten, *Unterricht von Auslegung*, 2.
[64] Baumgarten, *Unterricht von Auslegung*, 47–48: "*von algemeinen Wahrheiten sehr sinlich geredet wird; . . . gantz einerley Ausdrucke oder doch sehr änliche und gleichgültige wiederholt werden; . . . sonderlich abwesende Personen auch wol unvernünftige und leblose Dinge angeredet werden;*

internally contradictory passages could not be proven to be divinely inspired. Hence his defense of "strong, sensible emotion" as a consequence of divine inspiration.

Baumgarten saw the source of this danger, of course, in the work of biblical critics who had called the divine inspiration of biblical authors into question. One of the most prominent of these critics, and the most relevant to an investigation of Alexander Baumgarten's role in the controversy, was the Genevan theologian and man of letters Jean Le Clerc (1657–1736). In 1685, Le Clerc had published *Impressions of Some Theologians from Holland Concerning the Critical History of the New Testament* (*Sentiments de quelques Theologiens de Hollande sûr l'Historie Critique du vieux Testament*), a critique of Richard Simon's *Critical History of the Old Testament* in epistolary form.[65] In the eleventh and twelfth letters of the critique, published five years later in English as the first two chapters of Le Clerc's *Five Letters Concerning the Inspiration of the Holy Scriptures*, Le Clerc concedes that the "sense" of biblical authors' words was perhaps in some cases inspired, but not the words themselves. Contradictions in the historical books, haphazard variations in diction, and the vagueness about dates and numbers, Le Clerc explains, prove that the Holy Spirit cannot have dictated the biblical text to its human authors.[66]

Corresponding to Le Clerc's incredulity about the divine origins of most biblical words, it seems, was a presupposition that divinely inspired discourse must by its nature meet the standards to which Le Clerc thought human beings should aspire in their own use of language. One of the most important standards was "perspicuity of style."[67] In an essay on "True and False Eloquence," Le Clerc devotes ten pages to the discussion of the three canonical styles, but he virtually omits discussion of the "pleasing" and "sublime" styles, devoting far more space to praising the "simple and proper style," which he appears to take as a model of perspicuity:

> The principal rock, which we ought to avoid in this simple and natural language is obscurity, and 'tis for that reason that we carefully shun everything that may produce it, as equivocal terms, too great plenty of figures, and an ill disposition of words and thoughts.[68]

. . . *kurtz abgebrochene Sätze und Reden vorkommen; . . . Zueignungsworte vorkommen, die der Zusammenhang und die Volständigkeit des Verstandes eben nicht erforderte; . . . die Rede durch eingeschaltete Vorstellungen unterbrochen wird, die zur Verständlichkeit der vorgetragenen Sachen nicht gehören.*"

[65] Golden, *LeClerc*, 31.
[66] [Le Clerc], *Five Letters*, 20–41.
[67] [Le Clerc], *Parrhasiana*, 79.
[68] [Le Clerc], *Parrhasiana*, 82.

Among the several dangers of deviating from a perspicuous style, according
to Le Clerc, is the perpetuation of an ethical "disorder" that false eloquence
tends to produce. "If the end of the discourse be to correct the faults of the
readers and auditors," Le Clerc writes,

> the multitude of impertinent words, the weakness of the reasonings, and the
> [in]judicious choice of the thoughts, produce but very sorry effects. As we are
> pers[u]aded without knowing why or wherefore, and have no clear and contin-
> ued principles to preserve ourselves from errour, and to regulate our conduct
> aright, our manners will infallibly derive an unhappy tincture from the disorder
> of our minds; we do good and evil without discerning them so distinctly as we
> ought to do, and our lives become a perpetual mixture of a little virtue and a
> great deal of vice. We know the general rules of good and evil confusedly, and
> we apply them almost by mere accident to the particular actions of life.[69]

Ethically effective eloquence, Le Clerc implies, ought to use a perspicuous
style to convey "general rules of good and evil" such that they can be understood distinctly. Le Clerc's reservations about poetry as an instrument of
moral edification therefore come as no surprise. Though he denies "that poets
are altogether unuseful,"[70] Le Clerc nonetheless expresses caution at every
turn: everything about a poem that produces sensible pleasure—whether its
beautiful style, its power to arouse the passions, or the agreeable sounds of its
words and cadence—blind the audience to all the "false thoughts" the poem
contains.[71] Le Clerc moreover asserts that the intent of a poet to communicate
a particular moral lesson by means of a poem cannot be reliably discerned
from the poem itself. In his view,

> there never was any narration in the world from which some sort of a moral
> might not be deduced, altho' the author of it never dreamt of any such thing. . . .
> Therefore to be assured that any poet had a design to give us certain lessons, 'tis
> necessary that he should tell us so himself, or at least set it down in his writings
> after such a manner that no body cou'd doubt it.[72]

The effect of a poem on its reader's or listener's affects, in other words, is not
a sufficient indicator of the moral truth that the poet wished to convey. This
view distinguishes Le Clerc clearly from Francke and Rambach, who take
the affects aroused by divinely inspired words as themselves an important

---

[69] [Le Clerc], *Parrhasiana*, 65–66.
[70] [Le Clerc], *Parrhasiana*, 41.
[71] [Le Clerc], *Parrhasiana*, 6–7, 9–10, 20–21.
[72] [Le Clerc], *Parrhasiana*, 42–43.

"spiritual truth" and one of the indispensable indicators of the intended meaning of the words. Le Clerc's lack of interest in the sublime style and lack of firm confidence that poetry can be used for moral-educational purposes, moreover, stands in contrast to the defense of poetry in Rambach's *Poetic Thoughts*.

Le Clerc's challenge to the divine inspiration of the bible's human authors was answered by Alexander Baumgarten under the direction of Christian Benedict Michaelis, an open critic of Le Clerc. In 1733, Michaelis had assigned an older classmate of Alexander's, Johann Christian Meisner, the task of writing a dissertation defending the authorship of Exodus 36 by Moses, whose authorship had been called into question by Spinoza, Iitschakus, Richard Simon, and Jean Le Clerc. According to Michaelis, the danger of ascribing the chapter to an author other than Moses was twofold. First, it made the exegesis of all the other chapters uncertain, in so far as doubt could then be cast upon Moses's authorship of all the books traditionally attributed to him. Moreover, it seemed to cast doubt upon the divine inspiration of the author of the chapter in question, since God would not have driven anyone to add sections to the books of Moses without indicating their different authorship.[73] Michaelis continued his defense of the divine inspiration of the biblical authors in 1735, when he assigned Alexander Baumgarten the task of defending several verbal expressions whose usage in Genesis had been criticized—by Le Clerc, among others—as chaotic and imprecise, such that they seemed unbefitting an author inspired by a perfect God.[74] The result was Baumgarten's *Chorographic Dissertation* (*Dissertatio chorographica*), a defense of biblical authors' use of the words *superus* and *inferus* ("above" and "below") as internally consistent rather than haphazard, and by implication divinely inspired. The usage may appear haphazard to those interpreters who "scarcely blush at imputing the mark of invalidity to the style of the sacred book" (*stilo codicis sanctissimi ἀκυρολογία notam inurere haud eruberint*), but this appearance of haphazardness is simply the result of the words having been used in a variety of senses, depending on the context. Sometimes they refer to physical locations, sometimes to moral qualities, and sometimes the physical and the moral aspects are connected with each other.[75] Baumgarten presented this dissertation, apparently to great acclaim, six months before completing his *Reflections on Poetry*.[76]

---

[73] Michaelis, "J. C. Meisner, *Dissertatio Theologico-Historico-Critica,*" 553–556.

[74] Michaelis, "A.G. Baumgarten, *Dissertatio chorographica,*" 181–185.

[75] Baumgarten, *Dissertatio chorographica,* 401, 404–405.

[76] According to the records of the Philosophy Faculty at Halle, the text of Baumgarten's *Reflections on Poetry* was submitted to the faculty censor, Johann Heinrich Schulze, on August 9, 1735. *Halle Universitätsarchiv*, Rep. 21, III.261, f. 74.

That Baumgarten wrote his *Reflections on Poetry*, too, in sympathy with Francke and Rambach's defense of biblical authors' affect-laden and poetic discourse as divinely inspired cannot be inferred from unambiguous assertions by Baumgarten himself. Various arguments and allusions in the *Reflections on Poetry* nonetheless tend toward this conclusion. First, Baumgarten's assertion that a poem is capable of perfection and that a poem is perfect in proportion to its tendency to arouse affects in the reader through the presentation of indistinct ideas implies that the use of indistinct ideas to arouse affects also befits a perfect God, who would only use a perfect means of communication and edification. Baumgarten himself suggests this implication at several points. He describes miracles, for example, as well as prophetic predictions whose accuracy is verifiable (because the events they describe have already come to pass), as subjects that contribute to the perfection of a poem.[77] Baumgarten's allusions to biblical stories and prophecies, here, are undoubtedly intentional.[78] Baumgarten also describes the development of a poem's theme as similar to the creation of a world; the ideal ordering principle of representations in a poem, according to Baumgarten, corresponds to the order "in which things in the world follow one another, such that the glory of the Creator is revealed—the highest and ultimate theme of an immense poem, so to speak" (*quo in mundo sibi res succedunt, ad evolvendam creatoris gloriam, summum et ultimum thema immensi, liceat ita vocare, poematis*).[79] Baumgarten's sympathy with Francke and Rambach appears still more clearly in his call for an aesthetic philosophy at the end of the *Reflections on Poetry*. As he describes it, this philosophy is meant to aid in the use of the lower cognitive faculties for the attainment of knowledge (*scientia*), or, in other words, for the perception of truth (*veritas*).[80] The correspondence between this truth and the "spiritual truth" invoked by Francke and Rambach, which is also transmitted by the arousal of affects, is clear.

Nor can Baumgarten's heavy use of a philosophical vocabulary—above all, the words, *clarus, confusus,* and *distinctus* in the technical senses delineated by Leibniz—have been as alien to Francke, Rambach, and other Pietists as one might suppose. The suitability of Baumgarten's philosophical terms for describing ideas of moral education like Francke's and Rambach's is

---

[77] Baumgarten, *Reflections on Poetry*, §64.
[78] At any rate, Baumgarten cannot have mentioned prophecies and miracles simply because the poetic rules to which they relate follow from his criteria of perfection in a poem. For he tests neither every possible subject of a poem nor every possible poetic rule against those criteria. I must therefore disagree with Werner Strube's assertion that Baumgarten purports to present a theory of poetry that is complete in so far as Baumgarten "derives all specific poetic rules from the basic principle—or at least, this is his idea or intent." Werner Strube, "Die Entstehung der Ästhetik als einer wissenschaftlichen Disziplin," 15.
[79] Baumgarten, *Reflections on Poetry*, §71, cf. §68.
[80] Baumgarten, *Reflections on Poetry*, §115.

revealed clearly by Alexander's brother, Siegmund Jacob. In his *Instruction in Lawful Christian Conduct* (*Unterricht vom recht-mäßigen Verhalten eines Christen*), Siegmund Jacob Baumgarten explains the process of conversion (*Sinnesänderung* or *Bekehrung*), described in Francke's *Delineatio* as a replacement of carnal by spiritual desires. Employing terms different from Francke's, Baumgarten characterizes it as a replacement of pseudo-virtue (*Scheintugend*) by genuine virtue (*Tugend*). But Francke would immediately have recognized Baumgarten's description of conversion as a moral transformation. Baumgarten describes the aim of the transformation as the development of a *habitus*, calling virtue at various points a "state of the heart" (*Gemüthsfassung*) or a "capacity" (*Fertigkeit*)—more specifically, a "capacity to observe the law as strictly as possible" (*Fertigkeit zur möglichsten Beobachtung des Gesetzes*).[81] "Natural virtue" (*natürliche Tugend*) refers to natural law, and "Christian virtue" (*christliche Tugend*) refers to divine law.[82] The difference between virtue and merely apparent virtue or "pseudo-virtue" (*Scheintugend*) is the motivation (*Beweggrund*) for observing the law in question: pseudo-virtue is motivated by an overbearing self-love (*Eigenliebe*), the various forms of which include sensual desire, pride, and greed (*Wollust*, *Hochmut*, and *Geiz*), whereas genuine virtue is motivated by an "inclination of one's character toward God, such that a man takes God to be his God and his highest good, and expects his well-being to come from Him."[83] The correspondence between Baumgarten's two sets of motivations and Francke's two types of desires, natural and spiritual, is unmistakable.

Also like Francke, Siegmund Jacob Baumgarten repeatedly emphasizes that the perception of "divine truths" (*göttliche Wahrheiten*) by the intellect alone is not sufficient for the genuine improvement of one's character (*Gemüthsfassung*) and for the replacement of natural desires by spiritual ones. In Baumgarten's words:

> The inner working of God . . . extends not only to distinct ideas [*deutliche Vorstellungen*] and therefore the higher powers of the soul, but also to indistinct [*undeutliche*] and dark [*dunkele*] [ideas] . . . , which not only make the necessary impression of distinct perception onto the heart, but are also indispensable in the special case of children before they can use their reason.[84]

[81] Baumgarten, *Unterricht vom recht-mäßigen Verhalten eines Christen oder Theologische Moral*, 594.
[82] Baumgarten, *Unterricht vom recht-mäßigen Verhalten eines Christen*, 600–601.
[83] Baumgarten, *Unterricht vom recht-mäßigen Verhalten eines Christen*, 115–116: "*Neigung des Gemüths gegen Gott, daß ein Mensch Gott für seinen Gott und höchstes Gut annimmt, und seine Wohlfahrt von demselben erwartet.*"
[84] Baumgarten, *Unterricht vom recht-mäßigen Verhalten eines Christen*, 680: "*Die innere Wirckung Gottes . . . [erstreckt] sich nicht nur auf deutliche Vorstellungen, und folglich obere Kräfte der Seele, sondern auch auf undeutliche und dunckele [Vorstellungen] . . . , die sowol bey erwachsenen*

Siegmund Jacob Baumgarten uses terms recognizable from his brother's *Reflections on Poetry*, referring to the higher faculties of the soul and to obscure and distinct ideas, in order to advance a theory of moral education similar to that of Francke and Rambach. Whereas Francke and Rambach assert that spiritual truths must be grasped through sensation (*Empfindung*)— in other words, a receptiveness to, and imitation of, the affects of the authors who give voice to those spiritual truths—Siegmund Jacob Baumgarten insists that God's "inner effect" (*innere Wirkung*) on one's character works through indistinct and obscure ideas, graspable by the lower rather than the higher cognitive faculties.[85]

Alexander Baumgarten applies in his 1735 *Reflections on Poetry* a philosophical vocabulary similarly to his brother's, but it is not clear whether he also meant to advance a similar position. He expressly claims to have written the *Reflections on Poetry* "in order to make it clear that philosophy and the knowledge of how to construct a poem, which are often held to be entirely antithetical, are linked together in the most amiable union," a formulation that echoes his call for philosophers to inquire into the means of improving the lower cognitive faculties.[86] "[A]nyone who knows our logic," Baumgarten writes, "is not unaware of how uncultivated this field is." This comment in turn finds echoes in Baumgarten's other writings.[87] In his *Philosophical Letters* (*Philosophische Brieffe*), for example, Baumgarten remarks that logic "seems to promise more than it delivers, when it pledges to improve our cognition as a whole," since "we possess far more cognitive faculties of the soul than can simply be placed in the category of reason or intellect."[88] But here, too, the ethical implications of the attention Baumgarten draws to the deficiencies of logic as taught by many of his contemporaries, and to the consequent need for an aesthetic philosophy that inquires into the improvement of indistinct rather than distinct perception, are not obvious.

The ethical implications become more obvious in *The Force and Efficacy of Ethical Philosophy* (*De vi et efficacia ethices philosophiae*), a dissertation written under Baumgarten's supervision by Samuel Wilhelm Spalding in

---

Personen den nötigen Eindrück der deutlichen Erkentnis ins Gemüt verursachen, als sonderlich bei Kindern vor dem Gebrauch des Verstandes unentberlich sind."

[85] In general, the use of a philosophical vocabulary to describe what earlier Pietists tended to describe in other terms is characteristic of Siegmund Jacob Baumgarten, according to Bühler and Cataldi Madonna, "Von Thomasius bis Semler. Entwicklungslinien der Hermeneutik in Halle," 61–62.

[86] Baumgarten, *Reflections on Poetry*, 36: "*[u]t . . . philosophiam & poematis pangendi scientiam habitas saepe pro dissitissimis amicissimo iunctas connubio ponerem ob oculos.*"

[87] Baumgarten, *Reflections on Poetry*, §115: "*[Q]ui nostram scit logicam, quam incultus hic ager sit, non nesciet.*"

[88] [Baumgarten], *Philosophische Brieffe*, II.6: "*Weil wir nun aber weit mehrere Vermögen der Seelen besitzen, die zur Erkenntnis dienen, als die man bloß zum Verstande oder der Vernunfft rechnen könne, so scheint ihm [Baumgarten] die Logik mehr zu versprechen, als sie halte, wenn sie unsere Erkenntnis überhaupt zu verbeßern sich anheischig macht.*"

1741, a year after Baumgarten had taken up an *ordinarius* professorship in Frankfurt (Oder).[89] The dissertation, according to Spalding, is based on Baumgarten's *Ethics* (1740) and *Metaphysics* (1739), and its aim is to demonstrate that the truths one learns by studying ethics have an effect on one's behavior, even when those truths are not perceived distinctly. Indistinct ideas about ethics may be incapable of the same force as distinct ideas—which, unlike indistinct ideas, can be technically described as "effective" (*efficax*) and "motivating" (*movens*)—but Spalding argues that they nonetheless provide the motivation for most people's behavior.[90] The practical effect of indistinct ideas of ethical truths, Spalding points out, is easily noticeable among people who are unaccustomed to behaving virtuously and who obviously have no distinct ideas about ethics, but who nonetheless display an internal resistance to wrongdoing when they apologize for their transgressions and ask for forgiveness.[91] The practical effect of indistinct ideas of ethics is also detectable among those who call themselves Christians and appear to behave accordingly: "Many if not most good actions," Spalding writes, "not only of human beings but even of those who take their name from Christ, rest on a foundation of confused perception of ethical things, the things demonstrated in ethical philosophy."[92] More precisely, confused perceptions of ethical matters provide people with a "sufficient reason" for the various appetites and aversions associated with good actions.[93]

The connection between Spalding's dissertation and Baumgarten's *Reflections on Poetry* becomes clearer in Spalding's assertion that the confused perception of ethics is made practically more effective by a "good and virtuous education" (*bona et virtuosa educatio*). Such an education works, according to Spalding,

> by increasingly developing and strengthening good instinctive desires and aversions as well as their roots, exciting the corresponding affects, [and] more often restraining contrary affects, by means of stories, histories, comedies, tragedies, custom, proverbs, homilies, and so on.[94]

---

[89] Spalding, resp., *De vi et efficacia ethices philosophiae* (1741).
[90] Spalding, *De vi et efficacia ethices philosophiae*, §21, §26. Like Francke, Spalding uses *efficax* to refer to the effectiveness of God's word. See above, n. 34.
[91] Spalding, *De vi et efficacia ethices philosophiae*, §22.
[92] Spalding, *De vi et efficacia ethices philosophiae*, §26: "*Sublatis vero his praeiudiciis quisque videbit, multas, nisi plurimas, actiones bonas non hominum solum, sed et eorum, qui a Christo nomen habent, fundamento confusae Ethicorum, quae in Ethica Philosophica demonstrantur, cognitionis niti.*"
[93] Spalding, *De vi et efficacia ethices philosophiae*, §19.
[94] Spalding, *De vi et efficacia ethices philosophiae*, §23: "*instinctus fugasque bonas, earumque radices sensim evolvens, et corroborans, effectus conformes excitans, saepius contrarios refrenans, fabulis, historiis, comoediis, tragoediis, consuetudine, proverbiis, homiliis, etc.*"

The usefulness of these various forms of literature, Spalding further explains, depends on their producing in the mind of their readers or auditors ideas whose various characteristics correspond to the characteristics of the ideas Baumgarten says a perfect poem tends to produce: clarity and vividness. "The more steady, clear, and vivid an idea of something is to me," Spalding writes,

> the greater my cognition becomes—since if it already had force when it was obscure, this, too, increases along with the increasing clarity. And so from a good education, from fables, histories, and so on, I acquire a greater degree of motivating cognition.[95]

The usefulness of this mechanism in moral education, Spalding concludes, should not be underestimated:

> The ancient philosophers' custom of presenting morals by such diverse means should not only not be rejected, but rather it should be recommended to the greatest extent possible. Indeed, in Paschius, too, you find the words: "that there is almost no subject in moral philosophy that cannot be illustrated from the poets." And Conrad Durrius shows the same thing more fully in his work, *On the Hidden Poetic Philosophy* (*De recondita philosophia poëtica*). Even Horace himself says about Homer, "He explains what is beautiful, what is base, what is convenient, and what is not, in a fuller and better way than Chrysippus and Crantor." What's more, the scandalous poets often contain the best teachings, such that reading them is unjustly considered useless to everyone or entirely to be rejected.[96]

Spalding's defense of moral education through the communication of steady, clear, and vivid—but not distinct—ideas implies a defense of poetry as an instrument of moral education, an instrument whose effectiveness should not be ignored. In this way, Spalding's dissertation casts light upon an

---

[95] Spalding, *De vi et efficacia ethices philosophiae*, §24: "*Quo enim frequentior, clarior et vividior de aliqua re mihi est repraesentatio, eo maior mea redditur cognitio, quae si vim iam habuit obscura, crescet et haec crescente luce, hinc bona educatione, fabulis, historiis, etc. maiorem acquiro cognitionis moventis gradum.*"

[96] Spalding, *De vi et efficacia ethices philosophiae*, §24: "*[E]t ideo[ ]non modo non reiiciendus mos veterum Philosophorum, moralia tam diverso modo proponendi, sed etiam quam maxime suadendus. Ita et in iam allegato Paschio, verba invenies: 'Nullum fere caput esse philosophiae moralis, quod ex Poëtis non possit illustrari.' Quod et Conr. Durrius in oratione de Recondita Philosophia Poëtica amplius ostendit. Jam et ipse Horatius de Homero dicit, quod 'Hic, quid sit pulchrum, quid turpe, quid utile, quid non, Plenius ac Melius Chrysippo ac Crantore dicat.' Immo optimas saepe obscoeni Poëtae continent doctrinas, inde horum lectio inutilis omnibus, aut omnino reiicienda haud iuste deprehenditur.*"

ethical implication of Baumgarten's call for an aesthetic philosophy in his *Reflections on Poetry*.

The various ways in which Baumgarten agreed with his Pietist teachers should not obscure the ways in which he deviated from them. Baumgarten's use of the word, *aisthētikē*, for example, does not necessarily imply his agreement with Francke and Rambach's view that *aisthēsis*, a perceptive ability available only to the reborn on account of their experience of spiritual affects, was absolutely indispensable for biblical exegesis. Unambiguous signs of Baumgarten's disagreement with them are not obvious either, but his brother Siegmund Jacob Baumgarten does deviate slightly from Francke and Rambach's position. While allowing that experience of the things described in the Bible makes the perceptions of a biblical exegete clearer and more reliable, Baumgarten denies that it is indispensable, asserting in fact that "an unconverted person as well as a converted one can discern the correct sense of holy scripture."[97] This deviation from Francke and Rambach may explain Siegmund Jacob Baumgarten's avoidance of the word *aisthēsis* in his own hermeneutic writings. Whether Alexander Baumgarten shared his brother's reservations is difficult to discern.

A deviation from Rambach is easier to discern in Baumgarten's endorsement of mythological figures as the subject of a poem, an endorsement echoed by Samuel Wilhelm Spalding's indirect praise of Homer as an effective moral teacher. In his *Poetic Thoughts*, Rambach worries that the "heathen religion" promotes a "disposition toward fleshly desire" (*Neigung zur fleischlichen Wohllust*).[98] To be fair, as one contemporary reviewer noted, Rambach himself does not always avoid mythological subjects in his own poems; in one of them he "forgets" himself, making reference to Apollo and the Muses.[99] In general, though, his wariness of mythological subjects stands in clear contrast with Baumgarten's enthusiasm for them.[100]

But even if Baumgarten did not simply endorse Francke's and Rambach's ideas about poetry and moral education in every detail, he nonetheless learned much from their writings while studying in Halle. Francke and Rambach had taken what they themselves portrayed as a controversial position in a debate about biblical hermeneutics: the spiritual meaning of a biblical text consists of its power to reform the affects of a reader who has had the experience of conversion. This position, marked by Francke's and Rambach's references to *aisthēsis*, presupposed that divine inspiration reforms rather than suppresses

---

[97] Siegmund Jacob Baumgarten, *Öffentliche Anzeige seiner diesmaligen Akademischen Arbeit* (Halle, 1734), §10; Baumgarten, *Unterricht von Auslegung der Heiligen Schrift*, 18.

[98] Rambach, *Poetische Fest-Gedancken, Vorrede*, §3.

[99] [Anonymous], "Johann Jacob Rambach, *Geistliche Poesien*," 785–787.

[100] Baumgarten, *Reflections on Poetry*, for example, §36.

the human affects of the people subject to it. Furthermore, Francke and Rambach conceived of moral education in general as a process of reforming one's own affects, and they considered imitation of other people's spiritual affects to be one of this education's important methods. In Rambach's view, poetry, too, can have an edifying effect on the affects of its audience. In other words, Rambach and Francke may very well have urged the "suppression of evil sensuality" and considered darkness a metaphor for the defectiveness of the unconverted soul, as Wilhelm Ludwig Federlin points out, but in the idiom of Leibniz, as employed by Siegmund Jacob Baumgarten, they were describing divine inspiration, biblical interpretation, and moral education as processes that make use of "indistinct" and "dark" ideas.[101]

Alexander Gottlieb Baumgarten absorbed all this. By the time he called for philosophers to study the method of perfecting the lower cognitive faculties of the soul, he had become well acquainted with Francke's and Rambach's ideas of hermeneutics and moral education as a student in Francke's Latin School and the University of Halle. He had written a dissertation in defense of the divine inspiration of the Bible under Christian Benedict Michaelis, and he was aware of the controversy over poetry's suitability as a means of divine communication. His 1735 *Reflections on Poetry* reflects all this, in part by its use of the word *aesthetica* and in part by its implications for the nature of divine inspiration. If Baumgarten's sympathy with Francke and Rambach's general view of moral education appears only indirectly in the *Reflections on Poetry*, it becomes more obvious in Spalding's *The Force and Efficacy of Ethical Philosophy*. There is of course still far more to be learned about Baumgarten's relationship to his Pietist teachers, but one thing is clear: his conception of an aesthetic philosophy with a moral purpose took inspiration from their ideas.

---

[101] For the opportunity to conduct the research for this article in summer 2007 in Halle, I thank the Francke Foundations, the Interdisciplinary Center for European Enlightenment Research, and the Interdisciplinary Center for Pietism Research for a Fritz Thyssen Fellowship. For advice about the article's subject, I am indebted above all to Alexander Aichele, Ulrich Barth, Thomas A. Brady Jr., Ulrich Diehl, Hans-Joachim Kertscher, Boris Maslov, Udo Sträter, Kelly Whitmer, and Johan van der Zande. I am especially obliged to Alexander Aichele for inviting me to publish the article in German in 2008. For indispensible help with the German translation I thank Peter Grote, Christoph Schmitt-Maaß, and Hugo Stockter. In retranslating the article into English for the current publication, I have made small changes necessitated by the volume's style sheet and have silently corrected several errors, most of which were introduced during the editorial process in 2008. A thoroughly revised version of the article, expanded and otherwise modified in light of further research, can be found in Grote, *The Emergence of Modern Aesthetic Theory,* 67–101.

Chapter 6

Wolffian Rationalism and Baumgarten's Aesthetics

J. Colin McQuillan

INTRODUCTION

Since its inception, Baumgarten's aesthetics has been seen as an example, expression, or extension of Wolffian rationalism. In this chapter, I argue that there are a number of important differences between Wolffian rationalism and Baumgarten's aesthetics that raise questions about Baumgarten's Wolffianism and the rationalism of his aesthetics. After surveying the literature on the subject and establishing the context in which the Wolffianism of Baumgarten's aesthetics has been discussed, I highlight two key features of Wolffian rationalism—the mathematical method and the marriage of reason and experience. I then show that Baumgarten equivocates about the mathematical method, limits the scope of logic, and distinguishes the perfections of sensible and intellectual cognition in his aesthetics, separating what Wolff sought to combine in his marriage of reason and experience. I conclude that historians of philosophy and contemporary philosophers should take note of the differences between Wolffian rationalism and Baumgarten's aesthetics, while resisting the tendency to see Baumgarten as an irrationalist or treat his aesthetics as part of an attack on the authority of reason.

CONTEXT

Shortly after Baumgarten published his *Reflections on Poetry* (*Meditationes philosophicae de nonnullis ad poema pertinentibus*, 1735), the dissertation in which he introduced aesthetics as a new science and a new part of philosophy, Carl Günther Ludovici included the work in a catalog of Wolffian

texts.[1] Two biographies published shortly after his death—one by his former
student and friend, Georg Friedrich Meier, and another by a former colleague
at the University of Frankfurt an der Oder, Thomas Abbt—also emphasize
Baumgarten's Wolffianism. According to Meier, Baumgarten undertook a
careful study of Wolff's philosophy when he was a student, during a time
when many of Wolff's works were banned, and found that they contained
"nothing dangerous."[2] Abbt goes even further, suggesting that Baumgarten
was one of the young people in Halle that learned about "genuine" philosophy
from Wolff's "precise analysis and correct determination of concepts" and
who came to reject as "unnecessary or even harmful" everything that could
not be demonstrated through reason.[3] Meier's successor at the University of
Halle, Johann August Eberhard, also treated Baumgarten as a representative
of Leibnizian-Wolffian rationalism in his polemics against Kant, who agreed
that Baumgarten was a rationalist and a discipline of Leibniz and Wolff.[4] This
helps to explain the footnote to the 'Transcendental Aesthetic' in the *Critique
of Pure Reason*, where Kant objects to "the failed hope, held by the excellent analyst Baumgarten, of bringing the critical estimation of the beautiful
under principles of reason and elevating its rules to a science."[5] Kant rejected
Baumgarten's aesthetics because he thought Baumgarten was a dogmatic
rationalist like Wolff and, as such, never questioned the validity of the a priori
principles he employed.[6]

   The apparent consensus of his contemporaries allowed later philosophers and
historians to take the Wolffianism and rationalism of Baumgarten's aesthetics
for granted. In his lectures on the philosophy of art, Schelling claims that "all
pre-Kantian doctrines of art in Germany were merely children of Baumgarten's
Aesthetics," which was, in turn, "an offspring of Wolffian philosophy."[7] Hegel
likewise says that aesthetics became "a philosophical discipline in the school of
Wolff," without mentioning Baumgarten by name, in his lectures on the philosophy of fine art.[8] Hegelian and Neo-Kantian historians of philosophy defended
the same view throughout the nineteenth century. In the volume of his *History
of Modern Philosophy* devoted to Leibniz and his followers (*Geschichte der
neuern Philosophie*, Vol. 2: *Leibniz und seine Schule*, 1867), Kuno Fisher says

[1] Ludovici, *Neueste Merckwürdigkeiten aus der Leibnitz-Wolffischen Weltweisheit*, §232.
[2] Meier, *Baumgartens Leben*, 356.
[3] Abbt, *Vermischte Werke*, Vol. 4 *(Leben und Charakter Alexander Gottlieb Baumgartens)*, 219.
[4] See, for example, Eberhard's essays, originally published in the *Philosophisches Magazin*, now
   included in Kant, *Der Streit mit Johan August Eberhard*, 44, 62, 72, 76. See also Kant, *Lectures on
   Logic*, 535 and Kant, *Lectures on Metaphysics,* 249.
[5] Kant, *Critique of Pure Reason*, A21/B35.
[6] I argue against Kant's characterization of Wolff as a "dogmatic" rationalist in McQuillan, "Wolff's
   Logic, Kant's Critique, and the Foundations of Metaphysics," 217–239.
[7] Schelling, *Philosophy of Art,* 11.
[8] Hegel, *Aesthetics,* Vol. 1, 1.

that it was "first in the school of Wolff that Alexander Baumgarten founded the new aesthetics."[9] Eduard Zeller also discusses Baumgarten's aesthetics in a chapter devoted to "the Wolffian school" in his *History of German Philosophy Since Leibniz* (*Geschichte der deutschen Philosophie seit Leibniz*, 1873).[10] Anglophone scholars in the twentieth and twenty-first centuries have defended this view as well. Lewis White Beck deals with Baumgarten's aesthetics under the heading "The Extension of Wolffianism into the Theory of Art" in *Early German Philosophy* (1969).[11] Paul Guyer employs a similar convention in *A History of Modern Aesthetics* (2014), where he discusses Baumgarten and Meier in a chapter on "The First Generation of Wolffian Aesthetics."[12] Finally, in his book *Diotima's Children* (2009), Frederick Beiser includes Baumgarten's aesthetics in the tradition of German aesthetic rationalism, which he traces back to Wolff.[13]

Despite the judgment of his contemporaries, and the agreement of later scholars, I think there are good reasons to doubt Baumgarten's Wolffianism and the rationalism of his aesthetics. In the *Philosophical Letters from Aletheophilus* (*Philosophische Brieffe von Aletheophilus*, 1741), Baumgarten says he laughed when he found his dissertation included in Ludovici's catalog of Wolffian texts. He jokes that his work had only been included because "I had divided my text into §s and referred in each [section] to the previous one."[14] Baumgarten's own account of his experience with Wolffian philosophy in Halle also seems to be at odds with Meier's and Abbt's biographies. In the 'Preface' to the third (1750) edition of the *Metaphysics* (*Metaphysica*, 1739), Baumgarten says he is thankful "for having grown up surrounded by others hostile to this way of philosophizing," referring to Wolffian rationalism. He also notes that he "first imbibed almost exclusively whatever could be objected to it, rather than its own doctrines."[15] Baumgarten then says that he "made some—no, on the contrary, many—of these same teachings my own, but only after an intense and careful investigation of the truth," which suggests that studying Wolff's philosophy convinced him that at least some of Wolff's doctrines were true, though he never abandoned his Pietist religiosity.[16] Meier tells us that Baumgarten insisted on his deathbed that only

---

[9] Fisher, *Geschichte der neuern Philosophie*, Vol. 2, 571.
[10] Zeller, *Geschichte*, 285–289.
[11] White Beck, *Early German Philosophy,* 278–288.
[12] Guyer, *A History of Modern Aesthetics*, Vol. 1, 318–340.
[13] Beiser, *Diotima's Children,* 48, 118–155.
[14] Baumgarten, *Philosophische Brieffe*, 3. This remark suggests that the mathematical method that Baumgarten says he employs in the *Reflections* only concerns the manner in which his dissertation is presented and not the philosophical substance of his work. See Baumgarten, *Reflections*, §21.
[15] Baumgarten, *Metaphysics*, 77.
[16] Baumgarten, *Metaphysics*, 77. Baumgarten specifically identifies "the first principle of knowing," "the first contingent principles of becoming . . . i.e., monads or simple beings," and the universality

Christian faith, and not philosophy, could bring peace to one's soul.[17] As a result, Brandon Look has recently argued that Baumgarten's rationalism was "tempered" by his religious commitments.[18]

Similar considerations have led a number of scholars to question the Wolffianism and rationalism of Baumgarten's aesthetics. One of the most radical challenges can be found in Alfred Baeumler's *The Problem of Irrationality in Eighteenth-Century Aesthetics and Logic* (*Das Irrationalitätsproblem in der Ästhetik und Logik des 18. Jahrhunderts*, 1923/1967). Baeumler treats Baumgarten's aesthetics as an attempt to address the "individuality" and "determinacy" of sensible phenomena, which cannot be captured by universal laws and general principles.[19] Baumgarten's aesthetics represents, for Baeumler, "the first and deepest protest against abstract rationalism, upon whose rationalistic foundations the history of philosophy up to that point had been constructed."[20] It is interesting to note that Baeumler does not condemn Wolff for his "abstract rationalism," though his reasons for calling Wolff the "grandfather" of Baumgarten's aesthetics are transparently nationalistic.[21] As a Nazi ideologue, Baeumler sought to cast German philosophers like Wolff and Baumgarten as a bulwark against the abstract intellectualism of other European philosophical traditions. Ernst Cassirer's judgment is more moderate, and certainly more cosmopolitan, but not entirely different. In *The Philosophy of the Enlightenment* (*Die Philosophie der Aufklärung*, 1932), Cassirer praises Baumgarten as the only one of Wolff's students that had "really mastered the logical technique which Wolff taught and by which he first gave German philosophy a definite shape of its own."[22] Yet he also indicates that Baumgarten's "real intellectual accomplishment consists in the fact that, through his mastery of the subject, he became especially conscious of both the intrinsic and the systematic limitations of formal logic."[23] Thus, Cassirer argues, "aesthetics evolves from logic, but this evolution discloses the immanent weakness of traditional scholastic logic," so that "this casting

---

of the principle of sufficient reason as teachings of the Leibnizian-Wolffian philosophy whose truth he came to accept after studying Wolff's philosophy for himself. See Baumgarten, *Metaphysics*, 77–78.

[17] Meier, *Leben Baumgartens*, 356.

[18] Look, "Baumgarten's Rationalism," 10–22. Similar concerns have led scholars to describe Baumgarten as a "pietist enlightener." On Baumgarten's relation to pietism and its influence on his philosophy, see Schwaiger, *Alexander Baumgarten*, 27–29; Borchers, *Die Erzeugung des ganzen Menschen*, 136–164; Grote, *The Emergence of Modern Aesthetic Theory*, 87–146; and Dyck, "Between Wolffianism and Pietism," 78–93.

[19] Baeumler, *Irrationalitätsproblem*, x.

[20] Baeumler, *Irrationalitätsproblem*, 224.

[21] Baeumler places particular emphasis on Leibniz's and Wolff's monadology, which he regards as an attempt to philosophically reconcile the universal (reason) and the individual (the irrational). See Baeumler, *Das Irrationalitätsproblem*, 5–6.

[22] Cassirer, *The Philosophy of the Enlightenment*, 338.

[23] Cassirer, *The Philosophy of the Enlightenment*, 339.

off of traditional logical and metaphysical fetters was the historical and systematic condition which permitted aesthetics to find its place in the sun and to constitute itself as a philosophical discipline in its own right."[24] More recently, Hans Rudolf Schweizer and Ursula Franke have characterized Baumgarten's account of sensible cognition as an objection to the "one-sidedness" of rationalist epistemology, while Martin Seel has described his aesthetics as a struggle for "freedom of movement" within the strictures of enlightenment rationalism.[25] Contemporary scholars like Clemens Schwaiger have maintained that Baumgarten's aesthetics should be regarded as an attempt to "attenuate" and "improve" Wolff's rationalism by reining in its "intellectualizing tendencies."[26]

I agree with these scholars that there are important differences between Wolffian rationalism and Baumgarten's aesthetics. The differences between them are subtle, so readers will not find passages in Baumgarten's works in which he expresses explicit disagreement with Wolff, rejects his terminology, points out the shortcomings of his arguments, or disparages his system. This should not be surprising, since Baumgarten's main publications are academic textbooks and treatises. Instead of writing polemics, or engaging in public controversies with other philosophers, he articulates his dissatisfaction with Wolffian rationalism through selective appropriation, variations in the way he defines technical terms, and in the novel ways in which he characterizes the relationship between the different parts of philosophy.[27] When we compare Wolff's and Baumgarten's works, however, we see that Baumgarten equivocates about the mathematical method, limits the scope of logic, and undermines, through his aesthetics, the "marriage of reason and experience" (*connubium rationis et experientiae*) in which Wolff sought to unite rational philosophy and experimental natural science by combining cognition derived from the senses and the understanding. If I am right, then the objections Kant raises against Baumgarten in the first *Critique* are essentially backward—the problem is not that Baumgarten extended Wolff's dogmatic rationalism to matters of taste by applying a priori principles to aesthetic judgment. The problem is that Baumgarten distinguishes the aesthetic perfection of sensible cognition from the logical perfection of intellectual cognition because he

---

[24] Cassirer, *The Philosophy of the Enlightenment*, 339, 341–342.

[25] Schweizer, *Ästhetik als Philosophie der sinnlichen Erkenntnis,* 66–67, 93; Franke, *Baumgartens Erfindung der Ästhetik,* 9; Seel, *Die Kunst der Entzweiung,* 28.

[26] Schwaiger, *Alexander Baumgarten,* 6, 22–26.

[27] Baumgarten implores God "never to give me so much spare time that I could while it away, squander it, and waste it through quarrels" in the 'Preface' to the third (1750) edition of the *Metaphysics*, emphasizing his unwillingness to engage in public controversies. See Baumgarten, *Metaphysics,* 75–76.

feared that unchecked Wolffian rationalism would be a threat to theological authority and Christian faith.

WOLFFIAN RATIONALISM

In order to understand the relationship between Wolffian rationalism and Baumgarten's aesthetics, it is important to establish what kind of rationalist Wolff is. This is not an easy task, because there are so many different kinds of "rationalism" in early modern European philosophy—the new methods proposed by Bacon and Descartes are very different, but they both have strong claims to being rational; Cartesian nativism and Lockean empiricism are antithetical to one another, yet neither of them is irrational; Spinozist monism and Leibnizian pluralism are both rationalist, even though they present dramatically opposed pictures of the world. Wolff's philosophy has much in common with all of these different kinds of rationalism and he draws liberally from other early modern rationalists—even those that later historians of philosophy considered "empiricists." At the most basic level, however, Wolff's rationalism is distinguished by his commitment to the mathematical method as well as the "marriage of reason and experience" in which he sought to unite rational philosophy and experimental natural science.

Wolff's commitment to the mathematical method should not be surprising. He was trained as a mathematician and was originally hired at the University of Halle as a professor of mathematics. The first textbook he published was the *Foundations of all Mathematical Sciences* (*Anfangs-Gründe aller mathematischen Wissenschafften*, 1710). The text is preceded by Wolff's 'Short Lesson on the Mathematical Method' (*Kurzer Unterricht von der mathematischen Methode oder Lehrart*), which performs a function similar to the 'Preliminary Discourse on Philosophy in General' (*Vorbericht von der Welt-Weisheit/Discursus Praeliminaris de Philosophia in Genere*) that precedes his *German Logic* (*Rational Thoughts on the Powers of the Human Understanding, Vernünftige Gedanken von den Kräften des menschlichen Verstandes*, 1713) and, later, in an expanded and more elaborate form, his *Latin Logic* (*Rational Philosophy or Logic, Philosophia rationalis sive Logica*, 1728). According to Wolff's 'Short Lesson,' the mathematical "method" (*Lehrart*) is "the order that mathematicians follow in their lectures, which begins with definitions, proceeds to axioms, and from there to theorems and problems."[28] Over the course of the 'Short Lesson,' Wolff distinguishes between definitions of words (nominal definitions) and things (real definitions), though he insists that mathematical sciences must

---

[28] Wolff, *Anfangsgründe*, §1.

employ "distinct and complete concepts" in both kinds of definitions.[29] After explaining how to formulate these definitions, Wolff defines an axiom as a conclusion that follows immediately from a definition.[30] A theorem is defined as a conclusion derived from the comparison of different definitions, which was impossible to draw from any one of the definitions by itself.[31] Finally, a problem "concerns how a thing should be done or made," meaning that it explains how a particular conclusion can be derived from a definition in order to demonstrate a theorem.[32] Wolff's account of the mathematical method is clearly based on Euclid's *Elements* and a variety of other works in early modern science and philosophy—Spinoza's *Ethics* (1677) and Newton's *Principia Mathematica* (1687) are only the most prominent examples. Like his predecessors and many of his contemporaries, Wolff regarded mathematics as an "epistemic ideal"—a model of reasoning that could be extended from mathematical demonstrations to other parts of philosophy.[33]

As Wolff expanded his teaching and began to publish textbooks on logic, metaphysics, ethics, politics, natural science, and other philosophical topics, he continued to argue that mathematics "leads us to the most accurate and perfect knowledge that it is possible to attain."[34] Yet he also began to characterize the mathematical method in more general terms than he had employed in the *Foundations*. The fullest account of his mature method can be found in the 'Preliminary Discourse' that precedes his *Latin Logic*.[35] In a chapter on 'The Method of Philosophy,' Wolff defines "philosophical method" as "the order which the philosopher ought to use in treating dogmas."[36] In this context, "dogmas" (*dogmata*) are simply the truths that philosophers seek to demonstrate. To "treat" these dogmas is to demonstrate with certainty that they are true. Such a demonstration must begin with accurately defined terms, "since philosophy is a science" and "whatever it affirms must be demonstrated."[37] "Since a thesis obviously cannot be demonstrated unless its meaning is certain, and since the

---

[29] Wolff, *Anfangsgründe*, §12.
[30] Wolff, *Anfangsgründe*, §29.
[31] Wolff, *Anfangsgründe*, §37.
[32] Wolff, *Anfangsgründe*, §47.
[33] On mathematics as an "epistemic ideal" in early modern European philosophy, see Demeter and Schliesser, "The Use and Abuse of Mathematics in Early Modern Philosophy," 3161–3164, along with the other essays published in the special issue of the journal *Synthese* on the subject.
[34] Wolff, *German Logic, Preliminary Discourse*, §16.
[35] Curiously, this source is neglected in many discussions of Wolff's mathematical method. See, for example, Gava, "Kant, Wolff, and the Method of Philosophy," 271–303 and Frketich, "Wolff and Kant on the Mathematical Method," 333–356. However, it is discussed in detail in Tutor, *Die wissenschaftliche Methode bei Christian Wolff*, 68–86. Tutor also treats the marriage of reason and experience in Wolff's philosophy as a sign of the universality of his mathematical method. See Tutor, *Die wissenschaftliche Methode bei Christian Wolff*, 117–119.
[36] Wolff, *Preliminary Discourse*, §115.
[37] Wolff, *Preliminary Discourse*, §116.

meaning of every philosophical proposition should be certain," Wolff concludes that "only terms which have been explained with accurate definitions
should be used in philosophy."[38] Following the same line of argument, Wolff
asserts that "only principles which have been sufficiently proven should be
used in philosophy."[39] Doing otherwise would compromise the certainty of
the truths philosophers seek to prove, undermining their ability to respond to
skeptical objections. For the same reason, he maintains that "no proposition
should be admitted into philosophy unless it is legitimately deduced from
sufficiently proven principles."[40] This amounts to saying that all of the terms,
principles, and propositions that philosophers employ should be grounded in
prior demonstrations, so nothing unproven or uncertain enters into any demonstration in which they are used. The same methodological principle leads
Wolff to claim that philosophical demonstrations should be ordered so that
"those things should come first through which later things are understood and
demonstrated."[41] He even says that "the supreme law of philosophical method
is that those things must come first through which later things are understood
and established."[42] It might not seem as though this method has anything to do
with mathematics; yet Wolff insists that "the rules of philosophical method are
the same as the rules of mathematical method," since mathematics also depends
on accurate definitions, the demonstration of principles and propositions, and
the proper order of proofs. The identity of the philosophical and mathematical
methods is so obvious to Wolff that he thinks it would only surprise "someone
who does not know the common source from which the rules of both mathematics and philosophy are derived."[43] According to Wolff, both philosophy
and mathematics derive from "true logic"—the right use of the powers of the
human understanding.[44]

Given his commitment to the mathematical method and his identification of the methods of mathematics and philosophy, one might assume
that Wolff would treat sensibility, experience, and empirical knowledge
dismissively. Yet his account of the mathematical method and the method
of philosophy pays greater attention to these things than one would expect
from such an allegedly dogmatic rationalist. In the *Short Lesson*, Wolff says
that mathematicians should pay special attention to experience, because the
axioms and principles they employ are often "mixed in" with experience.[45]

---

[38] Wolff, *Preliminary Discourse,* §116.
[39] Wolff, *Preliminary Discourse,* §117.
[40] Wolff, *Preliminary Discourse,* §118.
[41] Wolff, *Preliminary Discourse,* §132.
[42] Wolff, *Preliminary Discourse,* §133.
[43] Wolff, *Preliminary Discourse,* §139*.
[44] Wolff, *Preliminary Discourse,* §139*.
[45] Wolff, *Anfangsgründe,* §33. This claim could, perhaps, be compared with Kant's claim that
"even among our experiences cognitions are mixed in that must have their origin *a priori*" in the

The main difference between them has to do with their quantity—experience concerns "individual things" and "special cases," while axioms and principles are more general. Experience is not useful in demonstrating the truth of general principles, because a preponderance of experiences establishes only the probability of a conclusion; however, their use poses no threat to the certainty of demonstrations, if one understands how to distinguish general principles from particular experiences.[46] Indeed, in the chapter on method in the *Preliminary Discourse*, Wolff agrees that philosophers can make use of hypotheses and merely probable knowledge, as long as they are carefully distinguished from certain truths. The use of such uncertain principles can be justified by their "usefulness in the affairs of life" as well as their importance for science. He recognizes that "certain knowledge cannot be acquired without previous probability," so the use of a philosophical hypothesis, which he defines as "an assumption which cannot yet be demonstrated but which provides a reason," is likewise justified.[47] Philosophical hypotheses "pave the way to the discovery of certain truth," particularly for "things which are observed to occur," but whose causes remain unknown to us.[48] Wolff notes that the use of philosophical hypotheses in astronomy has been particularly fruitful, because, "at first, the true theory of planetary motion could not be discovered."[49] This led astronomers to formulate "hypotheses to explain celestial motion," from which "they then deduced things which they compared with their observations."[50] "In this way," Wolff continues, "they had the opportunity to make observations which they would have never thought of, and continually and gradually to amend their hypotheses until they finally discovered the actual truth."[51] "As philosophers," he concludes, "we should imitate the astronomers whenever we are faced with problems in which we can establish the basis for discovering truth by making assumptions."[52]

Wolff also shows a surprising openness toward sensibility in his *German Logic* and *German Metaphysics* (*Rational Thoughts on God, the World and the Soul of Man, and on All Things in General, Vernünftige Gedanken von Gott, der Welt und der Seele des Menschen, auch allen Dingen überhaupt*, 1720). In the *Short Lesson*, he argues that mathematical sciences must employ distinct and complete concepts. Yet the opening chapter of the *German Logic*

'Introduction' to the first (A) edition of the *Critique of Pure Reason*. See Kant, *Critique of Pure Reason*, A2.
[46] Wolff, *Anfangsgründe*, §34.
[47] Wolff, *Preliminary Discourse*, §125–§127.
[48] Wolff, *Preliminary Discourse*, §125–§127.
[49] Wolff, *Preliminary Discourse*, §127.
[50] Wolff, *Preliminary Discourse*, §127.
[51] Wolff, *Preliminary Discourse*, §127.
[52] Wolff, *Preliminary Discourse*, §127.

suggests that these concepts can be derived from either sensibility or the understanding. A concept is, for Wolff, "any representation of a thing" that is present in our "understanding" or in our "thoughts."[53] Sensation is defined as the feeling or perception we have of an external object that is present to us, so Wolff infers that "the senses give occasion to thoughts of representations of things outside us" and, therefore, "lead us to concepts of them."[54] The task of logic is, he says, "to diligently attend to the thoughts to which our senses give occasion," which requires that we "carefully distinguish the objects that differ; and, as much as may be, observe what it is that makes us judge the one to differ from another."[55] Through this process, which Wolff naturally calls "analysis," we begin to clarify our concepts, rendering them less obscure, less confused, more distinct, more complete, and, in some cases, adequate— adequate concepts clearly and distinctly represent all of the predicates that belong to the definition of an object. Wolff acknowledges that it is "very rarely . . . possible, for us to bring this analysis to a conclusion, that is, to carry it on till we come to such concepts as cannot be further analyzed."[56] But he also does not think complete analysis and adequate concepts are necessary in most cases. What is important is whether we have a concept that is suf- ficiently distinct and complete for the purposes of the demonstration in which we are engaged, not whether we have enumerated every single predicate that is contained in the real definition of an object. Nor is the origin of the concept significant—it does not matter whether our concepts originate in the senses or in the understanding, since it is the distinctness and completeness of our con- cepts that matters in mathematical and philosophical demonstrations. In the *German Metaphysics*, and, later, in his *Empirical Psychology* (*Psychologia Empirica*, 1732), Wolff even suggests there is no real or essential differ- ence between the faculties of sensibility and the understanding—they do not have different kinds of objects and do not give rise to different kinds of cognition.[57] The difference between them is simply a function of the clarity and distinctness of the cognition with which they are concerned. Sensibility is the faculty of obscure, confused, and otherwise indistinct cognition, while

---

[53] Wolff, *Anfangsgründe*, §5; Wolff, *German Logic,* Ch. 1, §4.
[54] Wolff, *German Logic,* Ch. 1, §1–§5.
[55] Wolff, *German Logic,* Ch. 1, §7.
[56] Wolff, *German Logic,* Ch. 1, §28.
[57] Wolff even denies in the *German Metaphysics* that human beings possess a "pure understanding," because "much indistinctness and obscurity" remains among our distinct cognitions. He grants that we can find examples of "pure reason" in mathematics, where "all inferences proceed from distinct concepts and various principles which are abstracted from the senses," but even this suggests that human cognition will be bound up with sensation and imagination unless it is actively dissociated from them by abstraction. See Wolff, *German Logic,* §285, §382 (translation by Corey Dyck in Dyck, *Early Modern German Philosophy,* 113–114).

the understanding is the faculty of distinct cognition.[58] This means that, as analysis proceeds, and our concepts become clearer and more distinct, they also become less sensible and more intellectual. Nothing prevents a concept of an object that originates in the senses from becoming clear and distinct except incomplete analysis.

The rationalism of Wolff's mathematical method and his appreciation for sensibility and experience come together in the "marriage of reason and experience" that he promotes in a number of his works.[59] An important reference to Wolff's *connubium* is found at the end of the *German Logic*, where he explains how to develop habits of logical thinking.[60] After explaining how the study of mathematics can help to develop these habits, Wolff turns to the contributions of the natural sciences. He says that "particularly in the Essays towards a more accurate knowledge of Nature, or the Experimental Philosophy," he has "propounded everything in such a manner, as they might, on reflection, mutually arise from each other, on combining together the use of our Senses and Understanding."[61] The combined use of cognition derived from the senses and the understanding is crucial for Wolff, because he thinks it can give rise to "a Habit of drawing determinate propositions from Experience, and by means of some one of them, find out the ground or reason of the others, consequently combine Reason with Experience."[62] In other words, Wolff thinks people acquire a habit of thinking logically by combining reason and experience in the study of natural science, which gives rise to a disposition that "they may retain all their days."[63] In a similar context in his *Latin Logic*, Wolff singles out optics and astronomy as particularly good examples of the marriage of reason and experience, because they combine pure rational philosophy and experimental natural science, demonstration and observation, and a priori and a posteriori reasoning.[64] Whether we begin with direct observation and proceed inductively to generate more abstract principles or whether we begin with general principles and deduce from them truths about nature and morality, Wolff thinks experience and reason will lead us to the same conclusions in the end. Instead of asking us to choose between the two starting points, Wolff hopes to combine

---

[58] Wolff, *German Metaphysics,* §276–§277; Wolff, *Psychologia Empirica*, §275.

[59] Here I only mention references to Wolff's "marriage of reason and experience" in his logical works, but Wolff's *connubium* also plays an important role in his ethics, psychology, and natural philosophy. See Buschmann, *"Connubium rationis et experientiae,"* 186–207; Dyck, *Kant & Rational Psychology*, 19–42; and Vanzo "Christian Wolff and Experimental Philosophy," 225–255. See also the helpful discussion in Matt and Dyck, "Christian Wolff," (2019).

[60] Wolff added Ch. 16, "Concerning the Method of Acquiring Habit in the Practice of Logic," to the fifth (1727) edition of the *German Logic*. See Wolff, *German Logic*, lxii.

[61] Wolff, *German Logic,* Ch. 16, §11.

[62] Wolff, *German Logic,* Ch. 16, §11.

[63] Wolff, *German Logic,* Ch. 16, §11.

[64] Wolff, *Latin Logic,* §1232.

them in a marriage of reason and experience that will allow us to make progress in the sciences and cultivate habits of logical thinking.

Wolff's commitment to the marriage of reason and experience is also evident in the way he presents his philosophy in his textbooks. In addition to the chain of definitions he constructs through his propositions, Wolff includes a series of illustrative examples that clarify the nature and application of the claims he is making. For instance, when he explains what adequate concepts are and how they may be acquired in the *German Logic*, Wolff discusses lively knowledge ("that which inclines or influences the will, or yields a motive to will something"), usufruct ("the right to procure to one's self from the property of another, all the profit and advantage one will, yet consistently with the preservation of the thing itself, in use and enjoyment"), colic ("an acute and fixed pain in the bowels"), understanding ("the faculty of conceiving possible things"), dew ("a collection of very subtle vapors, which, in the absence of the sun, fall down gradually out of the air, and adhere to the upper surfaces of the bodies on the earth"), and covetousness ("a desire of having more than one's necessity requires, and than according to his circumstances he can lawfully earn, etc.") as examples to show what it means to possess an adequate concept.[65] In the same passage, he goes on to show that the definition of virtue ("the habit of regulating our actions by the law of nature") can be constructed from the definitions of habit, human action, and the law of nature.[66] This highlights the methodological function of Wolff's examples, which help to clarify the process by which one can demonstrate philosophical truths. Whether one reaches these truths rationally, by proceeding from definitions to axioms and theorems using the mathematical method, or through the consideration of examples with which one is familiar through experience, is immaterial for a rationalist like Wolff. Both reason and experience—the construction of definitions and the consideration of examples—lead us to the same truths in the end. Indeed, Wolff thinks our ability to discover and comprehend these truths will be increased if we employ both methods, and unite them, as he does in his textbooks.

BAUMGARTEN'S AESTHETICS

Baumgarten arrived in Halle in 1727, when he was only thirteen years old. The young Alexander and his older brothers were taken in and educated by August Hermann Francke, who was a friend of the Baumgarten family, one of the founders of the University, and the leader of the Halle Pietists.

---

[65] Wolff, *German Logic*, Ch. 1, §16.
[66] Wolff, German Logic, Ch. 1, §16.

Eating at Francke's table and studying in his *Waisenhaus*, Baumgarten was raised at the heart of the theological opposition to Wolffian philosophy in eighteenth-century Germany.[67] Indeed, Francke was one of the theologians that petitioned the King to have Wolff expelled from the University, the city of Halle, and the Kingdom of Prussia in 1723, only four years before Baumgarten's arrival. Another one of Baumgarten's teachers, Joachim Lange, was continuously engaged in polemics against Wolff and his philosophy throughout the 1720s and 1730s, when Baumgarten defended his dissertation, *Reflections on Poetry*, and began teaching at the University. At one point, shortly before Wolff's return to Halle, Lange even accused Baumgarten's oldest brother, Siegmund Jakob, by then a professor of theology in Halle, of incorporating too much philosophy into his lectures and employing a "Wolffian" pedagogical style.[68] These biographical details establish a context for Baumgarten's remarks in the *Philosophical Letters* and the Preface to the third (1750) edition of the *Metaphysics*, confirming that Baumgarten was surrounded by Pietists throughout his youth and that Wolff's critics supported his education and academic career. Yet his biography does not prove that Baumgarten rejected Wolff's philosophy or that his aesthetics is antirationalist—the truth is more complicated. Meier is correct that Baumgarten began to study Wolff's philosophy at a time when many of his textbooks were banned in Halle. It should also be noted that Baumgarten adopted the format of Wolff's textbooks for many of his own writings. Nor should we forget that he questioned the philosophical acumen of Wolff's critics in the same 'Preface' to the *Metaphysics* in which he says he is thankful for having been exposed to criticisms of Wolff before studying his philosophy for himself.[69] These considerations suggest that Baumgarten was sympathetic to at least some aspects of Wolff's philosophy and did not agree with all of the charges leveled against Wolff by the Pietists. If Baumgarten was indeed a critic of Wolffian rationalism, his criticisms were tempered by an appreciation of its form, a respect for its rigor, and support for some of its major doctrines.

To understand the relationship between Wolffian rationalism and Baumgarten's aesthetics, it is helpful to examine Baumgarten's views on the mathematical method and the implications of his aesthetics for the marriage of reason and experience that Wolff promoted. Although he adopted the form of Wolff's textbooks for his own writings, it is less certain that

---

[67] Meier, *Baumgartens Leben*, 355.
[68] See Sorkin, *The Religious Enlightenment*, 125–128 and Grote, *The Emergence of Modern Aesthetic Theory*, 120–128.
[69] Baumgarten, *Metaphysics*, 76–77.

Baumgarten accepted the identity between the mathematical method and the method of philosophy that Wolff defends in the *Preliminary Discourse*. Questions about Baumgarten's views on philosophical method arise from the *General Philosophy*, which was published posthumously in 1770, although its contents reflect Baumgarten's lectures at the University of Frankfurt an der Oder dating back to the 1740s.[70] In the fourth chapter, Baumgarten distinguishes philosophy from "non-scientific" disciplines, mathematics, and disciplines that are "superior" to philosophy. By "non-scientific" disciplines, Baumgarten means those disciplines that are "1) merely historical, 2) merely uncertain, and 3) not deduced from other, certain cognition."[71] As examples of such disciplines, he mentions lexicography, grammar, oratory, rhetoric, poetics, criticism, and hermeneutics. Baumgarten acknowledges that all of these disciplines can be "presented" in a philosophical manner, but still maintains that they fall "outside the sphere of human philosophy."[72] When he turns to disciplines that are "superior" to philosophy, Baumgarten discusses theology. Because theology is grounded in revelation, and its teachings are known through faith, Baumgarten denies that theology is a kind of philosophy.[73] Mathematics is situated between history and theology, because it is a science, because mathematical truths are demonstrated rather than revealed, and because they are known through reason rather than faith. Baumgarten also recognizes that mathematics and philosophy have same object—being (*res*).[74] Nevertheless, he insists that they must be distinguished, because he regards philosophy as a science of qualities and mathematics as a science of quantities.[75]

Baumgarten holds that qualities, quantities, and relations exhaust the possible determinations of things as well as our cognition of them. Relations can hold between qualities or quantities, so they can be addressed by either philosophy or mathematics, but mathematics concerns itself solely with quantities. Mathematics does not tell us anything about the qualities of things, so it must be distinguished from philosophy.[76] This follows naturally from the definition of philosophy that Baumgarten proposes in the first

---

[70] See Nannini, "Baumgarten and the Lost Letters of Aletheophilus," 25–26.

[71] Baumgarten, *Philosophia Generalis*, §158.

[72] Baumgarten, *Philosophia Generalis*, §159–§161.

[73] Baumgarten, *Philosophia Generalis*, §173.

[74] Baumgarten, *Philosophia Generalis*, §168.

[75] Baumgarten, *Philosophia Generalis*, §167. Wolff also defines mathematical knowledge as knowledge of quantity in the *Preliminary Discourse*, but he does not identify philosophical knowledge with knowledge of quality. Instead, he defines philosophical knowledge as "knowledge of the reason of things which are or occur." See Wolff, *Preliminary Discourse*, §6, §14.

[76] In the *General Philosophy*, Baumgarten also draws a distinction between the mathematics of extension and intension, which refers to a discussion of the mathematics of intensive quantities in the *Metaphysics*. See Baumgarten, *Metaphysics*, 21, §246–§249 and Baumgarten, *Philosophia Generalis*, §172.

chapter of the *General Philosophy*, where he says that philosophy is "the science of the qualities of things that are known without faith."[77] It also aligns with Wolff's definition of mathematical knowledge in the first chapter of *Preliminary Discourse* ("knowledge of the quantity of things"), though it is at odds with Wolff's definition of philosophy ("knowledge of the reason of things which are or occur") because it restricts the object of philosophy to "the qualities of things" (instead of everything that is or occurs), and implies that faith is a legitimate source of knowledge.[78] The differences between Wolff's definition of philosophy and Baumgarten's definition suggest that Baumgarten's definition is actually intended to set up the distinctions he draws between mathematics, philosophy, and theology; to limit the degree to which mathematics can serve as "epistemic ideal" for philosophy; and to ensure that neither mathematics nor philosophy threatens theological authority or Christian faith.

The seventh chapter of the *General Philosophy*, 'Concerning Philosophical Presentation' (*De ratione proponendi philosophica*) also includes a discussion of philosophical method that is markedly different from Wolff's *Preliminary Discourse*. Wolff treats method as a way to demonstrate philosophical truths—to establish with certainty that they are true.[79] Baumgarten treats method as one aspect of the "presentation" (*proponere*) of philosophical doctrines, so its role is limited to "producing cognition in [the mind of] another through speech."[80] Baumgarten uses the German *vortragen* ("to lecture") as a synonym for the Latin *proponere* ("to put forth"), so it is clear that he has a specifically pedagogical context in mind, in which a teacher communicates established truths to a student. Baumgarten explains that anyone lecturing about philosophical doctrines must have good reason to present them, must arrange them according to the proper method, and must employ the appropriate style in speaking about them. Interestingly, Baumgarten stipulates that teachers of philosophy should employ the mathematical method.[81] He does not define the mathematical method in the *General Philosophy*, where he mentions only the synthetic, analytic, and vulgar methods; yet he does refer to a definition in his *Lectures on Logic* (*Acroasis Logica*, 1761).[82] There Baumgarten says that the mathematical method is "the stronger method

---

[77] Baumgarten, *Philosophia Generalis,* §21. On Baumgarten's definition of philosophy in the *Philosophia Generalis,* see Aichele, "Wahrheit—Gewißheit—Wirklichkeit," 15–18.

[78] Wolff, *Preliminary Discourse,* §6, §14.

[79] See, for example, Wolff, *Preliminary Discourse,* §115–§118.

[80] Baumgarten, *Philosophia Generalis,* §249.

[81] Baumgarten, *Philosophia Generalis,* §249.

[82] Baumgarten, *Philosophia Generalis,* §249. The reference given in the text appears to be incorrect, referring to §286–§289, when the mathematical method is actually discussed in §298 in the 1761 edition of the *Acroasis Logica* and in §507 in the 1773 edition.

of the sciences," because mathematics follows the synthetic method.[83] According to Baumgarten, the synthetic method is the principal method of philosophy, because it uses established definitions of concepts to proceed from premises to conclusions.[84] And he considers the synthetic method to be more philosophical and more certain than the analytic method, which begins with conclusions and then tries to discern their premises.[85] Both are preferable to the vulgar or common method, which relies on sensation and imagination, often following particularly vivid examples.[86] The *Lectures on Logic* treats these methods as methods of reasoning, through which one cognition is derived from another, so it is perhaps closer to Wolff's account of method in the *Preliminary Discourse* than Baumgarten's discussion of method in the *General Philosophy*.[87] Still, the difference between the two conceptions of "method" that Baumgarten employs in the *Lectures on Logic* and the *General Philosophy*, and his suggestion in the *General Philosophy* that the mathematical method is really just a function of the "presentation" of philosophical doctrines, raise questions about the extent of his Wolffianism. If the mathematical method is one of the defining characteristics of Wolffian rationalism, and Baumgarten employs that method in a more limited and instrumental way than Wolff did, then it is perhaps because Baumgarten was less committed to philosophical rationalism than Wolff.

When we turn to his writings on poetics and aesthetics, we find further evidence that Baumgarten was not a Wolffian rationalist in the strict sense. Consider, for example, the passage that immediately precedes the introduction of aesthetics as a new science "guiding sensible discourse to perfection" in the *Reflections on Poetry*.[88] Baumgarten denies that logic is equal to this task, because he thinks "logic, by its very definition, should be restricted to the rather narrow limits to which it is as a matter of fact confined."[89] The "rather narrow limits" to which Baumgarten refers actually concern a definition of logic that is far more restrictive than the ones we find in Wolff. In the 'Preliminary Discourse' to *German Logic*, Wolff says that logic teaches us "the powers of the human understanding, together with their right use and

---

[83] Baumgarten, *Acroasis Logica*, §298. See also Meier, *Exerpt*, §426.
[84] Baumgarten, *Acroasis Logica*, §297 and Baumgarten, *Philosophia Generalis*, §250. See also Meier, *Exerpt*, §422, §424–§425.
[85] Baumgarten, *Acroasis Logica*, §299 and Baumgarten, *Philosophia Generalis*, §251. See also Meier, *Exerpt*, §422–§423.
[86] Baumgarten, *Acroasis Logica*, §295 and Baumgarten, *Philosophica Generalis*, §252. See also Meier, *Exerpt*, §415.
[87] This is to be expected, since the *Acroasis Logica* is based on Baumgarten's lectures on Wolff's *German Logic*. Baumgarten notes that while he was prohibited from teaching Wolff's metaphysics and ethics during his time in Halle, he was allowed to use Wolff's *German Logic* in his lectures. See Baumgarten, *Acroasis Logica*, Preface, 2.
[88] Baumgarten, *Reflections on Poetry*, §115.
[89] Baumgarten, *Reflections on Poetry*, §115.

application in the knowledge and search for truth."[90] In the same passage, Wolff defines the understanding as "the faculty . . . of perceiving possible things."[91] This definition implies that the human understanding is concerned with cognition that arises from the senses as well as from thought, insofar as sensation and thought both involve representations of things that are present to us and which are, therefore, possible. That Wolff had this broader conception of the understanding in mind seems to be confirmed by the *Latin Logic*, where he defines logic as "the part of philosophy that guides the use of the cognitive faculties in cognizing truth and avoiding error."[92] By appealing to the cognitive faculties in general, and not just the superior cognitive faculty of the understanding, Wolff indicates that logic is actually concerned with all the ways in which human beings come to know things, through all of the cognitive faculties they possess. This stands in sharp contrast to Baumgarten, who calls logic "the science of knowing things philosophically" and "the science for the direction of the higher cognitive faculty in apprehending the truth."[93] Baumgarten's definitions restrict the scope of logic, so that it only concerns the cognition of the superior cognitive faculty (the understanding) and the perfection of its cognition (clear and distinct knowledge of the truth). The constraints Baumgarten places on logic seem to be intentional—by limiting the scope of logic, excluding from logic all the cognition that arises from the inferior cognitive faculty (sensibility), and rendering logic incapable of guiding confused, sensible cognition to perfection, Baumgarten creates a space for aesthetics, as well as the need for his new science.

The distinction Baumgarten draws between aesthetics and logic in his *Reflections on Poetry* paves the way for a more radical separation of the cognitive faculties of sensibility and the understanding in his *Aesthetics*. Wolff had established in his empirical psychology the distinction between the inferior and the superior cognitive faculties of sensibility and the understanding that Baumgarten uses to define aesthetics and distinguish it from logic; yet he had also maintained that the cognition of the two faculties was only distinguished by its clarity and distinctness—a difference of degree, rather than a difference in kind. For Wolff, sensibility is the inferior cognitive faculty only because its cognition is obscure or confused, while the cognition of the superior cognitive faculty, the understanding, is clear and distinct. The difference between sensible and intellectual cognition is significant for Wolff, but he makes it very clear that the difference between them is not essential— the two kinds of cognition do not differ in kind, simply because they originate

---

[90] Wolff, *German Logic*, Preliminary Discourse, §10.
[91] Wolff, *German Logic*, Preliminary Discourse, §10.
[92] Wolff, *Latin Logic,* §61.
[93] Baumgarten, *Reflections on Poetry,* §115.

in different faculties. Obscure and confused cognition can be rendered clear and distinct through analysis, while distinct propositions can be presented in less precise ways that make them more accessible to the senses, as Wolff's use of examples in his textbooks demonstrates. Baumgarten radicalizes the distinction he draws between sensible and intellectual cognition in the *Reflections on Poetry* in his *Aesthetics* by postulating a separate perfection for sensible cognition. According to Baumgarten, the perfection of sensible cognition is "beauty" (*pulcritudo/Schönheit*), though he emphasizes that even beautiful sensible cognition remains confused, and cannot be distinct, because distinct cognition would no longer be sensible.[94] The significance of this gesture, for aesthetics and for philosophy in general, should not be overlooked. By postulating a separate perfection for sensible cognition and distinguishing that perfection from the perfection of intellectual cognition, Baumgarten makes the distinction between sensible and intellectual cognition into a qualitative difference—a distinction between *kinds* of cognition—rather than a quantitative difference—a difference in *degrees* of clarity and distinctness. Qualitative differences are essential differences, so, if sensible and intellectual cognition are really different in kind, it would no longer be possible to convert sensible cognition into intellectual cognition through analysis, nor would it be possible to translate intellectual cognition into sensible cognition through the use of examples. Instead, each of the two types of cognition would have to achieve their respective perfections independently of one another—"beauty" in the case of sensible cognition and "philosophical knowledge of the truth" in the case of intellectual cognition. Combining the perfections of these two kinds of cognition into what Baumgarten and Meier sometimes call "aesthetico-logical cognition" (*cognitio aesthetico-logica*)—cognition that is both aesthetic and logical, sensible and intellectual, beautiful and true—would be impossible, because it would result in a cognition that is obscure, confused, clear, and distinct, all at the same time.[95]

---

[94] Baumgarten, *Aesthetica/Ästhetik*, §14. It is curious that Baumgarten does not discuss the separate perfections of sensible and intellectual cognition in his *Metaphysics*, since he had already distinguished them at the end of the *Reflections on Poetry*. However, he does indicate that sensible cognition can be "livelier" and "stronger" than intellectual cognition in some cases. See Baumgarten, *Metaphysics*, §531–§532.

[95] Baumgarten, *Metaphysics*, §519–§521, §624; Baumgarten, *Aesthetica/Ästhetik*, §17. For discussions about the possibility of combining the perfections of sensible and intellectual cognition in *cognitio aesthetic-logica*, see Baumgarten, *Reflections on Poetry*, §14; Baumgarten, *Aesthetica/Ästhetik*, §556; and Meier, *Exerpt*, §24. Neither Baumgarten nor Meier seem to have appreciated the inherent contradiction in postulating a kind of cognition that would be both indistinct (sensible) and distinct (intellectual). Based on §522 of the *Metaphysics*, it appears that Baumgarten thought confused and distinct cognition could be combined without contradiction, though this does not imply that the resulting combination would be both confused and distinct—it would either be confused enough to be sensible or sufficiently distinct to be intellectual. Meier amends this passage in his translation to explain that "such a representation is distinct to the extent that it has clear notes, and at the same time sensible, to the extent that it has obscure notes," which

It might seem as if Baumgarten's equivocations about the mathematical method; the way he restricts the scope of logic in his *Reflections on Poetry*; and the way he separates the perfections of sensible and intellectual cognition in the *Aesthetics* are only small deviations from Wolff's methodology, logic, and psychology. This is true, to a certain extent; yet the effect of these differences should not be underestimated. By equivocating about the mathematical method, Baumgarten raises questions about one of the most distinctive features of Wolffian rationalism. If the mathematical method is merely a pedagogical device that teachers of philosophy employ in order to communicate philosophical doctrines to their students, as Baumgarten suggests in the *General Philosophy*, then it is not the source of the certainty that distinguishes philosophical knowledge from other kinds of cognition. Baumgarten would no doubt insist that philosophy is rational and that philosophical knowledge is both rational and certain; yet it is not clear that he thinks it is certain in the same way or for the same reasons as Wolff does, since, for Baumgarten, mathematics no longer serves as an "epistemic ideal" for philosophy. By restricting the scope of logic and introducing a new science to guide sensible cognition to perfection, Baumgarten also undermines the marriage of reason and experience that characterizes Wolff's rationalism. And he does that by converting what was, for Wolff, a difference in degrees of clarity and distinctness into an essential distinction between different kinds of cognition, arising from different faculties, with mutually exclusive standards of perfection.

Even though Baumgarten insists that aesthetics and logic are closely related to one another, calling logic the "older sister" of aesthetics, the way he distinguishes them suggests that aesthetics and logic are, at best, analogous to one another.[96] Baumgarten's introduction of an alternate standard for the perfection of sensible cognition implies that the kinds of cognition with which the two sciences are concerned differ essentially and in kind and not just in degrees of clarity and distinctness. And, because they differ in kind, any discussion of their similarities would be, at best, equivocal. It would no longer be possible to resolve sensible and intellectual cognition into one another through analysis or the use of examples. It would also be impossible to combine sensible and intellectual cognition without contradiction, since a cognition cannot be confused and distinct at the same time. One could almost

---

implies that any combination of confused and distinct representations would only possess a particular degree of confusion and distinctness, which may or may not be sufficient for the cognition as a whole to be distinct. I do not think this is sufficient to resolve the contradiction or explain the possibility of *cognitio aesthetico-logica*. See Baumgarten, *Metaphysics*, §522.

[96] Baumgarten, *Aesthetica/Ästhetik*, §14. On aesthetics as an "art of the analogue of reason" (*ars analogi rationis*) see Baumgarten *Aesthetica/Ästhetik*, §1. See also Franke, "Analogon rationis," 229–230 and Berndt, *Facing Poetry*, 15–21.

say that Baumgarten recreates in his aesthetics the divided line Plato used to separate the sensible and the intelligible world in the *Republic*, though his aim is not quite the same. While Plato's divided line is meant to inspire philosophical contemplation of the intelligible world of the forms, it seems that Baumgarten wants to limit the scope of reason and call our attention back to sensibility.

RATIONALISM AND AESTHETICS

In this chapter, I have argued that there are important differences between Wolffian rationalism and Baumgarten's aesthetics. While many of his writings superficially resemble Wolff's textbooks, Baumgarten equivocates about the mathematical method, restricts the scope of logic, and distinguishes between the perfections of sensible and intellectual cognition in ways that undermine Wolff's marriage of reason and experience. Baumgarten's views on these subjects challenge the most fundamental commitments of Wolffian rationalism—Wolff's methodology, logic, and psychology. Taken together, they constitute a new and different philosophical system, in which philosophy is a more limited science than it had been for Wolff. Instead of being the science of everything that is or occurs, philosophy is, for Baumgarten, merely the science of the qualities of things that are known without faith. The distinctions Baumgarten draws between history, mathematics, philosophy, and theology in the *General Philosophy* imply that philosophy is, in fact, subordinate to theology, because Christian faith is superior to philosophical knowledge. The distinction Baumgarten draws between aesthetics and logic also indicates that logic cannot be extended beyond the "rather narrow limits to which it is as a matter of fact confined."[97] So, in the same way that logic cannot be used to guide confused sensible cognition to its perfection in beauty, philosophical truths cannot be used to challenge the authority of Christian theology, because the truths with which theology is concerned are known through faith. If I am right about the implications of Baumgarten's departures from Wolff, and the consequences of his aesthetics, then he should probably be counted among the Pietist critics of Wolffian rationalism, instead of being seen as one of its advocates or defenders.

Still, the differences between Wolffian rationalism and Baumgarten's aesthetics should not lead us to conclude that Baumgarten or his aesthetics were irrationalist. Baeumler goes too far when he calls Baumgarten's aesthetics "the first and deepest protest against abstract rationalism," because

---

[97] Baumgarten, *Reflections on Poetry,* §115.

he ignores a substantial body of evidence to the contrary.[98] Baeumler's interpretation remains influential nonetheless, because it was for many years one of the very few surveys of the history of aesthetics that included a detailed account of Baumgarten's thought. It also has much in common with narratives about "the fate of reason" in German philosophy promoted by scholars like Frederick Beiser. According to Beiser, in the period immediately following the publication of Kant's *Critique of Pure Reason*, German philosophers "began to look critically at the fundamental article of faith of the European Enlightenment: the authority of reason."[99] In *Diotima's Children*, Beiser suggests that German philosophers were debating this subject even earlier in the eighteenth century.[100] Consequently, he regards the tradition of German aesthetic rationalism, which begins with Wolff and culminates in Lessing and Mendelssohn, as "an attempt to defend the borders of reason against the challenges of irrationalism."[101] Many find Baeumler's interpretation and Beiser's narrative appealing, but they can also be misleading.[102] The form of Baumgarten's works is not merely the rationalist "shell" surrounding the irrationalist "core" of his aesthetics. On the contrary, it reflects Baumgarten's genuine philosophical concern with definitions, demonstrations, order, and clarity. Nor does Baumgarten ever question the authority of reason as such, as Beiser claims many of Kant's contemporaries and successors did.[103] We see in the 'Preface' to the third edition of his *Metaphysics* that Baumgarten recognized the force of Wolff's arguments and did not reject his rationalism entirely. Instead, Baumgarten says he subjected Wolffian rationalism to exactly the kind of critical, philosophical investigation that Wolff himself would have demanded—despite Kant's erroneous claim that Wolff never

[98] Baeumler, *Das Irrationalitätsproblem*, 224. In *Diotima's Children*, Beiser calls Baeumler's book "one of the most brilliant works on eighteenth-century aesthetics," but agrees that Baeumler "failed to weigh carefully the evidence for the opposing interpretation." See Beiser, *Diotima's Children*, 23 n. 43 and 150 n. 71.

[99] Beiser, *The Fate of Reason*, 1.

[100] Beiser, *Diotima's Children*, 26, 105, 196–200, 231, 249.

[101] Beiser, *Diotma's Children*, 23. This thesis owes clearly owes a great deal to Baumler, whose *Irrationalitätsproblem* Beiser calls "one of the most brilliant works on eighteenth-century aesthetics." Although Beiser acknowledges that Baeumler was "a rabid national-socialist," he praises his work for "stressing the importance of the irrationality problem, and for recognizing its formative role in the development of rationalism." See Beiser, *Diotima's Children*, 23 n. 43.

[102] Beiser helpfully points out that Bauemler ignores evidence that does not support his thesis, neglecting Baumgarten's defense of general aesthetic norms and the scientific status of aesthetics. See Beiser, *Diotima's Children*, 124 n. 36, 149 n. 71. However, Beiser neglects the Pietist influence on and implications of Baumgarten's aesthetics. In *Diotima's Children*, he only mentions Pietism twice, in the same paragraph, in which he claims that Baumgarten "explicitly affirms Wolff's [mathematical] method" and employed it in his *Reflections* in order to "silence Wolff's vitriolic Pietist opponents." See Beiser, *Diotima's Children*, 124. Baumgarten's remarks on the inclusion of the *Reflections on Poetry* in Ludovici's catalog of Wolffian texts in the *Philosophical Letters* seem to contradict this interpretation.

[103] Beiser, *The Fate of Reason*, vii, 1–2ff.

thought to "prepare the field" for his rationalist philosophy with a critique of reason itself.[104] Baumgarten also justifies the introduction of his new science of aesthetics with reasoned arguments, which cannot be dismissed out of hand, simply because they may be motivated by religious concerns and advance a more limited conception of philosophy than we find in rationalists like Wolff. The rationality of Baumgarten's aesthetics has to be judged on its merits, the same way we judge other philosophical arguments and systems.

At the same time, I think contemporary philosophers should go beyond Baumgarten and explore the possibility of a genuine aesthetic rationalism. The restricted definition of logic that Baumgarten uses to make room for aesthetics in his *Reflections on Poetry* reminds philosophers of the value of sensible cognition; yet it does so by limiting the powers of the understanding. The introduction of a separate standard for sensible perfection in the *Aesthetics* sets beauty (sensible perfection) and truth (intellectual perfection) against one another in ways that make their combination contradictory—cognition cannot be confused (sensible) and distinct (intellectual) at the same time, so it also cannot be beautiful (sensibly perfect) and true (intellectually perfect) at the same time. It seems to me that a genuine aesthetic rationalism could follow the model of Wolff's "marriage of reason and experience" and reject the limitations, distinctions, and contradictions that Baumgarten introduces. A genuinely rationalist aesthetics could postulate, instead, that sensible and intellectual cognition are continuous with one another and not just analogous or complementary. This would not require philosophers to police the borders between two different kinds of cognition, because it would recognize that the difference between them is merely a matter of degree. And it would be able to resolve them into one another through analysis and examples, as Wolff does in his textbooks. Nor would genuine aesthetic rationalism require philosophers to set beauty and truth against one another, as if they were somehow contradictory values. Aesthetico-logical cognition may be impossible according to the definitions Baumgarten employs, but the contradiction disappears as soon as we reject the claim that sensible and intellectual cognition and their perfections, beauty and truth, differ in kind. I suspect this alternative has been overlooked because Wolff was depicted as a dogmatic rationalist throughout the nineteenth and twentieth centuries, partly because of Kant's objections against Wolffian dogmatism and his characterization of Baumgarten's aesthetics in the first *Critique*. Still, aesthetic rationalism may prove to be a viable course for contemporary aesthetics, if we are no longer satisfied with limited logic, constrained understanding, and contradictory values.

---

[104] Kant, *Critique of Pure Reason*, Bxxxvi. I call Kant's claim erroneous because Wolff presents his logic as an investigation of the powers of human reason that does exactly what Kant says Wolff never even attempted. See Wolff, *German Logic, Preliminary Discourse*, §10. See also McQuillan, "Wolff's Logic, Kant's Critique, and the Foundations of Metaphysics," 217–218.

Chapter 7

The Cofounding of Aesthetics

Baumgarten and Meier

Alessandro Nannini

INTRODUCTION

According to Kant, aesthetics, in the way in which it was introduced by the "excellent analyst" Baumgarten, is only an idiosyncratic way to call what other nations more consistently call "the critique of taste."[1] If Kant had been right, aesthetics hardly could have survived the exhaustion of the philosophical category of taste, which is already tangible in Hegel: "The development of taste only touched on what was external and meagre."[2] Baumgarten's aesthetics, though, was much wider than that.

For a long time, though, the breadth of his aesthetics was mostly ignored—for a number of reasons.[3] In the history of philosophy, the foundation of aesthetics as a philosophical discipline dates back to the period between Wolff and Kant—a period that received scarce attention from scholarship until very recently. It comes as no surprise that still in 1994 Wolfgang Riedel could rightly label it a "historical-philosophical *terra incognita.*"[4] As for the history of aesthetics, the "small" foundation of aesthetics achieved by Baumgarten and Meier is embedded within the "larger" process of the emergence of modern aesthetics, ranging roughly from French classicism to Hegel. Within this framework, Baumgarten and Meier's project is perceived as nothing but a stage in a much longer process leading to the identification of aesthetics with the philosophy of art. These heterogeneous approaches have long concurred that the most

---

[1] Kant, *Critique of Pure Reason*, 156 (A21/B35). This paper is part of the project PN-III-P4-ID-PCE-2020-2579: "Between Truth and Freedom: Enlightenment Answers to Thinking for Oneself," University of Bucharest.
[2] Hegel, *Aesthetics*, Vol. 1, 16.
[3] See the Introduction to this volume.
[4] Riedel, "Anthropologie und Literatur in der deutschen Spätaufklärung," 120.

remarkable contribution of Baumgarten to aesthetics was the naming of a discipline that did not take long to part ways from the philosophy of its first founder.

The Baumgarten renaissance of the past decades, accompanied by an increasing number of translations (to which, however, the English rendition of the *Aesthetics* is still missing), stems from a significant development in both historiography and aesthetics. On the one hand, a closer investigation of the "middle period" between Wolff and Kant, not only in the history of philosophy[5] but also in German studies[6] and intellectual history,[7] has focused attention on less well-known German thinkers, getting partially rid of the teleological fetters that committed scholars to a Kant-oriented narrative. On the other hand, a trend in (especially Continental) aesthetics has brought to the fore the problem of *aisthesis*, hence also its debt to the original project of "aesthetics."[8] The concurrence of these factors has fostered a reassessment of the founding of the discipline in all its breadth as well as in its fruitful relations with the early modern thought, from theology to rhetoric and logic.

One problem, though, still stands. If Baumgarten and Meier's project was quickly discarded, what is the relationship between the aesthetics they founded and the discipline we call "aesthetics" today? Through the reconstruction of the historical stages of the beginnings of scientific aesthetics, I intend to show in what follows that Baumgarten and Meier crucially contributed to making the newborn discipline a theoretical arena for what we now consider to be the "traditional streams" of aesthetics—sensible knowledge, beauty, and art.[9] In this way, it should be clear that the role of the "small" foundation of aesthetics for the "larger" history of modern aesthetics goes well beyond the coinage of a most fortunate term.

THE FOUNDING MOMENT

On September 23, 1735, at the *Fridericiana* University in Halle,[10] Alexander Gottlieb Baumgarten publicly discussed as *praeses* the disputation *Reflections*

---

[5] In addition to the numerous volumes published on central figures of that age (Meier, Hißmann, Tetens, Garve, etc.), see Dyck, *Early Modern German Philosophy* (2019).

[6] See the aforementioned article of Riedel and the debate about the "anthropological turn" in the mid-eighteenth century and its antedating, firstly proposed in Zelle, "Zwischen Weltweisheit und Arzneiwissenschaft," 35–44.

[7] See, for example, Buchenau, *The Founding of Aesthetics in the German Enlightenment* (2013) and Grote, *The Emergence of Modern Aesthetic Theory* (2017).

[8] Among the various philosophers, see, for example, Maurizio Ferraris, Wolfgang Welsch, and Martin Seel.

[9] Heinz Paetzold, "Einleitung," in Baumgarten, *Meditationes,* XLV. See in general Barck, "Ästhetik," 55–62.

[10] For the precise date, see the congratulatory letter of his brother Siegmund Jacob Baumgarten in Baumgarten, *Opuscula quae latine scripsit*, 300.

on Poetry (*Meditationes philosophicae de nonnullis ad poema pertinentibus*; *Philosophical Reflections on Some Aspects Concerning the Poem*),[11] which he had previously submitted to the Faculty of Philosophy on August 9 of the same year.[12] As he announced in the preface, the topic of this writing reflects his long-standing, double interest in poetry and philosophy, two subjects that, Baumgarten argues, have been inimical to each other for so long: "I wish to make it plain that philosophy and the knowledge of how to construct a poem, which are often held to be entirely antithetical, are linked together in the most amiable union."[13]

Actually, the need for a philosophical foundation of poetry was not really unheard of in the German context of the early Enlightenment, especially in the Wolffian camp.[14] In light of the modern reduction of rhetoric to mere *elocutio*, poetics was increasingly regarded as connected with logic.[15] This means, as Gottsched outspokenly declares, that a poem is made first of all of thoughts rather than of syllables and meters,[16] and that these thoughts must be conceived correctly. Even before Gottsched, the anonymous *Breslau Guide* (*Breslauer Anleitung*, 1725), the first poetics of the German Enlightenment, states that it is logic that must secure the verisimilitude of fictions.[17] The Swiss critics Bodmer and Breitinger, for their part, had outlined a broad plan aimed at a philosophical foundation of poetics and rhetoric in a letter-preface addressed to Christian Wolff in 1727.[18] The same need was briefly mentioned by Wolff himself in his logical treatise of 1728 as a desideratum of research.[19]

Against this backdrop, the original thesis that Baumgarten intends to uphold is that the majority of the thoughts in a poem are sensible

---

[11] Baumgarten, *Reflections on Poetry* (1954). With this writing, discussed with his younger brother Nathanael as *respondens*, Baumgarten obtained the *venia legendi*, see Buchenau and Marti, "Nr. 46 / Baumgarten," 444–454.

[12] Acta / in Collegio Ordinis Philosophici / Decano / Martino Schmeitzel [. . .] a die XI. Julii A. 1735. / ad diem XIII. Jan Anni 1736, University Archive in Halle, Rep. 21 Nr. 261.

[13] Herder will see this union as "an attempt to transplant Wolffian philosophy into the soil so dear to our Baumgarten, the soil of his childhood sweetheart, poetic art," see Herder, "A Monument to Baumgarten," 42.

[14] Ludovici, *Ausführlicher Entwurff*, §508–§509. See in general Buchenau, "Wolffs Rezeption in der Ästhetik," 405–426.

[15] On this aspect, see already Tonelli, "Zabarella inspirateur de Baumgarten," 182–192; see also Pimpinella, "Ragione e sensibilità," 121–150; Tedesco, *L'estetica di Baumgarten* (2000); Buchenau, "Die Einbindung von Poetik und Ästhetik in die Logik der Aufklärung," 71–84.

[16] See Gottsched's "Vorrede" to the second edition in Gottsched, *Versuch einer Critischen Dichtkunst* (2nd Ed., 1737).

[17] [Anonymous], *Anleitung zur Poesie*, 3. Another important work for the philosophical foundation of poetry, with which Baumgarten was familiar, is Daniel Heinrich Arnoldt's *Versuch einer systematischen Anleitung zur deutschen Poesie überhaupt* (1732).

[18] "Schreiben an Se. Excellentz Christian Wolffen," in [Bodmer and Breitinger], *Von dem Einfluß und Gebrauche der Einbildungs-Krafft* (1727).

[19] Christian Wolff, *Philosophia rationalis, sive Logica*, §72.

and should be philosophically grounded as such.[20] As is well known, Baumgarten defines poetry as a perfect sensible discourse (*oratio sensitiva perfecta*).[21] This means that poetic speech designates a series of sensible representations, that is, representations that are acquired through the lower cognitive faculty.[22] However, the sensible discourse is made up of not representations alone but also of their nexus and of the words designating them. Therefore, a sensible speech will be perfect, and, hence, poetic, when all of the three aspects contribute to the apprehension of sensible representations.[23]

From this point of view, the union between philosophy and poetry that Baumgarten is striving to achieve seems to point to a more ambitious framework than his merely personal tastes. For behind this biographical idiosyncrasy, Baumgarten is aiming at the convergence of two relatively distinct parts of the Aristotelian corpus: (1) the treatise *On the soul*, with the problem of *aisthetà*, which Baumgarten interprets within the Wolffian framework as indistinct or sensible representations rather than as sensations themselves, and (2) the treatise on *Poetics*. In Baumgarten, it is precisely the nature of the soul and the certain principles established by psychology that constitute the groundwork for any work of poetry.

Yet, insofar as *aisthetà* are bearers of knowledge, they do not only belong to psychology but also to logic.[24] If poetics must rest on logic, then the logic on which it depends is not the logic of the intellect, but the logic of *aisthetà*, hence, of the lower cognitive faculty. At the end of the disputation, Baumgarten takes note that this part of logic is regrettably the most neglected in his time.[25] Barely a year before, one of Baumgarten's professors at Jena, Johann Peter Reusch, had complained in his *Logical System* (*Systema logicum*) that logic tends to limit itself to the clarity of the intellect alone, thus failing to cover the

---

[20] It has been claimed that Baumgarten's aesthetics stemmed from the attempt, nurtured by a Pietist sensitivity, to theoretically justify the prophecies about Jesus Christ and the poetic dimension of the Old Testament against radical intellectualism, see Goldenbaum, "Mendelssohn's Spinozistic Alternative to Baumgarten's Pietist Project of Aesthetics," 299–328. On the importance of theology for the birth of aesthetics, see also Simon Grote in this volume; Fritz, *Vom Erhabenen*, Part 2, Ch. 2; and Borchers, *Die Erzeugung des "ganzen Menschen,"* Ch. 3.

[21] Baumgarten, *Reflections on Poetry*, §9.

[22] Baumgarten, *Reflections on Poetry*, §115. When Baumgarten only refers to the senses, he uses the adjective "sensuale," sensuous; when he refers to the knowledge acquired by the lower powers of the mind in general, he uses the term "sensitivum," sensible.

[23] Baumgarten, *Reflections on Poetry*, §7. For Baumgarten's theory of poetry, see Stefanie Buchenau, "Die Sprache der Sinnlichkeit," 151–173; Strube, "Alexander Gottlieb Baumgartens Theorie des Gedichts," 1–25.

[24] On the convergence of these disciplines in Paduan Renaissance Aristotelianism, see in general Sgarbi, "Renaissance Facultative Logic and the Workings of the Mind," 270–290.

[25] Baumgarten, *Reflections on Poetry*, §115.

entirety of its scope.[26] A hint as to how it could be complemented was already made by the Wolffian philosopher Georg Bernhard Bilfinger in a notorious passage of his *Dilucidationes*, where he expressed the wish that somebody could do for the lower faculties what Aristotle did for the intellect in his *Organon*, that is, lay down the rules for their correct usage and perfection.[27]

Like a new Aristotle,[28] the twenty-one-year-old Baumgarten takes up the challenge and proposes to distinguish logic into two parts, one concerning the lower cognitive faculty and the other the higher cognitive faculty. Since the lower faculty deals with *aisthetà*, its name will be "aesthetics," that is, the science of knowing something sensibly.[29] The philosophy of poetry resting on the logic of *aisthetà* thus becomes a springboard for a wider project that does not only apply to the making of a poem but acquires the scope of a new organon of knowledge, thereby paralleling the domain of logic in the strict sense.

The directions in which Baumgarten developed his research in the following years are therefore already contained *in nuce* in his *Reflections on Poetry*: first of all, the elaboration of a philosophy of poetry, which will subsequently expand into a philosophy of the liberal arts; second, the exploration of the psychological roots of the *aisthetà*; and lastly, the outline of an organon for thinking correctly through sensibility, which will culminate in the *Aesthetics* (1750–1758).

EARLY RECEPTION

The first person to understand the importance of this project was Alexander's elder brother, the theologian Siegmund Jakob Baumgarten, who was educated in the Pietist milieu, but also familiar with Wolffian philosophy,[30] and who played a central role in the philosophical education of Alexander.[31] In the congratulatory letter addressed to his brother on the occasion of the latter's graduation on February 26, 1735, Siegmund claims credit for introducing the young Alexander to literary studies well beyond the usual academic

---

[26] Johann Peter Reusch, *Systema logicum* (Jena: Cröker, 1734), 61–62. For a contextualization, see Nannini, "L'idea estetica di 'chiarezza estensiva' e la sua genesi nella filosofia wolffiana," 421–442.

[27] Bilfinger, *Dilucidationes philosophicae*, §268.

[28] The juxtaposition with the Stagirite was all but unusual in Baumgarten's day. Both Herder and Lambert, for instance, regarded him as a second Aristotle for his systematization of the field of aesthetics.

[29] Baumgarten, *Reflections on Poetry*, §115–§116.

[30] See in general Schloemann, *Siegmund Jacob Baumgarten* (1974).

[31] See Meier, *Alexander Baumgartens Leben*, 11.

curriculum.[32] Then, in the congratulatory letter for the defense of the *Reflections on Poetry*, Siegmund recalls the importance of the belles-lettres for both the *res publica* and the *civitas Dei*, praising his brother's attempt to "recast into a science a discipline [poetics] that was long discussed in the form of an art."[33] Small wonder, then, that Siegmund stresses the necessity of perfecting one's sensibility from a natural point of view in his *Theological Ethics* (1738).[34] In the preface to Samuel Gotthold Lange's poetic translation of the Psalms (1746), Siegmund will also theologically legitimize poetry and rhetoric, not least because they played a significant role in the writing of Scripture itself.[35] Against the refrain that Halle was a city hostile to the belles-lettres, in particular owing to its strict Pietist legacy,[36] Siegmund outspokenly argues for the reconcilability between devotion and good taste, thereby contributing to the promotion of the aesthetic project.[37]

If we consider that the *respondens* of the *Reflections on Poetry* was Alexander's and Siegmund's younger brother Nathanael, there is little doubt that aesthetics was originally a Baumgarten family business. Tentative signs of its early reception are not missing, however, as is witnessed by the positive review in the *Hamburg Reports* (*Hamburgische Berichte*) in November 1735[38] and by the insertion of the *Reflections on Poetry* in the repertoire of the Wolffian poetics in 1738.[39]

As for the elaboration of aesthetics in the years immediately after the *Reflections on Poetry*, evidence is rather poor. It is likely that the first development of Baumgarten's project took place in the *collegia privatissima* of aesthetics held in Halle in the late 1730s, where Baumgarten had the chance to expand on the general claims of his dissertation and survey the different poetic genres.[40] It comes as no surprise that the attendees that are known to

---

[32] Michaelis (praeses) and Baumgarten (respondens), *Disputatio chorographica inauguralis notiones superi et inferi*, 61–62.

[33] Cfr. Baumgarten, *Opuscula quae latine scripsit*, 300–303.

[34] See, for example, Baumgarten, *Unterricht vom rechtmässigen Verhalten eines Christen, oder Theologische Moral*, §125.

[35] See Baumgarten, "Vorrede," in [Lange], *Oden Davids* (1746). For the wider picture, see Gutzen, *Die Poesie der Bibel* (1972).

[36] See the letter of Johann Joachim Schwabe to Gottsched (January 5, 1738, in Gottsched, *Briefwechsel*, Vol. 5, 7–8.

[37] On Siegmund Jakob Baumgarten's role in the birth of aesthetics, see Nannini, "Da Baumgarten a Baumgarten," 67–90. Clemens Schwaiger rightly claims that the relationship between the brothers Baumgarten and Meier constitutes the inner core of nascent aesthetics, Schwaiger, *Alexander Gottlieb Baumgarten*, 20.

[38] *Hamburgische Berichte von gelehrten Sachen*, 92 (November 18, 1735), 749–750.

[39] Ludovici, *Neueste Merckwürdigkeiten*, §232. See also Ludovici, *Ausführlicher Entwurff*, Vol. 2, §509. Baumgarten seems to implicitly raise an objection to the straightforward attribution of his work to Wolffism in the first of the *Philosophical Letters from Aletheophilus* (1741).

[40] Ludovici, *Neueste Merckwürdigkeiten*, §232. See Schneider, "Das geistige Leben von Halle im Zeichen des Endkampfes zwischen Pietismus und Rationalismus," 162–163. As Ludovici

us, such as Immanuel J. Pyra[41] and the future Anacreontic circle of Halle (*in primis*, Johann Wilhelm Ludwig Gleim), took a sustained interest in poetry.[42]

Among these followers there must have been also the young student Georg Friedrich Meier (1718–1777). The son of a preacher, Meier began his studies at the University of Halle in 1735, where he attended, among others, the courses of logic, metaphysics, natural right, ethics, Hebrew grammar, and a *collegium philologicum* on the book of Isaiah by Alexander Baumgarten (who had been appointed Extraordinary Professor at the end of 1737[43]) and the courses of theology given by Siegmund. The relationship between Meier and both of the Baumgartens became so close that he soon regarded them as his true benefactors and promoters of his career.[44]

In the public disputation *On the Difference Between What is Called "Natural" and "Moral" in Theology* (*De discrimine ejus quod naturale et morale dicitur in theologia*, 1738), defended under the direction of Siegmund Jakob Baumgarten and written even before he became a *Magister* in philosophy (1739), Meier shows that he was well aware of the discussion about aesthetics that was in place in those years. Dealing with the concept of the force of Holy Scripture, Meier also mentions a rhetorical force, that is, a force addressing the lower powers of the mind. The reference to rhetoric, Meier argues, must be understood here as metonymical, in that it points to the whole aesthetics, which is "the science of the lower faculties and their perfection."[45]

In 1739, Alexander G. Baumgarten published his *Metaphysics*, where he lays the foundation that allowed him to claim a scientific status for aesthetics. After defining aesthetics as "the science of knowing and presenting sensibly,"[46] Baumgarten deals with the lower powers of the mind, which are also called the "analogue of reason":[47] the senses, (reproductive) imagination; perspicaciousness (wit and acumen); memory; the faculty of invention; foresight; taste; anticipation; and the faculty of characterization (which joins

---

witnesses, Baumgarten had the intention of publishing these thoughts, but was restrained by time issues.

[41] For references to the relevance of Baumgarten's mentorship, see Pyra, *Fortsetzung des Erweises*, 20; 39–40.

[42] For the reception of Baumgarten's *Meditationes* in the Anacreontic circle of Halle, see Verweyen and Witting, "Zur Rezeption Baumgartens bei Uz, Gleim und Rudnick," 101–119. On the link between aesthetics and the theory of literature in Baumgarten, see Berndt, *Facing Poetry* (2020).

[43] Meier, *Baumgartens Leben*, 18.

[44] Lange, *Leben Georg Friedrich Meiers*, 35. For a modern intellectual biography, see Schenk, *Leben und Werken des halleschen Aufklärers Georg Friedrich Meier* (1994). For the relationship between Meier and Halle, see Kertscher, "Georg Friedrich Meiers Platz im geistig-kulturellen Leben der Stadt Halle," 25–42.

[45] Meier (auctor) and Baumgarten (praeses), *Exercitatio theologica*, 33.

[46] Baumgarten, *Metaphysics*, §533.

[47] Baumgarten, *Metaphysics*, §640. Unlike reason, its analogue perceives confusedly the nexus of things. For the history of this concept, see Ferraris, "Analogon Rationis," 5–126; Buchenau, "Sinnlichkeit als Erkenntnisvermögen," 191–206.

signs with the signified). Aesthetics thus officially finds its foundation in the section of empirical psychology devoted to the lower powers of the mind. While the importance of refining the *analogon rationis* is already highlighted in his *Metaphysics*, Baumgarten develops it as a moral duty toward oneself in his *Philosophical Ethics* (1740).[48]

As a science of a certain kind of knowledge, aesthetics is considered to be an instrumental or organic philosophy, as Baumgarten will make clear in his lectures on philosophical encyclopedia, delivered in Halle in 1739/1740 and posthumously published by Johann Christian Förster as *Outline of Philosophical Encyclopedia* (*Sciagraphia encyclopaediae philosophicae*, 1769).[49] From the transcript of the course, we learn that since the instrument or the medium of all knowledge, hence also of philosophy, is the cognitive faculty and discourse, the science of knowing and presenting can be rightly called "organic philosophy."[50] Organic philosophy can thus be divided into the science of discourse in general (universal philology), and the science of knowledge, or gnoseology (logic in the broad sense). In turn, since any cognition is either sensible or intellectual, there will be a science of sensible and a science of intellectual knowledge. The former is aesthetics.[51]

In this way, the brief remarks about the parallelism between logic and aesthetics at the end of the *Reflections on Poetry* find their place within the general outline of philosophy. Precisely because of its instrumental role, aesthetics must serve as a foundation for all the disciplines resting on sensible knowledge.[52] By virtue of this encyclopedic approach, Baumgarten highlights the versatility of aesthetics that he will restate in his course on general philosophy of 1740/1741.[53] These lectures were already held at the University of Frankfurt on the Oder, where Baumgarten had just been appointed Full Professor, much to the chagrin of his students in Halle.[54] His courses in Halle were taken over by his pupil Meier, who probably already delivered lectures on Baumgarten's *Reflections on Poetry* soon after his master's departure.[55] In his first writings on aesthetics—an anonymous essay on mediocrity in

---

[48] Baumgarten, *Ethica philosophica*, §202–§220.
[49] These lectures were assiduously attended, among others, by the future "founder" of the art history, Johann Joachim Winckelmann. See Winckelmann, *Briefe*, Vol. 4, 173.
[50] Baumgarten, *Sciagraphia encyclopaediae philosophicae*, §7.
[51] Baumgarten, *Sciagraphia*, §25. Baumgarten here states that aesthetics rests on psychological and philological principles, in that knowledge must be thought and presented, see Baumgarten, *Sciagraphia*, §26.
[52] To foster the achievement of this task, in the *Outline*, Baumgarten joins each of the lower faculties to a specific branch of aesthetics (e.g., the senses with an *ars sentiendi* or "empirical aesthetics," taste with "critical aesthetics," etc.). Baumgarten will confirm these pairings between faculties and branches of aesthetics in his *Metaphysica* from the second edition (1743).
[53] Baumgarten, *Philosophia generalis*, §147.
[54] Meier, *Baumgartens Leben*, 18–19.
[55] See Verweyen and Witting, "Zur Rezeption Baumgartens."

poetry (1741), published in one of Gottsched's journals—Meier, while not mentioning the word "aesthetics," overtly employs the categories of Baumgarten, whose *Reflections on Poetry* are praised as the author's most important source.[56]

HALLE AND FRANKFURT

In this way, aesthetics began to spread through two channels, one in Halle, promoted by Meier under the guidance of Siegmund Jakob Baumgarten, and the other in Frankfurt on the Oder around Alexander Gottlieb Baumgarten. In the presentation of his teaching activities at the university in Frankfurt, Baumgarten immediately considered the possibility of giving lectures on aesthetics, which became a reality some years thereafter.[57]

Baumgarten's engagement with aesthetics, though, was not solely academic. A role in the promulgation of the new discipline is played by the journal he founded in 1741, *Philosophical Letters from Aletheophilus* (*Philosophische Brieffe von Aletheophilus*). Baumgarten, under the disguise of a pseudonym, pauses from the laconic style of his Latin treatises and assumes a more witty and friendly tone. In letter 11, in which he analyses in particular the stylistic perfections (purity, coherence, correspondence, and ornamentation),[58] Baumgarten proposes a slightly different definition of the poem from the one put forward in the *Reflections on Poetry*: no longer "perfect sensible discourse," but rather discourse so lively as to require the meter.[59] In the second letter, where he returns to the issue of philosophical encyclopedia, Baumgarten takes the opportunity to briefly present the new science of aesthetics in German, recalling the arguments of the *Reflections on Poetry* concerning the necessity of this new philosophical science. Baumgarten here details a specific branch of aesthetics, empirical aesthetics, which is essential to experimental physics, where observations and experiments presuppose a refined usage of the senses.[60] In this way, it is clear that aesthetics is not only useful to poets and artists.

---

[56] [Meier], "Versuch einer philosophischen Abhandlung von dem Mittelmäßigen in der Dichtkunst," 264–265. On the relevance of mediocrity as a philosophical theme in this period, see Arnold, *Rhetorik der Empfindsamkeit*, 44–52.

[57] Baumgarten, *Gedanken vom vernünfftigen Beyfall auf Akademien*, 36.

[58] [Baumgarten], *Philosophische Brieffe*, 29–32.

[59] [Baumgarten], *Philosophische Brieffe*, 31. See also Baumgarten, *Sciagraphia*, §106; and *Philosophia generalis*, §147. The presence of this doctrine in the *Sciagraphia* indicates that such a change probably derives from the *collegia privatissima* held in Halle.

[60] [Baumgarten], *Philosophische Brieffe*, 7–8. For more details, see Nannini, "Aesthetica experimentalis," 55–77.

The attention around Baumgarten's invention slowly increased. In 1742, Hermann Jacob Lasius, who graduated in Halle in 1740, wrote a long review (basically an abridged German version) of the *Reflections on Poetry* in the *Critical Attempts at a Survey of the German Language* (*Critische Versuche at a Survey of the German Language*), published in Greifswald.[61] This journal, to which Meier himself contributed, would become a seminal channel of the earliest dissemination of Baumgarten's project.[62] Thanks to the more accessible summary of the disputation, the Swiss critic Johann Jakob Breitinger became aware of Baumgarten's *Reflections on Poetry* and praised them in his *Defense of the Swiss Muse* (*Vertheidigung der schweitzerischen Muse*, 1744), in which he chastised the superficiality of the German literary world that had neglected Baumgarten's text for several years.[63] For his part, Carl Friedrich Brämer, the author of an important poetics from a Baconian perspective (1744), discusses Baumgarten's definition at length as one of the most relevant, albeit unsatisfying, theoretical options being considered at that time.[64]

Meanwhile in Frankfurt, a childhood friend and colleague of Baumgarten's, Friedrich Wilhelm Roloff, professor of antiquities, had founded a literary society to improve the German language.[65] Roloff's early death in 1741 led the members of the society to invite Baumgarten to take over the presidency. Baumgarten accepted the new position and broadened the scope of the society, so that in its weekly meetings the participants also tried their hand at the translation of poems from Greek, Latin, and French, hermeneutics, philosophy, rhetoric, epistolography, and so on, that is, all that can offer material to the *studia mansuetiora*—the study of the humanities. As Baumgarten conclusively argues, the society intended to deal with every learned and liberal subject that did not belong to the higher faculties (law, medicine, theology).[66] Since the perfection of these *studia mansuetiora* pertains to aesthetics,[67] it is not too far-fetched to consider this society as a practical and collective experiment in aesthetic education. Unsurprisingly, Baumgarten's literary society was already known in the eighteenth century as "society of aesthetics"—indeed, the first-ever society of aesthetics.[68]

---

[61] *Critische Versuche zur Aufnahme der Deutschen Sprache*, 6. Stück, 1742, 573–604. Baumgarten himself wrote a reply to Lasius's review in 1744. See Nannini, "Alexander G. Baumgarten and the Lost Letters of Aletheophilus," 36–37.

[62] The journal started from a position close to Gottsched and then became more independent, see Nannini, "Alexander G. Baumgarten and the Lost Letters of Aletheophilus," 37–38.

[63] Breitinger, *Vertheidigung der schweitzerischen Muse*, 5–7.

[64] Brämer, *Gründliche Untersuchung von dem wahren Begriffe der Dichtkunst*, 290–294.

[65] Baumgarten, *Scriptis*, §8.

[66] Baumgarten, *Scriptis*, §8.

[67] Baumgarten, *Scriptis*, §8.

[68] See the biographical note of one of its members, Christian Gottlob Stöckel, in Streit, *Alphabetisches Verzeichnis,* 129–130, here 130. The phrase "ästhetische Gesellschaft" also served to tell it

ACADEMIC RECEPTION

Precisely these "workshops" might have induced some students to beg Baumgarten to give proper lectures on aesthetics, which Baumgarten happily did in the winter semester 1742/1743.[69] In an academic report (1743), Baumgarten remarks that these lectures are all the more necessary because of the neglect that philosophers have for the humanities, leading to the corruption of the public taste.[70] In this short and rather overlooked text, Baumgarten mentions six categories as the ornaments with which we should adorn what we think beautifully: wealth and abundance, magnitude and dignity, verisimilitude, light, persuasion and, lastly, life, the highest kind of beauty—a beauty that is able to arouse emotions.[71]

Despite the indication of this list of categories, which will remain crucial up to the *Aesthetics* itself, the content of Baumgarten's notes for this course is not easy to determine. A precious hint is however available. Although the *Philosophical Letters from Aletheophilus* did not enjoy much success and ceased after less than a year, Baumgarten wrote three more issues for the journal, probably at the beginning of 1744.[72] One of these issues concerns aesthetics and is entitled *On Aesthetics, to Hamburg*, the city where the first review of the *Reflections on Poetry* had been published.

Here, Baumgarten sketches for the first time the core of his future *Aesthetics*. Aesthetics is defined as the science of sensible knowledge in the same way as logic is defined as the science of the understanding and reason. Baumgarten argues that only two branches of aesthetics have been developed in a detailed way over the centuries, namely, rhetoric and poetics. The importance of the beauty of the thoughts as the root of the beauty of discourse, however, has often been forgotten. To be sure, many attempts were made to gain better insight into the nature of taste, imagination, or beauty (Baumgarten mentions Bouhours, Pope, König, Bodmer, Crousaz). Yet, all these theoretical efforts proved to be unsatisfactory as to the discovery of the first principles of their subject. Even the proposal of a "logic of phantasy" put forth by Breitinger seems to Baumgarten as a mere portion of the whole aesthetic project, which must include a logic of sensibility in all its breadth. After the discussion about the refinement of the various lower powers of the

---

from the *Deutsche Gesellschaft* à la Gottsched founded in Frankfurt on the Oder by the successor of Roloff as professor of the antiquities Wolf Balthasar Adolf von Steinwehr at the end of 1743.

[69] Baumgarten, *Scriptis*, §15.

[70] Baumgarten, *Scriptis*, §15. On the aesthetic perfection of life, see Nannini, "Per una storia dell'idea di 'conoscenza viva.' Da Lutero all'estetica dell'Aufklärung," 381–402. and McQuillan, "The Aesthetic Perfection of Life," (Forthcoming).

[71] Baumgarten, *Scriptis*, §15.

[72] See Nannini, "Alexander G. Baumgarten and the Lost Letters of Aletheophilus."

mind, Baumgarten claims that aesthetics should include a general treatise on the (1) wealth, (2) nobility and greatness, (3) verisimilitude, (4) liveliness, (5) persuasiveness, and (6) movingness (or life) of beautiful thoughts,[73] as well as a doctrine of the method or order of the beautiful thoughts, and a treatise on the signs of the things being thought in particular words. After this theoretical part of aesthetics, Baumgarten intended to include a practical part, where the general theory of beautiful knowledge will be analyzed in its specific kinds, for example, by means of poetics and rhetoric.[74]

If we consider that this issue of the *Philosophical Letters* was contemporaneous with or slightly later than Baumgarten's course on aesthetics, it is likely that his lectures followed this plan. A further hint in this direction is provided by some references to this "proto-aesthetics" in a handwritten transcript of Baumgarten's lectures on dogmatic theology dating from the 1740s.[75] Unlike the published *Aesthetics*, this first version, albeit much shorter, was complete, at least in the theoretical part; hence it also contained the section on method and semiotics. The fact that Baumgarten proposed a course on "poetical philosophy" in the summer semester of 1743 seems to offer a supplement to the course given in the previous semester as to the practical section of aesthetics.[76] Be that as it may, Baumgarten sent his manuscript to Meier in 1745, who taught a course on aesthetics in Halle in the winter semester 1745/1746.[77] As early as the summer semester of 1748, Meier's student Christian Ernst von Windheim (1722–1766) delivered lectures on aesthetics (*Aisthetic* [*sic*]) in the newly founded University of Göttingen.[78]

While aesthetics thus began to receive academic recognition, Meier helped foster its spread through literary debates as well.[79] In his autobiographical memoir, Meier notes that his education in the belles-lettres was poor, so that he very soon decided to study Gottsched's writings.[80] However, the proximity to Gottsched, witnessed by a letter from November 1743,[81] soon faltered. His friendship with Samuel Gotthold Lange and, through him, with the Swiss

---

[73] On the genesis of these categories, see Nannini, "The Six Faces of Beauty," 477–512.

[74] Kliche, "'Ich glaube selbst Engel können nicht ohne Sinnlichkeit sein,'" 56–59.

[75] See Nannini, "Alexander G. Baumgarten and the Lost Letters of Aletheophilus," 32–34.

[76] *Rector et Senatus Academiae Regiae Viadrinae, Indices lectionum* (Francofurti ad Viadrum: Schwartz, 1743). The course on poetical philosophy was proposed as an alternative to a course on social right.

[77] See Lange, *Sammlung gelehrter und freundschaftlicher Briefe*, 1. Theil, 173.

[78] *Göttingische Zeitungen von gelehrten Sachen*, 31. Stück, March 1748, 247.

[79] See in general Meier, *Frühe Schriften zur ästhetischen Erziehung der Deutschen* (1999–2002).

[80] Lange, *Leben Georg Friedrich Meiers*, 31 and 40.

[81] The letter is published in Bergmann, *Die Begründung der deutschen Ästhetik*, 230–231.

critics Bodmer and Breitinger, led to a rapid defection from Gottsched's ranks, which will be evident at the end of 1744.[82]

It is during this time that Meier wrote important juvenile works arguing for the fecundity of aesthetics in different contexts: while in a long treatise on the affects Meier develops Baumgarten's suggestion about "aesthetic pathology," a doctrine that includes the arousal, the stilling, and the signs of passions,[83] in his thoughts on jesting he presents a critique of witty remarks, considering it as an integral part of aesthetics.[84] When Meier publishes his *Portrait of a Critic* (*Abbildung eines Kunstrichters*, 1745), where he develops a more general "logic of criticism," that is, the science of the rules of judgment applied to works of the liberal arts,[85] he already takes advantage of Baumgarten's manuscript on aesthetics and considers Baumgarten the model of the critic.[86] By contrast, Gottsched, while not overtly despised, is regarded as inferior to the Swiss critics.[87]

Gottsched's retaliation occurs in 1745 through one of his acolytes, Theodor Johann Quistorp, who attacked Baumgarten's *Reflections on Poetry* on the basis of the ideological misunderstanding of the definition of the poem.[88] While Baumgarten had written that a poem is a perfect sensible discourse, Quistorp interprets it as "perfectly sensible discourse," and accuses Baumgarten of subordinating reason to passions. Meier's impassioned defense, with a detailed summary of Baumgarten's position, and the subsequent reply by Quistorp fueled the controversy.[89] Baumgarten, for his part, decided to stay out of the feud and took a stance only in the preface to the third edition of his *Metaphysics* (1750).[90] It is not possible to follow here the "poets' war," which will be further revived by the dispute over occasional poems[91] and the dispute over the appraisal of the Christian *épopée*, in particular after the publication

[82] Lange, *Sammlung gelehrter und freundschaftlicher Briefe*, 176. The split with Gottsched is already tangible in Meier, "Gedanken über die Frage: Ob ein Kunstrichter seine Urtheile jederzeit erklären und beweisen müsse," 3–21.

[83] Meier, *Theoretische Lehre von den Gemüthsbewegungen überhaupt* (1744).

[84] Meier, *Gedancken von Schertzen*, §6. These writings can be better understood within the wider "Halle constellation" that brings about the contemporaneous emergence of anthropology and aesthetics: see the works of Carsten Zelle, in particular Zelle, "Sinnlichkeit und Therapie," 5–24. See also Borchers, *Die Erzeugung des "ganzen Menschen."*

[85] It is wrong to claim, as Bergmann does, that Baumgarten does not have a theory of taste, and that it is necessary to turn to Meier to find one, see Bergmann, Die Begründung der deutschen Ästhetik, 70 and 76. For Baumgarten's theory of taste, see Nannini, "Critical Aesthetics. Baumgarten and the Logic of Taste," (Forthcoming).

[86] Meier, *Abbildung eines Kunstrichters*, §60.

[87] Meier, *Abbildung eines Kunstrichters*, §48.

[88] Quistorp, "Erweis, daß die Poesie schon für sich selbst ihre Liebhaber leichtlich unglückselig machen könne," 433–452.

[89] Meier, *Vertheidigung der Baumgartischen Erklärung eines Gedichtes* (1746); for Quistorp's reply, see *Pommersche Nachrichten von gelehrten Sachen*, 8. April 1746, 28. Stück, 225–229.

[90] See Baumgarten, *Metaphysics*, 75–76.

[91] See Segebrecht, *Das Gelegenheitsgedicht*, 255 ff.

of the first three cantos of Klopstock's *Messiah* (1748).[92] What is certain is that while Gottsched and Meier agreed upon the importance of improving the taste of the German bourgeoisie, Gottsched could not subscribe to a logic of sensibility in the matters of taste that aimed to replace the logic of the intellect to which he still stayed true in his poetics.[93] As we shall see below, this rift will initiate another controversy between Gottsched and Meier, this time over the very concept of "aesthetics."

THE SYSTEMATIC PLAN

The science of aesthetics receives its first official, systematic exposition in Meier's *Foundations of All Beautiful Sciences (Anfangsgründe aller schönen Wissenschaften)*, which was published in three volumes between 1748 and 1750. It is mainly on the basis of Meier's work that the word "aesthetics" is included in the supplement to Zedler's grand *Lexicon* in 1751, thus obtaining an important intellectual recognition.[94] From the outset, Meier credits Baumgarten with being the authentic founder of aesthetics,[95] as he had already done in the *Portrait of a Critic*. For all the merits of previous theorists, Baumgarten must be granted the honor of having "outlined a systematic plan of aesthetics, achieved it, and enriched it with his inventions."[96] To dispel possible doubts about Meier's real contribution to the undertaking, the latter wishes that Baumgarten would soon publish his own treatise on this subject, so that the audience will be able to distinguish what belongs to the master and what belongs to the pupil.[97]

For his part, Baumgarten gave another course on aesthetics in 1749, once again at the request of his students.[98] Seizing this didactical opportunity, Baumgarten manages to finalize the text of the first volume of the *Aesthetics* in the winter 1749/1750.[99] The disease that struck him in 1751, probably tuberculosis, caused Baumgarten to publish only a thin second volume

---

[92] See Muncker, *Friedrich Gottlieb Klopstock,* 143–186; see also Gunzenhauser, *Seraphische Hexameterdichtung* (2020).

[93] See Mirbach, "Gottsched und die Entstehung der Ästhetik," 113–127; Pimpinella, "Ragione e sensibilità," 121–150.

[94] Zedler and Ludovici, *Nöthige Supplemente zu dem Großen Vollständigen Universal Lexicon,* Vol. 1, coll. 667–668.

[95] Meier, *Anfangsgründe aller schönen Wissenschaften,* Vol. 1, Vorrede and §6.

[96] Meier, *Anfangsgründe,* Vol. 1, §6.

[97] Meier, *Anfangsgründe,* Vol. 1, Vorrede. Some lines thereafter, however, Meier claims that he has combined Baumgarten's and his own thoughts in such a way that no reader will be able to say what is whose.

[98] See Fontius, "Baumgarten und die Literaturbriefe," 553–594, here 571. For the publication of the transcript of the course, see Baumgarten, *Kollegium über die Ästhetik,* 65–258.

[99] Baumgarten, *Aesthetica* (1750).

of the *Aesthetics* in 1758,[100] leaving the work unfinished. Apart from the prolegomena and the exposition of the character of the gifted aesthetician, Baumgarten develops the sections concerning the first five perfections of knowledge (wealth, magnitude, truth, light, persuasion), without even finishing the section on aesthetic persuasion. The further aspects of heuristic (the discovery of beautiful thoughts), the method and the signs of what is thought beautifully, as well as the practical part of aesthetics will never be written.

Unlike Baumgarten, Meier manages to finish his *Foundations* (in which the presentation of practical aesthetics is however omitted). Much easier to read and understand than Baumgarten's stodgy Latin, Meier's work overshadowed Baumgarten's *Aesthetics* in the short term, as is witnessed by the number of positive reviews.[101] While in the preface to the *Foundations* Meier clearly maintains that his work is not a simple translation or rephrase of Baumgarten[102] (as Baumgarten himself confirms[103]), the scholarly literature has often voiced the impression that Meier had just watered down Baumgarten's wine.[104] In this sense, Meier's real merit allegedly consists in the fact that he "read the mood of the age correctly."[105] Other authors such as Ernst Bergmann affirmed that Meier, while not being an original thinker, did more good for aesthetics than Baumgarten himself, thanks to his unfailing defense of this discipline against the attacks of Gottsched's followers and his alignment with the new trends in German literature (first of all, Anacreontism and Klopstock).[106] Meier's ties with the younger generation of German poets and his public presence in literary debates were certainly key to the success of aesthetics; yet, Meier can also boast of genuinely philosophical accomplishments in aesthetics, if only because he fleshes out several internal domains of aesthetics (aesthetic pathology, critical aesthetics, etc.) as well as several applications of the discipline (in hermeneutics, homiletics, etc.)[107] that Baumgarten had merely indicated as promising areas for research, but never fully developed.[108]

---

[100] Baumgarten, *Aestheticorum pars altera* (1758).

[101] See Bergmann, *Die Begründung der deutschen Ästhetik*, 173.

[102] Meier, *Anfangsgründe*, Vol. 1, §6.

[103] Baumgarten, *Aesthetica*, Praefatio.

[104] See Gesner, *Primae lineae isagoges in eruditionem universalem*, Vol. 1, 219; see also Reiss, "The Naturalization of the Term Ästhetik," 653.

[105] Reiss, "The Naturalization the Term Ästhetik," 656.

[106] See, for example, Bergmann, *Die Begründung der deutschen Ästhetik*, 23–24; 35–37.

[107] On hermeneutics, see Tedesco, "L'Ermeneutica Generale di Meier," 195–209; on homiletics, see Strassberger, *Johann Christoph Gottsched und die "philosophische" Predigt*, Ch. 5.1; Nannini, "Predicare per l'uomo," 29–42.

[108] The detailed analysis of Meier's merits in aesthetics goes well beyond the scope of this essay as well as the survey of his diverse essayistic production concerning aesthetic themes.

As for the *Foundations*, that explicitly rely on Baumgarten's plan, Meier develops a rather faithful, but still personal interpretation.[109] Alongside the differences in the structure with regard to the *Aesthetics* (e.g., the doctrine of the gifted aesthetician in Meier follows that of the kinds of beauty, a choice mildly criticized by Baumgarten[110]) and in the particular themes (e.g., the *analogon rationis* as the whole of sensibility is less evident in Meier than in Baumgarten), the two authors have different sensitivities in their own references (e.g., Meier is more indebted to contemporary poetic sources, while Baumgarten engages in a closer dialogue with ancient poetics and rhetoric) and in the development of their arguments (e.g., Meier is inclined to more articulated subdivisions for each topic and uses a more adorned style, thus targeting a wider readership).[111] It is doubtful that without either of them aesthetics could have asserted itself to the point of durably changing the very "genome" (*Chromosomensatz*)[112] of philosophy.

THE SCOPE OF THE PLAN

If one wants to mention an overarching theme going through Baumgarten's *Aesthetics* and Meier's *Foundations*, certainly the conceptualization and promotion of beauty is a good candidate. Baumgarten had already defined beauty in his *Metaphysics* as "phenomenal perfection," that is, a perfection insofar as it is accessible to taste as a sensible judgment[113]—a definition that Meier already resumes in his early essay on the mediocre in poetry in 1741. In the *Aesthetics*, Baumgarten clarifies that beauty can be referred not only to beings but also to the way we know them. In this second sense, beauty

---

[109] From this point of view, the accusations of falsifying Baumgarten's message (see Hans Reiss, "Georg Friedrich Meier (1718–77) und die Verbreitung der Ästhetik," 14; Haverkamp, "Wie die Morgenröthe zwischen Nacht und Tag," 8) or, at the other extreme, of being Baumgarten's "monkey"—a phrase often used by his opponents in the literary war with Gottsched and taken up again by Benedetto Croce—do not hit the mark. For a more balanced perspective, see Schwaiger, *Alexander Gottlieb Baumgarten*, 20–21.

[110] See Baumgarten, *Kollegium über die Ästhetik*, §27.

[111] More questionable is Reiss's thesis that Baumgarten neatly separates ethics from aesthetics, unlike Meier, and that Meier neglects the cognitive aspect of aesthetics, unlike Baumgarten. See Reiss, "Georg Friedrich Meier," 14; for the second remark, see also Witte, *Logik ohne Dornen*, 65–66. As a matter of fact, Baumgarten stresses the importance of aesthetics for one's conduct from the very beginning of his *Aesthetics*, hence a moral goal cannot be excluded. In addition, it must be recalled that Meier does not neglect the epistemic stakes of aesthetics throughout his works, see Borchers, *Die Erzeugung des "ganzen Menschen,"* 165–176, which also points out that for both authors the improvement of the lower powers of the mind, albeit differently justified, aims at the formation of the "whole man."

[112] Welsch, *Aisthesis*, 22.

[113] Baumgarten, *Metaphysics*, §662. For this definition of beauty and its relationship with the concept of taste, see Nannini, "Critical Aesthetics. Baumgarten and the Logic of Taste," (Forthcoming).

can be regarded as the perfection of sensible knowledge.[114] Thus, there can be a beautiful object that is thought in an ugly way and an ugly object that is thought in a beautiful way.[115] While sticking to the definition of beauty of Baumgarten's *Metaphysics*, Meier too will point out this duality of elements in his *Foundations*. In fact, if beauty is a perfection that is known sensibly, then beauty increases either with the increase of the perfection of the object or with the increase of the perfection of our sensible knowledge of that object.[116]

As for the object, Baumgarten claims that its beauty depends on the richness in characters and nobility, as well as on its metaphysical truth. Hence, those who intend to think beautifully should preferably choose to think about individual things, inasmuch as they are thoroughgoingly determined, hence more metaphysically true than abstractions.[117] As for the way we know the object, it must comply with one or more of the aforementioned six categories of aesthetic heuristics, with life being the highest beauty. Joining the two conditions in a singular statement, we could affirm that the fullest beauty we can experience is for Baumgarten and Meier the perfection of the sensible knowledge of perfection. Since the maximally perfect object is God in the way he manifests himself in creation, incarnation, and redemption, a poem like Klopstock's *Messiah*, which was able to propose and arouse "living," that is, emotional thoughts about the incarnated God, gained the enthusiastic approval of both Baumgarten and Meier; the latter will even devote a very positive book-length review to the first cantos of Klopstock's work in the late 1740s.[118]

The insistence on such high achievements of beautiful thinking, however, should not give the impression that aesthetics only deals with them. Baumgarten avowedly argues for the significance of aesthetics in everyday life;[119] similarly, Meier contends that the application of the correct principles of sensible thought and judgment runs the gamut "from the heroic poem to the curls of the fops and the rouge on the cheeks of the beauties."[120] In truth, the domain of aesthetics is even wider, if we take into account the fact that the sensible faculties, insofar as they are lower faculties, are regarded

---

[114] Baumgarten, *Aesthetica*, §14. On the importance of aesthetic perfection, see McQuillan, "Baumgarten, Meier, and Kant on Aesthetic Perfection," 13–27.

[115] Baumgarten, *Aesthetica*, §18.

[116] Meier, *Anfangsgründe*, Vol. 1, §23–§24.

[117] Baumgarten, *Aesthetica*, §440–§441.

[118] Meier, *Beurtheilung des Heldengedichts* (1749).

[119] Baumgarten, *Aesthetica*, §3; Baumgarten, *Kollegium über die Ästhetik*, §3.

[120] Meier, *Gedancken von Schertzen*, Vorrede. Aesthetics also spreads scientific and theological knowledge in a language that is accessible to a larger audience, exerting a strong influence on the establishment of popular philosophy. On this aspect, see Böhr, *Philosophie für die Welt* (2003); Nannini, "Johann August Ernesti e le origini della filosofia popolare tra neoumanesimo ed estetica," 117–127.

as the "foundations of the soul" (*Boden der Seele*;[121] the collection of obscure representations is called the *fundus animae* or "ground of the soul" by Baumgarten[122]), and must prepare the material that will be then further elaborated by the intellect and reason.[123] Aesthetics as "lower gnoseology" thus plays a key role in the development of intellectual thought as well.

This marks a different approach with regard to Wolff. In fact, what in Wolff was lower from the point of view of the hierarchy of the soul now discloses a genetic and topographical sense: hence, the sensible faculties are not inferior merely because they are less noble than the superior, but above all because they precede the development of the latter and, as it were, constitute their psychological roots. It comes as no surprise that Meier writes at the beginning of the second volume of his *Foundations* that aesthetics, "which deals with the emendation of the sensible faculties of knowledge, is still more necessary and useful than logic."[124] Aesthetics, which was built on the model of its "older sister,"[125] namely, logic, actually discovers that it constitutes the very basis of the latter.

AESTHETIC WAR

Meier was appointed Full Professor in Halle in 1748, enjoying a large success as philosopher and as the author of moral journals (with his friend Samuel Gotthold Lange).[126] His rising visibility and the lambasting review he addressed to Gottsched's poetics in 1747–1749[127] must have exacerbated the tense relationships between Halle and Leipzig, leading Gottsched to take up arms again in the preface to the fourth edition of his *Critical Poetics* (1751).[128] Despite Meier's protest against the vilifying attitude of his opponent,[129] the war was waged not only in a number of polemic pamphlets[130] but also in Gottsched's commentary on the German translation (1754) of excerpts of

---

[121] [Meier], "Gedanken von dem Werthe der freyen Künste und schönen Wissenschaften in Absicht auf die obern Kräfte der Seele," 134.

[122] Baumgarten, *Metaphysics*, §511. For this issue and the relevant bibliography, see the classical Hans Adler, "Fundus Animae," 197–220; Nannini, "At the Bottom of the Soul," 51–72.

[123] Meier, *Anfangsgründe*, Vol. 1, §13.

[124] Meier, *Anfangsgründe*, Vol. 2, §253.

[125] Baumgarten, *Aesthetica*, §13.

[126] On Meier's activity in the moral journals and the importance of aesthetics in them, see for instance, Martens, "Zur Thematisierung von schöner Literatur in Samuel Gotthold Langes und Georg Friedrich Meiers Moralischen Wochenschriften Der Gesellige und Der Mensch," 133–145. More in general, see Zenker, "Zwei Jahrzehnte Volksaufklärung (1748–1768)," 55–80.

[127] Meier, *Beurtheilung der Gottschedischen Dichtkunst* (1747–1748).

[128] Gottsched, *Versuch einer Critischen Dichtkunst* (4th Ed., 1751), Vorrede.

[129] Meier, *Vertheidigung seines Beweises des ewigen Lebens der Seele und seiner Gedancken von der Religion*, §33.

[130] See Bergmann, *Die Begründung der deutschen Ästhetik*, Ch. 12.

Batteux's *The Fine Arts Reduced to a Single Principle* (*Beaux-Arts réduits à un même principe*, 1746). Among the goals of this editorial undertaking, there is undoubtedly the attempt to condemn, under the aegis of Batteux, "the stream of erroneous doctrines that seek to find the nature of poetry not in imitation, but simply in the savage expression of unbridled imagination, which they call 'aesthetics.'"[131]

As a matter of fact, until the end of the 1750s "aesthetics" often turned into a sort of insult (*Schimpfwort*),[132] while the adjective "aesthetic" became synonymous with "senseless."[133] The values of phantasy and intuitiveness promoted by aesthetics became, in the eyes of the hostile critics, evidence of confusion in thought and turgidity in style.[134] Aesthetics was thus assimilated to the sensualism of the Pietist sect of Herrnhuters for their allegedly shared emphasis on the sensible and the individual, so that the advocates of aesthetics were also stigmatized as heretics or fanatics.[135] The endorsement of Klopstock's poetry as well as the attempts to interpret Scripture using the tools of aesthetics, promoted in particular by Siegmund Baumgarten's and Meier's pupil Gottlob Samuel Nicolai,[136] must have appeared to be a confirmation of this heterodoxy. Wolff himself harshly criticized this hermeneutical *hybris*,[137] going so far as to extend the condemnation to aesthetics as such: "The beautiful minds spoil everything in philosophy," he reportedly exclaimed on the occasion of the publication of his colleague Meier's aesthetic works.[138]

Similarly, in a eulogy for his late colleague Carl Gerhard Wilhelm Lodtmann, the first professor to lecture on Baumgarten's *Aesthetics* (University

---

[131] Review of the "Auszug aus den Herrn Batteux schönen Künsten," *Das Neueste aus der anmuthigen Gelehrsamkeit* (Wonnemonath 1754), 464–467, here 464.

[132] Nicolai, "Vorrede," in *Briefe über den itzigen Zustand der schönen Wissenschaften in Deutschland* (1755). See also Huber, "Fortsetzung der Geschichte der deutschen Dichtkunst," 422.

[133] Gesner, *Primae lineae isagoges in eruditionem universalem*, 243.

[134] Gottsched himself publicly endorses this misunderstanding in Gottsched, "Fortsetzung und Beschluß des neulichen Schreibens von der französischen und wälschen Musik [...]," 745–746 fn. Here aesthetic words are considered full of obscure and confused concepts.

[135] Aesthetic poets, Gottsched writes in the *Auszug*, would like to "turn the imitation of the beautiful nature into obscure alchemistical ramblings, worthy of Jakob Böhme and the Herrnhuters," see Gottsched, *Auszug aus den Herrn Batteux schönen Künsten*, 42. For the context of this criticism, see Müller, *Ästhetische Religiosität und Kunstreligion*, 53–63.

[136] See, for example, Nicolai, *Von der Verbesserung der sinlichen Erkentnis, als einem Hülfsmittel der Auslegung der Heiligen Schrift* (1748). For a more detailed analysis, see Nannini, "Biblical Hermeneutics in the Light of Aesthetics," 551–559; see also Nannini, "The Language of Affects. From Pathologia Sacra to Pathologia Aesthetica," (Forthcoming).

[137] See Oelrichs, "Tagebuch einer gelehrten Reise 1750, durch einen Theil von Ober- und Nieder-Sachsen," 62.

[138] The sentence is recorded in Johann Christoph Schwab's essay in the collective volume *Welche Fortschritte hat die Metaphysik seit Leibnitzens und Wolffens Zeiten in Deutschland gemacht?*, 23–24. On the difference between Wolff's and Baumgarten's approach on taste, see Nannini, "Critical Aesthetics. Baumgarten and the Logic of Taste" (Forthcoming).

of Helmstedt, winter semester 1751/1752),[139] the theologian Johann Benedikt Carpzov takes a stance against that "new art or wisdom, unknown to the Atticans, the Romans and, I believe, to those who claim to be its adherents, that has drawn its name from a Greek root."[140] Carpzov's disdain was certainly amplified by Meier's statement that Jesus himself was a practical aesthetician, since he narrated "the celestial truths, adapted to the folks' understanding, through parables, metaphors and allegories."[141] Carpzov's conclusion is that what is good in aesthetics has been borrowed from other disciplines (first of all from poetics and rhetoric) and what is new is sheer nonsense.[142] Against these misunderstandings, both Meier[143] and Nicolai[144] will stand up to show the erroneousness of these arbitrary condemnations (Baumgarten, by now sick, prefers once again to stay out of the feud).[145] Meier even goes so far as to devote a whole essay to the reasons why it seems to be useless to dispute with Gottsched in 1754. If we turn to the intellectual scene of the second half of the 1750s, the dispute in fact no longer had reason to continue. Aesthetics progressively asserted itself both as a word and as an academic discipline throughout the German-speaking universities.[146] When Baumgarten died in 1762, the "aesthetic war" was undoubtedly won.

AESTHETICS AND PHILOSOPHY OF THE ARTS

Even if the advocates of aesthetics defeated their opponents, it is worth asking what kind of aesthetics came out as the winner of this controversy. As we have suggested, for Baumgarten and Meier aesthetics was certainly a discipline that concerned a certain way of knowing things, more than a certain class of things. This does not mean, though, that this way of thinking lacks an elective terrain of application. Such a terrain is that of the "liberal arts."

---

[139] *Braunschweigische Anzeigen, Jahrgang* 7, Stück 68 (August 1751), col. 1373. The importance of cultivating the lower powers of the mind through aesthetics is advocated in Lodtmann, *Oratio aditialis [. . .] domini Ioannis Christiani Wernsdorfii* (1753).

[140] Carpzov, *Sempiternae memoriae*, V.

[141] Carpzov, *Sempiternae memoriae*, VII.

[142] Carpzov, *Sempiternae memoriae*, XI.

[143] Meier, *Vorstellung der Ursachen, warum es unmöglich scheint, mit Herrn Profeßor Gottsched eine nützliche und vernünftige Streitigkeit zu führen* (1754).

[144] Nicolai, "Vorrede."

[145] See Nannini, "Können Sie denn dergleichen schreiben, ohne in Wallung zu gerathen? Ich nicht," 205–227.

[146] See Weimar, *Geschichte der deutschen Literaturwissenschaft bis zum Ende des 19. Jahrhunderts*, 78–81; Reiss, "The Naturalization the Term Ästhetik"; Strube, "Die Entstehung der Ästhetik," 1–30. For the dissemination of aesthetics in France, see Décultot, "Aesthetik/esthétique: étapes d'une naturalisation (1750–1840)," 7–28.

As a matter of fact, Wolff had already expressed the need for a philosophy of the liberal arts (grammar, rhetoric, poetics, etc.), able to account for the rules of these arts and the judgment on their works.[147] Baumgarten himself seems to be willing to expand the poetical philosophy of his *Reflections on Poetry* in this direction as early as in the fifth of his *Philosophical Letters* (1741): "I am one of the philosophical eccentrics that consider a great part of the beautiful sciences [. . .] as an authentic issue of philosophy."[148] Needless to say, this philosophical demand should be now met through the discipline of aesthetics, which is also defined the "theory of the liberal arts."[149] Baumgarten clarifies in the *Aesthetics* that "the laws of the aesthetic art spread across all the liberal arts as a sort of North Star with regard to the individual arts."[150]

The new aesthetic framework, however, brings about a major change with regard to Wolff. In fact, the "liberal arts"[151] are no longer limited to the sole arts of discourse. From the first course of aesthetics in 1742/1743, an essential goal of the new discipline had been precisely to widen the narrowness of the laws of poetics and rhetoric, in order to discover—Baumgarten writes—the laws that also underlie painting, sculpture, and music. At the beginning of his second course on aesthetics, Baumgarten still wonders: "If I want to think in a sensibly beautiful way, why should I think only in prose or in verse? Where does the painter or the musician remain?"[152] The signs designating the beautiful thoughts in the *Aesthetics* and the *Foundations* thus no longer coincide with words as in the *Reflections on Poetry*, but include (at least) the signs employed by the painter and the musician.[153] Consequently, after explaining that aesthetics contains the principles of poetics and rhetoric, Meier clearly states in 1748 that "aesthetics also contains the grounds of the remaining fine arts (*schöne Künste*)."[154]

Although the fine arts are not regarded as a codified and closed system and although Baumgarten and Meier draw the greater part of their examples

---

[147] Wolff, *Philosophia rationalis*, §72. See Pimpinella, "La théorie wolffienne des arts à l'origine de l'esthétique," 9–22.

[148] [Baumgarten], *Philosophische Brieffe*, 15.

[149] Baumgarten, *Aesthetica*, §1.

[150] Baumgarten, *Aesthetica*, §71.

[151] Liberal arts are often used in a sort of hendiadys with the German term *schöne Wissenchaften* (beautiful sciences). For an overview of this fluctuating term, see Strube, "Die Geschichte des Begriffs 'schöne Wissenschaften,'" 136–216. In Meier's period the term usually indicated poetics and rhetoric. For the role of history in relation to the beautiful sciences and rational sciences in Baumgarten, see Nannini, "In the Wake of Clio. Baumgarten on History," 1–41.

[152] Baumgarten, *Kollegium über die Ästhetik*, §1. Referring to this course of lectures in a letter of 1749, Baumgarten's pupil Louis de Beausobre claims that the course deals with aesthetics or "the rules of the fine arts," see Fontius, "Baumgarten und die Literaturbriefe," 571.

[153] For the semiotics of the arts in Baumgarten, see, for example, Franke, "Die Semiotik als Abschluß der Ästhetik," 347–357.

[154] Meier, *Anfangsgründe*, Vol. 1, §19.

from rhetoric and poetics,[155] they both perceive the relevance of aesthetics for their philosophical foundation.[156] In his biography of Baumgarten (1763), Meier goes as far as to consider as the most urgent desideratum of research in aesthetics the fact that "philosophical minds, who understand music, painting and the remaining fine arts, besides oratory and poetics, [may] apply aesthetic principles to them."[157] The aesthetics coming out as winner from the disputes of its early history therefore points in the direction of a philosophy of the arts.

At the beginning of the nineteenth century (1806), an historian such as Johann Kaspar Friedrich Manso argues that it was precisely the theory of the fine arts, in particular Batteux's, that made it possible to flesh out the practical part of aesthetics that neither Baumgarten nor Meier had developed in their main aesthetic works.[158] Meier's wish thus came true in a sense. Its price, however, was the progressive neglect of the original framework of aesthetics as the science of sensible knowledge, which will become even more pronounced after Kant. Baumgarten and Meier's aesthetics, reduced to its contribution to the philosophy of (the) art(s), has long been predictably considered as unripe and defective.[159] It took the late-twentieth-century crisis of aesthetics as a philosophy of art for their "aesthetica" to be again regarded as fruitful food for thought to aesthetics at large.[160]

---

[155] See, for example, the criticism made in Mendelssohn, "Alexander Gottlieb Baumgarten, Aestheticorum Pars altera," 451 and Mendelssohn, "Georg Friedrich Meier, Auszug aus den Anfangsgründen aller schönen Wissenschaften," 133.

[156] The term "fine arts" even features in the title of Meier, *Betrachtungen über den ersten Grundsatz aller schönen Künste und Wissenschaften* (1757), on which I cannot linger.

[157] Meier, *Baumgartens Leben*, 43.

[158] Manso, "Übersicht der Geschichte der deutschen Poesie," 173–174.

[159] See, for instance, the first historian of aesthetics, Benedikt Josef Maria von Koller, *Entwurf zur Geschichte und Literatur der Aesthetik von Baumgarten bis auf die neueste Zeit*, 27–28 and also Kristeller, "The Modern System of the Arts: A Study in the History of Aesthetics (II)," 34.

[160] On the crisis of aesthetics, see, for example, Gołaszewska, *Crisis of Aesthetics?* (1979). More specifically, see Scheer, "Baumgartens Ästhetik und die Krise der von ihm begründeten Disziplin," 108–119. For a survey of Baumgarten's presence in today's aesthetic debate, see Nannini, "Postfazione, L'Aesthetica oggi," 361–370. On the importance of the historical roots of aesthetics for the future of the discipline, see Shusterman, "Back to the Future: Aesthetics Today," 104–124.

Chapter 8

An Exercise in Humanity

Baumgarten and Mendelssohn on the Importance of Aesthetic Training

Anne Pollok

In the first part of the *Aesthetics* (1750/58), Baumgarten considers the importance of "aesthetic training" (*exercitatio aesthetica*), which supports and enhances our natural capacities to realize beauty but also our sensible capacities in general. It is interesting how this 'training' reflects in Mendelssohn's later considerations on taste in his aesthetic writings (mainly *On Sentiments*, 1755/1761/1771[1] and *Rhapsody*, 1761/71), but also on exercise and habit in his essay *On Evidence*, which won the prize of the Prussian Royal Academy in 1763. For Mendelssohn, our sensible nature plays an important role in the realization of our vocation as a human being. It can support us in developing a sense of the true, good, and beautiful, respectively. This "gain in reality," however, can only be called a perfection if said gain is harmonious and encompasses both the higher and the lower faculties. Both Mendelssohn and Baumgarten are thus offering a rationalist account on aesthetics that allows to incorporate sensibility and emotion without succumbing to any form of irrationalism.

In his *Aesthetics*, Baumgarten presents the reader with an almost complete *gnoseologia inferior*, a science of our sensible cognition (as the inferior mode of cognition in comparison to our intellect). But Baumgarten goes even further than that, arguing that our sensible cognition is essential for us as human beings and needs to be considered in order to gain a complete and sufficient picture of all human faculties: "sensible cognition is the ground of distinct cognition: if the whole understanding is to be improved, aesthetics must come

---

[1] It should be noted that Mendelssohn's aesthetic writings changed rather decisively during the course of their various publications. I discuss this at length in my introduction to Mendelssohn, *Ästhetische Schriften*, xiii–xlviii.

to the aid of logic."[2] Perfection in aesthetics is extensive: a sensibly perfect representation contains more (confused and obscure) details than an intensively clear, intellectual representation that presents its formative aspects distinctly.[3]

This is an idea that all German philosophers with interest in the arts and in human sensibility more generally took up—most prominent among them Moses Mendelssohn. His views on aesthetics, in particular concerning the idea that aesthetics is indeed a self-standing philosophical project, are in large part due to Baumgarten's works. His separation of aesthetics from empirical psychology and the explicitly tripartite definition of the human faculties (and their respective division as higher and lower versions of these faculties in sensibility and the understanding) was important for Mendelssohn. Jean-Paul Meier even refers to the years around 1760 as a "*période Baumgartienne*."[4] In this chapter, I discuss the role of aesthetic training—the capacity to comprehend any given information with greater speed, ease, and elegance—that seems a perfect prerequisite for the common cry among German aestheticians of the eighteenth century: the perfection of the whole human being. Aesthetics thus becomes not only an instructional manual for the arts but also a tool to improve our mental capacities in general.

BAUMGARTEN: AESTHETIC EXERCISE AND ITS RELATION TO PERFECTION

As Stefanie Buchenau makes very clear in her excellent book on the emergence of aesthetics in the German enlightenment, the advent of a philosophy of the sentiments and the conditions of sensibility were by no means an outburst of irrationality.[5] It is true, she holds, that "Baumgarten's view profoundly *modifies* and *redefines* the traditional division of the faculties, and affects both the traditional doctrine of man's relation to the beasts and lower creatures, and to God and the higher creatures."[6] However, it also modifies our image of reason and its powers, in that it widens the scope of reason and makes it operational. In particular in those chapters of the *Aesthetics* that argue for such an operationalization of the sentiments, Baumgarten shows

---

[2] Baumgarten, *Kollegium über die Ästhetik*, 80.
[3] Baumgarten, *Reflections on Poetry,* §17; Baumgarten, *Metaphysics* §393, §531, or later: richness, *ubertas*, in Baumgarten, *Aesthetica/Ästhetik* §115. On this, see McQuillan, "Baumgarten on Sensible Perfection," 49.
[4] Meier, *L'esthetique de Moses Mendelssohn*, 229. The catalogue of Mendelssohn's books lists the *Aesthetics*, *Metaphysics*, and *Ethics*, see Mendelssohn, *Verzeichniß der auserlesenen Büchersammlung*, 36, #316; 48, #588; 50, #611, and #617.
[5] Buchenau, *Founding of Aesthetics*, Ch. 8.
[6] Buchenau, *Founding of Aesthetics,* 154.

how even seemingly irrational tendencies can be explained and improved upon by rational means. All faculties are rational: the lower ones follow the standard of poetry, the higher ones the standard of distinctness, and hence all of them are susceptible to such a form of transformation, and their respective form of perfection.[7] The lower ones in particular respond to a form of training that engages both understanding and sensibility.

For the most part, even Baumgarten, particularly in the *Metaphysics* (1739), champions the higher perfection of the higher faculties. However, he also seems to be very aware that most of our representations are not clear and distinct; he even acknowledges that in almost every (human) perception there is something confused or even obscure.[8] In §560 of the *Aesthetics*, he then asks, more or less rhetorically, "*quid enim est abstractio, si iactura non est?*" "What is abstraction, if not a loss?" In order to understand something clearly and distinctly, we need to get to its heart, to the important information that forms the fundamental structure of the issue at hand. Many times, the mass of this information, in particular when it comes to contingent truths, is still overwhelming and has to be captured in an abstraction, in its most condensed and still adequate form. But, as Baumgarten notes, there is a loss to be mourned. And at times, such a loss cannot be tolerated if we do want an adequate picture of the issue. In these cases, we have to leave abstract intellectual ideas behind and concern ourselves with the plenitude of lived experience.

The beauty of art, however, does not thrive on mere magnitude of impressions, but requires its own form of reduction. The beauty of a statue supersedes the beauty of the mere marble the beautiful object is made of: the fundamental and valuable aspects of the marble are retained, but also made more striking through its beautiful form, which is better suited to bring together all aspects under a single idea.[9] Hence, we can say that Baumgarten puts a different stress on aesthetics than Wolff (who rather viewed aesthetic as a sensible appreciation of rational perfection): "sensible knowledge has . . . its own kind of perfection," irreducible to rational perfection in logic, mathematics, and metaphysics, yet still according to rational principles in its own right.[10]

Baumgarten considers *cognitio sensitiva* mainly from two perspectives: (a) psychological, as the indistinct mode of perception in reference to Leibniz's definition as presented in the *Meditations on Knowledge, Truth, and Ideas*

---

[7] Buchenau, *Founding of Aesthetics*, 155.
[8] Baumgarten, *Metaphysics*, §207, §544, §624.
[9] Baumgarten, *Reflections on Poetry,* §95; Baumgarten, *Metaphysics,* §88.
[10] Makkreel, "The Confluence of Aesthetics and Hermeneutics," 66; Buchenau, *Founding of Aesthetics*, 151, 166–169.

(*Meditationes de cognitione, veritate et ideis*, 1684)[11] and (b) metaphysical, defining sensible cognition as one way to cognize the abundance of all things seen in their fundamental interrelatedness.[12] The lower faculties here encompass sensible memory, imagination, habit, wit, sensible perspicuity, sensible judgment or taste, and a sensible *facultas characteristica*.[13]

Sensible evidence comes with a form of evidence that we barely experience in regard to matters of logic, which are clear and distinct. Whereas those are defined by intensive clarity[14] (which goes inward: we do grasp the internal structure and clearly see the relations between the basic concepts), beauty offers extensive clarity.[15] It captures the abundance of life, the complexity of contingent aspects of our reality. One important marker of this kind of cognition is its liveliness, and with this comes a certain kind of efficacy[16] and determinacy. Concerning the latter, Baumgarten follows Leibniz that the more aspects of a representation are given, the more we can see its individuality: the object becomes "more clearly distinguishable from without," the abundance of information even "more suggestive of order."[17] Concerning the former, he seeks to establish ways of training for the improvement of the lower faculties *without turning them into higher ones*.

Sensible cognition represents its object as meaningful and full of hidden facets, satisfying the power of the soul as a *vis repraesentativa universi*—a force that aims at representing the universe as a whole. Since we as human beings are limited in our capacities, our idea of the universe can consist in a limited number of clear and distinct ideas, but will include many more confused or even obscure ones. It will be, in short, a more aesthetic than intellectual idea overall. But as this is the world in which we live, we better know our way around in it, and thus form as adequate ideas as possible about it—may these capture only portions of it. The way Baumgarten presents the *Aesthetics*, our knowledge of the inferior modes of understanding, but even more so, our incorporation of these modes through aesthetic training into our habits and our personality—to form the *felix aestheticus*[18]—is key to this knowledge.

---

[11] See Leibniz, *Philosophical Essays*, 23–27. In the same volume, see *Discourse on Metaphysics*, §24; *Monadology*, §13–§28, and *Principles of Nature and Grace*, §4–§5.

[12] See Franke, *Kunst als Erkenntnis*, 41.

[13] I follow Buchenau's interpretation that Baumgarten not only considered the (higher) capacity for formal universal concepts, but more generally the use of language for communication as characteristic for humankind. See Buchenau, *The Founding of Aesthetics*, 167–170.

[14] A distinction introduced already in the Baumgarten, *Reflections on Poetry*, §16. See also Buchenau, *The Founding of Aesthetics*, 126–127.

[15] See FN 3.

[16] Baumgarten, *Metaphysics*, §517.

[17] Makkreel, "The Confluence of Aesthetics and Hermeneutics," 66.

[18] Baumgarten, *Aesthetica/Ästhetik*, §47.

The inner structure and (discernible) cohesiveness of the aesthetic object to be an apt instrument for the training of a *felix aestheticus* is of course essential. Poetic thinking is the reflection of the richness of this world; but it is a richness that is representative of an inner unity. Beauty is perfection that appears, that the senses can grasp and comprehend relatively easily and promptly. The beautiful world presented by the artist (as indeed a "second maker under Jove"[19]) is 'heterocosmic': built on the principles of world-formation by the principle of noncontradiction and sufficient reason. Seen this way, it becomes clear why beautiful cognition is still a part of reason.[20]

Baumgarten's *Reflections on Poetry* (1735) already goes in this direction, as they aim to develop the concept of poetry from the nature of the human soul.[21] At the same time, this reflection should reveal the possibilities of cultivating human cognition and representation in a way that enables us to comprehend the world at large more adequately. For this, a keen look at the conditions of human psychology is important. Baumgarten seems to have understood the dynamics of the functioning of the human psyche. And even if some of his discussions of this functioning still sound a bit mechanistic, he does embrace the dynamism of the activity of the Leibnizian monad.

Whereas intellectual cognition functions by way of abstraction, and by aiming at clear and distinct, general ideas, sensible cognition envisions the complexity of the world in its individual representations. Aesthetic thinking works within "concrete abundance," but this abundance seems not completely devoid of a more general structure: it is still an abundance that reflects the perfect order of the world according to ultimately rational principles. In a sensible representation, the given aspects appear interconnected, even though at many points we cannot concretely say why and how. We understand this obscure richness as part of the *fundus animae*, the obscure foundation of the soul as such.[22] These principles of connection are determined by association, and that is why aesthetic exercise can work. Baumgarten does not argue for *ambiguitas*, which rather obscures a meaning. He rather acknowledges that in most representations of reality, both clear and distinct as well as confused aspects are included. A representation too obscure is of little worth,[23] but the extensive richness of a plethora of confused markers can be rather valuable if it shows a degree of unity. It is a *perceptio praegnans*, a notion pregnant with meaning and life. The richness of such a representation is lively and has

---

[19] "Such a *Poet* is indeed a second *Maker*; a just PROMETHEUS under JOVE." See Shaftesbury, *Characteristicks*, 136.

[20] See Franke, "Baumgarten," 76.

[21] See Franke, *Kunst als Erkenntnis*, 18–19.

[22] Baumgarten, *Metaphysics*, §522. On clear and distinct rational representation as the "realm of light," see Baumgarten, *Metaphysics*, §518.

[23] Baumgarten, *Metaphysics*, §531.

a strong effect on both our soul and sentiments. Complexity is a powerful marker of the perfection of sensible cognition.

Cognitio sensitiva, paired with imagination, *phantasia*, and the capacity for aesthetic judgment are important aspects of the *analogon rationis*, the sensible analogue of reason. The power of imagination expresses itself in the free combination and distinction of its content. One of its highest expressions is wit. Through wit, we perceive more of the world, even though as a faculty, it lacks originality and can only reproduce—its creative spark comes through offering combinations of what is already known. But this may open up new avenues of understanding, of connecting to the world. Poetry should not, in the end, establish a new world, but enhance the one we have: and hence, "poetry is supposed to come as close as possible to sensation."[24] However, such poetry should not try to fabricate a new and different world that would only be a mere image, as imagined objects are less lively and convincing than experienced, felt sensations. Rather, imagined ideas should closely resemble "real" ones, offering a sense of inner unity (such as the Aristotelian norm of unity of place and time), which can also be used to "represent rare and uncomprehended objects so as to stir wonder and admiration."[25]

Aesthetics, the science of the lower faculties, should not just be read as a theoretical exercise of sensible cognition, but also taken seriously in its relation to poetry: it not only opens the way to perfect the lower faculties, but also offers ways to become a better artist, to become more sensible and keyed-in to the nuances of sensible cognition. In particular, aesthetic exercise shifts the focus from the constitution of aesthetic representations to our (hopefully imaginative and creative) dealings with them. The goal is the formation of the *felix aestheticus*, who, apparently, does not necessarily just spring from nature. As Baumgarten argues in the respective section of his *Aesthetics*, it also takes exercise.

In section 2, Part I of the *Aesthetics*, 'On Natural Aesthetics,' Baumgarten presents the *felix aestheticus* as someone who is born with a natural disposition for beautiful thinking that pervades their whole soul (*aesthetica naturalis connata*).[26] Such an elegant spirit[27] whose senses and sensibility are sharp and precise, but who also has a good feeling for one's inner dispositions, one's reactions to these feelings, and the way in which they change one's inner sense and position[28] is, of course, rare. But even such a character can be improved and honed. Sensibility works in tandem with the other faculties,

---

[24] Buchenau, *The Founding of Aesthetics*, 129.
[25] Buchenau, *The Founding of Aesthetics*, 130.
[26] Baumgarten, *Aesthetica/Ästhetik*, §28.
[27] Baumgarten, *Aesthetica/Ästhetik*, §29–§30.
[28] Baumgarten, *Aesthetica/Ästhetik*, §30.

rather than on its own. The artistic sensibility does not allow just any impression and feeling to pass through, but it filters them, and aptly suppresses those sensations that are too heterogeneous.

Thinking beautifully, Baumgarten assumes, in full Leibnizian fashion, is also sensitive to the history and future of its sensations—our presence and past is pregnant with the future, and we might even be able to feel that richness. The *felix aestheticus* who not only aims to feel, but also to express this richness must learn to turn imagination into (future) reality by envisaging their imaginative situation as one of the future, and orient their faculties (lower as well as higher) toward this future position. Their imaginative faculty makes this position graspable and offers them an inner direction, a drive toward more perfection in both sentiment and expression. The natural aesthetician will also have an apt temperament[29]—a drive toward what is grander, or perfect. The rich imaginative power of a *felix aestheticus* does not always drown out all other impressions, thoughts, and sensations, but collects them all and pulls them together.[30] We need *acumen* and *ingenium*[31] for this, and both can and should be trained and refined. The disposition to express (or signify) one's perceptions requires a refinement of these faculties more than if one is merely representing beautiful thoughts to themselves:[32] this means that the artist needs aesthetic training even more than a mere beautiful soul that represents the world to themselves alone. All in all, even though born with a good predisposition, a *felix aestheticus* also needs exercise as a frequent repetition of similar acts in order to achieve a fuller harmony among their faculties and the predispositions described in the preceding paragraphs.

Such frequent exercise is meant to bring spirit and character into harmony, to make the acquired and perfected acts of representation and expression more natural and flowing. Through exercise, so Baumgarten, we could learn step by step to think and express more beautifully.[33] In a section that Lessing repeats almost verbatim later,[34] Baumgarten holds that any trait, habit, or ability once acquired would need constant exercise in order to not diminish

---

[29] Baumgarten, *Aesthetica/Ästhetik*, §44. Baumgarten also seems to translate this temperament one paragraph later as a "magnanimity of the heart." See Baumgarten, *Aesthetica/Ästhetik*, §45.

[30] Baumgarten, *Aesthetica/Ästhetik*, §31.

[31] Baumgarten, *Aesthetica/Ästhetik*, §32.

[32] Baumgarten, *Aesthetica/Ästhetik*, §36–§37.

[33] Baumgarten, *Aesthetica/Ästhetik*, §47.

[34] In a letter to Mendelssohn from January 21, 1756, concerning Mendelssohn's critique of Rousseau's concept of perfection, Lessing envisages perfectibility not as an attempt to become ever better, but to stay good: we humans "did not receive perfectibility to become something better than a savage, but to not become anything worse than a savage." See Mendelssohn, JA 11, 34. See also Mendelssohn's positive reaction about this in a letter to Jacob Hermann Obereit, March 13, 1770, in Mendelssohn, JA 12.1, 217. To be sure, this idea they could also have gleaned from Leibniz.

again. Also, there are more or less adequate such exercises to keep beautiful thinking alive without deforming it.[35]

Exercises not only need to be rather uniformly performed repeatedly, but they should also be relatively similar to one another across the board. However, Baumgarten only requires a "certain" similarity.[36] They might sometimes even seem to promote something ugly, but, as long as they fit the character they train and as long as this ugliness is conscious, they might still work well enough. Baumgarten compares the established expectation of similar cases through exercise to Leibniz's image of music as unconscious counting:[37] the more intricate the exercises (of course, only by a person whose consciousness and taste matches the intricacy) and the more independence they allow for the performer, the better they work.

This could be connected to Baumgarten's considerations of aesthetic probability,[38] which again highlights the difference from Wolff: even in confused aesthetic representation there is an element of truth. Our sensible cognition already contains some of the "complete certainty" and enough knowledge to distinguish true from false objects. In the following section of the *Aesthetics* he refers to these as the truths of the *sensus communis*. To be reliable, Baumgarten cautions, such experience must be combined with sensations and "many other representations from the other lower faculties,"[39] so that we can think these contents more beautifully. Baumgarten himself, however, does not seem inclined to combine his thoughts on probability with aesthetic exercise; it took Moses Mendelssohn to develop these seeds further.

MENDELSSOHN: PREPARATION FOR THE VOCATION OF HUMANITY?

Mendelssohn always treats the conditions of beautiful thinking within the rationalist framework, but with significant nods toward more empirically inclined thinkers as Edmund Burke and David Hume,[40] and what I call his

---

[35] Baumgarten, *Aesthetica/Ästhetik*, §48.

[36] Baumgarten, *Aesthetica/Ästhetik*, §48.

[37] Baumgarten, *Aesthetica/Ästhetik*, §54.

[38] Baumgarten, *Aesthetica/Ästhetik*, Part I, Section XXIX. See, for instance, Baumgarten, *Aesthetica/Ästhetik*, §480.

[39] Baumgarten, *Aesthetica/Ästhetik*, §482.

[40] We should not completely ignore the influence of, to put it simplistically, British Empiricism on German Rationalism. In particular in ethics the fundamental differences between these two schools become visible, see Kuehn, *Scottish Common Sense,* 36–51 and Altmann, *Mendelssohns Frühschriften*, 347. Altmann holds that, all things considered, Baumgarten's influence is strongest—even though I would agree that thinkers like Mendelssohn and even Sulzer borrow heavily from Baumgarten, the influence of (Dubos and) Burke concerning the mixed sentiments, and the

"rational anthropology," that is, with clear consideration of the limits and conditions of human knowledge, and the ways in which we can improve it. The aesthetic dimension is of great importance in this regard—it is the obscuring speed and uniformity of sensible ideas that make them the ideal object for his version of exercise: it is through repetition and training that we can turn intellectual cognition back into sensible cognition in order to make it more *effective*. In a way, Mendelssohn represents a good kind of *Popularphilosoph*: a philosopher who promotes the improvement of the people through a clearer conception of their own condition. He focuses on the human being and its capacities to know and understand, within its limitations, and its ability to act on such knowledge. What are human epistemological standards, which areas of knowledge are even accessible to us, and what kind of conviction and security can we reach in each of these areas? The vocation of humanity which sits at the center of these questions ties knowledge to practicability and, ultimately, to the realization of happiness. Thus, Mendelssohn's philosophy stresses the human conditions of gaining and securing knowledge.

In this, he proves himself as a true student of Baumgarten. Mendelssohn makes it clear in his reviews of both the second part of the *Aesthetics* (1758) and Meier's *Foundations of All Beautiful Sciences* (*Anfangsgründe aller schönen Wissenschaften*, 1748–1750),[41] that he also reads Meier's work as an apt and faithful translation of Baumgarten. I will not discuss whether and to what extent he was justified to do so. However, in reference to McQuillan[42] I suspect that Mendelssohn got the basics of Baumgarten's view right: by including the concept of perfection very explicitly within aesthetics, even though Baumgarten abstained from this in the *Metaphysics*, and included this definition only in the *Reflections on Poetry* and the *Aesthetics*. This connection is important for Mendelssohn as he takes perfection to be the highest aim of humanity, which can only be achieved through the inclusion of our lower faculties. Even more, his version of aesthetic training makes it clear that the lower faculties might have some important advantages for ultimately reaching the goal of humanly possible perfection.

---

influence of Addison, Henry Homes, Alexander Gerard, and Shaftesbury to account for aesthetic enthusiasm and genius were also quite notable.

[41] Mendelssohn reviews a condensed version of the *Anfangsgründe aller schönen Wissenschaften* (1748) with a slightly expanded title: *Auszug aus den Anfangsgründen aller schönen Künste und Wissenschaften*. Even though Mendelssohn is supposed to discuss the shorter version, he constantly references the second edition of the *Anfangsgründe* from 1757 to 1759, see my commentary in Mendelssohn, *Ästhetische Schriften*, 301–302, see for Mendelssohn's reviews *Bibliothek der schönen Wissenschaften und freyen Künste*, Vol. 4.1 (1758), 438–456 in Mendelssohn, JA 4, 263–275 and *Bibliothek*, Vol. 3 (1758), 130–138, in Mendelssohn, JA 4, 196–201.

[42] Meier included the notion of perfection in his definition of aesthetics both in the *Anfangsgründe* and his translation of Baumgarten's *Metaphysics*, see McQuillan, "Baumgarten on Sensible Perfection," 52.

Mendelssohn's interest is to make rational considerations about the true, the good, and the beautiful *effective*, turn them into unconscious operations that are quicker, but also—if trained in the right way—as good and beneficial as painstaking considerations by the higher faculties. I should also note here that in one important regard Mendelssohn does not strictly follow Baumgarten, but stays within the so-called Leibnizian-Wolffian paradigm, and that is concerning the strength of the distinction between sensible and intellectual cognition: for Mendelssohn, the difference between them is indeed in degree (not, as for Baumgarten and later Kant, in kind[43]), so that, in his books, any cognition that is clear and confused is called sensible. However, he does allow for aesthetics to form a completely different philosophical discipline than logic—or any other part of the 'higher faculties,' for that matter. As I will show here, he develops a notion of "aesthetic exercise" that targets the lower, not higher, faculties, but that ultimately pulls them closer together and aims at making them pragmatically interchangeable. He remains convinced that the ultimate aim of perfection can only be reached if both lower and higher faculties are improved in their respective ways.[44] This is also why, to my mind, Mendelssohn distinguishes between an anthropological philosophy that addresses all issues in the living world, and a speculative metaphysics that concerns itself with the overall conditions for perfection (that cannot be reached within this world, but, under the assumption of immortality, might be fulfilled in another).

What sounds in Mendelssohn's philosophy like a precarious combination of rationalist metaphysics with a good portion of empirical psychology is actually not that far from what Baumgarten and other thinkers in Germany of the 1750–1770s were doing. One further and interesting example is Johann Georg Sulzer (1720–1779), a Swiss professor of Mathematics and director of the philosophical section of the Berlin Academy of Sciences, who wrote the highly influential *General Theory of the Fine Arts* (*Allgemeine Theorie der schönen Künste*, 1771–1774), with a heavy emphasis on aesthetic psychology. His views had a decisive influence on the prominence of this theory in

---

[43] See McQuillan, "Baumgarten on Sensible Perfection," 48; McQuillan, "The History of a Distinction," 182.

[44] With this, I do not claim to finally fix the nature of Mendelssohn's position. To me, it seems clear that he admired and utilized Baumgarten's aesthetics, but I also suspect that he did not quite see the radical difference—if, with McQuillan, there is indeed one—to the Leibnizian framework. Given Mendelssohn's views on human perfectibility, it seems that he indeed embraced the idea that *ultimately* all concepts will get cleared up into clear and distinct ones. On the other, he was well aware of the fundamentally limited nature of bodily notions, which then could either be given up, or must be retained. He would have embraced this concept, if just for this present world. Then, his philosophy would indeed be divided between general metaphysics of perfection and an anthropological philosophy of the whole human being.

the eighteenth century, and they certainly challenged Mendelssohn's more prevalent rationalism of the 1750s and 1760s.

In an anonymous review (attributed to Mendelssohn) of Sulzer's *Short Notion of All Sciences and other parts of learnedness, in which all parts are aptly described according to their respective content, usefulness, and perfection* (*Kurzer Begriff aller Wissenschaften Worinn die natürliche Verbindung aller Theile der Gelehrsamkeit gezeiget, auch ein jeder insbesondere nach seinem Inhalt, Nutzen und Vollkommenheit kürzlich beschrieben wird,* 1745/1759) the author cautions that Wolff had already discussed all clear and distinct notions, but insufficiently treated what is merely confused or obscure. The present work by Sulzer, so the reviewer continues, at least starts to make up for Wolff's one-sidedness in that it discusses, however briefly, the "swift judgments which result from intuitive cognition (*anschauende Erkenntnis*)."[45] Now we just needed to delve into this topic further and inquire why many activities cannot be improved by intellectual learning, but by aesthetic exercise, and why clear and distinct operations can be realized in tandem with obscure ones. This should be the topic of an "explanatory psychology" (*erklärende Psychologie*)[46]—a worthwhile topic even for the Academy of Sciences. Mendelssohn himself would have had more than enough material on this issue (some of which he brought to bear in his later prize essay). A first hint we get with his sketch "On Mastery Over the Inclinations" (*Von der Herrschaft über die Neigungen,* written around 1756/1757), the "Relation between the Beautiful and the Good" (*Verwandtschaft des Schönen und Guten*) from around the same time, as well as their more or less final form in the *Philosophical Writings* (*Philosophische Schriften,* 1761/1771) in particular the *Main Principles* (*Über die Hauptgrundsätze der schönen Künste und Wissenschaften*) and the *Rhapsody* (*Rhapsodie, oder Zusätze zu den Briefen über die Empfindungen*).

And indeed, under Sulzer's reign the academy did announce a prize topic regarding the influence of our sensations on our judgment. The winner, Johann August Eberhard (who also beat Herder),[47] stresses in his essay *General Theory of Thought and Sensation* (*Allgemeine Theorie des Denkens und Empfindens,* 1776) the importance of this topic: "The most important [subject of the] study of humanity is the human being itself, its inclinations, its passions. The most important observations that a human being could make of itself were those which it makes about its sensations and passions, about

---

[45] Mendelssohn, JA 5.1, 92. See also *Letters on Literature* [LB] 61/62 from October 11, 1759, in Mendelssohn, JA 5.1, 91–97.

[46] Mendelssohn, JA 5.1, 92.

[47] That Eberhard won might not quite be testament to his genius, but more due to the Wolffian politics of the *Academy* at that point, see Buschmann, "Philosophische Preisfragen und Preisschriften," 779–789.

their origin, their relations, their transformations, growth and decline; because on this depends all knowledge of ourselves insofar as they can be useful for our moral education, and for the guidance of our will."[48] As it so often happens, this is a perfect expression of the previous period, not necessarily for the times to come. But this somewhat backward programmatic sentence describes quite well Mendelssohn's interests in a notion of the unconscious as presented by Sulzer, according to whom not only representations or ideas, but many judgments themselves are determined by unconscious forces. Even more, Sulzer assumed that our emotions and unconscious sensations are more efficacious concerning our actions and motivations than any rational convictions.[49] Human beings can relate to and consciously evaluate their clear and distinct representations, but we cannot think away our feelings and sensations: their impression on us is stronger than any thought. Whenever thought and sensation collide, the latter takes the lead: "not a single distinct idea can move us,"[50] but confused or obscure representations can, and do. To develop a functioning moral psychology, Sulzer advises to investigate into the "traces of the presence of the depth of our soul"[51]—a somewhat circuitous way of describing the unconscious, the *fundus animae*. The clarification of its inner workings would help us to analyze inner conflicts, inexplicable inhibitions of action, emotional aversions, ambivalence, and inner contradictions within our soul. Sulzer was well aware of the Freudian slip (even though, of course, assuming somewhat different implications with it). Sulzer is not only, ever the psychologist, interested in the confused and obscure notions of sensible cognition, but also in the "particular kinds of confusions of spirit."[52] The titles of some of his essays already offer an apt description of his interests: whereas in his *Examination of the Origin of the Pleasant and Unpleasant Sentiments* (*Untersuchung über den Ursprung der angenehmen und unangenehmen Empfindungen*, 1751/52) he still tries a loose connection with Wolffian psychology, later works depart from this tendency. *Explanation of a Psychologically Paradoxical Statement: That man sometimes not only acts and judges without drive or apparent reasons, but even against pressing incentives or plausible reasons* (*Erklärung eines psychologisch paradoxen Satzes: Daß der Mensch zuweilen nicht nur ohne Antrieb und ohne sichtbare*

---

48 Eberhard, *Allgemeine Theorie*, 141.
49 Rand, "The Hidden Soul," 276 refers, of course, to Sulzer's reception of Hume's theory of association: "The mind makes its habit-driven transitions from one idea to the next so quickly that there is no time for reflexion."
50 Sulzer, *Vermischte philosophische Schriften*, Vol. 1. (*Anmerkungen über den verschiedenen Zustand*), 213.
51 Sulzer, *Vermischte philosophische Schriften*, Vol. 1. (*Anmerkungen über den verschiedenen Zustand*), 213.
52 Sulzer, *Kurzer Begriff aller Wissenschaften* (1745), §207. See Riedel, "Erkennen und Empfinden," 413.

*Gründe sondern selbst gegen dringende Antriebe und überzeugende Gründe
handelt und urtheilet*, 1759) tries to explain the all too common ways of acting
irrationally against one's better judgment; the *Notes Concerning the Various
States of the Soul when Exercising its Main Faculties, that is the faculty of
representation and the faculty of sensation* (*Anmerkungen über den verschiedenen Zustand, worinn sich die Seele bey Ausübung ihrer Hauptvermögen,
nämlich des Vermögens, sich etwas vorzustellen, und des Vermögens zu empfinden, befindet*, 1763) offer an account on human sensibility and representation, which is turned toward the unconscious in *On Consciousness and Its
Influence on our Judgements* (*Von dem Bewußtseyn und seinem Einfluße in
unsere Urtheile*, 1764). The earlier Sulzer had indeed rationalized the lower
faculties, but then he turns toward their inherent power,[53] ultimately denying
the higher faculty any persuasive force. In the end, he now decides, are we
moved "by forces that we do not know."[54] But instead to just giving in, we
should study these forces and learn how to control them. Sulzer was optimis-
tic that we could not only explain these baffling phenomena but also change
them. In this particular sense, he was a true *Aufklärer*, and his influence spans
well into the 1780s, when Karl Philipp Moritz develops the *Magazine for
Experiential Psychology*.[55] Mendelssohn was, as becomes evident in his later
discussions with Moritz during the planning of the *Magazine*, also interested
in the various forms of the unconscious and discusses its effects in his concepts of a sense for truth, conscience, and taste. How does he envisage the
mechanisms of turning anything intelligible into a sentiment? What are the
criteria for a successful transformation? What is the relation between knowing and acting, clear and distinct analysis and obscure activity?

Aesthetic training develops through exercise, habit, intuitive cognition, and
illusion.[56] He first develops these ideas in the aforementioned "On Mastery
Over the Inclinations," and later in the *Evidenzschrift* (*Abhandlung über die
Evidenz in Metaphysischen* Wissenschaften, 1763) under the headline of an
"applied [or: practical] ethics" (*ausübende Sittenlehre*).[57] Mendelssohn never
shies away from stressing the (anthropological) necessity of the lower faculties, since—again, in line with Sulzer—without them we would never act. In
the *Rhapsody* (1761/71, this aspect is already discussed in the first version)

---

[53] That he also "invented" a third state besides thinking and sensation, calling it *Betrachten*, contemplation, I discuss in Pollok, *Facetten des Menschen*, Ch. III.3.
[54] Sulzer, *Vermischte philosophische Schriften*, Vol. 1. (*Anmerkungen über den verschiedenen
Zustand*), 241.
[55] Moritz was the main editor of this journal from 1783 to 1793. Its subtitle is programmatic: "Gnothi
Sauton" ("Know Thyself"). The journal is accessible online through https://www.mze.gla.ac.uk/
[56] I discuss the intricacies of this transition in Pollok, *Facetten des Menschen*, 304–317, and, concerning Mendelssohn's concept of illusion, in Pollok, *Facetten des Menschen*, 196–203.
[57] Mendelssohn, JA 2, 323. On pleasurable sentiments, see Mendelssohn, JA 2, 328/Mendelssohn,
Philosophical Writings, 295.

he thus distinguishes between speculative and pragmatic knowledge: "Each insight that passes over into the [realm of the] capacity to desire and thus effects a desire, or aversion, is called *effective* (*wirksame*) or pragmatic *cognition*; whereas one that doesn't have a marked influence on the capacity to desire is called *ineffective*, or speculative *knowledge*."[58] If there is a conflict between different instances of effective knowledge, we become indifferent; but the moment one side has more such instances, this knowledge becomes lively and indeed leads to a respective action. This constant dynamic of balancing is the main subject of Mendelssohn's theory of sensible training. The efficacy of such *"vital forces"*[59] does not, Mendelssohn stresses, need to be consciously felt in order to lead to action. We are free if we can discern and compare the "compelling reasons for and against an action," in which some of these reasons are merely obscurely felt inclinations, others clear and distinct reasons. In an ideal case, we would combine both kinds of knowledge. However, we would not let the vital forces pass unexamined, but we would start to train our compelling reasons to feel like inclinations, in that we would learn to heighten the speed in which they pass through our mental apparatus.[60]

This encompassing idea of a pragmatic theory of association treats all four aspects as parts of the same underlying principle of quantification. The amassing of reasons deals explicitly with this sheer quantity of representations; exercise aims at the appropriate, yet only obscurely felt connection among these representations, and a fitting, responding action or an activity of some higher order (say, to play the piano)—it aims at establishing a habit. Pleasurable feelings are, as Mendelssohn puts it in the *Evidenzschrift*, the flowers put onto the hard road of doing the good, true, or beautiful thing;[61] "intuitive cognition" on its part offers images of the results that help us envisaging ourselves not only on the road toward, but already at the goal. In any instance, the process of judging, evaluating, and ratiocination is supposed to be circumvented by obscure representations.[62]

Taste in particular we have to understand as a certain interplay of the lower faculties. As Baumgarten defines genius in §8 of his *Metaphysics*, with his "usual curtness,"[63] as "such a proportion of the faculties of the soul which come together in such a way that the person who has them is especially apt for certain performances . . . in a word, a genius must be the master of his

---

[58] Mendelssohn, JA 1, 413/Mendelssohn, *Philosophical Writings*, 159 (trans. amended).

[59] Mendelssohn, JA 1, 413/Mendelssohn, *Philosophical Writings*, 159.

[60] Mendelssohn, JA 1, 414–415/Mendelssohn, *Philosophical Writings*, 160.

[61] Mendelssohn, JA 2, 328/Mendelssohn, *Philosophical Writings*, 295.

[62] Lessing develops a similar scheme: "The ideal of our actions consists in 1) a shortening of the time [it takes to comprehend all relevant information, A.P.] 2) the enhancement of our impulses (*Triebfedern*), and the exclusion of mere chance 3) the stimulation of our passions." See the paralipomena to the *Laokoon* in Lessing, *Werke* 5/2, 260.

[63] According to Mendelssohn in LB 92 from April 3, 1760. See Mendelssohn, JA 5.1, 166.

passions, his reason must within his temperament sit atop all others, so that even in the throw of passions it never loses the reigns."[64] Mendelssohn himself insists that genius in its best embodiment[65] brings "all faculties and capacities of the soul under the idea of an encompassing final goal to an extraordinary degree."[66] This idea is not merely an abstraction or reduction, but transcends them under an encompassing idea of wholeness, as a poetic idea that unifies a manifold of clear and confused representations in a pleasurable way.

In the sketch *Relation between the Beautiful and the Good* he considers the sense for truth, conscience, and taste as functions "through which we feel the true, good, and beautiful without distinct judgment."[67] All of them are equal regarding their level of clarity and are unequivocally among the lower faculties. They even work "according to similar rules" as their 'higher' counterpart. However, where the higher faculties work more exactly, but at a slower pace, "so that we can sense the middle-concepts" which justify the connections made, the lower faculties work "so fast that we cannot detain the complete order of concepts from beginning to end."[68] However, given ample time, we could ideally translate those fast obscure judgments into rational, clear, and distinct ones.[69] As it is, the impressions cannot be discerned and fully analyzed; the soul cannot oversee the mass and rapid succession of the motivational representations. "With every sensible emotion a sea of concepts streams into our soul. The soul thinks when it represents some of these concepts clearly; and it feels, once it gives itself over to the overall impression that encompasses all of them at once."[70] Ultimately, feeling and thinking both deal with such concepts or representations, but in a very different way. It may be that hearing and analyzing a tetrachord boils down to the same thing: a "sensation of certain relations."[71] However, when it is analyzed it doesn't have the same effect than when it is heard. Only in the latter case the whole human being is involved, as we feel and discern the aspects of this impression at the same time. A mere absence of such sensations, however, is never

---

[64] Mendelssohn, JA 5.1, 167–168, 170.

[65] Mendelssohn cautions that genius is not always tantamount to comprehensibility—at times, a genius seems to write "for children," at others "for angels" (Mendelssohn, JA 5.1, 558), as genius only follows its own rule. Only when their extraordinary creative ability is paired with taste can they create works that are comprehensible on a larger scale.

[66] LB 208, January 7, 1762, in JA 5.1, 484.

[67] Mendelssohn, JA 2, 182.

[68] Mendelssohn, JA 2, 183.

[69] Mendelssohn, JA 2, 184.

[70] Mendelssohn, JA 2. 183. A similar stance can be found in the *Main Principles*: "An instance of knowledge is called 'sensuous,' however, not simply if it is felt by the external senses, but in general whenever we perceive a large array of an object's features all at once without being able to separate them distinctly from each other." See Mendelssohn, JA 1, 430/Mendelssohn, *Philosophical Writings*, 172.

[71] Mendelssohn, JA 2, 184.

as intense nor motivational. Like Sulzer, Mendelssohn holds that "freedom has no immediate power over the senses."[72] This does not necessarily mean that rational considerations have no influence whatsoever, but that these considerations need an additional element to gain immediate influence—in the end, what matters is a harmonious connection of both thinking and feeling. Mendelssohn's theory of a sensualization of rational judgments is not tantamount to a mere amassment of obscure impressions, but a specific (and rationally guided) combination of representations.

The emotive force of such judgments works quantitatively: "The more good a representation of an object or a state contains, the more clearly we have insight into this good, and the less time we need to see it completely, the bigger is our desire, the more pleasurable its enjoyment."[73] Through habit, we can develop such a form of directed association—that whenever we are confronted with a certain state of affairs, we have already trained ourselves to respond with a certain set of actions.[74] The heightened efficacy of an "accumulation of compelling reasons (*Bewegungsgründe*)"[75] is used in an aesthetic training that connects pleasure and reason in one intuitive cognition. For instance, through the use of examples we can turn general reasons into such sensible intuitions. Then, a "*conscience* and a good *sense for the truth (bon-sens)*" could be defined as "a proficiency at correctly distinguishing good from evil by means of indistinct references,"[76] ultimately to be "incorporated into our temperament by constant practice, and, as it were, transformed into our sweat and blood."[77]

For Mendelssohn, there is no significant difference here between the three lower faculties of taste, moral sense, and sense for truth (*Wahrheitssinn*); all three might deal with different content but follow the same operations. However, *taste* is a somewhat special category, as it does not have a real counterpart in the higher faculties (as beauty is inherently reliant on confused perceptions), and is tied in a peculiar way to the audience, but even more to the creators of objects evoking said sentiments. This quasi-divine element might be called, in the higher faculties: contemplation (note the passive element), and in the lower: inspiration. There is a form of training for being a better connoisseur of art (oftentimes, academia is suspected of creating such an attitude); and, as we have seen, Baumgarten also assumes and develops

---

[72] Mendelssohn, JA 2, 184.

[73] Mendelssohn, JA 2, 149. From Mendelssohn's notes that prepared both the *Rhapsody* and *On Probability:* "On the Dominion over the Passions" from about 1756. Here he starts to wonder, in tandem with Sulzer, why we sometimes act against our better judgment: a competing, more obscure, but richer and faster idea overwhelmed our judgment.

[74] For references toward the British tradition, see Duncan, "*Sturm und Drang* Passions," 47–68, esp. 57 and Kuehn, "David Hume and Moses Mendelssohn," 197–220, esp. 211.

[75] Mendelssohn, JA 2, 327/Mendelssohn, *Philosophical Writings*, 305.

[76] Mendelssohn, JA 2, 325/Mendelssohn, *Philosophical Writings*, 303.

[77] Mendelssohn, JA 2, 325/Mendelssohn, *Philosophical Writings*, 303.

the regimen of such a training for the artist, or the creative *felix aestheticus*. Mendelssohn develops the methods in quite some detail, as discussed here.

We should stress again that Mendelssohn develops his theory under the general assumption of the human drive for (self-)perfection. In the end, all human activity is fundamentally oriented by the vocation of humanity: "The intellectual perfection illuminates the soul, and satisfies its original drive for cogent (*bündigen*) representations. If, however, it is to set in motion the impulses (*Triebfedern*)[78] of the capacity to desire (*Begehrungsvermögen*), then it must transform itself into a beauty; the individual concepts of the manifold must lose their tiresome distinctness so that the whole can shine forth in an all-the-more transfigured light."[79] Sensible cognition is not just what we discern with the external senses, but "whenever we perceive a large array of an object's features all at once without being able to separate them distinctly from each other."[80] This means that the attribute of effectiveness is included in the notion of beauty. And whenever we train ourselves to react more quickly, or to improve our actions, we are beautifying our decision-making process.

This also implies that the capacity or faculty of taste has no inherent strict connection to morality, other than the very general suggestion that we strive to become more perfect. For each and every representation and its connection to a motivation, a moral compass would have to be added.[81] But this is an issue that would lead us too far astray here. Nevertheless, it is important that Mendelssohn seeks to pair taste and perfection, as we see in his notes against Friedrich Justus Riedel's *On the Public* (*Ueber das Publikum*),[82] in which he argues against Riedel's idea of a merely subjective taste (even

---

[78] The notion of *Triebfeder* stems from the mechanics of clocks and refers to the spring that keeps the clock working. Sometimes *Triebfeder* is translated as "incentive," which misses the *internally driving* aspect of it; the word "spring" might evoke too mechanical associations, "drive" is too close to *Trieb*, which is the force itself, but not what sets it in motion. Here I followed Dahlstrom's translation, an "impulse" as the driving force behind an inner motion. However, I am still not completely happy with this either, as 'impulse' might also be associated with "thoughtless in-the-moment decision."

[79] Mendelssohn, JA 1, 430–431/Mendelssohn, *Philosophical Writings*, 172 (trans. amended). See also section 4 of the *Evidenzschrift*, Mendelssohn, JA 2, 316/Mendelssohn, *Philosophical Writings*, 296.

[80] Mendelssohn, JA 1, 430/Mendelssohn, *Philosophical Writings*, 172.

[81] A claim that I discuss in Pollok, *Facetten des Menschen,* 145–147 and Pollok, "Beautiful Perception," 274 in particular concerning Mendelssohn's early statement that tragedy has its own morality. In a nutshell, I take Mendelssohn to be arguing that in order to uphold the motivational effect of tragedy, the artist ought not turn it into an obviously ethical exercise, which would only engender lifeless but dutiful imitation. Instead, tragedy can make us feel how sublime human agency can be if it holds up against some wrong or evil agent or circumstance. Later we will find this stance in Schiller's work on tragedy.

[82] Mendelssohn, JA 3.1, 285–289. The exact date of this commentary is unclear, but the earliest possible year is 1768. It is even possible that Riedel sent his book to Mendelssohn for some comments, as there are some direct addresses in the text.

though Mendelssohn himself does not overlook the importance of the subjective in aesthetics). Generally, he holds, we take pleasure in whatever keeps
the natural capacity of our body and our soul, or even both at once, active
and engaged (he calls this *Übung und Beschäftigung*),[83] since that will render
them more perfect. We should hence improve our taste to that we indeed seek
those aesthetic experiences that improve us, not those that divert us too much.
"Our taste is correct," he continues, "if we judge an object to be more beautiful the more it engages, in a way that adequately supports our perfection,
our manifold capacities and powers, and the less it hinders the realization of
these capacities ad powers."[84] There is hence a taste conducive not only to our
personal well-being but also to our perfection. Such a taste cannot be merely
subjective, and it is also not bound to a particular time. We might mourn the
tastes of previous epochs. But, Mendelssohn asks, do we really want all the
concomitant conditions of those times back? Wouldn't it be better to improve
our perfection in this time, according to its present requirements and limitations? At least we would have a better, more correct taste if we did not let
it hinder our development. Whenever we allow ourselves to be distracted
by what is ugly or ridiculous (typical structures of our habits of consuming
social media come to mind), we demonstrate bad taste; instead, we should
train ourselves so that our attention toward the good and perfect survives the
inevitable crashes with the lower aspects of our reality.[85]

TASTEFUL GENIUS AND THE HUMAN
VOCATION: A PRELIMINARY RESULT

Mendelssohn's thoughts concerning the transformation of clear and distinct
ideas into effective, vital forces (the attempt at a sensualization) owe a lot to
Baumgarten's notion of aesthetic extensive clarity, in which many confused
representations are gathered together to form a particular kind of rich sensible
representation: all he did was offering a way to allow a transition of intellectual notions into sensible representations. As we have seen in Mendelssohn's
comments on Riedel, he is willing to go a long way against the subjective
dimension of taste in favor of its subservient role for the perfection of the
individual. Maybe it was Riedel's extreme position that lured Mendelssohn
into such a sharp attack on subjectivism, as many of his further considerations
of the inner workings of aesthetic appreciation are much more keenly invested
in the subjective, emotional side of art. However, I will not go in complete

[83] Mendelssohn, JA 3.1, 288.
[84] Mendelssohn, JA 3.1, 288–289.
[85] Mendelssohn, JA 3.1, 289.

opposition to Beiser's *Diotima's Children* and declare Mendelssohn a subjectivist. Rather, Mendelssohn took a serious interest in the individual's road to perfection: an interest that served him even as a main line of defense in the infamous Spinozism debate with Jacobi at the end of his life.[86] Everyone has the duty to fruitfully combine the higher and lower faculties in order to become more perfect. Maybe human beings can never fully leave the realm of the sensible[87]—the more important that our lower faculties receive an apt training. And this is the main reason why Mendelssohn hails the capacity for self-cultivation in his essay *On the question: what does to enlighten mean?* published, like Kant's enlightenment essay, in the *Berlinische Monatsschrift*. Our ability to transform sentiments into rational judgments and turn concepts of reason into sentiments[88] Mendelssohn here presents the practical dimension of Enlightenment as a form of culture. We can take this as the inheritance of Mendelssohn's aesthetics and practical philosophy for the era of Enlightenment: In a perfectly and encompassingly educated society, in which citizens have improved their thinking (what Mendelssohn here calls "enlightenment"), but have also taken care to improve their social interactions ("culture"), we finally find the perfect environment for the *felix aestheticus*.

---

[86] Atlas, "What God Does Not Possess," 26–59 is an excellent case in point for this. Regarding Beiser, see *Diotima's Children*, Ch. 7, and my reply in Pollok, "Beautiful Perception," 270–285, esp. 272–273.

[87] In his thoughts on the immortality of the soul, Mendelssohn discusses with Herder the idea whether the soul develops new 'senses,' accounting for all the yet confused notions the soul might still be experiencing. That there will be such notions must be a given, as Mendelssohn envisages the continuation of life after death not as a complete jump, but a further development toward ever higher forms of perfection. But this is another issue to discuss elsewhere, as it leads us into the most uncomfortable depths of eighteenth-century rationalism. See my introduction and the respective texts in Mendelssohn, *Phädon und einige Texte zur Bestimmung des Menschen,* vii–xlvi.

[88] A very loose translation of "*Empfindungen in Vernunftschlüsse aufzulösen, und Begriffe der Vernunft zu versinnlichen,*" Mendelssohn, JA 6.1, 162.

Chapter 9

Herder's Engagement with Baumgarten

Hans Adler

AISTHESIS AS THE POINT OF DEPARTURE

For Johann Gottfried Herder "aesthetics" is a concept that reaches far beyond the philosophical discipline of the doctrine of art. Humans designate (and know) "objects not as they have been *created*, but how they *appear* to them: not in their essence but in their form."[1] The form of truth is "beauty, this phenomenon of truth."[2] The material of truth is reality, insofar as it is accessible to humans. It is not possible for humans to circumvent the mode of sensibility, in which this material is given. All cognition which is not based on sensibility, any intuition that pretends to be without sensibility is surreptitious. In short, without *aisthesis* (sensate, sensuous, sensible perception/cognition) there is no self-knowledge and no knowledge of the world. Any separation of art and world, of artistic and philosophical aesthetics, will for Herder always be *willkürlich*, an arbitrary act of the will, in the sense that it is derived, artificial, and "scientific." But even the term "philosophical aesthetics" is itself inadequate as a description of what Herder's comprehensive concept of aesthetics intended, since "philosophy" for Herder is the systematic form of the scientific, the derived, with its tendency to an alleged independence that is alienated from reality and from life, and that Herder criticized time and again. "The wish always to establish a system is an inherent weakness of human nature. It is perhaps also inherent in its weakness to not to be capable

---

[1] Herder, "Von Baumgartens Denkart in seinen Schriften." *FHA* 1, 655.
[2] Herder, *Critical Forests. Fourth Grove*, 187. See also Herder, "Studien und Entwürfe zur Plastik," *SWS* 8, 112 and Adler, "Kritische Wälder," 443–469.

to ever establish it. Anyone who reveals this second weakness is more useful than the one who establishes three systems."[3]

For this reason it is historically more accurate with regard to Herder to speak of a "general aesthetics," whereby "general" does not mean that which is unspecific or imprecise, nor is it an *"aesthetica universalis"*[4] entirely divorced from phenomena, but instead it designates the claims that Herder attaches to the sensibility of living beings. It is on this basis that it becomes possible, via the encompassing validity claims of a general aesthetics, to establish a relationship between the philosophy of history and the concept of humanity, such that it is not the influence of the one on the other but the interweaving of the two that can be shown.

Time and again, we find in Herder's early works the *fundus animae*, the obscure ground of the soul, which Baumgarten had determined to be the complex of *"perceptiones obscurae."*[5] Where Johann Georg Sulzer had recommended in 1759 that empirical psychology concern itself with the "obscure regions of the soul,"[6] the realm has now become central for Herder. The *fundus animae* is for him the cornerstone of anthropology, "since our *strength as human beings* resides in the *grounds* of the soul"[7]—even if Herder has difficulty in specifying the measure of this strength. He thus sees the necessity in the *Fourth Critical Grove* of rendering visible the meaning of the *fundus animae* by seeing it as a compound in which there is a proportional dominance of that which is obscure. Herder's intentions can be clarified by looking at a comparison taken from physics and applied in the context of metaphysics (in another context, Rudolf Haym speaks of the "ambivalent ground" which Herder covers):[8]

> The whole ground of our soul consists of obscure ideas, the most vivid and most numerous ideas, the throng from which the soul prepares its more refined ones; these obscure ideas are the most powerful mainsprings of our life, make the greatest contribution to our happiness and unhappiness. If we imagine the integral parts of the human soul in physical terms, it possesses, if I may be permitted

[3] Herder, "Von Baumgartens Denkart," *FHA* 1, 657. "I have no greater horror than the hereditary defect of the Germans, the establishment of systems." Herder to Johann George Scheffner, Riga, October 31, 1767, in Herder, *HB* I, 92.
[4] Herder, "Kritik der '*Aesthetica*,'" *FHA* 1, 661.
[5] Baumgarten, *Metaphysics*, §511.
[6] See Sulzer's *Kurzer Begriff aller Wissenschaften und andern Theile der Gelehrsamkeit* [2nd ed., 1759] in Sulzer, *Gesammelte Schriften*, Vol. 1, 141 (§206).
[7] Herder, "Kritik der '*Aesthetica*,'" *FHA* 1, 665.
[8] Rudolf Haym, *Herder nach seinem Leben und seinen Werken*, Vol. 1, 257. Haym is referring to Herder's comments on music in the *Fourth Critical Grove*, where he speaks of the "inner physics of the mind," of "a material soul," and "the physiology of the human soul." See Herder, *Critical Forests. Fourth Grove*, 240 and 246.

to express myself in this way, a greater mass of powers specific to a sensuous being than to a pure spirit; the soul has therefore been granted to a human body [*einem Menschlichen Körper beschieden*]; it is a human being.[9]

What is noticeable compared to Wolff, Baumgarten, and Sulzer is that the *fundus animae* is no longer a *portion* of the obscure sensations, but its *"entire ground."* The coexistence of light and darkness, of *campus claritatis* and *campus obscuritatis* described by Baumgarten becomes for Herder a monistically[10] grounded succession, in which the coexistence is retained in an increasing degree of attenuation. The obscure is no longer given as that which can simply be considered in a field synchronous with light in order to give profile to that which has clarity and Enlightenment (*Aufklärung*) is no longer considered as a process whereby the obscure is reduced to a single point in this field. Herder understands the obscure as the origin, to which all human development has been and will remain bound. The process of becoming human begins there, and the development of a human being will never proceed beyond a "median position" (*Mittelstellung*), since it is in this that its "human-ness" consists. Herder uses a variety of modified organic metaphors and comparisons to present his understanding of the way a human being is bound to its origin. The conclusion that the *conditio humana* is determined by the coexistence of darkness and light is augmented by Herder to include a diachronic dimension that, in contrast to the synchronic model of the School Philosophers, does not allow the obscure to be excluded. Initially—that is *before* Herder's *Ideas for a Philosophy of the History of Humankind*— Herder attempts to do justice to this diachronic dimension with a model of speculative individual development. Conspicuous here is the stages-of-life analogy, which he frequently uses and which he himself criticizes

---

[9] Herder, *Critical Forests. Fourth Grove*, 193 (translation modified).

[10] Alongside the coincidence of sensory and the mental processes in the *fundus animae*, Panajotis Kondylis notes Herder's "adherence to the fundamental ontological heterogeneity of thought and matter." Kondylis gives tactical and pragmatic reasons in explanation of the "indecision" that Haym had already observed: "I [i.e., Kondylis] sense here the fear that the unifying approach could end up being interpreted in a materialist manner. To be quite clear, Herder does not abandon the dualist argument completely, although his main strategy in opposing materialism is the establishment of a monism whose portents are reversed, that is in the complete transformation of matter into mind." See Kondylis, *Die Aufklärung im Rahmen des neuzeitlichen Rationalismus*, 622. Kondylis's thesis of the "complete transformation of matter into mind" is scarcely defensible. Kondylis misunderstands the importance of analogy for Herder. I believe Haym to be more accurate when he writes that Herder "naturalizes [. . .] the mental by simultaneously spiritualizing the activity of nature [. . .] in order to demonstrate how A Single Thread, A Single Law, A Single Development extends from below to above." Haym, *Herder*, 1, 672. In his *Metakritik* Herder writes: "*A single* quiet thread ties the most obscure sensation to the clearest act of reason and all powers of cognition are concerned with the same works." Herder, *SWS* 21, 316. On analogy as a method in Herder, see Irmscher, "Beobachtungen zur Funktion der Analogie im Denken Herders," 64–97.

as his historical knowledge increases. In the *Fourth Critical Grove* he writes:

> Let us start somewhere in the middle and return to the time when man first became a phenomenon of our world, when he emerged from a state of having been merely a thinking and perceiving plant [*Pflanze*] and began to develop into an animal. Still he appears to be endowed with no sentiment other than the obscure idea of his ego, as obscure as only a plant can feel it [*so dunkel als sie nur eine Pflanze fühlen kann*]. Yet in this idea the concepts of the entire universe lie contained; from it, all of man's ideas evolve; all sentiments sprout forth from this vegetal feeling, just as in visible Nature the seed carries within it the tree and every leaf is an image of the whole.
>
> Now the embryo has grown into an infant who still experiences everything within himself; even that which he feels outside him lies in his interior. With every sensation he is roused as if from a profound dream to be reminded, as through a violent impetus, more vividly of an idea that his position [*seine Lage*] in the universe now occasions in him. Thus the infant's powers develop by suffering external influences, but the internal activity of development is his goal, his inward, obscure pleasure, and a constant perfection of himself.[11]

The cited passage offers more insight into Herder's position than is apparent at first glance. The history of philosophy, general aesthetics, and the concept of humanity are here, in a manner typical for Herder's early works, so intertwined that none of them can be determined without the others. The first sensation, "the obscure idea of his ego" is the certainty of Being, which is constitutive of subjectivity and which we know already from the *Essay on Being*.[12] It is the only truth of which the inner sense is aware without any mediation. "This inner feeling, then, is humanity's original and true *sensus communis*; it is acquired immediately, and without inferences and judgment."[13] This is the germ of the individuality of the species, whose core is force (*Kraft*), in other words the tendency to development.[14] It is possible to conceive of the being that represents this stage as a being without organs, as elementary and monadic. However, Herder makes reference to the biological metaphor of a plant and an animal, since the human being, as a "phenomenon

---

[11] Herder, *Critical Forests. Fourth Grove*, 194 (translation modified).
[12] Herder, *Critical Forests. Fourth Grove*, 194. "Properly speaking, there is nothing in the world of which I am immediately convinced by an inner feeling other than that I exist, that I feel. This truth alone is inwardly cognized without inferences." Herder, *Critical Forests. Fourth Grove*, 178. See Noyes, *Herder's Essay on Being* (2018).
[13] Herder, *Critical Forests. Fourth Grove*, 179.
[14] See Menke, *Kraft* (2008) and Adler, "Das neue Verhältnis von Vernunft und Sinnen: Ästhetik," (Forthcoming).

of our world," must be conceived already as a complex organic structure. The construct of an elementary subject immediately certain of its existence and considered as originary is followed by another speculatively deduced stage—the development of the plant-*like*, in which however "the concepts of the entire universe" are already contained. At this time (1769), Herder was already familiar with Leibniz, and this documents his affirmation of Leibniz's assumption that the universe is connected in its entirety, as well as the monadological assumption that in all things there is a unique form of consciousness and that these forms stand in a hierarchical relationship to one another. In his "Truths from Leibniz" Herder states: "The power of imagination of all elements is something that . . . Wolff did not want to accept, and yet the universe is an entirety, all of whose parts are intensely connected, attached in the same way to a spider's web as it is to the force that binds the planets to the sun. And so whatever befalls each individual thing in any one moment relates to the universe in such a way that the unending spirit sees therein the entire existent universe, in which only this individual alone fits, as it is."[15] Herder's reference to plants is in this way justified as an adaptation of Leibniz's assumption of a unified, harmonic, and hierarchically ordered universe.

As a gnoseological datum, the unanalyzable obscurity of the certainty of Being has a correlate in the philosophy of history in the category of force, which is the condition of possibility of development and history, whereby "force" is not cause, but a precausal tendency for causation. As such, it can only be hypothetically deduced by way of a sensually determined conclusion based on effect, on a "sensual phenomenon." The transformation of dynamic latency (force) into actuality (cause, effect) is the progression from a simple to a complex phenomenon.[16] Once it has become a "phenomenon of our world," the elementary subject becomes an embryo and then an infant, a process which leads from the nonextensive, disembodied to the bodily extended, from the state of only unmediated certainty of the self, to a mediated certainty of the other via the sensory organs and the external sense. The perception of the other requires the (developmental) constitution of space, in which each individual has its place. Assuming a place for each individual in turn determines the perspectivity of affectation of the individual. Finally, the perspectivity of affectation—what Baumgarten referred to as representation "*ex positu corporis mei in hoc universo*" ("from the position of my body in this universe")[17]—is responsible for deciding measure, number, and

---

[15] Herder, *SWS* 32, 211.
[16] See Herder's critique of School philosophy's doctrine of capacity in his *Treatise on the Origin of Language*, in Herder, *Philosophical Writings*, 86. Herder argues there that without force it is not possible for an ability to become a skill.
[17] Baumgarten, *Metaphysics*, §512.

importance in the development of forces capable of apprehending the other via the developing organs. This alone, the "internal activity of development," is the goal or purpose ("Zweck") of the human being, or to be more precise, of all individuality. The development of the individual is an end in itself in the sense that development is not a process with a result that devalues the unique sequence of events leading up to it; development is self-referential in its realization. This auto-referential quality of the developmental process has its subjective reality in *enjoyment*, "inward, obscure pleasure." "Perfection" is not the motion toward a state of being perfect, since the individual is always "perfect" at any one moment in its development, that is, at the stage it is capable of reaching at that point in its own evolvement.

This means first of all that the *historicity* of the individual gives it a historical-philosophical determination, since the individual is no longer simply the *"ens omnimode determinatum,"*[18] but that which occurs uniquely (a phenomenon). Second, it is determined by its *place*. There is only one place in which the individual can develop according to the measure of its perspectivally determined possibilities. And third, it is functionally determined by its *autarchy* ("self-sufficiency" is Herder's term). Nothing has determined the development of the individual except its inherent tendency toward development as such, which is experienced as pleasure. This means that unimpeded development is the only postulate in attaining happiness.[19] Thus, the only test to which the process of development can be put is aesthetic in nature. Here, it is only necessary to point to the fact that the amalgamation of aesthetics and the philosophy of history in Herder's concept of individuality comprises a concept of humanity as a qualitative concept that is as far as possible from any kind of sentimentality. It is also opposed in the extreme to the social and historical reality of the second half of the eighteenth century, something which cannot be further pursued here. Suffice it to say that this "individual" cannot be reduced to a subject of absolutism. It is clear that this is not an intellectual fantasy, but an articulated desire whose power over all attempts at deprivation has remained until today.

I have laid out the more general considerations concerning the context of Herder's ideas on aesthetics in his early works in order to provide an understanding of the "climate" in which his thoughts about aesthetics

---

[18] Wolff, *Philosophia rationalis sive Logica*, §74.

[19] This what J. G. Sulzer had developed in 1751 and 1752 in his voluminous inaugural lecture at the Académie Royale des Sciences et Belles Lettres in Berlin. See J. G. Sulzer, "Recherches sur l'origine des sentimens agréables et desagréables," in *Histoire de l'Académie Royale des Sciences et Belles Lettres* 1753, 57–75 (part 1); 76–100 (part 2); *Histoire de l'Académie Royale des Sciences et Belles Lettres* 1754, 350–372 (part 3); 373–390 (part 4). German translation: "Untersuchung über den Ursprung der angenehmen und unangenehmen Empfindungen." See Sulzer, *Vermischte philosophische Schriften*, 1–98.

flourish. This should at the same time foreground the fact that, for Herder, aesthetics as a doctrine of art is a special case in general, anthropological aesthetics. Thus, his investigations into Baumgarten's aesthetics may indeed be a thorough critique within the bounds of philosophical discourse, but its intention far exceeds this. The concern here is less with a fixation on philosophy as a corpus of insights, but with philosophy as a path to knowledge.

Originally, it was Herder's plan to compose a critical appraisal of Thomas Abbt, Baumgarten, and the theologian Johann David Heilmann.[20] Only the first part of this "Torso," *On Thomas Abbt's Writings*, was published.[21] The critical evaluation of Heilmann remained in the planning stages. Baumgarten, however, is the subject of a number of sketches, outlines, and drafts. This context makes it clear that the engagement with Baumgarten which interests me here is to be seen in a relationship (including a biographical one)[22] that underscores even more its exemplary generality.

A general opening section to a collection of drafts called "On Baumgarten's Way of Thinking in his Writings" (*Von Baumgarten's Denkart in seinen Schriften*) might originally have been Herder's own plan for giving shape to the segment on Baumgarten; in any event, Herder explains there his concept of "philosophizing." In philosophy he distinguishes between those who are like parrots and lack any independence of thought, and the "virtuosos,"[23] who reformulate what they find, and reconfigure it. The latter is "the lowest degree of this philosophical characteristic," of which, in that form, Herder has a very low opinion, and whose proponents he sees as the typical bearers of university office, calling them textbook writers and "philosophical tradesmen."[24] In contrast, "true philosophy" is interested in the new and seeks with conviction its own paths to truth. It requires tolerance, primarily because "wisdom is a goddess which no eye has ever beheld in its entire appearance, and perhaps no earthly eye is capable of seeing her."[25] Herder calls this power or force of independent thinking *Eigensinn*, characteristic/specificity, and regards it as the "sourdough that sets everything fermenting"[26] and keeps philosophy alive.

---

[20] See Haym, *Herder*, Vol. 1, 171–182; specifically on Baumgarten, 177–179.

[21] See Herder, *Ueber Thomas Abbts Schriften. Der Torso zu einem Denkmaal, an seinem Grabe errichtet* in *SWS* 2, 249–294. The second part was published posthumously in *SWS* 2, 295–363.

[22] With the planned "Memorandum" Herder sought closer contact to the circle of Berlin Enlightenment. See Herder to Nicolai, Riga, February 19, 1767, in Herder, *HB* 1, 70ff.

[23] See Herder's *Von Baumgarten's Denkart in seinen Schriften* (Erstes Fragment) in Herder, *Herders Lebensbild*, Vol. 1.3, 293.

[24] Herder, *Von Baumgarten's Denkart*, 293.

[25] Herder, *Von Baumgarten's Denkart*, 294.

[26] Herder, *Von Baumgarten's Denkart*, 295.

Baumgarten is a "second rate"[27] philosopher for Herder; his philosophy has shown independence in part, even if not in its entirety. To use more modern terms, it can be stated that the idea of aesthetics as a science of the lower faculties of cognition is grasped by Herder as a philosophical innovation whose elaboration has been hindered in Baumgarten's thinking by elements of tradition, not only in its objects but in its methodology. The first of these traditional elements is the Latin language, which, as a dead language, fundamentally hinders the development not only of philosophy but more essentially of *Bildung*, that is, development and self-realization. Herder repeats this same criticism time and again in various contexts.[28] Second, the "tinkering with words" (*Wortkrämerei*) arising from the nominal definitions and their syntactic linking in deductions prevents reaching conclusions about the reality of the matter at hand. Herder puts it succinctly in one of his drafts:

> Error of this wordy philosophy:
>
> a) no thought beneath the word
> b) very formal
> c) very academic, not free;
> d) prevents knowledge of the world.[29]

Here Baumgarten is implicated by Herder's critique of Wolff with the latter's "*artifice* in remaining faithful to the word," and his "arbitrary and willful definitions, repugnantly repeated demonstrations."[30] And yet this severe judgment is not a condemnation of School Philosophy as a whole. Herder is very well acquainted with its achievements, as he makes clear in his scathing critique of Justus Riedel's aesthetics. But in spite of his own criticism, there he takes sides against the "great anti-Wolffian thinkers" and "modern beauty-philosophers [*Schönphilosophen*]" to defend the rationalism of the School as a starting point. In his polemic against Riedel he writes: "If they do not even spare the first axioms of reason and desire to imbue everything—principles, method, reason itself—with a partisan spirit,

---

[27] Herder, *Von Baumgarten's Denkart*, 295. Abbt writes: "Experts know that this discipline [aesthetics] has placed Baumgarten's name among the ranks of second-rate inventors." See Abbt, "Leben und Charakter Gottlieb Alexander Baumgartens," 229.

[28] For example, see *Über die neuere deutsche Literatur*. Third collection (1767) in Herder, *FHA* 1, 374ff., 392ff. See also the second version of the first collection (1768). In Herder, *FHA* 1, 631ff.; Herder, "A Journal of My Voyage in the Year 1769," 281–284. Of immediate relevance in the present context is *Von Baumgarten's Denkart in seinen Schriften*, second Fragment. There Herder states: "His philosophy is veiled in the Latin [. . .] I would like to read it in German." See Herder, *Herders Lebensbild*, 1/3,1, 296; see also Herder, *FHA* 1, 653f.

[29] Herder, *Herders Lebensbild*, 1/3,1, 296.

[30] Herder, "Ueber Christian Wolfs [*sic*] Schriften. Erste Betrachtung," *SWS* 32, 156, 157.

then just look at what they replace it with, only to return to the principles of Wolffian philosophy."[31]

Herder labels Baumgarten's philosophy, or to be more exact, Baumgarten's poetics and aesthetics with the ambiguous term *Wolfische Poesie*, "Wolffian poetry."[32] With this he is referring to the fact that, as a philosopher, Baumgarten was a follower of Wolff, while his teacher Christgau insisted from very early on that he compose poetry in the Latin language, making *Wolfische Poesie* an amalgam of what was not possible in this form prior to Baumgarten. The immediate context suggests this interpretation. But it is also conceivable (and more likely) that Herder calls Wolff's philosophy "Poesie" in the same way he calls mathematics the dealing in fictions and Leibniz a poet of the monad poem. Thus, *Wolfische Poesie* is not necessarily to be seen as an oxymoron.[33] This would not really make sense in the given textual setting anyway. Applying *Wolfische Poesie* to the art of poetry results in Baumgarten's *Reflections on Poetry*, which Herder holds in high esteem, and which, in its capacity as the "outline of his [Baumgarten's] metapoetics,"[34] that is his *Aesthetics*,[35] Herder sees as an overarching theory.

HERDER'S CRITIQUE OF BAUMGARTEN'S *REFLECTIONS ON POETRY*

There are four reasons why Herder considers Baumgarten's *Reflections on Poetry* the "*most philosophical*"[36] explanation of poetry. First, he appreciates the derivation of poetry from psychology—that is, in the eighteenth-century understanding, the theory of cognition and knowledge (gnoseology)—or to put it in more general terms, the philosophical foundation of poetry as an anthropological datum. The clear and confused cognition has its objectification or practice in poetry, which is philosophically legitimated via

[31] Herder, *Critical Forests. Fourth Grove*, 184 and 185.
[32] Herder, *FHA* 1, 682. In Herder, *SWS* 32, 184 and Herder, *Herders Lebensbild*, 1.3, 1, 328 we find "Wolfische Philosophie." The manuscript definitely has "Poesie," that is, Ulrich Gaier's reading in *FHA* 1 is correct. See Herder, *Der handschriftliche Nachlass*, Vol. XXV, 63, fol. 2. Thanks to Heinrich Clairmont for drawing my attention to the differences between *FHA*, *SWS*, and *Herders Lebensbild*.
[33] See Herder, *FHA* 1, 1270.
[34] Herder, "A Monument to Baumgarten," 42. Herder's brief excerpt from Baumgarten's *Reflections on Poetry* (Herder, *Der handschriftliche Nachlass*, Vol. XXV, 56) refers to the first eleven sections, which he comments in keywords. In limiting himself in this way, it is possible that Herder took his cue from Baumgarten's exposition in the foreword of the *Reflections on Poetry*, where he writes: "... vsque ad §XI. in euoluenda poematis & agnatorum terminorum idea teneor."
[35] The fact that he is referring to the "*Aesthetica*" is evident from Herder's manuscript, where the "Metapoetics" is preceded by a deletion: "~~nachher~~[igen?]"
[36] Herder, "A Monument to Baumgarten," 42.

gnoseology. Second, Baumgarten lays the basic foundation for an independent poetics with his definition *"oratio sensitiva perfecta est POEMA."*[37] Next, Baumgarten has provided a prospect on aesthetics in the narrower sense. And finally, his clear determination of literature and poetry excludes "mechanically" composed poetry, for instance, that written under the guidance of compositional rules (*Regelpoetik*). Besides the criteria of simplicity and generality of the initial definition (*oratio sensitiva perfecta*) and the embedding of the partial theory (poetics) in a comprehensive theory (aesthetics) and the usefulness of the theory,[38] Herder is above all fascinated by the grounding of the poetic discourse in the psychological: "It must be possible— this was Baumgarten's great insight—to apportion to poetry its own domain in the human spirit, in the soul, and to demarcate its boundaries exactly. [. . .] We must journey into these dark regions."[39]

With this, Herder has arrived once again at the position where the *fundus animae* proves to be the point of departure for any form of cognition and practice. Poetry is an "effect" that points to "forces" of the soul, forces which are specific to humans: "In this realm [i.e., the soul] must reside powers that originally produced poetry and powers that are now in turn exercised by it [i.e., poetry]."[40]

It is the production and reception of poetry that are of interest to Herder, not its derivation from imitation, since that which is to be imitated, the "barren matter of the thing imitated in a poem,"[41] is in itself heterogeneous to poetry and to human beings. Poetry and aesthetics are both sciences of the "effects" of humans, by way of which humans come to know themselves. The Delphic saying *"gnothi seauton"* is also Herder's maxim for his journey in pursuit of the human forces at work in the obscure grounds of the soul. "This much is settled: by itself the principle *'imitate Nature!'* leads mostly to arid observations. But the principle *'pursue sensuous perfection!'* concentrates, as it were, all the rays of Nature in my soul and is nothing other than the application of the oracular injunction O mortal! Know thyself!"[42]

In this sense Baumgarten's philosophy is "human,"[43] and the "philosopher of feeling"[44] should depart from a fixed point in order to survey and fathom the "enormous ocean" of the soul's depths. This is to be done in such a way that that which is new and has hitherto been regarded as unworthy by philosophy

---

[37] Baumgarten, *Reflections on Poetry*, §9.
[38] See Adler, "Was ist ästhetische Wahrheit?" 49–66, esp. 51–53.
[39] Herder, "A Monument to Baumgarten," 43.
[40] Herder, "A Monument to Baumgarten," 43. Regarding Herder's fascination by the succinctness of Baumgarten's definition, see Irmscher, "Grundzüge der Hermeneutik Herders," 17–57, esp. 54.
[41] Herder, "A Monument to Baumgarten," 43.
[42] Herder, "A Monument to Baumgarten," 46.
[43] Herder, "A Monument to Baumgarten," 45.
[44] Herder, "A Monument to Baumgarten," 44.

is to be sought in the realm of feelings and sensations, regardless of whether a system is expected to emerge or not. What should prevail is the joy in *"examining, becoming acquainted"*[45] with the soul. What Herder is proposing here is once again an affront to the ideals of the *cognitio mathematica*, cognition based on reason and the third mental operation of conclusion. *Cognitio mathematica* is based on de-individuation for the purpose of comparing dimensions. Cognition based on reason (*Vernunft*) is knowledge of coherence which has been preceded by the intellectual (*Verstand*) comprehension of the individual, and the operation of conclusion assumes attention to the individual fact (*attentio*) followed by analysis of the individual's components (*reflexio*), which are compared to each other through judgment. Herder argues emphatically in favor of the lowest stage of cognition, the *cognitio historica*, as a foundation; of the first mental operation, attentiveness; and thus for the collection of qualitatively differing individuals as objects of knowledge.

In his critical appraisal of the *Reflections on Poetry*, Herder offers a challenge to School Philosophy in two respects. He revalues the lowest level of cognition, the *cognitio historica*. Psychology cannot be structured on the basis of alleged cognitive faculties, in order to subsume the affects and sensibilities beneath them. Instead, all factually occurring affects and sensibilities would first have to be observed and comprehended in their own right, as individual entities. "Not playing at reason, but collecting"[46] is Herder's demand on a "human science." In 1769, he then writes (referring to music): "The undiscovered country that we seek is no idle metaphysical chatter; it is an inner physics of the mind, a fertile and profitable territory in the psychology of the beautiful."[47]

This serious approach to the empirical finds its most succinct expression in psychology in Karl Philipp Moritz, whose statement: "What would our entire morality be if it were not taken from *individuis*?"[48] is yet further condensed in the *Magazine for Empirical Psychology*, where it becomes the maxim: "Facts, not moralizing prattle."[49]

But it is not only the revaluation of the individual that distinguishes Herder from School Philosophy. Systematically related to this is his revaluation of the senses as organs of the *cognitio historica*. In this respect, Herder is distancing himself not so much in the object itself, but in the traditional evaluation of the importance of the object. According to School Philosophy, sensory perception

---

[45] Herder, "A Monument to Baumgarten," 45.
[46] Herder, "Kritik der *Aesthetica*," *FHA* 1, 672.
[47] Herder, *Critical Forests. Fourth Grove*, 240.
[48] See Karl Philipp Moritz's "Vorschlag zu einem Magazin einer Erfahrungs-Seelenkunde [1782]," in Moritz, *Werke in zwei Bänden*, Vol. 1, 794.
[49] See Karl Philipp Moritz's *Vorrede zum Magazin der Erfahrungsseelenkunde* in Moritz, *Werke in zwei Bänden*, Vol. 1, 810.

is bound primarily to the presence of that which is perceived, and an actual, individual object has a stronger effect in perception than whatever is on the periphery of attention, or is reproduced. Sensory perception is therefore the mode of individuation in its presence. But since for Herder humans are "more animals than spirits,"[50] more importance is granted to sensory perception and the certainty of world and self provided by it than to understanding and reason. What Herder values in this respect in Baumgarten's *Reflections on Poetry* is its attempt to find a meta-linguistic, philosophical path to the individual phenomenon. The *Reflections on Poetry* provides for Herder the outline of a 'philosophy of acquaintance' which is opposed to the dominant trend toward deduction. But it is also not necessarily inductively oriented. He writes: "If experiences are dredged from the bottom of the soul [*attentio*], if sensations are rendered distinct [*intellectus*] to them [the readers], then these persons, who are untroubled by the question as to how these experiences can be accommodated within a system and how these individual sensations will accord with this and that object, will be satisfied by the examination of themselves and necessarily think subjective rather than objective philosophy of greater import."[51]

The cognition Herder has in mind here is not cognition of objects but cognition of cognitive processes, the meta-quality of whose *regressus in infinitum* was already countered by Herder in his "Essay on Being" by confirming the immediate certainty of Being.[52] The philosophy Herder is referring to is a subjective, but not an idiosyncratic or solipsistic philosophy, since it presupposes an objective reality and derives its object through the communication between the world and those who partake of it. But Herder sees it as *more* subjective than objective, because its object is not "all that is possible,"[53] but only that which can be experienced by human beings. This means that poetry is not primarily a part of metaphysics, but of anthropology.

HERDER'S CRITIQUE OF BAUMGARTEN'S *AESTHETICS*

When compared to his critique of the *Aesthetics*, Herder's commentary on Baumgarten's *Reflections on Poetry* is conspicuous not only because it is more extensive but also by the general tone of agreement.[54] It is not that the *Aesthetics* is completely rejected by Herder, but it is striking that, as a work that aspires to the status of a system, it meets with Herder's fundamental and

---

[50] Herder, "Kritik der *Aesthetica*," *FHA* 1, 660.
[51] Herder, "A Monument to Baumgarten," 45.
[52] "Real Being is the first absolute concept." See Herder, *Herder's "Essay on Being,"* 67.
[53] See Adler, *Die Prägnanz des Dunklen*, 13.
[54] In the fourth of the *Critical Forests*, Herder concentrates explicitly on the Prolegomena to the *Aesthetica*. See Herder, *Critical Forests. Fourth Grove*, 189.

serious objections. Here, once again, Herder's critique is closely bound to his own position, and here too, he is more interested in a programmatic critique than focusing on details, even if his own method seems at first to give the opposite impression. It was the first eleven paragraphs of the *Reflections on Poetry* that Herder concentrated on in his critical appraisal, and in the *Aesthetics* it is the first twenty-five paragraphs.[55] This text was not published during Herder's lifetime, and important new texts were only made available since Ulrich Gaier's transcription of 1985.[56]

Herder proceeds section by section, and yet from the very start any explanation and commentary is superimposed with his own elaboration and counterposition. This is a clear indication that Herder is approaching the text with a decisive sense of his own ideas on aesthetics. The differences are not only in the details, but—as the "Essay on Being" leads us to suspect—fundamental. As Ulrich Gaier has argued,[57] Herder's critique of Baumgarten's *Aesthetics* is best understood as a *radicalization of the concept of aesthetics*, a radicalization that must be seen in the context of his comprehensive critique of the School's conception of philosophy.

The project of a philosophical aesthetics meets with Herder's full approval. It is the realization of this project by Baumgarten and "those who parrot him"[58] that Herder dismisses as "in the highest degree unphilosophical."[59] This is the fundamental and most consequential criticism, since it involves the very concept of philosophy, and Herder is worth citing at length in this connection:

> If only we would learn from nature that our origins in thinking are not in playing at reason, but acquiring, and that reason is the mature age of humans, and that science completes (crowns, or deforms?) art. But that is *unphilosophical*? On the contrary, it is indeed philosophical, since, *in the end*, it derives or approaches an explanation through analysis. However, as far as an aesthetics of the author [i.e., Baumgarten] goes, it may be as true as it wants to be, is unphilosophical in the highest degree, since it presupposes from metaphysics all the philosophical concepts of aesthetics that it wants to develop. It parrots metaphysics, and extracts from it a bunch of empty, incorrect, and over-sophisticated conclusions. In its fundamental concepts it swallows camels and in the end it only catches gnats.[60]

---

[55] See Baeumler, *Das Irrationalitätsproblem*, 213.

[56] See Herder, *FHA* 1, 659–676.

[57] See Herder, *FHA* 1, 1236–1237.

[58] Herder, "Kritik der *Aesthetica*," *FHA* 1, 659.

[59] Herder, "Kritik der *Aesthetica*," *FHA* 1, 673.

[60] Herder, "Kritik der *Aesthetica*," *FHA* 1, 672–673. This refers to Matthew 23:24 where Jesus criticizes the Pharisees. In the King James version, this passage reads: "*Ye* blind guides, which strain

That is the polemic language of someone who holds a fundamentally different opinion without examining the opposing position in detail. In any event, Herder has not counted all the "gnats," and doubts have been raised as to whether he gave the *Aesthetics* in its entirety the same amount of careful attention he accorded to the *Metaphysics*. But it is precisely the detailed knowledge of the *Metaphysics* that gives Herder the certainty with which he criticizes the foundations of the aesthetics, using it as a basis for extrapolating what the system he describes *would have to* look like. The only thing is, the foundation of a philosophical aesthetics is the very thing he already found missing in Baumgarten's metaphysics: "A tower to the heavens is not possible because the earth is insufficient support for its foundation. [. . .] At the very least, it goes against humans to extend their buildings up to the heavens instead of being earth-animals."[61] In other words, there is no sense in taking as a starting point metaphysical conceptual constructions that may be possible and thinkable, when in fact the matter at hand is empirical science whose groundwork is to be undertaken in analogy to onto- and phylogenesis. Baumgarten built his aesthetics back to front by taking the foundational concepts as given without testing their reality. For Herder an aesthetics without knowledge of human beings, knowledge of the history of humanity as a species, and knowledge of cultural evolution would be without foundation. The nature, accomplishments, and significance of the senses and feelings are for Herder the regions that aesthetics in the first instance has to develop. For Herder, aesthetics becomes "philosophical" when it is capable of explaining the nature of human beings as *historical beings*. And he sees as "unphilosophical" the attempt to establish a system of aesthetics prior to any empiricism, and on the basis of defined but unverifiable concepts. Herder does not want any "gratuitous explanations," not "*qualitates occultas*" and none of the "unexplored forces"[62] that are brought to bear in the absence of real knowledge in traditional metaphysics, physics, and moral doctrines.

Aesthetics as Logic

Behind the keynote of de-metaphysicizing philosophy, there are three focal points in Herder's critique of Baumgarten's *Aesthetics*, which do not bear equal weight, but are closely related to one another. The most important criticism concerns the construction of aesthetics as a parallel to logic. Herder disapproves of, and to a certain extent he misunderstands Baumgarten's

---

at a gnat, and swallow a camel." Luther renders it in German as "Ihr verblendeten Leiter, die ihr Mücken seihet und Kamele verschluckt!"

[61] Herder, "Kritik der *Aesthetica*," *FHA* 1, 673.

[62] Herder, "Kritik der *Aesthetica*," *FHA* 1, 672.

statement that logic is the "older sister of aesthetics," and he considers this assertion an error that is connected to Baumgarten's "entire doctrinal edifice."[63] However, while Baumgarten understands logic as a science aimed at guiding the higher faculty of cognition, that is, he is thinking of the *discipline* of logic, Herder reads in this nothing of the discipline, but sees "logic" as "the higher faculty of cognition" itself. Since "there were humans before there were philosophers," and since reason characterizes the "maturity of humans," Baumgarten's assertion is false. Here Herder confuses *habitus* and *scientia*, which is disturbing, since just a little earlier he had accused Baumgarten of the very same confusion. However, this misunderstanding remains a (polemic?[64]) slip, since Herder's critique is aimed above all at logic as a discipline in a specific sense.

It is logic as organic philosophy which Herder rejects. Either the insights of knowledge are enhanced by "foreign *inspiration*,"[65] that is, by impulses, experiences that have nothing to do with the operations of cognitive processes themselves and their description. "*Common understanding*"[66] requires no rules to instruct it, neither to fulfill its functions, nor for its further development. Or else—and this is in Herder's view the claim logic makes—logic classifies and formalizes thought, and it attempts to influence thought by way of a body of rules. This is for Herder an unnecessary meta-linguistic reduplication of that which "common understanding" reliably achieves in any event. Finally, the "improvement" which logic offers to insights of knowledge is an unfounded assertion, since the question of how this improvement is to be monitored is something which cannot be answered by the logician. In order to avoid an endless *mise en abyme*, whereby a logic of logic monitors logic, and so on, Herder returns to the primary level of cognition: it is "either [. . .] common knowledge" that provides the instance monitoring logic "or nobody."[67] In short, *logica artificialis* as organic philosophy is in Herder's opinion a hybridization of philosophy, a sophistical irrelevancy.

Herder's critique is not however aimed at denying logic per se its right to exist. What he envisages is much more a logic that functions neither instrumentally nor prescriptively. Instead of prescriptively setting itself up as the cause of the forms of thought, logic should study the functions of thought.

---

[63] Herder, "Kritik der *Aesthetica*," *FHA* 1, 666.

[64] It may be that Herder made this mistake in the enthusiasm of his oppositional spirit. In terms of *value*, he writes, the higher cognitive faculties could not be more important, since the lower ones are "more practical and effective." In terms of *development*, the higher faculties follow the lower. In his critique of the latter point, Herder becomes abusive. He writes: "c) in terms of *nobility*, and this is superfluous if you *know* logic." See Herder, *FHA* 1, 666. In point c) he is thinking of logic as a philosophical discipline.

[65] Herder, "Kritik der *Aesthetica*," *FHA* 1, 666.

[66] Herder, "Kritik der *Aesthetica*," *FHA* 1, 666.

[67] Herder, "Kritik der *Aesthetica*," *FHA* 1, 662.

On the one hand this shifts the functional balance of logic from prescription to description, which cannot be equated with "theoretical logic." It no longer provides guidelines for how to think, but instead it "gathers" how thought actually proceeds. On the other hand, by describing and analyzing the "effects" of thought, logic provides a connection to the "causes" and thus the conditions of these causes, the "forces." It is immediately clear that "logic" in this sense is no longer the science of the higher faculty of cognition. Since, as "logic *of investigation*,"[68] it is assigned the task of inventory taking, analyzing, and providing an inverse genetic explanation (effect–cause–force) for "the experiences of my *thinking* self,"[69] it is in the final instance for Herder "science of the soul," a form of empirical psychology.[70] The descriptive-analytical path from the effects to the causes and from there in the direction of the forces is the path from the complex to the simple, which means that, as analysis advances, the analysandum withdraws ever more from intellectual access. Herder is claiming here nothing but the principal limitation of the human capacity for the analytic access to knowledge, while at the same time—and this is decisive—steering clear of praising stupidity, or taking recourse to the "philosophy of laziness" which Leibniz and Kant criticized. In Herder's conception, Baumgarten's dual division of logic into the higher and lower cognitive capacities becomes a *pluralization of logic*: "In the face of every force, a *logic* is possible."[71] This is Herder's *extensive* modification.

But, starting with effects, with phenomena, the closer the investigations come to the force of the soul, which itself can never be reached, the more alien logic becomes when compared to the common forms of logic. This is Herder's *intensive* modification of Baumgarten's conception. Herder is speaking here of a new kind of rationality. Measured against the logic of tradition, it is a logic of the a-logical, on the basis of which it is meaningless to speak of the "Other of Reason,"[72] since it lays claim to grasping all that is human by way of the human sensorium. The pleasure in "*examining, becoming acquainted* with a thing"[73] is intended to lead to methodically grounded certainty, even in those regions in which traditional science no longer holds sway. Now, however, object and method are no longer scientific when measured against the accepted concept of science. Herder formulates his affront

---

[68] Herder, "Kritik der *Aesthetica*," *FHA* 1, 667.

[69] Herder, "Kritik der *Aesthetica*," *FHA* 1, 667.

[70] This relationship is also at work in Herder's "Draft for the Implementation of three Academic Years for a Young Theologian," written in 1781–1782. According to this plan, philosophy is to be "a major exercise" in the first year of study. "If possible, one should begin with *psychology*, in which logic is also taught." Herder, *SWS* 30, 406. See also Herder, *SWS* 32, 38.

[71] Herder, "Kritik der *Aesthetica*," *FHA* 1, 667.

[72] It is important to emphasize this in contrast to Hartmut and Gernot Böhme's understanding of Enlightenment. See Böhme and Böhme, *Das Andere der Vernunft* (1983).

[73] Herder, "A Monument to Baumgarten," 45.

like this: "The *First* Logic should examine the *human being*, the animal that acts according to thoughts and instincts in a manner analogous to reason. It is the briefest, the most difficult, the most important, the foundation of the other one, of which we don't even possess the shadow, since the *truth* of the other one refers to it. *It has no scientific object and thus should not be scientific.*"[74]

Herder radicalizes Baumgarten's *ars analogi rationis* to the extent that he tendentially reduces that which is analogous to reason to the feeling of one's own Being, the original *aisthesis*. He calls his "*First* Logic" the "briefest" since the process takes place without mediation in the inner sense; it is the "most difficult" since it is in essence not accessible to "scientific" analysis; the "most important" since it forms the foundation of all further mental activity in the broadest sense. In this context, the expression "analogous to reason" is more a reference to Leibniz[75] than it is to Baumgarten.

But when the "*First* Logic" has an unanalyzable object and in consequence cannot itself proceed analytically, at least not in the sense of the accepted scientific concepts, then in this context "logic" can only mean the "logic of the matter at hand" and "examining and getting to know the matter at hand." The "*First* Logic" is the exploration of the *fundus animae*, the heuristics of the obscure, whose point of departure is the aesthetic act of recognizing the absolute pithiness (*Prägnanz*)[76] of Being.

Aesthetics as a discipline, however, only comes into its own in the analysis of differentiated forms of sensation. Here too, Herder insists on the independence of aesthetic discourse, "since the orders of *affect* and of *reason* are 2 extremes."[77] Analysis should mount from affect to sensation and from there to imagination, and from the imagination to consciousness, and it is only in the last of these that it is possible to speak of "actual *logic*."[78] Its field has however

---

[74] Herder, "Kritik der *Aesthetica*," *FHA* 1, 667 (emphasis added).

[75] See, for example, §65 of the preface to Leibniz's *Essais de Theodicee*: "Les sens *exterieurs*, à proprement parler, ne nous trompent point. C'est nostre *sens interne* qui nous fait souvent aller trop vite; et cela se trouve aussi dans les bêtes [. . .]: car les bêtes ont des *consecutions* de perception qui imitent le *raisonnement*, et qui se trouvent aussi dans le sens interne des hommes, lorsqu'ils n'agissent qu'en *empiriques*." See Leibniz, *Die philosophischen Schriften*. Vol. 6, 87 and Leibniz, *Theodicy*, 109 (§65). See also §5 of *Principes de la Nature et de la Grace*, where Leibniz asserts that three quarters of all human actions are to be called "empirical" in this sense. See Leibniz, *Die philosophischen Schriften*, Vol. 6, 600 and Leibniz, *Philosophical Essays*, 209 (§5) See also *Monadologie*, §26, §28ff. in Leibniz, *Die philosophischen Schriften*, Vol. 6, 611 and Leibniz, *Philosophical Essays*, 216–217ff.

[76] On the concept of "Prägnanz," see Adler, *Die Prägnanz des Dunklen*, Ch. III.A. Let it be noted here that the concept of "Prägnanz" plays an important role for Herder, who has received it from Leibniz via Baumgarten, and who is fully aware of its etymology: lat. praegnans, that is, pregnant. In this connection see Irmscher's observation: "Herder [. . .] replaces thinking (as his time understood *cogitare*) with the experience of one's own embodiment as the sole reliable origin of self- and world knowledge." Irmscher, "Grundzüge der Hermeneutik Herders," 33.

[77] Herder, "Kritik der *Aesthetica*," *FHA* 1, 667.

[78] Herder, *FHA* 1, 668.

been strongly reduced. The major portion of cognition in human cognitive processes is now accounted for by a "logic of affect"[79] and a "logic of the power of imagination"[80] that do recognize traditional logic neither methodologically as a guiding discipline, nor as a hierarchically more advanced discipline. They reassert their claim of being more appropriate for the investigation of the human. Herder has displaced if not upended the criteria for relevance.[81] Thus, his central criticism of Baumgarten's aesthetics is that it takes recourse to logic as a science, both as organon and as role model, which is heterogeneous to its object and which in meta-linguistic terms strives for an untenable compromise between the higher and lower faculties of cognition.

From this, Herder derives a second point of critique that is essentially reliant on the first one. Analogous to logic, Baumgarten had distinguished between *aesthetica naturalis* and *aesthetica artificialis* in such a manner that *aesthetica artificialis* as an instrumental complex should be in a position to have an improving influence on *aesthetica naturalis*. Herder denies this categorically. Naturally innate aesthetics[82] is according to Herder not only proper to all humans, "since they are *all born* as animals with sensation,"[83] but it also determines humans more than innate logic.

Aesthetics as "Mere Metaphor"

Herder agrees with the differentiation between natural and artificial aesthetics, and he accepts the differentiation within natural aesthetics between an innate aesthetic (*connata*) and one that has been developed through practice (*habitus*). There is a tone of approval, even if it is more severe than that of Baumgarten, in the formulations that give profile to a scientific aesthetics, that is, an *aesthetica artificialis*. Herder calls it an aesthetics in the objective sense and identifies it as "a *philosophical investigation* of sensory cognition as *its object*. And in this capacity it is the *science* that *Baumgarten* invented [. . .] and which must thus possess all the *qualities of philosophical investigation, proofs*, and *analytic method*."[84] It is a *meta*-language, "*de pulchris philosophice* cogitans scientia."[85] It "*instructs, convinces*" in "*propositions* and *clear concepts*."[86] In the *Fourth Critical Grove*, Herder becomes more

---

[79] Herder, "Fragments of a Treatise on the Ode," 44.
[80] Herder, *FHA* 1, 71 (Von der Ode). The expression is also in the critique of Baumgarten. See Herder, *FHA* 1, 663.
[81] Adler, *Die Prägnanz des Dunklen*, 59.
[82] See Adler, *Die Prägnanz des Dunklen*, 32–33.
[83] Herder, "Kritik der *Aesthetica*," *FHA* 1, 660.
[84] Herder, "Kritik der *Aesthetica*," *FHA* 1, 659.
[85] Herder, "Kritik der *Aesthetica*," *FHA* 1, 659.
[86] Herder, "Kritik der *Aesthetica*," *FHA* 1, 660. See also pg. 665 on *obiectio* 5). It should be noted expressly that the emphasis in the above three citations is Herder's own.

offensive in the delineation of his concepts, which is partly a result of the context, namely, his critique of Riedel. Here he calls artificial aesthetics "a great philosophy,"[87] which is concerned with taste, imagination, and the *analogon rationis*, "an analyzeress [*Zergliedererin, sic*] of the beautiful, wherever it is found, whether in arts and science, in bodies and souls,"[88] and whose goal is "a distinct concept of beauty."[89] And with a clear and decisive emphasis on the rationality of aesthetics as a science, he calls aesthetics "the most rigorous philosophy concerned with a worthy and very significant conspectus of the human soul and of the imitations of Nature; it is [. . .] a part, a significant part of anthropology, of the knowledge of humankind."[90]

Herder brings the most intense moment of his specification of aesthetics as a science to a close by describing the aesthetician (*aisthetikos*) and distinguishing him from the aesthete (*aisthetos*): "Our aesthetics is a science and aspires in no way to cultivate men of genius and taste; it aims only to cultivate philosophers."[91]

It is as a theoretical, scientific, non-prescriptive and non-propaedeutic discipline, but only in this respect, that Baumgarten's *Aesthetics* meets with Herder's near-complete approval. This is also the aspect not only of Baumgarten and the "Baumgarten School,"[92] but also of Christian Wolff, that Herder continuously praises, right up to his later writings. Time and again, Herder highlights the succinctness, precision, and clarity of Baumgarten's conceptual language. Mercilessly, Herder criticized those "half-thinkers,"[93] those who "are limping along with fine words,"[94] the "*almost* philosophizing"[95] of the "beauty-philosophers,"[96] the mixing-up of philosophy and poetry, of meta-language and object-language. Herder's insistence on a sharp distinction between philosophical and poetic discourse is all the more noteworthy, since he himself has repeatedly been accused of this very same confounding.

Even though the differentiation between natural and artificial aesthetics is generally acknowledged, it is striking how decisively Herder draws this line. His critique is not aimed at the delimitation of these two fields, but at the *relationship* Baumgarten asserts they have to one another. When Herder

---

[87] Herder, *Critical Forests. Fourth Grove*, 189.
[88] Herder, *Critical Forests. Fourth Grove*, 189 (translation modified).
[89] Herder, *Critical Forests. Fourth Grove*, 191.
[90] Herder, *Critical Forests. Fourth Grove*, 191.
[91] Herder, *Critical Forests. Fourth Grove*, 191.
[92] This is what Herder calls the contributors to *Briefe, die neueste Literatur betreffend* as distinct from the "Gottschedians" and the "Swiss faction Bodmer and Breitinger." See Adler, "Das neue Verhältnis von Vernunft und Sinnen: Ästhetik" (Forthcoming).
[93] Herder, "On the Cognition and Sensation of the Human Soul," *Philosophical Writings*, 227.
[94] Herder, *Critical Forests. Fourth Grove*, 193 (translation modified).
[95] Herder, *Fragmente* 1, 2nd edition. See Herder, *FHA* 1, 633.
[96] Herder, *Critical Forests. Fourth Grove*, 185.

reproaches Baumgarten's student Georg Friedrich Meier, claiming that his aesthetics is nothing but "regurgitated logic,"[97] his accusation focuses on the parallel construction of aesthetics and logic, whereas in fact the discourse of logic is heterogeneous to the objects of aesthetics. Herder rejects in principle the possibility of employing *aesthetica artificialis* as an *aesthetica emendans*, an organic aesthetics, in analogy to logic. In this respect, Baumgarten's aesthetics is a "mere metaphor"[98] in the literal sense. It is the central concept of *"cognitio"* in its specification as *"cognitio sensitiva"* that Herder objects to. It should be clear by now that, as a philosophical discourse, artificial aesthetics is indebted to the analysis of the "confused" and "obscure" to the point of clear and distinct concepts, judgments and statements. However, the object of the discourse, its "material" is not *cognitio*, not the realm of *noeta*,[99] as can be added from Baumgarten's *Reflections on Poetry*, but the realm of *aistheta*. This is what is meant when Herder censures a conception of *aesthetica theoretica* "whose material [. . .] is much too narrow, since it speaks only of *cognition*; in contrast, it is almost inessential, since *thoughts* already partake of the least aspect of the *aesthetic*; and it is at the very least unfathomable, since the beautiful already precedes in sensation."[100]

That which is figurative and metaphorical in Baumgarten's concept of aesthetics arises in Herder's view out of the transposition (*metaphorá*) of the logical paradigm onto the objects of sensory perception so that aesthetics thus conceived only takes cognizance of a fraction of the *aistheta*, and of these, only a very limited aspect. A reductionism that speaks the language of logic while at the same time claiming to grasp the entirety of *aesthesis*—this is the central focus of Herder's criticism. But there are two aspects to this reductionism. On the one hand, logic as the "formal" element reduces the quantity of all possible objects ("material") to that which is accessible, an observation that is trivial. On the other hand, it is worth considering that logic as *habitus* developed later than sensation. Sensation is the basis of logic, and thus logic as an independent discourse is a reduction of the modes of human perception. In this way, Herder's critique of reductionism in the guise of logic combines a systematic line of argument with a historical-genetic one. The systematic reduction is legitimate as long as it remains conscious of its reduction. In this respect, *"there is* indeed a logic"[101] that is not metaphorical but "actual *logic*."[102] In contrast, the illegitimate form of logic is that which

---

[97] Herder, *Critical Forests. Fourth Grove*, 192. Alexander Aichele states that Meier "removed the core" of Baumgarten's philosophy. See Aichele, *Wahrscheinliche Weltweisheit*, 346, note 74.
[98] Herder, *Critical Forests. Fourth Grove*, 210.
[99] See Baumgarten, *Reflections on Poetry*, §116.
[100] Herder, "Kritik der *Aesthetica*," *FHA* 1, 668.
[101] Herder, "Kritik der *Aesthetica*," *FHA* 1, 667.
[102] Herder, "Kritik der *Aesthetica*," *FHA* 1, 668.

denies its origin and equates "the *scholar's* knowledge with *the human being's knowledge*,"[103] while proud of the artifact of scientific logic that it has constituted through its "*own* work."

The main reason why artificial aesthetics cannot "improve" natural aesthetics is that the process of evolution (in the sense Herder understood it) is irreversible. In more general terms, it can be said that philosophical reflection about sensory perception is a *genus novum* that is heterogeneous to *genus vetus* or natural aesthetics.[104] For Herder, natural and artificial aesthetics hold the same relationship as object and description, facts and diagnosis, but not a relationship of patient and therapy. As Herder emphasizes, this observation applies to general aesthetics, but not to theories specific to individual media or senses. Here, Herder writes that aesthetics "acquaints us with faculties of the soul with which logic did not acquaint us. In individual theories its observations may subsequently give rise to practical rules of thumb." However, this is neither "the primary aim of aesthetics," nor does it seek "to provide a new beautiful nature or a feeling that we did not have before."[105]

For systematic reasons, Herder does not allow for any emending influence of *aesthetica artificialis* on *aesthetica naturalis connata*. These reasons are guaranteed by the philosophy of history, in that effects cannot act as causes for modifying their own causes. Causal connections are thought as an irreversible historical process, and historically subsequent events are evidence of earlier ones, but they are not their yardstick.

It goes without saying that the meta-linguistic reduction of "confused" sensory experience to yield clear and distinct concepts is achieved by abstracting from the "material" of the beautiful in a way that it becomes discursively adequate. The abstraction accomplished by artificial aesthetics is such that the "material" of the beautiful gives way to the "formal," whose purpose is truth, represented in clear and distinct concepts. The concern of artificial aesthetics is not wholeness but "the elements of beauty."[106] These do not function as beautiful in themselves, but as elements of true statements about beauty. Herder grounds this view in the distinction between object-language and meta-language, but also in Leibniz's recognition that clear and distinct human cognition is *always* partial cognition, while confused cognition always tends toward infinity and totality. Hansjörg Salmony's "impression of incompleteness, indeed contradiction"[107] in the aesthetics of the young Herder is the result of his ignorance of its gnoseological implications, but also of his

---

[103] Herder, "Kritik der *Aesthetica*," *FHA* 1, 668.
[104] See Herder, "Kritik der *Aesthetica*," *FHA* 1, 661.
[105] The previous three citations are from Herder, *Critical Forests. Fourth Grove*, 192.
[106] Herder, *Critical Forests. Fourth Grove*, 190.
[107] Salmony, *Die Philosophie des jungen Herder*, 160.

disregard for the need to think of artificial and natural aesthetics in simultaneous mutual competition.[108]

Herder understands this simultaneous competition as an inherently risky relationship to the extent that artificial aesthetics suppresses natural aesthetics, or, as he states on the basis of his own position, sensation is weakened by reflection.[109] In Herder's view, however, this does not only apply to the artist in the moment of production, but this weakness is also a characteristic of the situation of art and literature in the eighteenth century. This is the result of a long development which Herder understands in terms of his philosophy of history, and which he attempts to render intelligible phylogenetically as a weakening of natural aesthetics through scientific reflection. Aesthetics has its own history, which is irreversible and thus not open to critique, and which is so intimately entwined in human history that it takes on the role of a guiding principle for development. This means that categories of general aesthetics provide structural elements for Herder's philosophy of history. The tension between natural and artificial aesthetics within the modern artist's concrete process of creation is augmented by a tension between these two within the history of humanity, and it is this that provides the conditions for the "current" tension. The immediate result is what Herder sees as a perilous dominance of artificial aesthetics in the so-called philosophical age of Europe.

The issues hinted at here make it clearer why Herder so adamantly holds his position on the relationship of *aesthetica naturalis* and *artificialis*. The dominance of philosophical discourse is a loss that is not compensated by new knowledge; it is a loss that uses an illegitimate transgression (*metaphorá*) of the limits of a discourse in order to mask the suppression of sensuality. What is illegitimate here is not the development of scientific discourse; on the contrary, Herder has an impressive list of desiderata for sciences that are yet to be established! What is illegitimate is the "rationalist imperialism" whose gains Herder counts against the loss of any specifically human, holistically oriented dispositions. In this respect, what Leibniz wrote about the monads also applies to Herder's concept of humanity: they possess different

---

[108] In addition, Salmony does not comprehend Herder's distinction between object-language and meta-language. The beautiful as object of sensation and sensation of the beautiful as object of analysis are two qualitatively distinct dimensions or aspects of a matter. The reason Salmony does not come to grips with this problem is, among other things, his vague conception of the gnoseology of Herder's time. See Salmony, *Die Philosophie des jungen Herder*, 145ff., especially 151 and 155–160.

[109] See, for example, Herder, *FHA* 1, 661 and 664: "I thought that the *metaphysical knowledge* of the beautiful weakened sensation"; "The greater the poet [. . .], the less he vitiated himself by working with distinct, debilitating, wearying rules; and when the greatest of all was inspired by the Muse, he was conscious of no law." Herder, *Critical Forests. Fourth Grove*, 187.

limits in terms of their clear and distinct perceptions, however "elles vont toutes confusement à l'infini, au tout."[110]

Aesthetics as "Mere Theories of the *Sciences* of the Arts"

The two points of critique outlined above concern first the structural foundation of Baumgarten's *Aesthetics*, and second the relationship between natural disposition and scientific discourse. Herder's third point of critique is aimed at the extension of the *Aesthetics*. He writes: "*His* [i.e., Baumgarten's] *Aesthetics*, and by necessity the works of those who parrot him, are mere *theories* of the *sciences* of the arts, of *rhetoric* and *poetry*; *all the fine arts* are missing, and with them the most objective of aesthetics."[111]

This is a reference to Baumgarten's first "synonym"—*theoria liberalium artium*—for the term *aesthetica* in the first section of his *Aesthetics*.[112] In Herder's opinion it does not serve well in the context of modern aesthetics to continue to speak of the *septem artes liberales*. It would be advisable instead to take as the starting point that which is understood as the fine arts (*beaux arts*) and the sciences of the arts. For this reason, section 1 of the *Aesthetics* should refer to (if at all) *theoria liberalium artium et scientiarum*, or to be more precise and more in keeping with the intentions of a "*general* aesthetics": *theoria summa artium et scientiarum liberalium*.[113] This is *Herder's* suggestion, and it is important to bear in mind that his concept of *ars* differs from Baumgarten's in that Herder separates it strictly from *scientia*. Herder escalates this difference to the point where he claims that Baumgarten's *Aesthetica* has nothing to do with the fine arts, but only with the sciences of the arts. However, in §39–§41 of the *Reflections on Poetry*, Baumgarten deals with painting, and in the *Aesthetics* Baumgarten himself discusses the hypothetical objection that his aesthetics are nothing but rhetoric and poetics, that is the doctrine of the liberal arts. Here he claims a broader field for aesthetics, but at the same time he derives criteria from rhetoric and poetics which he sees as transferable onto the arts.[114] This is the reason for Herder's curt

---

[110] Leibniz, *Philosophical Essays*, 220 (§60).
[111] Herder, "Kritik der *Aesthetica*," *FHA* 1, 659.
[112] See my comments concerning the expressions in parentheses in the first paragraph of the *Aesthetica* in Adler, *Die Prägnanz des Dunklen*, 30.
[113] In the *Fourth Critical Grove*, Herder glosses over this when he states that Baumgarten "calls his work a *Theory of the Fine Arts and Sciences of the Arts*" (Herder, *SWS* 4, 22). The reason may lie in Herder's desire for what he saw as a broad-stroke "simplification" in his polemic against Riedel. For Herder, any convergence of *ars* and *scientia* is out of the question. On *ars–scientia*, see Jäger, *Kommentierende Einführung in Baumgartens Aesthetica*, 25–27. On *theoria liberalium artium*, see Jäger, *Kommentierende Einführung in Baumgartens Aesthetica*, 8–10.
[114] See Baumgarten, *Aesthetica/Ästhetik*, section 5, obiectio 2.

objection that Baumgarten's aesthetics are nothing but rhetoric and poetics.[115] But the claim that aesthetics is too broadly conceived, which Baumgarten makes in another hypothetical objection,[116] is vehemently contradicted by Herder. A "true aesthetics"[117] would encompass "arts and science within itself," and thus Baumgarten's *Aesthetics* is much too narrowly conceived. But a "true aesthetics" would also be more general. It would not examine that which is specifically beautiful only in the individual arts, but the beautiful in so far as it belongs to all the arts and sciences together, and the sensation of the beautiful. In short, Herder criticizes the rhetorical-poetological design of the *Aesthetics* as well as its theoretical narrowness. These are both connected. The limitation of its object leads to a narrowness and narrow-mindedness of its perspective, and the narrow perspective means that certain objects are not even taken account of. In Herder's opinion, Baumgarten's aesthetics finds itself in a kind of limbo, since it lacks a firm foundation and an adequate conclusion. In its given form, Herder sees only a provisional appraisal comprising various theories but lacking a "*theoria summa*"[118] that encompasses all individual theories of the arts. This is what Herder understands by a "*general aesthetics*,"[119] which he also calls "the most objective aesthetics."[120]

Surveying Herder's critique of Baumgarten, there are two questions that become unavoidable, but that can be resolved with a single answer. The first question pertains to the contradiction between Herder's praise for Baumgarten and his at times devastating critique of his aesthetics. How does the claim that Baumgarten can be called "the father of a School of genuine critique"[121] and "the real *Aristotle* of our time"[122] fit together with his censure of the *Aesthetics* for its lack of a foundation and a conclusion, as well as for the fundamental errors in the structure it employs? Is the critique of the aesthetics only a matter of detail which bears no weight in the overall appraisal of Baumgarten's philosophy? If this were the case, then Herder would have to be in agreement with Baumgarten's metaphysics. However, this is not the case. Instead, it is

---

[115] See Herder, *FHA* 1, 665. The position of the *Aesthetica* within the tradition of rhetoric has been discussed on many occasions in the commentaries, and I will not repeat their positions here. See my discussion of the literature in Adler, *Die Prägnanz des Dunklen*, 28f., note 199.

[116] See Baumgarten, *Aesthetica/Ästhetik* section 5, obiectio 1.

[117] Herder, "Kritik der *Aesthetica*," *FHA* 1, 665.

[118] Herder, "Kritik der *Aesthetica*," *FHA* 1, 660.

[119] Herder, "Kritik der *Aesthetica*," *FHA* 1, 660.

[120] Herder, "Kritik der *Aesthetica*," *FHA* 1, 659. In his commentary, Gaier has a different interpretation of this statement, claiming that Herder makes room for "more objective and more subjective aesthetics, according to the medium in which the beautiful is produced" (Herder, *FHA* 1, 1247). I agree with this, but it does not explain the superlative. The "most objective aesthetics" is not that of a more or less "objective" art, but the most general theory, the theory most suitable for covering the entire field of objects of sensory perception (*aisthesis*).

[121] *Briefe zu Beförderung der Humanität*, eighth collection in Herder, *SWS* 18, 126.

[122] Herder, "Fragments of a Treatise on the Ode," 50.

on the basis of his critique of metaphysics that his critique of the aesthetics is established. In other words, Herder's critique of Baumgarten's aesthetics is a fundamental critique that takes issue with the aesthetics in its own right, but moves beyond it in order to engage with School Philosophy in general, helping provide a newly defined role for aesthetics and from there arriving at a philosophy that is framed by what is humanly possible. Just because a philosophy that extrapolates and systematizes all that is possible (*omne possibile*) in keeping with the meaning of the concepts [*wortgerecht*], it does not mean that, by virtue of its internal consistency alone, it does justice to the matter itself [*sachgerecht*]. Philosophy only does justice to the matter itself if it secures its empirical foundation, not only with respect to the field of philosophy's object, but also with respect to the one who philosophizes. Aesthetics receives special attention from Herder because any ratiocination issues from inner sensations of Being, and all forms of external sensation provide the basis for perceiving the world. It is Herder's intention to move *aisthesis* from the periphery to the center and make it the starting point of scientific concern. His initial aim is to "become acquainted with" and to "collect" the foundational forms of sensory perception. This gives psychology and physiology a new weight as empirical sciences, and, since the types and forms of perception have a history, they become objects of central interest not as timeless, constant faculties, but as historically developing and changing. This is not Herder's plea for the subjective arbitrariness of an 'emotional philosophy,' but his attempt to gain philosophical and—*cum grano salis*—scientific mastery over a region of human qualities and conditions of perception and cognition that has hitherto been regarded by philosophy with mistrust. It is apposite to Herder's haptics when, taking account of the constitution of the self in experiences of Being, Hans Dietrich Irmscher speaks of Herder's design for an "*ontology* based on the sense of feeling."[123] In Herder's view, aesthetics should become a foundational philosophy sui generis. It should approach "objects" on the basis of the historical and sensory determinations of the subject of cognition and the composition of the "objects" available to it, without leaning on the crutch of an inadequate master discourse.

Thus, Herder sees Baumgarten's achievement as having established the lower faculties as objects of philosophical concern. But what is important is not the manner in which he set about doing this. It is here that Herder focuses his acute criticism. Of importance is the fact *that* Baumgarten devoted his philosophical attention to sensuality, thereby helping this field attain philosophical respectability. Herder regards Baumgarten's "scientific framework"[124] as the auspicious dawn of a philosophy that is adequate to

---

[123] Irmscher, "Herder," 528.
[124] Herder, *Critical Forests. Fourth Grove*, 187.

the whole human being. This is also borne out by the fact that Baumgarten was "the first to develop philosophical concepts of beauty,"[125] that he leads the way "into the profoundest secrets of our soul," and that he teaches us "to make a psychological discovery with each rule of beauty."[126] For theoretical and pragmatic reasons, and in spite of all his reservations and his fundamental criticisms, Herder is forced into a laborious engagement with Baumgarten's sophisticated paradigm of School Philosophy.

From a *theoretical* perspective, Herder sees Baumgarten's *Aesthetics* as the philosophical position that develops the problem of sensuality most clearly and comprehensively. Over and above the various pragmatic and personal aversions Herder held for Riedel and Klotz, they both represent a philosophy of "lazy hypotheses"[127] and bad reductionism, and thus they fall victim to Herder's sharp criticism and his derision. Baumgarten presented an approach that needs to be overcome, while Herder sees Riedel's position as obsolete from the very beginning. This overcoming of aesthetics thus aims at its foundations, beginning with metaphysics, and it radicalizes Leibniz's critique of Descartes's nominalist determination of truth.[128] In the first instance, Herder's thoughts on general aesthetics are neither "aesthetics of art,"[129] nor are they a "philosophy of art,"[130] but fundamental considerations concerning ontology and gnoseology from an anthropological perspective.

From a *pragmatic* point of view, Herder is interested in Baumgarten in order to obtain access to the circle of intellectuals involved in the *Letters on the Most Recent Literature*. Penniless and ambitious, Herder is in pursuit of not just any public, but the public that is defined by Nicolai, Lessing, and Mendelssohn, that is the "Baumgarten School."

The second question that arises when perusing the critique of Baumgarten concerns Herder's knowledge of the *Aesthetics*. It is striking that his excerpt from the *Reflections on Poetry* comprises only the first eleven paragraphs, that is, *grosso modo*, little more than the exposition with a definition of the poem. In Herder's notes, the critique of the *Aesthetics* extends to section 25,

---

[125] Herder, "Entwurf der Anwendung dreier Akademischer Jahre für einen jungen Theologen," *SWS* 30, 407.

[126] Herder, "A Monument to Baumgarten," 45.

[127] In connection with his critique of occasional causes, Leibniz speaks in the Preface to his *New Essays* of a "Hypothese faineante [qui . . .] detruiroit egalement nostre Philosophie qui cherche des raisons, et la divine sagesse qui les fournit." See Leibniz, *Die philosophischen Schriften*, Vol. 5, 59. See also Leibniz, *New Essays, on Human Understanding*, 66. On the personal motivation behind Herder's critique of Riedel, see Wilhelm, *Friedrich Justus Riedel und die Ästhetik der Aufklärung*, 121–123. Regarding Riedel's position, see Seiler, *Die Stellung Friedrich Just(us) Riedels in der Literaturgeschichte und sein Einfluß auf die Literaturtheorie unter besonderer Berücksichtigung seiner Ästhetik* (1998).

[128] See Adler, *Die Prägnanz des Dunklen*, 5.

[129] Salmony, *Die Philosophie des jungen Herder*, 148.

[130] Gulyga, *Johann Gottfried Herder*, 98.

and in the *Fourth Critical Grove*, it is explicitly confined to the prolegomena of the *Aesthetics*, that is to the section dealing with the definition of aesthetics, hypothetical criticism, and the outline of the discipline. It is unclear whether Herder worked his way through the entirety of the *Aesthetics*, and it is also not certain if his critique takes account of Baumgarten's various concepts of truth (*veritas aesthetica, aestheticologica*, etc.). Without being able to offer an answer, the question of Herder's habits in dealing with the literature may be posed, particularly since this is not an isolated case. Is it possible that his stupendous knowledge rests upon a precise knowledge of the texts in their entirety? Or is it not perhaps the case that—at least on occasion—he was satisfied to use the exposition of the text as *dispositio* for the purpose of an independent *inventio* and *elocutio*? If this is indeed the case—and this would have to be subjected to scrutiny in individual instances—it would mean that, in dealing with the literature, Herder proceeds in analogy to his interest in the seed or the sprout [*Keim*], in the 'pregnancy' of exposition of an idea that is to be developed via "independent" or "self-thinking" [*Selbstdenken*]. In this sense, caution is advised when claiming that Herder read everything in its entirety. It is however also justified in this sense to note that Herder's polemic uses the arguments he encounters as a vehicle for refining his own ideas.[131]

Both questions—that concerning Herder's "contradictory" evaluation of Baumgarten and that concerning his knowledge of Baumgarten's texts on aesthetics—may be answered with reference to the perspective Herder adopts in his writings. Herder's critique of aesthetics is a critique of science and philosophy which takes as its point of departure the critique of aesthetics as a discipline and the discussion surrounding its position in philosophy. In the *Journal of My Voyage* he writes: "But in particular I want to resist the German disease of deriving everything, whether it really follows or not, from purely verbal explanations."[132] The intended point of departure is the certainty of aisthesis, formulated in analogy to Descartes's "Cogito, ergo sum": 'Sentio, ergo sum.'—"I have a sensation of myself! I am!" [*Ich fühle mich! Ich bin!*][133] The certainty of Being—Gaier speaks of a "bodily *a priori*,"[134] probably making reference to Karl Otto Apel—is developed on the basis of internal and external feeling and is differentiated by way of reflection and abstraction: "the first ontology of sensation: of Being, Being-beside-ourselves [*Außer uns seyn*], space, time, force [*Kraft*], body, etc."[135]

---

[131] This is seen frequently in Salmony, *Die Philosophie des jungen Herder*.

[132] Herder, "Journal meiner Reise im Jahr 1769," *SWS* 4, 383.

[133] Herder, "Zum Sinn des Gefühls," *SWS* 8, 96.

[134] Gaier, "Der frühe Herder," *FHA* 1, 817. See Apel, "Das Leibapriori der Erkenntnis," 152–172.

[135] Herder, "Philosophie des Wahren, Guten und Schönen aus dem Sinne des Gefühls," *SWS* 8, 104.

Herder's promise, however, is that the foundation and the endpoint are one and the same. Originary *aisthesis* and highest abstraction are the starting and finishing points of philosophy combined into one. In other words, Herder's general aesthetics is not part of philosophy in the sense of a discipline, but the onto-gnoseological condition for philosophizing: "The apex of philosophy is at once the beginning and the well-known" [*das Erste und bekannt*].[136]

On first sight, this is certainly confusing. When, as a holist, Herder reduces philosophy to sensuality, is this a simple reversal of the intellectual reductionism of School Philosophy? But Herder continues the previously cited passage: "And so everything else must likewise depart from and return to sensation. What a splendid undertaking, to thus reduce all concepts to it in this way! To sensation and the senses."[137]

Translated by John K. Noyes

---

[136] Herder, "Zum Sinn des Gefühls," *SWS* 8, 96.
[137] Herder, "Zum Sinn des Gefühls," *SWS* 8, 96.

Chapter 10

The Majesty of Cognition

The Sublime in Baumgarten, Mendelssohn, and Kant

Robert R. Clewis

At first glance, it might seem odd to look to Alexander Baumgarten for thoughts on the sublime. After all, his contributions to aesthetic theory, associated with his views of beauty as the perfection of sensible cognition, appear to leave little room for it. But in fact a significant portion of the *Aesthetics* (1750) is devoted to the sublime. It is not just tucked away in this influential work, but explicitly discussed in numerous sections on "aesthetic magnitude" (Sections 15–26; paragraphs §177–§422). At almost 250 paragraphs, it is in fact his book's longest chapter.[1]

Since the author of the *Aesthetics* counts as one of the modern founders of the discipline called aesthetics, it is surprising that Baumgarten's theory of the sublime has been largely overlooked. After all, the sublime has been one of the core concepts in aesthetics since at least the 1690s (for instance in the work of John Dennis), which is itself almost a century and a half after numerous Latin and Greek editions of Longinus's *On the Sublime* appeared in the middle of the 1500s.[2] Nevertheless, Baumgarten's view of the sublime has been far less examined than that of Mendelssohn and, needless to say, of Kant.

Nearly all of the histories of the sublime either skip over Baumgarten's theory or mention him in passing as one of the founders of "aesthetics," without any substantial discussion of his theory of the sublime, aesthetic dignity, or aesthetic majesty. Dagmar Mirbach, who translated the *Aesthetics*

---

[1] The passages on the sublime range from Section 15 on "aesthetic magnitude" starting at §177, through Section 26, the "greatest magnanimity in aesthetics" ending with §422. Section 21 is given the title, "The Sublime Way of Thinking."

[2] On this history, see the texts collected in *The Sublime Reader* as well as my Introduction to it.

into German, observes that the chapter devoted to *magnitudo aesthetica* (§177–§422) is "hitherto almost unread."[3] Since nearly all of the histories of the sublime overlook Baumgarten on the sublime and how he fits into that history,[4] there is a need to understand his contribution better. The present chapter begins to fill in this gap.

According to a narrative of early modern aesthetics that is starting to become more prevalent, Baumgarten plays a more central role. Within this perspective, the practical and ethical aspects of his aesthetics receive more attention.[5] In keeping with this realignment, I will also explore the connection between the sublime and the moral and practical aspects of his thought, especially his views on freedom and the moral sublime. I will also consider how this sublime-moral relation is handled by Mendelssohn and Kant and thereby observe to what extent they are influenced by or instead depart from Baumgarten's account.

This naturally raises the issue of what is meant by the "sublime." There is no final, once-and-for-all definition of the term, but instead there are various historically situated answers, instantiated in different particular cultures and times. Still, let it be (provisionally) submitted that the experience of the sublime is paradigmatically a "mixed" yet pleasing aesthetic experience in response to an object or event that exhibits striking vastness or power. (This leaves open whether or not this greatness and/or power has moral qualities.) The experience of the sublime, then, is "mixed," which means that the experience has both negative and positive elements or aspects, even if on the whole it is gratifying and even exhilarating: people find the experience pleasant overall and want to continue having it. So, the experience of the sublime is an intense feeling of uplift and elevation in response to the powerful or vast object, which otherwise can be experienced as menacing or threatening— capable of eliciting fright or a sense of being overwhelmed.[6] While undergoing the overall positive experience, a person thinks they are safe (whether they actually are is another matter); otherwise they would simply feel a mode

---

[3] Mirbach, *"Magnitudo aesthetica,"* 103. Her article, based on the Introduction to her 2007 German translation of the *Aesthetics*, is one of the few scholarly (philosophical) studies devoted to Baumgarten on aesthetic magnitude or the sublime. For a historically and theologically oriented overview mentioning Baumgarten and the sublime, see Fritz, *Vom Erhabenen*, 230–283. Guyer briefly discusses Baumgarten on aesthetic magnitude in Guyer, *History of Modern Aesthetics*, vol. 1, 333–335, as does Beiser, *Diotima's Children*, 122.

[4] Neither Philip Shaw nor James Kirwan's overviews of the topic, *The Sublime* and *Sublimity*, respectively, discuss Baumgarten on the sublime, nor does Timothy Costelloe's collected edited volume of essays on the sublime. And while one would expect a book entitled *The Sublime from Longinus to Kant* to cover the sublime in Baumgarten, no such discussion is to be found in this somewhat uneven book by Robert Doran.

[5] For example, see Mirbach, "Aesthetic Greatness"; Grote, *Emergence of Modern Aesthetic Theory*, and Buchenau, *The Founding of Aesthetics*.

[6] Clewis, "Towards a Theory of the Sublime and Aesthetic Awe," 346.

of *fear*, plain and simple. The objects eliciting the experience need not be visual (though that is perhaps the easiest case of perception to discuss) but can be construed to include music or poetry. The elicitors can be conceptual too: grand ideas and mind-boggling physical theories, not just what is perceived as vast or powerful, can evoke the response.

By comparing Baumgarten's account with that of Mendelssohn and Kant and some post-Kantians, we can see which elements are distinctive or original in Baumgarten. Rather than attempting to give a comprehensive overview of the account of the sublime in these thinkers, I will center my discussion on two main themes, the subject-object relation and the moral sublime.[7] In presenting their thoughts about the sublime, I shall address how their accounts handle the relation between seeing the sublime as a feeling or sensible cognition, on the one hand, and the quality or feature of an object, on the other. I will also address whether they think there is something called a moral sublime, and if so, describe what that is.

BAUMGARTEN

Since the sublime is a "majestic" cognition, we would do well to begin by reviewing Baumgarten's conception of aesthetics as "the science of sensible cognition."[8] Sensible cognition is clear and confused, rather than (like intellectual cognition) clear and distinct. According to Baumgarten's (1735) *Reflections on Poetry*, an idea is *clear* in that it allows us to recognize what thing is being represented, because it contains representations of those characteristics of the thing that allow us to distinguish it from other things. An idea is *confused*, as opposed to distinct, in that those distinguishing characteristics are not made explicit, so that the thing represented cannot immediately be classified according to a definition.[9] To put it more simply, when we have a *clear* idea of a thing, we know what a thing is and can identify it. But when we have a clear cognition that is also *distinct*, we know not only what the thing is but also why it is that way or what makes it what it is.

Beauty, Baumgarten claims, arises from the presence of six qualities or criteria of sensory cognition: richness/abundance/wealth (*ubertas*), magnitude/greatness (*magnitudo*), truth (*veritas*), light or clarity (*lux*), certainty

---

[7] While there will be some reference to their other works, my focus will be on Baumgarten's *Aesthetics*; Mendelssohn's "On the Sublime and Naïve in the Fine Sciences," and Kant's *Critique of the Power of Judgment*.

[8] Baumgarten, *Aesthetica/Ästhetik*, §1. Unless stated otherwise, translations of Baumgarten are my own.

[9] Grote, *Emergence of Modern Aesthetic Theory*, 73. Baumgarten, *Reflections on Poetry*, §13–§14.

(*certitudo*), and life (*vita*). He examines these six criteria (though the sections on life were never written) under the heading "heuristics" in the *Aesthetics*. Magnitude is discussed second and, as mentioned, at the greatest length. The six qualities are mentioned at §22:

> The richness, magnitude, truth, clarity, certainty, and life of cognition constitute the perfection of every cognition, insofar as they are in a representation and in agreement with each other; for example, richness and magnitude in agreement with clarity, truth and clarity with certainty, and all of the rest in agreement with life, and insofar as the various different parts of cognition agree with it (§18–§20), they constitute the perfection of every cognition (*Metaphysics* §669, §94). As phenomena they constitute the beauty of the sensible (§14), namely a universal beauty (§17), especially of the things and the thoughts (§18), in which please [*iuvat*]: copiousness [*copia*], nobility [*nobilitas*], and the certain light of the moving truth.[10]

The concept of the "sublime" in Baumgarten can be broadly construed to include his references to aesthetic magnitude/greatness (*magnitudo*), aesthetic dignity or nobility, and aesthetic majesty. Although at some level there may be minor differences between the concepts of the aesthetic great, dignified, noble, majestic, and sublime, he appears to use them as near synonyms or very closely related terms.[11]

Since the sublime cognition requires the perfection of the sensible, Baumgarten sees the sublime as a kind of *beauty*. As he puts it, "The sublime way of thinking is beautiful in the fullest sense."[12] This seems to follow from its being a sensible perfection of cognition that is combined with, or exhibits, aesthetic magnitude. Of course, not all beauty is or should be rendered sublime, and in that same paragraph Baumgarten claims that it is an error to attempt to render everything that is beautiful as also sublime.

As might be expected, Baumgarten does not come up with his theory in an intellectual vacuum. But what is somewhat surprising is that he engages more with ancient authors than with his contemporaries. Mirbach observes that Baumgarten does not offer "argumentative reflection," but rather a "rich fund of metaphors and quotations" from (mostly) ancient Roman poetry and rhetoric.[13] The account of the sublime in the *Aesthetics* contains many quotes from

---

[10]　Baumgarten, *Aesthetica/Ästhetik,* §22. Cf. Baumgarten, *Metaphysics*, §515, §531, §669.

[11]　Buchenau makes this point too. See Buchenau, *The Founding of Aesthetics*, 141. Baumgarten never describes the sublime's phenomenology and his discussion is not centered on pleasure or on identifying its sources. He never says that in the sublime there is a play between imagination (or a lower faculty) and reason.

[12]　Baumgarten, *Aesthetica/Ästhetik* §319.

[13]　Mirbach, "Aesthetic Greatness," 114.

classical authors such as Longinus, Cicero, Seneca, Horace, Virgil, Pliny, and Catullus. With his concern for literary style and how to make thoughts great in readers or listeners, Baumgarten writes in the rhetorical tradition associated with Longinus and Cicero. The editor and translator of the Italian edition of the *Aesthetics*, Salvatore Tedesco, views the pages specifically dedicated to the sublime as "surprisingly underdeveloped" with respect to the contemporaneous European debates about the sublime, and attributes this to the fact that Baumgarten's method of proceeding and theoretical apparatus can sometimes come across as "mechanistic."[14] Baumgarten's method and technical apparatus, Tedesco suggests, may have hindered his ability to connect to the debate about the sublime that was prevalent during his time. Perhaps, we might also add, he was not very familiar with contemporary contributions to arts and ideas. Whatever the reason, it is true that Baumgarten sometimes writes as if he were insulated from contemporary debates about the sublime. If and when current writers influenced his ideas on the sublime, he usually does not acknowledge it explicitly.

In presenting his own views, Baumgarten frequently cites Longinus, the pseudonymous author of the first (or possibly third) century treatise, *On the Sublime*. In the important opening of Section 15 ("Aesthetic Magnitude"), for instance, we can see how Baumgarten approvingly quotes from Longinus.

> The second concern, in thinking of things in a graceful way (§115), is magnitude (*Metaphysics* §515), that is, the one that is aesthetic. We understand by this designation (§22): 1) the importance [*pondus*] of the objects (§18) and their relevance/gravity [*gravitatem*] (*Metaphysics* §166); 2) the importance and gravity of the thoughts proportionate to these objects; 3) and the fruitfulness of both of these (*Metaphysics* §166). *Because what is truly great* [vere magnum] *is what enriches thoughts and is difficult, even impossible, to put out of mind, but instead leaves an enduring, firm, and indelible memory* (Longinus 7.3).[15]

As he often does in the *Aesthetics*, Baumgarten here refers to his own works, above all, the *Metaphysics*. Moreover, the referenced passage in the *Metaphysics* suggests that *gravitas*, *dignitas*, and *nobilitas* are used as near synonyms: "The magnitude of a ground stemming from the number of

---

[14] See Tedesco's introduction in Baumgarten, *L'Estetica*, 15. For an earlier (complete) translation into Italian, see Baumgarten, *L'Estetica*, translated by Piselli.

[15] Baumgarten, *Aesthetica/Ästhetik*, §177. Following Mirbach's Latin-German edition, I reproduce as closely as possible the references Baumgarten provides to his own works and to those of others (i.e., internal and external references). For another translation of the Longinus quote (from a volume edited by Donald Andrew Russell and Michael Winterbottom in 1972), see Clewis, *The Sublime Reader*, 19–20: "Real sublimity contains much food for reflection, is difficult or rather impossible to resist, and makes a strong and ineffaceable impression on the memory."

consequences is FECUNDITY, and from the magnitude of these, is WEIGHT (gravity, dignity, nobility)."[16]

In the following paragraph, *Aesthetics* §178, Baumgarten distinguishes *absolute* from *relative* aesthetic magnitude.[17] When the aesthetic magnitude is "absolute," it is necessary for every beautiful cognition (*omni pulcre cogitando*). But the relative or comparative kind is only a degree of the absolute kind. Furthermore, Baumgarten makes a similar absolute/relative distinction with regard to aesthetic *dignity*. The latter, he clarifies, is a part and species of aesthetic magnitude.[18] Even if he does not do much with this specification of a part/whole relation in the *Aesthetics*, Baumgarten appears to be claiming that artworks may, but need not, portray moral subjects that have aesthetic dignity. In other words, they can exhibit aesthetic magnitude in some other manner.

For Baumgarten, "magnitude" refers to the number of "internal characteristics" that allow a thing to be distinguished from another.[19] According to *Metaphysics*, a multitude of parts is "magnitude" or continuous quantity.[20] A "greater magnitude" is a "comparative multitude" while a smaller one is "fewness."[21] The more distinguishing characteristics (*determinationes, notae, predicata*), the greater the magnitude of the idea (of a thing). And the greater the magnitude of the idea, the greater the idea's force (*vis*) or strength (*robur*), or the *idea's power to change the state of mind* of the person in whose mind the idea arises.[22]

On such grounds it is fair to call Baumgarten's account in part an *aesthetics of truth* (even if he might to some extent recognize the emotional impact of art).[23] Baumgarten's cognitivism is also evident in a relevant passage from *Metaphysics*:

> Therefore, the truer the knowledge is of more and greater beings, the greater it is (§160) until it is the greatest, which would be the truest knowledge of the most and greatest beings. The degree of KNOWLEDGE in which it knows more things [*plura*] is its RICHNESS [*ubertas*] (copiousness [*copia*], extension [*extensio*], riches [*divitiae*], vastness [*vastitas*]); the degree in which it knows fewer things is its NARROWNESS; the degree in which it knows greater things

---

[16] Baumgarten, *Metaphysics*, §166.

[17] Baumgarten, *Aesthetica/Ästhetik*, §178.

[18] Baumgarten, *Aesthetica/Ästhetik*, §185. For brief discussion of aesthetic dignity, see Guyer, *History of Modern Aesthetics*, 335.

[19] Grote, *Emergence of Modern Aesthetic Theory*, 104.

[20] Baumgarten, *Metaphysics*, §159.

[21] Baumgarten, *Metaphysics*, §161.

[22] Grote, *Emergence of Modern Aesthetic Theory*, 104–105.

[23] Guyer thinks Baumgarten combines an aesthetics of truth (a kind of cognitivism) with a recognition of the emotional aspect of art. Guyer, *A History of Modern Aesthetics*, vol. 1., 323.

[*maiora*] is its DIGNITY [*dignitas*] (nobility [*nobilitas*], magnitude [*magnitudo*], gravity [*gravitas*], majesty [*maiestas*]); the degree in which it knows smaller things [*minora*] is its WORTHLESSNESS (meagerness, shallowness).[24]

While his use of the word dignity or majesty might at first seem to suggest a connection to the *moral* sublime, we see here that he is only speaking of *cognition*. The parenthesis—"dignity (nobility, magnitude, gravity, majesty)"—again suggests that these terms are being used as near synonyms, at least in this context. It seems that the nobility or dignity pertaining to or contained within a degree of (true) cognition is due to the magnitude of the *objects* being thought or cognized. The "greater" things (*maiora*) (containing a multitude of predicates under them) give any cognition of them dignity or majesty of cognition.

As we can see in the previously cited block quote from §177, Baumgarten touches on the difficult issue of whether the sublime is to be predicated of the subject (or something in the subject, i.e., cognition) or of the object. Is the sublime in the subject's thoughts (way of thinking)—or even in the subject/mind itself—or in the value/importance (*pondus*)[25] located in the object? But it is not clear that he works out the tensions within his position. Aesthetic greatness, in his view, seems to lie in the object, in the subject's way of thinking that is nonetheless tied to the object, and, finally, in the subject who thinks.[26]

When it comes to the subject-object relation, one philosophical option is to focus on the subjective pole and claim that the aesthetic attribute or quality in question is really (or only) a modification of the subject. For instance, one could speak of a sublime way of thinking, as Baumgarten does in the title of Section 21 (*sublime cogitandi genus*). If the sublime is a way of thinking, it is clearly not a property of a (great) object.

A subset of this approach would tie the sublime to our *free* way of thinking.[27] Baumgarten sometimes takes this route too, and thinks of the sublime as based in a way of thought in which reason is in harmony with

---

[24] Baumgarten, *Metaphysics*, §515; translation slightly altered. For a German translation of this passage, see Baumgarten, *Texte zur Grundlegung der Ästhetik*, 7.

[25] Baumgarten himself translates *pondus* with *Wichtigkeit* (importance). See Mirbach's introduction in Baumgarten, *Aesthetica/Ästhetik*, LXVIII, fn 98.

[26] As Mirbach succinctly puts it, in his chapters on aesthetic magnitude, Baumgarten distinguishes systematically between the greatness of the *object* that is thought (*magnitude materiae*, §191–§216), the greatness of the *way of thinking according to the respective greatness* of its objects (*ratio cogitationum*, §217–§328), and finally the greatness of the *subject who thinks* (*magnitudo personae*, §§352–422). Mirbach, "Aesthetic Greatness," 114.

[27] For Descartes, for instance, the will is free; in fact—in comparison to matter—it is *infinitely* so. One could say this counts as a kind of sublimity. The will (*ego*) experiences its own freedom, as being superior to matter. Incidentally, in the *Meditations*, *Discourse on Method*, and *The Principles of Philosophy*, Descartes never (as far as I can tell) uses the term *sublime* or its relatives.

sensibility, a kind of "psychological and inner freedom."[28] Freedom, according to *Metaphysics*, is the dominion of the mind or soul over *itself* (not over the sensory per se), in which sensory desires and rational motives work together harmoniously.[29]

Alternatively, one could instead see the *object* as sublime. Here the object that is said to be "sublime" can be construed broadly. The most obvious object or elicitor (as found in the accounts of Dennis and Shaftesbury) is the divine being: God is the example here, the most sublime object (however different from all other ones). In medieval and early Renaissance thought, the experience of the sublime was closely connected to religious feelings in response to the God of the Christian philosophers. Bonaventure and Aquinas refer to the sublime (*sublimis* and its linguistic relatives) in a theological context, where God, above all, is sublime. For instance, Aquinas defines such *admiration* as a species of fear that results from the apprehension of the sublime truth (*sublimis veritatis*), or God, in which our contemplative faculty is exceeded.[30] Baumgarten probably would not deny that God is sublime, but he does not really emphasize it either.

Another obvious candidate for a sublime "object" is a marvel of nature. But Baumgarten's examples of the sublime tend to be, not natural objects, but *poetic* descriptions and citations of Latin authors. Even if it is compatible with his account for the sublime object to be a natural wonder, he does not emphasize this kind of case either.

Other sublime objects would include great acts of virtue, or supererogatory acts, as well as the agents performing them. It would also include works of art and poetry *describing* such acts, that is, poetic descriptions of moral greatness. Baumgarten takes this approach above all. In short, for Baumgarten, the object is typically a virtuous act and agent, and their representation in works of art.

To see some of the tensions within his account, we can look at *Aesthetics* §18, §118, and §189. He notes—in agreement with Aristotle—that ugly things can be thought (*cogitari*) in a beautiful manner, and beautiful things can be cognized in an ugly way.[31] This implies that beauty/ugliness lies not exclusively in the object, but in the manner of presentation or depiction.[32] At §118, discussing aesthetic richness or abundance (*ubertas*), he mentions what turns out to be *objective* elements. They are either in the thing or material ("There are objects that as it were present themselves in their own richness") or in the artist (in the

---

[28] Baumgarten, *Aesthetica*, §414. Mirbach translates all of §414 in Mirbach, "Aesthetic Greatness," 116–117.

[29] Mirbach, "Aesthetic Greatness," 114. See Baumgarten, *Metaphysics*, §725, §730.

[30] See Introduction, in Clewis, *The Sublime Reader*, 10. Mendelssohn will call this admiration *Bewunderung*.

[31] Aristotle, *Poetics*, 1448b.

[32] Baumgarten, *Aesthetica/Ästhetik*, §18.

person or mind [*ingenii*], i.e., one's *capacity to represent* the object richly).[33] (As we will see, Mendelssohn accepts a very similar distinction.) In §189, Baumgarten applies this distinction to aesthetic magnitude and dignity (i.e., the sublime). Both the *object* (*rerum, materiae*) *depicted* artistically and the *manner of representation* adopted by the subject or person (*personae*) can appropriately be qualified as having aesthetic magnitude and dignity.[34]

This brings us back to the question of objects that are moral or have moral qualities, including when the object, thing, or subject matter is virtue. At §203 he first agrees with Seneca that "every kind of vice is limited, dismal, and base" and that "virtue alone is sublime [*sublimis*] and elevated (from a moral perspective too)." But he adds, "But for us this discourse concerns objective magnitude and dignity, not insofar as they are inherent [*inhaeret*] in the objects" but rather insofar as "the objects, whatever they might be, contain in themselves a ground on which great and dignified cognitions can be formed, in conformity with the object."[35] Baumgarten thus walks a very fine line. Unlike extension or shape, the sublime is not strictly inherent in the objects or an "objective" quality (i.e., what the moderns like Locke called "primary qualities"). If the object is a kind of magnitude, in turn defined by the number and properties it contains (or by the predicates contained in its definition), the great or sublime can be called a capacity in the object to give evoke thoughts in us (observers, readers) or in artists depicting (*pingi*) them. The thoughts so elicited need to be "in conformity with or appropriate for" the object. But even if it is somehow in the object, the sublime quality is still response dependent and requires someone to think it and/ or to depict or represent it in artistic forms such as poetry. In other words, the "great and dignified cognitions" have to be "formed."

Since poetry is the perfection of sensible cognition, it is no surprise that majestic cognition can be found in it. In fact, majestic cognition is not limited to great objects of nature and natural wonders, but seems to be found in poetry above all. (He appears to offer no discussion of the sublime in music.) Baumgarten often cites poetry in his chapters on the sublime in the *Aesthetics*.

About nine years before the publication of the *Aesthetics*, he even wrote a poem that mentions the sublime, claiming that it is reason that makes souls sublime (noble, great). I translate it as follows:

Reason and virtue make souls
sublime, noble, great, and free,
swift in thinking and clever in choice.
Yet one thing is not there to see:

---

[33] Baumgarten, *Aesthetica/Ästhetik*, §118.
[34] Baumgarten, *Aesthetica/Ästhetik*, §189.
[35] Baumgarten, *Aesthetica/Ästhetik*, §203.

souls live in bodies here;
whatever moves body, moves soul too.
For the soul to be free of care,
the body has the first move to do.

Baumgarten published this poem in 1741, it implicitly argues for being *moved* by feeling and sentiments, that is, love and beauty.[36] He here appears to argue *against* a (stoic) view that sees affects as something to be controlled or tamed: the body has to make the "first move," even if reason and virtue make souls "sublime." And in the *Aesthetics* he appears to repudiate stoicism ("not the one of the wise stoic") in a description of sublime magnanimity that includes a quotation from Horace:

Although a mind which has enough greatness for sublime things is not the one of
   the wise stoic, who,
if the universe crashes down shattered,
keeps intrepid in face of the smashing wreckage (§353),
it will nonetheless never be tormented by minor troubles nor will it be deprived of
   its calm serenity which emulates the life of the gods.[37]

Baumgarten's poem from the *Philosophical Letters* and his apparent repudiation of stoicism in the *Aesthetics* leads to the question of the moral sublime. It should be recalled (as recent scholarship has begun to emphasize) that Baumgarten's aesthetics has a practical (and religious) dimension. An aim of aesthetics, he thinks, is to exhibit virtue (good morals) in its various sensible forms or ways of being expressed.[38] Aesthetics is part of cultivating the whole person.[39]

This practical-religious aspect of aesthetics is evident in the case of the sublime.[40] Sublime magnanimity turns out to be a community of the virtuous person with the divine.[41] At §181, Baumgarten puts the moral in "connection" with freedom (*libertate connectuntur*):

Furthermore, *aesthetic magnitude* (§177), both absolute (§178) and relative (§180), is either *natural*, which pertains to what is not closely connected with

---

[36] Baumgarten, *Philosophische Brieffe*, 90 (my translation). Grote cites, translates, and comments on the poem in Grote, *Emergence of Modern Aesthetic Theory*, 140.
[37] Baumgarten, *Aesthetica/Ästhetik*, §403; translated in Mirbach, "Aesthetic Greatness," 115.
[38] Marbach, in Baumgarten, *Aesthetica/Ästhetik*, 966, fn 3, on §211.
[39] See Anne Pollok's contribution to this volume.
[40] Tedesco claims that, in constant dialogue with Longinus, Baumgarten uses the concept of "aesthetic magnitude" to promote this ethical dimension. Tedesco, "Introduction," in Baumgarten, *L'Estetica*, 15.
[41] Mirbach, "Aesthetic Greatness," 119.

freedom, or *moral*, which applies to objects and cognitions insofar as they are more closely connected with freedom [*libertate connectuntur*].[42]

First, it is worth noting that cognitions can be "connected" with freedom, since we will come back to this point when we turn to Kant, where it is not entirely clear whether, with his theory of the "dynamical" sublime as opposed to the "mathematical" sublime, Kant is extending and building on Baumgarten's view that there can be an aesthetic magnitude that is "moral" rather than "natural," or instead repudiating Baumgarten's category of a moral aesthetic greatness by replacing it with a pure aesthetic judgment of the power of nature (which in the end, however, is based on an estimation of our *own* power and thus presupposes our status as presumably free beings, which for Kant, implies being subject to the moral law). Second, by "nature" Baumgarten is not here referring to natural marvels as such. When he gives an example of the "natural," it is not a natural wonder but a *description* from Virgil's *Aeneid* of Entellus's bodily strength and large muscles. Likewise, he mentions a poet (Lucretius) who says "great things" about Sicily, when describing nature ("great Charybdis" and "menacing Etna").[43] It is a *poet* writing about aesthetically great objects of nature. In §182, he further describes "moral" aesthetic magnitude as the kind "that is possible due to (*per*) the freedom that is determined in conformity with moral laws." He adds that *moral* aesthetic magnitude can also be called "aesthetic dignity" (*dignitatem aestheticam*).[44]

Equipped with this distinction between the moral and the nonmoral (or natural), Baumgarten employs a distinction between positive and negative dignity. Great natural objects (described by the poets) might seem "insignificant from a moral point of view," because they are just objects of nature. Nonetheless, they still belong to the sphere of "dignity," even if it is a "negative" kind.[45] He continues in the next paragraph: "Among these same objects possessing generically the greatest magnitude (§203), sometimes emerge ones that have, in addition to natural magnitude and negative dignity (which can be said to pertain to the great), a certain positive dignity (§193)."[46] Divinely inspired people—he mentions Socrates—can have such positive dignity. A connection to the divine thus surfaces here. He claims that the "first law of the positive dignity for sublime things [*per sublimia*]" is: "Everything human [*humana*], whatever it is, even the great [*maxima*] in a specific manner, is to

---

[42] Baumgarten, *Aesthetica/Ästhetik,* §181. Guyer claims that this natural/moral distinction, even if Baumgarten applies it mainly to artworks, "anticipates Kant's later distinction" between the "mathematical" and the "dynamical" sublime. Guyer, *History of Modern Aesthetics*, vol. 1, 333.
[43] Baumgarten, *Aesthetica/Ästhetik*, §205.
[44] Baumgarten, *Aesthetica/Ästhetik*, §182.
[45] Baumgarten, *Aesthetica/Ästhetik*, §205.
[46] Baumgarten, *Aesthetica/Ästhetik*, §206.

be subordinated to the divine [*divinis*]."[47] So it turns out that positive dignity lies not only in the moral but also in the divine or divinely inspired: there is an overlap of the ethical and the theological.

Like his Italian contemporary Vico (whom he apparently never mentions in the *Aesthetics*), Baumgarten thinks that heroic actions and qualities are sublime.[48] Using his view that heroic virtue is sublime, Baumgarten offers a scale of the "aesthetic dignity" of ways of life: the honest, noble, and heroic.[49] He then matches these with the simple/plain, medium/moderate, and sublime way of thinking (in other words, the low, medium, and high). Thus, the scale proceeds from the simple, honest way of life (which corresponds to the modest or plain), to the noble way of life (analogous to the moderate), to the heroic way of life full of virtue.[50] The heroic corresponds to the "sublime" (*heroicum: sublimia*). The sublime style and discourse (or way of speaking) best suits the heroic way of life.

If temperament is an inclination to desire certain kinds of objects, the *aesthetic* temperament desires the great. We ascribe to the "aesthetic temperament" an "inborn magnitude of the heart" and "an instinct for the great [*magna*]," he claims.[51]

This applies to both the heroic and the tragic: tragedy too can represent the sublime. A "sublime manner of thinking" is required by dramatic tragedy. Baumgarten refers to tragedies by the "buskins" or boots worn by the ancient Greek actors performing tragedy: "Who doesn't know that slippers of comedy require the simple/plain [*tenue*] way of thinking, while buskins of tragedy require the sublime way of thinking [*sublime cogitandi genus*]?"[52] Unfortunately, it is not very clear whether he means—by "requiring" (*postulare*: require, need) the sublime way of thought—to claim that tragedians need to have a sublime way of thought in order to compose their works, or instead that spectators and readers typically respond to tragedies with the feeling of the sublime.

In any case, to conclude this overview, we can say that Baumgarten's thoughts on the sublime fit in with the practical aims of his aesthetics. Poetry (and tragedy) can not only depict but even *extol* virtue (the morally good), and thus represent it in a manner that has great "magnitude." The poet is to

---

[47] Baumgarten, *Aesthetica/Ästhetik*, §399.

[48] Giambattista Vico, "On the Heroic Mind," 69–77. Nicolas Boileau likewise calls the father in Corneille's *Horace* an "old hero" who elicits our "heroic grandeur." See Boileau Despréaux, "Preface to his Translation of Longinus on the Sublime," in Clewis, *The Sublime Reader*, 60.

[49] Baumgarten, *Aesthetica/Ästhetik*, §214.

[50] Baumgarten, *Aesthetica/Ästhetik*, §213. On heroic virtue or way of living, see also Baumgarten, *Aesthetica/Ästhetik*, §281, §363.

[51] Baumgarten, *Aesthetica/Ästhetik*, §45.

[52] Baumgarten, *Aesthetica/Ästhetik*, §236. At §294, he mentions tragedy in its sublimity (*tragodiae cum sublimitate*).

take what is great and make it greater (*augere*), which is indeed the topic of Section 23 (*argumenta augentia*). This point is summarized in the direct and personal advice Baumgarten offers at the end of Section 26, which concludes the discussion on the great or "sublime" in the *Aesthetics*:

> So that you love the truth in beautiful thoughts, here is what you have to do to augment (sec. 23) what is great (sec. 15) in an absolute way (sec. 16), according to its relative magnitude (sec. 17), using thoughts proportionate to the matter (sec. 18)—either in a lowly (sec. 19), or moderate (sec. 20), or sublime manner of thinking (sec. 21)—without the defects that are often quite conspicuous in the greatest things (sec. 22): You have to build up, with absolute importance [*gravitatem*] (sec. 24), that inborn greatness of heart that to a certain degree you must have (§45), and elevate it as much as you can (sec. 25). You are fortunate [*felix*] if this is sufficient and you are able to touch the sublime (sec. 26).[53]

The sublime is central to the project of helping shape a person into a *felix aestheticus*.

MENDELSSOHN

Let us now turn to the reception of Baumgarten's theory of aesthetic magnitude, dignity, and the sublime, beginning with Mendelssohn, one of the foremost German aesthetic theorists following Baumgarten.

In this section, I explore the question of the sublime and its possible relation to morality by examining an essay in Mendelssohn's *Philosophical Writings* (1761). I will not try to explain Mendelssohn's *entire* theory of the sublime and "mixed sentiments" ("mixed," in the sense that we take pleasure in what is otherwise unpleasant or even shocking and astonishing, e.g., when we viewing a dramatic tragedy). Rather, I will address the question of the moral sublime and the sublime's relation to virtue, by examining the essay "On the Sublime and Naïve in the Fine Sciences."[54] It may well be true that, as one scholar claims,[55] in order to understand properly Mendelssohn's theory

---

[53] Baumgarten, *Aesthetica/Ästhetik*, §422.

[54] An excerpted version of the essay (translated by Dahlstrom) can be found in Clewis, *The Sublime Reader*, 91–101, which will be cited here. The complete version (of the same translation) is found in Mendelssohn's "On the Sublime and Naïve in the Fine Sciences." See Mendelssohn, *Philosophical Writings*, 192–232. On the essay, see also Guyer, *History of Modern Aesthetics*, vol. 1, 361–363, and Beiser, who discusses Mendelssohn on the sublime in Beiser, *Diotima's Children*, 217–224.

[55] Pollok, "Mendelssohn's Notion of Admiration," 92 n. 30. The essay examined here was published as the penultimate essay in the 1761 *Philosophical Writings*, but a version of it had been published anonymously in 1758 in *Library of the Fine Sciences and Free Arts* under the title "Considerations of the Sublime and the Naïve in the Fine Sciences." See Mendelssohn, *Philosophical Writings*, xxxvi and Beiser, *Diotima's Children*, 219. Mendelssohn reworked the essay yet again for the 1771 edition of *Philosophical Writings*.

of "mixed sentiments" in their final version, one needs to read "Rhapsody," "On the Main Principles," and "On the Sublime" together (all published in *Philosophical Writings*). Yet my aim is more limited and I am focusing only on "On the Sublime and Naïve in the Fine Sciences." This essay, as its title suggests, examines the representation of the sublime in the fine arts, by which is meant poetry, tragedy, painting, music, and architecture. Mendelssohn quotes poets and tragedians, and in this sense he is like Longinus and Baumgarten. Yet Mendelssohn gives more attention to music and architecture than Baumgarten.

Mendelssohn conceives of the moral sublime (if I can put it this way) under what is called the sublime of power, or intensive magnitude, a category that includes virtue. Awe (*Bewunderung*) is the response to such perfection, which is found in a sublime object, person, or act. To see this, let us examine his views of the sublime more generally.

Mendelssohn, having published in 1758 a review of Burke's *Enquiry*, was familiar with the latter's empirical, psychological account of the sublime. As Pollok observes, Mendelssohn takes over many of Burke's examples while applying or appealing to his own theory of perfection and mixed sentiments.[56] Indeed, there are differences between their accounts. Whereas Mendelssohn concentrates on (objective) sublimity and the largely positive *Bewunderung* (awe) it inspires, Burke focuses more on the fearful jolt that verges on terror.[57] They also come from different intellectual frameworks. Beiser helpfully observes: "Mendelssohn continued to uphold the aesthetics of perfection of Leibniz, Wolff, and Baumgarten, according to which all aesthetic experience is a sensible perception of rational structure."[58] Mendelssohn draws from this German scholastic tradition (filled no doubt with internal philosophical differences) to discuss the admiration felt before an object or person exhibiting a kind of "perfection."

First, Mendelssohn distinguishes beauty from immensity. Whereas beauty is *bounded* and can therefore be taken in by the senses all at once, immensity ("gigantic or enormous in extension")[59] is *unbounded*. But when "the boundaries of this extension are deferred further and further, then they ultimately disappear completely from the senses and, as a result, something *sensuously immense* emerges."[60] This typically gives rise to a pleasing shudder. The

---

[56] Pollok, "Mendelssohn's Notion of Admiration," 85.

[57] Pollok, "Mendelssohn's Notion of Admiration," 85. See also Koller, "Mendelssohn's Response to Burke on the Sublime," 331.

[58] Beiser, *Diotima's Children*, 196. In comparison with the Mendelssohn-Burke relation, there is little scholarship on Mendelssohn's response to Baumgarten on the aesthetically great. For passing discussion of Mendelssohn and Baumgarten, see Koller, "Mendelssohn's Response to Burke on the Sublime," 335, 337, 342.

[59] Mendelssohn, "On the Sublime," 93.

[60] Mendelssohn, "On the Sublime," 93.

"objects of nature" that elicit such an "alluring" trembling are vast or extensive: the vast sea, far-reaching plain, innumerable stars, heights and depths that cannot be comprehended, eternity.[61]

Artists, meanwhile, imitate nature: art, for Mendelssohn, is mimetic. Art, through imitation, can elicit this pleasing shudder or "mixed" sentiment. "Because of the pleasantness of these sentiments art also makes use of them, seeking to produce them through imitation."[62] Such art is able to awaken this response because it *appears* boundless; it is not itself an unlimited magnitude (*Größe*). For instance, the uniform repetition of temporal intervals in music can represent the experience of an extended immensity.

Mendelssohn identifies two kinds of *immensity* in such art: extended and nonextended ("intensive"). The *extensively* immense can be called the *enormous*, while the *intensively* so can be called the *strong*. The extensively immense is the vast or great in size, the intensive one is the mighty, the great in strength or power. Moreover, "the enormous is for the outer sense precisely what the sublime is for the inner sense."[63] The sublime in art falls under the latter. When the strength is "a matter of a perfection," it is said to be *sublime*. As he summarizes it, "In the fine arts and sciences the sensuously perfect representation of something immense will be *enormous*, *strong*, or *sublime* depending upon whether the magnitude concerns an extension and number, a degree of power, or, in particular, a degree of perfection."[64]

> The term commonly applied to what is intensively enormous is "strength," and strength in perfection is designated "the sublime." In general, one could also say: each thing that is or appears immense as far as the degree of its perfection is concerned is called *sublime*.[65]

In particular, virtue—including *artistic* virtue or genius—can be seen as a display of intensive immensity. It is a kind of capacity or power.

Whereas *Bewunderung* (awe) is the feeling we have before the sublime, the sublime is characterized as being an objective quality. The sublime is in the object, and its effect on subjects is the feeling of *Bewunderung*.[66] He defines the *sublime in art* as a "sensuously perfect representation" of something immense, one that is capable of inspiring *Bewunderung*.

---

[61] Mendelssohn, "On the Sublime," 93.
[62] Mendelssohn, "On the Sublime," 93. He uses the term "mixed" here.
[63] Mendelssohn, "On the Sublime," 95.
[64] Mendelssohn, "On the Sublime," 94.
[65] Mendelssohn, "On the Sublime," 94.
[66] The sublime is the "object of awe" according to Mendelssohn. Mendelssohn, "On the Sublime," 96. Dahlstrom sometimes translates *Bewunderung* as "awe" and sometimes as "awe or admiration."

All these sentiments blend together in the soul, flowing into one another, and become a single phenomenon which we call *awe*. Accordingly, if one wanted to describe the sublime in terms of its effect, then one could say: "It is something sensuously perfect in art, capable of inspiring awe."[67]

Bewunderung, he specifies, is a "debt" we owe to the "extraordinary gifts of spirit" or genius creating the work.[68] *Bewunderung* is the soul's condition when it looks at the "unexpectedly good,"[69] the good in turn being another kind of perfection. The sublime experience, Pollok observes, must "contain some reference to a higher perfection" either in the "grandness of the object that overwhelms our sensible apparatus" or in the "genius of the artistic presentation of a subject."[70]

Pollok attributes to Mendelssohn the view that the awe response or *Bewunderung* is "a necessary ingredient in the experience of the sublime." It seems that this "ingredient" of the experience of the sublime is why Mendelssohn considers the experience to be positive and pleasing.[71] (In contrast, Baumgarten does not really explain the sources of the pleasure in the sublime.) In a moment I will suggest two further reasons why, for Mendelssohn, the experience might be pleasant.

Mendelssohn identifies more value in nonextended, *intensive* immensities. Presumably he does so because of their clearer link to *perfection* (on the objective side) as opposed to an imperfection on our part (a limited cognitive-perceptual faculty), as when we cannot comprehend or fully take in a seemingly unbounded object. He claims that mere vastness, magnitude, or greatness (*Größe*), by itself, can start to feel monotonous. The extensively great must contain some kind of order and structure if it is to "awaken a pleasant shudder."[72] It must be the great multitude in a vast unity that hints at a harmonious whole (even if we struggle to comprehend it).[73]

In contemplating the sublime, the mind shares in the object's strength (*Stärke*) and perfection. One feels a union or connectedness with the object, "latching on" to it. "The sentiment produced by the sublime is a composite one. The *magnitude* captures our attention, and since it is the magnitude of a perfection, the soul enjoys latching on to this object so that all adjoining

---

[67] Mendelssohn, "On the Sublime," 94.
[68] Mendelssohn, "On the Sublime," 98.
[69] Mendelssohn, "On the Sublime," 95n.
[70] Pollok, "Mendelssohn's Notion of Admiration," 85.
[71] Pollok, "Mendelssohn's Notion of Admiration," 85. For a defense of the claim that the sublime experience is instead a kind of awe, see Clewis, "Why the Sublime is Aesthetic Awe" (Forthcoming).
[72] Mendelssohn, "On the Sublime," 93. Pollok, "Mendelssohn's Notion of Admiration," 86.
[73] Pollok, "Mendelssohn's Notion of Admiration," 86. See also Koller, "Mendelssohn's Response to Burke on the Sublime," 340 and Beiser, *Diotima's Children*, 223.

concepts in the soul are obscured."[74] In the experience of the sublime we identify with the power and perfection of the object, and this is one reason why it is uplifting or why the "mixed" experience is ultimately pleasant. We take pleasure in the assumed perfection of the sublime object. In addition, the *imagination* is engaged in (or even expanded by) the sheer number of impressions, producing a "sweet shudder." The passage continues: "The *immensity* arouses a sweet shudder that rushes through every fiber of our being, and the *multiplicity* prevents all satiation, giving wings to the imagination to press further and further without stopping."[75] This seems to be another reason why (for Mendelssohn) the experience is pleasing.

The intensively great is less likely than the extensively great to lead to satiation and disgust:

> Power, genius, virtue have their unextended immensity that likewise arouses a spine-tingling sentiment but has the advantage of not ending, through tedious uniformity, in satiation and even disgust, as generally happens in the case of the extended immensity.[76]

As can be seen from this passage, Mendelssohn places moral qualities such as "virtue," as well as artistic ones such as "genius," alongside "power": these are all kinds of capacity or strength. When we behold the creative genius, stunning virtuoso, or wholly virtuous person, whom we admire precisely because we know we cannot achieve what they do, we sometimes feel a pleasant shudder or even a delightful dizziness.

The perfect representation of intensive immensity (in response to the sublime) produces *Bewunderung* because it passes beyond our ordinary, customary expectations. Echoing Baumgarten, there are two kinds of *Bewunderung*, one felt in response to the *perfection in the object represented* and the other at the *perfection in the artist*. The second kind is a response to the artist's powers of representation and artistic abilities: the artist represents ordinary objects in an extraordinary way. In the perfection in the presentation, we discern the stamp or footprint of genius.

> In the works of fine arts and sciences, the awe, like the perfection which it presupposes, belongs to two different genera. Either the object to be represented possesses awesome properties in and for itself, in which case the awe at the object becomes the dominating idea in the soul; or the object in itself is not so

---

[74] Mendelssohn, "On the Sublime," 94.
[75] Mendelssohn, "On the Sublime," 94. Kant will also identify an expansion of imagination in the sublime.
[76] Mendelssohn, "On the Sublime," 93–94.

extraordinary, but the artist possesses the skill of elevating its properties and showing them in an uncommon light. In this case the awe is directed more at the imitation than at the original, more at the merits of the art than at the merits of the object.[77]

In the sublime in art in which the artist represents a sublime object (the first kind of sublimity, "in which the basis for awe is to be found in the very matter to be represented"[78]), the *naïve and unaffected* expression and presentation are most appropriate. The artist (e.g., Klopstock and Shakespeare) need not and should not embellish the magnitude represented. "It becomes clear from this that excessive embellishment in the expression of things is not compatible with something sublime of the first type."[79] Rather, "in representing something sublime of this type, the artist must devote himself to a naïve, unaffected expression which allows the reader or spectator to think more than is said to him."[80]

But in the second type of sublimity (concerning the perfection of the *artist*) matters are different. Here the poet's *manner of presentation* can make use of "embellishments" and "beauties," for instance, in the selection of adjectives that designate "the most sensuous properties," in word combination, and in melody and harmony.[81] This view of the combination of "objective sublimity" and "subjective sublimity" is summarized in the following:

Hence, subjective sublimity can in many cases be combined with objective sublimity. Depending, however, upon whether the awe [*Bewunderung*] redound more to the object itself or to the skill of the artist, the expression can be more or less embellished, something that must be judged in each case on the basis of the makeup of the subject treated or of the aim of the artist.[82]

Moreover, the distinction between sublimity in the matter or object represented, on the one hand, and the intentions of the artist to represent it in a certain way, on the other, turns out to be useful. Toward the end of the essay,

[77] Mendelssohn, "On the Sublime," 95.
[78] Mendelssohn, "On the Sublime," 97.
[79] Mendelssohn, "On the Sublime," 96.
[80] Mendelssohn, "On the Sublime," 96–97. The representation of the objective sublime in mimetic or representational art can be contrasted with the representation by what Lyotard's calls "avant-garde" art, where this is a *negative* presentation of the infinite or transcendent, and the image (in part) represents what cannot be fully represented. Lyotard writes, "The avant-gardist attempt inscribes the occurrence of a sensory *now* as what cannot be presented and which remains to be presented in the decline of great representational painting." See Lyotard, "The Sublime and the Avant-Garde," in Clewis, *The Sublime Reader,* 268.
[81] Mendelssohn, "On the Sublime," 99.
[82] Mendelssohn, "On the Sublime," 99.

Mendelssohn makes use of it in proposing a way to resolve certain aesthetic disagreements when judging the sublimity of a line or phrase. For instance, a long-standing debate surrounding the Biblical passage from Genesis, "God said, Let there be light," can be resolved by appealing to this distinction. According to Mendelssohn, some "art critics" are focusing on the "intention" of the author (which was *not* to utter a sublime statement). Other critics, meanwhile, are paying attention to the "action" or "event" described; on this view, the passage would be sublime.[83]

What of the moral sublime? As we can see from the passages cited so far, Mendelssohn's account contains something we can call the moral sublime, in that he considers virtue to be a sublime quality. Virtue includes both moral and artistic displays of excellence. As a kind of power or intensive sublime, virtue can be a sublimity: it is a kind of power or capacity to perform the morally great act. Note that the felt *Bewunderung* is a *response* to observing virtue, not the sentiment one feels when being virtuous.

To be sure, Mendelssohn does not use the terms "noble" or "moral" sublime. He does not identify a unique subspecies of sublimity to account for remarkable, stirring displays of virtue. Rather, he places such sublimity at the very heart of his theory. The moral sublime is already captured by his conception of the sublime as a strong, intensive immensity, a kind of perfection in the object. There is no need to carve out a subspecies named the "moral sublime."

Finally, let us consider the question of the divine. Recall that according to the Judeo-Christian tradition, God is seen as the most divine being; this is reflected in the theories ranging from the Christian scholastics (writing on *sublimis* and its relatives) to Dennis and Burke. Mendelssohn continues this line of thinking in a passage that was partially quoted above and continues as follows:

> In general, one could also say: each thing that is or appears immense as far as the degree of its perfection is concerned is called *sublime*. God is called "the most sublime being." A truth is said to be "sublime" if it concerns a quite perfect or complete entity such as God, the universe, the human soul and if it is of immense use to the human race or its discovery would require a great genius.[84]

After giving a working definition of the sublime ("in general, one could also say"), he observes that God is called the most sublime being. This is very much like Aquinas's claim about reverence for the sublime truth (God). And a few lines later Mendelssohn writes: "The properties of the

---

[83] Mendelssohn, "On the Sublime," 100.
[84] Mendelssohn, "On the Sublime," 94.

Supreme Being which we recognize in his works inspire the most ecstatic awe [*Bewunderung*] because they surpass everything that we can conceive as enormous, perfect, or sublime."[85]

On this issue, Mendelssohn is largely in agreement with the preceding theological-aesthetic tradition. To see a more radical turn on the moral sublime and God, we will have to go to Kant.

KANT AND POST-KANTIAN GERMAN AESTHETICS

We now turn to the sublime in general in Kant's third *Critique*. He famously divides the sublime into two forms, the dynamical and the mathematical, the mathematical form of the sublime being a response to extent or vastness and the dynamical a response to great power. It may well be, as Guyer suggests, that Baumgarten's distinction between natural and moral kinds of aesthetic magnitude, on the one hand, and Mendelssohn's distinction between extensive and nonextensive immensities, on the other, anticipated or even influenced Kant's subsequent division of the sublime into the mathematical and dynamical forms of sublimity.[86] Since Kant's theory of the sublime has been the object of a vast scholarly literature, the following discussion will indeed focus on the similarities and differences between Kant and his predecessors on the sublime (i.e., Baumgarten and Mendelssohn).

Unlike both Baumgarten and Mendelssohn, Kant does not think of the sublime as an objective quality. The sublime is in the mind. "Thus sublimity is not contained in anything in nature, but only in our mind, insofar as we can become conscious of being superior to nature within us and thus also to nature outside us (insofar as it influences us)."[87] We, not the object, are sublime. Accordingly, nature is only *improperly* called sublime. The next sentence continues: "Everything that arouses this feeling in us, which includes the *power* of nature that calls forth our own powers, is thus (although improperly) called sublime."[88] And at the end of his discussion of the sublime (§30), Kant writes: "the sublime in nature is only improperly so called, and should

---

[85] Mendelssohn, "On the Sublime," 94.

[86] "This [Mendelssohn's] distinction [between extended and unextended immensity], like Baumgarten's distinction between 'natural' and 'moral magnitude,' anticipates Kant's subsequent distinction between the 'mathematical' and the 'dynamical' sublime, and while it was not uncommon in British discussions of the sublime, Mendelssohn may be Kant's most likely source for it." Guyer, *History of Modern Aesthetics*, vol. 1, 361–362. For references to two further scholars (Braitmeier and Goldstein) who hold that Mendelssohn's account anticipates Kant's, see Koller, "Mendelssohn's Response to Burke on the Sublime," 348 n. 86.

[87] Kant, *Critique of the Power of Judgment*, §28 (AA 5:264), 136—the last page reference listed in Kant citations will be to the selection in Clewis, *The Sublime Reader*.

[88] Kant, *Critique of the Power of Judgment*, §28 (AA 5:264), 136 (emphasis in the original).

properly be ascribed only to the manner of thinking, or rather to its foundation in human nature."[89] If we actually think of the sublime as an objective
property, he holds, we commit a mistake in reasoning.[90]

The sublime lies in the subject in at least two ways for Kant. First, it is
a feeling. He often writes about the *feeling* of the sublime, a feeling of our
own greatness and power. Second, he holds it is the mind, reason, or way of
thinking (*Denkungsart*) that is sublime (or that "introduces" sublimity). We
seek a ground of the sublime, he writes, merely "in ourselves and in the way
of thinking that introduces sublimity" into a representation.[91]

Another key divergence from Baumgarten and Mendelssohn is that (at
least in the *Critique of the Power of Judgment*) Kant does not typically have
in mind the sublime in art or the artistic sublime. Almost all of Kant's examples come from nature: they are natural wonders such as overhanging cliffs,
ravines, mountain chains, and the innumerable stars in the night sky. (This is
one reason why his work on the sublime is widely invoked in recent environmental aesthetic theory.) Indeed, many of Kant's examples from nature are
the same as those mentioned by his predecessors, including Mendelssohn.
They are stock examples.

Kant is not so much concerned with the artistic representation of such
object, at least not in the third *Critique*. (In the *Observations on the Feeling
of the Beautiful and Sublime*, by contrast, many of his examples come from
literature and poetry.) He is interested in the natural object itself as giving
rise to an experience of the sublime, the purposiveness of which is found not
in the object but in the use we make of it, namely, as it reveals our human
freedom and (what he thinks this ultimately implies) our moral vocation or
calling. This is not to say that the natural object plays no role in his account.
The object plays a role in Kant's systematic aims in that an object of nature
gives rise to an experience that is taken to be an experience of freedom. For
Kant, this allows philosophers to forge a bridge (in a way of thinking, if not
in an ontological sense) from nature to freedom.[92]

But Kant does not completely overlook the artistic sublime and he does
not deny its possibility.[93] The *Anthropology from a Pragmatic Point of view*
(1798), a handbook published toward the end of Kant's life on the basis of

---

[89] Kant, *Critique of the Power of Judgment*, §30 (AA 5:280), 146.
[90] Although I am striving to summarize Kant's account as clearly as possible, it is worth pointing out
that Kant is not consistent about what the predicate "sublime" properly applies to and picks out—a
distinct kind of *feeling* or experience, the rational *mind*, *reason*, an *idea of reason* such as the idea
of *freedom* or *infinity* (what is beyond all measure, that which is absolutely great), *freedom* itself as
a capacity to set ends, the human moral *calling*, to name just a few candidates.
[91] Kant, *Critique of the Power of Judgment*, §23 (AA 5:246), 124.
[92] See Clewis, "The Place of the Sublime in Kant's Project," 149–168.
[93] For a defense of the possibility of artistic sublimity in Kant's account, see Clewis, "A Case for
Kantian Artistic Sublimity," 167–170.

his handwritten notes for his anthropology course, contains claims about representing the sublime in art, which for Kant (as for Mendelssohn) should be both beautiful and mimetic. The section, "On Taste with regard to the Sublime," states:

> The *sublime* is the counterweight but not the opposite of the beautiful; because the effort and attempt to raise ourselves to a grasp (*apprehensio*) of the object awakens in us a feeling of our own greatness and power; but the representation in thought of the sublime by *description* or presentation can and must always be beautiful. . . . The artistic presentation of the sublime in description and embellishment (in secondary works, *parerga*) can and should be beautiful, since otherwise it is wild, coarse, and repulsive, and, consequently, contrary to taste.[94]

This position seems quite similar to Mendelssohn's claims about the latter's second form of the sublime. Even if (unlike Mendelssohn) Kant does not focus on the perfection of the *artist*, he agrees that the artist can, even should, appeal to embellishments and various ways of making it more beautiful. Yet such a discussion of the beautiful representation of the sublime in art is not found in the third *Critique* account (although it is consistent with it).

In his 1790 discussion (unlike Baumgarten and Mendelssohn) Kant rarely quotes from other authors who wrote about the sublime. Kant gives what might be called a phenomenological description of the experience of the sublime, and in addition offers a transcendental explanation of the conditions that make that phenomenological experience possible: the interplay between reason and imagination.

There are two possible exceptions to this lack of references: first, when Kant writes that "we call" something sublime, and, second, his citation of the Exodus injunction against making images of God. Given his focus on experience, Kant never really clarifies what he means when he says that *we call* something *sublime*, a phrase that occurs several times (e.g., first paragraph of §24, opening line in §25, title of §30). In the end, though, it is not really a genuine citation. A rare instance of quotation occurs, however, when Kant refers to the prohibition of image-making of the divine (Exodus 20:4). "Perhaps there is no more sublime passage in the Jewish Book of the Law than the commandment: Thou shalt not make unto thyself any graven image, nor any likeness either of that which is in heaven, or on the earth, or yet under the earth."[95]

If God cannot be represented, what about freedom? This leads to the question of the moral sublime. Here we see a further difference between Kant and his predecessors. In his work of 1764, the *Observations*, Kant identifies a type

---

[94] Kant, *Anthropology*, §68 (AA 7:243), 147.
[95] Kant, *Critique of the Power of Judgment*, "General Remark" (AA 5:274), 142.

of sublimity called the noble (*edel*) sublime.[96] But when he publishes on the same topic some twenty-five years later, there are only two kinds of sublime (mathematical, dynamical), not three. And the noble sublime drops out—at least officially.

Even if Kant does not use the term "noble" sublime or "the moral sublime" in 1790, there are two senses in which Kant can be said to have something like it. First, he describes our responses to virtue as sublime, offering the example of the fearless, virtuous soldier who evokes our admiration. Second, he holds that the sublime is based or grounded on "moral feeling" and freedom: in a loose sense, the sublime already is moral.

Let us examine the first of these. Kant thinks that we can respond with *Bewunderung* to the virtuous soldier who displays fearlessness before death.

> For what is it that is an object of the greatest admiration [*Bewunderung*] even to the savage? Someone who is not frightened, who has no fear, thus does not shrink before danger but energetically sets to work with full deliberation. And even in the most civilized circumstances this exceptionally high esteem for the warrior remains, only now it is also demanded that he at the same time display all the virtues of peace, gentleness, compassion and even proper care for his own person, precisely because in this way the incoercibility of his mind by danger can be recognized.[97]

Observers can here feel a sublime response to the compassionate soldier's embodiment of virtue. The soldier is not the one feeling the sublime; instead, with "full deliberation," he feels apathy. He is unmoved. He possesses self-rule and self-control ("incoercibility of his mind"), rising above nature. (This is yet *another* sense of *Erhabenheit*—he has sublimity in that he is raised above nature, and it should not be confused with the claim that he makes a pure aesthetic judgment of the sublime or has the feeling associated with that judgment. Not everyone who is raised in this sense *feels* the sublime.) It is we who observe the soldier's rising above nature who can feel the sublime and thereby make an aesthetic judgment of the sublime. The structure of this observer-object relation seems similar to Mendelssohn's account where we feel *Bewunderung* in response to a display of virtue.[98]

---

[96] Kant, *Observations*, 106 (AA 2:209). In this "pre-critical" treatise, *Observations on the Feeling of the Beautiful and Sublime*, Kant distinguishes the sublime and the beautiful in terms of their phenomenology and qualities. He identifies and gives examples of three kinds of sublimity (noble, terrifying, magnificent). In addition to identifying a form of the sublime that is moral (noble), he discusses moral feeling in terms of sublimity.

[97] Kant, *Critique of the Power of Judgment*, §28 (AA 5:262), 135.

[98] For a classification of the various solicitors of the moral sublime, see Appendix 3 in Clewis, *The Kantian Sublime and the Revelation of Freedom*, 233.

Let us turn to the second instance. In the third *Critique* Kant clearly connects the sublime to freedom. He bases the sublime on a shared human feature, our own practical freedom (even if we cannot *prove* our freedom—neither to ourselves nor to anyone else). Since for Kant freedom is a moral concept, then, if he grounds the sublime on freedom, he is grounding it on a moral concept. In this important passage, Kant claims that the judgment on the sublime in nature is founded on human nature, namely, freedom, which in turn demands the cultivation of moral feeling.

> But just because the judgment on the sublime in nature requires culture (more so than that on the beautiful), it is not therefore first generated by culture and so to speak introduced into society merely as a matter of convention; rather it has its foundation in human nature, and indeed in that which can be required of everyone and demanded of him along with healthy understanding, namely in the predisposition to the feeling for (practical) ideas, i.e., to that which is moral. . . . But because the latter [i.e., the sublime] relates the imagination to reason, as the faculty of ideas, we require it only under a subjective presupposition (which, however, we believe ourselves to be justified in demanding of everyone), namely that of the moral feeling in the human being, and so we also ascribe necessity to this aesthetic judgment.[99]

Kant grounds the necessity that we attribute to claims of the sublime, to our having a capacity for moral feeling, namely, on our human constitution as (presumably) free beings. ("Presumably" means: we operate under the idea of freedom and take ourselves to be free whenever we act, but we cannot prove that we are free.) The experience is grounded on our being rational and finite beings who are aware of the moral law through the "moral feeling" of respect. This way of thinking (*Denkungsart*) is capable of being shared by all human beings. It is a way of thinking that everyone *should* have (even when they do not): the sublime is grounded in this feature of human nature. (Kant's unfortunate claim, above, that the judgment of the sublime in nature "requires" culture seems to be in direct tension with an assertion in that same sentence, viz., that it is "not therefore first generated by culture." The culture requirement seems inconsistent with his appeal to human nature and freedom. As Koller observes, "Kant's explanation of the sublime seems to require too much acculturation," and such a requirement does not seem essential to Kant's account of the sublime).[100] The experience of the sublime is based on our shared capacity and disposition to hold other people accountable for

---

[99] Kant, *Critique of the Power of Judgment*, §29 (AA 5: 265–266), 137.
[100] Koller, "Mendelssohn's Response to Burke on the Sublime," 349.

our feelings and actions, and to do so on the basis of reasons. The sublime is grounded in our status as normative beings.

Kant's account of the sublime shows one sense in which Kant is a dialectical thinker (if I can put it this way). At first, Kant separates interest from the sublime: the pure aesthetic judgment of the sublime in nature is disinterested. But after conceptually distinguishing or separating them, he then reunites interest and the sublime. "Even that which we call sublime in nature outside us or even within ourselves (e.g., certain affects) is represented only as a power of the mind to soar above *certain* obstacles of sensibility by means of moral principles, and thereby to become interesting."[101] We can here discern a distinction between first-order and second-order. On the first-order, a pure aesthetic judgment of the sublime is disinterested,[102] but on the second-order we can take an interest in it—just as we can take an interest in the experience of beauty which is itself disinterested.[103] Reason always has an interest in such demonstrations of claims to universal validity (an "interest in disinterestedness," as it were), in claims to intersubjectivity and agreement, since such demonstrations can promote one of the ends of reason, morality. If the sublime is a sensible expression of ideas of reason and an experience of freedom, it is evidence of the presence of reason in the world, and as such, can be taken to support and promote reason's practical-moral interests.

Finally, when it comes to the question of God and the sublime, Kant rejects the traditional view. It is not God who is sublime, it is *we* (our reason, etc.) who are. It is not God who is truth; it is *we* who, by virtue of our faculties of intuition and categories, are capable of making true judgments. Moreover, he holds that we should not adopt a slavish or fearful attitude toward God, but should feel self-respect and self-esteem, based on our status as (presumably) free beings capable of morality.[104]

As for freedom, there is no risk that freedom, which cannot be put into an image, will not motivate us via the moral law. "It is utterly mistaken to worry that if it were deprived of everything that the senses can recommend it would then bring with it nothing but cold, lifeless approval and no moving force or emotion."[105] Freedom is always strong enough to act as a motive, since we are constituted so as to feel pure respect for freedom in the form of the moral law. While it is impossible for us to have a sensible intuition of freedom (for reasons Kant gives in the first *Critique*), freedom can be represented symbolically or analogically. In fact, one of the aims of art is to provide sensible

---

[101] Kant, *Critique of the Power of Judgment*, "General Remark" (AA 5:271), 141.

[102] Kant, *Critique of the Power of Judgment*, §24 (AA 5:247), 125.

[103] On the intellectual interest in beauty, see Kant, *Critique of the Power of Judgment*, §42 (AA 5:298).

[104] Kant, *Critique of the Power of Judgment*, §28 (AA 5:263), 136.

[105] Kant, *Critique of the Power of Judgment*, "General Remark" (AA 5:274), 143.

symbols of freedom, and the artist represents symbols of freedom in various ways—a point that Schiller and other post-Kantian philosophers will take up.

Let us thus briefly explore some of their ideas, to glimpse how the concept of the sublime will develop in the German aesthetic tradition after Baumgarten, Mendelssohn, and Kant.

Friedrich Schiller shares some of the psychological elements deriving from Burke and Mendelssohn, offering vivid, rich descriptions of the experience of the sublime. Unlike Mendelssohn, however, Schiller accepts the Kantian transcendental arguments for the view that the sublime is grounded on freedom and moral feeling. For instance, Schiller emphasizes the "practical" sublime over the "cognitive" sublime.[106] Like Baumgarten and Mendelssohn, Schiller views the sublime as a paradigmatic response to tragedy. Like them, then, Schiller emphasizes sublimity in art.

G. W. F. Hegel repudiates an anthropological-psychological orientation, whether non-transcendental (as in Baumgarten and Mendelssohn) or transcendental (as in Kant and Schiller). He construes the sublime ontologically.[107] In his lectures on fine art (published posthumously in 1835), Hegel rejects seeing the sublime as a merely subjective state and more generally is critical of psychological accounts of the sublime. Accordingly, Hegel offers scant reference to the moral or to moral greatness in his account of the sublime. Rather, the sublime consists in an attempt to grasp God (the infinite) in finite expression, that is, in poetry. This attempt necessarily fails, he thinks, and thereby turns into the next stage of the dialectic.

If Hegel makes freedom a core notion of his view of the sublime, it is in a sense that differs from the transcendental-psychological one found in Kant and Schiller. For *this* freedom is not a subject's freedom of the will. If Hegel makes any connection of the sublime to freedom, it is only insofar as Hegel's philosophy itself is posited as an expression of freedom, namely, the idea coming to know itself in and through external forms, distinct from itself, or: spirit knowing itself in the form of spirit (in and for itself). The sublime is for Hegel a stage in the "Symbolic" form of art that will pass into "Classical" form of art. In turn, the Absolute (the idea) will find a deeper expression in religion than in art, before being grasped most fully in conceptual thought by philosophy.

Arthur Schopenhauer, finally, proposes that a person perceiving the sublime feels a connectedness or union with a world-whole or universe. Unlike

---

[106] See Schiller's 1793 essay, "On the Sublime: (Toward the Further Development of Some Kantian Ideas)"—not to be confused with his 1801 essay "Concerning the Sublime"—in Clewis, ed., *The Sublime Reader*, 150–160.

[107] For the account of the sublime found in Hegel's lectures on fine art, see Clewis, *The Sublime Reader*, 200–210.

Baumgarten and Mendelssohn, however, Schopenhauer does not describe this union (a bond with the world-whole, not to be confused with the object) in terms of *perfection*. The experience, involving a loss of self, reveals the world as pure striving or willing, which in his view is blind, not guided by the morally good or any kind of perfection. Schopenhauer would question Baumgarten's and Mendelssohn's appeals to a scholastic notion of perfection. For related reasons, Schopenhauer rejects what he perceived as Kant's moral "scholastic philosophy," although he accepts Kant's conception and division of the mathematical and dynamical sublime.

> The impression of the sublime can arise in quite a different way by our imagining a mere magnitude in space and time, whose immensity reduces the individual to nought. By retaining Kant's terms and his correct division, we can call the first kind the dynamically sublime, and the second the mathematically sublime, although we differ from him entirely in the explanation of the inner nature of that impression, and can concede no share in this either to moral reflections or to hypostases from scholastic philosophy.[108]

Since Kant's theory itself repudiates much of German scholasticism, Schopenhauer's remark seems rather unfair, even if he is honing in on an undeniable element of moralism in Kant's account. There may even be an element of scholasticism in Schopenhauer. Yet he prefers to look to the ancient religious texts of India (such as the *Upanishads*) rather than the theological texts of medieval philosophy or the Leibnizian tradition to which Baumgarten and Mendelssohn belonged and contributed.

Finally, it is worth mentioning Schopenhauer on the sublime and art. Like Baumgarten, Mendelssohn, and Schiller (to name a few from the German tradition alone), Schopenhauer sees a deep connection between dramatic tragedy and the sublime. Schopenhauer writes, "Our pleasure in tragedy belongs not to the feeling of the beautiful, but to that of the sublime; it is, in fact, the highest degree of this feeling." The effect of tragedy is "analogous to that of the dynamically sublime, since, like this, it raises us above the will and its interest, and puts us in such a mood that we find pleasure in the sight of what directly opposes the will."[109] So, whereas in the third *Critique* Kant does not present the sublime as one of the main ways to respond to dramatic tragedy, Schopenhauer does so by employing Kant's category of the dynamical sublime.

---

[108] Schopenhauer, *The World as Will and Representation*, Vol. 1, §39. See also Clewis, *The Sublime Reader*, 197.

[109] Schopenhauer, *The World as Will and Representation*, quoted from Clewis, *The Sublime Reader*, 194.

CONCLUSION: THE MORAL SUBLIME?

Baumgarten's theory is in part an *aesthetics of truth*, since the majesty of cognition is a perfection of sensible cognition. Baumgarten might not *deny* the emotive or affective side of the sublime, but in the *Aesthetics* he does not really emphasize it either, for he offers little to no description of the phenomenology of the sublime. In contrast, given the central role Mendelssohn gives to the notion of *Bewunderung* and his recognition of an expansion of imagination (pressing further on its "wings"), his account is in part a theory of emotion and of imaginative play. But it is *also* one of truth, since the sublime discloses goodness (to which "awe" is a response) and perfections in the world.

Both Baumgarten and Mendelssohn work with a conception of perfection, although not the same one. For Baumgarten the focus is on the perfection of *sensible cognition*. For Mendelssohn it is about the perfection of the *object*, whether in the object presented or in the artist representing.

Kant, in turn, rejects most of this perfectionism. To be sure, the third *Critique*'s notion of adherent or dependent beauty (§16) does recognize the active role played by concepts in the formation and articulation of disinterested and subjectively universal aesthetic judgments, and perhaps there could be said to be partially intellectualized aesthetic judgments of the sublime.[110] Nevertheless, Kant's aesthetic theory typically focuses on the free play of imagination and the mental faculties and, in the case of the sublime, on emotion (*Rührung*), more than on the perception of perfections in an object, even if this focus might later be complicated in interesting ways. If there is any perfectionism in Kant's 1790 view of the sublime, it lies above all (but not exclusively) in his claim that in sublime experiences we admire our own reason rather than a great objective perfection.[111]

Baumgarten has a version of the moral sublime, claiming that virtue alone is sublime (*sublimis*) and elevated. Here it would be useful to recall the practical ends of Baumgarten's aesthetic project, the second practical part of the *Aesthetics* that he never completed, as well as the practical thrust of his thinking as a whole. The ends of thinking are practical; the aim is to realize the talents God gave us.[112] In accordance with this, there is a religious-theological element in his thoughts on the sublime: Everything human, even the great, is to be subordinated to the divine. Aesthetic theory has practical, not just

---

[110] Though it is missed by most commentators, Kant suggests the possibility of partially intellectual (adherent) judgments of the sublime, though he adds that, given his aims, his analysis will not make use of such examples. Kant, *Critique of the Power of Judgment*, §29 "General Remark" (AA 5:269–270), 140.

[111] Guyer, *History of Modern Aesthetics*, vol. 1, 362–363.

[112] Baumgarten, *Aesthetica/Ästhetik*, §12.

theoretical, aims: to make individuals better through aesthetic exercises and practices. The goal is to acquire, among other things, an aesthetic habit.[113] Aesthetics should help cultivate the lower faculties of cognition for moral improvement. In this there is some affinity with Longinus, since one of the objectives of Longinus's *On the Sublime* is to help us improve our natural gifts and thereby elevate us.

Mendelssohn, we have seen, sees virtue as an objective sublimity. Virtue, including artistic virtuosity, is a kind of objective perfection, and we respond to it with *Bewunderung*.

When it comes to the moral sublime, Kant is more indirect. But even here, as we have seen, Kant thinks we respond with *Bewunderung* to the gentle, moral soldier. Moreover, Kant's theory of the sublime is clearly based on everyone's having a capacity for moral feeling. This is not to say it is the moral sublime in a way that will *reduce* the sublime to the moral feeling, but it does show that morality (like freedom) underlies this theory. This is after all what Schopenhauer found to be repugnant in Kant's moral "scholasticism."

How innovative is Kant here? Whether one thinks that Kant is innovative or not probably depends to some extent on one's preference for focusing on differences rather than continuities. At least in this case, I prefer to be a "lumper" rather than a "splitter" and to emphasize the continuities. As noted, Kant offers the examples of the virtuous soldier to which we respond with a feeling of the sublime; and he bases the sublime on our shared human freedom and moral feeling—a way in which the sublime could merit being called (in a loose sense) already a "moral sublime," though of course not in a way that reduces the aesthetic to the moral or that loses sight of Kant's distinctions between these spheres. Accordingly, when Baumgarten writes of the natural and moral forms of aesthetic magnitude, "lumpers" might be inclined to see these reemerge in Kant's theory of the pure aesthetic judgment of the mathematical and dynamical sublime in nature, seeing the dynamical as Kant's modified version of what Baumgarten called the "moral" kind of aesthetic magnitude. In contrast, "splitters" might instead wish to say that it is precisely Kant's *rejection* of and failure to defend a category of the "moral" sublime (at least in 1790) that constitutes his unique contribution to the aesthetics of the sublime. But, in addition to what has already been mentioned, splitters have the additional burden (to name just one) of having to explain the numerous passages in which Kant describes our aesthetic, disinterested experiences and responses to moral phenomena (the moral law itself and its embodiments and representations) in way that does not see these as merely experiences of the dynamical sublime or subsume these experiences under the dynamical.

---

[113] Grote, *Emergence of Modern Aesthetic Theory*, 128–141. Buchenau, *The Founding of Aesthetics*, 148.

Presumably such aesthetic (disinterested) responses to the moral law or its embodiments cannot be experiences of the dynamical sublime, since for Kant the moral law, unlike the menacing object that initiates an experience of the dynamical sublime, cannot elicit fear in us.

Other scholars might understandably stress what is new in the third *Critique* and insist that it contains no official concept of the moral sublime; technically they would be right. But I think it would be a mistake not to see, in Kant's writings, how freedom connects up with morality. In the 1764 *Observations*, he explicitly recognizes the moral or noble (*edel*) sublime, leading one to inquire whether or not it emerges in the other elements of his thought after all. And one might likewise wonder if Kant had in mind something like the intellectual interest in the sublime (on par with the beautiful) when he describes the "interest" we take in "enthusiasm" (where *Enthusiasm* is defined in the third *Critique* as "the idea of the good with affect"), both in 1790 and a few years later.[114] In a work published in 1798, *The Conflict of the Faculties*, he describes the intellectual interest we take in the sublime-like response of enthusiasm (*Enthusiasm*) for the first French Republic. He characterizes the distant onlookers' participation (*Theilnehmung*) as "exaltation" (*Exaltation*) and calls this response universal (*allgemein*) and disinterested (*uneigennützige*.)[115] The overlap with the experience of the sublime should be clear. Accordingly, Kant can be said to describe (or even himself take) an intellectual interest in something (i.e., enthusiasm) that shares some of the key features of the experience of the sublime; moreover, an experience that too is morally based.[116]

Before closing, it might be useful to mention how contemporary empirical research on the sublime (or aesthetic "awe") might be like or unlike the

---

[114] Kant, *Critique of the Power of Judgment*, "General Remark" (AA 5:272), 141. Immediately before that he had written: "Even that which we call sublime in nature outside us or even within ourselves (e.g., certain affects) is represented only as a power of the mind to soar above *certain* obstacles of sensibility by means of moral principles, and thereby to become interesting."

[115] Kant, *Religion and Rational Theology*, 301–303 (AA 7: 85–87). He writes at AA 7: 86, in my translation: "True enthusiasm moves only towards what is ideal and, indeed, purely moral, such as the concept of right, and it cannot be grafted onto self-interest." I give a fuller defense of the present interpretation in *The Kantian Sublime and the Revelation of Freedom*.

[116] The concept of enthusiasm (*enthousiasmos*, which Baumgarten writes in Greek) seems important to Baumgarten's thoughts on the sublime, in part because of the enthusiasm's traditional connection to artistic creation. In line with the pre-Kantian and modern stance on artistic creativity, Baumgarten believes in the compatibility of the idea of exercise and method with genius, or enthusiasm, impetus, and divine breath. Buchenau, *The Founding of Aesthetics*, 149. On *enthousiasmos*, see especially Baumgarten, *Aesthetica/Ästhetik*, §78, §95. At *Aesthetics* §416, Baumgarten even characterizes enthusiasm as having rational elements and as occurring "with the approval of reason" and "in the presence of rational conscience" before, during, and after the moving pathos. On such tranquility, see also Baumgarten, *Ethica philosophica*, §445. Whereas Baumgarten does little to define enthusiasm in terms of the morally good, Kant quite pointedly characterizes enthusiasm as "the idea of the good with affect."

accounts we have examined. Empirical studies hardly talk of the "perfection" of sensible cognition, like Baumgarten, or call the sublime the "majesty of cognition." But insofar as current empirical research in aesthetics looks at the psychological and physical responses to the sublime ("awe"), it follows the same path as Mendelssohn, who accepted much of the psychological account of Burke and used many of his examples. While Kant is still widely cited in philosophy, it is Burke above all who dominates (as citations and references attest) this subdiscipline of empirical research. The preference for Burke is perhaps due to Kant's transcendental (hence nonempirical) method and penchant for a philosophical system, and in part to the difficulty of the expression and presentation of his ideas (even in the German), not to mention the content. Specifically, I doubt many contemporary empirical researchers would accept Kant's thesis the experience of the sublime is based on and requires the notion of freedom, on the grounds that it is too hard to test empirically. (Incidentally, that freedom is not empirically verifiable is a point Kant would readily grant.)

For philosophers and aesthetic theorists, meanwhile, the question remains: is it fruitful to capture the morally noble or virtuous using the notion of the sublime?

It depends on which conception of the "aesthetic" we employ. If we regard the aesthetic as free from any practical-moral elements, there is hardly room for a *moral* sublime. In Baumgarten and Mendelssohn (like Shaftesbury and many others), however, there *is* room for a moral sublime, as well as, more generally, for blending virtue and beauty (and in turn beauty and the sublime), or the sublime and religious feeling. In short, there is room for combining the aesthetic and the moral.[117]

Today, the experience of the sublime tends to be seen as "aesthetic" in the sense that was developed and consolidated above all by Kant. For introducing and defending rigid distinctions and divisions among the aesthetic, moral, and religious spheres, it is common to blame Kant (or praise him, depending on one's view). It is widely accepted that Kant, at least according to a prominent interpretation of him, divided up these three spheres and, even more than Baumgarten, helped shape aesthetics into the discipline it is today. Hence Buchenau can justly claim: "While the practical origin of Baumgarten's

---

[117] On this issue, see Kathrine Cuccuru, "The Problem with the History of Aesthetics before Aesthetics." Mirbach concludes her article on Baumgarten with the following lines: "Man can come near to God by striving for the perfection not only of his cognitive, but also of his appetitive faculties. In this last point I believe there is *(especially in the chapter on aesthetic greatness) a fundamental ethical and theological meaning for aesthetics* as theory of sensory cognition. This ethical and theological import of aesthetics for Baumgarten has hitherto not been realized to the extent it deserves. But it opens up a new horizon for the understanding and the evaluation of the complexity of Baumgarten's aesthetic theory in the history of aesthetics." Mirbach, "Aesthetic Greatness," 120; emphasis added.

aesthetics has not completely escaped the notice of interpreters, these interpreters, paradoxically, have preferred to view its *primary impulse* as *incompatible* with modern aesthetics. In their account, Baumgarten's practical view
is a relic from pre-modern art theory, and one of the main *problems* immanent
in his aesthetics."[118] Whether one thinks that Kant improved Baumgarten's
account or (as she hints) made things worse, what seems true is that, had current aesthetic theory followed the author of the *Aesthetics*, there would now
be much less hesitation in accepting the blending of the aesthetic and the
moral found in accounts of the sublime. It is the (apparently) Kantian division
that makes us pause at the notion of a moral sublime or even view the concept
of a moral sublime as being in tension with itself.

As noted, such a judgment may well involve a caricature of Kant. As we
have seen, Kant reunites (after separating them) interest and disinterest in the
sublime. Moreover, he combines (after distinguishing) the aesthetic and the
moral features of the experience of the sublime, by claiming that the sublime
is based on freedom and a capacity for moral feeling. Nevertheless, for those
who prefer straightforward and non-dialectical blendings of the aesthetic and
the moral, rather than a distinguishing and reuniting, Baumgarten could function as a viable source of inspiration.

---

[118] Buchenau, *The Founding of Aesthetics*, 178.

Chapter 11

The Discipline of Aesthetics Is the Aesthetics of Discipline

Baumgarten from Foucault's Perspective

Christoph Menke

In the classical conception of political sovereignty that has been dominant since the sixteenth and seventeenth centuries, the relationship between art and power is regulated by the concept of representation [*Räpresentation*]. This guarantees here the political significance of art. For its central problem lies in the representation of sovereignty, of which Hobbes's *Leviathan* is especially emblematic—more in the title page, however, than in the text itself. This problem consists in the fact that there can only be political sovereignty through its representation, not prior to it and not independently from it. Sovereignty must constitute itself through its representation. But in the process it surrenders itself at once to a mechanism that it can never entirely control—its achievement of representation is its success among its spectators.[1]

"The spectacle of the scaffold" describes an art of sovereign self-presentation, in which the punishing sovereignty displays the "spectacle of power letting its anger fall upon the guilty person."[2] Among the people taken as spectators—who are the "main characters"—it ought to provoke "feelings of terror" [*Terrorwirkung*][3] through which representation gains the evidence of presence. However, something else frequently happens:

Since the poorest—it was a magistrate who made the observation (Dupaty, 1786, 247)—could not be heard in the courts of law, it was where the law was manifested publicly, where they were called upon to act as witnesses and almost

---

[1] See Menke, "Die Depotenzierung des Souveräns im Gesang," 281–296.
[2] Foucault, *Discipline and Punish,* 58.
[3] Foucault, *Discipline and Punish,* 58.

as coadjutors of this law, that they could intervene, physically: enter by force into the punitive mechanism and redistribute its effects; take up in another sense the violence of the punitive rituals.[4]

The excess of violence displayed by the spectacle of the scaffold, through which sovereignty exhibits the fact that its "superiority is not simply that of right, but that of the physical strength,"[5] can have contagious effects. In it, there is "a whole aspect of the carnival, in which the roles are reversed, authority mocked, and criminals transformed into heroes."[6]

In contrast, the "art of the human body" operates in the opposite direction. Through this art, the new form of power of disciplines, which "in the course of the seventeenth and eighteenth centuries [. . .] became general formulas of domination,"[7] dissolves the public spectacle of the bodily scaffolds. In this new art of disciplines, no sovereign central instance represents itself anymore, since "discipline is a political anatomy of detail."[8] Its art does not aim any longer at representing the body of the king in its splendor, nor to leave the mark of his power on the body of the subjugated, but rather makes "the mechanism itself [the body] more obedient as it becomes more useful, and conversely."[9] The new "art" of the body in disciplinary power serves the production of usefulness, of normality, and no longer the (punishing or overwhelming) representation of sovereignty. More precisely: it aims at producing bodies that are docile, useful for their functions, because they are capable of self-determination; disciplining [*Diziplinierung*] fulfills itself as subjectivation [*Subjektivierung*]. That way, the art of disciplining evades the danger of the carnivalesque contagion of the violence in which sovereignty represents itself: insofar as it does not concern the people anymore as the spectator of power, but as its subject.

Disciplines are the arts of subjectivation: this is the definition of the new technologies of power that constitute the social reality of the Enlightenment, and it is at once the definition of the arts throughout Enlightenment, whose systematic elaboration gained from Alexander Gottlieb Baumgarten the title of "aesthetics." Aesthetics no longer thinks of the arts as representations of sovereign power; aesthetics is the thinking of the arts of the production and reproduction of subjectivity. From the perspective of *Discipline and Punish*, this must be spelled out in the following way: aesthetics is the thinking of disciplines, of disciplinary power. Nevertheless, nowhere does Foucault's

---

[4] Foucault, *Discipline and Punish*, 61.
[5] Foucault, *Discipline and Punish*, 49.
[6] Foucault, *Discipline and Punish*, 60 (translation modified).
[7] Foucault, *Discipline and Punish*, 137.
[8] Foucault, *Discipline and Punish*, 139.
[9] Foucault, *Discipline and Punish*, 138.

book speak explicitly of aesthetics as the new thinking of arts; *Discipline and Punish* does not speak *about* aesthetics. Nor does it have to, for it is aesthetics that *models* Foucault's analysis of disciplines: the model after which Foucault thinks disciplinary power in *Discipline and Punish* is aesthetics.

AESTHETIC DISCIPLINE

Foucault describes the new art of the body, through which disciplinary power is practiced, as the basic change in the concept of the body that it presupposes or produces. The object of subjectivation is no longer the mechanical body, "the image of which had for so long haunted those who dreamt of disciplinary perfection. This new object is the natural body, the bearer of forces and the seat of duration."[10] The body of disciplining is "a describable, analyzable object, not in order to reduce the individual to 'specific' features, as did the naturalist in relation to living bodies, but in order to maintain him in his individual features, in his particular evolution, in his own aptitudes or capacities, under the gaze of a permanent corpus of knowledge."[11]

The central concepts through which Foucault determines a body of disciplinary power that is no longer mechanical are those of force and capacity, of dynamics and development [*Entwicklung*].[12] "Disciplinary power has as its correlative an individuality that is not only analytical and 'cellular,' but also natural and 'organic.'"[13] But this means nothing else than the fact that the matrix of disciplinary power is Leibniz's metaphysics, which had already determined the monad in the same way. The monad has appetite, it has forces, it is self-acting, it creates novelty; the monad is organic (in other words, it lives). Leibniz's image of the monad is the metaphysics of the new microphysics of disciplinary power. And at the same time, Leibniz's metaphysics is the starting point for the new philosophical discipline of aesthetics: Baumgarten's aesthetics unfolds the systematic consequences out of Leibniz's new determination of force.[14] Foucault's analysis of disciplinary power and the thinking of aesthetics operate, therefore, on the basis of the

---

[10] Foucault, *Discipline and Punish,* 155.
[11] Foucault, *Discipline and Punish,* 190 [Whereas Foucault writes "dans son évolution particulière, dans ses aptitudes ou capacités propres" (see Foucault, *Surveiller et punir,* 223), Menke quotes Walter Seitter's German translation: "in seinem eigentümlichen Entwicklung, in seinen eigenen Fähigkeiten und Fertigkeiten" (See Foucault, *Überwachen und Strafen,* 245).]
[12] Compare Foucault, *Discipline and Punish,* 156, 160, 162.
[13] Foucault, *Discipline and Punish,* 156.
[14] On this issue, see Menke, "Das Wirken dunkler Kraft," 73–115. On the significance of Leibniz for the development of aesthetics, see Cassirer, *Leibniz's System,* 458 ff. See also Cassirer, *Freiheit und Form,* 62 ff. as well as Cassirer, *Philosophie der Aufklärung,* 368 ff.

same conceptual layout. This made it possible for Foucault to describe the disciplinary power with aesthetic figures of thought.[15]

The body's dynamic constitution stands at the center of those figures. Following Foucault's description, the body as the target of disciplinary power, of which it is "its effect as much as its object,"[16] is essentially temporal. Such temporality is that of a "continuously progressive organization."[17] The disciplinary power controls the body in such a way that it instructs its capacities, "bending its behavior towards a terminal state."[18] Disciplinary power controls the body while *exercising* it: "Exercise is that technique by which one imposes on the body tasks that are both repetitive and different, but always graduated."[19] But exercise is just as central to disciplinary power as it is for philosophical aesthetics, which designates it as *askesis* or *exercitatio*. Hence, Baumgarten offers three determining features of the "character" that make up a well-instructed, good, or competent aesthetician ("*ad characterem felicis aesthetici requiritur*"[20]). They fall into the categories of nature, praxis or exercise, and theory. Exercise mediates between nature and theory: it takes exercise to train the "natural aesthetic dispositions" of the soul (*aesthetica naturalis connata*) into the habit of beautiful thinking (*habitus pulchre cogitandi*),[21] and exercises are required to achieve the *disciplina aesthetica*, the philosophical doctrine of "perfected" beautiful cognizing that overcomes in practice "ignorance or uncertainty."[22] In this way, Baumgarten defines exercise as a "frequent repetition of similar actions," so that a harmony (*consensus*) of the naturally given capacities with regard to a specific topic, a specific task, is attuned.[23] Baumgarten compares it with soldiers' training,[24] which is also a paradigm for Foucault.[25] Crucial for the aesthetic understanding of the exercises is the insight into the decline that occurs when the exercises are not carried out or are not conducted correctly—"correctly meaning, here: ceaselessly, again and again:

---

[15] Foucault himself discusses Cassirer's *Philosophie der Aufklärung* in Foucault, "Une histoire restée muette," 545–549, which analyses the "fundamental problem of aesthetics." There, Foucault criticizes the privilege in the order of a history of ideas that Cassirer concedes to "philosophy and reflection." But then, the philosophy that Foucault's analysis of disciplinary power puts into brackets as an object still remains determinant as a model, as a form of thought.
[16] Foucault, *Discipline and Punish,* 161.
[17] Foucault, *Discipline and Punish,* 161.
[18] Foucault, *Discipline and Punish,* 161.
[19] Foucault, *Discipline and Punish,* 161.
[20] Baumgarten, *Aesthetica/Ästhetik,* §28.
[21] Baumgarten, *Aesthetica/Ästhetik,* §47.
[22] Baumgarten, *Aesthetica/Ästhetik,* §62.
[23] Baumgarten, *Aesthetica/Ästhetik,* §47.
[24] Baumgarten, *Aesthetica/Ästhetik,* §49.
[25] Foucault, *Discipline and Punish,* 179.

The spirit may be occupied with lifeless and cold exercises, but if the kind of mind has been neglected or completely corrupted and disdained, e.g. into a dominant passion and an overwhelming craving for hypocrisy [. . .], then, while a meager insignificance of the heart appears everywhere, what may seem to be beautifully thought is deformed.[26]

As Baumgarten composes the *Aesthetics* as a theory of the conditions for *successful* aesthetic exercises, he does not merely describe the subjectivation practices that Foucault analyzes as disciplinary power. Rather, aesthetics is already *part* of the new program for the disciplining of the body.[27]

According to Baumgarten, the success of the exercises does not just depend on their repetition, but also the knowledge of the one who imposes and controls them. On the one hand, the aesthetic exercises require general knowledge of the natural dispositions of human beings—the *aesthetica naturalis*. But beyond that, the success of the exercises also requires that they be adjusted to the level of development of the practitioner. This requires individual knowledge. Such is the "DYNAMIC or critical AESTHETICS," "which deals with the forces of a given person that are sufficient to achieve the beauty of a given cognition."[28] Foucault speaks of the "characterization of the individual"[29] that takes place through exercise or which is presupposed by it, while he sees in it the origin of the forms of knowledge in the human sciences.[30] Therefore, what the disciplinary power produces through the new form of knowledge in the exercises is nothing different than the "human": "And from such trifles, no doubt," the multiple exercises, surveillances, and sanctions of which disciplinary power is made, "the man of modern humanism was born."[31] Another word for human, in this decidedly modern sense (which Foucault's "Archeology of Human Sciences" already deals with in *The Order of Things*)[32] is the "subject"; hence, the procedures of disciplinary power are procedures of "subjectivation":

At the heart of the procedures of discipline, it [the examination procedure] manifests the subjectivation of those who are perceived as objects and the objectivation of those who are subjected.[33]

---

26 Baumgarten, *Aesthetica/Ästhetik*, §50.
27 See Caygill, *The Art of Judgment*, 103 ff.
28 Baumgarten, *Aesthetica/Ästhetik*, §60.
29 Foucault, *Discipline and Punish*, 161.
30 Foucault, *Discipline and Punish*, 183.
31 Foucault, *Discipline and Punish*, 141 [181].
32 Foucault, *The Order of Things*, 303 ff.
33 Foucault, *Discipline and Punish*, 184–185 (translation modified). The ambiguity of Foucault's "subjectivation" (*assujettissement*) is retrieved by the German translation in the formula "subjektivierende Unterwerfung." See Foucault, *Überwachen und Strafen*, 238. The French text reads: "*Au*

This is how Foucault defines the new disciplinary power. Disciplining means subjection or domination, but subjection or domination of a new type: it is a domination that gives the subjected the form and status of subjects.

This is the new concept of the subject, whose origins are analyzed in Foucault's studies of disciplinary power and also where Baumgarten's aesthetics finds its systematic center. Baumgarten releases the expression "subject" from its traditional meanings, in which it denotes the object of a statement or speech as well as the addressees of commands and orders, and gives this expression its modern meaning as the instance that can success-fully execute actions through its own faculties [*Vermögen*]. This becomes tangible in an exemplary way in the psychology chapter of Baumgarten's *Metaphysics*,[34] where he draws from the determination of aesthetics that is given in the *Reflections on Poetry* consequences for philosophical "psychol-ogy," the doctrine of the soul. Here, Baumgarten conceives the soul as a "determinate subject" that has "forces" of different kinds and magnitudes, "by which each subject is strong [or weak]" or "of which each substance [that is: each subject] is in command."[35] These forces are necessary to "actualize" something (*actuare*). Through its strength or weakness in a subject, such an actualization is "easy" or "difficult," then, "for a certain subject." Therefore, the new use of the expression "subject" that Baumgarten employs here pro-vides an understanding of the subject as an actor [*Akteur*], who actualizes something through his forces (*vires*) or faculties (*facultates*). Moreover, Baumgarten's subject consists of an actor whose forces can be greater or lesser and who, therefore, can find it more difficult or easier to achieve such an actualization; in other words, it is about an actor who, being "determinate" and thus different from others, is also an individual.

This is the image of aesthetics that Foucault's analysis of the new, bour-geois form of disciplinary power inscribes: insofar as Baumgarten's aesthetics lays out the foundations for the modern discourse of subjectivity, this is not only the starting point for idealistic philosophy and the hermeneutic sciences of the spirit (according to Ernst Cassirer's and Alfred Baeumler's interpreta-tion of Baumgarten's aesthetics[36]). According to Foucault's power-theoretical

---

cœur des procédures de discipline, il [sc. L'examen] manifeste l'assujettissement de ceux qui sont perçus comme des objets et l'objectivation de ceux qui sont assujettis." See Foucault, *Surveiller et punir*, 217.

[34] Hereafter, I follow the German translation of the psychology-chapter found in Baumgarten, *Texte zur Grundlegung der Ästhetik* (1983).

[35] Baumgarten, *Aesthetica/Ästhetik*, §527.

[36] Ernst Cassirer reads Baugarten's *Ästhetik* from the perspective of Kant's theory of spontaneity and freedom of spirit, cf. *Freiheit und Form*, 62 ff. Alfred Baeumler interprets the *Ästhetik* as the begin-ning of the hermeneutic opening of the individual in the realm of the human sciences, which Kant conceived in the third *Critique*, cf. Baeumler, *Das Irrationalitätsproblem* (1974). On Cassirer's reading of Baumgarten, see Haverkamp, "Wie die Morgenröthe," 24–30.

analysis, this is due to the fact that philosophical aesthetics, as conceived by Baumgarten, is a strict correlate of the new technologies of power that unfold in the procedures of the disciplines. This correlation prevails on two levels: first, philosophical aesthetics is an instrument of disciplining, insofar as its exercises carry out the "colonization" of the sensible.[37] Second, philosophical aesthetics is the ideology of such a praxis, insofar as it conceives the concept of its subject in the image of the *felix aestheticus* as a whole human being in agreement with itself. Aesthetics *means* therefore ideology,[38] and thus Foucault's tacit use of aesthetic terminology for the analysis of disciplinary power can be read as a reversal (return) of the reversal in which all ideology consists. This is confirmed by the fact that Baumgarten conceives aesthetics not only as theory but as an "art," a guideline for aesthetic exercises and thus as part of the disciplining enterprise, whose ideology it provides. The discipline of aesthetics is the aesthetics of discipline.

AESTHETICIZING DISCIPLINE

Foucault's thesis, according to which subjectivation is subjection, signifies that domination in bourgeois society is exercised through self-control, through self-guidance, and through self-determination; dominion over the subjects is executed in the disciplinary power through the freedom of the subjects. Aesthetic exercises—the exercises to which aesthetics leads and whose concept is elaborated by aesthetics—are an essential condition of this subjection. For its performance consists in dissolving the dualism of sensibility and understanding that rationalist philosophy had declared insurmountable. While Pascal, "tragically" sharpening this dualism, declares that it is "rare," indeed impossible, that "mathematicians be perspicacious and [that] perspicacious brains be mathematicians,"[39] so this is for Baumgarten only a "prejudice: that by nature the beauty of the spirit is in conflict with the more serious gifts of conceptual understanding and reasoning, insofar as these are innately received as from nature."[40] For

> Higher and universal spirits or geniuses of all time, Orpheus and the founders of poetic philosophy, Socrates, who is called the ironic one, Plato, Aristotle, Grotius, Descartes, and Leibniz, they all teach even from experience that

---

[37] Cf. Eagleton, *The Ideology of Aesthetic*, Chap. 1.
[38] Cf. de Man, *Aesthetic Ideology*, 70–128 [German trans., de Man, *Die Ideologie des Ästhetischen*, Teil I].
[39] Pascal, *Pensées*, 20. Cf. Goldmann, *The Hidden God*, 62 ff.
[40] Baumgarten, *Aesthetica/Ästhetik*, §41.

the disposition for the beautiful and for fundamental thinking come together [*convenire*], and that these can also dwell in a common site, which is not too narrow, also in accord with the more serious discipline of philosophers and mathematicians.[41]

Because the universal shows itself in the perfect (whereas the imperfect remains concealed), what Baumgarten says here about the "higher and universal spirits or geniuses of all times" has general validity: the "subject" or the "human being" is that instance where sensibility and understanding "come together" (*convenire*). For they cannot be conceived (and exercised) independently from one other.

But this can be understood in two wholly different and even opposite ways. It is this contraposition that defines aesthetics: the logic of aesthetics is in itself the conflicting and ambiguous logic of the "coming together" of sensibility and understanding at the site of the subject. Aesthetics itself unfolds as dispute.

According to one interpretation, aesthetics is about establishing the sensible—following the first paragraph of Baumgarten's *Aesthetics*—as the "analogue of reason."[42] Ernst Cassirer, who traces aesthetics back to Leibniz and formulates the analogy-thesis with Leibniz in mind, understands it this way: as the thesis according to which the insight gained by rationalist philosophy in regard to understanding applies also to sensibility, namely: that the sensible is not an event to which we are passively exposed, but rather our own "action." Accordingly, the sensible is not, as Descartes and Pascal describe it, constituted by a causal-determined effect (from body to body) and the vanities of the imagination (in the processing of those causal-effectuated impressions into numerous fantastic images, without any real content). But rather, "the sensible 'reception' of the impression is [. . .] also a form of intellectual action; even that mere receptivity dissolves into spontaneity for a deeper insight."[43] According to Cassirer, it is first through this insight into the analogy of understanding and sensibility that the modern concept of the subject is won. Thus, while rationalist philosophy divides the field of (self-) ability and (self-)action in half, it has in view only the half of the understanding. Aesthetics extends itself to the operations of sensibility; for these are also our actions, what we can do ourselves—our own self-determined activity.[44]

---

[41] Baumgarten, *Aesthetica/Ästhetik*, §43.
[42] Baumgarten, *Aesthetica/Ästhetik*, §1.
[43] Cassirer, *Freiheit und Form*, 76.
[44] And only first through this consequent subjectivization, according to Cassirer's Kantian argument, can the objectivity of cultural configurations be understood: "But only when it is reckoned that the reality of natural phenomena remits back to the ego's own actions and, moreover, that in this the ethical personality and with it the actuality of history can be gained; only then can it be understood

What Cassirer understands as the content of a "deeper insight"—the analogy of sensibility and understanding—considers aesthetics itself to be the result of a praxis, that is to say: of *its* praxis, the praxis of exercise. Only through aesthetic exercises can the irritating strangeness and power of sensibility (as Descartes and Pascal had described it) be broken and the analogy with understanding be established. The sensible is not an action of the subject, but it first *becomes* one—it is *made* into it. Aesthetics knows: the sensible must be cultivated—educated, exercised—in order to turn into an action of the subject. And, as the aesthetic theory of exercises modeled by Foucault's analysis of the disciplines shows, this is not a one-time (one-off) deed, but an unceasing, never-ending effort. This separates aesthetic exercise from philosophical meditation, which, according to Descartes, should reform one's thoughts and make them into one's own actions: unlike Cartesian meditation, aesthetic exercises do not set the "being" of the subject free, but rather they ought to generate it. Philosophical meditation *re*-produces; aesthetic exercise produces. Philosophical meditation reconstitutes the essential subjectivity of understanding; aesthetic exercise, in contrast, produces subjectivity in the sensible.

If aesthetic exercise is to subjectivize the sensible and generate it as the analogue of the understanding in the first place, then it also presupposes that the sensible *is not yet* subjective: that it is essentially and irreducibly a-subjective. Due to the fact that it must be exercised, aesthetic subjectivation presupposes the a-subjective [*das Asubjetktive*] and, therefore, cannot be—or can not be completely—achieved. In aesthetic exercise, the sensible stands within the tension between the analogy of the form of the understanding and the "alogy" [*Alogie*] of formlessness.[45] If aesthetics is the theory and praxis of the exercise of the sensible; and if the exercise of the sensible is only possible because it is both analogous and opposed to the form of the understanding, then aesthetics is the theory and praxis of this difference within the sensible (in the words of Baumgarten: the difference between the sensible as the field of "clear" perceptions, however confused they might be, and the field of "obscure" perceptions; between the sensible as "faculty" and as "force"). Aesthetics as the theory and praxis of exercise is the thinking of this difference: that between the identity (or analogy) of sensibility and understanding and their difference.

---

that the factors of artistic configuration [*künstlerischen Gestaltung*], precisely insofar as they point more vigorously and necessarily at the foundations in the 'subject,' produce a new kind of being that, in contrast to the empirical existence of things, is nothing retroactive and accidental [*nichts Nachträgliches und Zufälliges*], but has an independent truth and objectivity." See Cassirer, *Leibniz's System*, 458.

45 See the concept of "latency" (*Latenz*) in Haverkamp, "Wie die Morgenröthe," 27–33 and 226–229. See also Campe, "Vier Tropen bei Vico und Baumgarten," 192–193.

The discipline of aesthetics is the aesthetics of discipline: this describes aesthetics as an ideology and instrument of disciplinary subjectivation. But, at the same time, aesthetics is the reflection of discipline: its folding into its ground, which at once makes it possible and never lets it reach its end. The aesthetic exercises of the sensible repeat subjectivation through discipline and unfold the "obscure perceptions" as the "ground of the soul [FUNDUS ANIMAE],"[46] which are at once the possibility and the counterforce of subjectivation. This applies to the philosophical discipline or the discipline of philosophy—to which aesthetics does not quite belong, nor from which it can ever escape—as well as to the procedures of disciplinary power. Disciplinary power neither *defines* aesthetics nor does aesthetics stand *outside* the disciplines. Disciplining through aesthetics is answered by the aestheticization of discipline.[47]

Translated by Mauricio González

---

[46] Baumgarten, *Metaphysik*, §511.
[47] Cf. Caygill, "Über Erfindung und Neuerfindungen der Ästhetik," 233–242 and Menke, "Zweierlei Übung," 283–299.

Chapter 12

The Happy Aesthetician and the Feminist Killjoy

Baumgarten and Ahmed

Amelia Hruby

In this chapter, I intend to reconsider Alexander Gottlieb Baumgarten's account of the "happy aesthetician" (*felix aestheticus*) using Sara Ahmed's critique of happiness and the character of the feminist killjoy. Ultimately, I intend to perform a killjoy reading of Baumgarten's texts by illustrating the ways that Baumgarten fails to define or thematize happiness—so much so that we must read the "happiness" of the happy aesthetician as a subversive character, perhaps even against Baumgarten's own reliance on harmony and agreement in the happy aesthetician's beautiful thinking.[1]

I will begin by examining where and how Baumgarten conceptualizes happiness; first, by reviewing the places in which happiness appears in *Reflections on Poetry* and *Metaphysics* and pointing to the lack of clarity in Baumgarten's use of the word happiness in those texts, and then, by turning to Baumgarten's late text, the *Aesthetics*, to understand the character of the happy aesthetician that he introduces. While Baumgarten's early writings emphasize perfecting

---

[1] While there is a vast body of philosophical literature on happiness, for the sake of this comparison I will be limiting my scope of understanding happiness to these two thinkers, only bringing in other philosophers where Baumgarten or Ahmed themselves are in direct conversation with those thinkers. I limit this scope deliberately, as there is minimal literature explicitly considering Baumgarten and happiness, and I find it valuable to consider his writings on happiness on their own terms and then to stage this conversation between Baumgarten and Ahmed in order to reconsider the role of happiness in his work on feminist terms. For general overviews of philosophical literature on happiness, I suggest Nicholas White's *A Brief History of Happiness* (2008) and Darrin McMahon's *Happiness: A History* (2006). Julia Annas's *The Morality of Happiness* (1993) is also useful in this context, as she develops a comprehensive study of ancient ethical theory that considers the relationship of ancient ethics with modern ethical theories in terms of happiness; as is Stephen Engstrom and Jennifer Whiting's *Aristotle, Kant, and the Stoics: Rethinking Happiness and Duty* (1998) for its many essays considering eudaimonism in this historical context.

cognition vis-à-vis extensive clarity, the happy aesthetician is one who thinks *beautifully* (and thus happily), which in the *Aesthetics* means with richness, greatness, truth, clarity, certainty, and life. Neither Baumgarten's earlier texts nor the *Aesthetics* provide a definition of happiness or an argument for why happiness would result from beautiful thinking, but in his *Elements of First Practical Philosophy* (*Initia Philosophiae Practicae*, 1760), Baumgarten does more clearly suggest that the aesthetician's happiness seems to be the result of achieving the perfection of thinking beautifully. In this first part of this chapter, I aim to illustrate how Baumgarten fails to define happiness and to consider more precisely what Baumgarten has in mind when he designates the aesthetician as happy.

Having considered such questions, I will then contrast Baumgarten's happy aesthetician with Sara Ahmed's feminist killjoy. In her book *The Promise of Happiness*, Ahmed is deeply critical of happiness and the role it plays in modern society and philosophy. Ahmed is not concerned with what happiness *is*, but rather with raising the question of what work happiness *does* both for philosophers and contemporary political and social powers. In this second section of the chapter, I will turn Ahmed's question of what work happiness *does* back on Baumgarten, as I aim to reconsider what work happiness does in his texts in light of my previous critique of Baumgarten's failure to adequately define happiness. In doing so, I will propose that the work happiness does for the "happy" aesthetician is to cover up the ways in which her achieving the perfection of beautiful thinking must in some sense kill the joy of logic and introduce dissonance into the rationalist system through a proliferation of perfections. While Baumgarten himself seems to belie this dissonance by asserting the harmony and agreement of his system, I call this a killjoy reading so as to illustrate how I think we must undermine Baumgarten's own affirmations in order to uncover an implicit, aesthetic, and dissonant truth. Baumgarten's "happy" aesthetician is only "happy" in the subversively powerful way that Ahmed's feminist killjoy is joyous. Uncovering her subversive happiness allows us to also reconsider the subversive potential of Baumgarten's aesthetics.

HAPPINESS IN BAUMGARTEN

To begin, we must first consider where and how Baumgarten presents happiness in his philosophical writings, ultimately exploring how he fails to define the term in his early texts and provide a very undeveloped discussion of it in his later texts. In *Reflections on Poetry* (1735), Baumgarten uses the word happiness only once and only in its adverbial form. The word appears in the second to last section of the text where Baumgarten is explaining how aesthetics is the science of the lower cognitive faculty and should be considered as a science alongside logic, the science of the higher cognitive faculty. He argues that even though philosophers study the higher cognitive faculty, they "might still find occasion, not without ample reward, to inquire also into those devices by which they might improve the lower faculties of knowing, and sharpen them, and apply them *more happily* for the benefit of the whole world" (*Tunc enim daretur occasion philosophis non fine ingenti lucro inquirendi in ea etiam artificia, quibus inferiores cognescendi facultates expoliri possent, acui, & ad emolumentum orbis felicius adhiberi*).[2] At this point, Baumgarten does not explain how a philosopher might apply the lower faculties of knowing "more happily" for the benefit of the whole world. While this lack of explanation seems rather inconsequential in this text, it is an early sign of how Baumgarten is grappling with happiness in relation to aesthetics from the very beginning of his work and also shows the underdevelopment of happiness that remains throughout his work.

Happiness is not a major concept in Baumgarten's *Metaphysics* (1739) either, where it is included briefly in both the empirical and rational psychology chapters, without being thematized. In the empirical psychology—which is also where Baumgarten locates aesthetics—happiness is included as a quality of memory, particularly extensive memory. Baumgarten says there that "a greater memory is called GOOD and HAPPY, and insofar as it can recognize many great things, it is called EXTENSIVE (rich, vast)."[3] Here, Baumgarten is exploring what it means to recognize a representation that one had previously produced (to remember it), and happiness is a marker of a memory that can recognize many things. The ability to recognize many things is then named extensive, which echoes Baumgarten's discussion of extensive clarity in *Reflections on Poetry*, where he argues that extensively clear representations gather many things together. In this way, Baumgarten seems to connect happiness to aesthetics even in his discussion of memory.

Happiness, here, is also directly aligned with the good, as Baumgarten calls the greater memory "good *and* happy" (*bona & felix*).[4] Considering this *and*, it is also of note, that in this same section, Baumgarten identifies many other qualities of memory—firmness, tenacity, capability, vigorousness, and readiness[5]—each of which relate a single quality to a single function of memory: a memory that can recognize less intense representations among other representations is firm; a memory that can recognize something after a long time is tenacious; a memory that can recognize something reproduced only rarely is

---

[2] Baumgarten, *Reflections on Poetry*, §115 (emphasis added).
[3] Baumgarten, *Metaphysics*, §585.
[4] Baumgarten, *Metaphysics*, §585 (emphasis added).
[5] Baumgarten, *Metaphysics*, §585.

capable; a memory that can recognize more intensely is vigorous; and a memory that requires little for it to remember is ready. It is only with extension that a memory is one thing *and* another. "Good and happy" are the only two qualities of memory that come together, and Baumgarten provides no reasoning why goodness might imply happiness or vice versa. As in the *Reflections on Poetry*, the lack of explanation of happiness is rather inconsequential in this text, but it does provide another data point illustrating the vagueness that pervades Baumgarten's discussions of happiness—a concept which he seems to relate to aesthetics and the good without exploring what happiness itself may be or how this relationship works.

As mentioned previously, happiness is also included in the rational psychology of Baumgarten's *Metaphysics*. In that section of the text, it is used to describe nonhuman spirits. Baumgarten says, "The SPIRITS endowed with a higher essential degree of intellect than human beings are SUPERIOR, whereas those that have a lower grade are INFERIOR. They are both finite, and either happy or unhappy (§790). The former are GOOD SPIRITS (beautiful spirits), and the latter, EVIL SPIRITS."[6] Once again, happiness here is used as an adjective, to describe the quality of certain spirits. Finite spirits that are "happy" (*felices*) are "good spirits" (*agathodeamones/gute Geister*)— notably they are also "beautiful spirits" (*calodaemones*). While Baumgarten doesn't explain this parenthetical addition, it provides further support of the tentative connections Baumgarten is drawing between happiness, aesthetics, and the good in *Metaphysics*. It is also of note here that while happiness was a guiding motivation of many ethical theories that preceded Baumgarten, his own writings emphasize *obligation* rather than *happiness* as the motivating and regulating force of morality. In the context of his rational psychology, this even leads Baumgarten to argue that we have a certain kind of obligation toward happiness in our religious duties.[7] Perhaps it could even be said that Baumgarten's removal of happiness from moral philosophy allows him to relocate it in aesthetics, putting the concept of happiness to different work there. But that remains to be seen.

While happiness plays only very minor roles in *Reflections on Poetry* and *Metaphysics*, in the *Aesthetics* the concept of happiness is much more apparent in the character of the happy aesthetician, and it is in the discussion of this character that one can see the extent and effects of Baumgarten's failure

---

[6] Baumgarten, *Metaphysics*, §796.
[7] Clemens Schwaiger argues, for instance, that for Baumgarten, "the question of happiness is primarily a religious matter, which is why for him it is properly discussed in the context of rational psychology in relation to the 'last things.' In the domain of ethics itself, happiness is only mentioned in connection with our duties toward religion. Baumgarten even speaks explicitly of an obligation in relation to our happiness, something that would never even have occurred to Wolff." See Schwaiger, "The Theory of Obligation in Wolff, Baumgarten, and the Early Kant," 69.

to characterize happiness. Baumgarten first introduces this character in §27, where he proposes to explore "the genesis and the idea of the one who thinks beautifully, the CHARACTER OF THE HAPPY AESTHETICIAN, and enumerate the more closely related causes of beautiful thinking in a soul."[8] A primary focus of this text, then, is to define what it means to think beautifully such that one might cultivate the character of the happy aesthetician.

For Baumgarten, thinking beautifully means perfecting sensible cognition, and the beauty of thought is measured by its perfection. While it was suggested in *Reflections on Poetry* that the perfection of thinking beautifully is a matter of extensive clarity—which was seemingly a singular mode of perfection in that early text—in the *Aesthetics*, Baumgarten introduces a whole list of perfections of cognition: richness, greatness, truth, clarity, certainty, and life of cognition (*ubertas, magnitudo, veritas, claritas, certitudo, et vita cognitionis*).[9] To explain each briefly: by richness, Baumgarten has in mind the "copiousness, abundance, multitude, treasure, [and] wealth" of either a beautiful object (objective richness) or of a means of representing objects (subjective richness).[10] This category takes up Baumgarten's previous conception of extensive clarity to consider how much can be represented in a singular image. By greatness, Baumgarten means transcending simplicity of thought; akin to descriptions of the sublime, greatness entails both beautiful things that transcend the ability to be thought and an ability to think things bigger than oneself.[11] In the case of truth, Baumgarten distinguishes aesthetic truth from a logical truth[12] and requires the sensible recognition of the object's possibilities in their unity.[13] Aesthetic truths are not entirely divorced from logical truths, but rather in these sections, Baumgarten creates the category of the aestheticological truths, which suggests that sensible and intellectual truth can be combined.[14] The final perfection Baumgarten addresses in the first volume of the *Aesthetics* is clarity. This category hearkens again to his earlier discussions of extensive clarity, but in this instance describing how ways of thinking that represent many in the singular "shine with a beautiful shimmer," representing the multiplicity of cognition intuitively rather than just discursively.[15]

---

[8] Baumgarten, *Aesthetica*, §27.
[9] Baumgarten, *Aesthetica*, §22. These six perfections will only be explained in brief in this chapter. For further explanation, see Guyer, *A History of Modern Aesthetics*, 331–336 and Buchenau, *The Founding of Aesthetics*, 139–145.
[10] Baumgarten, *Aesthetica*, §115.
[11] Baumgarten, *Aesthetica*, §364–368, §422.
[12] Baumgarten, *Aesthetica*, §424, §429.
[13] Baumgarten, *Aesthetica*, §439.
[14] Baumgarten, *Aesthetica*, §440, §443.
[15] Baumgarten, *Aesthetica*, §618, §631.

By the time Baumgarten actually writes of certainty in the second volume of the *Aesthetics*, certainty (*certitudo*) has been replaced in his table of contents by persuasion (*persuasio*). The two, however, are related for Baumgarten. Certainty in logical truth, he argues, is *conviction*; certainty in aesthetic truth is *persuasion*.[16] The aesthetic perfection of certainty is a beautiful object or beautiful thought's ability to persuade. The final perfection of aesthetic cognition necessary for thinking beautifully is "life," but Baumgarten did not complete the sections of the *Aesthetics* on life before he died. While he describes the qualities of "lively" works of art in *Reflections on Poetry*[17] and aligns lively cognition with extensive clarity in the *Metaphysics*,[18] he never produced an extended discussion on what liveliness in aesthetic cognition might entail.[19]

While Baumgarten was unable to complete his Aesthetics, readers can perhaps see how he might have explored the concepts of life and liveliness further through the discussion of life in the work of his student Meier. Like Baumgarten, Meier aligns liveliness with extensive clarity.[20] He also goes on to explain the aesthetic life of cognition in terms of the powers of desire and the ability of beauty to evoke emotion.[21] Additionally, Meier emphasizes life as a preeminent perfection of aesthetic cognition, and for Meier aesthetic liveliness becomes the ultimate perfection of beautiful thinking.[22] Baumgarten himself does refer to life as "the foremost gift of beautiful cognition" in the *Aesthetics*,[23] but it is unclear whether he would have given it the ultimate status that Meier did.

Considering these six perfections of aesthetic cognition, however, does not seem to take Baumgarten (or the reader) any closer to a definition of happiness. Nothing in the *Aesthetics* makes an argument for why the happy aesthetician would be happy or why happiness would be the result of beautiful thinking. One way to attempt to resolve this question may be to turn to Baumgarten's late work *Elements of First Practical Philosophy* (*Initia Philosophiae Practicae*, 1760), where Baumgarten comes the closest to actually defining happiness. In this text, he distinguishes between theoretical and practical philosophy to consider human obligation. In §98, he defines complete law, which requires him to distinguish between human and divine law.[24] He then distinguishes between external happiness and internal happiness, arguing that the perfection of divine law yields external happiness and the

[16] Baumgarten, *Aesthetica*, §832.
[17] Baumgarten, *Reflections on Poetry*, §112.
[18] Baumgarten, *Metaphysics*, §517.
[19] See McQuillan, "The Aesthetic Perfection of Life," (Forthcoming).
[20] Meier, *Anfangsgründe*, Vol. 1, §33.
[21] Meier, *Anfangsgründe*, Vol. 1, §180.
[22] For more on this point, see Guyer, *A History of Modern Aesthetics*, 337.
[23] Baumgarten, *Aesthetica*, §188.
[24] Baumgarten, *Elements of First Practical Philosophy*, §98.

perfection of human law yields internal happiness.[25] Happiness is obtained by fulfilling different kinds of law, and the achievement of happiness is what makes the law complete. In other words, happiness is the result of a perfection—here, the perfect fulfillment of human or divine law.[26]

While this is not exactly a definition of happiness, it is the closest thing to a definition of happiness that Baumgarten has provided thus far. Carrying this notion of happiness as the effect of achieving perfection into Baumgarten's aesthetic texts suggests that *happiness is the result of the perfection of aesthetic cognition.* Having just reviewed Baumgarten's list of cognitive perfection in the *Aesthetics*, this raises the immediate question of "which perfection?" Does Baumgarten intend that the happy aesthetician perfect all six of the cognitive perfections he lists? Must the happy aesthetician perfect richness, greatness, truth, clarity, certainty, and life of cognition? Or might Baumgarten have had in mind what Meier later argues and thought that life (or one of the other perfections) was preeminently important? These questions are not clarified in Baumgarten's texts.

Additionally, there seems to be a deeper problem at stake in Baumgarten's utilization of happiness: that in the *Aesthetics* Baumgarten has no mechanism through which to explain *how* or *why* happiness would be the result of beautiful thinking. Baumgarten's aesthetic theory is based on aesthetic cognition, and his definition of beauty is based on the perfection of aesthetic cognition. The beauty of cognition itself, for Baumgarten, is the result of the perfection of beautiful thinking, as it is comprised of the agreement of the six aesthetic perfections he introduces in the *Aesthetics*.[27] In fact, Baumgarten opens §27, where he introduces the happy aesthetician, by saying "because the beauty of cognition is an effect of the one who thinks beautifully. . ." In reading Baumgarten, then, it is unclear how happiness is an additional, cognitive result of the perfection of aesthetic cognition when the beauty of cognition already results from this same cognitive perfection. This further raises the question, that if we are to rely on this understanding of happiness as a cognitive perfection, why would a purely cognitive conception of happiness be satisfactory in the first place? Does happiness require an affective dimension? And if so, does Baumgarten have the means in his texts to explain or explore one?

One can perhaps turn again to Baumgarten's student Meier to gain some clarity around how happiness might be a result of beautiful thinking and whether it is purely cognitive. The place of affect in philosophy and particularly aesthetics was a focus of Meier's work, and the ways in which Meier imports it into Baumgarten's system of cognitive perfections can be seen in the following excerpt of Meier's *Considerations on the First Principle of all Fine Arts and Sciences (Betrachtungen über den ersten Grundsatz aller*

---

[25] Baumgarten, *Elements of First Practical Philosophy,* §98.
[26] Baumgarten, *Elements of First Practical Philosophy,* §98.
[27] Baumgarten, *Aesthetica,* §22.

schönen Künste und Wissenschaften, 1757) where he recounts Baumgarten's aesthetic perfections and then adds new emphases and perfections of his own:

> For sensible representation to enjoy the greatest possible beauty, the following is required: 1) The wealth of these representations. A beautiful cognition must represent a great variety in a single image. Variation is pleasing. And the most beautiful cognition is to be considered like a broad region that contains infinitely many and different treasures. 2) The magnitude of cognition, the noble, the sublime, etc. For the sake of this beauty sensible cognition must not only represent great, suitable, important, noble objects, and so on, but must represent them in a way that is suitable and proportionate to their magnitude. 3) The truth of cognition. Without truth cognition is mere illusion, and thus the sensibly beautiful cognition must be as true as possible. 4) The liveliness and brilliance of cognition. 5) Its certitude. A sensible cognition, when it is to be properly beautiful, must not only produce conviction of its own beauty, but also conviction of the correct representation of its object. 6) The touching. A beautiful cognition must not only itself be as delightful as possible, but must also produce a proper gratification or dissatisfaction with its object. 7) The beautiful order in the entire fabric of a sensible representation, and in the interconnection and interweaving of all the individual representations, insofar as a whole is composed out of them. 8) The beautiful designation of sensible cognition. We can hardly ever or never think if we do not attach our thoughts to certain signs, which are related to the thoughts as the body is related to the soul. And thus if sensible cognition is to be as beautiful as possible, then so to speak not only its soul but also its body must have the greatest possible beauty.[28]

Wealth (richness), magnitude, truth, liveliness, and certitude are aesthetic, cognitive perfections that Meier takes from Baumgarten, but he also adds touching, order, and designation to this list. His emphasis on touching is particularly important for understanding how the perfection of aesthetic cognition may result in happiness as it considers the affective relationship between beautiful cognition and a beautiful object. For Meier, a key aspect of aesthetic perfection is the ability of beauty to "touch" us, to evoke feeling in the aesthetician who shall then feel gratification or dissatisfaction as a result of the experience.

Meier develops his discussion of how we are "touched" by beauty in his explanation of the "sensible life" of cognition in the first volume of the *Foundations*. There he argues that "a cognition is alive when it causes pleasure or pain, desire or aversion, through the intuition of a perfection or

---

[28] Meier, *Betrachtungen*, §22. Quoted and translated in Guyer, *A History of Modern Aesthetics*, vol. 1, 313.

imperfection."[29] Here Meier directly connects the cognitive faculty to the faculty of desire, bridging the divide between thought and feeling. He explains later in the *Foundations*, that just like the faculty of cognition is divided into higher and lower faculties which provide for the science of logic and the science of aesthetics, the faculty of desire is divided into higher and lower faculties—the will and feelings of pleasure and pain.[30] Meier then argues that beautiful objects (and other, particular kinds of representations) can evoke these feelings, either through distinct living cognition which excites the will or indistinct living cognition which produces pleasure or pain.[31]

Something akin to this appears in Baumgarten's *Reflections on Poetry* where he discusses the pleasure and pain associated with sensible representations[32] and explores this pleasure of the perfection of sound.[33] Baumgarten expands on this in the empirical psychology of the *Metaphysics* where he considers pleasure and pain in relation to the appetitive faculty.[34] That said, while Baumgarten emphasizes throughout his works that poetry arouses affects, these discussions largely disappear in the *Aesthetics* as Baumgarten emphasizes the cognitive perfection at stake in aesthetics. If anything, for Baumgarten, perfection is related to the good rather than to happiness ("Something is good if, when it is posited, a perfection is also posited"),[35] and the perfection of cognition to which pleasure is attached would be a marker of goodness and not happiness. Thus, there is still a missing link between beautiful thinking and a conception of happiness that extends beyond the cognitive. Baumgarten fails to provide a connection between the cognitive faculty and the faculty of desire that would definitively explain how thought and feeling—and more specifically, how beautiful thinking and happiness— are connected in the *Aesthetics*.[36]

It is worth noting here that unlike Baumgarten, Meier does follow through this connection between perfection, goodness, and happiness by connecting thought and emotion vis-à-vis the will or pleasure and pain. In the *Foundations*, Meier goes a step beyond Baumgarten in that he includes rules for the arousal of "aesthetic affections"[37] that explicitly connect pleasure,

---

[29] Meier, *Anfangsgründe*, Vol. 1, §35.

[30] Meier, *Anfangsgründe* Vol. 1, §178. Baumgarten also divides the faculty of desire into higher and lower faculties, but he does not align them with the will and pleasure and pain as Meier does. See *Metaphysics* Sections XVII and XVIII.

[31] Meier, *Anfangsgründe*, §178.

[32] Baumgarten, *Reflections on Poetry*, §24–§25.

[33] Baumgarten, *Reflections on Poetry*, §91–§97.

[34] Baumgarten, *Metaphysics*, §656–§662.

[35] Baumgarten, *Metaphysics*, §100.

[36] It should be noted that Baumgarten might have done this work if he had finished writing the *Aesthetics*. This is particularly relevant here because Baumgarten left the sections on sensible life unwritten which is where Meier makes the connection between thought and feeling.

[37] Meier, *Anfangsgründe*, §181–§187.

aesthetic cognition, and goodness (or badness). As a result, Meier creates the sorts of mechanisms necessary to understand how happiness would be the result of beautiful thinking (even though he does not use the concept of happiness to characterize beautiful thinking) and how happiness has both affective and cognitive dimensions. With the mechanism of aesthetic affections, Meier gives us the means to understand *how* the happy aesthetician would be happy as a result of beautiful thinking. And notably, Meier provides no such character as the "happy aesthetician" in his own work. Rather for Meier, the analogous character becomes the "beautiful spirit."[38]

Resolving the question of *how* the happy aesthetician might be happy vis-à-vis Meier still leaves the lingering question of *why*. In other words, knowing that the aesthetician *could* be happy still leaves the question of whether she actually *would* be. While it is possible to see how Baumgarten's aesthetician might become happy as a result of perfecting beautiful thinking, why happiness? Just as Baumgarten provides no argument for how the aesthetician might be happy, he also does not suggest why happiness is important for aesthetics. If anything, one might argue that Baumgarten is relying on an earlier strain of moral philosophy that would understand happiness to be an obvious goal or sign of moral goodness. But this is particularly ill-suited to Baumgarten, as Clemens Schwaiger points out, because his understanding of morality precisely rejects happiness as an aim and considers obligation to be foundational for ethics, presenting happiness most explicitly in connection with duty and goodness.[39] What then are we to make of happiness in Baumgarten? To begin to answer this question, we will now turn to contemporary feminist philosopher Sara Ahmed to see how her critique of the concept of happiness can be applied to Baumgarten.

HAPPINESS IN AHMED

Sara Ahmed opens her book *The Promise of Happiness* (2010) by raising a series of important questions about happiness. She argues that while happiness is often posited as a universal human desire, it is rarely defined in its own right and the *communal* nature of the desire for it is more often assumed than justified. And while Ahmed does not cite Baumgarten or Meier, she does reference their most famous reader—Immanuel Kant—on

---

[38] Meier's conception of the beautiful spirit here is not the same as the citation of Baumgarten's discussion of beautiful spirits previously. There Baumgarten was talking about spirits in the sense of incorporeal, thinking substances (human souls, angels, God, etc.) and here Meier is talking about the character of the aesthetician.

[39] Schwaiger, "The Theory of Obligation in Wolff, Baumgarten, and the Early Kant," 69.

the opening page of the book to consider his presumption of the universal striving toward happiness and mournful recollection of its indeterminacy.[40]

Ahmed notes from the very opening of the book that she is not concerned with what happiness *is* but rather with what happiness *does* in the world—precisely the question I want to ask of Baumgarten in this chapter (after explaining Ahmed's work). Raising the question of happiness, for Ahmed, means interrogating all of the things that (supposedly) make us happy and why we desire to be happy in the first place. She is particularly concerned with the idea that things "make" us happy, and the first chapter of the text considers how our colloquial idea of being "made happy" recognizes that happiness comes from outside ourselves. To explain this, Ahmed must note that she has "taken it as a given that happiness involves good feeling" and that (regardless of various other arguments in the history of philosophy) she finds it "hard to think about happiness without thinking about feeling."[41]

Ahmed's task then, as she sets it for herself in *The Promise of Happiness*, is "to think about *how* feelings make some things and not others good."[42] One can see then, that Ahmed is situating herself, very critically, in the midst of the many concepts that this chapter has shown are tenuously related in Baumgarten's work—happiness, goodness, and feelings. Therefore, understanding Ahmed's critiques of these concepts and returning to Baumgarten with them in mind may prove particularly fruitful in the efforts to understand Baumgarten's happy aesthetician.

As mentioned, Ahmed's interest in happiness is to trace the philosophical gestures through which happiness becomes aligned with the good.[43] To do so, she suggests returning to the root of the English word happiness, which is "hap," in order to recover the archaic sense of the word that emphasizes luck

---

[40] Ahmed, *The Promise of Happiness*, 1.

[41] Ahmed, *The Promise of Happiness*, 13. One of these various other arguments that Ahmed does not engage with here is the discussion among Artistotelians about Aristotle's distinguishing between the happy life and the life of pleasure, which Ahmed connects or seemingly conflates here (more on her discussion of Aristotle in footnote 13). For those interested in attending to Aristotle's distinction between happiness and pleasure, see Gosling and Taylor, *The Greeks on Pleasure* (1982); Owen, "Aristotelian Pleasures," 135–152; Rorty "The Place of Pleasure in Aristotle's Ethics," 481–493; Urmson, "Aristotle on Pleasure," 323–333; and Wolfsdork, *Pleasure in Ancient Greek Philosophy* (2013).

[42] Ahmed, *The Promise of Happiness*, 13.

[43] Ahmed clearly notes in her work that she is not claiming that "the Aristotelian [or, I would add, Kantian] approach to *eudaimonia* can be reduced to this critique" (Ahmed, *The Promise of Happiness*, 227). Rather, she says, "I am simply questioning *the gesture* that idealized classical happiness over contemporary happiness." To question this gesture, she puts into conversation more contemporary, societal and cultural conversations surrounding happiness with classical notions of happiness. To understand her accounts of Aristotle and Kant's work on *eudaimonia* and happiness, see Chapter 1 of *The Promise of Happiness*.

or good fortune.[44] Rather than happiness being an earned result of hard work, as it is often thought of now, happiness, Ahmed argues, must be realigned with its original notion of chance and contingency. Doing so, she says, will allow us to reconsider how happiness happens in the world rather than imagining happiness as something we produce or make.[45] Ahmed appeals to John Locke to illustrate the ways in which we make judgments of objects based on whether they produce pleasure or pain and that we call those objects that produce pleasure "good." She argues, however, that this association of pleasure with the good often moves too quickly and takes pleasure to be too permanent. Instead, she says that "it is not that good things cause pleasure, but that the experience of pleasure is how some things become good for us over time."[46]

Ahmed also wants to emphasize that in this schema happiness is conceived of simply as a particularly great form of pleasure. As we experience that pleasure, we begin to seek it out, and happiness becomes a particular orientation toward objects that produce pleasure for us. Thus, Ahmed defines happiness as "an orientation toward the objects we come into contact with."[47] Happiness is not a property of an object nor is it produced by the subject, rather it has a double or reciprocal mode. When we say that something "makes us happy," it is not that the thing has caused our happiness, but that the pleasure we take in the thing involves a happy orientation toward it, just as the experience of happiness registers that pleasure. As Ahmed argues, "We are moved by things [and] in being moved, we make things."[48] Certain things make us happy and in being happy we make those happy things. If we briefly consider this in Baumgarten aesthetic terms, certain beautiful objects affect us (richly, greatly, truthfully, clearly, lively-ly) and in being affected we cognize them beautifully. This double or reciprocal mode becomes one part of beautiful cognition that Baumgarten calls "the beauty of things and thoughts."[49] It denotes how the relationship between object and cognition of the object becomes a site of aesthetic perfection itself, and how—akin to what Ahmed argues with happiness—this makes beauty appear to be only a matter of cognition and not objects (or for Ahmed a matter of our orientation toward the object rather than any particular object itself).

---

[44] A similar association between happiness and luck can be found in the Latin *felix* and its cognates in Romance languages (*félicité* in French, *felice* in Italian, *feliz* in Spanish, etc.) as well as "felicity" in English.

[45] Ahmed, *The Promise of Happiness*, 22.

[46] Ahmed, *The Promise of Happiness*, 23.

[47] Ahmed, *The Promise of Happiness*, 24.

[48] Ahmed, *The Promise of Happiness*, 25.

[49] Baumgarten, *Aesthetics*, §18.

One of the problems with happiness, for Ahmed, is the way it takes on a futural quality. Ahmed argues that throughout the history of philosophy happiness has been an end rather than a means. Happiness, she seems to think (following philosophers like Aristotle), is always teleological, always a desired end—and often the ultimately desired end. As a result, objects become good insofar as they provide a means to happiness. These objects are simply instrumental. Ahmed also interprets the teleological quality of happiness temporally, arguing that insofar as happiness is always something pointed-toward then it is always, in a certain sense, futural. Thus, "we arrive at some things *because* they point us toward happiness . . . [but] an object can point toward happiness without necessarily having affected us in a good way."[50] In that happiness is the ultimate goal, objects can become markers that point toward happiness without actually producing any pleasure. And as a result "happiness becomes a question of following rather than finding."[51] What Ahmed wants to point out here is that if happiness is taken as the ultimate end of desire, and as such maintains this futural quality, then happiness is forever a forward direction that can never be perfectly or entirely achieved. It is only a promise, never actually a reward.

The second problem with happiness that Ahmed wants to emphasize is precisely the status of this "reward" and how happiness comes to be equated with goodness. Following Locke again, Ahmed argues that if happiness is an orientation toward objects, it becomes an orientation toward particular objects that are regulated by taste. It is here, Ahmed points out, that happiness loses its "hap," as taste is not simply a matter of chance but a matter of innate sense and cultural training over time. The concept of taste illustrates how the pleasure we take in objects is not just a matter of personal affect and orientation but also of social discourses and expectations.[52] These expectations teach or train us in regard to what objects to orient ourselves toward and what objects we should find pleasure in since they are accepted markers of happiness. Thus, Ahmed argues, "we acquire habits, as forms of good taste that differentiate between objects in terms of their affective as well as moral value. We have to work on the body such that the body's immediate reactions, how we sense the world and make sense of the world, take us in the 'right' direction."[53] Here Ahmed points out how happiness evolves from a simple taking pleasure in an object to an intensive social training of what

---

[50] Ahmed, *The Promise of Happiness*, 27.
[51] Ahmed, *The Promise of Happiness*, 32.
[52] One might think of Hume's discussion of taste here in which he articulates taste as a "natural equality" but then argues that it is in agreement among critics who have developed and perfected their sense of taste in which the "true standard of taste and beauty" is found. See Hume, "On the Standard of Taste," 137.
[53] Ahmed, *The Promise of Happiness*, 34.

objects are not only pleasurable but also good. When the good feelings of happiness become a matter of good taste, then the objects take on a social quality in which they are identified as good separately from their evocation of pleasurable feelings. The goal of happiness then becomes not seeking pleasure but cultivating the habit of identifying the good or moving in the "right" direction.

Ahmed's final point of critique in this chapter, though, is not simply that happiness becomes a habit as a matter of taste, but rather the ways in which that habit disappears and happiness appears to be free again. Ahmed explores how "to have good habits is to be oriented in the right way toward the right objects (not to insist on being proximate to objects that insist on enjoyment)."[54] What the emphasis on taste in relation to pleasure does, Ahmed argues, is attempts to "liberate" happiness from the body by making happiness merely a matter of cultivating a particular cognitive relation to an object, separate from sensory enjoyment of the object. "To work on the body such that you have the right reactions," Ahmed argues, "allows the body to disappear from view" in that the work of the body in reacting comes to appear as "natural" or "given."[55] Thus, happiness, which was originally rooted in the sensation of pleasure prior to a logical cognition of that sensation, through certain readings of aesthetics becomes almost entirely divorced from sensual experience of the world. Rather "happiness is about learning to be affected by objects in the right way. The very possibility that we can affect our affections by action, or through will or reason, becomes the basis of an ethical imperative."[56] Here Ahmed shows again how happiness is aligned with the good, this time, however, appearing as self-evidently good. We do not just follow our pleasure toward happiness, rather we establish what makes us happy by cultivating our affects in the right way. This is an ethical or moral imperative masked as simply a sensory drive. Thus that which appears to be a "natural" or "given" reaction of the body may in fact be a socialized response.

---

[54] Ahmed, *The Promise of Happiness*, 34.

[55] Ahmed, *The Promise of Happiness*, 34.

[56] Ahmed, *The Promise of Happiness*, 56. When reading Ahmed on this point, I think about Wesley Morris's 2018 essay for *New York Times Magazine* in which he recounts a conversation with another black man where he admitted to questioning the believability of Issa Rae's popular show *Insecure*. As a result, Moore was admonished by his conversation partner for failing to recognize the cultural importance of the show and Rae's status as a black woman. Moore says, "My tablemate insisted that who and what the show represents are more important than whether the show works *for me*." This is exactly what I think Ahmed is talking about when she critiques how aesthetics becomes a matter of taste at the expense of pleasure—how Moore's experience of the show (his lack of pleasure, in this instance) becomes irrelevant in the face of a larger cultural narrative of taste (which in this case must consider racial representation and its rarity) that argues he *must* enjoy the show. Wesley Morris. "Should Art Be a Battleground for Social Justice?" *The New York Times*, October 03, 2018.

REREADING HAPPINESS IN BAUMGARTEN

At this point, Ahmed's critique of happiness can be brought to bear on Baumgarten, to see how her reading of the function of happiness is and is not operative in his work. Remembering that Ahmed's question is not "what is happiness?" but "what does happiness do?" it seems evident from the work in this chapter that Baumgarten is precisely one of the thinkers who presume the universality of happiness while failing to define the term. As has been shown, he repeatedly uses the concept of happiness in relation to the beautiful and the good without giving a definition of what happiness is. What, however, does happiness *do* for Baumgarten? That's not entirely clear either. In reading his work, there is no argument for why the concept of happiness emerges to describe the aesthetician. In fact, what the aesthetician does is think beautifully, not happily. Why not call her the beautiful aesthetician, then? As readers, we must then ask what implicit work the concept of happiness is doing for Baumgarten when he describes the aesthetician as happy.

While Baumgarten provides no answer, I would like to suggest (following Ahmed's general critique) that he describes the aesthetician as happy in order to align aesthetics with goodness. It behooves him to mark the aesthetician as happy in order to elevate the status of the science of aesthetics. Since introducing aesthetics in *Reflections on Poetry*, Baumgarten consistently argues that aesthetics is necessary to understand the lower faculties of cognition. In the opening of the *Aesthetics*, he spends a dozen sections defending aesthetics as a true science, and he argues that it serves as a "sister" to logic.[57] If Baumgarten identifies happiness with aesthetics (rather than logic, which he identifies with knowledge of the truth), then he gives aesthetics a stronger valence of the good and makes it a more desirable category. There is no "happy logician" for Baumgarten, but he argues that there is a "happy aesthetician." As Ahmed says, "When happiness is assumed to be a self-evident good, then it becomes evidence of the good."[58] Insofar as Baumgarten saw happiness to be a self-evident good, then branding the aesthetician as happy provides evidence of the good in aesthetics. It seems that Baumgarten precisely uses happiness in the way that Ahmed critiques. By failing to provide any substantive definition of or function for the concept, he employs it instrumentally for external aims.

Ahmed's critique of happiness, of course, extends beyond this use of happiness as evidence of the good, and she is also concerned with how happiness becomes a habit that makes it appear as a free affect when it is

---

[57] Baumgarten, *Aesthetica*, §13.
[58] Ahmed, *The Promise of Happiness*, 13.

in fact a cultivated reaction. Baumgarten's happy aesthetician is certainly actively cultivating her aesthetic habits. Baumgarten devotes a large part of his plan for the *Aesthetics*, in fact, to outlining the habits of the happy aesthetician in terms of innate aesthetic temperament, aesthetic exercises, aesthetic teaching, aesthetic enthusiasm, and aesthetic improvement.[59] All of these, he suggests, are means of thinking beautifully as one develops the perfections of sensible cognition that is rich, great, truthful, clear, certain, and lively.

The problem with happiness in relation to habit for Ahmed, however, is not simply that habits exist but the way that they disappear as cultivated responses and appear to be free reactions. As previously mentioned, Ahmed is openly critical of aesthetic thinking that locates the aesthetic in the disappearance of consciously cultivated good habits into the "freedom" of disinterested aesthetic experience and taste.[60] Baumgarten's continual emphasis on habit, however, does not allow it to disappear so easily. To achieve the perfection of beautiful thinking the happy aesthetician must cultivate a number of aesthetic habits. One might be able to see how the disappearance of those habits may be an ultimate goal for Baumgarten, as those habits would perhaps be less necessary or appear given where perfection to be obtained, but Baumgarten himself makes no such assertion.[61] Therefore, while one can see in Baumgarten's presumption of happiness the implicit suggestion of an aesthetic good, there is not yet the more dangerous (for Ahmed) articulation of aesthetics in which the habitual cultivation of happiness is mistaken for free sensation.

Using Ahmed's critique of happiness to reread Baumgarten's underdeveloped account of happiness provides new understanding of the work happiness does for Baumgarten, even if it still fails to define the concept of happiness in his work. Following Ahmed through her critique of happiness and taste, however, also severely undermines the value of Baumgarten's aesthetic project if his assertion that the aesthetician is happy only serves to align his aesthetics with the good. To perhaps reclaim some of the value for Baumgarten's aesthetic system, this chapter will conclude by reconsidering his happy aesthetician alongside Ahmed's feminist killjoy to better understand the status of "happiness" and "joy" for these two figures.

---

[59] Baumgarten, *Aesthetica*, Sections II–VII.
[60] Ahmed, *The Promise of Happiness*, 35.
[61] In fact, Kant has to get rid of the notion of perfection all together in order to establish his aesthetic system that frees aesthetics from habit (as Ahmed claims), so this liberatory quality that Ahmed critiques which conceals habit as freedom doesn't seem to be at play in Baumgarten because of his reliance on perfection.

THE HAPPY AESTHETICIAN AND
THE FEMINIST KILLJOY

The character of the feminist killjoy is introduced in the second chapter of Ahmed's *The Promise of Happiness* to explore the consequences of refusing happiness in a society founded on the universal desire for it. Feminist consciousness, Ahmed argues, is not only consciousness of gendered experience but also "consciousness of the violence and power that are concealed under the languages of civility and love."[62] Throughout her critique of happiness, Ahmed strives to show how it "provides as it were a cover, a way of covering over what resists or is resistant to a view of the world, or a worldview as harmonious."[63] The feminist, in her awareness of this covering-over, must then always be uncovering the violence and power at stake in things in which people find pleasure or stability. She must be upsetting their happiness in order to show what lies beneath or within—always introducing dissonance to harmony. This certainly kills many peoples' joy. And, as Ahmed says, "feminists do kill joy in a certain sense: they disturb the very fantasy that happiness can be found in certain places."[64] Ahmed underscores just how widespread and pervasive these fantasies can be in *Living a Feminist Life* (2017). There she highlights how "you can cause unhappiness by noticing something. And if you can cause unhappiness by noticing something, you realize that the world you are in is not the world you thought you were in."[65] The feminist killjoy, in this sense, changes the world by noticing and uncovering something disturbing and painful, and insofar as she produces unhappiness in doing so, she becomes "bad." For her, the earlier-articulated process of how something pleasurable is transformed into something good occurs inversely or in the negative.

This may be precisely what Baumgarten is trying to avoid when he affixes the label of "happy" to the aesthetician. From the moment Baumgarten establishes "aesthetics" as a science alongside logic, he initiates a certain kind of break within a tradition that has emphasized the pervasiveness of logic. In articulating why and how aesthetics is a "sister science" to logic, he attempts to elevate what has forever been a "lower" faculty. He marks thinking *beautifully* as just as important as thinking *logically*, and in doing so he reorganizes and introduces dissonance into a system that has always emphasized harmony and completeness.

---

[62] Ahmed, *The Promise of Happiness,* 86.
[63] Ahmed, *The Promise of Happiness,* 83–84.
[64] Ahmed, *The Promise of Happiness,* 66.
[65] Ahmed, *Living a Feminist Life,* 62.

That being said, it must be noted that Baumgarten also works to uphold the values of harmony and completeness in his aesthetic science. He keeps the emphasis on perfection, and he considers beauty a matter of not only one but three agreements ("the unified agreement of thoughts among themselves" is the beauty of things and thoughts or the beauty of appearance; "the agreement of the order in which we think about beautiful things" is the beauty of order; and "the internal agreement of signs" is the beauty of signification).[66] Baumgarten's idea of "the beauty of sensible cognition and the tastefulness of things" emphasizes "the maximal possible agreement of the appearances,"[67] and his description of beautiful thinking demands the agreement of six aesthetic qualities.

But even in consistently affirming the importance of harmony and agreement, Baumgarten always seems to belie this harmony within his system. If we understand happiness (for Baumgarten) to be a matter of the increased perfection of cognition as was explored in previous sections, in the case of aesthetics it is still a *different* kind of perfection for a *different* kind of cognition than in the logical traditions. While Baumgarten affirms the value of harmony, his valorization of the lower faculty still belies its difference as he works to explain the *aesthetic* perfections of the qualities of richness, greatness, truth, clarity, certainty, and life that he introduces. In the case of certainty, this difference even slips into his organization of the system, where he renames the category persuasion to highlight *aesthetic* certainty, which is different than logical certainty which he calls conviction. The six qualities that comprise the perfection of cognition themselves also seem to introduce difference into Baumgarten's system, as it never becomes clear how to value them in relation to each other and which one or another may be more important. Baumgarten emphasizes that they must all be "in agreement with each other in a representation" but what does that actually look like? He certainly has a drive to perfection, order, and agreement in his system, but he himself cannot seem to realize this ideal and the workings-out of his system betray his emphasis on perfection always defined as agreement. Therefore, while Baumgarten is certainly not a thinker of radical difference on its own terms (as he attempts to uphold values of harmony and agreement in his philosophy), it is notable that his system introduces difference and dissonance in many places where there had previously only been sameness by consistently articulating and elevating the sensuous and sensible nature of aesthetics in a philosophical framework that traditionally valued logic over sensation.

Thus, perhaps describing the aesthetician as happy is precisely a way to mask the disagreement Baumgarten introduces in his thought and to cover

---

[66] Baumgarten, *Aesthetica,* §18–§20.
[67] Baumgarten, *Aesthetica,* §24.

up the ways that his aesthetics and the aesthetician are resistant to a more exclusively logical view of the world. Were the aesthetician to truly fulfill Baumgarten's articulations and introduce new modes of perfection, new standards for cognition, and new emphases on the lower faculties, she would likely not be happy or would at least not find her happiness in the world because she would be resisting dominant constructions of happiness as agreement and perfection. In fact, following Ahmed's killjoy, she would likely be causing unhappiness as she noticed something lacking in an emphasis on logic in life or a system that valorized the higher faculties.

By performing this killjoy reading that uncovers the work of happiness to cover unhappiness and disturbs the happy fantasy of Baumgarten's happy aesthetician, we have now aligned her with the feminist killjoy. Insofar as the aesthetician would end up disturbing long-held truths about the world, she would kill a certain kind of joy in a world that conceives of itself through those terms. Unlike the rationalist and aesthetic thinkers that create various constellations of beauty, goodness, and happiness based on harmony and agreement, she would revel in modes of dissonance that elevate the sensible as equal to the logical. She would expose the limitations of logic to explain all modes of experience, and she would propose her own sensible understandings beyond those limitations.

And while the "happy" aesthetician might create unhappiness, this does not necessarily mean that she would be unhappy. Rather as Ahmed admits, the "happy" aesthetician would find that "there can even be joy in killing joy."[68] For Ahmed, killing joy is a matter of uncovering false truths and living outside their harmonies; it is a matter of standing in opposition to a culture that covers up unhappiness with happiness. The feminist killjoy finds joy in reclaiming her experience outside the agreement of oppressive narratives. Analogously, the "happy" aesthetician can take joy in uncovering the value of sensible cognition and challenging the dominance of logic. She would not be happy in the way that Baumgarten seems to posit as a self-evident result of beautiful thinking, but she would be "happy" in her own subversive (rather than harmonious) way.

CONCLUSION

In conclusion, in reading Baumgarten we must take seriously his claim that the aesthetician would be happy and equally seriously his failure to explain how or why. This failure calls us to read his text as killjoys and to critique

---

[68] Ahmed, *The Promise of Happiness*, 87.

his use of the concept of happiness in order to consider what other work his "happy" aesthetician does. As Ahmed argues, "If we [feminist killjoys] do not assume that happiness is what we must defend, if we start questioning that happiness we are defending, then we can ask other questions about life, about what we want for life, or what we want life to become."[69]

Reconsidering how Baumgarten's aesthetic thought conceives of happiness allows us to better consider the differences he introduces by elevating the lower faculties of cognition, by articulating how sensuous experience may have its own perfections, and by considering a world in which thinking beautifully is as important as or even more important than thinking logically. Once we consider these differences, we are better able to understand what work happiness does for Baumgarten. While he seems to designate the aesthetician as happy in order to mask her subversive potential, perhaps she is "happy" precisely because she has reorganized the hierarchy of philosophical sciences and her own experience of the world. If we reread Baumgarten as killjoys, we uncover dissonance where there was once only harmony and agreement and rediscover the aesthetician's "happiness" alongside the subversive potential in Baumgarten's aesthetics.

---

[69] Ahmed, *The Promise of Happiness*, 218.

Permissions

This volume contains revised versions of the following material, reproduced here with permission:

Buchenau, Stefanie. "Baumgarten's Aesthetics: Topics and the Modern Ars Inveniendi" in *The Founding of Aesthetics in the German Enlightenment.* Cambridge: Cambridge University Press, 2013 © Stefanie Buchenau 2013, published by Cambridge University Press. Reproduced with permission of the Licensor through PLSclear.

Franke, Ursula. *Baumgartens Erfindung der Ästhetik.* Münster: Mentis Verlag, 2018. (Originally published in German)

Grote, Simon. "Pietist Aisthesis and Moral Education in the Works of Aelxander Gottlieb Baumgarten" in *Alexander Gottlieb Baumgarten: Sinnliche Erkentnis in der Philosophie des Rationalismus*, edited by Alexander Aichele and Dagmar Mirbach. Hamburg: Felix Meiner Verlag, 2008. (Originally published in German)

Adler, Hans. "Herder's Engagement with Baumgarten" in *Die Prägnanz des Dunklen: Gnoseologie - Ästhetik - Geschichtsphilosophie bei Johann Gottfried Herder.* Hamburg: Felix Meiner Verlag, 1990. (Originally published in German)

Menke, Christoph. "The Discipline of Aesthetics is the Aesthetics of Discipline: Baumgarten from Foucault's Perspective" in *Baumgarten-Studien: Zur Genealogie der Ästhetik*, edited by Rüdiger Campe, Anselm Haverkamp, and Christoph Menke. Berlin: August Verlag, 2014. (Originally published in German)

Bibliography

[Anonymous]. "Johann Jacob Rambach, *Geistliche Poesien*." In *Unschuldige Nachrichten von Alten und Neuen Theologischen Sachen*, edited by Valentin Ernst Löscher. Leipzig: Jacobi, 1736, 785–787.

[Anonymous]. *Index acroasium ex omni scientiarum et disciplinarum bonarum genere*. Halle, September 1735.

[Anonymous]. *Catalogus lectionum aestivalium*. Halle, April 1732.

[Anonymous]. *Anleitung zur Poesie*. Breßlau: Hubert, 1725.

Abbt, Thomas. *Vermischte Werke*. Berlin/Stettin: Friedrich Nicolai, 1780–1782.

Abbt, Thomas. "Leben und Charakter Gottlieb Alexander Baumgartens." In *Vermischte Werke*. Berlin/Stettin: Friedrich Nicolai, 1780, Vol. 4, 215–244.

Abbt, Thomas. *Briefe die neueste Literatur betreffend*. Berlin: Friedrich Nicolai, 1759–1767.

Adler, Hans. "Das neue Verhältnis von Vernunft und Sinnen: Ästhetik." In *Handbuch Literatur und Philosophie*, edited by Andrea Allerkamp and Sarah Schmidt. Berlin: Walter de Gruyter, forthcoming.

Adler, Hans. "Was ist ästhetische Wahrheit." In *Schönes Denken. A.G. Baumgarten im Spannungsfeld zwischen Ästhetik, Logik und Ethik*, edited by Andrea Allerkamp and Dagmar Mirbach. Hamburg: Felix Meiner Verlag, 2016a, 49–66.

Adler, Hans. "Kritische Wälder." In *Herder Handbuch*, edited by Stefan Greif, Marion Heinz, and Heinrich Clairmont. München: Fink, 2016b, 443–469.

Adler, Hans. "Aisthesis, steinernes Herz und geschmeidige Sinne. Zur Bedeutung der Ästhetik-Diskussion in der zweiten Hälfte des 18. Jahrhunderts." In *Der ganze Mensch. Anthropologie und Literatur im 18. Jahrhundert*, edited by Hans-Jürgen Schings. Stuttgart/Weimar: J.B. Metzler, 1994, 96–111.

Adler, Hans. *Die Prägnanz des Dunklen. Gnoseologie – Ästhetik – Geschichtsphilosophie bei J. G. Herder*. Hamburg: Felix Meiner Verlag, 1990.

Adler, Hans. "Fundus Animae – Der Grund der Seele. Zur Gnoseologie des Dunklen in der Aufklärung." *Deutsche Vierteljahrsschrift für Literaturwissenschaft und Geistesgeschichte* 62 (1988): 197–220.

Adler, Hans, and Wolff, Lynn L. *Aisthesis und Noesis. Zwei Erkenntnisformen vom 18. Jahrhundert bis zur Gegenwart*. Paderborn: Fink, 2013.

Ahmed, Sara. *Living a Feminist Life*. Durham: Duke University Press, 2017.

Ahmed, Sara. *The Promise of Happiness*. Durham: Duke University Press, 2010.

Aichele, Alexander. "Wahrheit – Gewißheit – Wirklichkeit. Die systematische Ausrichtung von A. G. Baumgartens Philosophie." In *Alexander Gottlieb Baumgarten: Sinnliche Erkenntnis in der Philosophie des Rationalismus*, edited by Alexander Aichele and Dagmar Mirbach. Hamburg: Felix Meiner Verlag, 2008, 13–36.

Aichele, Alexander. "Die Ungewißheit des Gewissens. Alexander Gottlieb Baumgartens forensische Aufklärung der Aufklärungsethik." *Jahrbuch für Recht und Ethik* 13 (2005): 3–30.

Aichele, Alexander. "Sive vox naturae sive vox rationis sive vox Dei? Die metaphysische Begründung des Naturrechtsprinzips bei Heinrich Köhler, mit einer abschließenden Bemerkung zu Alexander Gottlieb Baumgarten." *Jahrbuch für Recht und Ethik* 12 (2004): 115–135.

Aichele, Alexander. "Die Grundlegung einer Hermeneutik des Kunstwerks. Zum Verhältnis von metaphysischer und ästhetischer Wahrheit bei Alexander Gottlieb Baumgarten." *Studia Leibnitiana* 31 (1999): 82–90.

Aichele, Alexander, and Mirbach, Dagmar. *Alexander Gottlieb Baumgarten: Sinnliche Erkenntnis in der Philosophie des Rationalismus*. Hamburg: Felix Meiner Verlag, 2008.

Aichele, Alexander, and Theis, Robert. *Handbuch Christian Wolff*. Wiesbaden: Springer, 2018.

Allerkamp, Andrea. "Onirocritica und mundus fabulosus. Traum und Erfindung." In *Schönes Denken. A. G. Baumgarten im Spannungsfeld von Ästhetik, Metaphysik und Naturrecht*, edited by Andrea Allerkamp and Dagmar Mirbach. Hamburg: Felix Meiner Verlag, 2016, 201–221.

Allerkamp, Andrea, and Mirbach, Dagmar. *Schönes Denken. A. G. Baumgarten im Spannungsfeld von Ästhetik, Metaphysik und Naturrecht*. Hamburg: Felix Meiner Verlag, 2016.

Allison, Henry E. *Kant's Transcendental Idealism: An Interpretation and Defense (Revised and Enlarged Edition)*. New Haven: Yale University Press, 2004.

Allison, Henry E. *Kant's Transcendental Idealism: An Interpretation and Defense*. New Haven: Yale University Press, 1983.

Alsted, Johann Heinrich. *Encyclopaedia*. Herborn, 1630.

Altmann, Alexander. *Moses Mendelssohns Frühschriften zur Metaphysik*. Tübingen: Max Niemeyer Verlag, 1969.

Annas, Julia. *The Morality of Happiness*. Oxford: Oxford University Press, 1993.

Apel, Karl Otto. "Das Leibapriori der Erkenntnis. Eine Betrachtung im Anschluß an Leibnizens Monadenlehre." *Archiv für Philosophie* 12.1/2 (1963): 152–172.

Aristotle. *Poetics*. Translated by Richard Janko. Indianapolis: Hackett Publishing, 1987.

Arnold, Antje. *Rhetorik der Empfindsamkeit: Unterhaltungskunst im 17. und 18. Jahrhundert*. Berlin: Walter de Gruyter, 2012.

Arnoldt, Daniel Heinrich. *Versuch einer systematischen Anleitung zur deutschen Poesie überhaupt.* Königsberg: Stelter, 1732.

Assmann, Aleida. *Einführung in die Kulturwissenschaft. Grundbegriffe, Themen, Fragestellungen.* Berlin: Schmidt, 2008.

Assunto, Rosario. *Die Theorie des Schönen im Mittelalter.* Köln: Verlag M. DuMont Schauberg, 1963.

Atlas, Dustin N. "What God Does Not Possess: Moses Mendelssohn's Philosophy of Imperfection." *Journal of Jewish Thought and Philosophy* 27 (2019): 26–59.

Badura, Jens. "Erkenntnis (sinnliche)." In *Künstlerische Forschung. Ein Handbuch*, edited by Jens Badura, Selma Dubach, Anke Haarmann, Dieter Mersch, Anton Rey, Christoph Schenker, and Germán Toro Pérez. Zürich/Berlin: Diaphanes, 2015, 43–48.

Baeumler, Alfred. *Das Irrationalitätsproblem in der Ästhetik und Logik des 18. Jahrhunderts bis zur Kritik der Urteilskraft.* Darmstadt: Wissenschaftliche Buchgesellschaft, 1967.

Baeumler, Alfred. *Kants Kritik der Urteilskraft. Ihre Geschichte und Systematik.* München: Max Niemeyer, 1923.

Bahr, Petra. *Darstellung des Undarstellbaren. Religionstheoretische Studien zum Darstellungsbegriff bei A.G. Baumgarten und I. Kant.* Tübingen: Mohr Siebeck, 2004.

Barck, Karlheinz. "Ästhetik. Wandel ihres Begriffs im Kontext verschiedener Disziplinen und unterschiedlicher Wissenschaftskulturen." *Archiv Begriffsgeschichte* (Sonderheft, 2000): 55–62.

Barck, Karlheinz, and Kliche, Dieter. "Ästhetik/ästhetisch." In *Ästhetische Grundbegriffe*, edited by Karlheinz Barck, et al. Stuttgart/Weimar: J. B. Metzler, 2000, Vol. 1, 308–400.

Barck, Karlheinz, Fontius, Martin, Schlenstedt, Dieter, Steinwachs, Burkhart, and Wolfzettel, Friedrich. *Ästhetische Grundbegriffe.* Stuttgart/Weimar: J. B. Metzler, 2000.

Barth, Heinrich. *Philosophie der Erscheinung.* Basel: Schwabe Verlag, 1947/1959.

Baumgarten, Alexander Gottlieb. *Aesthetica – Ästhetik.* Translated by Constanze Peres. Paderborn: Wilhelm Fink, Forthcoming.

Baumgarten, Alexander Gottlieb. *Elements of First Practical Philosophy.* Edited and translated by Courtney D. Fugate and John Hymers. London: Bloomsbury, 2020.

Baumgarten, Alexander Gottlieb. *Estetica* (New Edition). Edited by Alessandro Nannini, translated by Salvatore Tedesco. Palermo: Aesthetica, 2020.

Baumgarten, Alexander Gottlieb. *Métaphysique.* Translated by Luc Langlois and Émilie-Jade Poliquin. Paris: Vrin, 2019.

Baumgarten, Alexander Gottlieb. *Metaphysics: A Critical Translation with Kant's Elucidations, Selected Notes, and Related Materials.* Edited and translated by Courtney D. Fugate and John Hymers. London: Bloomsbury Publishing, 2013.

Baumgarten, Alexander Gottlieb. "Aesthetics." In *Bloomsbury Anthology of Aesthetics*, edited by Joseph Tanke and Colin McQuillan. London: Bloomsbury, 2012, 158–162.

Baumgarten, Alexander Gottlieb. *Metaphysica/Metaphysik* (1st Ed., 1739 – 4th Ed., 1757, Lateinisch – Deutsch, Historisch-kritische Ausgabe). Edited and translated by Günter Gawlick and Lothar Kreimendahl. Stuttgart-Bad Cannstatt: Frommann-Holzboog, 2011.

Baumgarten, Alexander Gottlieb. *Aesthetica/Ästhetik*. Edited and translated by Dagmar Mirbach. Hamburg: Felix Meiner Verlag, 2007.

Baumgarten, Alexander Gottlieb. *Estetica*. Translated by Francesco Piselli. Milan: Vita e Pensiero, 1992.

Baumgarten, Alexander Gottlieb. *Esthétique*. Translated by Jean-Yves Pranchère. Paris: L'Herne, 1988a.

Baumgarten, Alexander Gottlieb. *Theoretische Ästhetik*. Edited and translated by Hans Rudolf Schweizer. Hamburg: Felix Meiner Verlag, 1988b.

Baumgarten, Alexander Gottlieb. *Texte zur Grundlegung der Ästhetik*. Edited and translated by Hans Rudolf Schweizer. Hamburg: Felix Meiner Verlag, 1983a.

Baumgarten, Alexander Gottlieb. *Philosophische Betrachtungen über einige Bedingungen des Gedichtes*. Edited and translated by Heinz Paetzold. Hamburg: Felix Meiner Verlag, 1983b.

Baumgarten, Alexander Gottlieb. *Reflections on Poetry*. Edited and translated by Karl Aschenbrenner and William B. Holther. Berkeley: University of California Press, 1954.

Baumgarten, Alexander Gottlieb. "Kollegium über die Ästhetik." In *Alexander Gottlieb Baumgarten. Seine Bedeutung und Stellung in der Leibniz-Wolffischen Philosophie und seine Beziehungen zu Kant. Nebst Veröffentlichung einer bisher unbekannten Handschrift der Ästhetik Baumgartens*, edited by Bernhard Poppe. Borna/Leipzig: Robert Noske, 1907, 59–258.

Baumgarten, Alexander Gottlieb. *Gedanken bei den Reden Jesu nach dem Inhalt der Evangelischen Geschichten*. Edited by Friedrich Gottlob Scheltz and Anton Bernhard Thiele. Pförten: Brükner, 1796.

Baumgarten, Alexander Gottlieb. *Metaphysica* (7th Ed.). Halle: Carl Hermann Hemmerde, 1779.

Baumgarten, Alexander Gottlieb. *Acroasis Logica* (2nd Ed.). Edited Johann Gottlieb Toellner. Halle: Carl Hermann Hemmerde, 1773.

Baumgarten, Alexander Gottlieb. *Philosophia Generalis*. Edited by Johannes Christian Foerster. Halle: Carl Hermann Hemmerde, 1770.

Baumgarten, Alexander Gottlieb. *Sciagraphia Encyclopaediae philosophicae*. Edited by Johann Christian Foerster. Halle: Carl Hermann Hemmerde, 1769.

Baumgarten, Alexander Gottlieb. *Metaphysica* (6th Ed.). Halle: Carl Hermann Hemmerde, 1768.

Baumgarten, Alexander Gottlieb. *Metaphysica* (5th Ed.). Halle: Carl Hermann Hemmerde, 1763.

Baumgarten, Alexander Gottlieb. *Acroasis Logica in Christianum L.B. de Wolff*. Halle: Carl Hermann Hemmerde, 1761.

Baumgarten, Alexander Gottlieb. *Aestheticorum pars altera*. Frankfurt an der Oder: Kleyb, 1758.

Baumgarten, Alexander Gottlieb. *Metaphysica* (4th Ed.). Halle: Carl Hermann Hemmerde, 1757.

Baumgarten, Alexander Gottlieb. *Aesthetica*. Frankfurt an der Oder: Kleyb, 1750a.

Baumgarten, Alexander Gottlieb. *Metaphysica* (3rd Ed.). Halle: Carl Hermann Hemmerde, 1750b.

Baumgarten, Alexander Gottlieb. *Metaphysica* (2nd Ed.). Halle: Carl Hermann Hemmerde, 1743a.

Baumgarten, Alexander Gottlieb. *Scriptis quae moderator conflictus academici disputavit*. Halle: Hemmerde, 1743b.

Baumgarten, Alexander Gottlieb. *Philosophische Brieffe von Aletheophilus*. Frankfurt and Leipzig, 1741a.

Baumgarten, Alexander Gottlieb. *Gedancken vom Vernuenfftigen Beyfall auf Academien* (2nd Ed.). Halle: Carl Hermann Hemmerde, 1741b.

Baumgarten, Alexander Gottlieb. *Ethica philosophica*. Halle: Hemmerde, 1740.

Baumgarten, Alexander Gottlieb. *Metaphysica*. Halle: Carl Hermann Hemmerde, 1739.

Baumgarten, Alexander Gottlieb. *Meditationes philosophicae de nonnullis ad poema pertinentibus*. Halle: Grunerti, 1735.

Baumgarten, Alexander Gottlieb, and Michaelis, Christian Benedict (praes). *Dissertatio chorographica notiones superi et inferi, indeque adscensus et descensus in chorographiis sacris evolvens*. Halle: Meyhii, 1735.

Baumgarten, Siegmund Jacob. "Vorrede." In *Oden Davids oder poetische Uebersetzung der Psalmen, Erster Theil*, edited by Samuel Gotthold Lange. Halle: Bauer, 1746.

Baumgarten, Siegmund Jacob. *Unterricht vom recht-mäßigen Verhalten eines Christen oder Theologische Moral*. Halle: Bauer, 1744.

Baumgarten, Siegmund Jacob. *Unterricht von Auslegung der heiligen Schrift*. Halle: Bauer, 1742.

Baumgarten, Siegmund Jacob. *Opuscula quae latine scripsit*. Halle: Bauer, 1740.

Baumgarten, Siegmund Jakob. *Unterricht vom rechtmässigen Verhalten eines Christen, oder Theologische Moral*. Halle: Bauer, 1738.

Baumgarten, Siegmund Jacob. *Öffentliche Anzeige seiner diesmaligen Akademischen Arbeit*. Halle: Bauer, 1734.

Beiser, Frederick C. *Diotima's Children: German Aesthetic Rationalism from Leibniz to Lessing*. Oxford: Oxford University Press, 2009.

Beiser, Frederick C. *The Fate of Reason: German Philosophy from Kant to Fichte*. Cambridge: Harvard University Press, 1987.

Belting, Hans. *Bild und Kult. Eine Geschichte des Bildes vor dem Zeitalter der Kunst* (3rd Ed.). München: Beck, 1993.

Bender, Wolfgang. "Rhetorische Tradition und Ästhetik im 18. Jahrhundert: Baumgarten, Meier, Breitinger." *Zeitschrift für Deutsche Philologie* 99 (1980): 481–506.

Bergmann, Ernst. *Die Begründung der deutschen Ästhetik durch Alex. Gottlieb Baumgarten und Georg Friedrich Meier*. Leipzig: Schunke, 1911.

Berndt, Frauke. *Facing Poetry: Alexander Gottlieb Baumgarten's Theory of Literature*. Berlin: Walter De Gruyter, 2020.

Berndt, Frauke. "Die Kunst der Analogie. A. G. Baumgartens literarische Epistemologie." In *Schönes Denken. A. G. Baumgarten im Spannungsfeld von*

Ästhetik, Metaphysik und Naturrecht, edited by Andrea Allerkamp and Dagmar Mirbach. Hamburg: Felix Meiner Verlag, 2016, 183–199.

Berndt, Frauke. "Ex marmore. Evidenz im Ungeformten bei J. J. Winckelmann und A. G. Baumgarten." In *Präsenz und Evidenz fremder Dinge im Europa des 18. Jahrhunderts*, edited by Birgit Neumann. Göttingen: Wallstein Verlag, 2015, 73–96.

Berndt, Frauke. *Poema/Gedicht. Die epistemische Konfiguration der Literatur um 1750.* Berlin: Walter de Gruyter, 2011.

Bezzola, Tobia. *Rhetorik bei Kant, Fichte und Hegel.* Tübingen: Max Niemeyer, 1993.

Bilfinger, Georg Bernhard. *Dilucidationes philosophicae de Deo, anima humana, mundo et generalibus rerum affectionibus.* Tübingen: Cotta, 1725.

Blänker, Reinhard "Die Viadrina und Alexander Gottlieb Baumgarten." In *Schönes Denken. A. G. Baumgarten im Spannungsfeld von Ästhetik, Metaphysik und Naturrecht*, edited by Andrea Allerkamp and Dagmar Mirbach. Hamburg: Felix Meiner Verlag, 2016, 299–316.

Blaschke, Bernd. "Leuchttürme und Irrlichter des Hässlichen. Ein Sammelband sucht ästhetische Alternativen zum Schönen." https://literaturkritik.de/id/9771 (2006).

Bloch, Ernst. *Das Prinzip Hoffnung.* Frankfurt am Main: Suhrkamp Verlag, 1959.

Bodmer, Johann Jakob, and Breitinger, Johann Jakob. "Schreiben an Se. Excellentz Christian Wolffen." In *Von dem Einfluß und Gebrauche der Einbildungs-Krafft.* Frankfurt und Leipzig, 1727.

Böhme, Gernot. *Aisthetik. Vorlesungen über Ästhetik als allgemeine Wahrnehmungslehre.* München, 2001.

Böhme, Hartmut, and Böhme, Gernot. *Das Andere der Vernunft. Zur Entwicklung von Rationalitätsstrukturen am Beispiel Kants.* Frankfurt am Main: Suhrkamp Verlag, 1983.

Böhr, Christoph. *Philosophie für die Welt. Die Popularphilosphie der deutschen Spätaufklärung im Zeitalter Kants.* Stuttgart/Bad Cannstatt: Frommann-Holzboog, 2003.

Boileau Despréaux, Nicolas. "Preface to his Translation of Longinus on the Sublime." In *The Sublime Reader*, edited by Robert R. Clewis. London: Bloomsbury Publishing, 2019, 57–61.

Borchers, Stefan. *Die Erzeugung des ganzen Menschen: Zur Entstehung von Anthropologie und Ästhetik an der Universität Halle im 18. Jahrhundert.* Berlin: Walter de Gruyter, 2011.

Bouhours, Dominique. *La manière de bien penser dans les ouvrages d'esprit, dialogues.* Paris: Mabre-Cramoisy, 1687.

Brämer, Carl Friedrich. *Gründliche Untersuchung von dem wahren Begriffe der Dichtkunst.* Danzig: Schreiber, 1744.

Breitinger, Johann Jakob. *Vertheidigung der schweitzerischen Muse.* Zürich: Heidegger, 1744.

Buchenau, Stefanie. "Wolffs Rezeption in der Ästhetik." In *Handbuch Christian Wolff*, edited by Robert Theis and Alexander Aichele. Wiesbaden: Springer, 2018, 405–425.

Buchenau, Stefanie. *The Founding of Aesthetics in the German Enlightenment: The Art of Invention and the Invention of Art*. Cambridge: Cambridge University Press, 2013.

Buchenau, Stefanie. "Die Einbindung von Poetik und Ästhetik in die Logik der Aufklärung." In *Kunst und Wissen. Beziehungen zwischen Ästhetik und Erkenntnistheorie im 18. und 19. Jahrhundert*, edited by Astrid Bauereisen, Stephen Pabst, and Achim Vesper. Würzburg: Königshausen & Neumann, 2009a, 81–84.

Buchenau, Stefanie. "Die Einbindung von Poetik und Ästhetik in die Logik der Aufklärung." In *Kunst und Wissen*, edited by Astrid Bauereisen, Stephan Pabst, and Achim Vesper. Würzburg: Königshausen & Neumann, 2009b, 71–84.

Buchenau, Stefanie. "Die Sprache der Sinnlichkeit. Baumgartens poetische Begründung der Ästhetik in den Meditationes philosophicae." In *Alexander Gottlieb Baumgarten: Sinnliche Erkenntnis in der Philosophie des Rationalismus*, edited by Alexander Aichele and Dagmar Mirbach. Hamburg: Felix Meiner Verlag, 2008, 151–173.

Buchenau, Stefanie. "Sinnlichkeit als Erkenntnisvermögen. Zum Begriff des Vernunftähnlichen in der Psychologie Christian Wolffs." In *Die Psychologie Christian Wolffs. Systematische und historische Untersuchungen*, edited by Oliver-Pierre Rudolph and Jean-Francois Goubet. Tübingen: Max Niemeyer, 2004, 191–206.

Buchenau, Stefanie, and Marti, Hanspeter. "Nr. 46/Baumgarten." In *Rhetorik, Poetik und Ästhetik im Bildungssystem des Alten Reiches*, edited by Hanspeter Marti, Reimund B. Sdzuj, and Robert Seidel. Köln/Weimar/Wien: Böhlau, 2017, 444–454.

Bühler, Axel. "Ein Plädoyer für den hermeneutischen Intentionalismus." In *Fiktion, Wahrheit, Wirklichkeit. Philosophische Grundlagen der Literaturtheorie* (3rd Ed.), edited by Maria E. Reicher. Münster: Mentis Verlag, 2016, 178–198.

Bühler, Axel, and Cataldi Madonna, Luigi. "Von Thomasius bis Semler. Entwicklungslinien der Hermeneutik in Halle." In *Hermeneutik der Aufklärung*, edited by Axel Bühler and Luigi Cataldi Madonna. Hamburg: Felix Meiner Verlag, 1993, 49–70.

Buschmann, Cornelia. "Connubium rationis et experientiae: Das Problem von Erfahrung und Theorie in seiner Bedeutung für den Denkeinsatz der Philosophie Christian Wolffs." In *Gottfried Wilhelm Leibniz im philosophischen Diskurs über Geometrie und Erfahrung*, edited by Harmut Hecht. Berlin: Akademie Verlag, 1991.

Buschmann, Cornelia. "Philosophische Preisfragen und Preisschriften der Berliner Akademie, 1747–1768. Ein Beitrag zur Leibniz-Rezeption im 18. Jahrhundert." *Deutsche Zeitschrift für Philosophie* 35 (1987): 779–789.

Campe, Rüdiger. "Vier Tropen bei Vico und Baumgarten. Zur Inversion von Kulturwissenschaft und Ästhetik." In *Baumgarten-Studien, Zur Genealogie der Ästhetik*, edited by Rüdiger Campe, Anselm Haverkamp, and Christoph Menke. Köln: August Verlag, 2014a, 192–193.

Campe, Rüdiger. "Effekt der Form. Baumgartens Ästhetik am Rande der Metaphysik." In *Baumgarten-Studien, Zur Genealogie der Ästhetik*, edited by

Rüdiger Campe, Anselm Haverkamp, and Christoph Menke. Köln: August Verlag, 2014b, 117–144.

Campe, Rüdiger. "Bella Evidentia. Begriff und Figur von Evidenz in Baumgartens *Ästhetik.*" *Deutsche Zeitschrift für Philosophie* 49 (2001): 243–256.

Campe, Rüdiger, Haverkamp, Anselm, and Menke, Christoph. *Baumgarten-Studien. Zur Genealogie der Ästhetik.* Köln: August Velag, 2014.

Carpov, Jakob. *Ausführliche Erläuterung der Wolffischen vernünftigen Gedancken von der Menschen Thun und Lassen.* Frankfurt and Leipzig, 1735.

Carpzov, Johann Benedict. *Sempiternae memoriae spectabilis consultis et excellentis viri Carol Gerard Guilielmi Lodtmann.* Helmstedt: Schnorr, 1755.

Cassirer, Ernst. "Die Philosophie der Aufklärung." In *Werke* (*Hamburger Ausgabe*), edited by Claus Rosenkranz. Hamburg: Felix Meiner Verlag, 2003, Vol. 15.

Cassirer, Ernst. "Freiheit und Form. Studien zur deutschen Geistesgeschichte." In *Werke* (*Hamburger Ausgabe*), edited by Reinold Schmücker. Hamburg: Felix Meiner Verlag, 2001, Vol. 7.

Cassirer, Ernst. *Philosophie der Aufklärung.* Hamburg: Felix Meiner Verlag, 1998.

Cassirer, Ernst. *Freiheit und Form. Studien zur deutschen Geistesgeschichte.* Darmstadt: Wissenschaftliche Buchgesellschaft, 1994.

Cassirer, Ernst. *Leibniz' System in seinen wissenschaftlichen Grundlagen.* Hildesheim: Georg Olms Verlag, 1980.

Cassirer, Ernst. *The Philosophy of the Enlightenment.* Translated by Fritz C. A. Koelln and James P. Pettegrove. Princeton: Princeton University Press, 1951.

Casula, Mario. "A.G. Baumgarten entre G.W. Leibniz et Ch. Wolff." *Archives de Philosophie* 42.4 (1979): 547–574.

Caygill, Howard. "Über Erfindung und Neuerfindungen der Ästhetik." *Deutsche Zeitschrift für Philosophie* 49 (2001): 233–242.

Caygill, Howard. *The Art of Judgment.* Oxford: Basil Blackwell, 1989.

Chladenius, Johann Martin. *Einleitung zur richtigen Auslegung vernünftiger Schriften.* Leipzig: F. Lanckisch, 1742.

Cicero. *On Invention.* Translated by H. M. Hubbell. Cambridge: Harvard University Press, 1949.

Cicero. *On the Orator.* Translated by H. M. Hubbell. Cambridge: Harvard University Press, 1942.

Cicero. *Tusculan Disputations.* Translated by J. E. King. Cambridge: Harvard University Press, 1927.

Cicero. *On Ends.* Translated by H. Rackham. Cambridge: Harvard University Press, 1914.

Cicero. *On Duties.* Translated by Walter Miller. Cambridge: Harvard University Press, 1913.

Clewis, Robert R. "Why the Sublime is Aesthetic Awe." *Journal of Aesthetics and Art Criticism*, forthcoming.

Clewis, Robert R. "Towards a Theory of the Sublime and Aesthetic Awe." In *The Sublime Reader*, edited by Robert R. Clewis. London: Bloomsbury Publishing, 2019, 340–354.

Clewis, Robert R. *The Sublime Reader.* London: Bloomsbury Publishing, 2019.

Clewis, Robert R. "The Place of the Sublime in Kant's Project." *Studi kantiani* 28 (2015): 149–168.

Clewis, Robert R. "A Case for Kantian Artistic Sublimity: A Response to Abaci." *Journal of Aesthetics and Art Criticism* 68.2 (2010): 167–170.

Clewis, Robert R. *The Kantian Sublime and the Revelation of Freedom*. Cambridge: Cambridge University Press, 2009.

Costelloe, Timothy M. *The Sublime: From Antiquity to the Present*. Cambridge: Cambridge University Press, 2012.

Cuccuru, Kathrine. "The Problem with the History of Aesthetics Before Aesthetics." Unpublished manuscript.

De Man, Paul. *Aesthetic Ideology*. Edited by Andrzej Warminski. Minneapolis: University of Minnesota Press, 1996.

De Man, Paul. *Die Ideologie des Ästhetischen*. Edited by Christoph Menke. Frankfurt am Main: Suhrkamp Verlag, 1993.

Décultot, Elisabeth. "Aesthetik/esthétique: étapes d'une naturalisation (1750–1840)." *Revue de métaphysique et de morale* 34 (2002): 7–28.

Demeter, Tamás, and Schliesser, Eric. "The Use and Abuse of Mathematics in Early Modern Philosophy: Introduction." *Synthese* 196 (2019): 3461–3464.

Descartes, René. *Philosophical Writings*. Edited by John Cottingham, Robert Stoothoff, and Dugald Murdoch. Cambridge: Cambridge University Press, 1985–1991.

Dilly, Heinrich. *Kunstgeschichte als Institution. Studien zur Geschichte einer Disziplin*. Frankfurt am Main: Suhrkamp Verlag, 1979.

Doran, Robert. *The Theory of the Sublime from Longinus to Kant*. Cambridge: Cambridge University Press, 2017.

Duncan, Bruce. "Sturm und Drang Passions and Eighteenth-Century Psychology." In *Literature of the Sturm und Drang*, edited by David Hill. Rochester: Boydell & Brewer, 2002, 47–68.

Dyck, Corey W. *Early Modern German Philosophy*. Oxford: Oxford University Press, 2019.

Dyck, Corey W. "Between Wolffianism and Pietism: Baumgarten's Rational Psychology." In *Metaphysics in Baumgarten and Kant*, edited by Courtney Fugate and John Hymers. Oxford: Oxford University Press, 2018.

Dyck, Corey W. *Kant & Rational Psychology*. Oxford: Oxford University Press, 2014.

Eagleton, Terry. *The Ideology of Aesthetic*. Oxford, Cambridge: Basil Blackwell, 1990.

Eberhard, Johann August. *Allgemeine Theorie des Denkens und Empfindens*. Berlin: Christian Friedrich Voß, 1776.

Eco, Umberto. *On Ugliness*. Translated by Alistair McEwan. New York: Rizzoli, 2007.

Eco, Umberto. *On Beauty: A History of a Western Idea*. London: Secker & Warburg, 2004.

Ehrenspeck, Yvonne. "Aisthesis und Ästhetik. Überlegungen zu einer problematischen Entdifferenzierung." In *Aisthesis/Ästhetik. Zwischen Wahrnehmung und*

Bewußtsein, edited by Klaus Mollenhauer and Christoph Wulf. Weinheim: Deutscher Studien Verlag, 1996, 201–229.

Einem, Johann Justus von. *Martini Lutheri poemata*. Magdeburg: Siegler, 1729.

Emmel, Armin. "Logische, ästhetische und metaphysische Wahrheit bei Alexander Gottlieb Baumgarten." In *Identität – Logik – Kritik*, edited by Benedikt Fait and Danielz Zumpf. Berlin: Lit Verlag, 2014, 209–242.

Emmel, Armin. "Alexander Gottlieb Baumgarten, *Ästhetik*, übers. u. hrsg. von Dagmar Mirbach, 2 Bände, Hamburg 2007." *Zeitschrift für philosophische Forschung* 63 (2009): 342–346.

Engstrom, Stephen, and Whiting, Jennifer. *Aristotle, Kant, and the Stoics: Rethinking Happiness and Duty*. Cambridge: Cambridge University Press, 1998.

Ezell, Margaret. "John Locke's Images of Childhood: Early Eighteenth-Century Responses to Some Thoughts Concerning Education." *Eighteenth Century Studies* 17.2 (1983): 139–155.

Federlin, Wilhelm L. *Kirchliche Volksbildung und Bürgerliche Gesellschaft. Studien zu Thomas Abbt, Alexander Gottlieb Baumgarten, Johann David Heilmann, Johann Gottfried Herder, Johann Gerd Müller und Johannes von Müller*. Frankfurt am Main: Peter Lang, 1993.

Ferraris, Maurizio. "Analogon rationis." *Pratica filosofica* 6 (1994): 5–126.

Finsen, Hans Carl. "Evidenz und Wirkung im ästhetischen Werk Baumgartens. Texttheorie zwischen Philosophie und Rhetorik." *Deutsche Vierteljahrsschrift für Literaturwissenschaft und Geistesgeschichte* 70 (1996): 198–212.

Fischer, Kuno. *Gottfried Wilhelm Leibniz*. Heidelberg: Winter, 1920.

Fisher, Kuno. *Geschichte der neuern Philosophie* (Vol. 2: *Leibniz und seine Schule*, 2nd Ed.). Heidelberg: Friedrich Bassermann, 1867.

Flögel, Karl Friedrich. *Einleitung in die Erfindungskunst*. Breslau/Leipzig: Johann Ernst Mayer, 1760.

Foerster, Johann Christian. *Charaktere dreier berühmter Weltweisen der neueren Zeit, nämlich Leibnizens, Wolffs und Baumgartens*. Halle, 1765.

Fontius, Martin. "Baumgarten und die Literaturbriefe. Ein Brief aus Frankfurt an der Oder an Louis Beausobre in Berlin." *Deutsche Vierteljahrsschrift für Literaturwissenschaft und Geistesgeschichte* 80 (2006a): 553–594.

Fontius, Martin. "Wahrnehmung." In *Metzler Lexikon Ästhetik: Kunst, Medien, Design und Alltag*, edited by Achim Trebeß. Stuttgart/Weimar: J.B. Metzler, 2006b, 420–421.

Foucault, Michel. "Nietzsche, Genealogy, History." In *The Essential Works of Foucault, 1954–1984, Vol. 2: Aesthetics, Method, and Epistemology*, edited by James D. Faubion. New York: The New Press, 1998, 369–392.

Foucault, Michel. "Une histoire restée muette." In *Dits et écrits I, 1954–1969*, edited by Daniel Defert, François Ewald, and Jacques Lagrange. Paris: Gallimard, 1994a, 545–549.

Foucault, Michel. *The Order of Things: An Archaeology of the Human Sciences*. New York: Vintage Books, 1994b.

Foucault, Michel. *Discipline and Punish: The Birth of the Prison*. Translated by Alan Sheridan. New York: Vintage Books, 1991.

Foucault, Michel. *Überwachen und Strafen, Die Geburt des Gefängnisses.* Translated by Walter Seitter. Frankfurt am Main.: Suhrkamp Verlag, 1977.

Foucault, Michel. *Surveiller et punir.* Paris: Gallimard 1975.

Francke, August Hermann. "Manuductio ad lectionem scripturae sacrae, in Schriften zur biblischen Hermeneutik." In *Schriften zur biblischen Hermeneutik*, edited by Erhard Peschke. Berlin: Walter de Gruyter, 2003a.

Francke, August Hermann. "Einleitung zur Lesung Heiliger Schrift." In *Schriften zur biblischen Hermeneutik*, edited by Erhard Peschke. Berlin: Walter de Gruyter, 2003b.

Franke, Ursula. *Baumgartens Erfindung der Ästhetik.* Münster: Mentis Verlag, 2018.

Franke, Ursula. "Was sie verbindet und was sie trennt. Rückriems Gesteinsskulptur und Overtons Pickup – Versuch eines Brückenschlags." In *Ulrich Rückriem: "Granit (Normandie), gespalten, geschnitten, geschliffen," 1985.* Münster: Westfälischen Kunstverein, 2014.

Franke, Ursula. "Sinnliche Erkenntnis - was sie ist und was sie soll. A. G. Baumgartens Ästhetik-Projekt zwischen Kunstphilosophie und Anthropologie." *Aufklärung* 20 (2008a): 73–99.

Franke, Ursula. "Baumgarten, Alexander Gottlieb." In *Killy Literaturlexikon. Autoren und Werke des deutschsprachigen Kulturraums* (2nd Ed.), edited by Wilhelm Kühlmann. Berlin/New York: Walter de Gruyter, 2008b, Vol. 1, 367–371.

Franke, Ursula. "Nach Hegel. Zur Differenz von Ästhetik und Kunstwissenschaft(en)." In *Ästhetik in metaphysikkritischen Zeiten. 100 Jahre Zeitschrift für Ästhetik und Allgemeine Kunstwissenschaft*, edited by Josef Früchtl and Maria Moog-Grünewald. Hamburg: Felix Meiner Verlag, 2007, 73–91.

Franke, Ursula. "Jenseits von schön und häßlich. Eine Skizze im Blick auf die Gegenwartskunst." In *Im Schatten des Schönen. Die Ästhetik des Häßlichen in historischen Ansätzen und aktuellen Debatten*, edited by Heiner F. Klemme, Michael Pauen, and Marie-Luise Raters. Bielefeld: Aisthesis, 2006, 289–304.

Franke, Ursula, and Gethmann-Siefert, Annemarie *Kulturpolitik und Kunstgeschichte. Perspektiven der Hegelschen Ästhetik.* Hamburg: Felix Meiner Verlag, 2004.

Franke, Ursula. "Bildung/Erziehung, ästhetische." In *Ästhetische Grundbegriffe*, edited by Karlheinz Barck, Martin Fontius, Dieter Schlenstedt, Burkhart Steinwachs, and Friedrich Wolfzettel. Stuttgart/Weimar: J. B. Metzler, 2000, Vol. 1, 696–727.

Franke, Ursula. "Alexander Gottlieb Baumgarten." In *Ästhetik und Kunstphilosophie. Von der Antike bis zur Gegenwart in Einzeldarstellungen*, edited by Julian Nida-Rümelin and Monika Betzler. Stuttgart: Alfred Kröner Verlag, 1998a, 72–79.

Franke, Ursula. "Zeichenkonzeptionen in der Kunstphilosophie und Ästhetik von der Renaissance bis zum frühen 19. Jahrhundert." In *Semiotik. Ein Handbuch zu den zeichentheoretischen Grundlagen von Natur und Kultur*, edited by Roland Posner, Klaus Robering, and Thomas Sebeok. Berlin/New York: Walter de Gruyter, 1998b, 1232–1262.

Franke, Ursula. "Ein Komplement der Vernunft. Zur Bestimmung des Gefühls im 18. Jahrhundert." In *Pathos, Affekt, Gefühl. Philosophische Beiträge*, edited by Karl Albert and Ingrid Craemer-Ruegenberg. Freiburg im Breisgau/München: Alber, 1981, 131–148.

Franke, Ursula. "Die Semiotik als Abschluß der Ästhetik. A. G. Baumgartens Bestimmung der Semiotik als ästhetische Propädeutik." *Zeitschrift für Semiotik* 1 (1979): 347–357.

Franke, Ursula. "Von der Metaphysik zur Aesthetik. Der Schritt von Leibniz zu Baumgarten." *Studia Leibnitiana* 14.3 (1975): 272–278.

Franke, Ursula. "Ist Baumgartens Ästhetik aktualisierbar? Bemerkungen zur Interpretation von H. R. Schweizer." *Studia Leibnitiana* 6 (1974): 272–278.

Franke, Ursula: *Kunst als Erkenntnis. Die Rolle der Sinnlichkeit in der Ästhetik des Alexander Gottlieb Baumgarten* (Studia Leibnitiana Supplementa IX). Wiesbaden: Franz Steiner Verlag, 1972.

Franke, Ursula. "Analogon rationis." In *Historisches Wörterbuch der Philosophie*, edited by Joachim Ritter, Karlfried Gründer, and Gottfried Gabriel. Basel: Schwabe Verlag, 1971–2007, Vol. 1, 229–230.

Frey, Christiane. "Zur ästhetischen Übung: Improvisiertes und Vorbewusstes bei A. G. Baumgarten." In *Schönes Denken. A. G. Baumgarten im Spannungsfeld von Ästhetik, Metaphysik und Naturrecht*, edited by Andrea Allerkamp and Dagmar Mirbach. Hamburg: Felix Meiner Verlag, 2016, 171–181.

Freylinghausen, Johann Anastasius, and Francke, Gotthilf August. *Ausführlicher Bericht von der Lateinischen Schule des Wäysenhauses zu Glaucha vor Halle zum Dienst derer die Nachfrage zu tun pflegen*. Halle: Verlegung des Wäysenhauses, 1736.

Fritz, Martin. *Vom Erhabenen. Der Traktat 'Peri Hypsous' und seine ästhetisch-religiöse Renaissance im 18. Jahrhundert*. Tübingen: Mohr Siebeck, 2011.

Frketich, Elise. "Wolff and Kant on the Mathematical Method." *Kant-Studien* 110. 3 (2019): 333–356.

Gabriel, Gottfried. *Logik und Rhetorik der Erkenntnis. Zum Verhältnis von wissenschaftlicher und ästhetischer Weltauffassung*. Paderborn: Mentis Verlag, 1997.

Gabriel, Gottfried. "Nelson Goodman, Weisen der Welterzeugung. Übers. v. Max Looser, Frankfurt am Main 1984." *Philosophische Rundschau* 33 (1986): 48–55.

Gaede, Friedrich. *Poetik und Logik. Zu den Grundlagen der literarischen Entwicklung im 17. und 18. Jahrhundert*. Bern/München: Francke, 1978.

Gaier, Ulrich. "Der frühe Herder." In *Werke in zehn Bänden* [FHA], edited by Günter Arnold, et al. Frankfurt am Main: Deutscher Klassiker Verlag, 1985–2000, Vol. 1, 813–832.

Garin, Eugenio. *Die Theorie des Schönen im Humanismus und in der Renaissance*. Köln: Verlag M. DuMont Schauberg, 1969.

Gava, Gabriele. "Wolff, Kant, and the Method of Philosophy." In *Oxford Studies in Early Modern Philosophy* (Vol. 8), edited by Daniel Garber and Donald Rutherford. Oxford: Oxford University Press, 2019.

Gawrilowitsch, Nikolai. *Die ästhetischen Beziehungen der Kunst zur Wirklichkeit. Mit einem einführenden Essay von Georg Lukács*. Berlin: Aufbau, 1954.

Gesner, Johann Matthias. *Primae lineae isagoges in eruditionem universalem*. Leipzig: Fritsch, 1774

Gethmann-Siefert, Annemarie. *Einführung in die Ästhetik*. München: Fink, 1995.

Gilbert, Katharine Everett, and Kuhn, Helmut. *A History of Esthetics*. New York: Macmillan, 1939.

Gołaszewska, Maria. *Crisis of Aesthetics?* Translated by Ewa Lech-Piwowarczyk. Cracow: Jagiellonian University, 1979.

Golden, Samuel L. *Jean LeClerc*. New York: Twayne, 1972.

Goldenbaum, Ursula. "Mendelssohn's Spinozistic Alternative to Baumgarten's Pietist Project of Aesthetics." In *Moses Mendelssohn's Metaphysics and Aesthetics*, edited by Reiner Munk. Dordrecht: Springer, 2011, 299–328.

Goldman, Lucien. *The Hidden God: A Study of Tragic Vision in the Pensées of Pascal and the Tragedies of Racine*. London: Routledge, 1964.

Gombrich, Ernst H. "Hegel und die Kunstgeschichte." *Neue Rundschau* 88.2 (1977): 202–219.

Goodman, Nelson. *Languages of Art: An Approach to a Theory of Symbols* (2nd ed.). Indianapolis: Hackett Publishing, 1976.

Gosling, J. C. B., and Taylor, C. C. W. *The Greeks on Pleasure*. Oxford: Oxford University Press, 1982.

Gottsched, Johann Christoph. *Briefwechsel. Historisch-kritische Ausgabe*. Edited by Detlef Döring, Rüdiger Otto, and Michael Schott. Berlin: Walter De Gruyter, 2011.

Gottsched, Johann Christoph. "Life of Baron Wolfius." In *Christian Wolff, Vernünftige Gedanken von den Kräften des menschlichen Verstandes und ihrem richtigen Gebrauche in Erkenntnis der Warheit (German Logic)*, edited by Jean École, et al. Hildesheim: Georg Olms Verlag, 2006, i–lii.

Gottsched, Johann Christoph. *Erste Gründe der gesamten Weltweisheit, darinn alle philosophische Wissenschaften in ihrer natürlichen Verknüpfung abgehandelt warden*. Frankfurt am Main: Minerva, 1965.

Gottsched. Johann Christoph. *Auszug aus den Herrn Batteux schönen Künsten, aus dem eintzigen Grundsatze der Nachahmung hergeleitet*. Leipzig: Breitkopf, 1754.

Gottsched, Johann Christoph. "Fortsetzung und Beschluß des neulichen Schreibens von der französischen und wälschen Musik [. . .]" *Das Neueste aus der anmuthigen Gelehrsamkeit* (1753): 738–756.

Gottsched, Johann Christoph. *Versuch einer Critischen Dichtkunst* (4th Ed.). Leipzig: Breitkopf, 1751.

Gottsched, Johann Christoph. *Versuch einer Critischen Dichtkunst* (2nd Ed.). Leipzig: Breitkopf, 1737.

Grassi, Ernesto. *Die Theorie des Schönen in der Antike* (2nd Ed.) Köln: Verlag M. DuMont Schauberg, 1980.

Gregor, Mary. "Baumgarten's Aesthetica." *Review of Metaphysics* 37.2 (1983): 357–385.

Gross, Steffen. "The Neglected Programme of Aesthetics." *British Journal of Aesthetics* 42.4 (2002): 403–414.

Gross, Steffen W. *Felix Aestheticus: Die Ästhetik als Lehre vom Menschen. Zum 250. Jahrestag des Erscheinens von Alexander Gottlieb Baumgartens 'Aesthetica.'* Würzburg, 2001a.

Gross, Steffen W. *"Felix Aestheticus* und *animal symbolicum.* Alexander G. Baumgarten – die 'vierte' Quelle der Philosophie Ernst Cassirers?" *Deutsche Zeitschrift für Philosophie* 49 (2001b): 275–298.

Grote, Simon. *The Emergence of Modern Aesthetic Theory: Religion and Morality in Enlightenment Germany and Scotland.* Cambridge: Cambridge University Press, 2017.

Grote, Simon. "Vom geistlichen zum guten Geschmack? Reflexionen zur Suche nach den pietistischen Wurzeln der Ästhetik." In *Schönes Denken. A. G. Baumgarten im Spannungsfeld von Ästhetik, Metaphysik und Naturrecht,* edited by Andrea Allerkamp and Dagmar Mirbach. Hamburg: Felix Meiner Verlag, 2016, 365–380.

Grote, Simon. "Pietistische Aisthesis und moralische Erziehung bei Alexander Gottlieb Baumgarten." In *Alexander Gottlieb Baumgarten: Sinnliche Erkenntnis in der Philosophie des Rationalismus,* edited by Alexander Aichele and Dagmar Mirbach. Hamburg: Felix Meiner Verlag, 2008, 175–198.

Gulyga, Arseni. *Johann Gottfried Herder. Eine Einführung in seine Philosophie.* Translated by Günter Arnold. Frankfurt am Main: Röderberg, 1978.

Gunzenhauser, Isabel. *Seraphische Hexameterdichtung: Friedrich Gottlieb Klopstocks Messias und die Ependiskussion im 18. Jahrhundert.* Göttingen: Vandenhoeck & Ruprecht, 2020.

Gutzen, Dieter. *Die Poesie der Bibel.* Dissertation, University of Bonn, 1972.

Guyer, Paul. *A History of Modern Aesthetics* (3 Vols.). Cambridge: Cambridge University Press, 2014.

Haller, Rudolf. "Das 'Zeichen' und die 'Zeichenlehre' in der Philosophie der Neuzeit." *Archiv für Begriffsgeschichte* 4 (1959): 113–158.

Harrison, Charles, Wood, Paul, and Gaiger, Jason. *Art in Theory, 1648–1815: An Anthology of Changing Ideas.* Malden: Blackwell Publishing, 2000.

Haverkamp, Anselm. "Alexander Gottlieb Baumgarten als Provokation der Literaturgeschichte." In *Schönes Denken. A. G. Baumgarten im Spannungsfeld von Ästhetik, Metaphysik und Naturrecht,* edited by Andrea Allerkamp and Dagmar Mirbach. Hamburg: Felix Meiner Verlag, 2016, 35–48.

Havercamp, Anselm. "Empson's Type IV. Avantgarde der Kritik und Vorgeschichte der Ästhetik." In *Baumgarten-Studien, Zur Genealogie der Ästhetik,* edited by Rüdiger Campe, Anselm Haverkamp, and Christoph Menke. Köln: August Verlag, 2014a, 203–230.

Haverkamp, Anselm. "Wie die Morgenröthe: Baumgartens Innovation." In *Baumgarten-Studien, Zur Genealogie der Ästhetik,* edited by Rüdiger Campe, Anselm Haverkamp, and Christoph Menke. Köln: August Verlag, 2014b, 15–47.

Haverkamp, Anselm. "Wie die Morgenröthe zwischen Nacht und Tag. Alexander Gottlieb Baumgarten und die Entstehung der Kulturwissenschaften in Frankfurt an der Oder." *Deutsche Vierteljahrsschrift für Literaturwissenschaft und Geistesgeschichte* 76 (2002): 3–26.

Haverkamp, Anselm. "Metaphora dis/continua: figure in de/construction. Mit einem Kommentar zur Begriffsgeschichte von Quntilian bis Baumgarten." In *Allegorie. Konfiguration von Text, Bild und Lektüre,* edited by Eva Horn and Manfred Weinberg. Opladen/Wiesbaden: VS Verlag, 1998, 29–45.

Haym, Rudolf. *Herder nach seinem Leben und seinen Werken*. Berlin: Rudolph Gaertner, 1880–1885.

Hegel, Georg Wilhelm Friedrich. "Symbolism of the Sublime." In *The Sublime Reader*, edited by Robert R. Clewis. London: Bloomsbury, 2019, 200–210.

Hegel, Georg Wilhelm Friedrich. *Einleitung in die Ästhetik*. Edited by Wolfhart Henckmann. München: Fink, 1985.

Hegel, Georg Wilhelm Friedrich. *The Difference Between Fichte's and Schelling's System of Philosophy*. Translated by H. S. Harris and Walter Cerf. Albany: SUNY Press, 1977.

Hegel, Georg Wilhelm Friedrich. *Aesthetics: Lectures on Fine Arts*. Translated by T. M. Knox. Oxford: Clarendon Press, 1975.

Hegel, Georg Wilhelm Friedrich. *Vorlesungen über die Ästhetik*. Edited by Rüdiger Bubner. Stuttgart: Reclam, 1971.

Hegel, Georg Wilhelm Friedrich. *Differenz des Fichte'schen und des Schelling'schen Systems der Philosophie in Beziehung auf Reinhold's Beyträge zur leichtren Übersicht des Zustands der Philosophie zu Anfang des neunzehnten Jahrhunderts*. Edited by Georg Lasson. Leipzig: Felix Meiner Verlag, 1928.

Heimsoeth, Heinz. *Die Methode der Erkenntnis bei Descartes und Leibniz*. Gießen: A. Töpelmann, 1912/1914.

Heineccius, Johann Gottlieb. *Elementa philosophiae rationalis et moralis*. Frankfurt an der Oder: Conrad, 1728.

Heinrich, Gerd. "Frankfurt an der Oder. Universität." In *Theologische Realenzyklopädie*. Berlin/New York: Walter de Gruyter, 1983, Vol. 11, 335–342.

Henckmann, Wolfhart. "Wahrnehmung, ästhetische." In *Lexikon der Ästhetik* (2nd Ed.), edited by Wolfhard Henckmann and Konrad Lotter. München, 2004, 385–389.

Henckmann, Wolfhart. "Neue Ausgaben von Baumgartens Ästhetischen Schriften." *Philosophisches Jahrbuch* 93 (1986): 420–423.

Herder, Johann Gottfried. *Herder's "Essay on Being." A Translation and Critical Commentary*. Edited and translated by John K. Noyes. Rochester: Camden House, 2018.

Herder, Johann Gottfried. *Selected Writings on Aesthetics*. Translated by Gregory Moore. Princeton: Princeton University Press, 2006a.

Herder, Johann Gottfried. "Critical Forests, Fourth Grove." In *Selected Writings on Aesthetics*, translated by Gregory Moore. Princeton: Princeton University Press, 2006b, 177–290.

Herder, Johann Gottfried. "A Monument to Baumgarten." In *Selected Writings on Aesthetics*, translated by Gregory Moore. Princeton: Princeton University Press, 2006c, 41–50.

Herder, Johann Gottfried. *Philosophical Writings*. Edited and translated by Michael Forster. Cambridge: Cambridge University Press, 2002a.

Herder, Johann Gottfried. "On the Cognition and Sensation of the Human Soul." In *Philosophical Writings*, edited and translated by Michael Forster. Cambridge: Cambridge University Press, 2002b, 187–243.

Herder, Johann Gottfried. "Fragments of a Treatise on the Ode." In *Selected Early Works*, edited and translated by Ernest A. Menze and Karl Menges. University Park: Pennsylvania State University Press, 1992, 35–52.

Herder, Johann Gottfried. *Werke in zehn Bänden* [FHA]. Edited by Martin Bollacher, et al. Frankfurt am Main: Deutscher Klassiker Verlag, 1985–2000.

Herder, Johann Gottfried. "Kritik der *Aesthetica.*" In *Werke in zehn Bänden* [FHA], edited by Martin Bollacher, et al. Frankfurt am Main: Deutscher Klassiker Verlag, 1985, Vol. 1, 659–676.

Herder, Johann Gottfried. "Von Baumgartens Denkart in seinen Schriften." In *Werke in zehn Bänden* [FHA], edited by Martin Bollacher, et al. Frankfurt am Main: Deutscher Klassiker Verlag, 1985, Vol. 1, 653–658.

Herder, Johann Gottfried. "Begründung einer Ästhetik in der Auseinandersetzung mit Alexander Gottlieb Baumgarten." In *Werke in zehn Bänden*, edited by Martin Bollacher, et al. Berlin: Deutscher Klassiker Verlag, 1985, Vol. 1, 651–694.

Herder, Johann Gottfried. *Sämtliche Werke* [SWS]. Edited by Bernhard Suphan. Hildesheim: Georg Olms Verlag, 1978/1979a.

Herder, Johann Gottfried. "Ueber Christian Wolfs Schriften. Erste Betrachtung." In *Sämtliche Werke* [SWS], edited by Bernhard Suphan. Hildesheim: Georg Olms Verlag, 1978/1979b, Vol. 32, 156–158.

Herder, Johann Gottfried. "Entwurf der Anwendung dreier Akademischer Jahre für einen jungen Theologen." In *Sämtliche Werke* [SWS], edited by Bernhard Suphan. Hildesheim: Georg Olms Verlag, 1978/1979c, Vol. 30, 402–423.

Herder, Johann Gottfried. "Philosophie des Wahren, Guten und Schönen aus dem Sinne des Gefühls." In *Sämtliche Werke* [SWS], edited by Bernhard Suphan. Hildesheim: Georg Olms Verlag, 1978/1979d, Vol. 8, 104.

Herder, Johann Gottfried. "Zum Sinn des Gefühls." In *Sämtliche Werke* [SWS], edited by Bernhard Suphan. Hildesheim: Georg Olms Verlag, 1978/1979e, Vol. 8, 96.

Herder, Johann Gottfried. "Ueber Thomas Abbts Schriften. Der Torso zu einem Denkmaal, an seinem Grabe errichtet." In *Sämtliche Werke* [SWS], edited by Bernhard Suphan. Hildesheim: Georg Olms Verlag, 1978/1979f, Vol. 2, 249–363.

Herder, Johann Gottfried. *Briefe. Gesamtausgabe 1763–1803* [HB]. Edited by Wilhelm Dobbek and Günter Arnold. Weimar: Hermann Böhlaus Nachfolger, 1977–2016.

Herder, Johann Gottfried. *A Journal of My Voyage in the Year 1769*. Translated John Francis Harrison. Dissertation, Columbia University, 1952.

Herder, Johann Gottfried. "Von Baumgarten's Denkart in seinen Schriften." In *Johann Gottfried Herders Lebensbild*, edited by Emil Gottfried von Herder. Erlangen: Theodor Bläsing, 1846.

Hettche, Matt, and Dyck, Corey. "Christian Wolff." In *The Stanford Encyclopedia of Philosophy,* edited by Edward N. Zalta, 2019. https://plato.stanford.edu/archives/win2019/entries/wolff-christian/.

Holloran, John Robert. *Professors of Enlightenment at the University of Halle, 1690–1730*. Dissertation, Department of History, University of Virginia, 2000.

Horace. *Satires, Epistles, The Art of Poetry*. Translated by H. R. Fairclough. Cambridge: Harvard University Press, 1926.

Hornig, Gottfried. "Perfektibilität II." In *Historisches Wörterbuch der Philosophie*, edited by Joachim Ritter, Karlfried Gründer, and Gottfried Gabriel. Basel: Schwabe Verlag, 1971–2007, Vol. 7, 241–244.

Hornuff, Daniel. "Kann Kunst forschen?" *Zeitschrift für Ästhetik und Allgemeine Kunstwissenschaft* 59 (2014): 225–233.

Huber, Michael. "Fortsetzung der Geschichte der deutschen Dichtkunst." *Hannoversches Magazin* 27. Stück (1 April 1768): 417–432.

Hume, David. "On the Standard of Taste." In *Selected Essays*, edited by Stephen Copley and Andrew Edgar. Oxford: Oxford University Press, 1998, 133–153.

Irmscher, Dietrich. "Beobachtungen zur Funktion der Analogie im Denken Herders." *Deutsche Vierteljahrsschrift für Literaturwissenschaft und Geistesgeschichte* 55 (1981): 64–97.

Irmscher, Dieter, and Adler, Emil. *Der handschriftliche Nachlass Johann Gottfried Herders.* Wiesbaden: Harrassowitz, 1979.

Irmscher, Hans Dietrich. "Johann Gottfried Herder." In *Deutsche Dichter des 18. Jahrhunderts. Ihr Leben und Werk*, edited by Benno von Wiese, et al. Berlin: Erich Schmidt, 1977.

Irmscher, Hans Dietrich. "Grundzüge der Hermeneutik Herders." In *Bückeburger Gespräche über Johann Gottfried Herder 1971*, edited by Johann Gottfried Maltusch. Bückeburg: Grimme, 1973, 17–57.

Jaeger, Friedrich, and Rüsen, Jörn. *Handbuch der Kulturwissenschaften.* Stuttgart/Weimar: J.B. Metzler, 2004.

Jäger, Michael. *Die Theorie des Schönen in der italienischen Renaissance.* Köln: DuMont Buchverlag, 1990.

Jäger, Michael. *Kommentierende Einführung in Baumgartens Aesthetica.* Hildesheim: Georg Olms Verlag, 1980.

Jahn, Johannes, and Haubenreisser, Wolfgang. "Kunstgeschichte." In *Wörterbuch der Kunst* (12th Ed.) Stuttgart: Kröner Verlag, 1995.

Kant, Immanuel. "Observations on the Feeling of the Beautiful and Sublime." In *The Sublime Reader*, edited by Robert R. Clewis. London: Bloomsbury Publishing, 2019, 105–112.

Kant, Immanuel. *Anthropology from a Pragmatic Point of View.* Translated by Robert Louden. Cambridge: Cambridge University Press, 2006.

Kant, Immanuel. *Critique of the Power of Judgment.* Translated by Paul Guyer and Eric Matthews. Cambridge: Cambridge University Press, 2000.

Kant, Immanuel. *Critique of Pure Reason.* Translated by Paul Guyer and Allen W. Wood. Cambridge: Cambridge University Press, 1998a.

Kant, Immanuel. *Der Streit mit Johan August Eberhard.* Edited by Manfred Zahn. Hamburg: Felix Meiner Verlag, 1998b.

Kant, Immanuel. *Lectures on Metaphysics.* Edited and translated by Karl Ameriks and Steve Naragon. Cambridge: Cambridge University Press, 1997.

Kant, Immanuel. *Religion and Rational Theology.* Edited and translated by Allen W. Wood and George di Giovanni. Cambridge: Cambridge University Press, 1996.

Kant, Immanuel. *Lectures on Logic.* Edited and translated by J. Michael Young. Cambridge: Cambridge University Press, 1992.

Kant, Immanuel. "Gesammelte Schriften (AA)." In *Preussische Akademie der Wissenschaften, Deutsche Akademie der Wissenschaften zu Berlin, Akademie der Wissenschaften zu Göttingen*, and *Berlin-Brandenburgische Akademie der Wissenschaften*. Berlin: Georg Reimer/Walter de Gruyter, 1900ff.

Kater, Thomas. "Brückenschläge. Eine wissenschaftstheoretische Perspektive auf die empirische Ästhetik." *Zeitschrift für Ästhetik und Allgemeine Kunstwissenschaft* 62 (2017): 171–176.

Kern, Andrea, and Sonderegger, Ruth. *Falsche Gegensätze. Zeitgenössische Positionen zur philosophischen Ästhetik*. Frankfurt am Main: Suhrkamp Verlag, 2002.

Kertscher, Hans-Joachim. *Er brachte Lichte und Ordnung in die Welt. Christian Wolff – eine Biographie*. Halle: Mitteldeutscher Verlag, 2018.

Kertscher, Hans-Joachim. "Georg Friedrich Meiers Platz im geistig-kulturellen Leben der Stadt Halle." In *Georg Friedrich Meier (1718–1777): Philosophie als wahre Weltweisheit*, edited by Frank Grunert and Gideon Stiening. Berlin: Walter De Gruyter, 2015, 25–42.

Kirwan, James. *Sublimity: The Non-Rational and the Irrational in the History of Aesthetics*. New York: Routledge, 2005.

Kleinschmidt, Nicolas. "Die Vermessung des Sinnlichen. Zur Etablierung der empirischen Ästhetik und ihrer Bedeutung für die Kunstpädagogik." *BDK-Mitteilungen* 4 (2017): 37–39.

Kliche, Dieter. "'Ich glaube selbst Engel können nicht ohne Sinnlichkeit sein'. Über einen Fund aus der Frühgeschichte der Ästhetik im Werner-Krauss-Archiv." In *Genuß und Egoismus. Zur Kritik ihrer geschichtlichen Verknüpfung*, edited by Wolfgang Klein and Ernst Müller. Berlin: Akademie Verlag, 2002, 54–65.

Klemme, Heiner F., and Kuehn, Manfred. *The Bloomsbury Dictionary of Eighteenth-Century German Philosophers*. Bloomsbury Publishing. Kindle Edition, 128.

Kliche, Dieter. "Sinnliche Erkenntnis. Erkenntnis. Über gemeinsame Gegenstände von Ästhetik und Literaturforschung." In *Literatur-Forschung Heute*, edited by Eckart Goebel and Wolfgang Klein. Berlin: Walter de Gruyter, 1999, 51–60.

Kliche, Dieter. "Ästhetik und Aisthesis. Zur Begriffs- und Problemgeschichte des Ästhetischen." *Weimarer Beiträge* 44 (1998): 485–505.

Köhne, Werner. *Das letzte Wort der Ästhetik ist die menschliche Freiheit*. Christoph, 2009.

Koller, Aaron. "Mendelssohn's Response to Burke on the Sublime." In *Moses Mendelssohn's Metaphysics and Aesthetics*, edited by Reinier Munk. Dodrecht: Springer, 2011, 329–350.

Koller, Benedikt Josef Maria von. *Entwurf zur Geschichte und Literatur der Aesthetik von Baumgarten bis auf die neueste Zeit*. Regensburg: Montag und Weiß, 1799.

Kondylis, Panajotis. *Die Aufklärung im Rahmen des neuzeitlichen Rationalismus*. München: DTV, 1986.

Kristeller, Paul Oskar. "The Modern System of the Arts: A Study in the History of Aesthetics (II)." *Journal of the History of Ideas* 13.1 (1952): 17–46.

Kuehn, Manfred. "David Hume and Moses Mendelssohn." *Hume Studies* 21 (1995): 197–220.

Kuehn, Manfred. *Scottish Common Sense in Germany, 1768–1800: A Contribution to the History of Critical Philosophy*. Kingston and Montreal: McGill-Queen's University Press, 1987.

Kulenkampff, Jens. "Metaphysik und Ästhetik: Kant zum Beispiel." In *Falsche Gegensätze. Zeitgenössische Positionen zur philosophischen Ästhetik*, edited by Andrea Kern and Ruth Sonderegger. Frankfurt am Main: Suhrkamp Verlag, 2002, 49–80.

Kwon, Jeong-Im. *Hegels Bestimmung der Kunst. Die Bedeutung der 'symbolischen Kunstform' in Hegels Ästhetik.* München: Fink, 2002.

Lamarque, Peter. "Analytic Aesthetics." In *The Oxford Handbook of the History of Analytic Philosophy*, edited by Michael Beaney. Oxford: Oxford University Press, 2013, 770–794.

Lange, Samuel Gotthold. *Leben Georg Friedrich Meiers.* Halle: Gebauer, 1778.

Lange, Samuel Gotthold. *Sammlung gelehrter und freundschaftlicher Briefe.* Halle: Hemmerde, 1769.

Lange, Samuel Gotthold. *Oden Davids oder poetische Uebersetzung der Psalmen, Erster Theil.* Halle: Bauer, 1746.

Lange, Thomas, and Neumeyer, Harald. *Kunst und Wissenschaft um 1800.* Würzburg: Königshausen & Neumann, 2000.

Langen, August. *Der Wortschatz des Deutschen Pietismus* (2nd Ed.). Tübingen: Max Niemeyer, 1968.

Le Clerc, Jean. *Parrhasiana.* London: Churchil, 1700.

Le Clerc, Jean. *Five Letters Concerning the Inspiration of the Holy Scriptures.* London: [Anonymous], 1690.

Leibniz, Gottfried Wilhelm. *Die philosophischen Schriften.* Edited by Carl Immanuel Gerhardt. Hildesheim: Georg Olms Verlag, 2008.

Leibniz, Gottfried Wilhem. *New Essays on Human Understanding.* Edited and translated by Peter Remnant and Jonathan Bennett. Cambridge: Cambridge University Press, 1996.

Leibniz, Gottfried Wilhelm. "Preface to an Edition of Nizolius." In *Gottfried Wilhelm Leibniz: Philosophical Papers and Letters* (2nd ed.), edited by Leroy Loemker. Dodrecht: Kluwer, 1989a.

Leibniz, Gottfried Wilhelm. *Philosophical Essays.* Edited and translated by Roger Ariew and Daniel Garber. Indianapolis: Hackett Publishing, 1989b.

Leibniz, Gottfried Wilehlm. *Theodicy.* Translated by E. M. Huggard. La Salle: Open Court Publishing, 1985a.

Lessing, Gotthold Ephraim. *Werke und Briefe in zwölf Bänden.* Edited by Wilfried Barner. Frankfurt am Main: Deutscher Klassiker Verlag, 1985b.

Liebsch, Dimitri. "Karlheinz Barck u. a. (Hrsg.), Ästhetische Grundbegriffe – Historisches Wörterbuch in sieben Bänden. Metzler Verlag, Stuttgart 2000 ff." *Zeitschrift für Ästhetik und allgemeine Kunstwissenschaft* 48 (2003): 135–145.

Linn, Marie Luise. "A.G. Baumgartens Aesthetica und die antike Rhetorik." In *Rhetorik: Beiträge zu ihrer Geschichte in Deuschland vom 16.-20. Jahrhundert*, edited by H. Schanze. Frankfurt am Main: Athenaion, 1974, 105–126.

Lodtmann, Carl Gerhard Wilhelm. *Oratio aditialis [. . .] domini Ioannis Christiani Wernsdorfii.* Helmstedt: Schnorr, 1753.

Look, Brandon. "Baumgarten's Rationalism." In *Metaphysics in Baumgarten and Kant*, edited by Courtney Fugate and John Hymers. Oxford: Oxford University Press, 2018.

Lucretius. *On the Nature of Things*, translated by W. H. D. Rouse, revised by Martin F. Smith. Cambridge: Harvard University Press, 1924.

Ludovici, Carl Günther. *Neueste Merckwürdigkeiten aus der Leibnitz-Wolffischen Weltweisheit*. Frankfurt and Leipzig, 1738.

Ludovici, Carl Günther. *Ausführlicher Entwurff einer vollständigen Historie der Wolffischen Philosophie*. Leipzig: Löwe, 1737.

Lyotard, Jean-François. "The Sublime and the Avant-Garde." In *The Sublime Reader*, edited by Robert R. Clewis. London: Bloomsbury Publishing, 2019, 259-270.

Makkreel, Rudolf A. "The Confluence of Aesthetics and Hermeneutics in Baumgarten, Meier, and Kant." *Journal of Aesthetics and Art Criticism* 54.1 (1996): 65–75.

Manso, Johann Kaspar Friedrich. "Übersicht der Geschichte der deutschen Poesie seit Bodmers und Breitingers kritischen Bemühungen." In *Nachträge zu Sulzers allgemeiner Theorie der schönen Künste*. Leipzig: Dyk, 1806, Vol. 8, Part I, 173–174.

Martens, Wolfgang. "Zur Thematisierung von schöner Literatur in Samuel Gotthold Langes und Georg Friedrich Meiers Moralischen Wochenschriften Der Gesellige und Der Mensch." In *Dichtungstheorien der deutschen Frühaufklärung*, edited by Theodor Verweyen. Tübingen: Niemeyer, 1995, 133–145.

Martens, Wolfgang. *Literatur und Frömmigkeit in der frühen Aufklärung*. Tübingen: Max Niemeyer, 1989.

McMahon, Darrin. *Happiness: A History*. New York: Grove Press, 2006.

McQuillan, J. Colin. "The Aesthetic Perfection of Life in Baumgarten, Meier, and Kant." In *Kant and the Feeling of Life: Beauty and Nature in the Critique of Judgment*, edited by Jennifer Mensch. Albany: SUNY Press, Forthcoming.

McQuillan, J. Colin. "Baumgarten, Meier, and Kant on Aesthetic Perfection." In *Kant and his German Contemporaries*, edited by Daniel O. Dahlstrom. Cambridge: Cambridge University Press, 2018, 13–27.

McQuillan, J. Colin. "Wolff's Logic, Kant's Critique, and the Foundations of Metaphysics." In *Christian Wolff's German Logic: Sources, Significance and Reception*, edited by Arnaud Pelletier. Hildesheim: Georg Olms Verlag, 2017a.

McQuillan, J. Colin. "Kant on the Science of Aesthetics and the Critique of Taste." *Kant Yearbook* 9 (2017b): 113–132.

McQuillan, J. Colin. "Kant's Critique of Baumgarten's Aesthetics." *Idealistic Studies* 45.1 (2015): 69–80.

McQuillan, J. Colin. *Early Modern Aesthetics*. London: Rowman & Littlefield, 2015.

McQuillan, J. Colin. "Baumgarten on Sensible Perfection." *Philosophica* 44 (2014): 47–64.

McQuillan, J. Colin. "The History of a Distinction: Sensible and Intellectual Cognition from Baumgarten to Kant." In *Rethinking Kant* (Vol. 3), edited by Oliver Thorndike. Cambridge: Cambridge Scholars Press, 2011, 180–199.

Meier, Georg Friedrich. *Excerpt from the Doctrine of Reason*. Translated by Aaron Bunch. London: Bloomsbury Publishing, 2016.

Meier, Georg Friedrich. "Alexander Gottlieb Baumgartens Leben." In *Alexander Baumgarten: Sinnliche Erkenntnis in der Philosophie der Rationalismus*, edited by Alexander Aichele and Dagmar Mirbach. Hamburg: Felix Meiner Verlag, 2008, 351–373.

Meier, Georg Friedrich. *Frühe Schriften zur ästhetischen Erziehung der Deutschen.* Edited by Günter Schenk and Hans-Joachim Kertscher. Halle: Hallescher Verlag, 1999–2002.

Meier, Georg Friedrich. *Versuch einer allgemeinenAuslegungskunst.* Edited by Axel Bühler and Luigi Cataldi Madonna. Hamburg: Felix Meiner Verlag, 1996.

Meier, Georg Friedrich. *Versuch einer allgemeinen Auslegungskunst.* Edited by Lutz Geldsetzer. Düsseldorf: Stern Verlag, 1965.

Meier, Georg Friedrich. *Alexander Baumgartens Leben.* Halle: Hemmerde, 1763.

Meier, Georg Friedrich. *Betrachtungen über den ersten Grundsatz aller schönen Künste und Wissenschaften.* Halle: Hemmerde, 1757.

Meier, Georg Friedrich. *Vorstellung der Ursachen, warum es unmöglich scheint, mit Herrn Profeßor Gottsched eine nützliche und vernünftige Streitigkeit zu führen.* Halle: Hemmerde, 1754.

Meier, Georg Friedrich. *Vernunftlehre.* Halle: Johann Justinus Gebauer, 1752a.

Meier, Georg Friedrich. *Vertheidigung seines Beweises des ewigen Lebens der Seele und seiner Gedancken von der Religion* Halle: Hemmerde, 1752b.

Meier, Georg Friedrich. *Beurtheilung des Heldengedichts, Der Meßias.* Halle: Hemmerde, 1749.

Meier, Georg Friedrich. *Anfangsgründe aller schönen Wissenschaften.* Halle: Hemmerde, 1748–1750.

Meier, Georg Friedrich. *Beurtheilung der Gottschedischen Dichtkunst.* Halle: Hemmerde, 1747–1748.

Meier, Georg Friedrich. *Vertheidigung der Baumgartischen Erklärung eines Gedichtes.* Halle: Hemmerde, 1746.

Meier, Georg Friedrich. *Abbildung eines Kunstrichters.* Halle: Hemmerde, 1745a.

Meier, Georg Friedrich Meier. "Gedanken von dem Werthe der freyen Künste und schönen Wissenschaften in Absicht auf die obern Kräfte der Seele." *Critische Versuche zur Aufnahme der Deutschen Sprache* 14. Stück (1745b): 131–141.

Meier, Georg Friedrich. *Gedancken von Schertzen.* Halle: Hemmerde, 1744a.

Meier, Georg Friedrich. *Theoretische Lehre von den Gemüthsbewegungen überhaupt.* Halle: Hemmerde, 1744b.

Meier, Georg Friedrich. "Gedanken über die Frage: Ob ein Kunstrichter seine Urtheile jederzeit erklären und beweisen müsse." *Critische Versuche zur Aufnahme der Deutschen Sprache* 13. Stück (1744c): 3–21.

Meier, Georg Friedrich. "Versuch einer philosophischen Abhandlung von dem Mittelmäßigen in der Dichtkunst." *Beyträge zur Critischen Historie der Deutschen Sprache* 7 (1741): 242–286.

Meier, Georg Friedrich (auctor), and Baumgarten, Siegmund Jakob (praeses). *Exercitatio theologica de discrimine ejus quod naturale et morale dicitur in theologia.* Halle: Hendel, 1738.

Meier, Jean-Paul. *L'esthétique de Moses Mendelssohn (1729–1786).* Paris: Atelier Reproduction des Thèses, 1978.

Meier-Oeser, Stephan. *Die Spur des Zeichens. Das Zeichen und seine Funktion in der Philosophie des Mittelalters und der frühen Neuzeit*. Berlin/New York: Walter de Gruyter, 1997.

Mendelssohn, Moses. "The Sublime and the Naïve in the Fine Sciences." In *The Sublime Reader*, edited by Robert R. Clewis. London: Bloomsbury Publishing, 2019, 92–100.

Mendelssohn, Moses. *Phädon und einige Texte zur Bestimmung des Menschen*. Edited by Anne Pollok. Hamburg: Felix Meiner Verlag, 2013.

Mendelssohn, Moses. *Philosophical Writings*. Edited and translated by Daniel O. Dahlstrom. Cambridge, 2009.

Mendelssohn, Moses. *Ästhetische Schriften*. Edited by Anne Pollok. Hamburg: Felix Meiner Verlag, 2006.

Mendelssohn, Moses. *Gesammelte Schriften: Jubiläumsausgabe (JA)*, edited by Ismar Elbogen, Julius Guttmann, and Eugen Mittwoch, later Alexander Altmann and Eva J. Engel. Stuttgart-Bad Cannstatt: Frommann-Holzboog Verlag, 1971.

Mendelssohn, Moses. *Verzeichniß der auserlesenen Büchersammlung des seeligen Herrn Moses Mendelssohn*. Edited by the Soncino-Gesellschaft der Freunde des jüdischen Buches. Berlin/Leipzig, 1926.

Mendelssohn, Moses. "Alexander Gottlieb Baumgarten, Aestheticorum Pars altera." *Bibliothek der schönen Wissenschaften und der freyen Künste* 4 (1758a): 438–456.

Mendelssohn, Moses. "Georg Friedrich Meier, Auszug aus den Anfangsgründen aller schönen Wissenschaften." *Bibliothek der schönen Wissenschaften und der freyen Künste* 3 (1758b): 130–138.

Menke, Christoph. "Die Disziplin der Ästhetik ist die Ästhetik der Disziplin. Baumgarten in der Perspektive Foucaults." In *Baumgarten-Studien. Zur Genealogie der Ästhetik*, edited by Rüdiger Campe, Anselm Haverkamp, and Christoph Menke. Köln: August Velag, 2014a, 233–247.

Menke, Christoph. "Das Wirken dunkler Kraft: Baumgarten und Herder." In *Baumgarten-Studien, Zur Genealogie der Ästhetik*, edited by Rüdiger Campe, Anselm Haverkamp, and Christoph Menke. Köln: August Verlag, 2014b, 73–115.

Menke, Christoph. *Kraft der Kunst*. Berlin: Suhrkamp Verlag, 2013.

Menke, Christoph. *Kraft. Ein Grundbegriff ästhetischer Anthropologie*. Frankfurt am Main: Suhrkamp Verlag, 2008.

Menke, Christoph. "Die Depotenzierung des Souveräns im Gesang. Claudio Monteverdis *Die Krönung der Poppea* und die Demokratie." In *Literatur als Philosophie*, edited by Eva Horn, Bettine Menke, and Christoph Menke. München: Fink, 2005, 281–296.

Menke, Christoph. "Zweierlei Übung: Zum Verhältnis von sozialer Disziplinierung und ästhetischen Existenz." In *Michel Foucault. Zwischenbilanz einer Rezeption*, edited by Axel Honneth and Martin Saar. Frankfurt am Main: Suhrkamp Verlag, 2003, 283–299.

Menke, Christoph. "Wahrnehmung, Tätigkeit, Selbstreflexion: Zu Genese und Dialektik der Ästhetik." In *Falsche Gegensätze. Zeitgenössische Positionen zur philosophischen Ästhetik*, edited by Andrea Kern and Ruth Sonderegger. Frankfurt am Main: Suhrkamp Verlag, 2002, 19–48.

Menke, Christoph. "Schwerpunkt: Zur Aktualität der Ästhetik von Alexander G. Baumgarten." *Deutsche Zeitschrift für Philosophie* 49 (2001): 229–232.

Menke, Kraft. "Ein Grundbegriff ästhetischer Anthropologie." *Deutschlandfunk* 11 (2009). https://www.deutschlandfunk.de/das-letzte-wort-der-aesthetik-ist-die-menschliche-freiheit.700.de.html?dram:article_id=84070.

Menninghaus, Winfried. *Das Versprechen der Schönheit*. Frankfurt am Main: Suhrkamp Verlag, 2007.

Menzel, Norbert. *Der anthropologische Charakter des Schönen bei Baumgarten*. Dissertation, Pontificia Universita Gregoriana, 1969.

Menzer, Paul. "Zur Entstehung von A. G. Baumgartens Ästhetik." *Zeitschrift für Deutsche Kulturphilosophie* 4 (1938): 288–296.

Mersch, Dieter. "Nicht-Propositionalität und ästhetisches Denken." In *Ästhetisches Denken, Nicht-Propositionalität, Episteme, Kunst*, edited by Forian Dombois, et al. Zürich: Diaphanes, 2014, 28–55.

Meyer, Herman. "Schillers philosophische Rhetorik." *Euphorion* 53 (1959): 313–350.

Michaelis, Christian Benedict. "A.G. Baumgarten, *Dissertatio chorographica*." *Wöchentliche Hallesche Anzeigen* 11 (March 14, 1735): 166–171; (March 21, 1735): 181–185.

Michaelis, Christian Benedict. "J. C. Meisner, Dissertatio Theologico-Historico-Critica." *Wöchentliche Hallesche Anzeigen* 35 (August 24, 1733): 553–556.

Michaelis, Christian Benedikt (praeses), and Baumgarten, Alexander Gottlieb (respondens), *Disputatio chorographica inauguralis notiones superi et inferi, indeque adscensus et descensus, in chorographiis sacris occurrentes*. Halle: Meyhius, 1735.

Mirbach, Dagmar. "Gottsched und die Entstehung der Ästhetik." In *Johann Christoph Gottsched (1700–1766): Philosophie, Poetik und Wissenschaft*, edited by Eric Achermann. Berlin: Akademie Verlag, 2014, 113–127.

Mirbach, Dagmar. "Die Rezeption von Leibniz' Monadenlehre bei Alexander Gottlieb Baumgarten." In *Der Monadenbegriff zwischen Spätrenaissance und Aufklärung*, edited by Hans-Peter Neumann. Berlin/New York: Walter de Gruyter, 2009, 271–300.

Mirbach, Dagmar. "*Magnitudo aesthetica*, Aesthetic Greatness: Ethical aspects of Alexander Gottlieb Baumgarten's Fragmentary *Aesthetica* (1750/58)." *The Nordic Journal of Aesthetics* 36–37 (2008/2009): 102–128.

Mirbach, Dagmar. "Ingenium venustum und magnitudo pectoris. Ethische Aspekte von Alexander Gottlieb Baumgartens Aesthetica." In *Alexander Gottlieb Baumgarten: Sinnliche Erkenntnis in der Philosophie des Rationalismus*, edited by Alexander Aichele and Dagmar Mirbach. Hamburg: Felix Meiner Verlag, 2008, 199–218.

Mirbach, Dagmar. "Neue Beiträge der italienischen Forschung zu Alexander Gottlieb Baumgartens Ästhetik." *Zeitschrift für philosophische Forschung* 56 (2002): 606–621.

Mirbach, Dagmar, and Allerkamp, Andrea. "Ale.Theophilus Baumgarten/Wenn die Magd in den Brunnen fällt." In *Schönes Denken. A. G. Baumgarten im Spannungsfeld von Ästhetik, Metaphysik und Naturrecht*, edited by Andrea Allerkamp and Dagmar Mirbach. Hamburg: Felix Meiner Verlag, 2016, 317–340.

Moritz, Karl Philipp. *Werke in zwei Bänden.* Edited by Heide Vollmer and Albert Meier. Frankfurt am Main: Deutscher Klassiker Verlag, 1999.

Morris, Wesley. "Should Art Be a Battleground for Social Justice?" *The New York Times* (October 3, 2018). https://www.nytimes.com/interactive/2018/10/03/mag azine/morality-social-justice-art-entertainment.html.

Müller, Ernst. *Ästhetische Religiosität und Kunstreligion.* Berlin: Akademie Verlag, 2004.

Muncker, Franz. *Friedrich Gottlieb Klopstock.* Stuttgart: Göschen, 1888.

Nannini, Alessandro. "Critical Aesthetics. Baumgarten and the Logic of Taste." *Aesthetic Investigations* 4.2 (Forthcoming).

Nannini, Alessandro. "The Language of Affects. From pathologia sacra to pathologia aesthetica." In *Gefühl und Norm. Pietismus und Gefühlskulturen im 18. Jahrhundert*, edited by Daniel Cyranka, Thomas Ruhland, Christian Soboth, and Friedemann Stengel. (Forthcoming).

Nannini, Alessandro. "Aesthetica experimentalis. Baumgarten and the Aesthetic Dimension of Experience." In *The Experiential Turn in Eighteenth-Century German Philosophy*, edited by Karin de Boer and Tinca Prunea. New York: Routledge, 2021, 55–77.

Nannini, Alessandro. "At the Bottom of the Soul. The Psychologization of the Fundus Animae between Leibniz and Sulzer." *Journal of the History of Ideas* 82.1 (2021): 51–72.

Nannini, Alessandro. "Postfazione, L'Aesthetica oggi." In *Alexander Gottlieb Baumgarten, Estetica*, edited by Salvatore Tedesco and Alessandro Nannini. Milan: Mimesis, 2020a, 361–370.

Nannini, Alessandro. "Johann August Ernesti e le origini della filosofia popolare tra neoumanesimo ed estetica." In *Popolo e cultura popolare nel Settecento*, edited by Anna Maria Rao. Rome: Edizioni di Storia e Letteratura, 2020b, 117–127.

Nannini, Alessandro. "The Six Faces of Beauty. Baumgarten and the Perfections of Knowledge in the Context of the German Enlightenment." *Archiv für Geschichte der Philosophie* 102.3 (2020c): 477–512.

Nannini, Alessandro. "In the Wake of Clio. Baumgarten on History." *Deutsche Vierteljahrsschrift für Literaturwissenschaft und Geistesgeschichte* 93 (2019): 1–41.

Nannini, Alessandro. "From the Density of Sense to the Density of the Sensible: The Emergence of Aesthetic Pregnancy from the Spirit of Hermeneutics." *Archiv für Begriffsgeschichte* 60/61 (2018/2019): 163–186.

Nannini, Alessandro. "Predicare per l'uomo. Sensibilità e intelletto nell'omiletica di Georg Friedrich Meier." In *Il Settecento e la religione*, edited by Patrizia Delpiano and Marina Formica. Rome: Edizioni di Storia e Letteratura, 2018b, 29–42.

Nannini, Alessandro. "'Können Sie denn dergleichen schreiben, ohne in Wallung zu gerathen? Ich nicht'. A Commented Edition of an Unknown Letter of Baumgarten to Meier." *Diciottesimo secolo* 3 (2018c): 205–227.

Nannini, Alessandro. "Alexander G. Baumgarten and the Lost Letters of Aletheophilus. Notes on a Mystery at the Origins of Modern Aesthetics." *Diciottesimo secolo* 2 (2017): 23–43.

Nannini, Alessandro. "Biblical Hermeneutics in the Light of Aesthetics. The Case of Gottlob Samuel Nicolai." In *Religion und Aufklärung*, edited by Albrecht Beutel and Martha Nooke. Tübingen: Mohr Siebeck, 2016, 551–559.

Nannini, Alessandro. "L'idea estetica di 'chiarezza estensiva' e la sua genesi nella filosofia wolffiana." *Rivista di storia della filosofia* 69.3 (2014a): 421–442.

Nannini, Alessandro. "Per una storia dell'idea di 'conoscenza viva'. Da Lutero all'estetica dell'Aufklärung." *Intersezioni. Rivista di storia delle idee* 34 (2014b): 381–402.

Nannini, Alessandro. "Da Baumgarten a Baumgarten. Siegmund Jakob Baumgarten e la fondazione dell'estetica moderna." In *Premio Nuova Estetica*, edited by Luigi Russo. Palermo: Aesthetica, 2013, 67–90.

Neumaier, Otto. *Grenzgänge zwischenWissenschaft und Kunst*. Wien/Münster: Lit Verlag, 2015, 25–52.

Neumann, Birgit. *Präsenz und Evidenz fremder Dinge im Europa des 18. Jahrhunderts*. Göttingen: Wallstein Verlag, 2015.

Nicolai, Gottlob Samuel. "Vorrede." In *Briefe über den itzigen Zustand der schönen Wissenschaften in Deutschland*, edited by Friedrich Nicolai. Berlin: Kleyb, 1755.

Nicolai, Gottlob Samuel. *Von der Verbesserung der sinlichen Erkentnis, als einem Hülfsmittel der Auslegung der Heiligen Schrift*. Halle: Fürst, 1748.

Niehues-Pröbsting, Heinrich. "Rhetorische und idealistische Kategorien der Ästhetik." In *Ästhetische Erfahrung*, edited by Willy Oelmüller. Paderborn: Schöningh, 1981, 94–110.

Nivelle, Armand. *Kunst- und Dichtungstheorien zwischen Aufklärung und Klassik*. Berlin: Walter de Gruyter, 1960.

Nünning, Ansgar. *Grundbegriffe der Kulturtheorie und Kulturwissenschaften*. Stuttgart/Weimar: J.B. Metzler, 2005, 125–130.

Oelmüller, Willi, Dölle-Oelmüller, Ruth, and Rath, Norbert. *Diskurs: Kunst und Schönes*. Paderborn: Schöningh, 1982.

Oelrichs, Johann Karl Konrad. "Tagebuch einer gelehrten Reise 1750, durch einen Theil von Ober- und Nieder-Sachsen." In *Sammlung kurzer Reisebeschreibungen*, edited by Jean Bernoulli. Berlin-Dessau: Buchhandlung der Gelehrten, 1782, Vol. 5, 1–152.

Orth, Ernst Wolfgang. "Ernst Cassirer als Kulturwissenschaftler." In *Kulturwissenschaften. Konzepte, Theorien, Autoren*, edited by Iris Därmann and Christoph Jamme. München: Fink, 2007, 269–291.

Ortland, Eberhard. "Ästhetik als Wissenschaft der sinnlichen Erkenntnis. Ansätze zur Wiedergewinnung von Baumgartens uneingelöstem Projekt." *Deutsche Zeitschrift für Philosophie* 49 (2001): 1–18.

Osawa, Toshiro. *Perfection and Morality: A Commentary on Baumgarten's Ethica Philosophica and its Relevance to Kantian Ethics*. Dissertation, Department of Philosophy, Macquarie University, 2013.

Ostermann, Eberhard. *Die Authentizität des Ästhetischen. Studien zur ästhetischen Transformation der Rhetorik*. München: Fink, 2002.

Owen, G. E. L. "Aristotelian Pleasures." In *Logic, Science, and Dialectic: Collected Papers in Greek Philosophy*, edited by G. E. L. Owen and Martha Nussbaum. Ithaca: Cornell University Press, 1986.

Paetzold, Heinz. "Rhetorik-Kritik und Theorie der Künste in der philosophischen Ästhetik von Baumgarten bis Kant." In *Von der Rhetorik zur Ästhetik: Studien zur Entstehung der modernen Ästhetik im 18. Jahrhundert*, edited by Gérard Raulet. Rennes: Centre de Recherches Philia, 1995, 9–40.

Paetzold, Heinz. *Ästhetik des deutschen Idealismus. Zur Idee ästhetischer Rationalität bei Baumgarten, Kant, Schelling, Hegel und Schopenhauer*. Wiesbaden: Steiner Verlag, 1983.

Park, Peter K. J. *Africa, Asia, and the History of Philosophy: Racism in the Formation of the Philosophical Canon*. Albany: SUNY Press, 2013.

Parret, Herman. "De Baumgarten à Kant: sur la beauté." *Revue Philosophique de Louvain* 90 (1992): 317–343.

Pascal, Blaise. *Pensées*. Heidelberg: Lambert Schneider, 1978.

Paul. "Letter to the Philippians and II Corinthians." In *The Greek New Testament*, edited K. Aland, et al. Stuttgart: Württemberg Bible Society, 1966.

Peres, Constanze. "Die Doppelfunktion der Ästhetik im philosophischen System A. G. Baumgartens." In *Schönes Denken. A. G. Baumgarten im Spannungsfeld von Ästhetik, Metaphysik und Naturrecht*, edited by Andrea Allerkamp and Dagmar Mirbach. Hamburg: Felix Meiner Verlag, 2016, 89–116.

Peres, Constanze. "Komplexität und Mangel ästhetischer Zeichen – Baumgartens (proto)semiotische Theorie und Goodmans Symptome der Kunst." *Studia Leibnitiana* 32 (2000): 215–236.

Perpeet, Wilhelm. *Vom Schönen und von der Kunst. Ausgewählte Studien*. Bonn: Bouvier, 1997.

Perpeet, Wilhelm. *Das Kunstschöne. Sein Ursprung in der italienischen Renaissance*. Freiburg im Breisgau/München: Alber, 1987.

Peters, Hans-Georg. *Studien über die Ästhetik des Alexander Gottlieb Baumgarten unter besonderer Berücksichtigung ihrer Beziehungen zum Ethischen*. Berlin: Junker und Dünnhaupt Verlag, 1934.

Pimpinella, Pietro. "La théorie wolffienne des arts à l'origine de l'esthétique." *Revue germanique internationale* 4 (2006): 9–22.

Pimpinella, Pietro. "Hermeneutik und Ästhetik bei A. G. Baumgarten." In *Die Hermeneutik im Zeitalter der Aufklärung*, edited by Manfred Beetz and Guiseppe Cacciatore. Köln/Weimar/Wien: Böhlau Verlag, 2000, 265–283.

Pimpinella, Pietro. "Ragione e sensibilità nelle poetiche critiche di Gottsched e Breitinger e nell'estetica di Baumgarten." *Lexicon philosophicum* 10 (1999): 121–150.

Pimpinella, Pietro. "Truth and Persuasion." *Lexicon Philosophicum* 6 (1993): 21–49.

Piselli, Francesco. "Einige philologische und theoretische Überlegungen zu A.G. Baumgartens Aesthetica." In *Schönes Denken. A. G. Baumgarten im Spannungsfeld von Ästhetik, Metaphysik und Naturrecht*, edited by Andrea Allerkamp and Dagmar Mirbach. Hamburg: Felix Meiner Verlag, 2016, 67–70.

Piselli, Francesco. "Ästhetik und Metaphysik bei Alexander Gottlieb Baumgarten." In *Alexander Gottlieb Baumgarten: Sinnliche Erkenntnis in der Philosophie des Rationalismus*, edited by Alexander Aichele and Dagmar Mirbach. Hamburg: Felix Meiner Verlag, 2008, 101–116.

Pollok, Anne. "Gazing Upwards to the Stage: Mendelssohn's Notion of Admiration and Its Consequences." In *The Moral Psychology of Admiration*, edited by Alfred Archer and André Grahle. London: Rowman & Littlefield, 2019, 79–94.

Pollok, Anne. "Beautiful Perception and its Object. Mendelssohn's theory of mixed sentiments reconsidered." *Kant-Studien* 109.2 (2018): 270–285.

Pollok, Anne. *Facetten des Menschen. Zu Moses Mendelssohns Anthropologie.* Hamburg: Felix Meiner Verlag, 2010.

Poppe, Bernhard. *Alexander Gottlieb Baumgarten. Seine Bedeutung und Stellung in der LeibnizWolffischen Philosophie und seine Beziehungen zu Kant.* Borna/ Leipzig: Robert Noske, 1907.

Pyra, Jacob Immanuel. *Fortsetzung des Erweises, daß die G*ttsch*dianische Sekte den Geschmack verderbe.* Berlin: Schütze, 1744.

Quintilian. *The Orator's Education.* Translated by Donald A. Russell. Cambridge: Harvard University Press, 2002.

Quistorp. Theodor Johann. "Erweis, daß die Poesie schon für sich selbst ihre Liebhaber leichtlich unglückselig machen könne." *Neuer Büchersaal der schönen Wissenschaften und freyen Künste* 5. Stück (1745): 433–452.

Rambach, Johann Jacob. *Erläuterung über seine eigene Institutiones hermeneuticae sacred.* Edited by Ernst Friedrich Neubauer. Gießen: Krieger, 1738.

Rambach, Johann Jacob. *Poetische Fest-Gedancken.* Jena: Rittern, 1727.

Rambach, Johann Jacob. *Institutiones hermeneuticae sacrae.* Jena: Hartungiana, 1723.

Rand, Nicholas. "The Hidden Soul: The Growth of the Unconscious in Philosophy, Psychology, Medicine, and Literature, 1750–1900." *American Imago* 61 (2004): 257–289.

Raulet, Gérard. "Logica inventionis und episteme esthetike. Die leisen Übergänge eines bahnbrechenden Umbruchs." In *Alexander Gottlieb Baumgarten: Sinnliche Erkenntnis in der Philosophie des Rationalismus*, edited by Alexander Aichele and Dagmar Mirbach. Hamburg: Felix Meiner Verlag, 2008, 127–148.

Recki, Birgit. *Ästhetik der Sitten. Die Affinität von ästhetischem Gefühl und praktischer Vernunft bei Kant.* Frankfurt am Main: Vittorio Klostermann, 2001.

Reicher, Maria E. *Fiktion, Wahrheit, Wirklichkeit. Philosophische Grundlagen der Literaturtheorie* (3rd Ed.). Münster: Mentis Verlag, 2016.

Reimann, Albert. *Die Ästhetik Alexander Gottlieb Baumgartens.* Halle: Max Niemeyer, 1928/1973.

Reiss, Hans. "Georg Friedrich Meier (1718–77) und die Verbreitung der Ästhetik." In *Geschichtlichkeit und Gegenwart*, edited by Hans Esselborn und Werner Keller. Köln: Böhlau, 1994a, 13–34.

Reiss, Hans. "The Naturalization of the Term Ästhetik in Eighteenth-Century German: Alexander Gottlieb Baumgarten and His Impact." *The Modern Language Review* 89.3 (1994b): 645–658.

Reiss, Hans. "Die Einbürgerung der Ästhetik in der deutschen Sprache des achtzehnten Jahrhunderts oder Baumgarten und seine Wirkung." *Jahrbuch der deutschen Schillergesellschaft* 37 (1993): 110–138.

Reusch, Johann Peter. *Systema logicum.* Jena: Cröker, 1734.

Riedel, Wolfgang. "Anthropologie und Literatur in der deutschen Spätaufklärung. Skizze einer Forschungslandschaft." *IASL* (Sonderheft 6, 1994a): 93–157.

Riedel, Wolfgang. "Erkennen und Empfinden. Anthropologische Achsendrehung und Wende zur Ästhetik bei Johann Georg Sulzer." In *Der ganze Mensch. Anthropologie und Literatur im 18. Jahrhundert*, edited by Hans-Jürgen Schings. Stuttgart: Verlag J.B. Metzler, 1994b, 410–439.

Riemann, Albert. *Die Ästhetik A.G. Baumgartens, unter besonderer Berücksichtigung der 'Meditationes philosophicae de nonnullis ad poema pertinentibus' nebst einer Übersetzung dieser Schrift*. Halle: Max Niemeyer, 1928.

Ritter, Joachim. *Vorlesungen zur Philosophischen Ästhetik*. Edited by Joachim von Bülow and Mark Schweda. Göttingen: Wallstein Verlag, 2010.

Ritter, Joachim. *Subjektivität. Sechs Aufsätze*. Frankfurt am Main: Suhrkamp Verlag, 1974.

Ritter, Joachim, Gründer, Karlfried, and Gabriel, Gottfried. *Historisches Wörterbuch der Philosophie*. Basel: Schwabe Verlag, 1971–2007a.

Ritter, Joachim. "Ästhetik, ästhetisch." In *Historisches Wörterbuch der Philosophie*, edited by Joachim Ritter, Karlfried Gründer, and Gottfried Gabriel. Basel: Schwabe Verlag, 1971–2007b, Vol. 1, 555–580.

Rorty, Amélie Oksenberg. "The Place of Pleasure in Aristotle's Ethics." *Mind* 83 (1974): 481–493.

Rosenkranz, Karl. *Ästhetik des Hässlichen*. Edited by Dieter Kliche. Stuttgart: Reclam, 2015.

Rueger, Alexander. "Enjoying the Unbeautiful: From Mendelssohn's Theory of 'Mixed Sentiments' to Kant's Aesthetic Judgments of Reflection." *Journal of Aesthetics and Art Criticism* 67.2 (2009): 181–189.

Rüsen, Jörn. "Sinnverlust und Transzendenz. Kultur und Kulturwissenschaft am Anfang des 21. Jahrhunderts." In *Handbuch der Kulturwissenschaften*, edited by Friedrich Jaeger and Jörn Rüsen. Stuttgart/Weimar: J.B. Metzler, 2004, 533–544.

Salmony, Hansjörg A. *Die Philosophie des jungen Herder*. Zürich: Vineta, 1949.

Scheer, Brigitte. *Einführung in die philosophische Ästhetik*. Darmstadt: Wissenschaftliche Buchgesellschaft, 1997.

Scheer, Brigitte. "Baumgartens Ästhetik und die Krise der von ihm begründeten Disziplin." *Philosophische Rundschau* 22 (1976): 108–119.

Schelling, Friedrich Wilhelm Joseph von. *The Philosophy of Art*. Edited and translated by Douglas W. Stott. Minneapolis: University of Minnesota Press, 1989.

Schelling, Friedrich Wilhelm Joseph von. *Philosophie der Kunst. Unveränderter reprographischer Nachdruck der aus dem handschriftlichen Nachlass herausgegebenen Ausgabe von 1859*. Darmstadt: Wissenschaftliche Buchgesellschaft, 1966.

Schenk, Günter. *Leben und Werken des halleschen Aufklärers Georg Friedrich Meier*. Halle: Hallescher Verlag, 1994.

Schiller, Friedrich, "On the Sublime: (Toward the Further Development of Some Kantian Ideas)." In *The Sublime Reader*, edited by Robert R. Clewis. London: Bloomsbury Publishing, 2019, 150–160.

Schloemann, Martin. *Siegmund Jacob Baumgarten*. Göttingen: Vandenhoeck & Ruprecht, 1974.

Schmidt, Horst-Michael. *Sinnlichkeit und Verstand. Zur philosophischen und poet-ologischen Begründung von Erfahrung und Urteilin der deutschen Aufklärung. Leibniz, Wolff, Gottsched, Bodmer und Breitinger, Baumgarten.* München: Fink, 1982.

Schmidt, Johann Andreas (praes.), and Gelhud, Ludovicus Guntherus (def.). *Dissertatio historico-theologica de modo propagandi religionem per carmina.* Helmstedt: Georg Wilhelm Hammii, 1710.

Schmitt, Arbogast. "Schönheit: Gegenstand der Sinne oder des Denkens? Zur Theorie des Schönen im 18. Jahrhundert und bei Platon." In *Kunst und Wissen. Beziehungen zwischen Ästhetik und Erkenntnistheorie im 18. und 19. Jahrhundert*, edited by Astrid Bauereisen, Stephen Pabst, and Achim Vesper. Würzburg: Königshausen & Neumann, 2009, 49–70.

Schmitt, Arbogast. "Die Entgrenzung der Künste durch ihre Ästhetisierung bei Baumgarten." In *Ästhetische Erfahrung im Zeichen der Entgrenzung der Künste. Epistemische, ästhetische und religiöse Formen von Erfahrung im Vergleich*, edited by Gert Mattenklott. Hamburg: Felix Meiner Verlag, 2004, 55–71.

Schmücker, Reinold. "Künstlerisch forschen. Über Herkunft und Zukunft eines ästhetischen Programms." In *Wie verändert sich Kunst, wenn man sie als Forschung versteht?* edited by Judith Siegmund. Bielefeld: Transcript Verlag, 2016, 124–144.

Schmücker, Reinold. *Was ist Kunst? Eine Grundlegung (Neuausgabe).* Frankfurt am Main: Klostermann, 2014.

Schmücker, Reinold. "Funktionen der Kunst." In *Wozu Kunst? Die Frage nach ihrer Funktion*, edited by Bernd Kleimann and Reinold Schmücker. Darmstadt: Wissenschaftliche Buchgesellschaft, 2001, 13–33.

Schnädelbach, Herbert. "Geist als Kultur? Über Möglichkeiten und Grenzen einer kulturtheoretischen Deutung von Hegels Philosophie des Geistes." *Zeitschrift für Kulturphilosophie* 2 (2008): 187–207.

Schneider, Ferdinand Josef. "Das geistige Leben von Halle im Zeichen des Endkampfes zwischen Pietismus und Rationalismus." *Sachsen und Anhalt* 14 (1938): 137–166.

Scholz, Oliver R. "Die Allgemeine Hermeneutik bei Georg Friedrich Meier." In *Unzeitgemäße Hermeneutik. Verstehen und Interpretation im Denken der Aufklärung*, edited by Axel Bühler. Frankfurt am Main: Klostermann, 1994, 158–191.

Schopenhauer, Arthur. *The World as Will and Representation* (Vol. 1). Edited and translated by Judith Norman, Alistair Welchman, and Christopher Janaway. Cambridge: Cambridge University Press, 2010.

Schurz, Gerhard. "Erklären und Verstehen. Tradition, Transformation und Aktualität einer klassischen Kontroverse." In *Handbuch der Kulturwissenschaften*, edited by Friedrich Jaeger and Jürgen Straub. Stuttgart/Weimar: J.B. Metzler, 2011, Vol. 2, 156–175.

Schwab, Johann Christoph. "Welches sind die wirklichen Fortschritte, die die Metaphysik seit Leibnitzens und Wolffens Zeiten in Deutschland gemacht hat?" In *Welche Fortschritte hat die Metaphysik seit Leibnitzens und Wolffens Zeiten in*

Deutschland gemacht?, edited by the Royal Prussian Academy of Sciences. Berlin: Friedrich Maurer, 1796, 1–170.

Schwaiger, Clemens. *Alexander Gottlieb Baumgarten - Ein intellectuelles Porträt.* Stuttgart-Bad Cannstatt: Frommann-Holzboog, 2011.

Schwaiger, Clemens. "The Theory of Obligation in Wolff, Baumgarten, and the Early Kant." In *Kant's Moral and Legal Philosophy*, edited by Karl Ameriks and Otfried Höffe. Cambridge: Cambridge University Press, 2009.

Schwaiger, Clemens. "Ein 'missing link' auf dem Weg der Ethik von Wolff zu Kant. Zur Quellen- und Wirkungsgeschichte der praktischen Philosophie von Alexander Gottlieb Baumgarten." *Jahrbuch für Recht und Ethik* 8 (2000): 247–261.

Schweizer, Hans Rudolf. *Vom ursprünglichen Sinn der Ästhetik.* Oberwil: Verlag Rolf Kugler, 1976.

Schweizer, Hans Rudolf. *Ästhetik als Philosophie der sinnlichen Erkenntnis. Eine Interpretation der Aesthetica A. G. Baumgartens.* Basel/Stuttgart: Schwabe Verlag, 1973.

Seel, Martin. *Die Kunst der Entzweiung. Zum Begriff der ästhetischen Rationalität.* Frankfurt am Main: Suhrkamp Verlag, 1985.

Segebrecht, Wulf. *Das Gelegenheitsgedicht. Ein Beitrag zur Geschichte und Poetik der deutschen Lyrik.* Stuttgart: J.B. Mezler, 1977.

Seiler, Kristin. *Die Stellung Friedrich Just(us) Riedels in der Literaturgeschichte und sein Einfluß auf die Literaturtheorie unter besonderer Berücksichtigung seiner Ästhetik.* Ph.D. thesis, Martin-Luther-Universität Halle-Wittenberg, 1998.

Sgarbi, Marco. "Renaissance Facultative Logic and the Workings of the Mind: The Cognitive Turn." In *Philosophy of Mind in the Late Middle Ages and Renaissance*, edited by Stephan Schmid. London: Routledge, 2018, 270–290.

Shaftesbury (Anthony Ashley Cooper). *Characteristics of Men, Matters, Opinions, Times.* Edited by Lawrence E. Klein. Cambridge: Cambridge University Press, 1999.

Shaw, Philip. *The Sublime.* London: Routledge, 2005.

Shusterman, Richard. "Back to the Future: Aesthetics Today." *The Nordic Journal* 43 (2012): 104–124.

Siebert, Irmgard. "Jacob Burckhardts Konzeption einer historisch fundierten Kunstgeschichtsschreibung." In *Zwischen Philosophie und Kunstgeschichte. Beiträge zur Begründung der Kunstgeschichtsforschung bei Hegel und im Hegelianismus*, edited by Annemarie Gethmann-Siefert and Bernadette Collenberg-Plotnikov. München: Fink, 2008, 107–119.

Solms, Friedrich. *Disciplina aesthetica. Zur Frühgeschichte der ästhetischen Theorie bei Baumgarten und Herder.* Stuttgart: Klett-Cotta, 1990.

Sonderegger, Ruth. "Die Kunst als Sphäre der Kultur und die kunstwissenschaftliche Transformation der Ästhetik." In *Handbuch der Kulturwissenschaften*, edited by Friedrich Jaeger and Jörn Rüsen. Stuttgart/Weimar: J.B. Metzler, 2004, 50–65.

Sorkin, David. *The Religious Enlightenment: Protestants, Jews, and Catholics from London to Vienna.* Princeton: Princeton University Press, 2008.

Spalding, Samuel Wilhelm (auct.), and Baumgarten, Alexander Gottlieb (praes.). *De vi et efficacia ethices philosophiae.* Frankfurt an der Oder: Hübner, 1741.

Spener, Philip Jacob. *Pia Desideria*. Edited and translated by Theodore G. Tappert. Minneapolis: Fortress Press, 1964.

Spree, Axel. "Cassirers Baumgarten." *Monatshefte* 95 (2003): 410–420.

Spree, Axel. "Die Aktualität der Ästhetik Baumgartens." In *Aktualität der Aufklärung*, edited by Ryszard Rózanowski. Breslau: Wydawnictwo Uniwersytetu Wrocławskiego, 2000, 155–165.

Stein, Karl Heinrich von. *Die Entstehung der neuern Aesthetik*. Stuttgart: J.G. Cotta, 1886.

Stemmrich, Gregor. *Das Charakteristische in der Malerei. Statusprobleme der nicht mehr schönen Künste und ihre theoretische Bewältigung*. Berlin: Verlag für Wissenschaft und Forschung, 1994.

Stöckmann, Ernst. "Steffen W. Groß, Felix aesthicus. Die Ästhetik als Lehre vom Menschen. Zum 250. Jahrestag des Erscheinens von Alexander Gottlieb Baumgartens ›Aesthetica‹." *Arbitrium* 3 (2001): 294–298.

Strassberger, Andres. *Johann Christoph Gottsched und die "philosophische" Predigt*. Tübingen: Mohr Siebeck, 2010.

Streit, Karl Konrad. *Alphabetisches Verzeichnis aller im 1774 lebenden in Schlesien lebender Schriftsteller*. Breslau: Korn, 1776.

Strieder, Friedrich Wilhelm. *Grundlage zu einer hessischen Gelehrten-und-Schriftsteller-Geschichte*. Hessen: Griesbach, 1797.

Strube, Werner. "Die Entstehung der Ästhetik als einer wissenschaftlichen Disziplin." *Scientia poetica* 8 (2004): 1–30.

Strube, Werner. "Alexander Gottlieb Baumgartens Theorie des Gedichts." In *Dichtungstheorien der Frühaufklärung*, edited by Theodor Verweyen. Tübingen: Niemeyer, 1995, 1–25.

Strube, Werner. "Ästhetische Wertäußerungen. Eine sprechakttheoretische Analyse." In *Perspektiven der Kunstphilosophie. Texte und Diskussionen*, edited by Franz Koppe. Frankfurt am Main: Suhrkamp Verlag, 1991, 240–257.

Strube, Werner. "Die Geschichte des Begriffs 'schöne Wissenschaften'." *Archiv für Begriffsgeschichte* 33 (1990): 136–216.

Strube, Werner. "Jörg Zimmermann, Sprachanalytische Ästhetik. Ein Überblick." *Philosophische Rundschau* 29 (1982): 157–160.

Sulzer, Johann Georg. *Gesammelte Schriften*. Edited by Hans Adler and Elisabeth Décultot. Basel: Schwabe Verlag, 2014ff.

Sulzer, Johann Georg. *Vermischte philosophische Schriften,* Vol. I, II. Hildesheim: Georg Olms Verlag, 1974.

Sulzer, Johann Georg. *Vermischte philosophische Schriften*. Leipzig: Weidmanns, Erben and Reich, 1773.

Sulzer, Johann Georg: *Kurzer Begriff aller Wissenschaften Worinn die natürliche Verbindung aller Theile der Gelehrsamkeit gezeiget, auch ein jeder insbesondere nach seinem Inhalt, Nutzen und Vollkommenheit kürzlich beschrieben wird*. Frankfurt and Leipzig, 1745/1759.

Tanke, Joseph, and McQuillan, J. Colin. *The Bloomsbury Anthology of Aesthetics*. London: Bloomsbury Publishing, 2012.

Tedesco, Salvatore. *L'Estetica di Alexander Gottlieb Baumgarten*. Palermo: Aesthetica Edizioni, 2000.

Tedesco, Salvatore. "L'Ermeneutica Generale di Meier. I rapporti tra estetica e ermeneutica nella scuola di Baumgarten." *Studi di estetica* 26 (1998): 195–209.

Tetens, Johann Nicolas. *Philosophische Versuche über die menschliche Natur und ihre Entwickelung*. Leipzig: Weidmanns, Erben, and Reich, 1777.

Tonelli, Giorgio. "Zabarella inspirateur de Baumgarten, ou l'origine de la connexion entre esthétique et logique." *Revue d'esthétique* 9 (1956): 182–192.

Trinius, Johann Anton. *Beytrag zu einer Geschichte berühmter und verdienter Gottesgelehrten auf dem Lande*. Leipzig: Jacobi, 1751.

Trop, Gabriel. *Poetry as a Way Of Life – Aesthetics and Askesis in the German Eighteenth Century*. Evanston: Northwestern University Press, 2015.

Tutor, Juan Ignacio Gómez. *Die wissenschaftliche Methode bei Christian Wolff*. Hildesheim: Georg Olms Verlag, 2004.

Ueding, Gert. *Einführung in die Rhetorik*. Stuttgart: J.B. Metzler, 1976.

Urmson, J. O. "Aristotle on Pleasure." In *Aristotle: A Collection of Critical Essays*, edited by J.O. Urmson. New York: Palgrave Macmillan, 1967.

Vanzo, Alberto. "Christian Wolff and Experimental Philosophy." In *Oxford Studies in Early Modern Philosophy* (Vol. 7), edited by Daniel Garber and Donald Rutherford. Oxford: Oxford University Press, 2015.

Velthusen, Johann Caspar, et al. *Commentationes theologicae*. Leipzig: Barth, 1798.

Verweyen, Theodor, and Witting, Gunther. "Zur Rezeption Baumgartens bei Uz, Gleim und Rudnick." In *Dichtungstheorien der deutschen Aufklärung*, edited by Theodor Verweyen. Tübingen: Niemeyer, 1995, 101–119.

Vico, Giambattista. "On the Heroic Mind." In *The Sublime Reader*, edited by Robert R. Clewis. London: Bloomsbury Publishing, 2019, 69–77.

Virgil. *Aeneid: Books 7–12*. Translated by H. Rushton Fairclough. Revised by G. P. Goold. Cambridge: Harvard University Press, 1918.

Virgil. *Eclogues, Georgics, Aeneid: Books 1–6*. Translated by H. Rushton Fairclough. Revised by G. P. Goold. Cambridge: Harvard University Press, 1916.

Vogt, Wilhelm. *Die ästhetische Idee bei Kant*. Gütersloh: C. Bertelsmann, 1906.

Waetzoldt, Wilhelm. *Deutsche Kunsthistoriker* (3rd Ed.). Berlin: Wissenschaftsverlag Spiess, 1986.

Walch, Johann Georg. *Philosophisches Lexicon* (2nd Ed.). Leipzig: Johann Friedrich Gleditsch, 1733.

Weimar, Klaus. *Geschichte der deutschen Literaturwissenschaft bis zum Ende des 19. Jahrhunderts*. München: Fink, 1989.

Wellek, René. *A History of Modern Criticism, 1750–1950*. New Haven: Yale University Press, 1955–1992.

Welsch, Wolfgang. *Blickwechsel. Neue Wege der Ästhetik*. Stuttgart: Reclam, 2012.

Welsch, Wolfgang. "Erweiterungen der Ästhetik. Eine Replik." In *Bild und Reflexion. Paradigmen und Perspektiven gegenwärtiger Ästhetik*, edited by Birgit Recki and Lambert Wiesing. München: Fink, 1997, 39–67.

Welsch, Wolfgang. *Grenzgänge der Ästhetik*. Stuttgart: Reclam, 1996.

Welsch, Wolfgang. *Ästhetisches Denken*. Stuttgart: Reclam, 1990.

Welsch, Wolfgang. *Aisthesis. Grundzüge und Perspektiven der Aristotelischen Sinnenlehre.* Stuttgart: Klett-Cotta, 1987.

White, Nicholas. *A Brief History of Happiness.* New York: John Wiley & Sons, 2008.

White Beck, Lewis. *Early German Philosophy: Kant and his Predecessors.* Cambridge: Harvard University Press, 1969.

Wicks, Robert. "Nineteenth- and Twentieth-Century Continental Aesthetics." In *A Companion to Aesthetics* (2nd ed.), edited by Stephen Davies, et al. Malden: Wiley-Blackwell, 2009, 51–61.

Wilhelm, Richard. *Friedrich Justus Riedel und die Ästhetik der Aufklärung.* Heidelberg: Winter, 1933.

Williams, Bernard. *Descartes: The Project of Pure Enquiry.* London: Routledge, 2015.

Winkelmann, Georg Christoph. "Von der ohnlängst erfundenen Aesthetik." In *Altes und Neues von Schulsachen*, edited by Johann Gottlieb Biedermann. Halle: Johann Justinus Gebauern, 1754, Vol. 6, 149–164.

Winckelmann, Johann Joachim. *Briefe.* Edited by Walther Rehm. Berlin: Walter de Gruyter, 1957.

Witte, Egbert. *Logik ohne Dornen: Die Rezeption von A. G. Baumgartens Ästhetik im Spannungsfeld von logischem Begriff und ästhetischer Anschauung.* Hildesheim: Georg Olms Verlag, 2000.

Wolandt, Gerd. "Zur Aktualität der Hegelschen Ästhetik." *Hegel Studien* 4 (1967): 219–234.

Wolff, Christian. *Vernünftige Gedancken von Gott, der Welt, und der Seele des Menschen, auch allen Dingen überhaupt (German Metaphysics).* In *Christian Wolff: Gesammelte Werke* (Vol. I.2.1), edited by Jean École, et al. Hildesheim: Georg Olms Verlag, 2009.

Wolff, Christian. "Vernünftige Gedanken von den Kräften des menschlichen Verstandes und ihrem richtigen Gebrauche in Erkenntnis der Warheit (German Logic)." In *Christian Wolff: Gesammelte Werke* (Vol. I.1), edited by Jean École, et al. Hildesheim: Georg Olms Verlag, 2006.

Wolff, Christian. "Logic, or Rational Thoughts on the Powers of the Human Understanding (German Logic)." In *Christian Wolff: Gesammelte Werke* (Vol. III.77), edited by Jean École, et al. Hildesheim: Georg Olms Verlag, 2003.

Wolff, Christian. "Anfangs-Gründe aller Mathematischen Wissenschaften." In *Christian Wolff: Gesammelte Werke* (Vol. I.12), edited by Jean École, et al. Hildesheim: Georg Olms Verlag, 1999.

Wolff, Christian. "Discourse on the Practical Philosophy of the Chinese." In *Moral Enlightenment: Leibniz and Wolff on China*, edited and translated by Julia Ching and Willard G. Oxtoby. Nettetal: Steyler Verlag, 1992, 145–186.

Wolff, Christian. "Psychologia Empirica." In *Christian Wolff: Gesammelte Werke* (Vol. II.5), edited by Jean École, et al. Hildesheim: Georg Olms Verlag, 1986.

Wolff, Christian. "Philosophia rationalis sive logica (Latin Logic)." In *Christian Wolff: Gesammelte Werke* (Vol. II.1), edited by Jean École et al. Hildesheim: Georg Olms Verlag, 1983.

Wolff, Christian. *Preliminary Discourse on Philosophy in General.* Translated by Richard J. Blackwell. Indianapolis: Bobbs-Merrill, 1963.

Wolff, Christian. *Psychologia rationalis.* Frankfurt/Leipzig: Officina Libraria Rengeriana, 1734.

Wolff, Christian. *Ausführliche Nachricht von seinen eigenen Schrifften* (2nd Ed.). Frankfurt am Main: Andreä and Hort, 1733.

Wolff, Christian. *Philosophia rationalis sive logica* (2nd Ed.). Frankfurt/Leipzig: Officina Libraria Rengeriana, 1732.

Wolff, Christian. *Philosophia rationalis, sive Logica.* Frankfurt and Leipzig: Renger, 1728.

Wolfsdork, David. *Pleasure in Ancient Greek Philosophy.* Cambridge: Cambridge University Press, 2013.

Wolterstorff, Nicholas. *Art Rethought: The Social Practices of Art.* Oxford: Oxford University Press, 2015.

Zedler, Johann Heinrich. *Grosses vollständiges Universal-Lexicon aller Wissenschaften und Künste.* Halle and Leipzig: Zedler, 1732–1750.

Zedler, Johann Heinrich, and Ludovici, Carl Günther. *Nöthige Supplemente zu dem Großen Vollständigen Universal Lexicon.* Leipzig: Zedler, 1751.

Zelle, Carsten. "Sinnlichkeit und Therapie. Zur Gleichursprünglichkeit von Ästhetik und Anthropologie um 1750." In *Vernünftige Ärzte*, edited by Carsten Zelle. Tübingen: Niemeyer, 2001, 5–24.

Zelle, Carsten. "Zwischen Weltweisheit und Arzneiwissenschaft. Zur Vordatierung der anthropologischen Wende in die Frühaufklärung nach Halle (eine Skizze)." In *Formen der Aufklärung und ihrer Rezeption*, edited by Reinhard Bach, et al. Tübingen: Stauffenburg, 1999, 35–44.

Zeller, Eduard. *Geschichte der deutschen Philosophie seit Leibniz.* München: R. Oldenbourg, 1873.

Zenker, Kay. "Zwei Jahrzehnte Volksaufklärung (1748–1768). Meier als Herausgeber und Autor Moralischer Wochenschriften." In *Georg Friedrich Meier (1718–1777)*, edited by Frank Grunert and Gideon Stiening. Berlin: Walter De Gruyter, 2015, 55–80.

Zimmerli, Walter Christian. *Die Frage nach der Philosophie. Interpretationen zu Hegels Differenzschrift.* Bonn: Bouvier, 1974.

Zimmermann, Jörg. *Sprachanalytische Ästhetik. Ein Überblick.* Stuttgart/Bad Cannstatt: Frommann-Holzboog, 1980.

Index

Abbt, Thomas, 10, 150, 151, 219;
    Baumgarten's Life and Character, 10
absolute, 54, 266
absolutism, 218
abstraction, 14, 126, 187, 195, 207, 233,
    240
abundance, 73–75, 181, 196–97, 243,
    248, 287
academia, 208
accuracy, 142
action, 72–73, 81, 205, 209, 259, 296;
    act of compiling, 81; act of judging,
    81; being acted upon, 81; good, 145;
    heroic, 252; human, 160; intellectual,
    280; virtuous, 248
activity, 205, 209, 218, 280; human,
    209; internal, 218; obscure, 205; self-
    determined, 280
actuality, 217
acuity, 81
adequacy, 109
admiration, 198, 248, 263
Adorno, Theodor W., 68
aesthetics, 3, 9, 11–19, 21–25, 30–33,
    36, 45–46, 49–51, 55–62, 65–68,
    73, 77, 81, 83, 90, 105–23, 126–27,
    149, 153, 164, 169–70, 172, 177,
    179, 180, 182–83, 185, 189–90,
    192–201, 210, 213–14, 216,

219, 225–52, 261, 268–98, 301;
aesthete, 231; aesthetic affection,
291–92; aesthetic appreciation, 210;
aesthetic argument, 90; aesthetic
cognition, 32–33, 81, 288–90,
292; aesthetic discipline, 24;
aesthetic disposition, 276; aesthetic
education, 51; aesthetic empiric,
14; aesthetic enthusiasm, 298;
aesthetic exercise, 24, 193, 269,
279–82, 298; aesthetic experience,
32, 118, 210, 242, 254, 269, 298;
aesthetic expression, 108; aesthetic
falsity, 116; aesthetic habit, 82,
269, 298; aesthetic heuristic, 187;
aesthetic horizon, 82, 112, 118–19;
aesthetician/*aestheticus*, 114,
231; aesthetic idea, 43; aesthetic
improvement, 298; aesthetic
invention, 79; aestheticization of
discipline, 282; aesthetic judgment,
36, 67, 153, 198, 252, 264–65,
268–69; aesthetic knowledge,
105; aesthetic magnitude, 116,
120, 241, 244, 246, 249, 250, 260,
269; aesthetic majesty, 241, 244;
aesthetic meditation, 112; aesthetic
mind, 82; aesthetic nobility, 244;
aestheticological truth, 32, 77, 106,

108, 110, 113–14, 120–21, 239, 287; aesthetic pathology, 183, 185; aesthetic perfection, 19, 153, 288, 290, 294; aesthetic persuasion, 18; aesthetic presentation, 121–22; aesthetic probability, 200; aesthetic psychology, 202; aesthetic rationalism, 151, 169; aesthetic representation, 111, 113, 117, 198, 200; aesthetic response, 270; aesthetic richness, 116, 248; aesthetics of truth, 246, 268; aesthetic semiotics, 59; aesthetic signification, 51; aesthetic speech, 60; aesthetic spirit, 112; aesthetic striving, 113; aesthetic subjectivation, 281; aesthetic sublime, 244; aesthetic striving, 113; aesthetic teaching, 298; aesthetic temperament, 252, 298; aesthetic theory, 30–31, 36, 43, 45, 51, 62, 65–68, 126–27, 241, 261, 268, 272, 281, 289; aesthetic thinking, 117–18, 197; aesthetic training, 22–24, 193–96, 201; aesthetic truth, 21, 32, 65, 68, 77, 105–23, 239, 287–88; aesthetic value, 49; aesthetic war, 190; aesthetic wealth, 43; anthropological, 219; of art, 238; artificial, 230, 231, 233–34; as artificial art, 83; as art of the analogue of reason, 13, 50, 107, 229; as art of thinking beautifully, 13, 107; combining aesthetics and morality, 271; critical aesthetics, 185, 277; cultivating the whole person, 250; dynamic, 277; early modern, 3, 242; empirical aesthetics, 68, 179; environmental aesthetics, 261; general, 214, 216, 219, 233–34, 236; German, 243; and goodness, 297; happy aesthetician/*felix aestheticus*, 24–25, 283–84, 286–87, 292–93, 297, 301; history of, 172, 234;

as ideology, 279; as inferior gnoseology, 13, 107; innate, 230; as instrumental philosophy, 55–61; as insult, 189; as logic, 226–30; logic of, 280; as logic of the inferior cognitive faculty, 12; *mathesis aesthetica*, 83; Meier's definition, 177; as mere metaphor, 232; natural, 81, 198–99, 230–31, 233–34, 276–77; as new science, 9, 56, 107, 122, 149, 164, 169–70, 179; objective, 230, 236; as part of philosophy, 149; philosophical, 45–46, 213, 225–26, 279; as philosophical investigation of sensory cognition, 230; as philosophy of art, 192; as philosophy of graces and muses, 12; post-kantian, 243; practical, 15, 18, 81, 182, 185, 250, 268, 271–72; proto-aesthetics, 182; religious, 250; as science, 14, 17, 107, 127, 149, 177, 231, 243, 285; science of, 297; as science of improving sensible cognition, 127; as science of knowing and presenting sensibly, 177; as science of sensible cognition, 17, 107, 243; as science of the lower cognitive faculty, 285; as science of the lower faculties and their perfection, 177; society of aesthetics, 180; as special science, 14; theoretical, 14, 15, 73, 81, 182; as theory of cognition, 107, 117; as theory of the liberal arts, 107, 117, 123, 235; as thinking of disciplinary power, 274; true, 236; universal, 214

affect, 129, 132, 135, 140, 142, 144, 147, 194, 229, 291–92, 296, 297; aesthetic affection, 291–92; holy, 134; human, 134, 148; natural, 131, 133; private, 134; spiritual, 131, 133, 137

agreement, 48, 89, 93, 97–98, 100, 244, 265, 300–302; of manifold,

93, 97; maximum, 300; of order, 300; and perfection, 89–90, 93; of representations, 97; of signs, 300; of thought, 97–98, 300

Ahmed, Sara, 25, 284, 292–302; critique of happiness, 292–97, 299; *Living a Feminist Life*, 299; *The Promise of Happiness*, 284, 292, 299

aisthanomai, 34

aisthesis, 21, 31, 33–34, 130–31, 137, 147, 172, 213, 240; *vs.* spiritual sensation, 21–22

aistheta, 130, 174–75, 232

aisthetike, 130, 147

Allerkamp and Mirbach, *Schönes Denken*, 27

Alsted, Johann Heinrich, 56; *Encyclopaedia*, 56

ambiguity, 41, 135, 197

amplification, 74–75

anacreontic circle, 177

anacreontism, 185

analogy, 35, 36, 44, 111–12, 116, 131, 177–78, 186, 229–30, 281; *analogia fidei*, 131; *analogon rationis*, 35, 36, 44, 111–12, 116, 177–78, 186, 229–30

analysis, 39–40, 150, 158–59, 166, 170, 205, 223, 225, 228–29; analyzability, 39–40; clear and distinct, 205; incomplete, 159; scientific, 229; theoretical, 278–79

anatomy, political, 274

animals, 216, 230

anthropology, 23, 65, 201, 214, 224, 231; rationalist, 201

apathy, 263

Apel, Karl Otto, 239

Apollo, 147

appearance, 21, 87–91, 95, 98–99, 101–3, 300; perfect, 95

appetite, 145

approval, 265

aptness, 76

architecture, 68, 254

ardor, 74

argument, 50, 79, 80, 153, 170; aesthetic, 50; philosophical, 170

Aristotle, 15, 57–58, 80–81, 174–75, 236, 248, 279, 295; *Categories*, 81; *On the Soul (De Anima)*, 174; *Poetics*, 174

arithmetic, 49, 73

arrangement, 73

art, 22, 30, 44–47, 49, 53, 68–69, 73, 79, 106, 172, 194, 234, 248, 266, 273, 279; aesthetics of, 238; art criticism, 68; art history, 45–47; artistic ability, 257; art of recollection, 80; art of the human body, 274; art theory, 30, 45–46, 151, 272; art-world, 48, 53; autonomy of, 48–49, 53–54; beauty of, 195; Christian, 49; classical, 266; emotional, 210; fine arts, 22, 53, 190–91, 235, 255, 257; fine arts and sciences, 236, 255, 257; historiography, 46; individual, 236; liberal arts, 22, 31, 43, 58, 61, 72, 107, 175, 190–91, 235; and nature, 81; original, 83; philosophy of, 48, 171, 192; political significance, 273; religious function, 49; as research, 67–68; science of, 235; semantic, 79; subjective, 210; sublime, 255, 266; symbolic, 44, 266; visual art, 30, 49, 66

artifice, 220

Aschenbrenner, Karl, 1

askesis, 276

association, 41, 197, 206, 208, 294; of pleasure and the good, 294; pragmatic theory of, 206

astronomy, 118–19, 157, 159

attention, 14, 223–24, 256

attitude, 36–37, 75, 117; moral, 75; poetic, 117

autarchy, 218

authority, 128, 154, 274; theological, 154

autonomy, 61

aversion, 145

awareness, 127
awe, 254–58, 263, 268; aesthetic, 270;
    ecstatic, 260
axiom, 154–55

Bacon, Francis, 20, 154, 180
badness, 292
Baeumler, Alfred, 62, 86, 152, 168–69,
    278; *The Problem of Irrationalism in
    Eighteenth-Century Aesthetics and
    Logic*, 152
Barck, Karlheinz, 33
Barth, Heinrich, 32; *Philosophy of
    Appearance*, 32
Batteux, Charles, 189, 192; *The Fine
    Arts Reduced to a Single Principle*,
    189
Baumgarten, Alexander Gottlieb,
    4–11; Baumgarten School, 231,
    238; biographies of, 150, 151, 192;
    Choreographic Dissertation, 141;
    as Christian Philosopher, 10; as
    Christian Socrates, 10; cognitivism,
    246; death, 11, 151–52; definition
    of poetry, 12, 222; *Elements of First
    Practical Philosophy*, 1, 9, 284, 288;
    English translations of, 1; *General
    Philosophy*, 9–10, 162–64, 168;
    Lectures on Aesthetics (*Kollegium
    über die Ästhetik*), 16–17; *Lectures
    on Dogmatic Theology*, 9–11;
    Lectures on Logic (*Acroasis Logica*),
    9, 79, 163–64; *Metaphysics*, 1,
    12–13, 16–17, 20, 29, 48, 85,
    95, 97–102, 145, 151, 161, 169,
    178, 183, 186–87, 201, 206, 226,
    245, 248, 278, 283, 285–86, 288,
    291; misology, 11; *Outline of
    Philosophical Encyclopedia*, 9–10,
    56, 178; as Philosopher of Feeling,
    222; *Philosophical Ethics*, 8, 29,
    178, 245; *Philosophical Letters of
    Aletheophilus*, 7–8, 14–16, 55–56,
    151, 161, 179, 181–82, 190, 250;
    Pietist background, 4–8, 65–66,

137–38, 151, 160–61; *Reflections on
    Poetry*, 1, 7–8, 11, 15–17, 21–22, 55,
    58, 61, 71, 73, 83, 128, 137, 141–44,
    149, 170, 172–73, 176, 178–79, 181,
    183, 190, 197, 201, 221–24, 238,
    278, 283–86, 288, 291; as "second
    rate" philosopher, 220; *Thoughts on
    Rational Acclaim from Academies*,
    8, 57; *Thoughts on the Speeches
    of Jesus*, 9–10; Wolffianism, 7–8,
    149–54
Baumgarten, Jacob, 127
Baumgarten, Nathanael, 176
Baumgarten, Siegmund Jakob, 6, 65,
    125, 138, 143–44, 147–48, 161, 175–
    77, 179, 189; *Instruction in Lawful
    Christian Conduct*, 143; *Instruction
    in the Exegesis of Holy Scripture*,
    138; *Theological Ethics*, 176
beasts, 194
beauty, 16–17, 19, 20, 45–50, 55, 66,
    74, 79, 85, 92, 94–97, 121, 165,
    170, 172, 181, 185–87, 193, 196,
    202, 206–9, 213, 230, 232–33, 236,
    241, 244, 248, 250, 254, 258, 262,
    265, 271, 289, 301; adherent, 268;
    Baumgarten's Definition, 90–92, 95–
    103; beautiful things, 16; beauty of
    appearance, 300; beauty of cognition,
    16; beauty of expression, 73; beauty
    of order, 16, 73, 95, 100–102, 300;
    beauty of signification, 95, 102–3,
    300; beauty of things and thoughts,
    73, 95–100, 103, 300; as confused
    cognition, 166; counterimage of
    the absolute, 47; definition of, 87,
    90–92, 103; dependent, 268; of
    expression, 16; general, 74; Meier's
    definition, 92–95, 99, 103; of
    object, 87, 96, 187, 195; of objects
    and materials, 96; as perfection
    of an object, 90; as perfection of
    appearance, 85–86; perfection of
    order, 101; as perfection of sensible
    cognition, 85–86, 166, 241; as

perfection represented without distinctness, 92; philosophical concept of, 238; psychology of, 223; rational-objective definition, 85; rational-subjective definition, 85; representation of the whole, 47; rule of, 238; sensible appearance of the idea, 47; sensible cognition of perfection, 91; supersensible, 47; of thoughts, 16; universal, 16, 95, 244; Wolffian theory, 91–92, 99, 104

Beck, Lewis White, 151; *Early German Philosophy*, 151

behavior, 133

being, 109, 162, 216, 224, 237, 239; certainty of, 239; experience of, 237; highest, 114–15; necessary, 115; sensation of, 237

Beiser, Frederick, 86, 151, 169, 211; *Diotima's Children*, 151, 169, 211; *Fate of Reason*, 169

Bergmann, Ernst, 185

bias, 73

Bible, 131, 138, 147

Bildung, 53, 220

Bilfinger, Georg, Bernahrd, 15–16, 28, 175; *Philosophical Elucidations on God, the Human Soul, the World, and Things in General*, 15, 28, 175

biology, 65

Bloch, Ernst, 54

Bodmer, Johann Jacob, 15, 28, 173, 181, 183

body, 46, 93, 110, 210, 217, 230, 239, 250, 274, 276, 290, 296; art of the, 274; bodily *a priori*, 239

Bonaventure, 248

Bouhours, Dominique, 15–16, 181

Brämer, Carl Friedrich, 180

Breitinger, Johann Jacob, 15, 28, 173, 180–81, 183; *Breslau Guide*, 173; *Defense of the Swiss Muse*, 180

brevity, 74–75

brilliance, 290

Bubner, Rüdiger, 44

Buchenau, Stefanie, 20, 194, 271–72

Burke, Edmund, 200, 254, 259, 266, 271; *A Philosophical Enquiry into the Origin of Our Ideas of the Sublime and Beautiful*, 254

cadence, 140

Calov, Abraham, 79

Campe, Rüdiger, 63; *Baumgarten-Studien*, 63–65

capacity, 210, 255, 264, 272, 285

capacity, shared, 264

care, 263

Carpov, Jakob, 6–7; *Critical-Philosophical Meditation on the Perfection of Language*, 7

Carpzov, Johann Benedikt, 190

Cassirer, Ernst, 66–67, 152, 278, 280–81; *The Philosophy of the Enlightenment*, 152

categories, 265

catullus, 245

causation, 217, 228

certainty, 16–19, 68, 73–74, 155–57, 167, 200, 239, 243–44, 284, 287–88, 290, 298, 300; aesthetic, 300; logical, 300

chance, 294

character, 136, 143, 198, 283, 287

characteristic, 59–60, 88, 219, 243, 246, 277; characterization of the individual, 246; distinguishing characteristics, 129, 243, 246; heuristic, 59; internal characteristics, 246; philosophical, 219

chastity, 136

Chladenius, Johann Martin, 61; *Introduction to the Correct Interpretation of Rational Writings*, 61

Christgau, Martin, 4, 221

Chrysippus, 146

Cicero, 15, 71, 74, 80, 120–22, 245, 299; *On the Orator*, 72; *Tusculan Disputations*, 120

clarity, 13, 17–19, 40, 42, 68, 71, 73–
    75, 78–79, 142, 146, 169, 174, 194,
    196, 207, 210, 231, 243–44, 284,
    287, 288, 298, 300; aesthetic, 210;
    conceptual, 39, 88; extensive, 13, 17,
    42, 71, 73, 75, 196, 210, 284, 287,
    288; intensive, 13, 40, 42, 194, 196;
    superlative, 41
cliffs, 261
climate, 218
cognition, 94, 146, 162, 213, 222,
    251, 287; abstract, 80; aesthetic,
    32–33, 166, 292; aestheticological,
    166, 170; artistic, 30, 35, 48, 50;
    beautiful, 86, 95, 166, 197, 276;
    beauty of, 103, 289; brilliance, 290;
    clear, 166; clear and confused, 35,
    39, 221, 243; clear and distinct, 13,
    233, 243; cognitive process, 224,
    227; cognitivism, 246; conceptual,
    43; confused, 165–66; definition,
    93; dignity of, 247, 249; distinct,
    166, 193; distinct and adequate, 112;
    effective, 206; great, 249; historical,
    223; human, 112; indifferent, 80;
    intellectual, 37, 48, 117, 120, 149,
    153, 201, 243; intuitive, 68, 80, 203,
    206, 208; learned, 43; life of, 17;
    liveliness, 290; logical, 33, 80, 166,
    296; magnitude, 290; majesty, 243,
    247, 268, 271; mathematical, 223;
    mathematical ideal, 106; multitude
    of, 290; object of sensible, 103;
    object of sensible, 91, 103; obscure,
    166; obscure and confused, 13;
    perfection, 86, 92–93, 98, 100, 284,
    287; philosophical, 80; pleasurable,
    80; poetic, 42; pragmatic, 206;
    sensible, 17, 19, 30, 35, 37, 39, 44,
    48, 62, 65–68, 86–93, 149, 153,
    165–66, 170, 193, 196–98, 201, 209,
    243, 268, 271, 290; sublime, 244;
    symbolic, 80; theory of, 107–8, 221;
    as totality of representations, 93;
    true, 166, 290; vivid, 44

coherence, 179
cohesiveness, 197
colic, 160
color, 78
comedy, 145, 252
commandment, 262
communication, 58, 78, 134, 137, 142,
    178
community, 136
compassion, 263
completeness, 299–300
complexity, 196, 198
comprehensibility, 138
comprehension, 223
concept, 63, 92, 94, 155, 157–58, 160,
    164, 207, 230, 232–33, 237, 268;
    adequate, 158, 160; clear, 158, 230;
    clear and distinct, 232–33; complete,
    155, 157–58; confused, 158;
    definition, 158; distinct, 155, 158;
    middle, 207; obscure, 158; origin,
    158; philosophical, 238; scope of,
    63; universal, 92
concreteness, 114, 123
conduct, 136, 140
confusion, 142
congruity, 76, 109
connectedness, 256, 266
connoisseur, 208
conscience, 205–8
consciousness, 100, 229, 299; feminist,
    299
consistency, 121
contemplation, 208
content, 75, 76, 129; of a poem, 129
contingency, 294
contradiction, 233
convention, 264
conversion, 127, 143, 144
conviction, 78, 280, 290
cooking, 49
copiousness, 146, 244, 287
coriolan, 77
correction, 52, 74, 81
correspondence, 179

counting, 200
courage, 121
covetousness, 160
crantor, 146
creativity, 79, 82
creatures, 194
criminals, 274
Critical Attempt at a Survey of the German Language, 180
criticism, 162, 236, 259; art critics, 259
Crousaz, Jean-Pierre de, 15–16, 181
cultural studies, 67
culture, 46, 211, 265
custom, 72, 145

danger, 263
darkness, 40
death, 11, 263
decency, 136
deduction, 156, 224
definition, 154–56, 160, 164, 169, 220; accurate, 156; arbitrary, 220; nominal, 154; real, 154; of things, 154; of words, 154
deliberation, 263
delight, 290
demonstration, 78, 144, 156–59, 169, 220; mathematical, 155, 158; philosophical, 156, 158
Dennis, John, 241, 248, 259
Descartes, René, 16, 39, 106, 119, 154, 238–39, 279, 280; *Meditations on First Philosophy*, 119
description, 227–28, 262; phenomenological, 262
designation, 290
desire, 76, 131, 136, 143, 145, 147, 252, 292, 295; carnal, 136; fleshly, 147; instinctive, 145; natural, 143; to seek God's glory, 131; sensual, 143; spiritual, 143
detail, 274
determinacy, 152, 196
development, 215, 217
devotion, 176

dew, 160
dialectic, 266
dialogue, 55
difference, 25, 158, 165–67, 202, 281, 300; of degree, 165–67, 202; essential, 158, 165–66; in kind, 165–67, 202; qualitative, 166; quantitative, 166; radical, 300; real, 158
dignity, 75–76, 116–17, 121, 181, 241, 244, 246–47, 249, 251–52; aesthetic, 241, 244, 246, 249, 252; negative, 251–52; positive, 251–52
disagreement, 300
disciplines, 33–35, 46, 57–59, 64–65, 67, 72, 74, 81, 83, 150, 153, 162, 171–72, 190, 202, 213, 274–75, 279, 281–82; non-scientific, 162; philosophical, 33–35, 65, 150, 153, 171, 202, 213, 275, 282; superior to philosophy, 162
discourse, 12, 128, 131, 134, 142, 164, 174, 179, 181, 219, 222, 232, 234, 237, 252, 278, 295; beauty of, 181; limits, 234; lively, 179; master discourse, 237; modern, 278; philosophical, 219; poetic, 142, 222; sensible, 12, 128, 164, 174, 179, 183; social, 295; of subjectivity, 278; sublime, 252; verbal, 131
discovery, 185
disgust, 257
disinterestedness, 265, 269, 298
disorder, 140
disposition, 52, 82, 117, 139, 198–99, 234–35, 239, 264, 276; aesthetic, 276; inner, 198; natural, 198, 276; poetic, 117
dissonance, 284, 299–302
distinctness, 76, 88, 92, 142, 195; conceptual, 88, 92; philosophical, 76
divination, 77
dizziness, 257
dogma, 155
domination, 279

dualism, 279; of sensibility and understanding, 279
Durrius, Conrad, 146; *On the Hidden Poetic Philosophy*, 146
dynamics, 79

Eberhard, Johann August, 150, 203; *General Theory of Thought and Sensation*, 203
edification, 66, 131, 137, 140, 142; moral, 136, 140
education, 53, 134, 142, 144–48, 211; of humanity, 53; moral, 134, 142, 144–48; popular, 53
effect, 144–45, 196, 209, 228; inner, 144; practical, 145
effectiveness, 209
efficacy, 196
Einem, Johann Justus von, 135
elaboration, 75
elocution, 73, 173, 239
eloquence, 60, 139–40
embellishment, 258, 262
embodiment, 270
embryos, 216–17
emotion, 135, 138, 181, 193, 207, 268; ardent, 135; holy, 135; pious, 135; sensible, 138, 207
empiricism, 154, 200; early modern, 154
enjoyment, 218, 296
Enlightenment, 9, 11, 20, 24, 27, 68, 78, 126, 153, 169, 173, 194, 211, 215, 274; German Enlightenment, 9, 11, 20, 27, 173, 194
enormity, 255
entellus, 251
enthusiasm, 52, 83, 270, 298; aesthetic, 298
epistemology, 3
epistolography, 180
épopée, 183
Erasmus, 63; *On the Abundance of Words and Ideas*, 63
error, 140

erudition, 81, 83
esteem, 263
eternity, 255
ethics, 27, 61, 75, 145, 177, 205, 252, 292; applied/practical, 205
ethos, 75
etymology, 59
Euclid, 155; *Elements*, 155
evaluation, 206
event, 259
evidence, 51, 78–79; formal, 78; intuitive, 79; practical, 79; symbolic, 78
evil, 127, 140, 148
evolution, 226
exaltation, 270
examination, 277
examples, 108, 160, 164, 170
exegesis, 130, 147
exercise, 52, 64, 74, 81–82, 193, 198–99, 203, 276–82, 298; aesthetic, 193, 269, 279–82, 298
exodus, 262
expectation, 295
experience, 66, 118, 120–23, 131, 135, 149, 156–60, 195, 224, 228, 242, 255–57, 261, 267, 279, 302; aesthetic, 32, 118, 210, 242, 254, 269, 298; cognitive, 123; doctrine of, 127; of freedom, 261; horizon, 123; human, 118, 122–23; lived, 195; mixed, 242, 257; moral, 121–22; of myself, 228; particular, 157; pleasing, 242; plural, 123; poetic, 118, 120; sensuous, 302; subjective, 118; of the sublime, 168, 262, 270, 272; of thought, 228
experiment, 179
explanation, 61, 225
exposition, 122, 130, 239
expression, 48, 50, 73, 82–83, 108, 141, 189, 199, 258; aesthetic, 108; of freedom, 266; naïve, 258; natural, 83; unaffected, 258; verbal, 141
extension, 246, 255, 260

fable, 146

fact, 118, 122–34

faculties, 278, 281; acuteness, 35–38, 52; analysis, 79; anticipation, 15, 177; appetitive, 291; astuteness, 15; of beauty, 80; characteristic/characterization, 35, 37, 82, 102–3, 137, 177, 196; cognitive, 16, 79, 80, 82, 91, 106, 110, 111, 129, 144, 165, 227, 256, 285, 297; creative, 79; denotative, 37, 38; designation, 15; desire, 209; discursive, 79; division of, 194; expectation, 36, 37; foresight, 15, 82, 177; higher/superior, 82, 91, 106, 110–11, 126, 129, 144, 165, 193, 202, 207–8, 227; human, 126, 193, 194; imagination, 36, 38, 52–53, 177, 196, 199; intellectual, 103; intuition, 265; invention, 15, 82, 177; judgment, 15, 35, 52, 82, 90–91, 196; limited, 256; lower/inferior, 16, 91, 103, 106–7, 110–11, 129, 144, 165, 177, 187, 193, 196, 200, 202, 205, 285, 297, 299–301; memory, 35, 37, 82, 177, 196; mental, 111; moral sense, 208; natural, 82; perceptual, 256; perspicuity/perspicaciousness, 37, 177, 196; philosophical, 79; poetic, 35, 52, 79; power of judgment, 35, 52; rational, 79; reason, 79, 82; recognition, 82; sense for truth, 208; sense, 177; sensibility, 15–16, 79, 158, 193, 198–99; sensible, 91, 103, 187, 196; of the soul, 206, 233; taste, 15, 82, 177, 196, 208; tripartite division of, 194; of truth, 80; understanding, 15–16, 82, 156, 158–60, 164–65, 193, 195, 264, 280; wit, 15, 35–38, 52, 196, 198

faith, 46, 152, 154, 162–63, 168

fanatic, 189

fantasy, 299, 301

fear, 136, 243

fearlessness, 263

fecundity, 246

Federlin, Wilhelm Ludwig, 126–28, 130, 148; *Popular Religious Education and Civil Society*, 126–28

feeling, 126, 158, 164, 198–99, 204, 207–8, 216, 223, 226, 237, 243, 250, 260, 269, 271–73, 290, 293, 296; good, 293, 296; inner, 126, 216; moral, 264, 269, 272; religious, 271

felix aestheticus, 24–25, 52, 81, 196, 198, 209, 211, 253, 276, 283

feminism, 299; feminist killjoy, 25, 283, 298–302

fiction, 113, 116, 121, 123, 173, 221; aesthetic, 121; poetic, 113, 116, 123; truthful, 113

figures, 139

firmness, 285

Fisher, Kuno, 150–51; *History of Modern Philosophy*, 150–51

Flögel, Karl Friedrich, 58

focus, 78

force, 31, 43, 54, 64, 83, 145–46, 177, 204–5, 208, 210, 216–17, 222, 228, 246, 278, 281; effective, 210; emotive, 208; magnitude, 278; of the soul, 222; unconscious forces, 204; vital, 210

form, 75–76, 195, 213, 232, 266; beautiful, 195; external, 266; systematic, 213

formlessness, 281

Förster, Johann Christian, 178; *The Characters of Three Famous Philosophers of Modern Times*, 10

Foucault, Michel, 24, 275–82; *Discipline and Punish*, 24, 63–64, 274–83; *The Order of Things*, 63, 277

Francke, August Hermann, 4, 21, 65, 125, 127, 131, 137, 140, 142–44, 147–48, 160–61; *Guide to Reading Hold Scripture*, 130, 137–38; *Introduction to the Reading of Holy*

Scripture, 137; *Outline of a Doctrine Concerning Affects*, 130, 143
Franke, Ursula, 20, 30, 86, 153; *Art as Cognition*, 20, 30
Frankfurt an der Oder, 8–11, 15, 22, 28, 61, 87, 145, 150, 162, 178–80; University of (*Viadrina*), 8, 28, 61, 150, 162, 178
Franzius, Wolfgang, 133
Frederick Wilhelm I, 6
freedom, 46, 208, 242, 248, 251, 261–62, 264–66, 269–72, 298; experience of, 261; expression of, 266; human, 261; idea of, 264; inner, 248; practical, 264; psychological, 248
Freudian Slip, 204
Friedrich III, 5
Fromme, Valentin, 79
fruitfulness, 245
Fugate, Courtney, 1
fullness, 75
fundus animae, 23, 41, 66, 109, 188, 197, 204, 214–15, 222, 229, 282

Gaier, Ulrich, 225, 239
genesis, 259
genius, 83, 255–59, 279–80
gentleness, 263
german idealism, 30
german studies, 172
Gilbert, Katharine Everett, 2; Gilbert and Kuhn, *A History of Esthetics*, 2
Gleim, Johann Wilhelm Ludwig, 177
glory, 131–32
gnoseology, 13, 39–40, 79, 107, 178, 188, 193, 217, 221, 238
gnoseology, inferior, 40, 79, 107, 188, 193
god, 39, 49, 109, 115, 136, 141, 143, 187, 194, 248, 259, 262, 265, 268
goodness, 25, 140, 193, 202, 206–7, 210, 268, 286, 291–95, 301
Gottsched, Johann Christoph, 22, 28, 63, 91, 178, 182–85, 188, 190; *Critical Poetics*, 188

government, 72
grace, 132, 245
grammar, 49, 59, 162, 177, 190
gravity, 116, 245, 247
greatness, 15, 17–19, 182, 242–44, 251, 256, 266, 284, 287–88, 298, 300; aesthetic, 244, 251; moral, 266; moral-aesthetic, 251
greed, 143
Gregor, Mary, 86
Gross, Steffen, 126
Grote, Simon, 21–22
Grotius, 279
ground, determining, 89, 97
Guyer, Paul, 151, 246, 260; *A History of Modern Aesthetics*, 151

habit, 37, 52, 81–83, 131–32, 143, 159–60, 196, 199, 208, 227, 232, 276, 295–97; aesthetic, 82, 269, 298; of logical thinking, 159; spiritual, 132
Halle (Saale), 5–8, 15, 22, 28, 61, 65, 87, 125–28, 130, 133, 135, 137–38, 147–48, 150–51, 154, 160–61, 172, 176–80, 182, 188; University of (*Fridericiana*), 5, 61, 125, 127, 137, 148, 150, 154, 172, 177
Hamberger, Georg Erhard, 6
Hamburg Reports, 176
happiness, 25, 121–22, 201, 214, 283–302; affective dimension, 289; Ahmed's critique of, 292–97; cognitive conception of, 289; external, 288–89; and goodness, 297; indeterminacy of, 293; internal, 288–89
harmony, 19, 76–77, 89, 94, 97–98, 193, 217, 247, 258, 299–300, 302; of the manifold, 94, 98; of the poem, 77
Haverkamp, Anselm, 63; *Baumgarten-Studien*, 63–65
Haym, Rudolf, 214
Hegel, Georg Wilhelm Friedrich, 3, 45–46, 48, 53, 55, 150, 171, 266; *Aesthetics*, 44–45; *The Difference*

Between Fichte's and Schelling's Systems of Philosophy, 46

Heilmann, Johann David, 219

Heineccius, Johann Gottlieb, 126; *Elements of Rational Philosophy*, 126

Henckmann, Wolfhard, 34, 45

Herder, Johann Gottfried, 23, 28, 213–40; and "Baumgarten School", 231; critique of aesthetics, 239; critique of Baumgarten's *Aesthetics*, 224–26, 238–39; critique of Baumgarten's *Reflections on Poetry*, 221–24; critique of metaphysics, 237; critique of philosophy and science, 239; critique of school philosophy, 225; *Essay on Being*, 216, 224–25; *Fourth Critical Grove*, 214, 216, 230, 239; *Ideas for a Philosophy of the History of Humankind*, 215; *Journal of My Voyage*, 239; *Letters on the Most Recent Literature*, 238; *On Baumgarten's Way of Thinking*, 219; *On Thomas Abbt's Writings*, 219; *radicalization of the concept of aesthetics*, 225; *Truths from Leibniz*, 217

hermeneutics, 58, 60, 130–31, 147, 162, 180, 185; biblical, 147; hermeneutic circle, 60

heroes, 274

heroism, 252

herrnhuters, 189

heuristic, 17, 59, 73, 185, 187, 244; aesthetic, 187

historicity, 218

history, 63, 145, 162, 168, 172, 214, 216–17; historical determination, 237; history of philosophy, 2–3, 150, 171–72, 216; intellectual history, 172; literary history, 31, 63; philosophy of history, 214, 217–18, 233–34

Hobbes, Thomas, 273; *Leviathan*, 273

holism, 240

Holther, William B., 1

homer, 146–47

homiletics, 145, 185

honesty, 252

honor, 136

horace, 117–18, 146, 245, 250

horizon, 11–12, 82, 118–19, 123; aesthetic, 82, 112, 118–19; experiential, 118–19, 123; logical, 112

Hruby, Amelia, 25

humanities, 67–68, 180

humanity, 203, 214, 216, 226, 238; concept of, 214, 216, 234; history of, 226; whole human being, 23, 65, 194, 207, 238, 279

Humboldt, Wilhelm von, 53

Hume, David, 200

humility, 131

hybris, 189

hymers, john, 1

hypocrisy, 11, 277

hypotheses, 157

idea, 43, 108, 119, 128–30, 142–43, 146, 157, 195–97, 207, 214, 243, 257, 264, 266; abstract, 108, 195–96; aesthetic, 43; clear, 146, 243; clear and confused, 129; clear and distinct, 196–97; confused, 129, 243; dark, 143; distinct, 129, 243; of freedom, 264; indistinct, 142–43; intellectual, 108, 195–96; obscure, 66; obscure and confused, 196; poetic, 207; sensible, 128–30; vivid, 146

identity, 109, 281

ideology, 279, 282

ignorance, 276

illusion, 290

image, 122, 129, 262, 280, 290

imagination, 38, 76–77, 81, 121, 129, 164, 189, 198, 229, 257, 264, 267–68, 280

imitation, 74, 81–82, 128, 144, 222, 255, 262

immensity, 254–59, 267; extensive, 255, 257; intensive, 255–56, 259; sensuous, 254

immortality, 202

imperfection, 256

imperialism, 234

impetus, 74, 81, 83, 216

importance, 218, 245, 247, 253

impression, 199, 204, 208, 267

improvement, 135, 227, 298; aesthetic, 298; moral, 135

improvisation, 82

impulse, 209

inclination, 73, 203, 206, 252

incompleteness, 233

independence, 200

individual, 217, 223, 277

individuality, 123, 152, 196, 218

induction, 224

infant, 217

infinity, 266

influence, 216

ingenium, 35–36, 74, 81–83

inspiration, 134–35, 138–39, 141, 147–48, 208, 227, 251; divine, 134, 138–39, 141, 147–48, 251

intellect, 46, 117, 119, 144, 174, 252; intellectualism, 152–53

intention, 97, 132, 258–59; of the artist, 258; of the author, 259

interest, 30–31, 46, 265, 270; cognitive, 30–31, 46; intellectual, 270; practical-moral, 265

interpretation, 58, 60, 131–32, 148; biblical, 132, 148; learned, 60; rational, 60

intersubjectivity, 265

intuition, 208, 213, 265, 290–91; of freedom, 265; of imperfection, 291; of perfection, 290; sensible, 208, 265

invention, 38, 50, 73, 79–80, 239; aesthetic, 79; art of, 20, 80; logical, 79; method of, 79–80; philosophy, 79; poetry, 79

Irmscher, Hans Dietrich, 237

irrationalism, 149, 168–69, 193

Isaiah, 177

Jacobi, Friedrich Heinrich, 211

jesting, 183

Jesus, 136, 145, 190; as "practical aesthetician", 190

joy, 284, 298–99

judgment, 36–38, 67, 82–83, 91, 153, 186–87, 198, 205, 207–8, 232, 252, 264–65, 268–69; aesthetic, 36, 67, 153, 198, 252, 264–65, 268–69; clear, 207; distinct, 207; faculty of, 90; lower form of, 82; obscure, 207; of the poet, 83; power of, 35, 52; pure, 269; rational, 207–8, 211; sensible, 91, 186; subjectively universal, 268; of the sublime, 264; true, 265

juggling, 49

Kant, Immanuel, 3, 23, 27, 30, 45, 47–48, 53, 67, 91, 93, 123, 150, 171, 192, 202, 228, 241–43, 251, 260–71, 292–93; *Answer to the Question: What is Enlightenment?*, 211; *Anthropology from a Pragmatic Point of View*, 261; *The Conflict of the Faculties*, 270; *Critique of Pure Reason*, 23, 47, 150, 153, 169–70; *Critique of the Power of Judgment*, 23–24, 91, 260–70; *Observations on the Feeling of the Beautiful and Sublime*, 261–62, 270; transcendental aesthetic, 150; transcendental method, 271; transcendental theory, 123

Kliche, Dieter, 33, 52

Klopstock, Friedrich Gottlieb, 184–85, 187, 189, 258; *Messiah*, 184, 187

Klotz, Christian Adolph, 238

knowledge, 83, 105, 115, 121, 142, 156, 160, 167, 172, 195, 205–6, 213, 221, 227, 231, 233, 246, 297; aesthetic, 105; clear and distinct, 105;

common, 227; confused, 83; degree
of, 246; empirical, 156; God's, 115;
historical, 216; human, 115, 201,
233; of humankind, 231; lively, 160;
middle, 115, 121; philosophical, 167;
pragmatic, 206; scholar's, 233; self-
knowledge, 213; sensible, 172, 195;
speculative, 206; theory of, 221
Köhler, Heinrich, 6
König, Johann Ullrich, 181
Kuhn, Helmut, 2; Gilbert and Kuhn, *A
History of Esthetics*, 2

Lange, Joachim, 6, 161
Lange, Samuel Gotthold, 176, 182, 188
language, 131, 135, 139, 220, 226, 230–
31; dead, 220; meta-language, 230–
31; natural, 139; object language,
231; simple, 139
Lasius, Hermann Jacob, 180
latency, 217
law, 27, 72, 137, 152, 160, 180, 251,
265, 270, 273, 288; book of the,
262; divine, 137, 288; human, 288;
moral, 251, 265, 270; natural, 160;
universal, 152
learnedness, 52
learning, 203
Le Clerc, Jean, 139–41; *Five Letters
Concerning the Inspiration of the
Holy Scriptures*, 139; *Impressions
of Some Theologians From Holland
Concerning the Critical History of
the New Testament*, 139
Leibniz, Gottfried Wilhelm, 16, 20,
31, 36, 39–40, 64, 90, 106, 115–16,
129, 150, 154, 195–96, 199, 202,
217, 221, 228, 233–34, 238, 254,
267, 279–80; Leibnizian-Wolffian
philosophy, 13, 22, 28, 150, 202;
*Meditations on Knowledge, Truth,
and Ideas*, 195–96; metaphysics, 47
Lessing, Gotthold Ephraim, 169, 199,
238
lexicography, 162

liberal arts, 22, 31, 43, 58, 61, 72, 107,
175, 190–91, 235; philosophy of,
190; theory of, 190
life, 16–19, 55, 66, 68–69, 73–74, 78,
181–82, 196–97, 213–14, 244, 252,
284, 287, 288, 300; godly, 136;
heroic way of life, 252; honest way
of life, 252
light, 16, 18, 40, 78, 181, 185, 243
Linn, Marie Luise, 73
literature, 222, 234, 261; literary history,
31, 63; literary studies, 175
liveliness, 13, 15, 43, 179, 182, 196,
288, 290, 298
location, 81
Locke, John, 4, 154, 249, 294–95; *Some
Thoughts on Education*, 4
Lodtmann, Carl Gerhard Wilhelm, 189
logic, 12–14, 25, 27, 31, 35, 40, 56,
68, 129, 144, 149, 152, 156, 158,
164–65, 167, 172–74, 177, 181,
184, 188, 194–96, 202, 226–30,
232–33, 264–65, 284–85, 297, 299,
301; artificial, 227; Baumgarten's
definition, 164–65; discipline, 227;
dominance of, 301; first logic,
229; formal, 152; happy logician,
297; illegitimate form of, 232;
innate, 230; of the intellect, 184; of
investigation, 228; logical criterion,
39; logical empiric, 14; logical view
of the world, 301; logic of affect,
230; logic of logic, 227; organon/
organic philosophy, 14, 230; of
phantasy, 181; of the power of
imagination, 230; scholastic, 152; as
science, 230, 233, 285; as science
of the understanding and reason,
181; scope, 149, 153, 165, 167; of
sensibility, 181; traditional, 230;
true logic, 156; Wolff's definition,
164–65
Longinus, 133, 241, 245; *On the
Sublime*, 241, 245
loquacity, 76, 133, 241, 245

352   *Index*

love, 131, 136, 250, 299; of God, 131; of honor, 136; of money, 136
Lucretius, 251
Ludovici, Carl Günther, 7, 149–50; *Newest Curiosities of the Leibnizian-Wolffian Philosophy*, 7
Lull, Raymond, 81
Luther, Martin, 133, 135
Lutheran Confessions (Konkordienbuch), 4–5

magnanimity, 75–76, 82, 250; sublime, 250
magnitude, 68, 73–76, 117, 181, 185, 243–49, 255–56, 290; absolute, 246, 250; aesthetic, 116, 120, 241, 244, 246, 249, 250, 260, 269; of cognition, 290; moral, 75, 251, 260, 269; natural, 75, 250, 260, 269; objective, 249; relative, 76, 246, 250, 253; unlimited, 255
majesty, 136, 241, 244, 247; aesthetic, 241, 244
manifold, harmonious, 98
marble, 195
marriage of reason and experience, 22, 149, 153–54, 159–61, 168
marriage of science and art, 61
mathematics, 5, 118–19, 155, 162–64, 167–68, 195, 221, 279, 280; as epistemic ideal, 155, 163, 167; as science of quantities, 162; synthetic method, 164
matter, 46, 232
McAndrew, Matthew, 20–21
McQuillan, J. Colin, 22, 201
meaning, 60, 66, 102, 116, 131–35, 147, 197, 228; literal, 131; meaningfulness, 116, 228; spiritual, 132–33, 147
measure, 217
medicine, 65, 180
mediocrity, 178
meditation, 112, 281; aesthetic, 112; cartesian, 281; philosophical, 281

Meier, Georg Friedrich, 7, 10, 22, 35, 42, 51, 60, 87, 91, 103–4, 150–51, 161, 172, 177, 182–84, 188, 190, 192, 231, 288–92; *Attempt at a General Art of Interpretation*, 60; *Baumgarten's Life*, 7, 10, 192; *Considerations on the First Principle of all Fine Arts and Sciences*, 289–90; Defense of Baumgarten's Reflections on Poetry, 183–84; *Doctrine of Reason*, 93, 97; *Foundations of All Beautiful Sciences*, 7, 9, 15–16, 18, 60–61, 91, 99–100, 104, 184–88, 201, 290–92; *On the Difference Between What is Called Natural and Moral in Theology*, 177; *Portrait of a Critic*, 183–84
Meier, Jean-Paul, 194
Meisner, Johann Christian, 141
melody, 258
memory, 14, 130, 245, 285–86
Mendelssohn, Moses, 11, 22–23, 53, 91, 169, 193, 200–211, 238, 241–41, 249, 253–60, 263, 267–69, 271; *Main Principles of the Fine Arts and Sciences*, 203; *On Evidence*, 193, 205–6; *On Mastery Over the Inclinations*, 203, 205; *On Sentiments*, 193; *On the Question: What Does 'To Enlighten' Mean?*, 211; *On the Sublime*, 254; *On the Sublime in the Naïve and Fine Sciences*, 253–54; *Philosophical Writings*, 203, 253; *Relation between the Beautiful and the Good*, 203; *Rhapsody*, 193, 203–6, 254
Menke, Christoph, 24, 34, 54, 63; *Baumgarten-Studien*, 63–65
metaphor, 215–16, 232, 244; biological, 216; organic, 215
metaphysics, 3, 27, 177, 195, 202–3, 214, 224–26, 233; rationalist, 202; speculative, 202–3
meter, 12, 173, 179

method/methodology, 17, 73, 154–56, 162–64, 220, 271; analytic, 163–64, 230; common, 163–64; gnoseological, 81; mathematical, 5, 149, 153–56, 160–61, 163, 167–68; philosophical, 155–56, 162; proper, 163; synthetic, 163–64; transcendental, 271; vulgar, 163–64

metonymy, 177

Michaelis, Christian Benedict, 137–38, 141, 148

Mightiness, 255

mind, 82, 132; aesthetic, 82

miracle, 142

Mirbach, Dagmar, 1, 29, 86, 241–42

modification, 228

monad, 22, 197, 221

money, 136

monism, 154

morality, 72, 106, 121, 133, 209, 226, 251, 265, 269, 277; combining aesthetics and morality, 271; moral theory, 121; moral transformation, 133

Moritz, Karl Philipp, 205, 223; *Magazine for Experiential Psychology*, 205, 223

Moses, 137, 141

motion, 157

motivation, 143, 145

mountains, 261

movingness, 15, 182

multiplicity, 257, 287

multitude, 41, 246, 287

muses, 135, 147

museum, 55

music, 30, 44, 49, 58, 190, 192, 200, 223, 243, 254–55

Nannini, Alessandro, 22

narrowness, 236, 246

nationalism, 152

nativism, 154

nature, 61, 113, 159–60, 177, 198, 213, 216, 222, 231, 251, 260–61, 264, 279; human, 213, 261, 264; imitation of, 231; law of, 160; marvels of, 248, 251; natural law, 61; natural right, 177; natural theology, 61; power of, 251, 260; wonders of, 251, 261

necessity, 46, 205

Newton, Isaac, 155; *Principia Mathematica*, 155

Nicolai, Christoph Friedrich, 238

Nicolai, Gottlob Samuel, 189, 190

nobility, 15–16, 182, 187, 244, 247, 252; aesthetic, 244

noeta, 232

nominalism, 238

normality, 274

nuance, 198

number, 217, 249

Nuzzo, Angelica, 21

object, 46, 87, 93, 96, 109, 158, 187, 195, 221, 229, 243, 247–48, 251, 255, 258, 268, 277, 290, 294–95; beautiful, 187, 195, 294; beauty of, 87; external, 93, 158; great, 251, 290; important, 290; instrumental, 295; intentional, 96; natural, 255; noble, 290; *obiectum*, 96; object, magnitude, 247; objectification, 221; objectivation, 277; objectivity, 46, 109; perfection of, 268; scientific, 229; sublime, 248, 258; sublime as quality of, 243; unanalyzable, 229

obligation, 286, 288, 292

obscurity, 41, 215, 217

observation, 157, 159, 179

odysseus, 116

ontogenesis, 226

ontology, 237–39

optics, 159

oratory, 72, 162, 192

order, 76, 81, 100–102, 113, 156, 169, 196, 217; beautiful, 290; beauty of, 100–102

organization, 276

organon, 58

organs, 217
ornamentation, 179
orphanage, 5, 28, 65, 125–28, 137–38, 161
orpheus, 279
orthography, 59
Other of Reason, 228

Paetzold, Heinz, 73
pain, 129, 291, 299
painting, 44, 49, 68, 78, 190, 192, 235, 254
parallelism, 131, 178
participation, 270
Pascal, Blaise, 279, 280
Paschius, 146
passion/passions, 140, 183, 203, 206–7, 277
pathology, 183, 185
Paul, 131; *Letter to the Philippians*, 131
peace, 263
perception, 34, 36, 42–43, 107–8, 117, 119, 144, 158, 197–98, 208, 223–24, 232, 235, 281; clear, 281; clear and distinct, 235; confused, 208; distinct, 144; human, 232; inner, 36; obscure, 281; *perceptio praegnans*, 42–43, 197–98; sense, 107–8, 117, 119, 223–24
Peres, Constanze, 29
perfection, 19–21, 48, 54, 68, 79, 87–90, 93, 97, 100, 149, 153, 165, 170, 179, 185–86, 193–95, 201–2, 209–10, 216, 218, 222, 244, 254–57, 259, 267–68, 271, 276, 288–91, 300, 302; aesthetic, 19, 153, 290, 294; as agreement, 97; of appearance, 20; in the artist, 257; of cognition, 97, 100; degree of, 255, 288–91; determining ground of, 97; extensive, 194; as harmony, 93; higher, 195; highest aim of humanity, 201; intellectual, 209; of intellectual cognition, 149; Kant's rejection of perfectionism, 268; of knowledge, 185; Leibniz's

definition, 90; logical, 153; magnitude of, 256; in the object, 257; of the object, 268; objective, 20, 268; perfectionism, 268; phenomenal, 186; preeminent, 288; in presentation, 257; rational, 195; scholastic notion of, 267; sensible, 170, 222, 244; of sensible cognition, 68, 149, 165, 268; separate, 165; of speech, 79; stylistic, 179; subjective, 20–21; of the whole human being, 194; Wolff's definition, 90; of the world, 54
person, 249, 257
personality, 196
perspicuity, 78, 81
persuasion, 15, 18, 51, 74, 78, 181–82, 285, 288, 300; aesthetic, 18; persuasiveness, 15, 182
phantasy, 38, 181, 198
phenomenon/phenomena, 88, 152, 214, 216–17, 224, 269; individual, 224; moral, 269; sensible, 152, 217; of the world, 216–17
philology, 58–59, 178
philosophy, 2–3, 10, 14, 19, 31, 48, 55–61, 67, 71–72, 130, 144, 147–48, 150, 153–59, 162–63, 168, 171–72, 175, 178, 192, 201–2, 213–28, 231, 233–34, 237–38, 240, 248, 254, 259, 266–67, 278–80, 286, 288–89, 293, 295, 302; as academic discipline, 10; aesthetic, 130, 147–48; affect in, 289; anthropological, 202; as art of thought, 71–72; Baumgarten's definition, 162–63, 168; "beauty philosophers", 220, 231; Christian, 248, 259; concept of, 225; contemporary, 19; "de-metaphysicizing", 226; eighteenth century, 19; experimental, 159; foundational, 237; genuine, 150; german, 19, 254; hierarchy of philosophical sciences, 302; history of philosophy, 2–3, 150, 171–72,

216, 293, 295; human, 162, 222; "hybridization", 227; idealistic, 278; instrumental, 31, 55–61, 67; medieval, 267; method of, 162; moral, 286; objective, 224; object of, 237; organic philosophy, 14, 57–58, 178, 227; parts of, 155; as a path to knowledge, 219; philosophical encyclopedia, 57; philosophy of art, 48, 171, 192, 238; philosophy of culture, 31; philosophy of history, 214, 217–18, 233–34; philosophy of language, 3; "philosophy of laziness", 228; philosophy of poetry, 175; philosophy of science, 3; philosophy of the liberal arts, 175; poetic, 279; popular, 201; practical, 288; pre-socratic philosophers, 72; rational, 153–59; rationalist, 279–80; school philosophy/scholastic philosophy, 215, 220, 223, 237–38, 240, 254, 259, 266–67; as science, 10; as science of everything that is or occurs, 168; as science of qualities, 162, 168; science of wise thinking, 72; subjective, 224; as system, 10; theoretical, 288; true, 219; Wolffian, 221; Wolff's definition, 163, 168

phylogenesis, 226, 234

physics, 179, 223, 226; experimental, 179; inner, 223; of the mind, 223

physiology, 237

piano, 206

pictures, 122

pietism, 18, 65–66, 125, 151, 161, 176; Baumgarten's, 151; Halle, 125; Pietist theologians, 125

Piselli, Francesco, 62

pithiness, 229

place, 217–18

plants, 216

Plato, 48, 168, 279; *Republic*, 168

plausibility, 76–77

play, 268

pleasantness, 255

pleasure, 129, 131, 207–8, 216, 253, 255–56, 267, 291, 294–96, 299

plenitude, 42–44

pliny, 245

pluralism, 21, 106, 154

poetics, 11–12, 15, 22, 27–28, 50–51, 55, 58, 60, 62, 162, 173, 176, 181, 184, 190, 192; philosophical, 12; Wolffian, 176

poetry, 11–12, 19, 21, 28, 30, 42, 44, 49, 73, 78–79, 83, 117, 128–29, 135–36, 142, 146, 173–76, 183–84, 187, 198, 221–22, 224, 235, 243–44, 248–49, 252, 254, 261, 266, 291; Baumgarten's definition, 12, 128–29, 174; defense of, 135; heroic, 187; as instrument of moral education, 146; Latin, 117; occasional, 183; perfection, 129, 142; as perfect sensible discourse, 12, 128–29, 174; philosophy of, 175; poetry and philosophy, 11; poets' war, 183–84; practical value, 78; roman, 244; Wolffian, 221

politics, 72

Pollok, Anne, 22–23, 254, 256

polysemy, 41

Pope, Alexander, 181

Poppe, Bernard, 16

position, 198, 216, 217

possibility, 76–77, 237; moral, 77; natural, 77

potency, 102

power, 31, 44, 47, 64, 102, 134, 205, 210, 222, 242–43, 246, 254–55, 257, 273, 299; degree of, 255; disciplinary, 64, 277, 279; inherent, 205; of representation, 44, 47; sublime of, 254

practice, 128, 208, 221–22

praxis, 281

precision, 231

predisposition, 199

prejudice, 279

premonition, 77

prescription, 227–28
presentation, 12, 121–22, 163, 256–58, 262; aesthetic, 121–22; artistic, 256, 262; manner of, 258; perfected, 12; perfection in, 257; unperfected, 12
pride, 143
principle, 22, 41, 77, 150, 152–57, 195, 197, 220; abstract, 159; *a priori*, 150, 153–54; of association, 41; general, 152, 157; principle of consequence, 77; principle of contradiction, 77; principle of noncontradiction, 197; principle of sufficient reason, 22, 197; rational, 195
priority, 81
private, 69
probability, 15, 157, 200; aesthetic, 200
problem, 154–55
proficiency, 208
progress, scientific, 160
proof, 129, 155–56, 160, 209, 230; logical, 129; order of, 156
prophecy, 142, 249, 258, 294
prophet, 136
proportion, 19
propriety, 77
prosody, 59
proverbs, 145
Prussian Royal Academy, 193, 202–3
Psalms, 176
psychology, 13, 23, 36, 41, 51, 53, 91, 106, 111, 165, 174, 178, 188, 194, 197, 202–4, 214, 221–23, 228, 237, 278, 285, 291; aesthetic, 202; Baumgarten, 102–3; of the beautiful, 223; empirical psychology, 13, 36, 51, 53, 91, 165, 178, 194, 202, 214, 228, 285, 291; explanatory, 203; human, 197; moral, 204; rational, 285; scholastic, 106, 111; Wolffian, 204
public, 69, 238
purity, 179
purpose, 97
purposiveness, 261

Pyra, Immanuel J., 177

quality, 81, 162, 226, 242, 249, 252, 260; heroic, 252; moral, 242; objective, 260; occult, 226; primary, 249
quantity, 81, 157, 162, 246; continuous, 246
Quistorp, Theodor Johann, 183

Rambach, Johann Jacob, 133, 136, 140–42, 144, 147–48; *Elucidation of his own Institutes of Sacred Hermeneutics*, 133; *Institutes of Sacred Hermeneutics*, 133, 137–38; *Poetic Thoughts in Celebration of God's Supreme Benefactions*, 136, 141, 147
Ramus, Peter, 81
ratiocination, 206, 237
rationalism, 2, 22–23, 106, 123, 149–61, 164, 168, 170, 200; abstract, 152, 168–69; aesthetic, 151, 169; Baumgarten's, 152; dogmatic, 150, 156, 170; early modern, 154; German, 123; Leibnizian-Wolffian, 2, 22; philosophical, 164; Wolffian, 2, 22–23, 106, 149–51, 153–61, 164, 167–69
ravines, 261
reaction, 296
readiness, 285
reality, 55, 77, 122–23, 193, 197, 210, 213, 218
reason/reasons/reasoning, 46, 60, 89, 143–45, 149, 159–60, 169–70, 183, 194, 197, 206–8, 211, 220, 223, 229, 247, 262, 265, 268, 296; *a posteriori*, 159; *a priori*, 159; authority of, 149, 169; axioms of, 220; clear and distinct, 206; critique of, 170; ends of, 265; fate of, 169; general, 208; and imagination, 262; powers of, 194; scope of, 194; sufficient, 89, 145; unity of, 46

reborn, 131
recitation, 128
recollection, 80
reductionism, 232, 238, 240
reflection, 233–34, 244
Reid, Thomas, 34
relation, 81, 162, 196, 207, 243, 290, 296; affective, 290; cognitive, 296; to an object, 296; sensation of, 207; subject-object, 243
relevance, 245
religion, 137, 147, 266
renaissance, 248
repetition, 201, 276
representation, 40–42, 88–89, 93–94, 96–97, 109, 111, 113–14, 117, 119, 158, 174, 194, 197–98, 200, 204, 206–7, 209–10, 249, 255, 261, 265, 273, 285, 287, 290; act of representing, 93; aesthetic, 111, 113, 117, 198, 200; analogical, 265; clear, 88; clear and distinct, 111, 204; concept of, 273; confused, 89, 200; discursive, 287; individual, 197; intellectual, 194; intense, 285; intuitive, 287; lively, 197–98; logical, 113; manner of, 249; obscure, 40, 88, 206; obscure and confused, 111, 204; perfect, 194, 255; poetic, 119; quantity of, 206; representing a beautiful object as ugly, 97; representing an ugly object as beautiful, 96–97; sensible, 41–42, 88, 114, 174, 194, 197, 210, 255, 290; subjective, 109; symbolic, 265; wealth of, 290
research, 67–68, 270; art as, 67–68; empirical, 270
response, 270–71, 296; aesthetic, 270; disinterested, 270; physiological, 271; psychological, 271; socialized, 296
Reusch, Johann Peter, 6–7, 174; *Dissertation on the Beauty of Speech*, 7; *Logical System*, 174

revelation, 162
rhetoric, 15, 19, 21, 25, 27–28, 31, 50–52, 58, 60, 62–63, 71–72, 162, 172–73, 176, 180–81, 190; art of discourse, 72; elegant speaking, 72
richness, 16–19, 116–17, 187, 197, 199, 243–44, 246, 248, 284, 287–88, 298, 300; aesthetic, 116, 248; objective, 287; subjective, 287
ridiculousness, 210
Riedel, Friedrich Justus, 209–10, 220, 231, 238
Riedel, Wolfgang, 171
Riemann, Albert, 85
Ritter, Joachim, 32
Roloff, Friedrich Wilhelm, 180
Rousseau, Jean Jacques, 53
rule/rules, 83, 207, 222, 227, 233, 238; of beauty, 238; compositional, 222; of poetry, 83; practical, 233

Salmony, Hansjörg, 233
satiation, 257
Schiller, Friedrich, 266–67
Schiller, Friedrich Wilhelm Joseph, 45, 53, 150
Schmidt, Johann Andreas, 137; *On the Method of Propagating Religion by Means of Poems*, 137
Schopenhauer, Arthur, 266–67
Schwaiger, Clemens, 153, 292
Schweizer, Hans Rudolf, 31–33, 86, 90, 98, 101, 103, 153
science, 28, 31, 56, 58, 67–68, 83, 106, 153–54, 157, 159–60, 213, 227–28, 235; arts and sciences, 236; beautiful sciences, 28, 58; cultural, 31, 67–68; empirical, 237; experimental, 153, 159; hermeneutic, 278; human science, 223, 277; mathematical, 154, 157; *mathesis aesthetica*, 83; natural, 153, 159; progress in, 160; scholastic, 56; social sciences, 67; traditional, 228
scripture, 21, 51, 132, 134

sculpture, 44, 49, 68, 190
Seel, Martin, 27, 153
self, 136, 143, 211, 213, 220, 263, 265, 267, 279; self, loss of, 267; self-control, 136, 263; self-cultivation, 211; self-determination, 279; self-esteem, 265; self-knowledge, 213; self-love, 143; self-realization, 220; self-respect, 265; self-rule, 263
semiology/semiotics, 17, 50–51, 59, 73; aesthetic, 59; philosophical, 59
Seneca, 245, 249
sensation, 33–34, 89, 93–94, 134, 144, 164, 199–200, 203–4, 207–8, 223–24, 229–30, 232, 240, 296, 298; distinct, 224; inner, 34, 94, 237; obscure, 215; ontology of, 239; outer, 34; of perfection, 94; spiritual, 134
sense/senses, 93, 95, 134, 159, 179, 198, 208–9, 217, 226, 237, 240, 255; external, 93, 209, 217; good sense, 208; inner, 88, 95, 198, 255; internal, 93; outer, 93–94
sensibility, 13, 30, 34, 46, 50, 123, 156, 158, 165, 181, 185, 193, 195, 198–99, 213–14, 248, 280; artistic, 199; colonization of, 279; faculty of indistinct cognition, 158; human, 194
sensuality, 127, 148, 237; suppression of, 234
sensualization, 210
Sensus Communis, 200, 216
sentiment, 194, 198, 205, 211, 218, 250, 253–54, 257; mixed, 253–54; sentimentality, 218
serenity, 131, 250
Sextus Empiricus, 56
Shaftesbury (Anthony Ashley Cooper), 113, 248, 271
Shakespeare, William, 258
signification, 51, 102–3; aesthetic, 51; beauty of, 102–3; perfection of, 102
sign/signs, 15, 48, 59–60, 95, 182, 185, 290; art of, 59; beauty of, 60; linguistic, 95; theory of, 59

similarity, 200
Simon, Richard, 139, 141; *Critical History of the Old Testament*, 139
simplicity, 252
sin, 51
sincerity, 76
society, 211
Socrates, 71–72, 251, 279
Solms, Friedhelm, 90, 98, 101, 103
soul, 13, 21, 23, 41, 46, 66, 93, 102, 109–10, 127, 131, 143, 152, 188, 196–98, 204, 209–10, 214–15, 222, 224, 229–30, 250, 257, 282, 290; foundation of (*Fundus Animae*), 23, 41, 66, 109, 188, 197, 204, 214–15, 222, 229, 282; human, 197, 259; power of the, 196; santified, 21; science of the, 228
sound, 291
sovereignty, 273–74
space, 217, 239, 267
Spalding, Samuel Wilhelm, 144–47; *The Force and Efficacy of Ethical Philosophy*, 144–45, 148
specificity, 219
spectacle, 273–74
spectator, 9
speech, 60, 72–74, 174; aesthetic, 60; clear, 74; elegant, 72; explicit, 74; full, 74; perspicuous, 74; poetic, 174
Spener, Philipp Jacob, 1, 4, 133
Spener, *Pious Longing*, 4
Spinoza, Baruch, 141, 154–55, 211; *Ethics*, 155; Spinozism, 211
spirit, 46, 54, 112, 132, 134–36, 139, 198, 204, 215, 217, 255, 266, 277, 279, 286, 292; aesthetic, 112; beautiful, 279, 286, 292; confusions of, 204; elegant, 198; evil, 286; finite, 286; good, 286; holy spirit, 130, 134–36, 139; inferior, 286; superior, 286
stability, 299
stars, 261
state, 72

statement, sublime, 259
stirringness, 15
stoicism, 250
stories, 145
strength, 255–56, 274, 278
striving, 113, 267, 293; aesthetic, 113
style, 72, 74, 76, 136, 139–40, 163, 179,
    189, 252; appropriate, 163; artistic,
    74; flowing, 72; high, 76; literary,
    245; low, 76; medium, 76; ornate,
    74; perfection, 179; perspicuous,
    140; pleasing, 139; proper, 139;
    simple, 139; sublime, 136, 139, 141,
    252
subjection, 64
subjectivation, 274, 277, 281–82;
    aesthetic, 281; disciplinary, 282
subjectivity, 46
sublime, 23–24, 33, 76, 241–72, 287;
    aesthetic, 244; in art, 255, 266–67;
    cognitive, 266; counterweight to
    the beautiful, 262; dynamical, 251,
    260, 263, 267, 269; experience of,
    242, 262, 270, 272; feeling, 252,
    261; mathematical, 251, 260, 263,
    267, 269; moral, 242–43, 247, 250,
    253, 259, 263, 268, 270, 272; in
    music, 249; noble, 263, 270; object,
    248; objective, 258; of power,
    254; practical, 266; psychological
    accounts, 266; as quality of an
    object, 243; subjective, 258; theory
    of the sublime, 241
substance, 81
succinctness, 231
Sulzer, Johann Georg, 202–5, 208,
    214–15; *Examination of the Origin
    of the Pleasant and Unpleasant
    Sentiments*, 204; *Explanation of
    a Psychologically Paradoxical
    Statement*, 204; *General Theory
    of the Fine Arts*, 202; *Notes
    Concerning the Various States of
    the Soul*, 205; *On Consciousness
    and Its Influence on our Judgments*,
205; *Short Notion of All Sciences*,
    202
surveillance, 277
symbol, 265–66
symmetry, 19
sympathy, 75
syntax, 59
system, 10, 153, 170, 213, 224, 271,
    284, 300; philosophical, 170;
    rationalist, 284

talent, 268
taste, 82, 91, 103, 171, 176, 186, 205–
    10, 262, 295–96, 298; bad taste, 210;
    correct taste, 210; critique of, 171;
    subjective, 209–10
Tatler, 8
Tedesco, Salvatore, 62, 73, 245
teleology, 295
temperament, 81–82, 199, 207–8, 252,
    298; aesthetic, 252, 298
tenacity, 285
terminology, 71, 153
terror, 273
tetrachord, 207
theology, 61, 126, 128, 137, 162, 168,
    172, 177, 180, 252; Christian, 168;
    natural theology, 61; Pietist, 128;
    poetic, 137
theorem, 154–55
theory, 30–31, 36, 43, 45, 51, 62, 65–
    68, 126–27, 241, 243, 261, 268, 272,
    281, 286, 289; aesthetic, 30–31, 36,
    43, 45, 51, 62, 65–68, 126–27, 241,
    261, 268, 272, 281, 289; ethical, 286;
    physical, 243
thing, 96, 115, 157, 162; contingent,
    115; individual, 115, 157; *res*, 96
thinking/thought, 15, 25, 31, 35, 40,
    42–44, 62, 67–68, 73, 82, 96–100,
    105, 107–8, 117–18, 126, 132, 134,
    158–59, 182, 187, 190, 196–200,
    204, 207–8, 219, 232, 239, 244,
    247–48, 252–53, 261, 264, 276–77,
    280, 283–84, 287–91, 297–302;

aesthetic, 117–18, 197; agreement of, 97–100; beauty of/beautiful, 15, 25, 31, 35, 40, 42, 44, 62, 67–68, 82, 105, 107–8, 117, 182, 190, 198–200, 253, 276–77, 280, 283–84, 287–91, 297–302; beauty of things and thoughts, 73, 95–100, 103, 300; clear, 126; emotional, 187; free way of thinking, 247; habits of, 159, 297; independent, 219; logical, 126, 299, 302; poetic, 117–18, 197; self-thinking, 239; sublime way of thinking, 244, 247, 252–53; thinking, nonconceptual, 43; thinking beautiful things in an ugly way, 248; thinking ugly things in a beautiful manner, 248; way of, 247, 261, 264

Thomas Aquinas, 248, 259

Thomasius, Christian, 5

thoroughness, 16–18

Tibullus, 116

time, 81, 239, 267

topics, 20, 50

totality, 93

touchingness, 290

tragedy, 145, 252–54, 266–67

training, 22–24, 82, 193–96, 201, 206, 209, 295; aesthetic, 22–24, 193–96, 201; sensible, 206; social, 295; training for the artist, 209; training for the connoisseur, 209

trait, 199

transcendence, 54

transcendentals, 109, 193, 202, 206–7; The True, Good, and Beautiful, 193, 202, 206–7

transgression, 234

transposition, 232

truth, 16–19, 21, 25, 32, 65, 68, 73–77, 105–23, 131, 133, 138, 141–43, 156–57, 163, 166, 170, 185, 187, 193, 195, 200, 202, 205–8, 213, 238–39, 243–44, 246, 248, 259, 265, 268, 284, 287–88, 290, 297, 298, 300; abstract, 114; aesthetic,

21, 32, 65, 68, 77, 105–23, 239, 287–88; aestheticological, 32, 77, 106, 108, 110, 113–14, 120–21, 239, 287; aesthetics of, 246, 268; certain, 157; contingent, 195; determinate, 114; dissonant, 284; divine, 143; established, 163; of fact, 118, 121; factual, 120; form of, 213; general, 138; in general, 107; heterocosmical, 115; historical, 120; human, 110, 113; individual, 114; logical, 32, 105, 111–14, 287; metaphysical, 77, 109–14, 118, 187; objective, 77, 110; as perfection of intellectual cognition, 166; phenomenon of, 213; philosophical, 163; philosophical knowledge of, 166; plural, 110, 123; scholastic definition, 109; sensibly cognized, 117; singular, 114; spiritual, 131, 133, 141; subjective, 77, 110, 112; sublime, 248, 259; theory of aesthetic truth, 108; transcendental, 109; truthfulness, 298; unique, 110; universal, 114

Tschernyshevskij, Nikolai Gawrilowitsch, 55

Tschirnhaus, Ehrenfried Walther, 79

tuberculosis, 10, 184

turgidity, 189

ugliness, 16, 49, 92, 96–97, 200, 210, 248

uncertainty, 276

unconscious, 204–5

understanding, 15–16, 82, 156, 158–60, 164–65, 193, 195, 264, 280; faculty of distinct cognition, 159; faculty of perceiving possible things, 165; healthy, 264; human, 156, 164

unhappiness, 299, 301

uniformity, 257

uniqueness, 109

unity, 19, 76, 197–98, 207, 217, 256, 266; of action, 76; of clear and confused representations, 207; inner,

197; of a manifold, 207; of place and time, 76, 198; of the poem, 76; in variety, 19

University of Frankfurt an der Oder (Viadrina), 8, 28, 61, 150, 162, 178

University of Halle (Fridericiana), 5, 61, 125, 127, 137, 148, 150, 154, 172, 177

univocity, 42

Upanishads, 267

usefulness, 274

usufruct, 160

validity, 118–19, 122, 141, 214; cognitive, 122; experiential, 119; invalidity, 141; psychological, 122; subjective, 118

value, 49, 118, 247, 295; aesthetic, 49; affective, 295; cognitive, 118; moral, 295

variation/variety, 74, 290

Vasari, Giorgio, 46; *Lives of the Artists*, 46

vastness, 242–43, 246, 255, 260

Vergil/Virgil, 112, 119–20, 245, 251; *Aeneid*, 119–20, 251

verisimilitude, 173, 181–82

vice, 140, 249

Vico, Giambattista, 63, 252

vigorousness, 285

violence, 274, 299

virtue, 121–22, 140, 143, 160, 249, 250, 252, 255, 257, 263, 268, 271; artistic, 255; natural, 143; pseudo-virtue, 143; virtuous agent, 248

virtuoso, 219

vividness, 146, 214

vocation, 201, 209, 261; moral vocation, 261; vocation of humanity, 201, 209

Waisenhaus, 5, 28, 65, 125–28, 137–38, 161

weakness, 278

wealth, 15, 43, 68, 181–82, 185, 243, 287, 290; aesthetic, 43

weight, 246

well-being, 210

Wellek, René, 32

Welsch, Wolfgang, 33; *Aisthesis*, 33

wholeness, 207

will, 167, 204, 213, 267, 296

Winckelmann, Johann Joachim, 47; *History of Ancient Art*, 47

Windheim, Christian Ernst von, 182

Winkelmann, Georg Christoph, 43

wisdom, 72, 121, 131, 219

wisdom, divine, 131

wit, 15, 35–38, 52, 196, 198

Wolff, Christian, 5–6, 16, 20, 27, 36, 41, 51, 79, 82, 90, 92, 106, 125–26, 150, 152, 154–59, 165, 171, 173, 188, 190, 195, 200, 202–3, 215, 217, 254; *Empirical Psychology*, 82, 91, 159–60; *Foundations of all Mathematical Sciences*, 126, 154–55; *German Logic*, 154, 157–59, 164; *German Metaphysics*, 157–59; *Latin Logic*, 89, 154–56, 159–60, 165; Leibnizian-Wolffian Philosophy, 13, 22, 28, 150, 202; logic, 79, 167–68; methodology, 167–68; *On the Practical Philosophy of the Chinese*, 6; *Preliminary Discourse on Philosophy in General*, 154–64; psychology, 81, 92, 167–68; *Short Lesson on the Mathematical Method*, 154–56; Wolffianism, 8, 18, 149–52, 164; Wolffian Rationalism, 2, 22–23, 106, 149–51, 153–61, 164, 167–69

wonder, 198, 251

Zedler, 184; *Universal Lexicon*, 184

Zeller, Eduard, 151; *History of German Philosophy Since Leibniz*, 151

About the Contributors

Hans Adler is Halls-Bascom Professor Emeritus for Modern Literature Studies at the University of Wisconsin.

Stefanie Buchenau is Maître de conférences, Departement d'Etudes germaniques, Université Paris 8-Saint Denis.

Robert R. Clewis is professor of Philosophy at Gwynedd Mercy University.

Ursula Franke taught philosophy and was a member of the Leibniz-Forschungstelle at the Westfälische Wilhelms-Universität Münster.

Mauricio González is a translator and editor at the Max Planck Institute for Legal History and Legal Theory in Frankfurt am Main.

Simon Grote is associate professor of History at Wellesley College.

Amelia Hruby received her PhD in philosophy from DePaul University.

Matthew McAndrew teaches philosophy at The College of New Jersey

J. Colin McQuillan is associate professor of Philosophy at St. Mary's University.

Christoph Menke is Professor of Practical Philosophy at the Goethe-Universität Frankfurt am Main.

Alessandro Nannini is a research fellow in ICUB Humanities at the University of Bucharest.

John K. Noyes is professor of German at the University of Toronto.

Angelica Nuzzo is professor of Philosophy at the Graduate Center and Brooklyn College, City University of New York.

Anne Pollok is Wissenschaftliche Mitarbeiterin at the Johannes Gutenberg-Universität Mainz.

9 781538 146255